Apprenticeship

MW00713912

Level 3: Team Leader / Supervisor

Tim Webb
PGCE, FBII, FInstLM

THE CHOIR PRESS

Titles in the Apprenticeship Companion series

Level 3: Business Administrator
Level 3: Customer Service Specialist
Level 3: Team Leader/Supervisor
Level 5: Operations / Departmental Manager

Copyright © 2022 Tim Webb

All rights reserved. No part of this publication may be reproduced or transmitted in any form or by any means, electronic or mechanical including photocopying, recording or any information storage or retrieval system, without prior permission in writing from the publishers.

The right of Tim Webb to be identified as the author of this work has been asserted by him in accordance with the Copyright, Designs and Patents Act 1988

First published in the United Kingdom in 2022 by
The Choir Press

ISBN 978-1-78963-288-0

Foreword

Having already written one book you might think the endless hours of writing, researching and proof reading would deter any attempt to repeat the process. Given that this is the second book in the series, that clearly hasn't happened! This time the challenge has been a little easier. The benefit of 20:20 hindsight and a great deal of the research done previously, whilst it has been no walk in the park, it has certainly been very rewarding.

The time, effort and endeavour will all be worth it though, if just one of today's Leader/Supervisors find it a beneficial and effective support resource as they work towards the End Point Assessment of their Apprenticeship.

I have taken the materials and resources I have used and developed over the years I have taught leadership and management and recompiled it into a format which, I hope, will be of benefit to all who have the stamina to wade through the detail it contains. I have tried to steer clear of the traditional, drab, textbook style and have striven to lighten what can be a rather mundane subject, being so entrenched in theory.

It is no coincidence the book follows the delivery plan for the Level 3 Team Leader/Supervisor Apprenticeship Standard and has been designed to provide the reader with support through each module of the Standard.

I hope that everyone who delves into this document finds something of interest and reward and for those who use it to support their efforts to develop themselves and their career, I wish you every success.

Remember – you only get out, what you put in!

Contents

Contents

Contents

Contents

Chapter 1: Self-Awareness

Self-Awareness

The Concept of Self-Awareness

Self-awareness is knowing who we are – our character, desires, beliefs, qualities, motives and feelings. Having a good understanding and knowledge of these aspects can help in the workplace and in our private lives.

We can assess our personal growth and understanding through self-awareness by:

- *being aware of the influence of people and things around us*
- *learning about how we can influence and interact with others*

Developing self-awareness and understanding our own psychology is a skill that is part of our personal and professional development. Self-awareness can be applied in our working lives to help us to, for example:

- *understand emotions more clearly* – ours and other people's
- *improve our communication skills* – to interact with others in the workplace and resolve conflict
- *improve leadership skills* – and our general operational performance
- *improve job satisfaction* – by focusing on job roles and tasks that truly motivate us
- *maximise career development opportunities*

Without being aware of and understanding our emotions, it will be difficult for us to move into the other emotional competencies like self-management, social awareness, or team leadership.

> ### *Self-awareness can improve our judgment and help us identify opportunities for professional development and personal growth.*

Self-improvement is also referred to as self-development and may be described as the improvement to one's own mind and character through one's own efforts. It is a conscious process where a decision is made to take charge and change one's life and prospects for the better.

When you look in a mirror – what do you see?

- *Do you see the person you are?*
- *The person you want to be?*
- *or the person you think other people see?*

The very first step on the road to self-awareness is to recognise that the reflected image you see, is simply a reflection of the packaging you come in!

That packaging is about as relevant as the cardboard box your breakfast cereals are delivered in!! – You do not eat the box – it is what is inside the box that matters!!

Self-Awareness

Self-awareness is being aware of oneself including one's traits, feelings and behaviours.

We are disinclined to spend much time on self-reflection. We focus very much on our outer packaging but we seldom look inside it because we are afraid of what we might find. Without taking a long hard look and absolute honesty, you will never really know what is inside.

It is quite difficult today to find time to think about who we are.

When personal feedback is presented to us, we are not always open to it, because honest feedback is not always flattering.

Developing self – awareness starts with taking a long hard look at ourselves and be brutally honest about our true targets and expectations in life. What are our strengths and weaknesses, what about our personality, habits and values? We simply avoid asking these difficult questions and therefore have a very low level of self-awareness. If you don't know the problem – you can't fix it! Self-awareness is the essential first step toward maximising our capabilities and realising our true prospects.

If you cannot be totally honest with yourself – you will never be honest with anyone.

Soft Skills

Both self-awareness and Emotional Intelligence are associated with soft skills – There are thought to be five elements to this – Personality, Values, Habits, Needs and Emotions.

Personality: *– Personalities cannot be changed, but values and needs are based on what we learn about ourselves. Understanding our own personality can help us find in what environment we can be successful. Awareness of our personality helps us analyse such a decision.*

Values: *– It is important that we know and focus on our personal values. When we focus on our values, we are more likely to accomplish what we consider most important.*

Habits: *– Our habits are the behaviours that we repeat daily and often automatically. Although we would like to possess the habits that help us interact effectively with and manage others, we can probably all identify at least one of our habits that decrease our effectiveness.*
Needs: *– Maslow and other scholars have identified a variety of psychological needs that drive our behaviours such as needs for esteem, affection, belonging, achievement, self-actualisation, power and control.*

Emotions: *–Understanding your own feelings, what causes them and how they impact our thoughts and actions is emotional self-awareness. Persons with high emotional self-awareness understand the internal process associated with emotional experiences and, therefore, has greater control over them*

Self-Awareness

Improving Self-Awareness

As we get older, many of our actions, responses, attributes and behaviours are based on things we have learned, seen and told along the way. We might base our initial education and career choices on what family members did. However, such choices might not suit our real desires, beliefs or character and we need to develop self-awareness to discover more options which may be open to us.

There are many tests and techniques available that help us to identify and understand ourselves in greater depth. They look at our character, qualities, motivation, feelings and so on, so that we can access information about ourselves that is often hidden or undiscovered.

Techniques that can help us learn about how to reveal, recognise, evaluate and understand the different attributes and qualities that make us unique include, for example:

- *psychometric tests*
- *management tools*
- *coaching tools*
- *self-reflection tools*

Psychometric Tests

There are many psychometric tests available and they are easy to find online. They are designed to show personality, mental ability, opinions, strengths, weaknesses and preferences. They are often used by employers, or prospective employers, to see how an individual's own mix of natural skills and attributes will fit into what the organisation wants.

They can be used as a recruitment selection tool by employers, but they are also useful when developing self-awareness skills. They help to unmask our hidden qualities and habits and focus on our natural abilities and preferences.

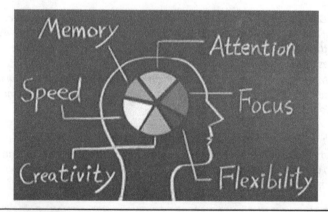

Self-Awareness

Myers-Briggs Type Indicator (MBTI)

The Myers-Briggs Personality Type Indicator is a self-assessment tool designed to identify a person's personality type, strengths and preferences.

The questionnaire was developed by Isabel Myers and her mother Katherine Briggs based on their work with Carl Jung's theory of personality types.

Today, the MBTI inventory is one of the most widely used psychological instruments in the world.

Have you ever heard someone describe themselves as an INTJ or an ESTP and wondered what those cryptic-sounding letters could mean? What the letters refer to is a personality type based on the Myers-Briggs Type Indicator (MBTI).

During World War II, Myers and Briggs began researching and developing an indicator that could be utilised to help understand individual differences. By helping people understand themselves, Myers and Briggs believed that they could help people select occupations that were best suited to their personality types and lead healthier, happier lives.

Myers created the first pen-and-pencil version of the MBTI during the 1940s and the two women began testing the assessment on friends and family. It took a further 20 years to fully develop it.

Based on the answers to the questionnaire, people are identified as having one of 16 personality types.

The goal of the MBTI is to allow participants to further explore and understand their own personalities including their likes, dislikes, strengths, weaknesses, possible career preferences and their compatibility with other people.

No one personality type is "best" or "better" than any other one.

It is not a tool designed to look for dysfunction or abnormality. Instead, its goal is simply to help people learn more about themselves.

The questionnaire itself is made up of four different scales:

Extroversion (E) - Introversion (I)
The extroversion-introversion dichotomy was first explored by Jung in his theory of personality types to describe how people respond and interact with the world around them. While these terms are familiar to most people, the way in which they are used here differs somewhat from their popular usage.

Extroverts are "outward-turning" and tend to be action-oriented, enjoy more frequent social interaction and feel energised after spending time with other people. Introverts are "inward-turning" and tend to be thought-oriented, enjoy

Self-Awareness

deep and meaningful social interactions and feel recharged after spending time alone. We all exhibit extroversion and introversion to some degree, but most of us tend have an overall preference for one or the other.

Sensing (S) - Intuition (N)

This scale involves looking at how people gather information from the world around them. Just like with extraversion and introversion, all people spend some time sensing and intuiting depending on the situation. According to the MBTI, people tend be dominant in one area or the other. People who prefer sensing tend to pay a great deal of attention to reality, particularly to what they can learn from their own senses. They tend to focus on facts and details and enjoy getting hands-on experience. Those who prefer intuition pay more attention to things like patterns and impressions. They enjoy thinking about possibilities, imagining the future and abstract theories.

Thinking (T) - Feeling (F)

This scale focuses on how people make decisions based on the information that they gathered from their sensing or intuition functions. People who prefer thinking place a greater emphasis on facts and objective data. They tend to be consistent, logical and impersonal when weighing a decision. Those to prefer feeling are more likely to consider people and emotions when arriving at a conclusion.

Judging (J) - Perceiving (P)

The final scale involves how people tend to deal with the outside world. Those who lean toward judging prefer structure and firm decisions. People who lean toward perceiving are more open, flexible and adaptable. These two tendencies interact with the other scales. Remember, all people at least spend some time extroverting. The judging-perceiving scale helps describe whether you extravert when you are taking in new information (sensing and intuiting) or when you are making decisions (thinking and feeling).

The MBTI Types

Depending on where you are on each scale, you will be assigned a letter for each category, to create the four-digit code. The resulting personality type can then be checked by the code formed.

Code		Personality Type	Code		Personality Type
ISTJ	=	The Inspector	ESTP	=	The Persuader
ISTP	=	The Crafter	ESTJ	=	The Director
ISFJ	=	The Protector	ESFP	=	The Performer
ISFP	=	The Artist	ESFJ	=	The Caregiver
INFJ	=	The Advocate	ENFP	=	The Champion
INFP	=	The Mediator	ENFJ	=	The Giver
INTJ	=	The Architect	ENTP	=	The Debater
INTP	=	The Thinker	ENTJ	=	The Commander

Self-Awareness

The test can be completed online and the results will be presented after the test for the personality type identified.

How MBTI differs from other personality tests

First, the MBTI is not really a "test." There are no right or wrong answers and one personality type is no better than any other type. The purpose of the indicator is not to evaluate mental health or offer any type of diagnosis.

Unlike many other types of psychological evaluation, the results are not compared against any norms. Instead of comparing a score to the results of other people, the goal of the MBTI is to simply offer further information about your own unique personality.

While there are many versions of the MBTI available online, only the real MBTI tool gives the most accurate results, most of the rest are simply weaker versions of the real thing.

The real MBTI must be administered by a trained and qualified practitioner that includes a follow-up of the results.

The current version of the Myers-Briggs Type Indicator includes 93 forced-choice questions in the North American version and 88 forced-choice questions in the European version. For each question, there are two options from which the participant must choose.

The 4 Cs' of Mental Toughness - Lyons (2015)

Mental Toughness is a personality trait that improves performance and well-being meaning that you are more likely to be successful in your personal and professional life.

Mental Toughness is defined as:

*Resilience - the ability to bounce back from setbacks and failures-
and Confidence -the ability to spot and seize opportunities.*

Mentally tough people are more outcome focused and better at making things happen, without being distracted by their own or other peoples' emotions.

The test is scientifically valid, reliable and based on a framework which measures four key components of mental toughness - Control, Commitment, Challenge and Confidence.

Control
Control is self-esteem.
It is your life's purpose and your sense of control over your life and emotions. It is the extent to which you feel you are in control of your life and that you can make a difference and change things. If you are high on Control, you have a good sense of who you are and what you stand for and are "comfortable in your own skin". You are also better able to

Self-Awareness

control your emotions meaning you can keep your anxieties in check and are less likely to be distracted by the emotions of others, or reveal your emotional state to other people.

Alternatively, if you are at the other end of the scale –and low on control –you will feel that events happen to you and are outside your personal control or influence.

Commitment
Commitment is your focus and reliability.
Scoring highly on commitment means that you can effectively set goals and targets and reliably and consistently achieve them without being distracted. You are strong at establishing routines and habits that enable you to be successful.

Alternatively, if you are at the other end of the scale – and low on commitment – you will sometimes fail or find it difficult to set goals and targets and then prioritise them. You may also find it difficult to focus and be easily distracted by other people and competing priorities. You rarely adopt routines or habits to make you successful.

Challenge
Challenge is your drive and adaptability.
Being high on challenge means that you are driven to be as good as you can be and to achieve your personal best. You see challenges, change, adversity and variety as opportunities rather than threats. You are likely to be adaptable and agile.

Alternatively, if you are at the other end of the scale – and low on challenge – you view change as a threat and avoid new and challenging situations for fear of failure or wishing not to expend what you perceive will be a wasted effort.

Confidence
Confidence is your self-belief and influence.
It describes to what extent you believe you can perform productively and proficiently and the ability to influence others. Being high on confidence means that you have the self-belief to successfully complete on tasks that other individuals with similar ability, but lower confidence would think beyond them.

Self-Awareness

In practice if you score high on Confidence, you will take setbacks, whether internally or externally generated, in your stride. You will keep your head, maintain your routine and often stiffen your resolve.

However, if you are low on confidence, you can easily be unsettled by the setback and feel undermined. Your head could drop. Your internal voice's positive commentary is vital here to counteract this loss of confidence and negativity.

The Challenge and Confidence scales together represent the Confidence part of the Mental Toughness definition.

It represents your ability to spot and seize an opportunity. This makes sense because, if you are a risk taker you see more situations more clearly as opportunities and are willing to embrace and explore them. If you are confident in your abilities and you easily engage with others, you are also much more likely to convert the potential opportunity of these situations into successful outcomes.

The Control and Commitment scales together represent the Resilience part of the Mental Toughness definition.

It is the ability to bounce back from setbacks and opportunities. This again makes sense because if you face a setback or failure your momentum slows or stops altogether and naturally question yourself and revisit your self-identity. You then need to re-affirm and reassess who you are and re-develop some momentum to enable you to bounce back. You can do this by setting and achieving a series of goals and targets, often small and simple at first, to rebuild your confidence and return to your chosen path.

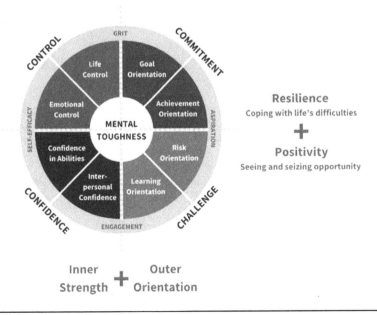

Self-Awareness

Management Tools

Many of the tools that we use in management can be useful to use when developing self-awareness. For example, we can learn from:

formal feedback from others – *e.g., formal reviews with a line manager*
informal feedback – *e.g., passing comments from colleagues or customers*
360-degree appraisals – *e.g., a formal review that takes comments from all stakeholders with whom we interact.*
learning activities – *e.g., courses on management or career development*
development activities – *e.g., working in a different department or role; taking on voluntary work*
attending counselling or mentoring sessions – *e.g., to focus on personal development*

> *By finding out how others view us, in a professional and controlled way, we can learn more about ourselves and the impacts we have on other people.*

Feedback Mechanisms

We all like to feel valued and that our opinions matter. We cannot force people to give us feedback, although we can follow the organisation's policies and procedures for giving and receiving feedback. As leader/supervisors developing self-awareness, we can actively seek out feedback from useful sources that will help us review our progress.

By understanding different feedback mechanisms, it helps to give insight into:

- *how to maximise the effectiveness of feedback we receive*
- *how to give effective feedback to others – particularly team members*

When giving feedback it is important to consider the person receiving the feedback. If the feedback is positive, it is a good opportunity to give praise and encouragement. This empowers and motivates the team member to continue doing well and not lose focus. They feel valued and respected and will benefit from feeling appreciated and recognised.

When we are asked to give feedback about someone else, it can be a good idea to only say things that we would say to that person's face. This helps us to keep the comment's objective, fair, valid and useful.

> *When delivered tactfully, constructive criticism and genuine praise are both valuable and welcome.*

There are many different mechanisms for giving feedback, including, for example:

Self-Awareness

Formal Reviews

These provide valuable, organised and focused opportunities for the individual to have detailed conversations with the line manager. Formal reviews usually start with a performance appraisal form that shows objectives, comments and maybe a rating system. The form is then discussed during a meeting when the individual and their line manager can:

- *give and receive feedback*
- *review progress so far*
- *discuss current strengths and issues*
- *set goals and targets for the next stage*

Informal Feedback

Informal feedback can be given at any time – e.g., on completion of a task, at the end of a shift, or when something good or bad happens at work. Opportunities to give informal feedback are usually unplanned and can just be a quick chat, a passing comment, or a spontaneous note or email.

360-Degree Feedback

360° appraisal is a process where feedback is gathered from peers, line manager and those who report to you, customers, suppliers – feedback from all directions. The 180° version does not include those who report to you. Both types can provide a great insight into the way your behaviour, attitude and approach is perceived by those on whom you have the biggest impact.

Some aspects of performance, impact and behaviour may have been identified through self-evaluation which you might wish to gather feedback about. Add a small number of other elements, specific to your role and context, to ensure the feedback is relevant and sufficiently comprehensive. Then consider your main stakeholders, internally and externally. What 3-5 things about you and your performance have the most critical impact on meeting their needs?

Feedback should be gathered from the right sources. It needs to come from those who have a valid opinion because they know you and are affected by your work and because they are an unbiased source. The feedback will not help if it is vague, distorted or misleading. Compile a list of people who are potential sources of feedback and seek their agreement to participating. Ensure the list of those who agree gives sufficiently comprehensive coverage and is representative of all 360°. If not, find some others.

Self-Awareness

Analyse the feedback to identify trends, contradictions and clues for your future development. Remember that the perceptions of others are their 'truth'. Whether you agree is irrelevant; this is what they see and how they feel, so take it seriously.

What is the feedback telling you about your behaviour, attitude, approach, impact and performance? What does it say about your style as a leader and manager? To further underpin your analysis of the latter you may wish to research and consider theories on leadership practice e.g., Adair's 'Action Centred Leadership, McGregor's Theory X & Y as well team theories such as Belbin's 'Team Roles'.

There are many more...

Gathering feedback from other sources

There are many sources of feedback and it can be collected from, for example:

line managers – e.g., in formal appraisals or informal chats
customers – e.g., in surveys, comments or complaints
team members and other colleagues – e.g., during appraisals or informal discussions
training providers – e.g., in reports and debriefing sessions after completing a unit of a training course or following an observation session
coaches and mentors – e.g., as part of a question and answer session after a learning activity or discussion

It is important to look at the feedback in detail and be objective about the comments. Some feedback will be reliable, useful and easily interpreted. Structured and informed feedback from a line manager, coach or training provider will be valuable as they have the skills to give useful and constructive criticism.

Good-quality feedback is likely to be based on good knowledge about:

- *the individual*
- *the workplace environment*
- *observations of the situation and task being reviewed*
- *the organisation's standards and requirements*

This means that the results can be interpreted as being valid and truthful and provides the individual with an honest view of themselves and they can:

be positive about the feedback – positive feedback is great for confidence and morale and negative feedback is useful
learn from the issues that need to be improved – and appreciate the opportunity to learn something about their performance they might not have seen before

enjoy and accept praise
take confidence from positive comments – **they are a guide that things are going well and need to continue to the same high standard**

Some feedback, however, is not reliable due to the inexperience of those taking part. There may be emotional and over-critical comments from some people due to personal reasons, which may not be honest, valid or useful. Customers sometimes leave feedback that is biased, emotional and subjective. When this happens, it is important to interpret the feedback in context, check the facts very carefully and look for useful and valid information that can be used as a guide for improving performance.

By gathering feedback from different sources, as happens in the 360-degree appraisal, we can:

- *create a three-dimensional picture of ourselves from other people's perspectives*
- *use reliable feedback to gain useful and valid insight and information*
- *recognise some feedback is unreliable and should not be taken too seriously or personally*

Self-Appraisal

Self-appraisal can also be part of the 360-degree appraisal process. It can be a surprisingly useful way of evaluating strengths and weaknesses. Self-appraisal can feel awkward or uncomfortable and people usually prefer their line manager to take responsibility for scoring their performance. Keeping a reflective diary to monitor activities is useful and can be brought into appraisal and reviews with the line manager.

This mechanism is particularly useful when evaluating skills, experience and knowledge connected with self-awareness. To maximise its effectiveness, it can be beneficial to compare self-appraisal with comments from other people to gain a more objective view.

Employee Engagement Surveys

Employee engagement is a workplace approach to create the right conditions for all members of an organisation to give of their best each day. As a result they will be committed to the organisation's goals and values, motivated to contribute to organisational success, with an enhanced sense of their own well-being.

> *"This is about how we create the conditions in which employees offer more of their capability and potential".* David Macleod

Employee engagement is based on trust, integrity, two-way commitment and communication between the organisation and its members. It is an approach which increases the chances of business success, contributes to organisational and individual performance and productivity and ensures the well-being of staff. The level of engagement can be measured and it can be nurtured and dramatically increased, or it can be lost and thrown away.

Self-Awareness

Delivering Negative Feedback

If some of the feedback to be delivered is negative, it needs to be delivered carefully and objectively. The best way to do this is to use a sandwich technique. Negative feedback is delivered in between two bits of positive feedback:

- **Positive** - *praise the individual for a good aspect of their performance*
- **Negative** - *mention and explain areas that need to be improved and provide guidance and support about how to improve*
- **Positive** - *finish with positive aspects, plans, hopes for future developments and improvements*

Coaching Tools

Johari Window

The Johari Window model was devised by American psychologists Joseph Luft and Harry Ingham in 1955, while researching group dynamics. *(How a group of individuals work and interact with each other)*

Today the Johari Window model is more relevant due to the emphasis on 'soft' skills such as behaviour, empathy, cooperation, inter-group development and interpersonal development.

The idea is that we examine information about ourselves and enter it into the relevant 'pane of the window'. The exercise of entering details can be revealing in itself, but we can work to change the sizes of the windowpanes as a focus for further analysis and personal development planning.

The Four Regions (or Panes)

The four Johari Window perspectives are called 'regions' or 'areas' or 'quadrants'. Each of these regions contains and represents the information - feelings, motivation, etc - known about the person, in terms of whether the information is known or unknown by the person and whether the information is known or unknown by others in the group.

Over the years, alternative terminology has been developed and adapted by different people - particularly leading to different descriptions of the four regions, hence the use of different terms in this explanation. Do not let it all confuse you - the Johari Window model is really very simple indeed.

- **what is known by the person about him/herself and is also known by others** - *open area, open self, free area, free self, or 'the arena'*
- **what is unknown by the person about him/herself, but which others know** - *blind area, blind self, or 'blind spot'*
- **what the person knows about him/herself that others do not know** - *hidden area, hidden self, avoided area, avoided self or 'facade'*

Self-Awareness

- *what is unknown by the person about him/herself and is also unknown by others*
  - unknown area or unknown self

	Known to self	Unknown to self
Known to others	1. Public Self *Open/free area / the "Arena"*	2. Blind Self *Blind area / "Blind Spot"*
Unknown to others	3. Private Self *Hidden area / "Façade"*	4. Unknown Self *Unknown area / "Unknown Self"*

Johari Quadrant 1 - **'Open self/area' or 'free area' or 'public area', or 'arena'**

Region 1 is also known as the 'area of free activity'. This is the information about the person - behaviour, attitude, feelings, emotion, knowledge, experience, skills, views, etc - known by the person ('the self') and known by the group ('others').

The aim in any group should always be to develop the 'open area' for every person, because when we work in this area with others we are at our most effective and productive and the group is at its most productive too. The open free area, or 'the arena', is the space where good communications and cooperation occur, free from distractions, mistrust, confusion, conflict and misunderstanding.
Established team members logically tend to have larger open areas than new team members. New team members start with relatively small open areas because little knowledge about the new team member is shared. The size of the open area can be expanded horizontally into the blind space, by seeking and actively listening to feedback from other group members. This process is known as 'feedback solicitation'. Also, other group members can help a team member expand their open area by offering feedback, sensitively of course.

The size of the open area can also be expanded vertically downwards into the hidden or avoided space by the person's disclosure of information, feelings, etc about him/herself to the group and group members. Also, group members can help a person expand their open area into the hidden area by asking the person about him/herself.

Self-Awareness

Managers and team leaders can play an important role in facilitating feedback and disclosure among group members and in directly giving feedback to individuals about their own blind areas. Leaders also have a big responsibility to promote a culture and expectation for open, honest, positive, helpful, constructive, sensitive communications and the sharing of knowledge throughout their organisation.

Top performing groups, departments, companies and organisations always tend to have a culture of open positive communication, so encouraging the positive development of the 'open area' or 'open self' for everyone is a simple yet fundamental aspect of effective leadership.

Johari Quadrant 2 - **'Blind self' or 'blind area' or 'blind spot'**

Region 2 is what is known about a person by others in the group but is unknown by the person him/herself. By seeking or soliciting feedback from others, the aim should be to reduce this area and thereby to increase the open area i.e., to increase self-awareness. This blind area is not an effective or productive space for individuals or groups. This blind area could also be referred to as ignorance about oneself, or issues in which one is deluded. A blind area could also include issues that others are deliberately withholding from a person.

We all know how difficult it is to work well when kept in the dark. No-one works well when subject to 'mushroom management'. People who are deemed to be 'thick-skinned' tend to have a large 'blind area'.

Group members and managers can take some responsibility for helping an individual to reduce their blind area - in turn increasing the open area - by giving sensitive feedback and encouraging disclosure.

Managers should promote a climate of non-judgemental feedback and group response to individual disclosure, which reduces fear and therefore encourages both processes to happen.

The extent to which an individual seeks feedback and the issues on which feedback is sought, must always be at the individual's own discretion.

Some people are more resilient than others - care needs to be taken to avoid causing emotional upset. The process of soliciting serious and deep feedback relates to the process of 'self-actualisation' described in Maslow's Hierarchy of Needs development and motivation model.

Johari Quadrant 3 - **'Hidden self' or 'hidden area' or 'avoided self/concealed' or 'facade'**

Region 3 is what is known to ourselves but kept hidden from and therefore unknown, to others. This hidden or avoided self represents information, feelings, etc, anything that a person knows about him/self, but which is not revealed or is kept hidden from others. The

Self-Awareness

hidden area could also include sensitivities, fears, hidden agendas, manipulative intentions, secrets - anything that a person knows but does not reveal, for whatever reason.
It is natural for very personal and private information and feelings to remain hidden, indeed, certain information, feelings and experiences have no bearing on work and so can and should remain hidden. However, typically, a lot of hidden information is not very personal, it is work- or performance-related and so is better positioned in the open area.

Relevant hidden information and feelings, etc, should be moved into the open area through the process of 'disclosure'. The aim should be to disclose and expose relevant information and feelings - hence the Johari Window terminology 'self-disclosure' and 'exposure process', thereby increasing the open area. By telling others how we feel and other information about ourselves we reduce the hidden area and increase the open area, which enables better understanding, cooperation, trust, team-working effectiveness and productivity. Reducing hidden areas also reduces the potential for confusion, misunderstanding, poor communication, etc, which all distract from and undermine team effectiveness.

Organisational culture and working atmosphere have a major influence on group members' preparedness to disclose their hidden selves. Most people fear judgement or vulnerability and therefore hold back hidden information and feelings, etc, that if moved into the open area, i.e., known by the group as well, would enhance mutual understanding and thereby improve group awareness, enabling better individual performance and group effectiveness.

The extent to which an individual discloses personal feelings and information and the issues which are disclosed and to whom, must always be at the individual's own discretion. Some people are more keen and able than others to disclose. People should disclose at a pace and depth that they find personally comfortable. As with feedback, some people are more resilient than others - care needs to be taken to avoid causing emotional upset. Also, as with soliciting feedback, the process of serious disclosure relates to the process of 'self-actualisation' described in Maslow's Hierarchy of Needs development and motivation model.

Johari Quadrant 4 - 'Unknown self' or 'area of unknown activity' or 'unknown area'

Region 4 contains information, feelings, latent abilities, aptitudes, experiences etc, that are unknown to the person and unknown to others in the group. These unknown issues take a variety of forms: they can be feelings, behaviours, attitudes, capabilities, aptitudes, which can be quite close to the surface and which can be positive and useful, or they can be deeper aspects of a person's personality, influencing his/her behaviour to various degrees. Large unknown areas would typically be expected in younger people and people who lack experience or self-belief.

Examples of unknown factors are as follows and the first example is particularly relevant and common, especially in typical organisations and teams:

- *an ability that is under-estimated or untried through lack of opportunity, encouragement, confidence or training*
- *a natural ability or aptitude that a person does not realise they possess*

Self-Awareness

- *a fear or aversion that a person does not know they have*
- *an unknown illness*
- *repressed or subconscious feelings*
- *conditioned behaviour or attitudes from childhood*

The processes by which this information and knowledge can be uncovered are various and can be prompted through self-discovery or observation by others, or in certain situations through collective or mutual discovery, of the sort of discovery experienced on outward bound courses or other deep or intensive group work. Counselling can also uncover unknown issues, but this would then be known to the person and by one other, rather than by a group.

Whether unknown 'discovered' knowledge moves into the hidden, blind or open area depends on who discovers it and what they do with the knowledge, notably whether it is then given as feedback, or disclosed. As with the processes of soliciting feedback and disclosure, striving to discover information and feelings in the unknown is relates to the process of 'self-actualisation' described in Maslow's Hierarchy of Needs development and motivation model.

Again, as with disclosure and soliciting feedback, the process of self-discovery is a sensitive one. The extent and depth to which an individual can seek out discover their unknown feelings must always be at the individual's own discretion. Some people are more keen and able than others to do this.

The idea is to enlarge the open/free area by:

reducing the blind area *– usually achieved through giving and receiving feedback*
reducing the hidden area *– through the process of disclosure*

A typical Johari Window would be as follows:

Self-Awareness

	Known to self	Unknown to self
Known to others	**1. Public Self** *Open/free area / the "Arena"* Known by the person Known by others Information about the person – *e.g., skills, knowledge, experience, behaviour, attitude, feelings*	**2. Blind Self** *Blind area / "Blind Spot"* Not known by the person Known by others Things that others know about the person that they do not know or realise themselves – *e.g., issues that are deliberately withheld from the person*
Unknown to others	**3. Private Self** *Hidden area / "Façade"* Known by the person Not known by others Information that is withheld from others – e.g., feelings, fears, worries, manipulative intentions, secrets	**4. Unknown Self** *Unknown area / "Unknown Self"* Not known to the person Not known by others Information that has not been recognised or revealed – *e.g., a young person's undiscovered talents and attributes that need to be revealed*

Johari Adjectives

The list below are the adjectives commonly used in a Johari Window. They are placed in the appropriate pane or quadrant in the window and when complete, will highlight areas where development is required.

Able	Empathetic	Logical	Responsive
Accepting	Energetic	Loving	Searching
Adaptable	Extroverted	Mature	Self-assertive
Bold	Friendly	Modest	Self-conscious
Brave	Giving	Nervous	Sensible
Calm	Happy	Observant	Sentimental
Caring	Helpful	Organised	Shy
Cheerful	Idealistic	Patient	Silly
Clever	Independent	Powerful	Spontaneous
Complex	Ingenuous	Proud	Sympathetic
Confident	Intelligent	Quiet	Tense
Dependable	Introverted	Reflective	Trustworthy
Dignified	Kind	Relaxed	Warm
Empathetic	Knowledgeable	Religious	Wise

Self-Awareness

The Wheel of Life

The Wheel of Life Exercise is a popular coaching assessment tool because it is a simple yet powerful diagnostic tool.

The Wheel of Life is based on the notion that there are specific categories - or **areas of focus** - that form the cornerstone of your overall life experience.

The Wheel of Life categories can include:

- **Health:** *Your physical health and well-being (can also include your emotional health).*
- **Relationships:** *Includes your primary intimate relationship, family and friends.*
- **Social:** *Includes religious/spiritual communities and other group activities.*
- **Financial:** *Your ability to manage your money effectively, save, budget and invest.*
- **Professional/Business:** *This is your work category, which can break out into a Wheel of Business.*
- **Personal Growth:** *Although not everyone might have an area of focus for personal development, anyone interested in Self-development does.*
- **Spirituality:** *This can be its own category or simply the driving force behind all your areas of focus.*

These are the basic categories of most people's Wheel of Life. Additional Wheel of Life categories might include:

Mental State
Attitude
Creativity
Contribution
Lifestyle
Recreation
.... or anything else that might play a dominant role in your life.

How to select Wheel of Life Categories

The key is to determine the areas that are most important to **you.**

We all tend to focus on certain areas at the expense of other areas. So, your areas of focus should include both your strengths AND your weaknesses. The reason why all the key areas are important is that many of them hit on basic human needs. Maslow suggests that, when we do not address these basic needs, our lives fall out of balance *(that is, we exhibit neurotic behaviour).*

Self-Awareness

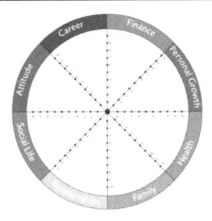

Assess your current level of fulfilment

After you have identified the major categories for your Wheel of Life, place them into a chart as if they are the pieces of a pie.

The entire circle represents your overall life and each piece represents a different area of focus. It might look something like this:

We all tend to have certain areas we are more proficient in and we all tend to spend time in these areas, neglecting our areas of weakness.

You may, for example, do an excellent job eating properly, exercising and staying active *(Health category)*, but you are hopeless at living within your means, paying off your credit cards, saving for the future and finding more ways to add value *(Financial category)*.

The Wheel of Life exercise brings these discrepancies to your conscious mind.

Generally, the reason why we fail to grow in particular areas of our lives is due to the subconscious limiting beliefs and a fixed mindset. Before you go through this process, it is important to address your mindset about your intelligence, your skills, your abilities and your personality.

The reason why many people fail to get to grips with these types of coaching exercises is that they start off with lots of preconceived notions. They answer questions based on what they think they "should" answer as opposed to what is actually true for them. The key to overcoming this tendency is to clear your mind before you do this exercise.

Self-Awareness

Self-Reflection

Reflecting helps to develop your skills and review their effectiveness, rather than just carry-on doing things as you have always done them. It is about questioning, in a positive way, what you do and why you do it and then deciding whether there is a better, or more efficient, way of doing it in the future.

In any role, whether at home or at work, reflection is an important part of learning. You would not use a recipe a second time around if the dish did not work the first time! You would either adjust the recipe or find a new and, hopefully, better one. When we do our job, we can become stuck in a routine that may not be working effectively. Thinking about your own skills can help you identify changes you might need to make.

Reflective questions to ask yourself:

> *Strengths* – *What are my strengths? For example, am I well organised? Do I remember things?*
> *Weaknesses* – *What are my weaknesses? For example, am I easily distracted? Do I need more practise with a particular skill?*
> *Skills* – *What skills do I have and what am I good at?*
> *Problems* – *What problems are there at work/home that may affect me? For example, responsibilities or distractions that may impact on study or work.*
> *Achievements* – *What have I achieved?*
> *Happiness* – *Are there things that I am unhappy with or disappointed about? What makes me happy?*
> *Solutions* – *What could I do to improve in these areas?*

Although self-reflection can seem difficult at first, or even selfish or embarrassing, as it does not come naturally. you will find it becomes easier with practise and the result could be a happier and more efficient you.

Self-Reflection Tools

Self-reflection is often used as a management or coaching tool and the process focuses strongly on self-awareness – e.g., keeping a journal, listening to the inner voice or practising mindfulness.

Keeping a journal can be a useful tool. Going through the process of writing down our thoughts, experiences and feelings on a regular basis can help us to understand more about ourselves, especially when we review entries later.

Listening to our inner voice can reveal things that we may not have realised previously. Just writing down some of the thoughts as they pass through our mind can be revealing, then reviewing them once a week can add to our self-awareness.

Self-Awareness

Practising mindfulness helps us to be aware of things going on in our minds, concentrate on the moment and allow unnecessary thoughts to pass through. There are many resources online, some of which are free, that help us to understand and train the mind, to improve concentration and aid stress management.

Strengths and Weaknesses (SWOT test)

Your strengths and weaknesses are the things which you are good at and things you are not so good at or need additional support or training to achieve a higher level of competence.

There are a few ways in which we can identify our strengths and weaknesses, but the most common is using a SWOT analysis. SWOT stands for Strengths, Weaknesses, Opportunities and Threats.

These are usually plotted on a chart with four sections.

Strengths (Current)	Weaknesses (Current)
an ability to get on with people *reliable* *hard-working* *able to take initiative* *honest* *research skills* *attention to detail* *analytical skills*	*timekeeping* *lack of confidence when dealing with people* *no work experience related to academic studies* *lack of spreadsheet and database skills*
Opportunities (Future)	**Threats (Future)**
gain experience of dealing with people *get experience of the world of work* *work abroad* *work in a team* *earn money*	*being unsupported at work* *fitting into the company culture* *transport problems may result in my unreliability*

The strengths and weaknesses are factors which affect you personally. The strengths are the things you are good at, things you can do without support or help. This could include literacy or numeracy, it could include being well organised, etc. Your weaknesses are things you need help or support to achieve. It may be that you can happily read a newspaper, but a textbook may be more challenging. You can perhaps deal with money including making payments and giving change, but more complex calculations you may find difficult and need help. It may also be that you are simply disorganised! These are your strengths and weaknesses!

Opportunities and threats are not about you personally, but about society in general. Opportunities are the things that help you to achieve your targets such as free training courses, help with childcare whilst studying, work experience opportunities, etc. Threats are the things which may prevent you from achieving your targets such as the economic

Self-Awareness

climate, lack of jobs, etc. Both opportunities and threats are matters outside of your control, but you should be aware of these issues.

Check you have included.....

Intellectual skills	**Personal and key skills**
Personal attributes and qualities	**Work experience issues**
Academic issues	**Future aspirations**

Reflect on how you are going to develop your strengths & weakness areas, minimise the potential threats and maximise future opportunities.

The close link between self-awareness and improved performance is almost irrefutable. Based on the outcomes of personal research, you will have found several instances where your performance falls into a weakness category and clearly needs to be addressed. Furthermore, the impact of your weaknesses will affect not just you and your career, but also the working lives of your team members, other teams and the wider stakeholders in the organisation and outside it.

Consequently, it is vital that performance is adapted to eliminate the weaknesses identified and immediate steps taken to develop these into strengths.

Self-Awareness

Reflective Practice

Reflective practice is thinking about or reflecting on what you do. It is closely linked to the concept of learning from experience, in that you think about what you did, what happened and decide from that what you would do differently next time.

Thinking about what has happened is part of being human. However, the difference between casual 'thinking' and 'reflective practice' is that reflective practice requires a conscious effort to think about events and develop insights into them. Once you get into the habit of using reflective practice, you will probably find it useful both at work and at home.

Reflective practice is excellent for increasing self-awareness and in developing a better understanding of others. Reflective practice can also help to develop creative thinking skills and encourages active engagement in work processes.

In work situations, keeping a learning journal and regularly using reflective practice, will support more meaningful discussions about career development and your personal development, including at appraisal time. It will also help to provide examples to use in competency-based interview situations.

Reflective Practice as a Skill

Various academics have touched on reflective practice and experiential learning to a greater or lesser extent over the years. They all seem to agree that reflective practice is a skill which can be learned and honed, which is good news for most of us.

> *Reflective practice is an active, dynamic action-based and ethical set of skills, placed in real time and dealing with real, complex and difficult situations.* Moon, J. (1999)

Reflective practice also bridges the gap between the 'high ground' of theory and the 'swampy lowlands' of practice. In other words, it helps to explore theories and to apply them to experiences in a more structured way. These can either be formal theories from academic research, or your own personal ideas. It also encourages us to explore our own beliefs and assumptions and to find solutions to problems.

Reflective Learning

Reflective learning is a learned process that requires time and practice. It is an Active process: involving thinking through the issues yourself, asking questions and seeking out relevant information to aid your understanding.

Reflective learning works best when you think about what you are doing before, during and after a learning experience. Reflective learning is therefore not only about recognising something new, but also about seeing reality in a new way.

Self-Awareness

Reflection is an important skill to develop and requires you to think about how you are personally relating to what is happening in the workshop or in your work.

The Reflective Learning Process

Identify a situation you encountered in a work or personal life that you believe could have been dealt with more effectively.

Describe the experience
What happened? When and where did the situation occur? Any other thoughts you have about the situation?
Reflection
How did you behave? What thoughts did you have? How did it make you feel? Were there other factors that influenced the situation? What have you learned from the experience?
Theorising
How did the experience match with your preconceived ideas, i.e., was the outcome expected or unexpected? How does it relate to any formal theories that you know? What behaviours do you think might have changed the outcome?
Experimentation
Is there anything you could do or say now to change the outcome? What action(s) can you take to change similar reactions in the future? What behaviours might you try out?

Developing and Using Reflective Practice

It is suggested that there are six steps to developing the critical, constructive and creative thinking that is necessary for reflective practice. These are:

Read - *around the topics you are learning about or want to learn about and develop*
Ask - *others about the way they do things and why*
Watch - *what is going on around you*
Feel - *pay attention to your emotions, what prompts them and how you deal with negative ones*
Talk - *share your views and experiences with others in your organisation*
Think - *learn to value time spent thinking about your work*

In other words, it is not just the thinking that is important. You also must develop an understanding of the theory and others' practice too and explore ideas with others.

Reflective practice can be a shared activity, it does not have to be done alone.

Self-Awareness

Some social psychologists have suggested that learning only occurs when thought is put into language, either written or spoken. This may explain why we are motivated to announce a particular insight out loud, even when by ourselves! However, it also has implications for reflective practice and means that thoughts not clearly articulated may not endure.

It can be difficult to find opportunities for shared reflective practice in a busy workplace. Of course, there are some obvious ones, such as appraisal interviews, or reviews of events, but they do not happen every day. So, you need to find other ways of putting insights into words.

Although it can feel a bit contrived, it can be helpful, especially at first, to keep a journal of learning experiences. This is not about documenting formal courses, but about taking everyday activities and events and writing down what happened, then reflecting on them to consider what you have learned from them and what you could or should have done differently.

It is not just about changing: a learning journal and reflective practice can also highlight when you have done something well.

Models of Reflective Practice

An implicit part of completing a reflection is an inner sense of discomfort (in fact the first stage of reflection as described by Boyd & Fales 1983). This is why many people put it off and may even try to avoid it, perhaps carrying out token reflections just to comply with CPD or course requirements.

In the early days reflecting on your actions is something that requires conscious effort after the event but eventually, according to Johns (2000), it will become an automatic thought process even when you are in the middle of experiencing the event.

When deciding which model to use, it can be helpful to find out which is your preferred learning style according to Honey & Mumford. You can relate these to the knowledge types shown in Carper/Johns' reflective models.

Below is an overview of the different models of reflection and which situations they are best geared towards.

Gibbs Reflective Cycle (1988)
Gibbs' Reflective Cycle was developed by Graham Gibbs in 1988 to give structure to learning from experiences. It offers a framework for examining experiences and given its cyclic nature lends itself particularly well to repeated experiences, allowing you to learn and plan from things that either went well or did not go well. It covers 6 stages:

- *Description of the experience*
- *Feelings and thoughts about the experience*
- *Evaluation of the experience, both good and bad*
- *Analysis to make sense of the situation*
- *Conclusion about what you learned and what you could have done differently*

Self-Awareness

- *Action plan for how you would deal with similar situations in the future, or general changes you might find appropriate*

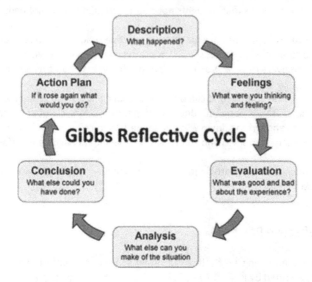

Positives: A basic, good starting point, six distinctive stages. Makes you aware of all the stages you go through when experiencing an event.

Negatives: superficial reflection- no referral to critical thinking/analysis/assumptions or viewing it from a different perspective (Atkins & Murphy 1993). Does not have the number or depth of probing questions as other models.

Kolb Reflective Cycle (1984)

Kolb's reflective model is referred to as "experiential learning". The basis for this model is our own experience, which is then reviewed, analysed and evaluated systematically in three stages. Once this process has been completed, the new experiences will form the starting point for another cycle.

Concrete experience:

You consciously and physically experience a situation, which makes you realise that you need to reflect systematically to learn something new or improve on your existing skill and practice. At this stage you will make a note of the specific situation and just describe what you see, how you feel and what you think.

Reflective observation:

Having written down the description of the experience, it is now time to reflect more deeply on what has happened in that situation. The questions you need to ask yourself are: what worked? what failed? why did the situation arise? why did others and I behave the way we did?

Self-Awareness

Abstract conceptualisation:
The guiding question for this stage leads on from the questions in the reflective observation stage: what could I have done better or differently? how can I improve? Initially, you try to find different ways for dealing with the situations and think up strategies for when you experience a similar situation again. Also, this is the stage where you should consult colleagues and literature to get a better understanding and further ideas.

Active experimentation:
This stage is now practising the newly acquired theoretical knowledge. You take your own reflections and thoughts about improvements as well as the theories back into your practice and try out the new strategies. Some of them will work, others will not, so this is then automatically the basis for the new cycle. As the experiences within the active experimentation stage become the new "concrete experiences".

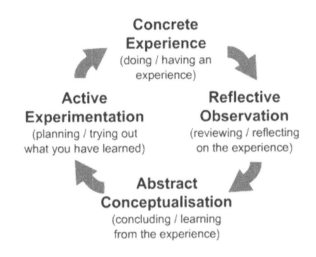

Positives: The reflective cycle. Consists of doing, asking how/why, making judgement, testing out.

Negatives: Superficial reflection- no referral to critical thinking/analysis/assumptions or viewing it from a different perspective (Atkins & Murphy 1993). Does not have the number or depth of probing questions as other models.

Writing a Reflective Journal

There is an old saying that "you can't teach an old dog new tricks" and it is certainly true when the "old dog" has a mind which is closed to new learning and experiences. A "old dog" with an open mind will analyse their experiences and use that analysis to influence their reaction and behaviour should the experience occur again.

Self-Awareness

A learning journal is a collection of notes, observations, thoughts and other relevant materials built-up over time and maybe a result of a period of study, learning and/or working experience. Its purpose is to enhance your learning through the process of writing and thinking about your learning experiences. Your learning journal is personal to you and will reflect your personality, preferences and experiences.

Why use a learning journal?

To provide a "live" picture of your growing understanding of a subject experience
To demonstrate how your learning is developing
To keep a record of your thoughts and ideas throughout your experiences
To help you identify your strengths, areas for improvement and preferences in learning

A learning journal helps you to be reflective about your learning, this mean that your journal should not be a purely descriptive account of what you did, but an opportunity to communicate your thinking process: how and why you did what you did and what you now think about what you did.

Structuring a learning journal

A learning journal may be called several different things: a learning log, a Field-work diary or personal development planner. Different subject areas may ask you to focus on different aspects of your experience and may have different formats.

A journal could be a notebook, an electronic document or sometimes recorded verbally on tape. Choose a method that works best for you!

Content of a learning journal

A learning journal should focus on your personal responses, reactions and reflections to new ideas or new ways of thinking about a subject that you have been introduced through:

Workshops, seminars, training sessions
Research and reading including any visual research including television, film and internet
Conversations and discussions with other participants, your Manager, Mentor, Coach and other colleagues
Significant experiences in the workplace

You will hear the term 'reflective writing' many times as part of your apprenticeship and indeed, it is an integral part of every successful apprenticeship. Without reflecting on something, how will you know whether to do the same thing again or maybe handle a situation differently next time? How will you know when something has gone well, but more importantly, why it went well?

Self-Awareness

Emotional Triggers and Inhibitors

Do you ever react with anger or fear and say or do things and then wish you had not? Do you end up wishing you could take it all back, or rewind it, or do it again?

An emotional trigger is when someone or something sets us off and our emotions are triggered.

We all have emotional triggers!

Emotional triggers consist of thoughts, feelings and events that seem to "trigger" an automatic response from us. The word "trigger" is important here because the idea is that our reaction occurs automatically. It might seem as if the emotional reaction is completely involuntary. The truth is that this reaction, like everything else that we do, is a choice. Learning how to identify our personal emotional triggers is the first step to taking control over how we choose to respond.

Have you ever been going through a relatively uneventful day, only to have something unexpected happen that seems to automatically turn your world upside down? You may be driving in the car in a good mood, only to have a sad or sentimental song come on the radio and hearing it instantly change your mood? Do you feel the overwhelming urge to do something that you know is not good for you when something upsetting happens? These are examples of being emotionally triggered.

The workplace can be a stressful environment and can involve many situations that may trigger strong negative feelings.

It is important for leader/supervisors not only to be in control of their own feelings, but also help workers de-escalate their emotional situations. This can help maintain workers morale, allow them to perform to their potential and contribute to a healthy work environment.

For most stressful situations, it is helpful when a leader/supervisor can respond in a calm rational and positive manner. This can help lessen the intensity of workers emotions and encourage them to see the situation more objectively. In contrast, it can be very unhelpful when leader/supervisors overreact or allow their own emotions into the mix, further fuelling workers emotions.

When leader/supervisors react in unhelpful ways, it can send a message to workers that they are incapable of remaining calm and leading the team through hard times. Conversely, managers who can help resolve an emotionally charged problem, or demonstrate empathy, can give workers confidence that they are overseen by strong, competent, leaders.

Below are some common situations in which workers may feel scared, angry or sad, as well as examples of unhelpful and helpful ways in which managers can respond.

Self-Awareness

Situations that trigger fear and ways to respond		
Situation	Response is more likely to trigger fear	Responses less likely to trigger fear
A worker makes a costly mistake at work	Blame the worker and question his or her ability to do the job properly	Remind the worker that mistakes happen, help to focus on problem solving
There have been talks about budget cuts and layoffs. Workers are asking you for information.	Thoughtlessly state: I think I have an idea who will be let go but I cannot talk about it	Empathise with their concern. Tell them you will share as much information as you can and keep communication ongoing. If layoffs are inevitable, talk about resources available to those who may need it e.g., Community resources and/or company benefits.
A worker is about to make a presentation but thinks that it will go poorly.	Urge the worker to make a good presentation no matter what, as the whole department depends on it. Reassure the worker that he has prepared well for the presentation, make encouraging comments	I am not concerned at all about your ability to give presentations, I have seen you speaking at meetings and you do a great job
A worker shows up in the manager's office for a performance review. The worker jokes nervously, okay so how bad is it this time?	Ignore the joke and maintain a serious look.	Keep a warm, relaxed expression. Ask if the worker is nervous. Remind them that a review is a positive, growth opportunity
It is a worker's second month on the job and she seems to have a hard time learning the tasks	Point out that most workers can learn the tasks by this time.	Show concern about the worker's progress, but focus on asking what you can provide to help her succeed
Workers on your team are unlikely to meet a looming deadline for an important project	Express your frustration openly to them: my reputation is on the line I will be hacked off if we do not meet the deadline.	Point out the problem in a calm manner, without placing blame on anyone. I accept responsibility as a manager for the delay. Focus on problem solving how can we work together to meet this deadline
A worker reports to you that another worker has been bullying him about his sexuality.	Ask the worker about his sexuality. Do not take his complaint seriously. Express doubt that he is telling the truth	Maintain a calm presence and do not act surprised or shocked. Assume the worker is telling the truth. Express empathy: I am sorry to hear what you are going through Thank the worker for informing. You indicate that you take these complaints seriously and inform the worker of your next steps and actions

Self-Awareness

Situations that trigger anger and ways to respond		
Situation	*Response is more likely to trigger anger*	*Responses less likely to trigger anger*
You had to choose one worker to promote from several qualified applicants. Today, you announce which worker received the promotion.	*Talk about workers in a disrespectful way: I know you have all been drooling over this job. Tell workers that only the successful applicant was qualified, whilst the rest were not good enough*	*Thank everyone for their interest. Acknowledge the efforts they put into their applications. Acknowledge that it was a tough decision. Remind workers that new opportunities may continue to arise*
Your team is delayed in finishing a project because of a worker's negligence	*Highlight to the team that it was one of the worker's fault. Show frustration my shaking your head, sighing and criticising the worker behind his back.*	*Show team spirit to the workers. De-emphasise the blame from the worker and focus on finishing the project team. Validate feelings of frustration: I can understand that everyone is frustrated they must work overtime. I really appreciate you for your professionalism and working through this as a team*
Your team is expanding and there are not enough offices for everybody.	*Allocate new offices to your favourite workers, without consulting the entire group of workers about space allocation.*	*Make sure the process is transparent as possible. Let workers know the criteria upon which you are basing your choices (possibly workload, seniority or job description). Thank the workers for understanding. Let them know that you are working on providing everyone the space they need.*
During a team meeting that you are chairing, two workers engaged in a debate that turns heated.	*Joining the argument. Say something disrespectful: okay let us not have a fight over this*	*Try to de-escalate with words in a calm light-hearted tone: I am glad to see that we all feel strongly about this issue. Retain control over the meeting. Unfortunately, we must move on to other topics. We might need to schedule another meeting just talk about this issue.*
A front-desk worker has just been verbally abused by a client and seems upset.	*Ask what happened and then walk away, without offering any words of comfort or care*	*Ask with a caring attitude what happened. Express concern about how the worker was treated. Show empathy to the worker: No one should be treated that way at work. We will need to file an incident report*
You and the worker are disagreeing over work-related issues. The worker seems to be getting frustrated and annoyed	*Keep emphasising your point and take on a hostile tone. Say something disrespectful: Whether you like it or not, this is how I want it maybe you still do not get it. Do I have to explain it again?*	*Pause the conversation. Acknowledge what you see: you seem really frustrated with this. It can help to get the emotions out before any rational thinking continues. Tell me what is going on. Why are you getting upset? Remain calm, keep focused and respectful*

Self-Awareness

Situations that trigger anger and ways to respond - Continued		
Situation	Response is more likely to trigger anger	Responses less likely to trigger anger
A worker has just ended a call with a customer and seems very frustrated	*Assume that the worker did not handle the call competently: do you need help with handling the phone calls?*	*Give the worker the benefit of the doubt. Ask what happened. Empathise with the worker. Sometimes it helps the worker, calm down when you paraphrase what they said simply using simpler, calmer words: So, the client got upset and called you stupid because he thought that you had lost his file?*
Its late Friday afternoon and you have just given a worker a large and important task which is due for completion by the end of the day.	*Tell the worker matter-of-factly about the last-minute task. It is her job, after all.*	*Recognise that workers need to leave work on time. Acknowledge late notice of the task and thank the worker for understanding. Plan for what is reasonable and feasible to complete.*

People tend to be triggered into an anger reaction if they feel:

- *Embarrassed*
- *Humiliated*
- *Insulted*
- *Afraid*
- *Rejected*

They can feel this if they feel someone is taking them down, ignoring them or not taking them seriously.

Any person who is not treated with respect could react to a trigger you give them.

Therefore, they will regard your actions as being the cause of their reaction, even though they may behave in a manner which is considerably worse than yours. The net result is, they will claim you started it!

Self-Awareness

Situations that trigger sadness (or hurt) and ways to respond		
Situation	Responses more likely to trigger sadness or hurt	Responses less likely to trigger sadness or hurt
One of your workers has just been rejected for a grant that he had worked hard to apply for and was hoping to get.	Dwell on the negatives and on the past. Say things that are unproductive: Wow that is too bad. That grant would have helped you a lot. You work so hard for it too. That is two weeks of your life you will never get back.	Empathise with the worker: that is frustrating, because you worked hard to apply for this. Focus on the positives: you did not get the grant, but you put together a good proposal that you can use for future projects.
During a team social event you notice that a worker is trying to mingle with others but is not being accepted	Ignore what you saw and go and mingle with other managers.	Try to make everyone feel included. Make small talk with the worker.
A worker seems ashamed as he is receiving negative feedback from you about his work	ignore what you see, thinking, "that's not my problem". Continue with the negative feedback.	Speak in a respectful, light-hearted tone. Acknowledge what you see. Express empathy with the worker's feelings: it is hard to hear this kind of feedback. But we know that it helps us be better in the long run. How can I help you make improvements?
A well-liked staff member is leaving and the workers seem sad to see her go	Do not acknowledge her upcoming departure	Acknowledge the situation and the worker's feelings: we are all sad to see her go. Focus on the positives: she is off to a very exciting new job. We will wish her all the best
There has been a massive layoff today in the company and some of the workers although spared, are quiet and sombre.	Focus on the negatives: it is so quiet in here now that some of you are gone. It is going to be a ghost town soon.	Empathise with the worker's feelings. Maintain a neutral attitude. Focus on the positives: the company always tries to find laid off staff other positions within the company.

Inhibitors are things which prevent people from completely losing their temper. Not everyone gets violent when they become angry and this is due to our inhibitions or our inhibitors.

- *self-control*
- *personal values*
- *fear that the other party may fight back*
- *social or legal consequences*
- *experience*
- *training*

Your choice of response is vitally important. You may even have passed the fight or flight stage, but we can still choose to escalate or de-escalate the situation. If you react at an emotional level, you could easily make the situation worse.

Self-Awareness

Your response such as pointing a finger could be a trigger which leads to an escalation to aggression and / or violence.

> *You must consciously choose to respond to the incident in a way which we de-escalate the situation by thinking about every step you take.*

As we become more aware of the triggers in our life which typically lead to an emotional reaction, so we can begin to find ways to manage them. These triggers can come in many forms. It may be the reaction to a mistake made by an employee, or a spill caused by a young child or a reaction to another driver who we consider has endangered us. Worse still it could be reaching out to an alcoholic drink or smoking a cigarette, after a trigger, both of which are highly addictive and can have seriously grave repercussions on our health and longevity.

It is therefore important that we recognise the triggers and we manage our emotional response to that trigger. It could be as simple as counting to ten before we react or learning strategies to deal effectively with the problem, so the trigger becomes irrelevant.

We know the problems of over-reacting, blowing things out of proportion, or lashing out in anger. But what can we do about it?

Notice when you get triggered

If you want to handle your emotional triggers better, you first need to notice when you get triggered. You need to become aware that you have been triggered and that your emotions are kicking in.

These are some helpful suggestions on things to look out for:

- **Body:** *Shallow breathing, rapid heartbeat and sick to the stomach*
- **Emotions:** *Experiencing a fight-or-flight response, either feeling like a 'deer in the headlights' or having an emotional outburst*
- **Thoughts:** *Feeling like a victim, thoughts of blame and judgment, difficulty paying attention*

Triggers almost always have long histories behind them. When we get triggered, it is very often because it brings back something from the past, that *"she's doing that, she's-doing-that-again feeling"*.

Triggers are also very often connected to a perceived inadequacy about ourselves that is a source of pain to us, like a raw nerve. This could be triggered by someone simply mentioning one of your identified weaknesses.
When you begin to feel a trigger, you need to manage your emotions and learn to master your responses to these negative events.

Self-Awareness

Impact of Own Behaviour on Others

Leader/supervisors always need to behave professionally and not let personal beliefs or opinions interfere with their judgment and actions. They need to lead by example and be aware of the strengths, weaknesses and needs of people around them.

The way in which you react to a person or situation will directly affect how they react back to you. This is known as stimulus and response. When we provide a stimulus, it will prompt a response from the person receiving the stimulus – how they respond will directly affect behaviour.

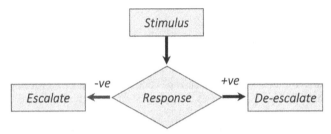

If the response is positive - the situation will de-escalate, whereas, if the response is negative - the situation has the potential to escalate and become more serious.

The Attitude and Behaviour Cycle

It is extremely unlikely that you will have a positive attitude towards everyone you meet. Some people, for any number of reasons, will cause you to have negative feelings towards them. If

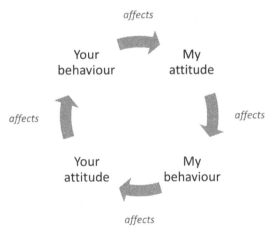

you have these negative feelings, you will communicate this unconsciously to them and their reaction will also be negative.

Once the person has become aware of your negative feeling, they will behave in a negative manner towards you. This will cause your negative feelings to cause you to behave in a negative manner. This will then cause them to behave in a negative way which will, in turn,

Self-Awareness

increase your negative feelings and behaviour and so, the cycle continues and the situation deteriorates even further.

It is very difficult to change your attitude towards someone. However, you can easily change your behaviour. You need to learn to behave in such a way that your negative feelings do not show and the behaviour does not reveal any negative traits. This will break the cycle and stop it getting worse.

In all activities, leader/supervisors need to think about how their behaviour:

- *is perceived by others*
- *impacts their own performance*
- *affects working relationships*

Any individual's performance and behaviour can affect other people, but a leader/supervisors role puts them in a responsible and influential position. Leaders are nearly always a focus for attention, which makes sense as being visible and vocal are important elements of the role.

However, people can judge leaders harshly and transfer their loyalty and support elsewhere very quickly. One only has to look at how often sports team managers and coaches are criticised or sacked to know how fragile a leader's position can be.

In the workplace, it is essential for leader/supervisors to make sure that their behaviour and leadership skills are of the highest standard so that they can provide effective leadership. As part of the leadership role, leader/supervisors need to be able to:

- *use good communication skills consistently*
- *lead and manage a stable, well-motivated and engaged team*
- *help their teams to meet organisational needs and objectives*
- *offer effective and imaginative solutions to problems*
- *bring energy, enthusiasm and a clear focus*
- *bring a balanced and positive attitude to change*

On a day-to-day level, examples of positive and inspirational leadership behaviour could include:

using excellent communication skills – *able to engage and inspire team members and make them feel valued*

being fair and consistent – *when making decisions or solving problems*

good timekeeping and attendance – *to show commitment to and respect for the team and its objectives*

performing at consistently high levels – *leading the way to achieve deadlines, targets and quality standards*

displaying good conduct and behaviour – *that minimise discomfort, stress, resentment and embarrassment for other team members*

following good working practices – *that avoid unnecessary harm or injury, lost work time or disciplinary procedures*

Self-Awareness

A leader/supervisor whose behaviour is positive, inspirational and professional will have the respect of team members, colleagues and other stakeholders. They will be able to deal with plans, strategies, decisions and problems with the positive support of those around them.

On the other hand, a leader/supervisor whose behaviour is negative for any length of time will soon lose the support of their team and colleagues. They will find it impossible to inspire and lead their team if they do not have their respect and cooperation. A leader/supervisor who is always late, loses their temper, acts unfairly and inconsistently, will quickly come up against complaints from customers, colleagues and others and find it very difficult to carry out their operational duties effectively.

From time to time, there will be unexpected circumstances that will adversely affect a good leader/supervisor's behaviour, such as sudden illness or bereavement. When this happens, because they have a good and loyal working relationship, team members will usually combine to support them and help them through the difficult time.

Adapting Behaviour

Using self-awareness, it is possible to understand the impact of our behaviour on others and take steps to adapt when necessary.

As the psychotherapist Carl Jung said:

> *"There is no cure and no improving of the world that does not begin with the individual himself"*.

Self-awareness helps us to consciously think about how we influence and interact with others. If things are going well, reflection still helps because it enables us to see what we need to keep doing to maintain good working relationships. If there are problems, however, we need to reflect to see if any of our behaviours are causing issues.

With the help of self-refection and maybe a discussion with the line manager, we can:

- *identify how our behaviours impact others* – *in positive or negative ways*
- *consider alternative ways of behaving* – *research other ways of behaving*
- *try new approaches*
- *collect feedback about effectiveness* – *with more reflection or discussion*
- *implement further improvements*
- *review regularly*

If team members and colleagues are having problems, the causes may be nothing to do with their leader/supervisors personally. However, the leader/supervisor still needs to investigate causes so that they can approach team members in an appropriate manner, to see if they can help or support them with external problems.

Self-Awareness

Emotional Intelligence

Self-awareness is the first building block of emotional intelligence.

Definition:

Emotional intelligence is the capacity of an individual to be aware of, control and express their emotions and use them effectively in interpersonal relationships. It is the ability to step into someone else's shoes' and see things from their point of view.

It was developed as a psychological theory by Peter Salovey and John Mayer in 1997. They asserted that it is "the ability to perceive emotions, to access and generate emotions so as to assist thought, to understand emotions and emotional knowledge and to reflectively regulate emotions so as to promote emotional and intellectual growth."

The ability to understand how people feel and react can be extremely useful when leading others and can be applied on two levels:

personal – *understanding our own feelings or reactions*
interpersonal – *understanding other people's feelings and reactions*

As leader/supervisors we often work as a team or develop relationships with colleagues, customers and other stakeholders. A reasonable degree of emotional intelligence can help leader/supervisors be:

empathetic – *e.g., able to put themselves in other people's shoes*
sensitive to others – *e.g., able to sense and respond to their needs, problems and feelings*
understanding and sympathetic – *e.g., able to understand the complexities of life and make allowances when things go wrong*
good at reading other people's emotions correctly – *e.g., able to identify the less obvious causes for emotional outbursts*

These skills give leader/supervisors a great advantage, especially when they are involved with functions that rely on relationship management. Leaders with good emotional intelligence skills instinctively know how to manipulate situations, inspire and motivate people and get the best out of them.

Salovey and Mayer's Emotional Intelligence Theory
According to their definition, emotional intelligence is the ability to process information about your own and other people's emotions. It is also the ability to process this information to guide your thoughts and behaviour.
By definition therefore:

Self-Awareness

*emotionally intelligent people pay attention to, use, understand
and manage their emotions.*

According to these two authors, for a person to be categorised as emotionally intelligent, they
must have four basic abilities:

- *Ability to perceive and correctly express their emotions and other people's.*
- *The ability to use emotions in a way that facilitates thought.*
- *Capacity to understand emotions, emotional language and emotional signals.*
- *The ability to manage their emotions to achieve goals.*

In this particular emotional intelligence theory, each ability has four different stages. However,
this process does not necessarily happen spontaneously. On the contrary, it usually requires a
conscious effort.

1. Emotional Perception and Expression
The first emotional intelligence skill is identifying your own emotions and other people's.
You should be able to understand what you are feeling. This includes thoughts as well as
your emotions.

In the second stage, you acquire the ability to do the same with the way other people think
and feel. In other words, you can understand other people's feelings, or the feelings
expressed by a piece of artwork.

In the third stage, you acquire the ability to correctly express your emotions. Not only that,
but you learn to communicate your needs.

In the fourth and last stage, you gain the ability to distinguish between correct and
incorrect emotional expressions.

Self-Awareness

2. Emotional Thought

In the first stage, emotions help you direct your thoughts to the most important information. In this stage, you are not yet able to take your own emotions into account.

During the second stage, your emotions start to intensify so you can identify them. As a result, you can use them to help you make decisions.

According to Salovey and Meyer, your emotions affect your mood in the third stage, meaning you can consider different points of view on a particular subject.

Lastly, in the fourth stage, your emotions help you make good decisions and think more creatively.

3. Understanding Emotions

You acquire the ability to distinguish between basic emotions and learn to use the right words to describe them. Then, this ability takes you to the second stage where you are able to place the emotion in your emotional state.

In the third stage, you can interpret complex emotions.

Lastly, you acquire the ability to detect the transitions between emotions. For example, the transition from anger to shame or surprise to joy.

4. Emotional regulation for intellectual and emotional growth

To begin, this ability requires your willingness not to limit the important role that your emotions have.

This is much easier to achieve with positive emotions than negative emotions. During this step, you will let yourself choose which emotions you want to identify with according to whether they are useful or not.

In the previous step, you acquire the ability to study emotions. This would happen according to how influential, reasonable, or clear the emotions are. Lastly, you would be able to regulate your emotions and other people's, moderating the negative ones and increasing the positive ones.

Goleman's Theory of Emotional Intelligence

One model that explains emotional intelligence was developed by Daniel Goleman, a psychologist and science journalist, following on from Salovey and Mayer's theory. The theory identifies four components:

> *Self-awareness* – *the conscious knowledge of our character, beliefs, emotions, qualities and desires*
> *Self-management and motivation* – *the ability to stay calm under pressure and stay motivated to achieve goals*
> *Social awareness* – *the ability to have empathy and understand other people's emotions and feelings*

Self-Awareness

Relationship skills – *the ability to influence, negotiate, communicate, build rapport and develop networks*

The diagram shows, the focus for emotional intelligence is relationship management. Emotional development can be achieved through:

- *team-building exercises*
- *coaching*
- *training in negotiation and communication skills*

In leadership roles, emotional intelligence can provide an extra insight into which approach will be most effective when guiding and inspiring the team to follow. By using emotional intelligence, leaders can:

read other people's feelings and reactions more accurately
adapt their approach
employ appropriate skills

According to Goleman, the higher someone goes in an organisation, the more the emotional skills matter.

Senior managers and directors can hire people with the skills and knowledge that the organisation needs, but they need to be very competent in emotional intelligence themselves. Good relationship capabilities become more critical as careers progress.

Self-Awareness

Qualities of people with high EI

1. They're not perfectionists.
Being a perfectionist can get in the way of completing tasks and achieving goals since it can lead to having trouble getting started, procrastinating and looking for the right answer when there is not one. Therefore, people with EI are not perfectionists. They realise that perfection does not exist and push forward. If they make a mistake, they will adjust and learn from it.

2. They know how to balance work and play.
Working 24/7 and not taking care of yourself adds unnecessary stress and health problems to your life. Because of this, people with EI know when it is time to work and when to play. For example, if they need to disconnect from the world for a couple of hours, or even an entire weekend, they will because they need the time to unplug to reduce the stress levels.

3. They embrace change.
Instead of dreading change, emotionally intelligent people realise that change is a part of life. Being afraid of change hinders success, so they adapt to the changes around them and always have a plan in place should any sort of change occur.

4. They do not get easily distracted.
People with high EI can pay attention to the task at hand and are not easily distracted by their surroundings, such as text or random thought.

5. They're empathetic.
Being able to relate to others, show compassion and take the time to help someone are all crucial components of EI. Additionally, being empathic makes people with EI curious about other people and leads them to ask lots of questions whenever they meet someone new.

6. They know their strengths and weaknesses.
Emotionally intelligent people know what they are good at and what they are not so great at. They have not just accepted their strengths and weaknesses; they also know how to leverage their strengths and weaknesses by working with the right people in the right situation.

7. They're self-motivated.
Were you that ambitious and hard-working kid who was motivated to achieve a goal--and not just because there was a reward at the end? Being a real go-getter, even at a young age, is another quality possessed by people with EI.

8. They do not dwell in the past.
People with high EI do not have the time to dwell in the past because they are too busy contemplating the possibilities that tomorrow will bring. They do not let past mistakes consume them with negativity. They do not hold grudges. Both add stress and prevent us from moving forward.

Self-Awareness

9. They focus on the positive.
Emotionally intelligent people would rather devote their time and energy to solving a problem. Instead of harping on the negative, they look at the positive and what they have control over. Furthermore, they also spend their time with other positive people and not the people who constantly complain.

10. They set boundaries
While people with high EI may seem like pushovers because of their politeness and compassion, they have the power to establish boundaries. For example, they know how to say no to others. The reason? It prevents them from getting overwhelmed, burned out and stressed because they have too many commitments. Instead, they are aware that saying no frees them up from completing previous commitments.

Self-Awareness

Inclusivity and Unconscious Bias

Unconscious Bias is related to equality and diversity and is therefore linked directly to inclusivity.

When we consider our self-awareness, we also need to examine our unconscious bias as it can affect all aspects of the work environment – e.g., management of individuals, recruitment, training, promotion opportunities, performance management or customer service.

Definitions

Being aware of the need for inclusivity in the workplace is important, as is an awareness that we need to avoid unconscious bias when making decisions that affect the workforce, customers and other stakeholders. But what do these terms mean?

Unconscious Bias

"the unintended inclination or prejudice for or against an individual or a group"

Everyone has unconscious bias. It is a natural and unintended influence on how we make decisions, based on unconscious preferences rather than careful, conscious consideration. We naturally favour others who are like us or share the same values – e.g., in looks, attitudes, education, accent, colour, ethnicity, beliefs or work ethic.

Information that influences us can come from many sources – e.g., our own experiences and upbringing; what we read, hear or see around us or in the media; other people we meet; education and family background; what we have seen and learned in the workplace. Our brains react to information all the time and they use unconscious shortcuts to speed up decision making processes.

Although unconscious bias can be useful in a dangerous situation, where we must make a split-second decision about survival, it is not a useful attribute when making decisions in the workplace. We need to overcome any instinctive judgements and make conscious, well-rounded and well considered decisions, especially when dealing with colleagues, customers and others.

Inclusivity

"the intention or policy of including people who might otherwise be excluded"

Self-Awareness

We often here about how something is exclusive and this is seen as something positive and desirable. It implies that it is a special privilege to be part of a select group that will only allow a few, carefully chosen people to join or be associated with it. However, this attitude is not helpful or desirable in the workplace. It leads to discrimination, which is illegal on certain grounds and has very negative impacts on the organisation and its stakeholders – anyone who has anything to do with it.

Instead, organisations need to be inclusive. They need to have policies of including people who might otherwise be left out.

An organisation that embraces inclusivity can have many benefits including:

a more diverse workforce – *e.g., people from many different backgrounds with a wide variety of attributes, experience, skills, knowledge and culture*

being able to tap into a wide of range human resources – *that may not seem obvious at first*

the ability to offer a diverse range of products and services – *to a diverse range of customers and service users*

more diverse opportunities to expand and stabilise its position in the market – *creating opportunities that a less inclusive organisation would miss*

being able to offer more secure employment – *due to its wide appeal to a broad range of customers*

Effects of Unconscious Bias on Inclusion

When considering our own self-awareness, we need to make sure that our words and actions support inclusivity and make sure that everyone feels valued and included – e.g., minority groups generally; people with disabilities; people from different cultures, ethnic groups or religions; people with unusual skills; people who have a great deal to offer but may not mix easily.

Whilst emotional intelligence can give valuable insight into working relationships, we need to make sure that we do not apply too much of ourselves and our experiences, when making decisions. This is particularly true when dealing with, for example:

- *recruitment of staff*
- *promotion and career development of team members*
- *evaluating team members and recognising their strengths and weaknesses*

For example, a manager who went to university may favour job candidates who also went to university, even though other candidates are just as suitable for the job. The manager unconsciously remembers how their own university experience shaped and helped them in their career and they assume that a degree is essential, even if it is not a mandatory requirement in the job description. This is called affinity bias, where the manager feels an affinity with people who have the same life experiences.

Self-Awareness

The university experience can be a harmless link that makes for easier communication when getting to know someone. However, if that manager fails to think consciously about all the candidates and just favours the graduates, when there is no operational reason to do so, their action would be discriminatory and potentially liable for legal action. They need to include all suitable candidates in their shortlist, not just the graduates.

Another form of unconscious bias is known as the halo effect, where a positive trait is transferred to someone without any evidence. For example, a team member who speaks with a 'posh' accent, uses body language very effectively and wears designer clothes may be considered as having better skills, knowledge and experience than they actually have. If selected for an unsuitable role, the manager and organisation could suffer:

> *complaints* – e.g., from dissatisfied colleagues or customers when the candidate proves unsuitable
>
> *increased costs* – e.g., from additional training or recruitment costs
>
> *a bad reputation* – e.g., from showing poor judgement

Where unconscious bias is against a protected characteristic under the Equality Act 2010, it can be discriminatory and possibly lead to legal action. The nine protected characteristics are:

> *age*   *race*
> *disability or impairment*   *religion or beliefs*
> *gender*   *sexual orientation*
> *gender reassignment*   *pregnancy or maternity*
> *marriage or civil partnership*

Discrimination based on these characteristics is illegal and complaints and legal action could be the serious consequences of forgetting about inclusivity and allowing unconscious bias to affect judgement.

Unconscious thoughts can be based on stereotypes and prejudices and unconscious bias when selecting people for promotion or recruitment can lead to:

- *discrimination in the workplace* – e.g., from allowing prejudices to affect judgement when selecting team members for promotion
- *possible legal action being taken* – e.g., if a team member is discriminated against on the grounds of a protected characteristic
- *a less diverse workforce* – e.g., if people of particular race are overlooked for promotion or recruitment
- *some people's talents being overstated* – e.g., if their image does not reflect the truth about their skills and attributes
- *some people's talents going unrecognised* – e.g., if they are awkward, shy and unable to 'sell' their considerable talents well

Self-Awareness

- *an inability to adapt to change* – e.g., from holding onto outdated, unhelpful and stereotypical ideas about people and their actions
- *an inability to exploit and develop new markets with diverse customers –* which restricts the chances of stability, success and sustainability for the organisation

Some of these effects apply to the organisation as a whole, but they can all be influenced by unconscious bias on a more personal level. A manager who is unaware of the impact of their own unconscious bias and how it affects their ability to be inclusive in their outlook, will have an effect on their team members, other teams and the organisation as a whole. Their inability to see how their instinctive prejudices affect people around them can easily lead to resentment, lack of respect and potentially serious consequences for all concerned.

Avoiding Unconscious Bias

Organisations usually have policies, procedures and training to help their staff treat colleagues, customers and other stakeholders equally and fairly. The main themes are to encourage respect and inclusion and to make it clear that discrimination will not be tolerated.

To support these policies, we can avoid and overcome our own unconscious bias by:

- *being aware that unconscious bias exists*
- *taking our time when making decisions* – to consider issues carefully before making decisions
- *justifying decisions* – with evidence and reasons for making the choices we have made
- *following best practice in all aspects of our work*
- *working with a wide range of people* – **and getting to know them as individuals**
- *being fair and focusing on positive behaviour* – and not making assumptions that might be incorrect
- *challenging negative stereotypes and prejudices* – our own and other people's
- *attending training on diversity, equality and inclusion*

Respect and awareness are the foundations of all good relationships. It is not necessary for people to share beliefs, interests or personal characteristics, they just need to be able to be aware and respect differences without prejudice.

Self-Awareness

Learning Styles

As part of a self-awareness assessment, it is helpful to understand different learning styles.

We all have our own preferences and it is useful to understand which learning styles apply to us so that we can use them during our career development.

We all have our preferred learning styles that we use to develop our skills, experience and knowledge.

Some people like to learn by reading about things, others need to see a demonstration to understand something and others need to try the activity themselves before they remember everything.

We often need repetition before new information can be absorbed and used – e.g., needing several driving lessons before using the car controls become simple to us. Adults usually need more repetition than children, so we should not be embarrassed if we do not understand something straightaway.

There are many theories about learning styles and here are some brief details about some of the most used theories:

VARK – Visual, Auditory, Reading/writing, Kinaesthetic

People have favourite ways of learning and training needs to be adapted to accommodate these preferences where possible. These four styles are:

Visual – **seeing and watching** – *e.g., seeing pictures of how to make the product, or watching instruction videos*
Auditory – **listening and speaking** – *e.g., being told how to make the product*
Reading/writing – *e.g., reading instructions and writing personal notes*
Kinaesthetic – **touching and doing** – *e.g., touching the components and making the product under supervision*

According to this model, people have a dominant or preferred learning style. When training team members, leader/supervisors need to be prepared to use a combination of all four skills so that everyone is learning style needs can be met.

- Aural (8%)
- Visual (32%)
- Kinesthetic (32%)
- Read/Write (28%)

Self-Awareness

- *A visual learner will learn about a subject by looking at graphs, pictures and diagrams, or watching videos or demonstrations. Just being told about what to do will not register. Touching and doing the new activity will help to reinforce the learning at a basic level, but they will need to observe and read up on the details.*
- *A reading/writing learner will learn best from reading instructions, research and information about the subject and writing notes to help them remember important details.*
- *An auditory learner will absorb the information by listening to their tutor or colleague, asking questions, then listening carefully to the answers.*
- *A kinaesthetic learner needs to touch and do the activity. They may absorb a reasonable amount of information from listening to the tutor or watching a demonstration, but they will not truly understand the subject or activity until they do it for themselves.*

VARK	*Very likely to appeal*	*Activity likely to appeal*
Visual *– benefit from seeing materials and watching others*	*Demonstrations Shadowing Computer-based training Internet-based training*	*Delegation Role-play Classroom-based training courses Blended learning Distance learning Workplace training*
Auditory *– benefit from being able to listen and discuss training*	*Demonstrations Shadowing*	*Classroom-based training courses Blended learning Workplace training*
Reading/writing *– benefit from reading training materials and making notes*	*Training manuals Reference books and journals Taking notes Computer-based training Internet-based training*	*Classroom-based training courses Blended learning Distance learning Workplace training*
Kinaesthetic *– benefit from being able to touch and handle items*	*Demonstrations Role-play Computer-based training Internet-based training*	*Job rotation Blended learning Workplace learning*

Self-Awareness

Gardner's Multiple Intelligences

In 1983, Harvard psychologist, Howard Gardner, developed a theory that stated there are several principles people use to understand and perceive the world.

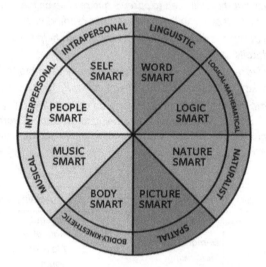

The theory has been refined since and the main principles are that people use these eight 'intelligences', as can be seen on Gardner's website – www.multipleintelligencesoasis.org:

linguistic – *the ability to use spoken or written words, sounds, rhythms or inflections*

logical-mathematical – *using reasoning and logic as well as numbers and abstract patterns*

spatial – *spatial awareness and the ability to mentally visualise objects – e.g., as used by an airline pilot or an architect*

bodily-kinaesthetic – *the ability to use the body control physical movements – e.g., using hands to solve problems*

musical – *the ability to master beats, tones and rhythms as well as music*

interpersonal – *the ability to communicate effectively with other people – e.g., to negotiate or develop workplace relationships*

intrapersonal – *understanding our own emotions, motivation and self-reflection*

naturalistic – *the ability to make distinctions in the world of nature – e.g., between different types of plants*

Self-Awareness

Gardner's Multiple Intelligences	Very likely to appeal	Quite likely to appeal
Linguistic – like to use words, sounds and rhythms	Delegation Demonstrations Role-play Shadowing Coaching and mentoring	Classroom-based training Computer-based training Internet-based training Blended learning Distance learning Workplace training Job rotation Project work
Logical-mathematical – like to use reasoning, numbers and abstract patterns	Training manuals Reference books and journals Taking notes Computer-based training Internet-based training	Classroom-based training courses Blended learning Distance learning Workplace training
Spatial – use spatial awareness and mental visualisation	Role-play Demonstrations Project work Delegation	Classroom-based training Blended learning Workplace training Job rotation
Bodily-kinaesthetic – benefit from being able to touch and handle items	Delegation Role-play Demonstrations Taking notes	Classroom-based training courses Job rotation Blended learning Workplace learning
Musical – benefit from responding to beats, rhythms, tones and music	Role-play Demonstrations Shadowing	Classroom-based training courses Blended learning Workplace training
Interpersonal – benefit from being able to communicate with other people and develop relationships	Role-play Coaching and mentoring Delegation Job rotation Project work	Demonstrations Shadowing Classroom-based training courses Blended learning
Intrapersonal – benefit from self-reflection and understanding their own emotions	Computer-based training Coaching and mentoring	Internet-based e-training Distance learning
Naturalistic – able to make distinctions in the world of nature	Demonstrations Shadowing Project work	Blended learning Delegation

Self-Awareness

Felder-Silverman Learning Style Model

This model was developed to help engineering students and their tutors, but it can be applied to other industries. The model shows four areas of personality that contribute to learning. A combination of these styles makes up an individual's learning preferences:

active or reflective – **how people prefer to process information** – *e.g., active people like to try things out and work with others in a group; reflective people prefer to think things through and work alone or with a familiar partner*

visual or verbal – **how people prefer information to be presented** – *e.g., visual learners prefer videos, pictures and charts; verbal learners prefer written and spoken explanations*

sensing or intuitive – **how people prefer to perceive or take in information** – *e.g., sensing learners prefer practical thinking, facts and procedures; intuitive people prefer conceptual thinking, theories and meanings*

sequential or global – **how people prefer to organise and progress towards understanding** – *e.g., sequential learners prefer linear thinking and small, incremental steps; global learners prefer holistic thinking, systems and learning in big steps*

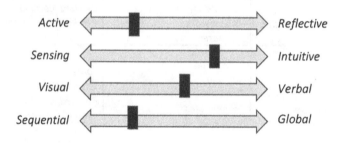

Self-Awareness

Felder-Silverman	Very likely to appeal	Quite likely to appeal
Active *– likes to work things out and work with others in a group*	*Delegation* *Demonstrations* *Role-play* *Job rotation* *Project work*	*Classroom-based training* *Computer-based training* *Internet-based training* *Blended learning* *Distance learning* *Workplace training*
Reflective *– likes to think things through and work alone or with a familiar partner*	*Computer-based training* *Coaching and mentoring*	*Internet-based e-training* *Distance learning* *Workplace training*
Visual *– benefit from seeing materials and watching others*	*Demonstrations* *Shadowing* *Computer-based training* *Internet-based training*	*Delegation* *Role-play* *Classroom-based training courses* *Blended learning* *Distance learning* *Workplace training*
Verbal *– benefit from written and spoken explanations*	*Delegation* *Demonstrations* *Role-play* *Shadowing* *Coaching and mentoring* *Classroom-based training* *Workplace training* *Job rotation* *Project work*	*Computer-based training* *Internet-based training* *Blended learning* *Distance learning*
Sensing *– prefer practical thinking, facts and procedures*	*Demonstrations* *Classroom-based training* *Workplace training* *Job rotation* *Project work* *Delegation*	*Computer-based training* *Internet-based training* *Blended learning* *Distance learning*
Intuitive *– prefer conceptual thinking, theories and meanings*	*Classroom-based training courses* *Role-play* *Computer-based training* *Internet-based training*	*Blended learning* *Workplace learning* *Distance learning*
Sequential *– prefer linear thinking and small, incremental steps*	*Computer-based training* *Internet-based training* *Blended learning* *Distance learning* *Coaching and mentoring*	*Workplace training* *Shadowing* *Demonstrations*
Global *– prefer holistic thinking, systems and learning in big steps*	*Shadowing* *Demonstrations* *Workplace training* *Delegation Role-play*	*Computer-based training* *Internet-based training* *Blended learning* *Distance learning*

Self-Awareness

Kolb's Experiential Learning Cycle

David Kolb developed this theory in 1979. It looks at four points to identify the way people learn:

experiencing – *learning and what was felt during the period of learning – e.g., having the first driving lesson and assessing it*

reflecting – *thinking about how useful the session was – e.g., learned to stop and start safely, learned to change gear smoothly*

thinking – *looking at ideas and theories that relate to the learning experience – e.g., looking at the functions of the car and the Highway Code*

acting – *testing the learning – e.g., practising using the gears smoothly when out with an experienced driver*

Part of Kolb's theory was that this process represents a circle or a spiral where people touch all the bases – i.e., a cycle of experiencing, reflecting, thinking and acting.

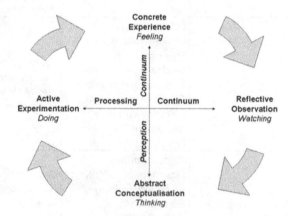

Self-Awareness

Kolb's Learning Cycle	Very likely to appeal	Quite likely to appeal
Experiencing *– having a go and assessing the experience*	*Delegation* *Demonstrations* *Role-play* *Job rotation* *Project work*	*Shadowing* *Blended learning* *Workplace learning*
Reflecting *– thinking about how useful the new subject or skill will be*	*Coaching and mentoring*	*Job rotation* *Shadowing* *Project work* *Classroom-based training* *Blended learning* *Distance learning* *Workplace learning*
Thinking *– looking for related ideas, theories and different approaches*	*Job rotation* *Shadowing* *Coaching and mentoring* *Project work*	*Demonstrations* *Role-play* *Classroom-based training* *Blended learning* *Distance learning* *Workplace learning*
Acting *– testing the learning and practising*	*Delegation* *Demonstrations* *Role-play* *Job rotation*	*Project work* *Classroom-based learning* *Blended learning* *Workplace learning*

Self-Awareness

Honey and Mumford's Learning Cycle

Peter Honey and Alan Mumford created a learning cycle as a variation of Kolb's theory in 1986. It is based on four approaches to learning:

activists do something – *these people actively enjoy challenges and learning new things*
reflectors think about it – *these people like to stand back and review learning experiences in a thoughtful manner*
theorists make sense of it – *these people like to think things through in logical steps*
pragmatists test it out – *these people like to try new ideas; they enjoy solving problems and making decisions as part of the learning process*

These are not seen as fixed personality characteristics. They can be changed at will or through changed circumstances, so each person can go through all four stages:

Honey and Mumford	Very likely to appeal	Quite likely to appeal
Activists *– like to do something*	Delegation Demonstrations Role-play Job rotation Project work	Classroom-based training Computer-based training Internet-based training Blended learning Distance learning Workplace training
Reflectors *– review progress, analyse and consider options*	Delegation Shadowing Coaching and mentoring	Project work Classroom-based training Computer-based training Internet-based training Blended learning Distance learning Workplace training
Theorists *– make sense of the options*	Shadowing Coaching and monitoring Classroom-based training Blended learning Workplace training	Demonstrations Computer-based training Internet-based training Distance learning
Pragmatists *– try out the options, evaluate the experience and progress, then decide how to proceed*	Delegation Demonstrations Role-play Job rotation Project work Blended learning	Classroom-based training Workplace training

Self-Awareness

Conscious Competence Learning Model

The conscious competence theory and related matrix model explain the process and stages of learning a new skill (or behaviour, ability, technique, etc.) The concept is commonly known as the 'conscious competence learning model', or 'conscious competence learning theory'; sometimes 'conscious competence ladder' or 'conscious competence matrix'.

Occasionally in more recent versions a fifth stage or level is added to the conscious competence theory, although there is no single definitive five-stage model, despite there being plenty of very useful and valid debate about what the fifth stage might be. The fifth stage is commonly represented, among other suggestions, as:

Conscious competence of unconscious competence, which describes a person's ability to recognise and develop unconscious incompetence in others.

Arguably this is a development in a different direction. The ability to recognise and develop skill deficiencies in others involves a separate skill set altogether, far outside of an extension of the unconscious competence stage of any skill.

Whether four or five or more stages and whatever people choose to call it, the 'conscious competence' model remains essentially a very simple and helpful explanation of how we learn and also serves as a useful reminder of the need to train people in stages. This is a summary of the usage of the 'conscious competence' learning theory, including the 'conscious competence matrix' model, its extension/development and origins/history of the 'conscious competence' theory.

The earliest origins and various definitions of the 'conscious competence' learning theory are uncertain and could be very old; indeed, perhaps thousands of years.

Several claims of original authorship exist for the 'conscious competence' model's specific terminology, definitions, structure, etc., the most notable is Martin M Broadwell as originator and seems to be the earliest.

Four Stages of Competence

Learners tend to begin at stage 1 - *'unconscious incompetence'*
They pass through stage 2 - *'conscious incompetence'*
then through stage 3 - *'conscious competence'*
And ideally end at stage 4 - *'unconscious competence'*

If the awareness of skill and deficiency is low or non-existent - i.e., the learner is at the unconscious incompetence stage - the learner will simply not see the need for learning.

It is essential to establish awareness of a weakness or training need (conscious incompetence) prior to attempting to impart or arrange training or skills necessary to move trainees from stage 2 to 3. People only respond to training when they are aware of their own need for it and the personal benefit they will derive from achieving it.

Self-Awareness

Conscious Competence Learning Matrix

Learner progression is from quadrant 1 through 2 and 3 to 4. It is not possible to jump stages. For some skills, especially advanced ones, people can regress to previous stages, particularly from 4 to 3, or from 3 to 2, if they fail to practise and exercise their new skills. A person regressing from 4, back through 3, to 2, will need to develop again through 3 to achieve stage 4 - unconscious competence again.

For certain skills in certain roles, stage 3 (conscious competence) is perfectly adequate and in some cases for the reasons which follow, may be desirable.

Interestingly, progression from stage to stage is often accompanied by a feeling of awakening - 'the penny drops' - things 'click' into place for the learner - the person feels like he/she has made a big step forward, which of course they have.

	Competence	*Incompetence*
	3 - conscious competence	**2 - conscious incompetence**
Conscious	*The person achieves 'conscious competence' in a skill when they can perform it reliably at will. The person will need to concentrate and think to perform the skill. The person can perform the skill without assistance the person will not reliably perform the skill unless thinking about it - the skill is not yet 'second nature' or 'automatic' the person should be able to demonstrate the skill to another but is unlikely to be able to teach it well to another person. The person should ideally continue to practise the new skill and if appropriate commit to becoming 'unconsciously competent' at the new skill practise is the most effective way to move from stage 3 to 4*	*The person becomes aware of the existence and relevance of the skill the person is therefore also aware of their deficiency in this area, ideally by attempting or trying to use the skill the person realises that by improving their skill or ability in this area their effectiveness will improve ideally the person has a measure of the extent of their deficiency in the relevant skill and a measure of what level of skill is required for their own competence the person ideally makes a commitment to learn and practice the new skill and to move to the 'conscious competence' stage*
	4 - unconscious competence	**1 - unconscious incompetence**
Unconscious	*The skill becomes so practised that it enters the unconscious parts of the brain - it becomes 'second nature' common examples are driving, sports activities, typing, manual dexterity tasks, listening and communicating it becomes possible for certain skills to be performed while doing something else, for example, knitting while reading a book the person might now be able to teach others in the skill concerned, although after some time of being unconsciously competent the person might actually have difficulty in explaining exactly how they do it - the skill has become largely instinctual this arguably gives rise to the need for long-standing unconscious competence to be checked periodically against new standards*	*The person is not aware of the existence or relevance of the skill area the person is not aware that they have a particular deficiency in the area concerned the person might deny the relevance or usefulness of the new skill the person must become conscious of their incompetence before development of the new skill or learning can begin the aim of the trainee or learner and the trainer or teacher is to move the person into the 'conscious competence' stage, by demonstrating the skill or ability and the benefit that it will bring to the person's effectiveness*

Self-Awareness

Identifying Learning Styles

Our preferred learning styles help us to make the most of the opportunities we have for working towards achieving our goals. We can, for example:

- *get the most out of learning and development activities*
- *enjoy the learning process more*
- *increase the chances of successful completion of training courses and programmes*

To address our learning styles in training and development, we need to:

- *find out about the learning and development activities that are available for our learning objectives*
- *select the best ones for our personal requirements*

Educational organisations have learning style questionnaires to help identify the preferred learning styles of individuals. By analysing the results, they can make sure that the learning materials and activities are compatible with each individual learner's preferences, where possible.

Questionnaires have a range of questions, which can be targeted on the workplace tasks and learning opportunities, or on general activities. For example, when trying a new recipe, tick which way you prefer to learn:

- *By reading the recipe in a book or online (visual)*
- *By watching a TV chef make the recipe (visual + auditory)*
- *By phoning a friend to ask for instructions (auditory)*
- *By having a go, following my instinct, tasting as I go (kinaesthetic)*

When analysing the results of learning style questionnaires, a mixture of styles is identified, selected according to the skills and knowledge we need to learn.

When learning about a concept or theory, we may prefer to read about it (visual), look at graphs and graphics (visual), then write our own notes by hand to consolidate our understanding (kinaesthetic).

For a more practical skill, such as learning about how to use a new and complicated photocopier, we may listen to someone else's tips (auditory), watch them use the machine (visual), try it for ourselves (kinaesthetic) and read the instruction manual for more advanced settings (visual).

The Chinese philosopher, Confucius, is thought to have said over two thousand years ago:

I hear and I forget

Self-Awareness

I see and I remember
I do and I understand

For many people, the learning is not successful until they have done the task themselves, which is something we need to consider when choosing development activities.

Appropriate Activities for Learning

By considering preferred learning styles it can help to select the most effective learning and development activities. There are many learning and development options, based inside or outside the workplace. A combination of activities can be put together to suit the individual's needs, as well as the organisational objectives.

Activity	Advantages	Disadvantages
Coaching	*can be arranged very quickly does not always detract from the workload specific to the individual*	*personality clashes difference of opinions maybe time constraints due to logistics*
Internal training course	*usually, low-cost can be arranged quickly*	*Time away from workload Familiarity*
External training course	*usually leads to a formal qualification individual can take some time away from the office environment*	*Cost time away from work*
On-the-job shadowing	*immediate sharing ideas and resources*	*Personality clashes difference of opinions possible conflict*
Secondment	*retained within the business broadens experience within the company*	*Time away from main work role possible conflict-of-interest, dependent on work areas involved*
Special assignment	*provides ownership and accountability interesting and varied*	*Time required to monitor and review*

Self-Awareness

Personal Development Planning (PDP)

It has never been more important that your personal skill set is developed to meet the demands of today's leader/supervisor.

There is little point in focussing on developing a team if there is no focus on personal development.

In reality, one could continue to develop a team until, at a personal level, one makes one is self-redundant!

All leader/supervisors need a broad range of skills in order to lead others effectively.

Personal and Professional Development

There was a time when personal and professional development was provided and managed by the employer. You went on a few courses chosen by your company, said yes when you were offered the chance to take on a new project and waited until the time was right to move up or move on. It is not like that anymore.

These days, **you** are responsible for your personal and professional development and **you** need to look for your own opportunities.

In order to achieve this, you need to know what needs to be changed and what needs to be developed. The only way to do this is to take a deep and thorough look at ourselves, not just at work, but personally too.

How can you manage and direct others if you do not have knowledge of your own weaknesses and inadequacies?

Professional Development
Professional Development can be defined as:

"the process of improving and increasing capabilities through access to education and training opportunities in the workplace, through outside organisations, or by watching others perform the job."

Self-Awareness

Professional Development is focused on gaining new capabilities and experience and improving the knowledge and skills that improve your potential in your work environment. These are the skills that make you more efficient and effective at your job. It is also suggested that it helps build and maintain the morale of staff members and is thought to attract higher quality staff to an organisation.

This means professional development is either related to the current role or the role you want next.

With changes to our working lives happening every day, be it economic change, amendments in legislation or even the advance of technology, it is important to develop your skillset to remain effective in your career.
Effective professional development involves ensuring your knowledge and understanding of your area of expertise for your career is always at the highest possible level. It is the process of gaining skills and knowledge to advance a career, but it also includes an element of personal development.

Broadly speaking, it may include formal types of vocational education or training that leads to a career related qualification. It can also include informal training and development programmes, which may be delivered on the job in order to develop and enhance skills.

Some examples of professional development are:

- *IT training*
- *Health and Safety*
- *Accountancy or budgeting*
- *Legal knowledge or expertise*

These could be delivered in many different methods, such as classroom-based learning, eLearning, coaching, consultation, mentoring and more.

Professional development is not only about climbing the "greasy pole" or earning more money. It is also about avoiding stagnation in your career and futureproofing yourself. When you expand your skills beyond your current role, you are preparing yourself for more and that makes you more valuable to employers.

Professional Development Opportunities
An opportunity either enhances your brand or takes your career where you want to go. Opportunities include:

- *Managing bigger budgets, more people or larger projects*
- *Attending professional training or gaining sought-after qualifications*
- *Volunteering as a buddy or taking on corporate charity work*
- *Taking on a role to gain specific experience, knowledge or skills*
- *Raising your profile by public speaking or leading a sales presentation*

Self-Awareness

Benefits of Professional Development

Offering professional development allows employees to perform better and prepares them for positions of greater responsibility. It can also help employers attract top job candidates, retain their best workers and identify future leaders. Moreover, ongoing professional development is very appealing to many employees today who are looking to keep their skills relevant in a rapidly changing world.

Investing in workers is beneficial to the whole organisation and can boost the bottom line. The list below identifies the organisational benefits which can be expected as a result of effective professional development training initiatives:

Increase the collective knowledge of the team

Encouraging employees to train in relevant subjects and applications — an advanced course in a software program they use daily, for example — can have an immediate effect on productivity. Professional development can also help raise overall staff expertise when employees with vastly different backgrounds and levels of experience are encouraged to share information.

Increase job satisfaction

When staff members can do their jobs more effectively, they become more confident. This leads to greater job satisfaction and improved employee retention. There are a range of low-cost professional development training options to choose from, including mentorships, job shadowing and cross training.

Improve the brand image

When training and development opportunities are on offer, they build a positive reputation as an employer that cares about its workforce and strives to employ only the best. Customers and clients will benefit too, from the high level of efficient service they receive. Keep in mind that employees are the brand ambassadors. When they attend conferences and seminars, they represent and reflect all that is good about an organisation.

Attract the right kind of applicant

To attract the most highly driven and career-focused candidates when advertising a job applicants want more than a competitive salary and benefits. They want the opportunity to grow professionally or expand their career options if they come to work for you. Development opportunities provide that.

Improve retention

Workers want to feel like they are appreciated and making a difference. But they also want to feel like they are gaining expertise and becoming more well-rounded. If team members do not feel challenged, or they sense stagnation in their careers, they will look for advancement opportunities elsewhere. Lifelong learning exposes employees to new experiences and keeps them engaged in their work. Professional development training helps build and maintain enthusiasm, but it also inspires loyalty.

Succession planning

Self-Awareness

Some employees will clearly fall into the management material category. Professional development programs are tools for grooming future leaders for the organisation. In order to promote internally to managerial positions in the future, targeted training now can help ensure the best and brightest are ready to move up.

Personal Development

Personal development is about improving talents and potential, both in and out of the workplace.

Personal Development can be defined as:

> *"the process of improving oneself through such activities as enhancing employment skills, increasing consciousness and building wealth."*

Personal development sits alongside professional growth —To progress in a career, personal development will be needed first. That is the only way to handle your fears, take on more responsibility and succeed with greater challenges. Personal Development requires development and broadening of knowledge, improvement and development of skills and refinement of behaviours to ensure optimum performance and professionalism.

This is illustrated in this example:

> *There are two people in your team, both of whom are great at their job. They are both accurate, detail-oriented and deliver the results needed. However, one of them is a real people person. Their interpersonal and communication skills are fantastic and, as a result of this, they have no problem getting the information they require quickly from colleagues at any level. The other person does not have this skill and often encounters conflict from colleagues, perhaps for many different reasons.*

Which of these people needs personal development?

Both can do their jobs. Both have the skills required on a professional level to deliver results, however, with the benefit of excellent relationship building skills one of them will always be one step ahead.

Examples of personal development are:

- *Leadership training*
- *Management training*
- *Time management*
- *Handling difficult situations and conflict management*
- *Communication skills*

Self-Awareness

Personal development relates to life skills. These are what you need in order to achieve your life goals. It focuses on helping you improve your talents, whether they are related to your work or not.

Personal and professional development courses can improve your motivation and help you excel in your domain.

Personal development offers some major benefits:

- *Boosting self-awareness*
- *Increasing self-knowledge*
- *Developing your existing skills or learning new ones*
- *Renewing or building your self-esteem or identity*
- *Developing pre-existing talents or strengths*
- *Enhancing your employability*
- *Improve the quality of your life*
- *Positively affecting your social status and wealth*

Focusing on your personal development will effectively ensure the right skill sets are in place.

Activities suitable for Personal and Professional Development

Personal Development	Professional Development
Emotional Wellbeing	Management Training
Health and fitness	Skill-based training
Communication	Internal Assessment
Motivation	Conflict Resolution
Spirituality	Online Education
Self-belief	Networking
Journaling	Research

The Difference between Personal and Professional Development

It is clear from the definition that professional development pertains to enhancing a workforce and/or an individual within a workforce. Often the objectives here are specific to an organisation and its goals at a specific time and the skills that would be required to deliver their products/services.

The second definition indicates that personal development is required where employees, as individuals, seek to update their own knowledge and learn skills that they would like to have.

Self-Awareness

Personal Development is more unique to the individual and his/her objectives.

When contrasting personal versus professional development, it is probably easy to see the connection rather than trying to identify differences.

There is a link in that both professional and personal development are similar regarding a drive towards improvement, greater understanding and better effectiveness of individuals' (either an individual or a group).

Additionally, they are alike in that both require effort, time and resources (often money) to get involved in and both regularly reoccur for all individuals and not just professionals.

Whilst personal development might seem separate from professional life, it could in reality be a great way to achieve career objectives. It is not just what is learnt that could drive success at work; by making a commitment to personal development it is clear to the employer, there is a willingness to demonstrate dedication and an ability to learn and grow.

Personal development makes a difference in life on a daily basis. At almost every stage of life, there will be new learning which will help to develop and grow as a person.

There is no need to specifically pick one over the other. Personal development plans might have many aspects of professional development too. Sometimes, the issues can be interlinked as well.

The key to managing personal development is knowing strengths and areas for improvement. Knowing these can help develop weaknesses and turn them into strengths.

An accurate self-assessment will identify areas for improvement and it is important to be totally honest in order to improve the biggest weaknesses.

Personal Development also has a number of business benefits. A study reported that 42% of companies do not believe in using personal development coaches, yet the same study revealed that if these companies had used a coach, they would have increased their income by 46%!

Of those who had received coaching, the survey revealed:

- *62.4% of employees got smarter in goal setting*
- *52.4% of employees became more self-confident*
- *57.1% of employees experienced the lowest levels of stress*
- *25.7% of them left their vices and bad habits behind*
- *33% of employees say they are unlikely to fulfil their career aspirations in their current organisation*

Not only does personal development benefit the business in many ways, it can also benefit each individual employee in different ways:

Mental health/self-esteem – Personal development not only improves work life; it also can helps develop personal life in a variety of different ways. Keeping track of positive and negative behaviours can help manage them better, preventing negative behaviours and encouraging positives ones. This can help to, improve self-confidence and performance at work, whilst developing self-esteem and mental health.

Productivity/motivation – Personal development can increase productivity. Becoming aware of strengths and weaknesses can encourage the production higher quality work – seeing improvements can give a confidence boost and the motivation to achieve more.

Personal development will also help turn weaknesses into strengths, a poor attitude can be turned into a positive one –by recognising the impact and consequences of attitudes and how it can affect others around you. It is certainly not easy but becoming more aware of how others respond to or absorb moods/behaviours may encourage turning it into a positive attitude in order to encourage others in the workplace! This should provide the drive needed to become more productive and work harder to achieve personal objectives.

Improves Skills – improving your areas of development will also improve your skills, for example, if you are trying to improve your telephone manner, you can use your personal development tools to keep track of this in order to develop the skill. This could make you a more competent worker and your colleagues may even recognise that you are becoming more dynamic. This could open up opportunities for career growth and promotions. When you are able to identify these needs, you are able to work towards a personal development plan.

Which is more important?

Personal development is the foundation for everything that follows. Focussing on developing the core aspects first will allow greater forward movement professionally and with greater ease. This is because personal development is where core habits of success are first formed.

Consider this quote by author and speaker, Brian Tracy:

> *"Personal development is a major time-saver. The better you become, the less time it takes you to achieve your objectives."*

You cannot help others until you have helped yourself. If you have ever flown on a plane, you will know that you must put on your own oxygen mask first!

There are no quick fixes in growth and development. It is a continuous cycle of reflection and self-improvement. It never ends and that is the whole point.

Neither Personal nor Professional development can be completed satisfactorily without a depth of self-awareness which is far greater than we currently have. By having a thorough understanding of what you need to achieve and how to achieve it, you can develop the necessary skills by way of a solution.

Self-Awareness

The Need to Change

When thinking about changes to yourself, or to a team, it can be helpful to use Marshall Goldsmith's 'Wheel of Change'. The need to change can come about from the results that you obtain from a personal or team SWOT, feedback, not hitting KPI's, or as part of the self-assessment processes.

Marshall Goldsmith refers to the wheel of change as:

> *"the variety of options that are presented when wanting to become a better version of ourselves. It illustrates "the interchange of two dimensions we need to sort out before we become the person we want to be: The Positive to Negative axis tracks the elements that either help us or hold us back. The 'Change to Keep' axis tracks the elements that we determine to change or keep in the future. Thus, in pursuing any behavioural change we have four options: change or keep the positive elements, change or keep the negative."*

- **Creating:** *This is about all of the positive things that you want to create for yourself (Adding, Inventing) e.g. "I want to go for the promotion in 3-months-time – how do I add to my skills?"*
- **Preserving:** *These are the elements that we wish to keep in the future (Improving, Maintaining) e.g. "I know that I am good at communicating with key stakeholders – I want to keep improving this"*
- **Eliminating:** *These are the things that we wish to eliminate in the future (Eradicating, Reducing) e.g. "My time management is not effective because I spend too much time micro-managing my team – I need to let go"*
  Accepting: *The things that we need to accept in the future (Delaying, Making Peace) e.g., "There are certain things that I cannot influence or control – I need to accept this"*

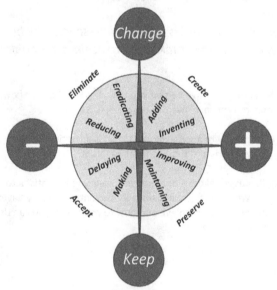

Self-Awareness

The Cost of Personal and Professional Development

Anything which is beneficial in life almost always comes at a cost and that is also true of Development.

There can be a personal cost as well as a cost for the organisation. It is, however, true to say that the cost of development is often far outweighed by the benefits it brings. The costs of development can include any or all of the following:

- *Financial cost of the training*
- *Time spent on training*
- *Expenses involved in attending the training*
- *The cost of providing mentors and coaches*
- *Loss of production whilst training*
- *Cost of replacement staff*

There may also be additional cost with regard to resources. It maybe that new software or machinery needs to be purchased in order to facilitate the development. It may be that structural alterations may be needed to facilitate this or additional resources such as PPE may need to be purchased. It may require that other staff need to be trained first to bring them to a standard whereby they can perform the task being left vacant by another staff member taking up their development.

Resources and Support Mechanisms

Resources and support mechanisms that suit the individual needs, objectives, circumstances and organisation need to be arranged. These include, for example:

- *development activities*
- *support mechanisms*
- *time and money*

Development Activities

Activities may include, for example:

delegation – e.g., *offering tasks to challenge the individual and give them the opportunity to develop their skills and experience*

demonstrations – e.g., *watching demonstrations about how a new piece of equipment is used, then trying it out*

role-play – e.g., *to practise how to deal with angry customers' complaints*

job rotation – e.g., *training team members on all the tasks performed by the team so that they can develop their skills, keep their interest and motivation levels up and be able to cover for each other*

Self-Awareness

shadowing – *e.g., arranging for a trainee to follow an experienced member of staff for a week*

coaching and mentoring – *e.g., giving intensive one-to-one support and guidance; having a senior member of staff as a role model*

project work – *e.g., expanding knowledge and experience by following through all aspects of a project and not just isolated tasks*

classroom-based training courses – *e.g., a first-aid course at the local college*

computer-based training – *e.g., induction courses to give an overview of the organisation and its policies and procedures*

Internet-based e-training – *e.g., food safety knowledge, followed by an exam at an assessment centre to gain the full certificate*

blended learning – a mixture of different methods – *e.g., a computer-based course in Spanish as well as conversation lessons at the local college*

distance learning – *e.g., a course done at work or at home, with the assistance of an assessor or a tutor who may be based miles away*

workplace training – *e.g., internal training sessions on equality and diversity given by colleagues or external trainers*

Support Mechanisms

The support mechanisms that people need will vary, but it is important to plan them in advance wherever possible. Support can come from, for example:

- *the line manager* – *e.g., to arrange access to new experiences; to give permission for study time in work hours; to act as a mentor or coach*
- *the HR and training departments* – *e.g., to help with access to courses; to access advice or counselling if there is a problem*
- *an outside training provider* – *e.g., allocating a course tutor or assessor to guide through a training programme*
- *colleagues* – *e.g., to help with developmental activities or provide cover during study periods*
- *family and friends* – *e.g., to give support at home during intense periods of study*

Time and Money

It is also important to organise time and money before starting on a major programme of career development. Time management is critical and deadlines need to be managed, so that ordinary activities can continue and still be productive. Finances may also need attention and preparation – e.g., to pay for fees ourselves; to apply for funding via an employer; to arrange for funding via a training provider such as a university or college; to replace income if we have to work part time for a while.

Self-Awareness

Personal Development Plans

A Personal Development Plan is usually created within the workplace or when studying (with guidance from your manager or tutor) and works by allowing you to establish your aims, recognise your strengths and weaknesses and identify the need for improvement.

Objectives are put in place based on the areas you would like to improve on and the plan consists of your own personalised actions that will help you to achieve them.

When creating a Personal Development Plan, it is essential to make sure it accurately outlines personal goals, why they are important and how it is planned to achieve them.

Although all PDPs are specific to each individual, the plan will generally detail an ideal future based on short and/or long-term ambitions. Areas of development will be specific and could be centred on work, education, or self-improvement.

It should also always recognise the potential obstacles you might face and how it is proposed to overcome them – and if the roadblocks cannot be tackled, include a contingency plan to the career keep moving forward.

One of the most important things to consider when creating a PDP is an accurate way of measuring success.

Not only will this be a great way to prove knowledge and skills development, but it will also maintain the motivation to succeed – and give the incentive to adapt the plan if things are not moving in the right direction.

Goals must be realistic and set in a clear timeframe.

A PDP can be used to plan for a variety of things, including career progression, career change, moving into further education, or to organise the actions needed to gain a new skill for self-improvement. However, in order to reach long-term goal, short-term goals must also be completed in the process. These would typically be based on the specific areas of improvement planned – with the eventual goal in mind.

These areas are normally based around learning and development, such as taking courses or professional qualifications, but may include things such as workshops, independent study, networking, on-the-job training, joining a club/support group, or something more directly linked to a current job or the company.

In a working environment, a PDP will be put together in conjunction with a manager to identify weaknesses, allow improvement on them and identify any key areas for further progression. They can then assist in whatever way they can, to make sure progression is continuing in the chosen direction. .

They can even be a useful tool if you are currently between roles. With a clear set of objectives, you will be able to make the most of your time off and add real value to your CV. You can even take it with you to an interview to demonstrate your enthusiasm to your potential employer.

Self-Awareness

A PDP is a logical way of accomplishing a range of different objectives.

It can help define a particular career path or area of study and give a realistic and well-thought-out goal to aim for. Not to mention making sure motivation is maintained and career progression is tracked.

Documenting individual development, will demonstrate dedication, enthusiasm and ability to learn and plan – all being key skills for any job.

Content of a Personal Development Plan

A Personal Development Plan should contain the following headings: -

Goal: (What do you want to achieve / change?)	Objectives: (How are you going to do this? SMART)	Resources: (What will you need to do this?)	Performance indicators: (How will you measure the impact?)	Target date: (When will you complete this?)	Review date:

You may have several different actions necessary to achieve one goal.

- *How will you know if you have been successful with each action?*
- *How will you measure success?*
- *When should you have achieved your goal?*
- *Do some goals need to be addressed before others?*

A clear Personal Development Plan is important. Check that your goals are SMART and that your plan is complete. You may find it helpful to discuss your plan with your employer and your tutor.

Please note:

You need to return to your Personal Development Plan on a regular basis to review your progress in completing your goals. If you are able to achieve a goal completely you should give evidence of how you have assessed that it is completed. You may also identify the need for other goals throughout the progression. Any new goals should be added to your development plan. Please also remember that, if a goal needs several actions, each action will need success criteria and a target date.

Self-Awareness

Creating a Personal Development Plan

A Personal Development Plan will include personal goals and objectives. The analysis of your learning styles, personal & key skills and SWOT should all have helped you to identify areas that you need to develop. You may also have evidence from other sources, such as tutor feedback. Use the development needs list below to help you identify your goals for the plan.

Development needs can be identified through

- *analysis of learning styles and personal and key skills*
- *SWOT analysis*
- *Psychometric tests*
- *Self-assessment*
- *Academic study and research*
- *Workplace goals*
- *Future career, employment/self-employment goals and direction*
- *Personal and social goals*

Creating a Personal Development Plan not only helps effectively plan for the future and manage learning and development, but it can also help give career direction and progression.

At the heart of the process, there are three questions:

Where am I now?
To answer this question, look at your current, personal, situation – e.g., your skills, knowledge and experience; qualifications; job description and tasks; salary package; grade or position at work.

Where do I want or need to be?
Where would you like to be in the future? This can be six months ahead, a year, five years or a period that fits logically into future plans. Consider your goals,– *e.g., a higher salary; promotion; increased knowledge and skills in specific areas at work; greater job satisfaction; improved job security; improve employability prospects.*

How will I get there?
The route to achieving this is what will be recorded in your Personal Development plan. Identify the steps you need to take to begin to work towards your goals. This may include qualifications, a career review, doing voluntary work to gain specific experience, broadening experience within your current work role, shadowing colleagues to learn from them - consider the best learning options for you personally.

Remember! This is about focussing on your personal goals and setting targets that are specific to you and your needs.

Self-Awareness

Identifying Development Needs and Setting Objectives

The normal process for analysing current skills, knowledge and experience is to use a skills audit. This is a simple process which identifies what you are good at, what you are not so good at, as well as things you may not have done before.

> ### *A skills audit is a simple process to identify strengths and weaknesses.*

A definitive list is made of the skills that are relevant to the role and it is essential that this list comprehensively covers all the appropriate criteria, otherwise its benefit and effect will be nullified. The existing skill set is then compared to the list and a simple rating system needs to be applied which shows the level of skill for each criterion.

Having analysed where we are now, we can work out where we want to be, then set personal objectives to plan how to improve our performance at work. When setting personal work objectives, it is important to have a realistic number of goals. If overloaded, people feel overwhelmed and are more likely to fail, give up and lose confidence. Honesty about achievements and expectations is important. It can be useful to support this process with personal reflection and discussions with senior colleagues, maybe during the appraisal process. Once you have established the needs, you can set objectives that support your strengths, address your weaknesses and help you improve your performance.

When deciding which skills to audit, the details can be taken from a variety of sources – e.g., the organisation's own policies, procedures and standards; national occupational standards; essential standards; professional bodies' standards; qualification specifications from awarding bodies. The job description and person specification should go some way to providing some of the elements for this, but the final list should be checked by all parties concerned or involved.

Below are two samples of skills audits:

Personal Audit		*1*	*2*	*3*	*4*	*5*
1	Lack confidence in expressing my needs		✓			
2	Manage time effectively			✓		
3	I am competent to lead		✓			
4	I cope with stress well				✓	
5	I do not have the confidence to give presentations			✓		
6	I am patient when teaching and coaching others		✓			
7	I can handle a number of tasks		✓			
8	I do not have the confidence to influence others			✓		
9	I can motivate others			✓		
10	I do not make people do tasks			✓		

Self-Awareness

Professional Skills Audit		
Skills required	Ability (1–5)	Action to be taken
Computing skills	4	Undertake short courses (if possible) to enhance computing skills
Leadership skills	4	Get more involved in communities/societies
Numeracy skills	4	Discuss with lecturers and fellow students on ways to improve
Revision and exam techniques	3	Learn from lecturers and fellow students on techniques to revise and answer exam questions.
Time-management and organisation skills	2	Jot down all activities that need to be done accordingly in a diary
Oral presentation skills	4	Learn to fully utilise and use other presentation aids that are available besides PowerPoint
Critical analysis and logical argument skills	3	Get more involved in group discussions
Selecting and prioritising information when reading	3	Listen to lectures and identify which are the important points
Referencing skills	3	Write more essays and get used to the Harvard referencing style
Summarising skills	4	Need to fully understand the topic
Developing appropriate writing style	3	Read more articles and journals to get used to the writing style so that it can be implemented
Search skills (library and e-resources)	3	Fully utilise the library's 'resources and support' section
Utilising and comprehension	5	Listen more to the way people converse with each other and try and pick up whatever necessary
Proofreading and editing	3	Take another look at the work

Identifying Goals

First things first, you need to define your goals.

Some goals could have been set in the back of your mind for years, just waiting for the right time to make an appearance – but for others, it could take a bit of soul-searching.

If you are stuck, ask yourself the following questions: 'where do you want to progress in your career?', 'will you be happier in a different job?', 'what new skills and knowledge would make you more fulfilled?' and most importantly, 'what type of achievements are most significant to you?'

Once you have set aside your goals, consider prioritising them – and try not to tackle too many at once. Be realistic with what you want to achieve and remember that these goals can be anything from short-term to long-term, big or small.

Example:

Self-Awareness

'I want to become a Primary School Teacher'

'I want to move up in my career as a Sales Assistant and eventually progress into a management role'

Once you have decided on your main goals, it is time to consider your relevant strengths.

Identify Current Strengths

What attributes do you already have that could help this goal become a reality? Are there any transferrable skills you could utilise?

Even if you do not have any direct experience in the field your goals are based in, a strength can be anything from dedication, a creative mind and a keen interest in a particular area of academia, through to excellent people skills or a knack for numbers.

Identifying your strengths can also lead you to potential areas for improvement. For example, it might be that you have a range of experience in HR roles (strength), but no qualifications to quantify your skills (weakness).

This is where the areas for development come in...

Examples:

'I'm great at talking to people and understanding their needs and have a range of experience in Customer Service based roles'

'I often draw in my spare time and have a keen interest in creative projects'

Decide on the key areas for development

If you often draw a blank when it comes to the common interview favourite, 'what are your weaknesses?' – this section of your PDP could help with that.

Identify the main areas of your career, or skills that will need improvement to be able to achieve your goals and from there, you will be able to come up with realistic actions to turn your weaknesses into strengths.

Make sure the areas that need work are linked directly to your main objectives, so you will actually be motivated to improve on them.

Self-Awareness

Examples:

'I lack accredited qualifications to be able to enter a career in accounting'

'My web design skills are basic and will need to be more advanced to progress in this field'

Research the skills needed to achieve the goals

Do some in-depth research on what is needed to achieve your goals and what kind of skills, knowledge, or qualifications will help overcome the weaknesses identified.

If you want to become a Social Worker, but you have no previous experience, you will probably need to consider gaining a specialised qualification by doing a course, or perhaps taking a more full-on approach and studying a related subject at university.

Alternatively, it could be that you just need to gain some practical, hands-on experience in the area you would like to progress in.

Examples:

'I will need to gain a an NVQ level 3 in Beauty and Make-up'

'I will need to be able to demonstrate at least a year's experience in Marketing, before I can progress further'

By identifying the development needs, you set some actions that will put you on the right track to achieving your goals.

The actions should be heavily based on the identified weaknesses and areas of improvement and the skills you will need to go ahead with fulfilling your ambitions. The number of actions you set for each objective is solely dependent on you, your individual plan and the complexity of your aims.

Academia is not for everyone and neither is a practical approach, so do your research and choose the one that suits you best. These actions could range from reading up on a particular topic, doing an apprenticeship or taking a course or learning a new skill.

Examples:

'Study a personal fitness trainer course'

'Gain three month's unpaid experience in a publishing house'

Setting a deadline for each one of your goals will give you a visible target to reach for, not to mention ensure you are on the right track throughout your career.

Self-Awareness

Set a clear timeframes for each goal

Be realistic with your timeframes and consider how long each individual action will take. You should also consider the potential obstacles that could delay you along the way, because things may not always run as smoothly as you hope.

Track progress

Finally, always track progress and development.

Not only does this help to emphasise areas of improvement (which boosts confidence and motivation), it also shows the which areas you are excelling in and which areas might need additional work.

By recognising the obstacles, you will be able to put in place new actions or alter your current ones in a way that better fits in with your main objective.

The personal development plan (PDP) is simply the tool to bring all of this together and record progress.

Setting SMART Objectives

Once areas for personal development have been identified, it is important to set targets. By having goals and objectives clearly in mind, there is a much greater chance of success. One good way to set goals is to use SMART objectives:

SMART is an acronym that you can use to guide your goal setting.

Its criteria are commonly attributed to Peter Drucker's Management by Objectives concept.

SMART has come to mean different things to different people, as shown below. To make sure your goals are clear and reachable, each one should be:

> *Specific* **(simple, sensible, significant)**
> *Measurable* **(meaningful, motivating)**
> *Achievable* **(agreed, attainable)**
> *Relevant* **(reasonable, realistic and resourced, results-based)**
> *Time bound* **(time-based, time limited, time/cost limited, timely, time-sensitive)**

Some authors have expanded it to include extra focus areas.

SMARTER, for example, includes Evaluated and Reviewed

Specific

Your goal should be clear and specific, otherwise you will not be able to focus your efforts or feel truly motivated to achieve it. When writing your goal, try to answer the five "W" questions:

Self-Awareness

- *What do I want to accomplish?*
- *Why is this goal important?*
- *Who is involved?*
- *Where is it located?*
- *Which resources or limits are involved?*

Example

Imagine that you are currently a marketing executive and you would like to become head of marketing. A specific goal could be, "I want to gain the skills and experience necessary to become head of marketing within my organisation, so that I can build my career and lead a successful team."

Measurable

It is important to have measurable goals, so that you can track your progress and stay motivated. Assessing progress helps you to stay focused, meet your deadlines and feel the excitement of getting closer to achieving your goal.

- *A measurable goal should address questions such as:*
- *How much?*
- *How many?*
- *How will I know when it is accomplished?*

Example
You might measure your goal of acquiring the skills to become head of marketing by determining that you will have completed the necessary training courses and gained the relevant experience within five years' time.

Achievable

Your goal also needs to be realistic and attainable to be successful. In other words, it should stretch your abilities but still remain possible. When you set an achievable goal, you may be able to identify previously overlooked opportunities or resources that can bring you closer to it.

An achievable goal will usually answer questions such as:

- *How can I accomplish this goal?*
- *How realistic is the goal, based on other constraints, such as financial factors?*

Example
You might need to ask yourself whether developing the skills required to become head of marketing is realistic, based on your existing experience and qualifications. For example, do you have the time to complete the required training effectively? Are the necessary resources available to you? Can you afford to do it?

Relevant

This step is about ensuring that your goal matters to you and that it also aligns with other relevant goals. We all need support and assistance in achieving our goals, but it is important to

Self-Awareness

retain control over them. So, make sure that your plans drive everyone forward, but that you are still responsible for achieving your own goal.

A relevant goal can answer "yes" to these questions:

- *Does this seem worthwhile?*
- *Is this the right time?*
- *Does this match our other efforts/needs?*
- *Am I the right person to reach this goal?*
- *Is it applicable in the current socio-economic environment?*

Example
You might want to gain the skills to become head of marketing within your organisation, but is it the right time to undertake the required training, or work toward additional qualifications? Are you sure that you are the right person for the head of marketing role? Have you considered your spouse's goals? For example, if you want to start a family, would completing training in your free time make this more difficult?

Time-bound

Every goal needs a target date, so that you have a deadline to focus on and something to work toward. This part of the SMART goal criteria helps to prevent everyday tasks from taking priority over your longer-term goals.

A time-bound goal will usually answer these questions:

- *When?*
- *What can I do six months from now?*
- *What can I do six weeks from now?*
- *What can I do today?*

Example
Gaining the skills to become head of marketing may require additional training or experience, as we mentioned earlier. How long will it take you to acquire these skills? Do you need further training, so that you are eligible for certain exams or qualifications? It is important to give yourself a realistic time frame for accomplishing the smaller goals that are necessary to achieving your final objective

Monitor Progress and Overcome Barriers

SMART objectives help us to monitor progress against the targets mapped out in the PDP. Progress needs to be monitored so that we can, for example:

- *assess progress against specific targets – to measure development* – e.g., looking at dates for handing in assignments and seeing if they are on time
- *adjust elements of objectives – to keep them achievable and realistic* – e.g., changing timescales following illness

Self-Awareness

- ***allocate or seek additional resources*** – *e.g., arranging for one-to-one tuition to learn a language needed for work on time for a newly signed project*
- ***agree further development activities*** – *e.g., work tasks have been done early and there is scope to help out in a different department for a few days*

A PDP needs to be monitored regularly to keep things on track so that problems do not get out of hand. If everything is going well, the positive feedback will be a boost and help to motivate you to carry on. If there are problems, it is vital to catch them early so that they can be dealt with quickly and keep the rest of the PDP intact.

Monitoring can be quite informal because it is really keeping an eye on the smaller elements and details of the PDP.

There can be barriers to learning that can stop people engaging in learning and career development activities. Potential barriers or threats to progress must be identified so they can be eliminated or by passed.

Some potential barriers to learning and some suggested ways to overcome these barriers are listed below:

Self-Awareness

Barrier:	Ways to overcome it:
Lack of time	Work out exactly how much time will be needed and agree realistic goals Discuss doing some study during working hours Arrange cover when the individual is in college or doing internal courses Create development activities that can be done on the job during normal hours Arrange to do part-time courses over a longer period
Lack of confidence	Have one-to-one meetings with a mentor or coach (maybe the line manager) to identify the causes of lack of confidence Seek positive feedback to reinforce the positive aspects of performance, skills etc. Find small learning and development activities to build confidence – e.g., several short courses and seminars rather than a 9-month diploma course
Fear about standing out from colleagues	Use positive feedback to reinforce the positive aspects of performance, skills etc. Check how well performance measures up against the organisation's standards and expectations Encourage team spirit and mutual support between individual team members Watch for any bullying or harassment from other team members – act as required
Worrying about being overworked or overloaded	Develop time-management skills Examine the current and expected workload and check timescales that are realistic Make sure that the workload is fair and arrange for extra assistance or cover from others if necessary Do not worry if it is necessary to step back and take a break
Learning styles are incompatible	Consider changing the development activities – e.g., introduce new activities; appoint different tutors; use different formats to appeal to different learning styles Make sure that the content is relevant to the individual and the organisation
Fear of change – e.g., in technology	Review the benefits of change, job security, the future of the company etc. Find out about all aspects of the plans for change Ask to be kept informed and keep others informed Have one-to-one discussions with the mentor/coach/line manager to identify causes of fear and ask for appropriate reassurance and support

Self-Awareness

Continuing Professional Development (CPD)

It is important to review career development and goals as an ongoing process. This is often referred to as continuing professional development (CPD). CPD links learning directly to working practices. Each time an activity is undertaken that increases skills, knowledge or experience, make a note of it in the CPD log. This helps to show how learning activities work towards achieving the goals we have set out in our overall personal development plan.

A CPD log, will capture useful experiences and assess the practical benefits of what has been learned.

CPD allows us to:

- *review the interrelationship of values* – *e.g., ambition, discipline, effectiveness and efficiency*
- *review and measure career direction and progress* – *e.g., promotion, remuneration, job satisfaction, qualifications and work-life balance*
- *measure goals against success*

The CPD Cycle
During the CPD process, we frequently check:

- *where we are* – *examining the current role in detail and identifying any skills gaps*
- *where we need to be* – *working out where we need or want to be, deciding and defining ambitions in a clear way*
- *how we plan to get there* – *identifying the learning and development activities and resources that we need to achieve our goals*

As managers, we need to do this for ourselves and our team members.

Self-Awareness

The CIPD use a seven-stage CPD cycle to illustrate the process:

Identify – *where you have been, where you are now and where you want to be*

Plan – *how to get these, using clear objectives and monitoring of progress*

Act – *do the development activities and be open to new experiences*

Reflect – *routinely reflect upon day-to-day activities*

Apply – *put theory into practice*

Share – *share learning experiences and generate insight and support with others*

Impact – *measure the overall impact of learning on work activities*

Using a CPD Log

Keeping a log to track CPD activity is widespread and many organisations have their own policies and procedures for this.

There are many ways of making a CDP log. The main thing to bear in mind is that we may need to show our log to someone else, so it is important to make sure that it is clear and contains sufficient information. It is a record of evidence that we can use to back up our claims that learning activities have been performed – either in the course of our normal duties or as extra activities.

Some people create their own records, maybe using Word, Excel or Evernote. Some organisations and professional bodies have paper-based or electronic templates or forms for people to use. This is particularly true when there is a legal or contractual requirement for staff or members to maintain evidence about how they keep their skills up to date – e.g., teachers, vets, architects or health professionals. They can be asked at any time to provide their CPD log to prove that their ongoing learning and development are appropriate and up to date. In many cases, it is important to show the number of hours of CPD that have taken place to comply with the organisation's requirements.

Typically, a CPD log needs to show:

- *the person's name*
- *the date of the activity*
- *the type of activity* – **e.g., attending a course, reading professional journals or performing a work activity**
- *details of the activity* – *e.g., the subject covered, or task performed*
- *how it addresses skills gaps*
- *duration* – *e.g., the study hours*

Self-Awareness

Name: Alex Smith				
Date of the activity	Type of learning activity – e.g., course	Details of the activity	Skills gaps addressed	Duration
8 Oct	*Evening class – Business English L3 – new course, week 1*	*Writing informal business emails and reports Grammar & spelling*	*Email etiquette Using graphs for reports Improved general business writing skills*	**2.0 hours**
10 Oct	*Refresher training at work*	*H&S practices and fire safety*	*Reminder re fire evacuation procedures Updated knowledge about dangerous cleaning chemicals*	**1.5**
11 Oct	*Fire drill*	*Had to clear my section and hand over to fire marshal*	*Consolidated training from yesterday Understand fire exit routes better*	**0.5**
15 Oct	*Bus English L3 week 2*	*Writing formal business letters and reports Apostrophes and other punctuation*	*Business report writing General business writing skills*	**2.0**
17 Oct	*Reading professional journal*	*Impact on customers of new consumer laws*	*Knowledge of legal processes*	**0.5**
19 Oct	*Presentation by Sales Director, Q&A*	*Organisation's approach to changes in consumer laws*	*Knowledge of legal processes and employer's policies*	**1.5**
			Total CPD Hours:	**8.0**

Self-Awareness

Evaluating CPD

The development process needs to be monitored and reviewed to check progress and identify any barriers to learning. The same applies to CPD as well. Whenever we commit time, effort and resources to improvement, it is important to ensure that we are achieving something of value.

We need to check:

- *progress* – *against agreed SMART objectives*
- *strengths* – *so that we can be confident in our abilities and continue to provide excellent goods and services*
- *areas that need further attention or support* – *so that we can give time, attention and resources to address areas that are weak or unresolved*

In a similar way, organisations also review progress on a wider scale, to make sure that they are getting a return on investment (ROI). Evaluating outcomes and reviewing progress helps individuals and organisations to, for example:

- *measure the additional skills, knowledge and experience gained*
- *identify actual benefits* – **e.g., in terms of output, earnings or increased opportunities**
- *identify potential future benefits* – *e.g., from more courses or putting more people through the same training*
- *identify problem areas as soon as possible* – *e.g., to be able to divert resources and support if required*
- *check that the commitment is still worthwhile and relevant*
- *justify continuing support* – **e.g., in terms of time, money and physical resources**

New skills can be tested in a variety of ways, for example:

- *demonstrating the new skill to an experienced colleague or trainer*
- *measuring feedback* – *e.g., from customers, colleagues or managers*
- *increased output* – *e.g., an increase in sales following training*
- *passing a practical test, exam or appraisal*

New knowledge can be tested with other methods, for example:

- *informal diagnostic tests* – *e.g., quizzes and multiple-choice tests online where the answers are given afterwards*
- *formal multiple-choice exams or tests* – *e.g., under strict exam conditions at work or place of study*
- *assessment by a tutor, assessor or trainer*
- *essays or dissertations*
- *questions in appraisal interviews*

Self-Awareness

Results cannot always be measured in terms of numbers, quantities or physical evidence. Along the way, managers and their team members may also:

- *define or redefine their limits of authority, now and in the future*
- *improve decision-making processes* – *due to the openness developed when discussing and agreeing objectives with others*
- *identify areas for improvement for individuals, teams and the organisation that lead to increased productivity and quality*
- *develop better working relationships* – **by working together on ways to move forward**
- *develop clarity and focus*
- *gain a deeper knowledge of the organisation's operations, policies and procedures*
- *feel engaged in their rules as they focus attention on their goals and feel motivated to improve and develop*

When evaluating the outcomes of CPD, the development activities which have been used need to be considered as well. This is to ensure any future development need is met with the most effective delivery method.

Learning activity	Outcome of learning activity	How this was evaluated and/or measured – plus further action if required
L3 Business English course	*Passed course* *Improved, shorter emails to colleagues* *Improved formal report presentation skills* *Grammar and spelling still a bit rusty at times*	*3 exam papers marked externally* *Positive feedback from line manager and colleagues* *Feedback and comments at the time and during annual appraisal* *Keep doing quizzes and online exercises to improve and develop knowledge*
Fire drill and H&S ongoing training	*Much faster response and more confident in fire evacuation procedures* *Better knowledge of dangerous chemicals*	*During drills* *Knew how to deal with actual dangerous spillage on my shift*
Sales legislation training by sales director	*Understand consumer rights better* *Able to deal with complaints more confidently* *Need to double-check equality and diversity policy at work*	*Passed online quiz on subject, got 97%* *Positive feedback from customers when dealing with queries. Line manager pleased with outcome of complaints* *Check policy against government website on equality and diversity*

Self-Awareness

CPD should become a routine task at work, especially if a role demands compliance with legal or contractual requirements, to log the ongoing learning activities. Many elements of workplace knowledge and skills need to be kept up to date on a regular basis. CPD, when it is done thoroughly, can provide a useful focus as well as evidence that this is being done.

Chapter 2: Managing Self

Managing Self

Time Management

Definition

Time management is the process of organising and planning how to divide your time between specific activities.

Good time management enables people to work smarter – not harder – so they get more done in less time, even when time is tight and pressures are high.

Failing to manage time damages effectiveness and causes stress.

Effective Time Management

An important skill when developing our careers is time management. It is the process of arranging and controlling how we spend our time, in or out of work.

A study in 2007 covering 2,500 businesses over 4 years in 38 countries identified that wasted time costs UK businesses £80bn per year, which was equivalent to 7% of the gross domestic product (GDP) at the time.

Their findings showed the causes of wasted time were:

- *inadequate workforce supervision – 30%*
- *poor management planning – 30%*
- *poor communication – 18%*
- *IT problems, low morale and lack or mismatch of skills – 21%*

It is very important to make a workforce as efficient as possible to maximise the organisation's investment in human resources. A 7% increase in productivity and efficiency would be a significant improvement for many organisations.

Effective time management at work can benefit individuals too and can help workers at all levels to, for example:

- *cut out non-essential activities*
- *be more productive and achieve more within work hours*
- *enhance career development prospects*
- *make tasks more enjoyable and rewarding*
- *meet deadlines more easily*
- *achieve a better work-life balance*

Managing Self

Many managers and team leaders have heavy workloads, considerable responsibility and big demands on their time and expertise. If time is not managed properly, these factors can lead to excessive strain and lack of performance.

On a personal level, effective time management can help managers to, for example:

- *be more organised on a day-to-day basis*
- *be in control of upcoming projects and tasks*
- *have a clearer view of their objectives in the short, medium and long term*
- *maximise efficiency and productivity*
- *enjoy better health as a result of lowering stress and anxiety*

Time Management Mistakes

Many people know that they could be managing their time more effectively; but it can be difficult to identify the mistakes that are being made and to know how improvements could be made.

When time is well managed, productivity soars and stress levels drop. This in turn allows time to be devoted to the interesting, high-reward projects that can make a real difference to a career. In short, happier!

1: Failing to Keep a To-Do List
Do you ever have that nagging feeling that you have forgotten to do an important piece of work? If so, you probably do not use a To-Do List. (Or, if you do, you might not be using it effectively!)

Using To-Do Lists effectively relies on prioritising the tasks on the list. Many people use an A – F coding system (A for high priority items, F for very low priorities). Alternatively, you can simplify this by using A - D, or by using numbers.

If you have large projects on your list, then, unless you are careful, the entries for these can be vague and ineffective. For instance, you may have written down "Start on budget proposal." But what does this actually entail? The lack of specifics here might cause you to procrastinate or miss key steps. So, make sure that you break large tasks or projects down into specific, actionable steps – then you will not overlook something important.

2: Not Setting Personal Goals
Do you know where you would like to be in six months? What about this time next year, or even 10 years from now? If not, it is time to set some personal goals!

Personal goal setting is essential to managing your time well, because goals give you a destination and vision to work toward. When you know where you want to go, you can manage your priorities, time and resources to get there. Goals also help you decide what is worth spending your time on and what is just a distraction.

3: Not Prioritising

Managing Self

Think about a situation where a team member walks into your office with a crisis that they need you to deal with right now. You are in the middle of brainstorming ideas for a new client. You are confident that you have *almost* come up with a brilliant idea for their marketing campaign, but now you risk losing the thread of your thinking because of this "emergency."

Sometimes, it is hard to know how to prioritise, especially when you are facing a flood of seemingly urgent tasks. However, it is essential to learn how to prioritise tasks effectively if you want to manage your time better.

4: Failing to Manage Distractions

Distractions lead to the loss of up to two hours productivity a day. Think how much more could be done if you had that time back!

Whether they come from emails, IM chats, colleagues in a crisis, or phone calls from clients, distractions prevent us from achieving that seemingly effortless and satisfying flow of work which can be achieved when 100 percent engaged in a task.

If you want to take control of your day and deliver the best work, it is vital to know how to minimise distractions and manage interruptions effectively. Turn off your social media and chat channels when you need to focus and tell people when they are distracting you too often.

You should also learn how to improve concentration, even when faced with distractions.

5: Procrastination

Procrastination occurs when you put off tasks that you should be focusing on now. When you procrastinate, you feel guilty that you have not started; you come to dread doing the task; and eventually, everything catches up with you when you fail to complete the work on time.

One useful strategy is to tell yourself that you are only going to start a project for ten minutes. Often, procrastinators feel that they have to complete a task from start to finish and this high expectation makes them feel overwhelmed and anxious. Instead, focus on devoting a small amount of time to starting. That is all!

6: Taking on Too Much

Are you the type who has a hard time saying "no" to people? If so, you probably have far too many projects and commitments on your plate. This can lead to poor performance, stress and low morale.

You might be a micromanager: someone who insists on controlling or doing all of the work themselves, because they cannot trust anyone else to do it correctly. (This can be a problem for everyone – not just managers!)

Either way, taking on too much is a poor use of your time and it can get you a reputation for producing rushed, sloppy work.

Managing Self

To prevent this, learn the subtle art of saying "yes" to the person, but "no" to the task. This skill helps you assert yourself, while still maintaining good feelings within the group. If the other person starts leaning on you to say "yes" to their request, learn how to think on your feet and stay cool under pressure.

7: Thriving on "Busy"

Some people get a rush from being busy. The narrowly met deadlines, the endless emails, the piles of files needing attention on the desk, the frantic race to the meeting... What an adrenaline buzz!

The problem is that an addiction to "busy" rarely means that they are effective and it can lead to stress. Instead, try to slow down and learn to manage time better.

8: Multitasking

To get on top of her workload, Linda regularly writes emails while she chats on the phone to her clients. However, while Linda thinks that this is a good use of her time, the truth is that it can take 20-40 percent more time to finish a list of jobs when you multitask, compared with completing the same list of tasks in sequence. The result is also that she does both tasks poorly – her emails are full of errors and her clients are frustrated by her lack of concentration.

So, the best thing is to forget about multitasking and, instead, focus on one task at a time. That way, work quality will be higher.

9: Not Taking Breaks

It is nice to think that you can work for 8-10 hours straight, especially when you are working to a deadline. But it is impossible for anyone to focus and produce really high-quality work without giving their brains some time to rest and recharge.

So, do not dismiss breaks as "wasting time." They provide valuable down-time, which will enable you to think creatively and work effectively.

If it is hard for you to stop working, then schedule breaks or set an alarm as a reminder. Go for a quick walk, grab a cup of coffee, or just sit and meditate at your desk. Take a five-minute break every hour or two. Make sure that you give yourself ample time for lunch – you will not produce top quality work if you are hungry!

10: Ineffectively Scheduling Tasks

Are you a morning person, or do you find your energy picking up once the sun begins to set in the evening? All of us have different work rhythms at different times of the day when we feel most productive and energetic.

You can make the best use of your time by scheduling high-value work during your peak time and low-energy work (like returning phone calls and checking email), during your "down" time.

Managing Self

Prioritise Work Activities and Improve Time Management

Looking at the causes of wasted time again, we can see ways to help us prioritise work activities and improve our time management. The main word to learn when developing our ability to prioritise is probably 'no'. This can be surprisingly difficult, but it is worth learning how to say it politely and effectively. It can help us manage interruptions and keep workloads under control.

Analyse how time is used

Breaks for coffee, tea etc.
Just being aware of how long we spend chatting by the kettle can make us realise where we might be losing an hour or two a week. Social interaction and breaks away from the desk or static work area are extremely important and we should move around at regular intervals. Walking around the office, going to fetch something or popping out for some fresh air are all activities that help maintain good physical and mental health.

However, we might need to change our visits to the kitchen to quieter times when we need to focus and avoid distractions. On other occasions, we can use body language and words to express how busy we are and that we are not stopping to chat today – e.g., avoiding too much eye contact; being polite, friendly and quick; avoiding asking any unnecessary questions. It is a question of balance and being aware of time.

Meetings and appointments
Well-run meetings can be very effective and useful for developing relationships. The person in charge of the meeting needs to be very clear and assertive about:

- *the objectives of the meeting* – running to a clear and simple agenda who needs to be there?
- *the time allocated to the meeting* – giving a strict timeframe at the beginning of the meeting and making sure that it winds up on time
- *keeping the meeting going* – to make sure that all points are covered and that no one is allowed to 'waffle' too much
- *how to deal with outstanding points that need action or attention* – e.g., setting the time for the next meeting, producing and reviewing an action plan

Informal meetings or chats with colleagues
Being friendly, cooperative and approachable is important, but managers can improve their own time management by, for instance:

- *making sure that people know about other sources of information and advice* – e.g., encouraging them to look up information themselves
- *making sure that delegation has been done correctly* – e.g., if the manager feels 'pestered' by colleagues who are afraid to make a decision
- *setting some parameters about interruptions* – e.g., having a policy of closing the door when privacy is needed to deter non-urgent interruptions

Managing Self

- *setting aside time for the team to discuss their views and queries* – *e.g., just after the team briefing at the beginning of the shift*

It is all about setting reasonable and balanced boundaries so that people can respect the manager's time and space and not burden them with unnecessary interruptions at inappropriate times.

Workload and task allocation
Some tasks land on us at work that are not even part of our job description, action plan or objectives – e.g., being asked to organise an event that would not be part of our normal duties or covering for a colleague who is off work due to long-term sickness.

When this happens, we can usually cope in the short term. However, we need to be proactive and find solutions if the excessive drain on our time, energy and resources continues. Actions could include open discussions with our own line manager about, for example:

- *the current task allocation* – *e.g., discussing how the new tasks impact on other commitments*
- *reviewing and amending action plans, objectives and priorities* – *e.g., to agree how long extra work will be needed; to agree changes in work rate or areas of responsibility; to see how to incorporate new tasks into future plans*
- *asking for help and support* – *e.g., arranging agency cover in the short term; arranging to delegate some tasks to others; agreeing overtime until longer-term solutions can be found; finding other colleagues who can help to share the load*

Insufficient preparation and organisation
Preparation is key to getting the most out of a meeting, task or work opportunity. We need to:

- *focus on each meeting, task or project* – *so that we know exactly what is expected of us and others*
- *do the necessary research in advance* – *so that we have all of the facts, figures, ideas and plans ready*
- *be well-prepared before we meet and discuss the task with others* – *with all of the necessary resources, notes and data ready to use*
- *let people know about progress or delays* – *it can be better to delay a meeting if something cannot be done in time, rather than waste everyone's time if things are not ready*

If we put in the effort to be well-prepared and organised, we can do our job well, be efficient, show our professionalism, inspire trust, make good use of other stakeholders' time and make a valued contribution to the team and organisation.

Deadlines
When prioritising deadlines, it is important to focus on all deadlines for all tasks and objectives and not just concentrate on the nearest deadline. A Gantt chart can be a useful tool when trying to work out exactly what needs to be done to achieve each deadline.

Managing Self

If a deadline is impossible despite good planning and organisation, it is important to let people know and negotiate:

- *extensions of the deadlines*
- *the priority of different stages and tasks* – and agree the delivery dates that are achievable
- *extra resources* – maybe more staff, money or physical resources

It is important to reassure other stakeholders that everything possible is being done and that they will be kept informed about progress.

Inefficient communication

To keep emails under control, we can, for example:

- *keep our emails brief and to the point*
- *only send out emails and other messages that need to be sent*
- *only copy messages to people who really need to see them*
- *put a clear description in the subject box to help others to prioritise our emails*
- *discourage others from sending emails that we do not need to see*
- *only open our inbox at set times* – rather than having it open all of the time so that we are distracted by new messages
- *have separate folders for emails* – to prioritise some and keep the rest to be read when time allows

Paperwork can be prioritised by putting papers in different folders as soon as they arrive. For example, we can have folders marked:

- *urgent* – deal with today
- *for action, this week*
- *for information only* – for things that we need to glance through quickly before filing them away for reference
- *bills to pay*
- *filing*

Files can also be allocated to specific tasks, projects or subjects – e.g., customer queries, or interviewees for a job.

To prioritise telephone calls, it is better to find a good time to get hold of the person we need rather than wait on hold for a long time. If receiving too many calls, managers can sometimes ask the reception staff to take messages at certain times or put the caller through to voicemail.

Managers can also make sure that reception staff know how to direct calls to the right person.

Managing Self

Tools and Techniques

When developing time-management skills, there are several tools and techniques that can help. Having identified how various things and people can waste our time, here are some examples of recommended time management techniques to solve those problems:

Set SMART objectives

When addressing issues of time management, one useful technique is to use SMART objectives. Set SMART objectives to prioritise and achieve team goals. By having personal objectives that align with the goals of the team and the organisation, you can work towards a common purpose and increase the chances of the punctual delivery of successful outcomes.

Leader/supervisors can set their own SMART objectives, integrate these with individual team members' objectives and make sure that all of them work together to achieve the wider goals for the team.

Breaking tasks and targets down into small, measurable stages can help each person to focus on the important deadlines and goals that need to be achieved, so that the whole task can move on smoothly. It is like having a three-dimensional view of a team objective, with all of the individual goals ending up in the same place.

Write activity logs

It is important to analyse how time is really spent. Keeping an activity log will show what is **actually** being done with time each day, rather than what we **think** we are doing with our time.

Note each activity, when it started and finished and whether we had planned to do it at that time. This may seem like a tie intensive activity, but it is a short-term investment in time, to analyse data that can be used to save time and energy in the long term.

Once complete, go through the list and categorise each task in order to identify where you expend most time and energy and tick each task off as you complete it. This may give you a sense of satisfaction and control.

Core tasks are the things you do which make up the bulk of your job description. For a leader/supervisor this may be updating daily sales figures, completing floor walks, or signing of work carried out by those they supervise. These can be easily predicted and planned.

Episodic tasks are those which occur at irregular intervals or only occasionally. An example of this might be a monthly health and safety review, annual staff appraisals, or a stock take.

Interruptions are anything we cannot plan for in frequency or duration. These include phone calls, emails and other demands of your time, such as covering staff absence.

Managing Self

Every time you do something different, even chatting at the coffee machine, write it down so that you can analyse what you spend your time on throughout the day.

Also log how motivated you feel at different times of the day and on different tasks. This way you can easily evaluate the low value tasks that you spend time on and this will help prioritise where you should be focusing your priorities.

Example:

Activity	Start Time	Finish Time	Time Spent	Planned task?	Notes

Assess activities using the Pareto Principle

The Pareto Principle, also known as the 80-20 rule, is a method which can be used to assess efforts and activities to see which are the most productive. This can be applied to time management and many other aspects of business – e.g., planning, decision-making, leadership or project management.

The 80 20 rule states that:

> *"80% of the output or results will come from 20% of the input or action"*

In other words, the little things are the ones that account for the majority of the results.

This is one of the best time management techniques you can use to help you regain focus and work on the things that bring the most impact.

> *Do 20% of your tasks bring 80% of the results?*

Then prioritise your time to work on them.

Use the 80/20 rule across your life and work to prioritise the inputs that deliver the majority of the output.

Here are some questions to ask yourself to use this rule:

- *Is 80% of value achieved with the first 20% of effort?*
- *Are 20% of the emails 80% of the important conversations?*
- *Do 80% of your distractions come from 20% of sources?*

Managing Self

- *Do 20% of your tasks give you 80% of the pleasure in your job?*
- *Is 20% of your team completing 80% of the work?*
- *Do 80% of problems originate with 20% of projects?*
- *Are 80% of customers only using 20% of services?*
- *Do 20% of customers make 80% of the complaints?*

Spend half an hour at the beginning of the day to plan activities

Use a diary or a planner to schedule when to do things. It is worth setting time aside each morning to do this, so activities are focused and clear. You need to:

- *go through everything very quickly*
- *make a list of what needs doing and when*
- *avoid handling the piece of paper more than once* – *e.g., avoid picking up a job, doing a bit and then putting it back on the pile*
- *avoid starting lots of jobs at the same time* – *multitasking is usually considered to be inefficient*
- *plan and schedule planning, preparation and creative time for long-term projects* – *otherwise short-term urgent tasks will always use up all of our time*
- *batching similar tasks together also saves time* – *e.g., setting aside half an hour to make all telephone calls, regardless of their subject.*

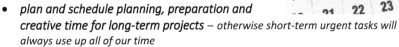

Accept that emails and telephones do not have to be answered immediately

Emails and telephone calls must be managed to prevent them managing us. Have set times for dealing with these and not let them disturb you when you need to focus and concentrate without interruptions. Even if leader/supervisors have a customer-facing role, they still need to have time when they are not available, so that they can catch up on other tasks and be proactive about objectives and plans.

The growing trend of dealing with work emails and other messages during time off should also be avoided. Some people spend hours each week dealing with emails before or after work. If this is a regular or ongoing occurrence, it is an indication that time management and a workload review are urgently needed.

Factor in some time for interruptions and unplanned activities

By leaving some time available for unplanned activities, important things will not need to be pushed out of the way when something turns up needing attention.

Managing Self

Be prepared to say 'No'!

It is important to examine tasks before saying 'Yes'. Find out what is involved, expectations and deadlines before committing to saying 'Yes'. Saying 'Yes' does not always work in the long run as the obliging person will often be given too many tasks and not be respected. Someone who says 'No' from time to time, in a firm, fair and objective way, will be taken more seriously and people around them tend to respect their decisions and parameters.

Accepting new challenges without question, particularly when adopting new technology that helps others but not us, opens the way for new demands on our time, new interruptions, new tasks and new obligations.

Before each meeting or call, plan exactly what needs to be achieved

This helps to focus time and effort on what needs to be achieved and you are less likely to be distracted. Being organised before a call or meeting means that you feel more confident about the objectives, give a more professional impression of the organisation and are comfortable about moving things along quickly to achieve your goals.

Delegate effectively

Delegate appropriate tasks, especially if you have a deputy or assistant within the team. They need to be in a position to take over sometimes and delegation can help them to learn the tasks and take some of the pressure off you. When delegation is not appropriate, you can just ask someone nicely if they will help or take over a task for which they are suitably experienced.

When delegating tasks effectively, the leader/supervisor needs to:

- *identify the work that needs to be delegated*
- *identify the team member's ability to take on the task*
- *identify any skills gaps before they delegate anything*

The leader/supervisor needs to keep an eye on things to make sure that the delegation has been successful. They need to monitor and review overall progress and discuss feedback with the team member to identify strengths, weaknesses and avoid unnecessary problems. If delegation is unsuccessful, it will not be an effective time-management tool for the leader/supervisor, so it needs careful planning and monitoring.

Be firm about time spent in meetings

When you take control and explain how you are going to use the meeting and keep it to time, people generally understand and respect you for it. You just need to make it clear at the beginning of the meeting so that people are not offended if you start to bring the conversations and discussions to an end.

Managing Self

Remove distractions when focus is needed

If possible, you need to be able to close the door on people and
interruptions when you need to work closely on something and
give it your complete focus. You can allocate time when you do
not wish to be disturbed and let colleagues know so that they can
protect and respect your privacy. Just having a rule about a closed
door meaning 'I'm busy, please don't come in unless it's urgent'
can work if people are told.

If you cannot stop interruptions in your normal workplace, it is worth finding somewhere
else to work when you need to be focused. Working in a large, noisy open-plan office,
especially if you do not have your own desk, can be a nightmare and an impossible place to
work.

Working from home can be an option with some organisations and you need to discuss
your needs and problems with line managers to find a solution when your time is being
wasted due to lack of space and privacy.

Prioritising Work

Individuals, teams and organisations all benefit from people being organised and prioritising
work. Benefits include:

- *more efficient use of time* – e.g., by only touching each file once
- *improved communication* – e.g., from everyone knowing and feeling confident about
  their position and the protocols for communication
- *improved customer service* – e.g., from customers knowing that urgent work will be
  given top priority
- *fewer complaints* – e.g., from urgent work being done first
- *a calmer work environment* – e.g., from people working more efficiently
- *respect from colleagues and others* – e.g., once they accept and understand the
  rules about interruptions and knowing how and when their issues will be dealt with
- *better mental and physical health* – e.g., from not having to 'firefight' all the time
- *fewer interruptions* – e.g., as people learn to leave others alone at certain times, or if
  the door is closed
- *faster meetings* – e.g., by being more focused and stricter about how the meeting is
  run
- *more time to deal with the unexpected* – e.g., having some flexibility to be able to
  cope with unplanned tasks and problems
- *improved promotion prospects* – e.g., from senior managers being aware of
  improvements in output or communication skills and achieving objectives and meeting
  deadlines with ease.

It is also easier for someone else to take over our work allocation if everything is organised and
prioritised, which can be useful for holiday cover, for instance.

Managing Self

Techniques for Prioritising Work

In addition to the practical steps which can be taken to manage time more efficiently, work can be prioritised using one of four methods. This can be a useful exercise that focusses attention:

- *at the beginning of each week, day or month*
- *at the beginning of a new project*
- *when deciding how to prioritise objectives*
- *if new tasks suddenly demand attention and need to be fitted in*
- *after an emergency or major interruption* – to reprioritise work
- *when events overtake and overcome us* – to help us refocus and get back on track

When you have the activity log data, you can analyse how you prioritise activities. This gives the information needed to be able to stand back, review everything objectively and then make adjustments to target efforts and time more effectively. There are four suggested methods for doing this:

To-Do Lists

To-Do lists are the key to efficiency!

Do you often feel overwhelmed by the amount of work you have to do? Do you find yourself missing deadlines? Do you sometimes just forget to do something important, so that people have to chase you to get work done?

All of these are symptoms of not keeping a proper "To-Do List." They are simply prioritised lists of all the tasks that need to be done. They list everything that has to be done, with the most important tasks at the top of the list and the least important tasks at the bottom.

By keeping such a list, you make sure that tasks are written down all in one place, so nothing important is forgotten. By prioritising tasks, you plan the order in which you will do them, so that task which need immediate attention and those which can be deferred until later are identified.

To-Do Lists are essential if you are going to beat work overload. When you do not use them effectively, you will appear unfocused and unreliable to the people around you.

When used effectively, you will be much better organised and much more reliable.

You will experience less stress, safe in the knowledge that you have not forgotten anything important. If you prioritise intelligently, you will focus your time and energy on high-value activities, which will mean that you are more productive and more valuable to your team.

Keeping a properly structured and thought-out list sounds simple enough. But it can be surprising how many people fail to use them at all, never mind use them effectively.

Managing Self

In fact, it is often when people start to use them effectively and sensibly that they make their first personal productivity breakthroughs and start making a success of their careers.

Step 1:
Write down all of the tasks that you need to complete. If they are large tasks, break the task down and write down the first action step along with the rest of the broken down steps. *(Tasks or action steps should take no longer than 1-2 hours to complete.)*

Note:
You may find it easier to compile several lists (covering personal, study and workplace, for example). Try different approaches and use the best for your own situation.

Step 2:
Run through the list of tasks allocating priorities from A (very important, or very urgent) to F (unimportant, or not at all urgent). If too many tasks have a high priority, go through the list again and demote the less important ones. Once you have done this, rewrite the list in priority order.

Using a To-Do List
To use a list, simply work your way through it in order, dealing with the A priority tasks first, then the Bs, then the Cs and so on. As you complete tasks, tick them or cross them off.

What you put on your list and how you use it will depend on your situation. If you are in a sales role, a good way to motivate yourself is to keep the list relatively short and aim to complete it every day.

If you are in an operational role, or if tasks are large or dependent on too many other people, then it may be better to focus on a longer-term list and "chip away" at it day-by-day.
Many people find it helpful to spend 10 minutes at the end of each day, organising tasks on their list ready for the next day.

Using Software
Although using a paper list is an easy way to get started, software-based approaches can be more efficient in spite of the learning curve. These can remind you of events or tasks that are close to being overdue and they can also be synchronised with your phone or email and shared with others on your team.
There are many time management software programs available. At a simple level, you can use MSWord or MS Excel to manage your lists. Some versions of Microsoft Outlook and other email services such as Gmail™, have task lists as standard features. Remember the Milk is another popular online task management tool that will sync with your smartphone, PDA, or email account. It can even show you where your tasks are on a map.

Managing Self

One of the biggest advantages of a software-based approach is that you can update it easily. Instead of scratching off tasks and rewriting the list every day, software allows you to move and prioritise tasks quickly.

Tip: *All of us think, plan and work differently. A program that works well for a colleague might not work well for you simply because you learn and think in your own way. This is why it is useful to research and try several different ways of compiling your list before deciding on a single system.*

Allen's Input Processing Technique

It is very easy to be distracted from tasks in the increasingly demanding environment we operate in today.

If distraction is an issue for you, Allen's Input Processing Technique may help to improve your productivity.

The model is not complicated, yet it has the potential to help save a significant amount of time every day.

Inputs are the demands which are placed on your time and attention. The way in which these 'inputs' are dealt with will determine how efficiently you utilise your time. Are some inputs allowed to distract you from the task at hand? If they completely ignored, does it mean you are missing out on important information? Whichever you chose you will not be operating at an optimum level.

Using this technique will put a plan in place for how each new input will be processed. Once the plan becomes second nature, there will be no need to waste time analysing every new input – quick decisions will be made allowing you to move on the other matters.

Collecting Inputs

The technique starts with collecting the inputs. They will arrive in different forms and through a variety of forms and formats.   An email is a clear form of input along with a phone message, a text message, a request for a meeting, a new bill, a customer complaint, etc. It does not matter what form an input is presented –is how you respond that matters

Critical Question

When a new input is received, in whatever form, there is one question which is going to determine how you process it and this is critical. That question is –

Will I act on this?

It is as simple as that. This one question starts the entire process.

Managing Self

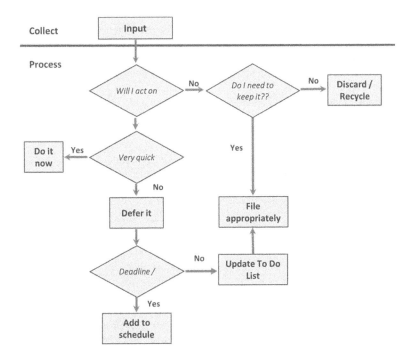

If the answer is 'no', then decide whether it is something that needs to be saved for later. If it is to be saved, file it appropriately and move on. If it does not need to be saved – delete it and move on.

Deciding immediately if a new input needs action, avoids having a pile of information which needs wading through. People fall behind on processing inputs and reach the point where they simply do not have sufficient time to get back on top of it.

Taking Action

If an input needs action, the next question to ask is does it need an immediate response? If the issue is urgent, the decision is simple –complete the task immediately. The urgent inputs are the easiest to deal with as there is no doubt as to when the task should be actioned.

When an input arrives which needs attention, but not immediate attention, it should be deferred to a later time/date. Respond immediately by setting a time and date for the task to be completed.

Consider what needs to be done, when it needs to be completed, and how long it will take complete.

When a time and date has been set add it to a calendar or to-do list.

Managing Self

Consistency is Key

Allen's Input Processing Technique helps to deal with inputs in the office, but only if it is consistently applied. It is the kind of tool that must be used every time if it is to save time effectively. Not using it for a day or two will cause a back log and it will be challenging to get back on top once again. Failing to deal with inputs will also result in missing something important – a mistake which could cost money in the long term.

Many people think they are sufficiently organised not to need the benefits of this kind of tool, but rarely is that the case. With an increasing number of inputs using an organisational tool is a good choice.

Allen's Input Processing Technique saves time, it can help to reduce stress levels and it can ensure information and assistance needed is received in a timely manner.

Eisenhower Grid

Another tool which can be used is the Eisenhower Grid or Matrix (also known as Stephen Covey's Time Management Matrix) can help manage available time more efficiently. The matrix allows you to organise priorities more effectively than before.

The grid makes use of four different quadrants that allow tasks to be prioritised in relation to their importance and urgency, helping to decide whether a task needs to be addressed immediately or if it can be postponed. As can be seen in the graphic below, the matrix is divided into four quadrants that are organised by importance and urgency.

- *Important responsibilities contribute to the achievement of your goals.*
- *Urgent responsibilities require immediate attention.*

These activities are often tightly linked to the accomplishment of someone else's goal. Not dealing with these issues will cause immediate consequences.

	Urgent	*Not urgent*
Important	Do Now	Plan to Do
Not Important	Reject and Explain	Resist and Cease

Managing Self

The grid is made up of four time-management quadrants

Quadrant 1 – urgent and important
The activities in quadrant 1 can be differentiated into items that could not have been foreseen and those items that could. The latter can be avoided by developing plans and paying close attention to their execution.

The first quadrant should only contain those activities and responsibilities that require your immediate attention. The space is reserved for emergencies and extremely important deadlines. Should a major crisis arise, you will have to postpone other tasks. When to use:

- *Crises*
- *Pressing problems*
- *Projects that are deadline driven*
- *Emergencies*
- *Last-minute preparations*

Quadrant 2 – not urgent but important
The items found in quadrant 2 do not have a high urgency but can play an important role in the future. This quadrant is not only reserved for strategic planning, but also to items related to health, education, exercise and career. Investing time in these areas might not be urgent at the present day, but in the long term, it will be of the greatest importance.

Pay close attention that you have scheduled enough time for quadrant 2 activities, in order to avoid them to become quadrant I items. Doing so will increase your capability of finishing tasks in time. When to use:

- *Planning*
- *Preparing*
- *Training*
- *Exercise, health and recreation*

Quadrant 3 – urgent but not important
The third quadrant summarises items that appear to have a high urgency but are not at all important. Some of these activities might be entirely ego-driven, without contributing any value. In fact, these activities are obstacles that stand between you and your goals. If possible, try to delegate these items or consider rescheduling them.

If another person is causing you quadrant 3 tasks it could be appropriate to decline their request politely. If this is not an option, try to avoid being constantly interrupted by appointing timeslots to those that often need your help. This way, you can address all their issues at once, without regularly interrupting your concentration. When to use:

- *Interruptions*
- *Meetings*

Quadrant 4 – not urgent and not important

The fourth and last quadrant contains all those activities that do not contribute any value at all—the obvious time wasters. All the activities contained therein are nothing more than distractions; avoid them as much as you can. You should also try to eliminate all the items in this list, no matter how entertaining. When to use:

- *Trivia*
- *Time wasters*
- *Surfing the Internet without purpose*
- *Watching TV for hours*

Applying the Time Matrix

When using the matrix it is recommended to try to maximise the time spent on quadrant II activities. This will allow you (in the long run) to reduce quadrant I activities, as many of them could have been quadrant II activities if better planning had been implemented at the start.

The objective of using the time management matrix is to question whether a certain activity brings you closer to your goals or not. If this is the case, these responsibilities need to be prioritised over those tasks that might demand your time but do not contribute to your goals. Delay activities that do not contribute any significant output, until more important tasks are finished.

Reprioritising your current 'to-do' list

The time matrix can be applied as a tool that allows you to reprioritise tasks by their importance and urgency. By sorting the tasks and responsibilities into the appropriate quadrant you will be able to quickly identify activities that need your immediate attention and those which can be safely put to one side.

One-week assessments

The second approach of using the time management matrix requires a weekly assessment.

You will need six blank copies of the matrix, five for each workday and one for your weekly assessment. At the end of each workday, you list all tasks and responsibilities and the amount of time spent. At the end of the week, you summarise the five days of your week in one matrix. Make sure to summarise the amount of time spent on a given task.

After you have summarised the week, you can then evaluate how well the time was spent and whether or not you need to make any adaptations.

Managing Self

Lakein ABC Priority System

Another theory is the Lakein ABC priority system, a technique used by Alan Lakein, a management consultant. When using this system, you need to have a brainstorming session and write down everything that you need to do – e.g., as a series of spider grams or in lists.

Then allocate each task a value: **A** (high value), **B** (medium value) or **C** (low value). The categories can be broken down further – e.g. A1, A2, B1 and B2. This helps you to remember to:

- *include odd items that we might otherwise forget*
- *focus on the whole workload*
- *prioritise each item so that we can concentrate and not be distracted by less important tasks*

Lakein Prioritised Activity List		
Task	Priority	Allocate
Book dentists	medium value	B1
Pay final reminder gas bill	medium value	B2
Finish report for line manager	high value	A1
Arrange to go to Cinema	low value	C1

The 4 D's of Time Management

Simply put, they are do, delete, defer or delegate.

Do it.

If a task can be completed there and then in a few minutes, then just do it.
Provided of course it is not a task to delete, delegate or defer. In other words, if it is important for you to do it and you have the time available to do it, then get it done straight away.

Postponing important tasks often leads to procrastination or feelings of anxiety or stress.

Defer it.

There are some tasks that you may not be able to deal with straight away. It might be an email about booking a family holiday. It is not important during your working day but is important to get done. So, you can defer it and look at the email later in your free time.

Similarly, you might need to meet with a team member to discuss how they can achieve better results in their sales. A very important task, yet it might be able to wait until the sales meeting in a few days. That way you can spend the time until then planning the sales meeting and getting the things done that are more important at that particular point in time.

Delegate it.
Is it important or necessary for you to do the task? Is it your responsibility to do it? If the answer is no, then delegate it. You will still be ultimately responsible for the task being done; however, it is better to delegate the task if there is someone who can complete it as well as you can. Often people choose to do tasks which are easier than others they need to do and not getting done what is really important.

There is a fine line between delegation and abdication.

Ensure that there is some measure in place to check that the task has been completed by the person to whom you have delegated. At the same time empower them to do the task and be understanding if the task has not been completed in quite the way you would have done it yourself.

Delegation does not only have to be to subordinates. You can delegate across, upwards and across departments as well.

Delete it.
Check whether the task actually requires your attention or whether it is worth your time. If it does not, then simply delete it. An example would be looking at all the email received during the day. Delete all of those which are spam or you have no interest in. Mail clients like Outlook provide a preview of emails so a decision can be made without having to open and read the whole email.

Defer any emails which are important but can be dealt with later. Remember the Pareto principle (80/20 rule) that people spend 80% of their time on activities that are a complete waste of time.

Implementing the 4 Ds' of time management
A great way to implement this is to look at your to do list on a daily basis. See which tasks need to be deleted, done, delegated or deferred. Then do the same thing with each task that comes across your desk during the day. Some tasks may simply keep on moving on to another day. Ask yourself if that task really is important for you to do. Chances are it may not be. If so, delegate it or delete it. Similarly, it might be a task that you are just procrastinating on in which case ask yourself what it is about the task that is stopping you from just doing it.

Managing Self

Delegation

Getting someone else to do the work is a great solution in everyone's book, however, there is the risk it can go horribly wrong leaving you with an even greater problem than when you started, which you will still have to resolve. That is, unless you understand the art of delegation!

The steps of successful delegation

1. Define the task

Confirm in your own mind that the task is suitable to be delegated. Does it meet the criteria for delegating?

2. Select the individual or team

What are your reasons for delegating to this person or team? What are they going to get out of it? What are you going to get out of it?

3. Assess ability and training needs

Is the other person or team of people capable of doing the task? Do they understand what needs to be done? If not, you cannot delegate.

4. Explain the reasons

You must explain why the job or responsibility is being delegated. And why to that person or people? What is its importance and relevance? Where does it fit in the overall scheme of things?

5. State required results

What must be achieved? Clarify understanding by getting feedback from the other person. How will the task be measured? Make sure they know how you intend to decide that the job is being successfully done.

6. Consider resources required

Discuss and agree what is required to get the job done. Consider people, location, premises, equipment, money, materials, other related activities and services.

7. Agree deadlines

When must the job be finished? If it is a long-term task, when are the review dates? When are the reports due? If the task is complex and has parts or stages, what are the priorities? At this point you may need to confirm understanding with the other person of the previous points, getting ideas and interpretation. This helps to reinforce commitment as well as showing you that the job can be done,

Methods of checking and controlling must be agreed with the other person. Failing to agree this in advance will cause this monitoring to seem like interference or lack of trust.

8. Support and communicate

Think about who else needs to know what is going on and inform them. Involve the other person in considering this so they can see beyond the issue at hand. Do not leave the person to inform your own peers of their new responsibility. Warn the person about any

Managing Self

awkward matters of politics or protocol. Inform your own boss if the task is important and of sufficient profile.

9. Feedback on results
It is essential to let the person know how they are doing and whether they have achieved their aims. If not, you must review with them why things did not go to plan and deal with the problems. You must absorb the consequences of failure and pass on the credit for success.

The Action Priority Matrix
Whether they are bright ideas to pursue, exciting opportunities, or interesting possibilities, most of us have many more activities on our to-do lists than we have time available to work on them.

By choosing activities intelligently, we can make the most of time and opportunity, however, by choosing badly, it is easy to become bogged down in time consuming tasks which prevent you moving forward.

This is where an "Action Priority Matrix" can be useful. These simple diagrams help you choose the activities you should prioritise and the ones you should avoid if you want to make the most of your time and opportunities.

Prioritising a To-do List
Action Priority Matrices are another way to show you how can prioritise activities to make the most of your time, energy and talents.

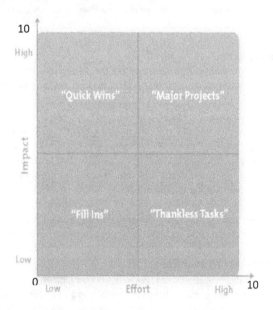

Managing Self

This is useful, because we rarely have time to complete all of the tasks which are outstanding. The matrix allows more of time to be spent on the high-value activities that keep us moving forwards and drop tasks that contribute little.

To use the matrix, you score tasks based on their impact and secondly on the effort needed to complete them.

You then use the scores to plot the activities into one of four quadrants:

Quick Wins (High Impact, Low Effort)
Quick wins are the most attractive tasks, because they give you a good return for relatively little effort. Focus on these as much as you can.

Major Projects (High Impact, High Effort)
Major tasks give good returns, but are time-consuming. This means that one major task can "crowd out" many quick wins.

Fill Ins (Low Impact, Low Effort)
Do not worry too much about doing these tasks – if you have spare time, do them, but drop them or delegate them if something better comes along.

Thankless Tasks (Low Impact, High Effort)
Try to avoid these tasks. Not only do they give little return, but they also soak up time that you should be using on quick wins.

Once you understand the principles behind the Action Priority Matrix, you will probably find that you apply it quickly and intuitively to new tasks and projects.

Workload Management Strategies
At some point, everyone feels as though they have more work than they can cope with. However, not all stress is bad and it is often cited as a key factor in helping people respond to crises, adapt to change and excel when a peak performance is required, for example, in an interview or presentation.

When coping with stress at work, the important thing is not to let your workload grow to the point where you are completely overloaded.

The most common sources of work-related stress include:

Plan Your Work and Work Your Plan

Managing Self

- *Continuous and tight deadlines.*
- *Dealing with crises on a daily basis.*
- *An excessive workload.*
- *Role ambiguity and conflict.*
- *Constant negative feedback.*
- *Inadequately trained support staff.*

If you are overloaded, then you need some workload management strategies to remedy the situation.

This will be easier if you have the facts to back up your case and are confident that you are working as effectively as possible by using an appropriate workload management strategy. The most common sources of work-related stress include continuous and tight deadlines, an excessive workload, role ambiguity and conflict and the need to deal with crises on a daily basis.

Avoid taking on too much

A significant contributor to workplace stress and overload is the inability to say no, which results in people taking on far more work than they can realistically manage. It is a natural response to want to accommodate requests made by others. We do not want to disappoint them, let them down, give the impression that we cannot be bothered or are too lazy to help.

Sometimes tasks may sound so enticing that we are tempted to take them on and worry about finding the time for them later, this is especially true for work that is some time in the future. However, it is important to think realistically about your workload.

Ask yourself:

> *"are you likely to have any more spare time in the future than you have at the moment?"*

One of the major factors in developing the ability to say no is to realise that if you take on things that you subsequently have not got time to do well, you will be letting everyone down. A job done badly will reflect poorly on you, your colleague and perhaps the whole organisation.

It is very easy to agree to take on more responsibility, to be seen as a keen and competent employee. It is much more difficult to admit that overload is a problem and then to take action to remedy the situation. If you feel that you are becoming overloaded, then you may decide to try to negotiate a reduction in your workload.

Managing Self

Negotiating Workload

If you have never questioned the demands of your manager or organisation before then this may be rather daunting. The most effective tactic may be to restrict your negotiations to a specific task or project that you identify as causing you the worst problem.

Below are some important guidelines to consider when assessing workload management strategies:

Specify your objectives precisely

If you feel deluged by low-level customer enquiries, you might suggest delegating the handling of first line customer enquiries to the receptionists. This approach provides a framework for the negotiation and prevents the risk of your request being mistaken for a general complaint.

Prepare your evidence

If you can produce a time log detailing the amount of time that a particular task has taken you and can show the associated cost, this will often make for a more convincing case.

Prepare counter arguments to the likely objections

The best way to prepare counter arguments is to look at the situation from your manager's perspective. Seeing things from your manager's viewpoint should help you to devise a solution that they will find acceptable.

Decide in advance what compromise you would accept

If both you and your manager are going to be happy with the outcome over the long-term, then there may need to be some form of compromise. Decide in advance what issues you are likely to need to give ground on.

Become more task-oriented

Some people are primarily task-orientated, whilst others are primarily people-orientated. Task orientated people often find it easier to say no, as they tend to evaluate requests against task related criteria. They will ask themselves whether or not they are capable of and willing to perform the requested task. This enables them to make a more objective decision in response to a request.

People-orientated individuals are more likely to ask questions relating to their relationship with other people and their desire not to disappoint them. If you feel that you would like to become more effective at saying no, then try prompting yourself to think more carefully about the task involved each time you are requested to take something on.

Ask yourself questions like:

1. *Can you tackle this task?*
2. *Are you clear about precisely what it entails?*
3. *Have you got the time to take it on?*
4. *Can you do the job well?*
5. *Is there someone else better equipped to do it?*

6. *What happens if you need to disengage from the task due to other commitments?*

If your responses lead you to believe that you would be unwise to take it on, then it is in nobody's interest for you to agree to it. Try to clarify your reasons and explain these in a clear and concise way when declining the request.

Be prepared to say 'No'

In most circumstances you have every right to decline a request. However, if you let yourself worry or dwell on past occasions where you have declined a request then you are more likely to accept future requests, regardless of their importance.

Consider your response

Try to predict circumstances in which you are likely to be asked to take on extra commitments and prepare some form of response. When requests arrive unexpectedly, ask for time to think about the request before responding.

Do not apologise

Do not fall into the trap of being over-apologetic. Say what you want to say in a clear and concise way but do not sound like you are making excuses. If people get the idea that they can talk you round, then they may persist until they are successful. The other drawback with adopting an apologetic approach is that the requester may feel that your reasons for declining are tenuous and doubt the reasons you have given.

Think ahead

It is a natural assumption that it is easier to book the time of a busy person well in advance and it is all too easy to accommodate such requests. However, are you likely to be any less busy in 6 months' time than you are in three weeks' time? If your future commitments are uncertain then be very careful about agreeing to things even if they seem to be a long way off.

Saying 'No' to your boss

There are three common reasons why saying no to your boss is a different proposition to declining requests from colleagues or clients:

Firstly, it may appear as though you are refusing to do the normal activities of your job.
Secondly, you may worry about giving the impression of not being as keen as your peers.
Finally, your boss may just overrule your objections and make you do it anyway.

Generally speaking, there are only two valid reasons for declining work that is passed down.

Managing Self

Firstly, that your existing work will suffer and secondly that the work is beyond your level of competence. This means that any workload management strategies you use must be based on one of these reasons.

It is important to construct a good case to support your argument. You should put your points clearly and concisely and do not offer too many objections. This invites your boss to use the weakest one to undermine your whole case, without giving you the opportunity to counter with your stronger points.

Another useful approach can be to devise a plan for how the task could be tackled, without taking the full responsibility upon yourself. You might even turn a request from your boss into an opportunity to offload some routine work, thereby freeing yourself to address the current request properly. It can assist you greatly to get the boss on-side by sowing the germ of an idea and letting them come up with the plan, before endorsing it as a great way to proceed.

The Pomodoro Technique

Getting things done is hard, especially if you are self-employed or need to do things for yourself that you usually put off, like paying bills. There always seems to be something else to do: a

drawer that could be organised, a phone call to your sister or checking hotel prices on a trip you have no intention of taking.

Enter: the Pomodoro Technique!

This popular time-management method can help you power through distractions, hyper-focus and get things done in short bursts, while taking frequent breaks to come up for air and relax. Best of all, it is easy. If you have a busy job where you are expected to produce, it is a great way to get through your tasks.

What is the Pomodoro Technique?

The Pomodoro Technique was invented in the early 1990s by developer, entrepreneur and author Francesco Cirillo. Cirillo named the system "Pomodoro" after the tomato-shaped timer he used to track his work as a university student.

The methodology is simple: When faced with any large task or series of tasks, break the work down into short, timed intervals (called "Pomodoro's") that are spaced out by short breaks. This trains your brain to focus for short periods and helps you stay on top of deadlines or constantly refilling inboxes. With time it can even help improve your attention span and concentration.

Managing Self

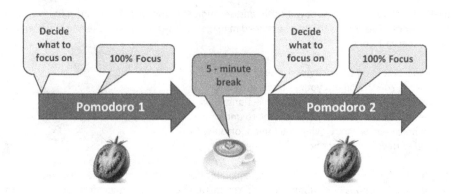

Pomodoro is a cyclical system. You work in short sprints, which makes sure you are consistently productive.

You also get to take regular breaks that bolster your motivation and keep you creative.

The Pomodoro Technique is probably one of the simplest productivity methods to implement. All you need is a timer. Beyond that, there are no special apps, books, or tools required (though plenty of them out there if you would like to go that route). Here is how to get started with Pomodoro, in five steps:

- *Choose a task to be accomplished.*
- *Set the Pomodoro to 25 minutes (the Pomodoro is the timer)*
- *Work on the task until the Pomodoro rings, then put a check on your sheet of paper*
- *Take a short break (5 minutes is OK)*

Every 4 Pomodoro's take a longer break

That "longer break" is usually in the order of 15-30 minutes, whatever it takes to make you feel recharged and ready to start another 25-minute work session. Repeat that process a few times over the course of a workday and you actually get a lot accomplished—and took plenty of breaks to grab a cup of coffee or refill your water bottle in the process.

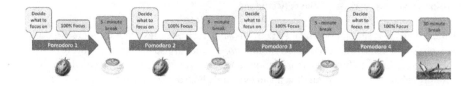

It is important to note that a pomodoro is an indivisible unit of work—that means if you are distracted part-way by a co-worker, meeting, or emergency, you either have to end the pomodoro there (saving your work and starting a new one later), or you have to postpone the

---

distraction until the pomodoro is complete. If you can do the latter, Cirillo suggests the "inform, negotiate and call back" strategy:

- *Inform the other (distracting) party that you are working on something right now.*
- *Negotiate a time when you can get back to them about the distracting issue in a timely manner.*
- *Schedule that follow-up immediately.*
- *Call back the other party when your Pomodoro is complete and you are ready to tackle their issue.*

Of course, not every distraction is that simple and some things demand immediate attention—but not every distraction does. Sometimes it is perfectly fine to tell your co-worker "I'm in the middle of something right now, but can I get back to you in....ten minutes?" Doing so does not just keep you in the groove, it also gives you control over your workday.

The Pomodoro Technique is often championed by developers, designers and other people who have to turn out regular packages of creative work. Essentially, people who have to actually produce something to be reviewed by others. That means everyone from authors writing their next book to software engineers working on the next big video game can all benefit from the timed work sessions and breaks that Pomodoro offers.

However, it is also useful for people who do not have such rigid goals or packages of work.

Anyone else with an "inbox" or queue they have to work through can benefit as well. If you are a customer support officer with enquiries to deal with, you can set a timer and start working through them until your timer goes off.

Then it is time for a break, after which you come back and pick up where you left off or start a new batch of enquiries. If you build things or work with your hands, the frequent breaks give you the opportunity to step back and review what you are doing, think about your next steps and make sure you do not get exhausted. The system is remarkably adaptable to different kinds of work.

Finally, it is important to remember that Pomodoro is a productivity system—not a set of shackles. If you are making headway and the timer goes off, it is OK to pause the timer, finish what you are doing and then take a break.

Managing Self

POSEC

The POSEC method is based loosely on Abraham Maslow's Hierarchy of Needs and it stands for 'Prioritising by Organising, Economising and Contributing'. This method can assist you to break down your goals into smaller targets and 'minor goals' and once you have achieved these, you are on your way to completing the bigger goals.

Prioritise – Using a robust tool to help you to prioritise what is urgent/important is the first step in using this method. This will help you to utilise your time wisely in the pursuit of achieving your goals.

Organise – This is about organising the things that you do on a regular basis to meet your basic needs. It could be planning in regular meetings or CPD sessions, or, on a more personal level, spending time with family.

Streamline – This applies to the tasks that you may not enjoy doing but that you must do. This is about managing your stability and security. Making this work simple and achieving it faster, will help your time management. On a personal level, this could be chores such as housework.

Economise – These apply to things that you would like to do, but do not have the time to devote to it. These are often not placed very high up on the importance list, such as CPD or socialising.

Contribute – This is the kind of work that may be over a period of time but have a positive long-term effect. These are the things that really make a difference and can contribute to your personal and organisational goals.

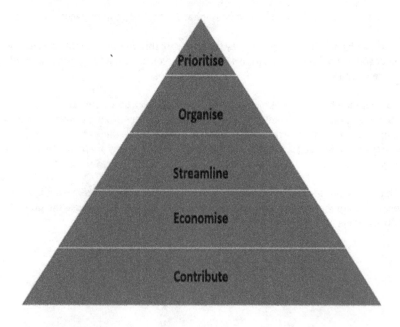

Managing Self

Getting Organised

Are you in control of everything you need for your job? Is the right information always at your fingertips? Do you have a clear plan of action every day?

Maybe your desk looks like it has been hit by a bomb and you are drowning in emails. You are in danger of missing a deadline, your important files are never where you thought they were and it is a lottery whether you will even have clean clothes to wear for work in the morning!

Your ability to organise yourself has a major impact on your success and it can have a knock-on effect on your team members and co-workers, too.

The following strategies will help to replace the mayhem and chaos in your life with a sense of calm.

Benefits of being more organised

You can lose a great deal of time to disorganisation. A minute here to find your keys, another there to track down an email… Those minutes quickly mount up to hours of lost productivity. Even if you do manage to get everything done, you are unlikely to have produced your best work.

The core benefits of being organised and operating in a generally clutter-free environment are increased productivity and improved performance. With those comes a greater sense of control, which is a vital part of stress management, resilience and overall well-being.

Good organisation can also lead to better thinking. Decision making and problem solving rely on a clear head, plus ready access to the right information and tools. An uncluttered approach improves concentration and your ability to learn.

Success at work also has a lot to do with how you are seen by others. If you are regularly late for meetings, careless with your responsibilities and seem out of control in your role, your reputation – and your chances of career progression – are at serious risk.

If you show yourself to be someone who manages their workload well and can be relied upon to help make your organisation or team run more smoothly, your competence and value will be clear for everyone to see.

Organise Your Workspace

To become more organised, a good place to start is at your desk – or wherever you do the majority of your work.

Does your workspace currently help you to be organised, or is it the source of many of your problems? You may work best with a little clutter – in which case, keep it there. But, if the state of your desk is spoiling your performance, it is time to make some changes.

What do you actually need to keep close by? If you spot anything that is no longer useful, or is just getting in the way, either store it carefully somewhere else, or get rid of it.

Managing Self

Try having an "action area" on your desk, where you keep the things you need for your current project or activity. This will help you to get started quickly, to avoid distractions and to stay focused on the task at hand. When one task is done, clear everything away to make room for the next.

When your workspace is sorted, keep it that way! At the end of every day, decide what needs to stay where it is and make everything else disappear.

Organise time

An uncluttered approach to work will not just save you time, it will also help you to use time more effectively. Good organisational habits are crucial for successful time management.

With easy access to everything you need, you will be confident about the amount of time each task should take. You will also have a clear idea of when to do it – to fit in with the rest of your work and to suit other people.

Most importantly, with a calm and controlled approach to each day, you will be able to make good use of all the time-management tools on offer.

Start every day as you mean to go on. Use the first 15 minutes to get organised. If you have an To Do List, go straight to the item at the top of your list.

Alternatively, write a To-Do List, with the day's priorities at the top. This will help you to see the best way to plan your day. You will know which tasks need to be done first and which can be left until the afternoon. You will also be able to match your most significant – or most challenging – work to the times of day when you are at your best.

Traditional Tools

For some people, a paper notebook is still the best way to stay in control of information, ideas, lists and plans. You can personalise it, carry it everywhere you go and it never needs recharging!

It is a good idea to start a new, dated page each day, so that you can easily go back and find the information you need.

You can use your notebook to record the key points from conversations and meetings. If an idea occurs to you while you are busy with a task, jot it down for later, so that you do not lose your flow.

Write To-Do Lists and reminders that will help you to stay in control of your working day. You can also add notes about your activities away from work, to make your whole day run more smoothly.

Other traditional tools can help, too:

Managing Self

Wall or desk calendars are great for keeping your schedule in front of you and they are easy to update.

Paper diaries give you a clear picture of your day, week, or even a whole year and help you to coordinate your work with everything else that is going on in your life.

Sticky notes allow you to leave yourself quick reminders – in useful places – as well as to mark key sections in books, separate out piles of documents, or help others to understand your systems.

Note:
Being organised is a personal responsibility, but it also benefits your team members and co-workers.

Following a file-naming convention, for example, saves you time and stress and it also makes the system effective for everyone else. Getting to appointments on time boosts your reputation and makes meetings more productive.

Even getting simple "housekeeping" responsibilities right, like keeping the printer paper topped up, for example, can have a major impact on the mood – and the performance – of your whole team.

Technology

Whatever system you use to communicate online, it will usually have many organisational features.

Consider the different options for labelling or filing emails. It helps to colour-code your online calendar (maybe red for urgent, green for extended deadlines and blue for low-priority tasks). Check that you know how to set electronic reminders.

Spreadsheets can be useful for keeping track of progress.

A smart phone also has plenty of useful tools built in. As well as making the most of the clock, alarm, calendar and reminder functions, you can use the voice recorder to capture your ideas. At other times, a simple photograph may be the best way to gather the information you need.

There are many apps geared to boosting your personal organisation skills. RescueTime, for example, monitors all your digital activity and provides detailed reports about how you are spending your time.

Managing Self

Time is finite!

We all have the same number of hours each day. You cannot store time, borrow it, or save for later use. You can only decide how to allocate it, spending it on activities of higher rather than low value.

Time management is a game of choices: projects to pursue, tasks to complete, routines to follow.

Adopting good time management techniques in your life is not about squeezing as many tasks as you can into your day. It is about simplifying how you work, getting things done faster and doing things better. By doing so, you will have more time to play, rest and doing the things you love. Do not try to work hard, invest in working smarter.

"Time management is not a peripheral activity or skill. It is the core skill upon which everything else in life depends." — Brian Tracy

Below, you will find a list of time management techniques. They are a set of principles, rules and skills that allow you to put your focus on the things that matter, get more done and help you be more productive.
Use them as a rulebook of your work. You will improve your productivity, accomplish more with less effort, improve your decision-making ability, reduce stress and ultimately become more successful in your career.

But remember everyone is different. These are the time management techniques that are useful in my life, but you might not. Adopt the ones that work for you and always seek to refine your own practices by regularly thinking about how to improve your time management skills.

By writing your own time management rulebook, you will discover that there are really enough hours in a day for everything you would like to do. It just takes a bit of rearranging and re-imagining to find them...

Organise Work Around Energy Levels
Productivity is directly related to your energy level. Find your most productive hours — the time of your peak energy — and schedule the most challenging work for those periods. Do low-value and low-energy tasks (also known as shallow work), such as responding to emails or unimportant meetings, in between those hours.

Example:
If you are a morning person, do your most critical work when you get in the office. After lunch, your energy might fall, so it is a great time to clean your desk, clear emails or update spreadsheets. Plan your work around your energy levels, scheduling critical work for peak productivity times.

You should also know your energy levels by day: Tuesday seems to be the most productive day for most people but find your own patterns. Here how the head of product marketing for Google Apps for Work, organises his week around his energy levels:

Monday: *Energy ramps out of the weekend — schedule low-demand tasks like setting goals, organising and planning.*

Tuesday, Wednesday: *Peak of energy — tackle the most difficult problems, write, brainstorm, schedule your Make Time.*

Thursday: *Energy begins to ebb — schedule meetings, especially when consensus is needed.*

Friday: *Lowest energy level — do open-ended work, long-term planning and relationship building.*

Map your work and energy levels in a spreadsheet for a couple of weeks until you uncover your productivity patterns.

Plan Your Day the Night Before
Before going to bed, spend 5 minutes writing your to-do list for the next day. These tasks should help you move towards your professional and personal goals. By planning ahead, the night before, you will be better prepared mentally for the challenges ahead and there will be no room for procrastination in the morning. As a result, you will work faster and smoother than ever before.

Start the day with critical work
This is a golden time management technique: Find your most important task for the day and tackle it first. Your most important task should be the one thing that creates the most impact on your work. Getting it done will give you the momentum and sense of accomplishment early in the day. That is how big life goals are achieved: small continuous efforts, day after day.

In Elon Musk's words:

> *"Focus on signal over noise. Don't waste time on stuff that doesn't actually make things better."*

Look at your to-do list and decide which tasks help you get close to your goals and make progress in meaningful work. Put these at the top of your list so you can focus on them first. Resist the temptation of tackling the easiest tasks first.

Prioritise tasks
Knowing how to prioritise your work is an essential time management technique. Projects, however small or large, need clear priorities. When everything is a priority, nothing is.

Managing Self

Prioritise the tasks that actually contribute achieving your goals. Use a productivity tool like the Eisenhower Matrix to identify the critical tasks.

Delegate tasks
The Eisenhower Matrix will identify tasks that are urgent but not important. These tasks are best delegated to someone who can complete these tasks for you. You do not have to do every task personally. Delegating some tasks can be a great way to multiply your efforts and get more done.

Automate repetitive tasks
Technology has now reached a point where wea great deal of our daily operations can be automated. By automating tasks, you save hours per week. You can then use that time for challenging tasks or taking breaks.

Set Time Constraints
You become more productive when you allocate a specific amount of time to complete a specific task. That is why we create deadlines.

Parkinson's law states:

"work expands so as to fill the time available for its completion".

If you reduce the time you have to complete a task, you force your brain to focus and complete it.
Set deadlines even when you do not need to. Scheduling less time to complete tasks and force your brain to focus.

Example:
You have to review and reply to an email, a task that normally takes you around 20 minutes. Reduce the time available to 10 minutes, set a countdown timer and work as hard as you can to beat it. The timer creates a sense of urgency and pushes you to focus and be more efficient, even if you end up having to go back and add a more time later. Even when you do not have a deadline, set one. Your brain will acknowledge it. Knowing you only have one hour to complete a report will ensure you do not waste 20 minutes on Facebook.

Eliminate Distractions
Distractions hurt your productivity and focus. A study found that it takes an average of 23 minutes and 15 seconds to get back to the task after getting distracted.

Make quick decisions on things that do not matter
You make hundreds of small, medium and big decisions every day. 90% of the decisions we make do not matter. Success comes from identifying and focusing your energy on the 10%.

The small decisions affect you for a day, such as what to wear or where to eat. Medium impact decisions affect your life for a year, such as deciding to go back to university or rent a different room. It is the big decisions that are worthy of serious pondering, discussion, investigation, investment and decision making.

Managing Self

Focus on the big decisions and make quick decisions on medium and small decisions.

A simple decision-making system utilises three questions.

How will I feel about this decision 10 minutes from now?
How will I feel about it 10 months from now?
And in 10 years from now?

Track Your Time
Do you know how much time you spend on each task? Most of us can guess, but the estimates are normally way off. A time-tracking app can help you take the guesswork out and provide real data on productivity.

After a couple of weeks, you will start noticing patterns and knowing where and how your time is leaking. By being aware of how exactly you are using your time, you can devise a plan to attack your leaks and how to get rid of them.

Beat Procrastination with the 2-Minute Rule
The "2-Minute Rule" is a great way to beat procrastination and get things done. It works for both your professional and personal life. There are two parts to the "2-Minute Rule":

Part 1: If it can be done in two minutes, just do it. Do not add it to your to-do list, put it aside for later, or delegate to someone else. Just do it.

Part 2: If it takes more than two minutes, start it. Once you start acting on small tasks, you can keep the ball rolling. Simply working on it for two minutes will help you break the first barrier of procrastination.

Say No More Often Than Yes
Most CEOs will tell you that saying "no" is one of the most important time management techniques. Saying "yes" often can be counterproductive, especially when you agree to do things that do not contribute to your work and goals. Time is a limited resource and you cannot let people set your agenda in life. Focus on doing great quality work rather than rushing through it all. Quality wins over quantity every single day.

Warren Buffet (4th richest man in the World!) said it best:

"The difference between successful people and very successful people is that very successful people say no to almost everything."

Take advantage of gap time
We have a lot of downtime throughout our days: commuting, waiting in line, waiting rooms, in-between tasks, small breaks in the schedule, etc. If we add all this time up, we have around 1–3 hours of "gap time" every day. Be as strategic about your breaks as you are about your day in general. While these short periods might not be enough to do Deep Work, we can still work on little things that contribute to your work, development and growth.

Managing Self

By taking advantage of your downtime, you end up getting more done and having more free time for fun after work.

Automate Decisions

Force your brain to make a lot of decisions and you end up depleting your willpower and suffering from decision fatigue. This hurts your decision-making ability. As the day wears on, you will start making fewer smart decisions. To avoid mental exhaustion, automate decisions to free yourself from cognitive burden and not rely solely on your self-discipline. Let decisions happen automatically and smart decisions will happen by themselves.

Single Task

Multitasking is a corporate myth that has evolved over time. The brain is designed to focus on one thing at a time. Switching between tasks can have damaging costs to our work and productivity. Develop the habit of single tasking by forcing your brain to concentrate on one task and one task only. Put your phone away, close all the browser windows and apps that you do not need. Immerse yourself in this task. Only move to the next one when you are done.

Break down big tasks

From Bird by Bird: Some instructions on writing and life by Anne Lamott:

> *"Thirty years ago, my older brother, who was ten years old at the time, was trying to get a report on birds written that he'd had three months to write, which was due the next day. We were out at our family cabin in Bolinas and he was at the kitchen table close to tears, surrounded by binder paper and pencils and unopened books on birds, immobilised by the hugeness of the task ahead. Then my father sat down beside him, put his arm around my brother's shoulder and said, 'Bird by bird, buddy. Just take it bird by bird.'"*

We all have huge tasks that we get tired just thinking about the amount of work needed to complete them. We procrastinate by doing mindless tasks instead of starting them. To avoid this, break down the larger goals into small manageable tasks with realistically achievable milestones. This will help you map out all the small activities that need to be done and creating a timeline to do them. As a rule of thumb, each small task should take less than one hour to complete.

Take fewer (but better) meetings

Meetings are the devil of the corporate world. Few people like meetings and most dread them.

Truth is that most things do not need a meeting. If the purpose of the meeting is neither to decide or complete an action together, cancel it and communicate over email (e.g., updates on a specific project). As for outside the office meetings, switch to phone calls or video conferences

As for the meeting that you do have to attend, make them highly efficient and productive by following these simple rules:

- *Do not schedule more time than needed. Most of the times 20 minutes is the sweet spot*

- *Keep the number of participants small.*
- *Send everyone an agenda and main points the day before*
- *Keep conversation on-track by reminding the participants of the topic: "Let's schedule another time to discuss that later if it's helpful since we only have 10 minutes left"*
- *Group your meetings back-to-back to have a clear start and end point for each one*

Only attend meetings that have a clear agenda and a decision that needs to be made. To run better meetings, have an end time and keep the number of participants small.

Let go of perfectionism
Perfectionism keeps you from being perfect. It is easy to get caught up in an endless cycle of trying to do everything perfectly. But being a perfectionist can delay your work and make you miss important deadlines. The sooner you realise that delivering high-quality work on time is the most important skill, the faster you will advance on your goals and career. Perfectionism is actually fear disguised in sheep's clothing, which shows itself as procrastination. Learn to accept that small details do not matter, ship faster and fix things afterward if needed. Aiming for perfection is a sure-fire way to delay or never complete a project. Choose to chase "good enough" instead.

In the words of Mark Twain:

"Continuous improvement is better than delayed perfection."

Have a To-Do not list
In Mathematics, there is a problem-solving technique called inversion. You start with results and work backward to calculate the causes. Inversion is a powerful tool because it forces you to uncover hidden beliefs about the problem you are trying to solve. You need to think how to minimise the negatives instead of maximising the positives. Let us say you want to improve productivity. Thinking forward, you would list all the things you could do to be more productive. But if you look at the problem by inversion, you would think about all the things you could do that would diminish productivity.

Enter..... the To-Do Not List.

Create your own To-Do Not list by writing down all the habits you want to quit and the activities you wish to eliminate from your life. Think about your possible workday — long meetings with people you do not like and boring repetitive tasks — and work from there. The reason why inversion works is simple: what you do not do, determines what you can do.

"People think focus means saying yes to the thing you've got to focus on. But that is not what it means at all. It means saying no to the hundred other good ideas that there are. Innovation is saying no to 1,000 things." — Steve Jobs

Managing Self

Batch Similar Tasks

What does processing all your emails in one sitting and cooking for an entire week on Sunday have in common? They use a productivity trick known as batching. The main idea behind this time management technique is to collect up a group of similar activities and do them all in one fell swoop. You can work efficiently on multiple tasks without losing your flow if the activities require similar mindsets. Batching forces your brain to be focused on one type of task at a time.

To process batches faster, work on similar tasks for a set period of time using the Pomodoro Technique.

Take time off to recharge

In today's hyper-connected world, it is easy to fall into the trap of being connected 24/7. We feel guilty during the weekend about not working ahead or completing an extra project. All the time our body and mind need rest to function properly. Taking time to recharge is crucial to sustaining motivation, passion and productivity. Quick breaks during a stressful deadline can help you maintain focus, renew creativity and make you feel more refreshed when you return to your task.

For longer periods of recharging, take regular holidays of at least a week throughout the year. Bill Gates, for example, went into seclusion for one week twice a year to focus and plan. Many of Microsoft's innovation ideas came from those "Think Weeks".

And finally.........

It is so easy to get caught up in our business that we forget to enjoy what we are doing. The ultimate goal of work is enjoyment. You want to spend more time doing things that you enjoy. Work can and should be fun. It is fun that drives motivation, passion, creativity and productivity. Dread your job and no time management technique in the world can help you.

Apply these management techniques as a way to maximise your happiness while at work, not the amount of time you spend working. Use the new found time in activities you value, such as spending time with your family, working on side-projects, practicing a hobby or developing your skills. The enjoyment you get from these other activities will in turn fuel your work productivity

Chapter 3: Communication

Communication

Communication

Have you ever thought about your most practised activity, one that you voluntarily exercise almost as often as your breathing?

If you have not guessed it already, it is "Communicating".

We are constantly communicating every moment, through various forms, channels, gestures and expressions, all as a natural reflection of our self. While it is completely voluntary, our communication is not always conscious. We sometimes communicate without our clear awareness, leading to misleading or even conflicting expressions of our self.

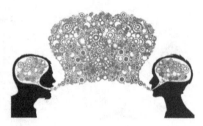

There lies the key to superlative communication: awareness.

If we can stay constantly aware of the subtle communication signals' we send out every moment, we can align this to reflect what we want to express. Our communication is then no longer accidental, it is thoroughly intentional!

The desired outcome or goal of any communication processes is mutual understanding.

Communication is defined as:

"the meaningful exchange of information between two or more participants"

A meaningful exchange involves 3 stages. The first stage is for the sender to determine

- *what the message will be*
- *who will be the recipient of the message*
- *and the best channel of communication to use*

The next stage is for the sender to actually send the message using

- *the appropriate channel of communication*
- *A clear unambiguous language*

The third stage is for the recipient to

- *Receive the message*
- *feedback to the sender*

Communication

Communication Models

The three most well-known models for communication are Linear, Interactional and Transactional. As West & Turner (2007) explain, each model sheds light on the development of communication, but emphasises different parts of the communication process.

The models provide pictures, or visual representations, of complex interactions. They are useful because they simplify the basic structure of communication and can help us to understand that structure not just verbal, but also visual. Most importantly, they identify the various elements of communication and serve as a kind of map to show how different parts of the communication process are interrelated.

Linear Models

Linear models explain one directional communication processes.

Originally developed by Shannon & Weaver in 1948, this model describes communication as a linear process. This model describes how a sender, or speaker, transmits a message to a receiver, or listener. More specifically, the sender is the source of the message. A message may consist of the sounds, words, or behaviours in a communication interaction. The message itself is transmitted through a channel, the pathway or route for communication, to a receiver, who is the target or recipient of the message. There may be obstacles in the communication process, or noise.

Noise refers to any interference in the channel or distortion of the message. This is a fairly simple model in which a message is simply passed from sender to receiver.

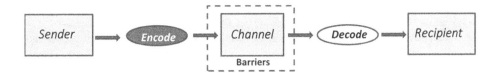

While the linear model was highly influential during the mid-20th century, this model is perhaps too simple. Its limitations are easy to see if you pause to think about the beliefs about communication, or assumptions, made in this model. First, this model assumes that communication only goes in one direction.

Here, a person can be a sender or receiver, but not both. This is problematic because communication in action is more dynamic than the linear model suggests. In action, communication involves a give and take between senders and receivers in which listeners are not simply passive receptacles for a sender's message. This model is also limited because it provides only one channel for only one message. Finally, it implies that messages themselves are clear-cut with a distinct beginning and a distinct end. However, communication is rarely, if ever, as neat and tidy as a linear model would suggest.

Communication

The three stages of communication form the basis for most models of communication and one such model is that of Claude Elwood Shannon and Warren Weaver. This is known as the Shannon Weaver model of communication and involves the following:

- **The sender (information source)** - *is the individual who creates a message and selects the channel and sends the message (the brain)*
- **encoder (transmitter)** - *the sender who uses the machine to transmit data in the appropriate form (via signals or code) (the mouth)*
- **channel** - *the medium which is used to send the message (the air)*
- **decoder (receiver)** - *the machine used to translate the message signals or codes (the ear receives the message in the brain decodes it)*
- **receiver (destination)** - *the individual receives the message or the location where the message arrives. The receiver provides feedback depending on the message (the receivers brain)*
- **noise** - *disturbances from people on the environment that can distract from the message*

The model has been widely used and adapted to different types of communication and is beneficial for identifying the causes of communication breakdowns. For example, messages that are received incomplete due to interference on a telephone line, or the sender and the receiver of an email interpreting its meaning differently.

Interactional Models

Interactional (Interactive) models are best for explaining impersonal two-way communication processes.

In the move to a more dynamic view of communication, interactional models follow two channels in which communication and feedback flow between sender and receiver. Feedback is simply a response that a receiver gives to a sender. Feedback can be verbal (i.e., "yes") or nonverbal (i.e., a nod or smile). Most importantly, feedback indicates comprehension. It can help senders know if their message was received and understood. By focusing on flow and feedback, interactional models view communication as an ongoing process.

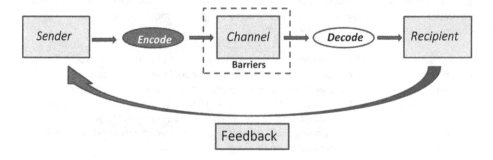

Communication

The final feature of this model is the field of experience. The field of experience refers to how environment, experiences, culture and even heredity can influence how a sender constructs a message. Keep in mind that each person brings a unique field of experience to an interaction. Likewise, each communication interaction is unique.

While the interactional model is more dynamic than the linear model, it still contains some limitations. For instance, this model implies that while people can be both senders and receivers, they cannot do so simultaneously. In real communication, roles are not quite so clear-cut and in fact are much more fluid.

Transactional Models

Transactional models explain direct personal communication processes where two-way feedback is immediate.

The transactional is the most dynamic of communication models. One notable feature of this model is the move from referring to people as senders and receivers to referring to people as communicators. This implies that communication is achieved as people both send and receive messages.

Fundamentally, this model views communication as a transaction. In other words, communication is a cooperative action in which communicators co-create the process, outcome and effectiveness of the interaction. Unlike the linear model in which meaning is sent from one person to another, also unlike the interactional model in which understanding is achieved through feedback, people create shared meaning in a more dynamic process in the transactional model.

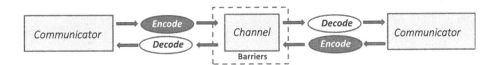

This model also places more emphasis on the field of experience. While each communicator has a unique field of experience, they must also inhabit a shared field of experience. In other words, communicators must share at least some degree of overlap in culture, language, or environment if people are to communicate at all.

This model also recognises that messages will influence the responses, or subsequent messages, produced in the communication interaction. This means that messages do not stand alone, but instead are interrelated. The principle of interrelation states that messages are connected to and build upon one another. The transactional model forms the basis for much communication theory because:

Communication

- *People are viewed as dynamic communicators rather than simple senders or receivers*
- *There must be some overlap in fields of experience in order to build shared meaning*
- *Messages are interdependent.*

Types of Communication

Take a step back and ask yourself:

- *Are you aware that you are communicating every moment? With yourself, with others, with nature?*
- *Are you aware of the various expressions of your communication?*
- *And finally, are you constantly communicating what you want to communicate, in the way you want to do it?*

"Communicating every moment? How is that even possible? I don't have my mouth open every minute?"

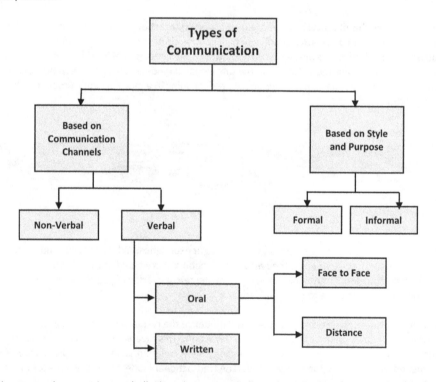

We communicate not just verbally, but also non-verbally and even informally. The entire gamut of the various types of communication channels and expressions we enjoy is outlined in this chart.

Communication

As you can see, there are at least 6 distinct types of communication: non-verbal, verbal-oral-face-to-face, verbal-oral-distance, verbal-written, formal and informal types of communication. Add to this the boundless opportunities the internet offers and you have an almost unlimited range of communication possibilities!

Formal Types of Communication

This type of communication is also referred to as "official communication" and covers the range of verbal expressions that address a formal need.

This communication is conducted through a pre-determined channel. For instance, a large number of your interactions within your profession, financial communication (from and to your bank, creditors, debtors, etc.) and legal expressions are examples of formal communication.

More time-consuming that non-formal communication, as it follows a particular communication protocol.

Even in cases of oral expressions (in meetings, seminars, etc.), it is often backed by written communication that can provide documentation evidence of the oral conversation. *(This written communication could be as simple as a minutes-of-meeting, to as complex as a detailed recording.)*

It is considered a reliable source of information. *(So, when you receive a letter from your bank, you had better take notice of it!)*

Formal communication forms the core of our professional lives (though not all professional communication is formal). Hence becoming an expert in this type of communication is central to professional advancement and success.

Below, are simple tips to excel in your expression and profession.

- *Begin by clarifying the purpose of your communication.*
- *Whether you use an oral or written expression, always follow a well-defined structure that can be easily understood by your audience.*
- *Keep your tone open, professional and friendly.*
- *End by re-iterating what you expect to cause through this communication:* clarification on your stance, answers to questions, a call to action, etc. Also clarify any constraints that apply to this communication (like confidentiality, time-limit for response, etc.)
- *Finally, thank your audience for their listening.* (*This works well for written communication too.*)

Communication

Informal types of Communication

Informal communication is surprisingly popular and often referred to as "the (unofficial) grapevine". This is often by word-of-mouth information. In fact, it is this type of communication that opens you up to unofficial yet provocative information.

- *Informal communication is spontaneous and free flowing, without any formal protocol or structure. Hence this type of information is also less reliable or accurate.*
- *A communication channel that spreads like wildfire, as there are no formal rules to follow.*
- *Mostly oral, with no documentation evidence. Due to this, many undermine the value of informal communication, terming it mere "gossip".*

Despite its drawbacks, informal communication is considered "user-friendly" and hence offers huge advantages when used wisely. For instance, a company is served by 3 different caterers. Employees may become aware of the timings of service, rules and regulations through a formal communication sent out by company management. But they will become aware of the preferred caterer of the day through informal communication from friends and colleagues. This type of communication serves well when you want to control or encourage positive opinions, ideas and expressions, without making them seem like they have been "thrust upon" by senior management.

Note: *More recently, social networks from "unofficial" sources (like your personal Facebook and Twitter feeds, LinkedIn, etc.) are powerful sources of informal communication and are often used to shape public opinion.*

Oral Communication (Face-to-face)

Face-to-face oral communication is the most recognised type of communication. Here, what you express comes directly from what you say. Again, this can be formal or informal: with your friends and family, in a formal meeting or seminar, at work with your colleagues and boss, within your community, during professional presentations, etc.

This type of communication gets better with practice.

- *The more you practice with awareness, the more control you will have on your oral expressions.*
- *Is vibrantly a-live! This means that despite all past rehearsals, oral communication offers you a present-moment opportunity to tune, revise, revoke and fix what you express. It is hence the most powerful type of communication and can work for or against you with every expression.*

Communication

- *Engages your audience more than other types of communication. The listener (or an audience) often expects to speak-back to you with oral communication, enabling two-way communication more than any other channel.*

For better face-to-face communication:

- *Always meet the eyes of your audience with confidence, conviction and openness.*
- *Practice before a mirror to perfect your tone and expressions, so they suit the message you want to convey. They two facets often convey more than your words do.*
- *Practice using role-play. This means that even when you rehearse before a mirror, candidly ask yourself, "Am I ready to receive this message with this tone and expression?" If you are not convinced, your audience will not be either. So, practice again until you get it right.*
- *Consciously engage your audience's participation. This is the strength of this type of communication, so never let your oral expression be a one-way rant to yourself. You can do this by asking questions, getting their opinion and encouraging expression of new ideas.*

Finally, become an active listener. An effective oral communicator not only speaks, but also actively listens to his audience.

Oral Communication (Distance)

Distance (oral) communication has made the world a smaller and more accessible place. Mobile phones, VOIP, video-conferencing, 2-way webinars, etc. are all modern expansions of distance communication, taking its expression to the next subtle level. And in this type of communication, your tone of voice and pace of delivery take priority over other expressions.

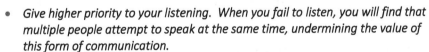

For effective oral communication over distance:

- *Give higher priority to your listening. When you fail to listen, you will find that multiple people attempt to speak at the same time, undermining the value of this form of communication.*
- *Speak slightly slower than you would in face-to-face communication. This will make sure that you remain aware of the subtle nuances of your tone and the receiver has time to grasp what you convey.*
- *Always re-iterate what you understand when you listen. This type of communication misses the non-verbal signals that you would receive in face-to-face communication (that can indicate subtle expressions like anger, friendliness, receptivity, sarcasm, etc.) So, paraphrase what you understand and confirm that this is indeed what the other party also meant to convey.*

Communication

- *Where appropriate, wear your friendly face with a smile on your lips and eyes. Feel this friendly face. Your tone will automatically convey your openness and receptivity to the other person. (This may not be appropriate if you expect to convey a warning on the phone, so ensure that your face suits your message.)*

Finally, back this up with written communication where possible. The intention is to confirm the take-away from the communication, so all parties are on the same page. This makes sense even for an informal call with your friend – perhaps you can send a quick text message to re-iterate how pleasurable it was to speak to him and then confirm the final call-for-action.

Written Communication

A few decades ago, written communication depended on the trusty old postman as we wrote to people who were far away. On rare occasions, this also included the formal note or legal notice from the bank, landlord, business client, etc. What a surprise then that this type of communication has now taken over every aspect of our world!

Think about it, if you group together the total written communication you engage with in a day – the text messages you send over your mobile, your Facebook and Twitter updates, personal and professional emails, maybe even the blogs you write – it would far surpass any other verbal communication you enjoy.

It is vital therefore that you are competent in this area and there are 3 rules that can help you get there:

- *Follow a clear structure so your communication is not all over the place. This can include a brief introduction, agenda, message body and conclusion. The cleverness and effectiveness of your communication lies in how you are able to capture this structure in your mode of communication (email, text message, quick status update on social media, etc.).*
- *Clarify the context of your communication where possible. This might seem like overkill for a harmless text message. But you would be amazed at the amount of seemingly harmless (written) communication that reaches the wrong eyes and ears. Take care to ensure that your context is reasonably clear, no matter who the recipient.*
- *Always err on the right side of caution. There are very few instances when written communication is purely formal (addressed to professional peers and seniors or third parties), or purely informal (addressed only to your immediate friend/family circle). More often, if falls between these two modes. Hence, play safe by adapting a semi-formal tone, keeping your communication clean (in language and expression) and open (without offending any group). It is far better to have your friends think of you as a "stiff" communicator, rather than have your boss view as an "offensive" communicator!*

Communication

Non-verbal Types of Communication

This type of communication is more subtle, yet far more powerful. It includes the entire range of physical postures and gestures, tone and pace of voice and the attitude with which you communicate.

> *"The most important thing in communication is hearing what isn't said"* - Peter Drucker

In the past few decades, body language experts have revealed how the posture you adopt, the hand gestures you endorse and other facets of your physical personality affect your communication. It is worthwhile to spend a few hours coming up to speed on basic body-language gestures, so you do not inadvertently send mixed messages with your gestures and speech. You can also use this to support your message, making it more impactful.

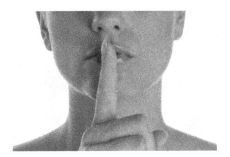

When communicating, always think about:

- *What you say with your words.*
- *What you share with your postures and gestures. (However, these can be learnt to express the right message).*
- *What you feel inside you and hence impacts the subtle message you feel compelled to share outside you.*

The first two can be learnt with a little bit of practice. But the third has to be consciously built so you constantly align yourself to what you want to express.

For instance:

- *When you want your peers to think of you as a friendly person, it is because you genuinely like and care for people.*
- *When you want your team to think of you as a strong leader, it is because you genuinely take responsibility for yourself and the team.*
- *When you want your peers, seniors and others to listen to you, it is because they are convinced that you will genuinely listen to them and factor their thoughts and opinions.*

Communication is a powerful activity that comes to us as naturally as breathing. With a little bit of awareness, our communication can be flawless, so the other person not only receives our message, but is also open to it.

Communication

"Communication begins with Listening!"
Paramahamsa Nithyananda

The next time you find yourself in the middle of a frustrating conversation, focus on your listening. This will help you grasp what your audience wants to hear from you, so you find a way to tailor your communication for your audience to become receptive to it too. When you listen and your audience also listens, you are engaged in the best form of communication!

Benefits of Effective Communication

In a work environment, when communication is effective, it means that we can:

- *send and receive information accurately*
- *share information effectively*
- *give a good impression of ourselves and the organisation*
- *deal with problems effectively*
- *develop useful and productive working relationships with colleagues, customers and others*

Communication is implicit in every function of management and communicating with people is essential in the workplace. These can include:

- *Running meetings and discussions* – e.g., agreeing objectives; discussing the allocation and progress of tasks; dealing with queries.
- *Motivating and leading the team* – e.g., having positive discussions about objectives; listening to feedback from the team and agreeing the way forward; organising team-building activities.
- *Sharing accurate information* – e.g., gathering accurate data from different people and departments; producing accurate leaflets, documents and websites for customers and others.
- *Delegating tasks and implementing plans* – e.g., passing responsibility to team members to move a project forward.
- *Training and coaching the team* – e.g., running training sessions for the whole team; giving one-to-one coaching to an individual to develop their skills.
- *Creating and delivering reports* – e.g., progress reviews sent by email to other managers, presenting a report to the team on PowerPoint.
- *Dealing with customers, visitors and the general public* – e.g., meeting, greeting and taking care of people visiting the workplace; answering questions and giving out information; dealing with complaints involving the team or its activities.
- *Giving and receiving feedback* – e.g., giving praise and support in a staff appraisal interview; receiving and dealing with feedback from customers.
- *Solving problems* – e.g., discussing options with the team and the rest of the organisation; monitoring and reviewing progress; negotiating for more time or resources.

Communication

- *Liaising with other managers and directors* – e.g., *discussing administration issues; revising organisational objectives; solving problems and making decisions about changes and progress.*

An organisation is a complex entity, with many stakeholders, each having an interest in how it is run.

Effective communication is vital to make sure that information is shared correctly and that working relationships are positive and well-supported. All stakeholders need to feel that their contributions and opinions matter and good communication enables information and views to be seen, heard, spoken and shared.

Formal and Informal Communication

Some workplace communication requires a formal approach, usually when information is important, sensitive or confidential – e.g., financial reports about the organisation or its customers; staff appraisal interviews; legal letters; formal letters to customers or colleagues; evidence to support a complaint or investigation.

Some workplace communication requires an informal approach, usually when information is not confidential and when it can be shared with people that we know – e.g., a quick question for a colleague or regular customer; sharing information and instructions; during a handover between shifts; announcements that can be made openly; reminders for colleagues or customers.

When choosing the most appropriate form of communication, we need to consider:

- *the type of information being sent*
- *the people who are going to read or hear it*
- *the security and confidentiality of the information*
- *how it will be circulated and shared*

Good communication skills are essential to make sure that:

- *errors and misunderstandings are kept to a minimum*
- *the right level of detail can be provided*
- *the organisation's positive and professional image is maintained*
- *the communication method follows good business practice and is in line with the organisation's policies and procedures*
- *confidentiality is protected, when appropriate*

Communication

Forms of written communication

In written communication, we need to think about reading, writing, pictures, symbols and other visual communication.

There are many instances when we need to use written information in the workplace – e.g., in notes, reports and emails. Written communication can be very important as it is often kept as evidence to show that policies and procedures have been followed.

Written communication can also include pictures, symbols and other visual communications – e.g., a scribbled drawing to explain something, or Braille versions of leaflets.

Methods of written communication can include:

Emails
May be formal or informal and are often used in the workplace to:

- *send information to one person* – e.g., **respond to a question**
- *send information to many people* – e.g., **inform all customers on a database about a product deal with customer's queries, complaints and comments**
- *plan a meeting*
- *report the outcome of a meeting*
- *circulate informal or formal reports*
- *share information*
- *make or confirm purchases and orders*

When used informally, emails are rather like postcards, memos or short notes. When used formally, emails need to be similar to formal letters. Organisations usually have their own styles, policies and procedures about how to write emails for different situations.

Notes and memos
Notes and memos in the workplace can be very quick and useful. They are generally informal and can be used to, for example:

- *leave notes in the work diary for the next shift* – e.g., **to report problems or make requests for someone to finish a task**
- *share information with colleagues and other stakeholders* – e.g., **to ask a colleague a question**
- *pass on a telephone message* – e.g., **to give a supplier's name, phone number and message to a colleague who was away from their desk**

- *remind people about something* – e.g., **the date, time and location of a meeting or training course**

Communication

Notes can be addressed personally or left for everyone to see, depending on who needs to see the contents.

Formal letters

These will be on headed notepaper and will be used in formal situations, especially if a permanent record is needed. They are particularly useful when information is confidential and sensitive and needs to be kept private, for example:

- *during disciplinary procedures*
- *when making a job offer*
- *when writing to customers, staff or other stakeholders about serious, confidential or sensitive matters*

Formal letters reflect the organisation at its most professional and serious, so good grammar, vocabulary and presentation are essential.

Reports

Reports can be formal or informal. An informal report can be, for instance, a completed paper or electronic form that is used for:

- *giving daily figures for sales or production*
- *reporting costs and other measurable statistics*
- *handover notes*

Formal reports can be printed or sent electronically and will cover subjects such as, for example:

- *annual accounts and accountants' reports*
- *directors' reports for shareholders*
- *research and development* – e.g., *test results for new equipment; detailed comparison between two production methods*
- *feedback and analysis prepared after an event or project* – e.g., *to show achievements, problems and opportunities for improvement*
- *staff appraisals*
- *analysis, strategies and plans on how to achieve objectives*

Spreadsheets and databases

Spreadsheets are used to bring numerical data together – e.g., to analyse expense claims for all employees under different headings, such as travel, subsistence, mileage and hotels.

Databases are used when names, addresses and other personal details and preferences need to be collected and used – e.g., for mailing lists.
Both systems are flexible and can be amended and updated by people who have authorised access to them.

Communication

Drawings, graphs and designs

Drawings and designs are used when information needs to be presented in a visual format – e.g., an architect's drawings; a graphic designer's brochure design; a fashion designer's sketches.

Graphs are used when presenting data in a visual and mathematical format – e.g., pie charts to show details of a company's expenditure.

Forms

Most organisations design and use their own forms. The idea is to simplify the process of sharing information so that the person completing the form can do so as easily as possible. The organisation can target the information that they need and want, so that time and resources are not wasted on processing unnecessary answers and data.

Forms can be used for many functions, including, for example:

- *timesheets, mileage and expenses claims from staff*
- *requests* – e.g., budgets, maintenance work, for leave and other time off, or new resources
- *surveys and feedback comments from customers*
- *job applications*
- *ideas and suggestions from staff*
- *orders and sales*
- *finance applications* – e.g., when asking for a loan or mortgage

Information signs and notices

Information signs need to be clear and very easy to understand. The language used needs to be straightforward and clearly written to maximise the chances of the message being understood, for example:

- *directions to different departments*
- *instructions about how to operate machinery* – e.g., how to use the photocopier
- *instructions about what to wear or how to behave* – e.g., please be quiet, exam in progress
- *information for visitors* – e.g., expected waiting times for their appointment's car park signs
- *prices and special offers in retail outlets*

Pictures and symbols can be really useful when the information is important, especially if language is an issue. We see them used on information signs all around us at work and in public places, for example:

Communication

- *health and safety information in green to imply safety* – e.g., emergency exit signs and first-aid signs
- *warning signs in yellow to show danger* – e.g., yellow trip hazard signs
- *fire information in red* – e.g., about fire extinguishers and fire alarms
- *mandatory (compulsory) information on blue signs* – e.g., about handwashing or instructions to wear personal protective equipment

Chemicals will also have symbols on the packaging to back up the information about the product.

Websites

Websites are now common in organisations and they are a useful way of communicating with an infinite number of people. They use language, pictures, symbols, graphs and other visual elements.

Websites can carry a vast amount of information, including, for example:

- *detailed information about products and services*
- *background information about the organisation and its structure*
- *policies and procedures*
- *photographs and other graphics to give visual examples of the organisation's products and services*
- *legal information*
- *testimonials and other feedback from customers and others*
- *links to related pages, websites or other information connected with the organisation*
- *availability and booking systems*
- *payment systems*
- *specifications and instruction manuals* – e.g., for staff or customers to use

Websites need to be well-presented and kept up to date. They can reach a wide number of people, so they need to give a good, professional impression of the organisation and its workforce.

Social media

A great deal of sales and marketing material is now shared using social media. Many organisations now have a team of people whose job is to monitor and manage social media communications so that an instant response can be given if necessary.

Social media can be used to, for example:

Communication

- *monitor and react to complaints* – *e.g., by train companies if their customers are complaining about a problem*
- *let followers and customers know the latest news* – *e.g., announcing a new participant at an air show or music festival*
- *offer promotions and special offers*
- *encourage followers and customers to engage with the organisation* – *e.g., to send their views to a live TV or radio programme, which shows advertisers the level of interest from different people in the audience*

Leaflets, newsletters and brochures

Leaflets, newsletters and brochures are generally quite formal and need to be factually correct. They can be illustrated and include graphs and technical information and have many uses – e.g., to give instructions and extra information about products and services; promote the organisation's image using glossy pictures, background information, logos and news; keep employees up to date.

Strengths and weaknesses of written forms of communication

Forms of written communication have different strengths and weaknesses. We need to consider the contents of our message and who is going to read it when we send written communication, including signs and symbols. This helps us to decide which form is most suitable and effective for the situation.

This table has some notes about some of the strengths and weaknesses of written forms of communication:

Communication

Form:	Strengths:	Weaknesses:
Emails	*Quick and simple* *Can be formal or informal* *Easy to keep a copy and track the messages coming in and going out* *Provide a clear record of what has been discussed*	*Cannot always get instant feedback or an answer from the other person – some people do not deal with emails every day, need to check this if the matter is urgent* *People often get too many emails, so hard to make important ones stand out*
Notes in the team diary	*Useful central place for handover notes for the next shift* *Can leave notes for many to see – e.g., manager, team leaders or team members* *Good way to flag up important dates, times and deadlines* *Good way to leave reminders – for self or others*	*Quite public* *Not suitable for confidential or awkward subjects and details*
Spreadsheets and databases	*Can be tailor-made for any situation where numerical data or contact details are recorded* *Can be simple or complicated* *Access can be open or restricted*	*Can be tricky to navigate and find if the data and details are not organised logically* *Some functions are complex and require thorough training and monitoring*
Drawings, graphs and designs	*Strong visual impact* *Can explain plans, results and achievements very quickly when data presented correctly* *Help people to imagine a three-dimensional plan or design*	*Often time-consuming to prepare* *Data and parameters can be hard to understand if people are not familiar with the format*
Forms	*Easy to complete* *Logical* *Designed for a specific purpose*	*Cannot always have room for additional information* *Questions and boxes might not be entirely suited to the nature of the answers needed*
Personal notes	*Can give specific information or request* *Person has a written record*	*Might be missed if left in wrong place* *Need to be aware of possible literacy or language issues*
Formal letters	*Suitable where very personal approach needed – e.g., with a job application Formal permanent record*	*Usually take longer to prepare, check and send*
Information signs and notices	*Can pass information to wide range of people – e.g., in the staffroom, customer waiting area, entrance to the building* *Symbols and colour-coding make them easy to understand* *Good for general information or announcements*	*Not suitable for personal or confidential information* *Some symbols can be harder to understand if they are unfamiliar*

Communication

Form:	Strengths:	Weaknesses:
Websites	Can be tailor-made for the organisation or department Relatively cheap and easy to use to reach a very wide audience Can hold a vast amount of data, pictures and information Can link to other pages, information and websites	The internal search engine within the website can be inadequate and make it hard to navigate Information can be irrelevant if not kept up to date Website can be hard to find on search engines – e.g., Google
Social media	Quick, easy and inexpensive to operate Can reach extremely large numbers of followers instantly Good for short messages	Needs to be monitored and updated all of the time – especially for customer comments that might need a response Bad news can travel fast – e.g., negative customer feedback or complaints
Leaflets, newsletters and brochures	Can be formal or informal Good for sending information in a permanent form to a large number of people Can be left for people to help themselves – e.g., in a doctor's surgery waiting area	Can go out of date quite quickly Often discarded unread, or hardly read, which is a waste of resources Expensive to produce and store

Forms of Verbal Communication

Forms of verbal communication between individuals and groups can be formal or informal and include:

Face-to-face conversations
Face-to-face conversations can take place in private or in a small group, including, for example:

- *informal and formal meetings to plan and agree objectives*
- *discussions about progress and potential problems*
- *team talks at the beginning of a shift*
- *handovers to other managers*
- *delegating tasks to team members*
- *monitoring and reviewing any workplace activity*
- *conversations with customers* – e.g., about sales or queries
- *conversations with suppliers* – e.g., to discuss problems or plans
- *staff appraisal discussions* – e.g., spontaneous feedback by the team member's workstation, or in a formal interview in the office

Face-to-face communication can be extremely effective, for example: questions can be answered straightaway and in a personal way; people can be reassured and made to feel valued and respected; training sessions can be lively and engaging. It is not always the

Communication

most time-efficient way of communicating with people, but the personal touch is hard to beat in most workplace situations.

Face-to-face conversations about sensitive, personal or private matters need to be conducted in private to protect dignity and confidentiality.

Telephone conversations

Telephone conversations can cover many of the topics that can be discussed face-to-face. However, in the workplace, telephone conversations can be much quicker and more efficient, especially when staff have additional information instantly available.

Telephone conversations are useful when two-way communication is needed – e.g., to get an answer or instruction from someone.

Typical tasks that can be performed using telephone conversations include, for example:

- *selling products and services* – e.g., cold calls to sell legal or insurance services
- *advising customers about problems* – e.g., bank staff calling about irregular activities on customers' bank accounts
- *dealing with customer complaints and comments*
- *ordering supplies and arranging delivery times*
- *dealing with supply problems* – e.g., chasing a late delivery
- *sharing information* – e.g., informing colleagues about meetings, changes or updates
- *initial interviews* – e.g., talking to potential job applicants in the early stages of recruitment

Structured formal meetings

Structured formal meetings can be for small or large numbers of people, generally following an established pattern where participants discuss the points listed on an agreed agenda, with someone taking and circulating the minutes (careful notes about the decisions and points made).

Examples of when structured formal meetings are used include, for example:

- *a small annual general meeting (AGM) for a family company with four directors*
- *a large AGM with thousands of shareholders of a public limited company (PLC)*
- *delivering formal reports to key stakeholders* – e.g., giving a quarterly report to trustees of a charity
- *formal disciplinary procedures* – e.g., delivering a final written warning to an employee

Communication

- **when accurate records of decisions are needed for legal and compliance reasons** – *e.g., if there is a health and safety investigation after an accident, if there is a financial investigation by auditors or a government department*
- **when members need to vote on an issue** – *e.g., shareholders of a small property company voting to increase funds to cover maintenance of shared areas*

Structured meetings show that the organisation is taking matters seriously and treating people and subjects with respect. The notes taken during these meetings can be used to show compliance with rules, regulations and legislation.

Training sessions and lectures

Verbal communication is a key element of training sessions, tutorials, seminars and lectures. The training can be given in person or using electronic devices that use videos of trainers presenting their topic or doing demonstrations. Examples of verbal training sessions include, for example:

- **induction training sessions in a training room at work**
- **'toolbox' talks in the work area** – *e.g., brief sessions on new equipment or procedures*
- **internal training courses** – *e.g., refresher training, short and long courses conducted by the organisation*
- **external training courses** – *e.g., attending colleges or other training providers; working with tutors and assessors when doing distance learning*
- **training DVDs, television programmes or online seminars (sometimes called webinars)** – *e.g., fire safety procedures; to show staff how to use new equipment; to increase background knowledge*
- **one-to-one shadowing or mentoring** – *e.g., following and observing an experienced colleague at work*
- **demonstrations** – *e.g., by the suppliers of new equipment and machinery*

Using the Internet

As technology increases its scope and capacity, the Internet is used for verbal communication more and more often. Organisations can use, for example:

- **Skype or other web-based communication systems that use speech – with or without video**
- **videoconferencing systems** – *e.g., to have international meetings without delegates needing to travel*
- **webinars** – *e.g., to learn about new products and services, then discuss them in detail with the supplier's sales team and technical specialists*
- **using tablets and other mobile devices for virtual meetings and conversations**

Communication

Internet-based communication is very flexible. It can be used in offices or out on the road, for example, with individual staff members having their own mobile devices to stay in touch. Reports can be made away from the office, research can be done and emails can be sent and received.

Announcements

From time to time, organisations need to make announcements. They are a one-way process to deliver messages, although there might be a questions and answer session straight after the announcement.

Organisations may wish to announce a variety of things, for example:

- *the appointment of key leaders*
- *the launch of new products and services*
- *problems with products that need to be recalled immediately*
- *their apologies and reactions to a disaster* – *e.g., following a major accident involving the organisation's customers, employees or products*

Announcements can be delivered through, for example:

- *giving interviews on television or the radio*
- *speaking to print and online journalists* – *e.g., giving interview to the local or national press, or to journalists who publish online articles*
- *at a meeting or conference* – *e.g., announcing changes in directors or objectives*

Presentations

Presentations are also a one-way verbal form of communication, although there is usually the time and opportunity for questions after a presentation. They can be given by one person or by a group of people, depending on the amount of information and the specialist knowledge needed. If the subject will take several hours to present, it can help everyone if there are several presenters – to keep the audience engaged and to give the presenters a break.

Organisations can use presentations for a range of reasons, including, for example:

- *training purposes*
- *to give an update on progress and objectives*
- *to sell products and services*
- *to inform stakeholders about different aspects of the operation*
- *as part of an application for finance* – *e.g., showing banks the current performance and future plans and projections*

Communication

Strengths and Weaknesses of Verbal Communication

As we have seen, different forms of verbal communication have different strengths and weaknesses and we need to consider the contents of our message and our audience.

Effective verbal communication relies on good speaking skills and good listening skills. The speaker has a responsibility to deliver messages that are clear, straightforward, appropriate and easy to understand.

The listener has the responsibility to concentrate and ask questions if they do not understand.

Form:	Strengths:	Weaknesses:
Face-to-face conversations with colleagues, customers or the public	Instant response Formal or informal Can be confidential if in private Can give good impression of self and organisation Focus on the information tends to be good People feel valued and respected when their views are taken seriously	Not always possible to be in private Timing can be tricky to arrange for formal meetings Can be time-consuming Limit to the number of people who can join in
Telephone communications	Can discuss, make decisions and arrangements in 'real time' People can be accessible – especially using mobiles Texts can be left for someone to read when they are ready – e.g., after a meeting or shift	Not always possible to get through to speak to the person needed Leaving messages is not always effective Texts do not always go through as expected and might not be read quickly
Structured formal meetings	Predictable structure with agenda and minutes Formal records kept and circulated Useful for legal and compliance reasons	Format can seem quite laboured and 'stuffy', using complicated language and procedures People will not always understand what is happening if the language and format are too difficult
Training sessions and lectures	Sessions can be lively and engaging for learners and tutors Instant response to queries and feedback Can be adapted to any subject, any learner and any situation Demonstrations help people to learn physical skills Mentoring and shadowing are personal and show current skills	Some people will not understand if the language or delivery are not clear and easy to follow People learn at different paces – some will find sessions too quick, others too slow Limits to the numbers that can be trained in each session Training DVDs and videos can leave learners uninterested and unable to engage

Communication

Form:	Strengths:	Weaknesses:
Using the Internet	*Relatively inexpensive to run once set up* *Can have international access* *Instant, real-time communication* *Staff can have their own mobile devices – e.g., phones or tablets*	*Staff can feel as though they are never off duty* *Some areas around the country do not have good mobile coverage* *Signals can be disrupted or disconnected at times*
Announcements	*Good for delivering a clear message* *Reduced chance of interruptions* *The speaker usually has control*	*A one-way process – there usually needs to be an opportunity for people to ask questions or give feedback*
Presentations	*Can be lively and engaging* *Formal or informal* *Can use pictures and other graphics to deliver messages* *Can be adapted to any topic, audience or situation* *Can be delivered with or without electronic support*	*Can be time-consuming to prepare, deliver and attend* *Not always relevant to people invited to attend* *Pace and level of information can be hard to judge – flexible approach needed*

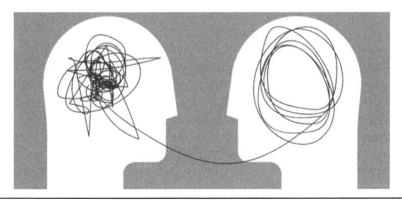

Communication

Speaking, Listening and Questioning Skills

To maximise the chances of successful verbal communication, it is important to use effective speaking, listening and questioning skills.

Speaking Skills

The speaker has the responsibility to deliver information and questions in ways that people can understand. If the listener does not fully understand what has been said, they may give inaccurate answers, feel embarrassed and anxious, or pretend that they know what was said. These consequences can affect working relationships, which can be critical when dealing with, for example, colleagues or customers. To aid communication, the speaker needs to:

- *speak clearly and slowly enough for everyone to understand*
- *keep their message simple and straightforward*
- *use language that is appropriate for the listener*
- *consider possible barriers to understanding* – e.g., hearing difficulties or having English as a second language
- *be prepared to repeat or explain if someone does not understand for any reason*
- *be ready to back up speech with hand signals, diagrams and other visual aids*

In addition, the speaker also needs to consider the tone, pitch and volume of their voice, as these will all affect the delivery.

Active Listening

Active listening is an integral part of effective communication. You will need to demonstrate active listening with your team members, colleagues, managers, customers and stakeholders in the role you hold.

Demonstrating active listening involves:

- *giving your full attention to the individual without interrupting them*
- *encouraging them to open up*
- *listening to what they say*
- *paying attention and reacting appropriately to their body language*
- *using your own body language, for example, head nodding, leaning forward and using gestures*
- *understanding their viewpoint and not your interpretation of it*
- *asking questions, if necessary, to gather further information*
- *repeating back phrases to provide confirmation that your listening*
- *summarising what they have told you to check that you fully understood them*

Communication

- *giving them the opportunity to let you know if you have not got it quite right*
- *empathising with them*

An effective listener needs to:

- *take ownership and not be afraid of chairing the meeting*
- *set high standards*
- *be on time*
- *be courteous*
- *encourage contributions*
- *listen carefully*
- *be fair but firm*
- *be able to work with, lead and manage people, especially during meetings*

Questioning Skills

Although there are numerous reasons for asking questions, the information we receive back (the answer) will depend very much on the type of question we ask.

Questions, in their simplest form, can either be open or closed - this section covers both types but also considers other question types and when it may be appropriate to use them, in order to improve understanding.

Questioning focuses the attention on the other person and selecting the right questioning technique for the situation can help us to collect the right information. We can use, for example:

- *closed*
- *open*
- *probing*
- *leading*
- *rhetorical*

It is important to use the right type of question for the individual and the situation to be able to obtain useful and relevant information. The following table suggests strengths and weaknesses for these different types of question:

Effective Questioning
Asking good questions is productive, positive, creative and can get us what we want!

Most people believe this to be true and yet people do not ask enough good questions. Perhaps one of the reasons for this is that effective questioning requires it be combined with effective listening.

Effective questions help you:

Communication

- *Connect with your team in a more meaningful way*
- *Better and more fully understand your team's problem*
- *Have employees experience you as an understanding, competent manager*
- *Work with your staff more effectively*
- *Help your staff take responsibility for their actions and solve problems within the workplace more easily*
- *Cross examine more effectively*
- *Gather better information*
- *Do more solution-oriented problem solving*
- *Improve your negotiating skills*
- *Reduce mistakes*
- *Take the sting out of feedback*
- *Defuse volatile situations*
- *Get cooperation*
- *Plant your own ideas*
- *Persuade people*

Effective Questions

Effective questions are questions that are powerful and thought provoking. Effective questions are open-ended and not leading questions. They are not "why" questions, but rather "what" or "how" questions. "Why" questions are good for soliciting information but can make people defensive so be thoughtful in your use of them. When asking effective questions, it is important to wait for the answer and not provide the answer.

When working with people to solve a problem, it is not enough to tell them what the problem is. They need to find out or understand it for themselves. You help them do this by asking them thought provoking questions. Rather than make assumptions find out what the person you are talking to knows about the problem.

Example:

> *"What do you think the problem is?"*

Behind effective questioning is also the ability to listen to the answer and suspend judgment. This means being intent on understanding what the person who is talking is really saying. What is behind their words? Let go of your opinions so that they do not block you from learning more information. Pay attention to your gut for additional information.

Powerful Questions

The following are examples of typical questions. These questions can help you improve your communication and understanding of the client or staff member.

Identification of issue:
These questions can be used in staff interviews and meetings, settlement negotiations and to work with others in solving problems.

Communication

What seems to be the trouble?
What do you make of _____?
How do you feel about _____?
What concerns you the most about _____?
What seems to be the problem?
What seems to be your main obstacle?
What is holding you back from _____?
What do you think about doing X this way?

Further information:

These questions can be used to find out what someone has already done to resolve a work problem.

What do you mean by _____?
Tell me more about _____
What else?
What other ways did you try so far?
What will you have to do to get the job done?

Outcomes:

These questions can be used in settlement negotiations or while working with staff to plan how to do something.

How do you want _____ to turn out?
What do you want?
What is your desired outcome?
What benefits would you like to get out of X?
What do you propose?
What is your plan?
If you do this, how will it affect _____?
What else do you need to consider?

Taking Action:

These questions can be used in working with staff.

What will you do? When will you do it?
How will I know you did it?
What are your next steps?

Communication

Listening as part of Effective Questioning

When staff are listened to, they feel understood and are more trusting of you. Effective listening is a skill that requires nurturing and needs development. Since managers are "smart", the temptation is to get by with listening at a minimal level. To connect with your staff and have them experience you as an effective manager requires you to maintain superior listening skills along with asking effective questions.

Consider the following different levels of listening:

Level 1 Listening:
When we are listening at level 1 our focus or attention is on how the words the other person is saying affect ourselves with minimal concern for the person talking. We listen for the words of the other person to see how they affect us. The attention is on me - what are my thoughts, judgments, issues, conclusions and feelings. There is no room to let in the feelings of the person being "listened" to. When listening at level 1 our opinions and judgments arise. Level 1 listening is appropriate when you are gathering information for yourself like getting directions or ordering in a restaurant or a store.

Level 2 Listening:
When we listen at level 2, there is a deeper focus on the person being listened to. This often means not even being aware of the context. Our awareness is totally on the other person. We notice what they say as well as how they say it and what they do not say. We listen for what they value and what is important to them. We listen for what gives them energy or sadness or resignation. We let go of judgment. We are no longer planning what we are going to say next. We respond to what we actually hear.

Level 3 Listening:
When we listen more deeply than the two levels described above, in addition to the conversation we take in all information that surrounds the conversation. We are aware of the context and the impact of the context on all parties. We include all our senses, in particular our intuition. We consider what is not being said and we notice the energy in the room and in the person we are listening to. We use that information to ask more effective questions.

Listening Skills as part of Effective Questioning include:

Articulating
Attention and awareness result in articulation and succinctly describing what we have learned from the employee. Sharing our observation clearly but without judgment does this. We can repeat back to our employee just what they said. We can expand on this by articulating back to them what we believe they mean. This helps a person feel heard. For example: "What I hear you saying is . . ."

Clarifying

Communication

Clarifying is a combination of asking and clearly articulating what we have heard. By asking questions the employee knows we are listening and filling in the gaps. When the employee is being vague, it is important for us to clarify the circumstances. We can assist them to see what they cannot see themselves by making a suggestion. For example: "Here's what I hear you saying. Is that right? "

Being Curious
Do not assume you know the answer or what the employee is going to tell you. Wait and be curious about what brings them to see you. What motivates them? What is really behind the meeting? Use your curiosity so that your next question can go deeper.

Silence
Giving the person we are listening to time to answer questions is an important aspect of listening. Waiting for the employee to talk rather than talking for them is imperative for an effective listener.

Question type	Description and examples	Strengths	Weaknesses
Closed	Answered with a 'yes' or 'no' – e.g. Do you work in the customer service department?	Useful when no further detail is required	Answers do not give many clues or depth The other person is not encouraged to give more detail or express an opinion
Open	They cannot be answered with a 'yes' or 'no' – e.g., Tell me about your recent experience in customer service	Useful when we want the other person to reflect and come up with their own ideas, opinions and suggestions	Answers can be long and may not be focused
Probing	Secondary questions that take the enquiry further – e.g. Following on from that point, can you explain why the customer reacted that way?	Useful to find out more detail and explore in depth Useful in investigations	Can be intimidating and uncomfortable for the other person, especially if they cannot answer
Leading	A question that prompts and suggests the desired answer – e.g. So, you are saying that you did remember to lock the door when you left? And weren't you going to tell us about next week's meeting?	Useful when we want to guide people to reflect on a particular problem or aspect Useful when reminding someone else to say something, maybe in a meeting or presentation	The questioner may be reinforcing their own opinion and may not get an accurate response or agreement
Rhetorical	When no actual answer is needed – e.g. That's better, isn't it?	Useful to help the other person to reflect and maybe commit to a course of action	The other person can feel pressurised

Communication

Non-Verbal Communication

A huge number of messages are sent non-verbally. These can be transmitted through, for example:

- *posture and body language*
- *gestures and touching*
- *physical appearance*

How people stand, how close they are 'in someone's space', eye contact, fidgeting and hand movements all add to the verbal messages.

A person who frowns, looks at the floor and sits with their arms folded gives off very negative messages. A person who sits or stands upright and who smiles and uses good eye contact, is far more approachable and less threatening.

Examples of good and useful body language include:

- *having an open and relaxed posture*
- *facing the person but not standing too close* – about an arm's length away is comfortable for most people
- *smiling when appropriate* – although it is important to be friendly, we need to show that comments are taken seriously
- *using facial expressions to show sympathy or reassurance*
- *using eye contact* – although we need to be aware that some people (and cultures) find too much eye contact inappropriate and threatening
- *being sensitive to the person's own body language*
- *being flexible about our own body language and gestures so that we do not appear threatening or unapproachable*

All gestures and body language support what we are saying and how we are listening. If we say positive things but use negative body language, people will not believe or trust us. They will think that the good things we are saying are untrue.

Conversely, if our verbal and non-verbal messages are compatible, our messages are far more convincing and acceptable. Someone who speaks enthusiastically, uses their hands expressively, moves around a stage and stands up straight will be a far more convincing and engaging communicator.

When touching other people, this needs to be appropriate and with the other person's permission if possible. Shaking hands is usually acceptable and encouraged but touching elsewhere needs to be done with caution. If a customer seems to need a helping hand to get up from a seat, for instance, we should offer help and ask if it is all right to hold their arm before we intervene.

Communication

If our job involves touching people as part of our everyday activities, we will have guidelines about how to ask for permission and deal with difficult situations. If touching is inappropriate or unwanted, it can make communication extremely difficult and ineffective.

Professional behaviour is another important non-verbal influence on communication. We all need to behave in a calm, polite and professional manner at all times in the workplace, however stressed or upset we might feel. This helps to gain respect and cooperation from other people and supports our verbal communication. For example, if staff members are seen running around, screaming and messing about, their words are less likely to be taken seriously. It would be hard to take them seriously if the behaviour is inappropriate and seemingly out of control.

The importance of good personal grooming should not be underestimated. Every member of the organisation needs to make sure that they are:

- *clean and fresh* – *body odour and bad breath are off-putting to colleagues, customers and others*
- *tidy and presentable* – *with clean and tidy hair*
- *correctly dressed* – *e.g., in clean uniform or other work clothes*
- *wearing the correct footwear* – *e.g., safety boots or smart, clean shoes*

A smart appearance supports the person delivering verbal messages in the same way that gestures and body language do. We all make conscious and subconscious judgments about each other, especially when we first meet, so it is important to come across as trustworthy, professional and capable in the workplace.

Non-verbal communication can influence verbal communication :

- *in a positive way* – *when gestures, appearance, posture and body language are positive and support the verbal messages*
  or
- *in a negative way* – *if gestures are negative and undermine the verbal messages*

The same applies in a customer service situation. Customers feel valued and respected if their feedback is taken seriously and they are more likely to have a favourable and positive impression of the organisation. This often leads to recommendations and continued support in the future.

Communication

Barriers to Communication

There are many barriers to communication and these may occur at any stage in the communication process. Barriers may lead to your message becoming distorted and you therefore risk wasting both time and/or money by causing confusion and misunderstanding. Effective communication involves overcoming these barriers in conveying the clear and concise message.

Common barriers to effective communication include:

- *The use of jargon. Over complicated, unfamiliar and/or technical terms.*
- *Emotional barriers and taboos. Some people may find it difficult to express their emotions and some topics may be completely off-limits or to boo to below difficult topics may include but are not limited to, politics, religion, disability is (mental and physical), sexuality and sex, racism and any opinion that may be seen as unpopular.*
- *Lack of attention, interest, distractions, or irrelevance to the receiver.*
- *Differences in perception and viewpoint.*
- *Physical disability such as hearing problems or speech difficulties.*
- *Physical barriers to non-verbal communication.* **Not been able to see the non-verbal cues, gestures, posture and general body language can make communication less effective. Phone calls, text messages and other communication methods that rely on technology are often less effective than face-to-face communication.**
- *Language differences and the difficulty in understanding unfamiliar accents.*
- *Expectations and prejudices which may lead to false assumptions or stereotyping.* **People often hear what they expect to hear rather than what is actually said and jump to incorrect conclusions.**
- *Cultural differences. The norms of social interaction very greatly different cultures, as do the way in which emotions are expressed. For example, the concept of personal space varies between cultures and between different social settings.*

A skilled communicator must be aware of these barriers and try to reduce their impact by continually checking understanding and by offering appropriate feedback

Communicating in Challenging Situations

Speaking, listening and questioning skills are essential when managing challenging conversations. As we saw earlier in the workbook, the person leading the meeting needs to, for example:

- *speak clearly and slowly enough for everyone to understand*

Communication

- *keep their message simple and straightforward*
- *use language that is appropriate for the listener*
- *consider possible barriers to understanding*
- *be prepared to repeat or explain*
- *be ready to back up speech with visual aids*
- *use active listening skills*
- *select appropriate question types – e.g., open, closed, probing, leading or rhetorical*
- *use the appropriate tone, pitch and volume for the situation*
- *support verbal communication with effective body language*

Once the person leading the meeting has planned their approach, they can decide on the speaking, listening, questioning and body language skills that will be most useful for the communication style they want to use.

For example, a manager who is dealing with a complaining customer needs to diffuse the situation, make the conversation less challenging and maximise the chances of a successful outcome. They may concentrate on:

- *having an open and non-confrontational posture*
- *being polite, courteous, patient, apologetic and confident – to inspire trust*
- *listening more than they speak – using active listening skills*
- *using a calm, polite, respectful but confident tone of voice*
- *using open, closed and rhetorical questions – maybe with probing questions if more detail is required*

On the other hand, a manager who is giving a second verbal warning to a team member may choose to use a more assertive approach. They still need to be polite, but they may also concentrate on:

- *using dominant body language – such as strong eye contact*
- *good speaking skills with a strong tone of voice*
- *being firm and assertive*
- *expressing their disappointment – that the first verbal warning did not seem to work*
- *a range of question types – including leading and probing questions*

Communication methods and styles need to be calm, fair and professional so that, for example:

- *everyone concerned can work together afterwards*
- *the challenging conversation is less likely to lead on to further complaints or accusations of harassment and bullying*
- *the good reputation of the individuals and the organisation are maintained*

Communication

Building a Rapport

Having the knack to get along with people is always an asset in building human relationships. More so if you work in a field that deals a lot with people, such as sales and marketing. Being able to 'hit it off' or 'get on well' with someone easily is about rapport building; an underlying communication skill for people to experience during personal interaction with strangers, acquaintances, colleagues and family members.

A quality that cannot be seen or measured although the impact can be felt when doing it well or otherwise, describing rapport building in the context of communication can be likened to warming up the engine a few moments before driving a car. Think also about the few minutes of heating an oven to a right temperature before baking in the kitchen. Even in sports, athletes are advised to warm up their body first. Within these example of daily life routines, the idea of rapport is simply about naturally warm people up to you first to pave a way for you to get along easily with someone or a group. In a way, it is like a prelude to the main music in orchestra or an appetite before the main course of a meal. It is an elegant introduction to the next heavy part of anything important and in this case, it is the entry point facilitated by social interaction to the main communication goal.

Understanding Rapport

Rapport is basically an emotional connection with other people.

An extended definition of rapport within human interaction was offered by Oxford Dictionaries (2018) through:

> *"A close and harmonious relationship in which the people or groups concerned understand each other's feelings or ideas and communicate well."*

Many definitions share key concepts within aspects of social interaction, interpersonal relationship, trust, respect, communication effectiveness. and harmonious environment.

Developing rapport is an essential skill

Developing rapport is an essential part of every relationship.

> *Without rapport, you would basically not have a relationship at all!*

Being able to build rapport consciously is therefore extremely useful both personally and professionally. As a skill, it means that you can build relationships faster and improve communication more rapidly. Your working relationships will be more effective and your personal relationships will be stronger as a result.

Communication

If you have ever heard the expression "doesn't meet a stranger," you likely know that the phrase describes someone who is unconditionally friendly and able to converse with anyone. Some people have this trait and others wish they did.

Why Does Rapport Matter?

Rapport is important in both our professional and personal lives.

Employers are more likely to employ somebody who they believe will get on well with their current staff. Personal relationships are easier to make and develop when there is a closer connection and understanding between the parties involved – i.e., there is greater rapport.

When we first meet someone new, we start to try to build rapport. Like it or not, this is why small talk exists: it is a way to try to find things in common with other people and build that shared bond. This bond is important because we all tend to want to be with 'people like us'.

It is much easier to build rapport with someone who is very like you, or who shares a lot of your interests.
You have shared ground and things to talk about. You also have a shared frame of reference. This makes both building a relationship and communicating more generally, much easier.

However, we have probably all found ourselves thinking:

"He/she is lovely, I'm sure, but we really have nothing in common."

Under those circumstances, working together is likely to be harder and communication more difficult, because you lack a shared frame of reference. You will need to work harder to build rapport and develop your relationship - but this is still possible.

Break the Ice

For many, starting a conversation with a stranger is a stressful event. We may be lost for words and awkward with our body language and mannerisms.

Creating rapport at the beginning of a conversation with somebody new will often make the outcome of the conversation more positive. However stressful and/or nervous you may feel, the first thing you need to do is to try to relax and remain calm. By decreasing the tension in the situation communication becomes easier and rapport grows.

When you meet somebody for the first time, there are some easy things that you can do to reduce the tension. This will help both of you to feel more relaxed and communicate more effectively. These include:

Use non-threatening and 'safe topics' for initial small talk. Talk about established shared experiences, the weather, how you travelled to where you are. Avoid talking too much about yourself and avoid asking direct questions about the other person.

Communication

Listen to what the other person is saying and look for shared experiences or circumstances. This will give you more to talk about in the initial stages of communication.

Try to inject an element of humour. Laughing together creates harmony, make a joke about yourself or the situation/circumstances you are in, but avoid making jokes about other people.

Be conscious of your body language and other non-verbal signals you are sending. Try to maintain eye contact for approximately 60% of the time. Relax and lean slightly towards them to indicate listening and mirror their body-language if appropriate.

Show some empathy. Demonstrate that you can see the other person's point of view. Remember rapport is all about finding similarities and 'being on the same wavelength' as somebody else. Being empathic will help to achieve this.

Make sure the other person feels included but not interrogated during initial conversations. Just as you may feel tense and uneasy meeting and talking to somebody new, so may they.

Put the other person at their ease. This will enable you to relax and conversation to become more natural.

Non-Verbal Rapport Building

Initial conversations can help us to relax. However, quite a lot of rapport-building happens without words and through non-verbal communication channels.

We create and maintain rapport subconsciously through matching non-verbal signals, including body positioning, body movements, eye contact, facial expressions and tone of voice with the other person.

Watch two friends talking when you get the opportunity and see how they sub-consciously mimic each other's non-verbal communication.

We create rapport instinctively. It is our natural defence from conflict, which most of us will try hard to avoid most of the time.

It is important to use appropriate body language. We read and instantly believe what body language tells us, whereas we may take more persuading with vocal communication. If there is a mismatch between what we are saying and our body language, then the person we are with will believe the body language. Building rapport, therefore, begins with displaying appropriate body language. This usually means being welcoming, relaxed and open.

As well as paying attention to and matching body language with the person we are with, it also helps to match their words. Reflecting back and clarifying what has been said are useful tactics for repeating what has been communicated by the other person. Not only will it confirm that you are listening but also give you opportunity to use the words and phases of the other person, further emphasising similarity and common ground.

Communication

The way we use our voice is also important in developing rapport. When we are nervous or tense, we tend to talk more quickly. This in turn can make you sound more stressed. We tend to vary our voices, pitch, volume and pace to make what we are saying more interesting, but it also has an effect on how we come across. Try lowering your tone and talk more slowly and softly. This will actually help you develop rapport more easily.

Helpful Rapport Building Behaviours

There are certain behaviours that are particularly helpful in building rapport. These include:

- *If you are sitting, then lean towards the person you are talking to, with hands open and arms and legs uncrossed. This is open body language and will help you and the person you are talking to feel more relaxed.*
- *Look at the other person for approximately 60% of the time. Give plenty of eye-contact but be careful not to make them feel uncomfortable.*
- *When listening, nod and make encouraging sounds and gestures.*
- *Smile!*
- *Use the other person's name early in the conversation. This is not only seen as polite but will also reinforce the name in your mind, so you are less likely to forget it!*
- *Try to ask the other person open questions (the type of questions that require more than a yes or no answer). These questions are more comfortable to answer, because you are not being put on the spot to give a clear opinion*
- *Avoid contentious topics of conversation. It is much easier to stick to the weather, the last speaker and travel arrangements than risk falling out over politics.*
- *Use feedback to summarise, reflect and clarify back to the other person what you think they have said. This gives opportunity for any misunderstandings to be rectified quickly.*
- *Talk about things that refer back to what the other person has said. Find links between common experiences.*
- *Try to show empathy*
- *Demonstrate that you can understand how the other person feels and can see things from their point of view.*
- *When in agreement with the other person, openly say so and say why.*
- *Build on the other person's ideas.*
- *Be non-judgemental towards the other person. Let go of stereotypes and any preconceived ideas you may have about the person.*
- *If you have to disagree with the other person, give the reason first, then say you disagree.*
- *Admit when you do not know the answer or have made a mistake. Being honest is always the best tactic and acknowledging mistakes will help to build trust.*
- *Be genuine, with visual and verbal behaviours working together to maximise the impact of your communication.*
- *Offer compliments, avoid criticism and be polite.*

Communication

How to build rapport

Shift your mindset to an "I am worthy" one
If you struggle with feelings of low-worth, you may have difficulty building rapport. You will wrongly believe that other people are better than you and perhaps that you do not deserve to be in communication with them.

You must believe that you are worthy in order to share your ideas, challenge ideas that are incongruent with your belief system and banter with others.

If you want to learn the skill of building rapport with anyone, you must first examine how you esteem or view yourself. At your core, you are worthy. You do not have to do or be anything to be worthy; you are worthy by virtue of your existence. You are worthy because you are living the human experience. If you can shift your mindset and truly embrace your worth, it will be easy to build rapport with others.

Ask some variation of "tell me about yourself"
The host of a TV chat show starts their interviews by asking subjects to tell them about themselves.

Opening interviews this way allows them to avoid mistakes that places subjects on the defence. They are also able to learn, via their own words, what is important to them. Conversationalists may consider doing the same way.

Look for indicators of shared humanity
At our core, we are all the same. When we feel anxious about being in a relationship or conversation with people who appear "perfect" or are very accomplished, remind yourself that at our core, we are all the same.

Regardless of how much money individuals have in the bank; they want to be treated with the same dignity and respect that each of us requires for ourselves. They want to be liked because of who they are, not because of what they have. If you can remember that, at our core, we are all the same, you will be better positioned to build rapport with anyone.

Identify one thing you can appreciate about the person with whom you are conversing
When children go to school, they commonly will have a favourite football team and will be able to talk about the players and the results they achieve. This can become quite partisan and over time they will become increasingly single minded about "their" team. Whilst they may well keep that team loyalty for the rest of their lives, as they mature, they will be happier to talk about football generally rather than their own team. Over time, they will learn that it does not matter which football team it is if they paid careful attention and tried hard, each speaker and each team had something unique and worthwhile to offer.

The same is true in conversation. Even your enemies have admirable traits. Even the colleague who annoys or triggers you in ways you did not know were possible, has something that is worthy of praise. If you approach every conversation with this mindset, you will indeed be able to build rapport with almost anyone.

Communication

Inquire about family, friends and pets only if your speaking partners introduce these areas first

If you feel stuck in a discussion and are not sure how to make a connection, look for cues that the person with whom you are speaking is open to discussing his or her family or pets. These areas are deeply personal and while most people gush when talking about their family and the animals that they adore, you have no idea what is happening in a person's life that may make him or her less than receptive to tackling these issues.

Not every person's life is filled with happy memories or experiences about family, friends or pets.

Research the person

To have substantive conversations, you must research the person or persons with whom you are engaging. You should know what drives them professionally and personally. This technique is more appropriate when you are attending an event and have a sense of who will be at the gathering.

In the age of social media, this information may be more readily accessible than you expect.

Listen to Understand

Listening is an underrated skill. As a society, we are intentionally taught how to listen well. Even when we invite colleagues or friends out for lunch or dinner, most of us struggle with the urge to check social media, text messages or email.

When we are not distracted by technology and devices, sometimes we prepare responses while the person with whom we are engaging is still speaking.

Listening highlights how you hold the other person in esteem. Since many people are poor listeners, when you exhibit good listening skills, you signal to other people that you are interested and that they are worthy.

They will respond in kind by having positive feelings about you and by wanting to be in conversation with you again.

Be the person who tells the truth

You will learn that people in authority or in great leadership positions do not always have people around them who are willing to tell them the truth.

Honesty requires courage and a willingness to take a chance. It requires diplomacy and wisdom – and you must understand the conditions that make different leaders more receptive to truth. But many leaders can come to appreciate someone who they know will be honest with them.

If a leader asks you how you truly feel, find the courage and the words to, diplomatically and carefully, tell the individual the truth. This will improve your rapport with the leader.

Be open

So many conversations at parties, receptions, conferences and events are transactional and shallow. One might be very sceptical that many result in genuine and authentic connections.

Communication

One of the reasons this happens is because everyone has a representative, the better version of ourselves, who we send to social events. When someone dares to send or show up as their real self, the decision is like a breath of fresh air. It allows others the freedom to shed the persona and the liberty to be themselves. This works in large settings and it can work as a technique to build rapport.

Communication

Emotional Intelligence

Emotional intelligence is the ability to understand the way people feel and react, then use the skill to make good judgements, avoid issues or solve problems. This ability can be extremely useful when managing and communicating with others and can be applied on two levels:

- *personal* – *understanding our own feelings or reactions*
- *interpersonal* – *understanding other people's feelings and reactions*

People with a reasonable degree of emotional intelligence can be, for example:

- *empathetic* – *able to put themselves in other people's shoes*
- *sensitive to others*
- *understanding and sympathetic*
- *good at reading other people's emotions correctly*

In the workplace, we often have to work as a team or develop relationships with colleagues, customers and other stakeholders. Being aware of how people think and react can be essential. When looking at different forms of communication and how they are used, emotional intelligence can provide an extra insight into which form and approach will be most effective.

Using Emotional Intelligence

Whatever our approach, we need make allowances for the other person's feelings when managing challenging conversations. The chances are that they will be nervous, afraid, uncomfortable, aggressive or defensive. By using our emotional intelligence, we can read their feelings and reactions more accurately and adapt our approach and employ appropriate skills.

People can be challenging to deal with for many reasons. They may have, for example:

- *additional needs or requirements* – *e.g., impaired vision, hearing or mobility issues*
- *poor communication skills* – *e.g., learning difficulties that make communication difficult*
- *language or cultural barriers* – *e.g., making them upset because they find it hard to express themselves in English*
- *personal problems* – *e.g., issues with alcohol, drugs or a medical condition; childcare or family problems; difficult living conditions*
- *they may have an incident, emergency or trauma* – *e.g., reacting badly if they (or a person close to them) have been involved in an accident, injury or serious illness*

Communication

- *dissatisfaction and disappointment* – *e.g., reacting emotionally when there is a problem with the product or service*
- *impatience* – *e.g., being short-tempered if they are not dealt with straightaway*
- *indecision* – *e.g., uncertainty about how to proceed, what they want or how to solve problems*
- *being overly assertive, confident or intimidating* – *e.g., coming across as a bully when talking*
- *being too talkative* – *e.g., making problems unnecessarily complicated, hard to identify and deal with*

By being aware of background information, it is possible to use our emotional intelligence to 'step into their shoes', understand their viewpoint and take appropriate measures to achieve the objectives of the conversation. This skill of using empathy and understanding can be extremely useful. It helps us to amend our approach, diffuse problems and use the listening, speaking and questioning techniques that will be most effective.

We also need to be aware that some people find it extremely hard to use and understand emotional intelligence and we cannot assume that we all have the same ability to 'put ourselves in someone else's shoes' when we are involved with challenging conversations.

Communication

Delivering Feedback

If you have been telling people the same things over and over again, it is possible you have not been telling them the right things.

It is vital when giving feedback to employees to make it so that it is useful to them. It is even more vital when this feedback goes to team members working on a project. Because successful project management requires good communication – both with stakeholders and with members of the team, then it is important to be able to give feedback to those individuals that reinforces the behaviour you would like to see them exhibit.

Delivering constructive feedback is an important element of effective communication, especially when managing challenging conversations.

There are many theories and versions of communication cycles that show how sharing information is a continuous process, but the principles are broadly the same:

There will be many types of feedback in the workplace – e.g., complaints and praise from customers, comments in staff appraisal interviews, or discussions in a progress review.

Feedback helps us to:

- *find out what went well – so that we know we are going in the right direction and can build on our strengths*
- *find out things that need to be improved*

Points to consider when giving feedback include, for example:

- *the value of constructive feedback*
- *following a feedback model*
- *how to give negative feedback*
- *environment and communication techniques*

Communication

Environment and Communication Techniques

As we have seen already, environment and communication techniques are important when managing challenging conversations and these apply when giving feedback too. For the feedback to be useful and well-received, discussions need to take place in private, where noise and distractions are kept to a minimum. The choice of speaking skills, active listening skills and questioning techniques need to be focused on the individual and a positive outcome.

Feedback Models

Feedback models help new managers and team leaders to develop their feedback skills. There are several different frameworks which can help guide managers and leaders.

STAR feedback Model

One type of effective model for such feedback is known as the STAR model. The purpose of this model is to help you to visualise a pattern of giving good positive feedback and encouraging individuals to take initiative and complete their tasks efficiently.

If you visualise a star, much like the one in the image to the right, you can divide that star into three sections. the top point of the star, the left two-star points and the right two-star points. The top point represents the situation or task at hand. the left two points refer to the action that was taken and the right two points stand for the result of that action.

ST – The Situation or Task

The first part of being able to interpret and use feedback given is to understand the situation or task. What happened that alerted you to the necessity of taking care of this situation? In order to be able to determine the sort of feedback that is appropriate, you will need to take a minute to define what happened and what that meant in terms of the project. By defining the situation or task that occurred, you can pinpoint exactly what it is you need to address when it comes to the individual to whom you are providing feedback. For example, a situation might involve an employee who has arrived late to work every day for a week.

A – The Action

What action was taken? Was that action good or bad? What action should have been taken? It is important to identify the action involved with the situation. When the action you are reviewing was positive, note that it was positive. When the action was negative, explain first what should have happened. In keeping with the current example, you would tell the tardy employee that he or she should have arrived on time. If it is a case of an employee who had provided outstanding ideas in a meeting, then point out the exact action that employee took that was worthy of praise.

Communication

R – The Results

Next, you need to look at the results that action lead to. What happened as a result of that action? For example, if the employee provided many good ideas during the brainstorming session that impressed stakeholders, tell them! By acknowledging the situation, action and results that turned out well, you will increase their motivation and commitment to the task.

When you are providing an employee with positive feedback using the STAR model, you will put everything together and deliver the feedback. For example, the following might be said when giving feedback using this model:

The other day, when things went wrong in the factory, you did not panic. Instead, you kept a calm head and patiently determined what the cause of the problem was. This resulted in keeping other employees calm and helped us to solve the problem much faster.

You can see in this example that by acknowledging the situation, identifying the action and praising the results, that you will be better able to encourage similar action in the future from employees.

When it comes to providing negative feedback, make sure you identify both the actual action and result and the desired action and result. For example:

When I sent this proposal back to you for adjustments and with questions, you did not correct the problems or respond to the questions and therefore I cannot accept the proposal. If you had made the needed adjustments and responded to the questions effectively, then I would have been able to approve the project proposal.

In this example, both the undesired and desired actions and results are identified. By doing this, it makes it much easier for employees, stakeholders and project team members to understand what needs to be done and why it needs to be done.

By providing effective feedback on a regular basis, you can improve the productivity and effectiveness of your team.

CORBS Feedback Model

The principles of CORBS feedback model are as follows:

- **Clear statement** – *give clear and concise information.*
- **Owned by the person speaking** – *your own perception, not the ultimate truth. How it made you feel. Use terms such as "I find" or "I felt" and not "You are".*
- **Regular** – *give immediately or as close to the event as possible. NEVER delay*
- **Balanced** – *balance negative and positive feedback. DO NOT overload with negative feedback.*
- **Specific** – *base your feedback on observable behaviour. Behaviours that the recipient can change.*

Communication

Situation, Behaviour, Impact Model

Imagine that you recently gave some feedback to a member of your team. You told him that his line KPI's are great, but he needed to improve his people skills.

You follow up a few weeks later to find out why he has not made any changes. You discover that he did not
understand what he could do to improve – your feedback simply prompted more questions. He was left thinking "What's good about achieving the KPI's and how can I do more?" and "What's wrong with my people skills?"

The Situation – Behaviour – Impact (SBI) Feedback tool helps people deliver more effective feedback. It focuses your comments on specific situations and behaviours and then outlines the impact that these behaviours have on others.

The SBI Feedback Tool outlines a simple structure that you can use to give feedback:

- *Situation.*
- *Behaviour.*
- *Impact.*

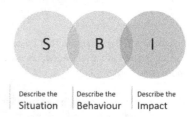

| Describe the Situation | Describe the Behaviour | Describe the Impact |

When you structure feedback in this way, people will understand precisely what you are commenting
on and why. When you outline the impact of their behaviour on others, you are giving them the chance
to reflect on their actions and think about what they need to change. The tool also helps you avoid making assumptions that could upset the other person and damage your relationship with them.

Applying the Tool

1. Situation
When you are giving feedback, first define the where and when of the situation you are referring to. This puts the feedback into context and gives the other person a specific setting as a reference.

2. Behaviour
Your next step is to describe the specific behaviours that you want to deal with. This is the most challenging part of the process because you must communicate only the behaviours that you observed directly.

You must not make assumptions or judgments about those behaviours. These could be wrong and this will undermine your feedback. For example, if you observed that a colleague made a mistake, you should not assume that they had not prepared thoroughly. You should simply comment that your colleague made mistakes – and, ideally, you should note what the mistakes were.

Communication

Do not rely on hearsay or gossip, as this may contain other people's judgments. Again, this could undermine your feedback and jeopardise your relationship.

The examples below include a description of behaviour:

- *"During yesterday morning's DRM, when you talked about the night shift KPI's, you were uncertain about why a line had a negative score and your calculations were incorrect."*

- *"At the team meeting on Friday afternoon, you ensured that the meeting started on time and all your research was correct and each of the managers' questions were answered."*

Aim to use measurable information in your description of the behaviour. This helps to ensure that your comments are unbiassed.

3. Impact
The last step is to use "I" statements to describe how the other person's action has affected you or others.

For example:

- *"During yesterday morning's DRM, when you talked about the night shift KPI's, you were uncertain about why a line had a negative score and your calculations were incorrect. I felt a bit embarrassed because my manager was there. I'm worried that this has affected the reputation of our team."*

- *"At the team meeting on Friday afternoon, you ensured that the meeting started on time and all your research was correct and each of the managers' questions were answered. I am proud that you did such an excellent job and put us in a good light. Keep up the great work!"*

Next Steps

Once you have delivered your feedback, encourage the other person to think about the situation and to understand the impact of his or her behaviour. Allow the other person time to absorb what you have said and then go over specific actions that will help him or her to improve.

Communication

Pendleton's Model of feedback

Pendleton's Rules are structured in such a way that the positives are highlighted first, in order to create a safe environment. Therefore, the learner identifies the positives first.

This is followed by the facilitator or group reinforcing these positives and discussing skills to achieve them.

"What could be done differently?" is then suggested, first by the learner and then by the person or group giving feedback.

The advantage of this method is that the learner's strengths are discussed first. Avoiding a discussion of weaknesses right at the beginning prevents defensiveness and allows reflective behaviour in the learner.

There are some deficiencies in the rules. They create artificiality and rigidity by forcing a discussion of the learner's strengths first. Therefore, an opportunity for an interactive discussion of topics that might be relevant to the learner is lost.

There is also inefficient use of time because the same topic is discussed twice in its entirety: first to discuss the strengths and then the weaknesses.

To someone expecting primarily negative feedback, the discussion of strengths may appear patronising, which makes the feedback more stressful and, perversely, a disproportionate amount of time may be spent discussing strengths to soften the impact of the negatives.

A judgemental tone may also creep into the feedback when "What was done correctly and what
was incorrect?" is discussed, which goes against the non-evaluative and formative nature of feedback.

Phase	Supervisor	Recipient
Positive Aspects		Tells what went well
	Complements on what went well	
Areas for Improvement		Tells what went wrong and what could be done better
	Complements on what could be done better	
Action Plan for Improvement		Tells action plan
	Approves action plan with modifications	
Summary		Summarises the key points
	Complements if necessary	

Communication

The Value of Constructive Feedback

For feedback to be useful, it needs to be constructive, not destructive. If there are problems and weaknesses that need to be addressed, people need to be advised of these tactfully and shown how to improve.

People can see feedback as criticism and may react negatively. They can become defensive, make excuses, choose not to hear or take the feedback seriously. Destructive or negative feedback that is handled poorly can leave people feeling bad, hopeless and worthless. They can feel they are left without any useful information or ideas on which they can build.

However, people often respond positively to constructive feedback because it concentrates on, for example:

- *the individual's needs and abilities* – *increasing self-awareness and offering them what they need to develop in the workplace*
- *positive messages* – *providing useful information about performance and how to develop*
- *being supportive* – *offering encouragement and developing working relationships and trust*
- *behaviours and actions rather than the person* – *making the issues less personal*
- *helping people to feel valued, respected and engaged in the workplace processes* – *to aid team building and motivation*

Delivering Negative Feedback

Negative feedback does not need to be avoided; it just needs to be handled well. If a manager only gives positive feedback, people will distrust their judgement after a while, as nobody is perfect and there must be some things that need correction and development. When giving negative feedback, it is useful to use a sandwich technique. For example:

- *give some positive comments about something that has gone well*
- *deliver the negative feedback tactfully, maybe following the CORBS model*
- *finish with some positive feedback and comments, maybe about the future*

This enables the recipient to be given the negative comments and end the conversation with an uplifting, positive comment that makes them feel valued and committed to the team.

Communication

Escalating Workplace Problems

Working within the limits of authority is important and this applies to managing challenging conversations as well. We all need to know when to escalate a problem to someone else. The limits of authority and how to escalate a problem that is outside those limits, will be set out in, for example:

- *the employment contract*
- *the job description*
- *organisational policies, procedures or standards*
- *training materials*

The organisation's procedures will show when staff need to escalate a problem. For example:

- *when a decision is needed that is outside their limits of authority*
- *when a customer or another stakeholder requests something that is outside the limits of their responsibility*
- *when dealing with complaints or problems that are outside the limits of authority*
- *when they do not have enough knowledge, experience or skill to be able to deal with something on their own*
- *when there is not enough time to deal with something properly*
- *when there is a threat to health and safety* – e.g., if someone becomes aggressive, very upset or unwell during a challenging conversation

The job titles can vary, but employment contracts, job descriptions and training materials should show the chain of command, or management structure, of the organisation. For example:

- *team members will usually escalate problems to their team leader, or supervisor*
- *team leaders and supervisors might refer a problem to their shift manager or a specialist from another department* – e.g., a quality control team leader for help with product testing
- *managers will escalate to more senior managers or subject specialists*

Working within the limits of authority and escalating problems when appropriate protects:

- *the people involved with the conversation* – by making sure that they act legally and are fully supported in their decisions and promises if they have worked in line with the organisational procedures; by making sure that their legal rights have been observed and respected
- *the organisation* – helping it to maintain a good reputation for being fair and consistent

Communication

Employers value employees who can operate independently and do not need to be micromanaged.

Similarly, particularly among employees with some level of management responsibility or who aspire to such responsibility, there is often a desire to handle things on their own without asking supervisors for help.

At the same time, managers are there for a reason and it is important for employees to know when they can and should escalate issues up the chain of command.

The employee has reached their level of authority

This is perhaps the most common situation when escalation is appropriate or necessary. Employees should not be expected to make decisions that are above their pay grade. Instead, they should bring these issues to their managers, who can make the call or escalate further as needed.

How do employees know when they are bumping up against their level of authority?

Their job descriptions should convey some indication. In addition, though, direct supervisors and managers need to help employees understand where their decision-making authority may end and when they need to turn to their managers for support. Citing specific examples and providing real-time feedback are both good ways of coaching employees.

Cross-department support is needed

Sometimes, the solution to a problem requires input across departments or business units and an employee may need to engage his leadership team to engage the appropriate resources.

Maintaining Relationships

It can be awkward for employees to be the ones to say "no" to an important customer. This is particularly true when employee-customer contact is frequent and long term. In these situations, it can help maintain that close relationship if the employee can take an issue to his manager and let the manager deliver the bad news—obviously with the appropriate explanation.

This lets the employee demonstrate that he advocated for the customer while insulating that employee from the unwelcome decision.

Again, supervisors and managers can help employees understand when this handoff is indicated by conveying clear expectations and providing feedback.

Independence is important for employees and employers alike, but there are always going to be situations when employees need to escalate issues to their boss, their bosses, etc. This is true at any level of the organisation.

Communication

Escalation of Customer Complaints

Reasons why Customer Complaints Require Escalation

Research has shown that the top seven reasons customers want to escalate complaints are:

- *staff lack of knowledge*
- *being told no without any apparent reason or explanation*
- *the employee lacking confidence*
- *the staff member having a negative or disagreeable attitude*
- *not receiving an apology*
- *the employee not communicating clearly and not adapting to the pace of the customer*

Strategize the way calls are handled

There should be a clear strategy in place for when complaints need to be escalated. The employee should be empowered to resolve an issue on their own in situations where senior intervention is unnecessary. Requiring managers to intervene in routine matters can be destructive rather than constructive. Staff should be trained in Active Listening so they can effectively understand and mitigate customer objections and satisfy their needs. Staff should be trained to understand they should never take things personally. A customer may be having a bad day or may just be a professional complainer! Staff should adopt a helpful mentality and treat customers with respect. This has the effect of disarming customers who may not be anticipating such a response.

Resolving the issues

The best resolutions to issues which arise with customers is to reach a win-win resolution. The customer service employee and the customer come to a consensus on what needs to be done to make the issue right. Once this has been verified with the customer that this will resolve the issue, immediately initiate the necessary steps to resolve the matter.

This is the opportunity to exceed customer expectations. It is already know their experience with the organisation has been less than ideal. Once steps have been taken to resolve the matter, verify that the customer is now satisfied. Ask whether the customer will continue to use the business after the resolution of the problem. This reminds the customer that apart from a minor hiccup to business as usual, their problems were swiftly and effectively resolved. This can actually prompt an even higher level of loyalty as the customer feels valued and respected.

Monitoring

All escalations within the business should be closely monitored. The need for escalation should be the exception not the rule. Monitoring escalations and the causes can identify the need for other corrective action to be taken further back in the customer journey. The root cause must be identified and remediated as soon as possible. The problem could be due to a customer message in advert which leads to a misunderstanding or it could be the actions of an overzealous employee who is overstating the performance of capability of the goods or services on offer. Once the root cause is identified, it should be resolved with whatever appropriate training, coaching or other activities necessary. Continued

Communication

monitoring should then evidence a decrease in escalations meaning the problem has been resolved.

Reasons why escalation does not take place

No one likes escalating problems as it suggests an inability to complete the task. It is vitally important however, that this attitude is dispelled and that all problems which are not immediately resolved are referred to a higher level. The customer is still waiting whilst the employee is deliberating and will continue to wait until the issue ahs been reviewed by the second line support. If the issue had been resolved immediately, the customer would not have had to wait so long, the problem would have been resolved more quickly and the reputation of the organisations would not be so badly damaged. It is also only by escalating issues that the need for training can be identified. If an employee is frequently escalating a specific problem, it is clear they require training and development in that area.

Communication

Chairing Meetings

Meetings offer the opportunity for employees to get together to share business information, generate ideas, plan future events and celebrate success. Whether meetings are face-to-face, by videoconference or webinars, employees have the chance to exchange information. You should make sure you are fully prepared for the meeting, carrying out any research in advance and making sure you have all the information that you need for each agenda item.

You need to create and communicate the agenda to all participants in good time, which enables them to plan their contribution, if required and add agenda items if they wish. Depending on the method you use for the meeting, you may need to check the availability of the meeting room and of any equipment you wish to use to enhance your communication and ensure that it set up and working correctly beforehand.

When chairing the meeting you should communicate clearly using the appropriate aspects of verbal and non-verbal communication. You will also need to actively listen to what is being said by members of the team and, if you are unsure of any points, ask questions to clarify your understanding.

Showing respect for other people's ideas and opinions is important, it is also important that you make sure you pass on your information in a clear and professional manner, using your own knowledge and experience.

As the chair of a meeting, you will be responsible for ensuring that it stays on track and does not stray too far from the agenda. Additional time should have been allowed at the end for any other business to be discussed, therefore some items can be added and anything nonurgent may be deferred to the next meeting or allocated to member of the team as an action.

You will need to agree for a participant of the meeting to take the minutes, recording the key items and actions to be taken, will be responsible for them and when they are to be completed by. The person produces the minutes will need to be able to use effective written communication and you may need to support them with this. You should clarify key points after each agenda item and check that all participants understand their roles. Meeting minutes should be checked for accuracy and then agreed or amended accordingly

Key Documentation

When organising a meeting, the person leading it will often generate and circulate an agenda in advance. This is a list of points that they are expecting to cover, in order, within the time allocated to the meeting.

The agenda is based on the organisational objectives that the people attending need to discuss, for example:

- *data to measure and evaluate progress so far in achieving objectives*
- *issues and problems*

Communication

- *possible solutions*
- *forecasts, plans and targets about how to achieve the next set of objectives*

For example, a quarterly meeting between department managers and team leaders to review activities could result in these items being on the agenda:

1. **Welcome and introduction** – *from the senior manager holding the meeting*
2. **Minutes from the last meeting** – *to be agreed and signed off as being accurate*
3. **Apologies** – *from people who cannot attend the meeting*
4. **Production output for the last two quarters** – *to compare and analyse*
5. **Problems arising** – *e.g., delays, staffing issues or problems with suppliers*
6. **Forecasts and targets for the next quarter**
7. **Anticipated resources needed and potential problems**
8. **Review draft targets for the following year**
9. **Recruitment plans for the following year**
10. **Training courses planned for the following year**
11. **Any other business (AOB)** – *for people to add things that need to be discussed*

It can be useful to put the expected time next to each item, so that people can see how long has been allocated. Also, it is helpful to show who will be leading each item. This helps to focus attention and identify speakers that may not be known to all of the attendees. For example, items 1, 2, 3 and 11 would be led by the chairperson, but items 7 and 8 about forecasts and targets would be led by the sales director.

It is important to have a meeting agenda that addresses the objectives of the organisation so that, for example:

- **the meeting is focused, structured and has direction** – *to keep things moving as people can see how much business needs to be covered and in what order; to avoid people spending valuable time talking about issues that are nothing to do with the objectives; to keep the meeting on time*
- **people can see what needs to be prepared before the meeting** – *e.g., reports and figures that are going to be discussed*
- **participants can anticipate questions they may want to ask** – *e.g., by having advance warning that they will discuss specific problems with other managers*

Having an agenda shows that the meeting is serious and will be run well. Everyone's time is precious and it is important to use the time wisely and efficiently, making the most of the opportunity to share information, review objectives and agree the ways forward.

During formal meetings, someone will usually take the minutes. These are brief or detailed notes that are written up after the meeting as a true representation of what was discussed and agreed. They are often sent out soon after the meeting, so that everyone can see the points that have been agreed. The minutes are checked and agreed at the next meeting to make sure

Communication

that they are accurate. They can also be used when writing the agenda for the next meeting, to check that actions have been completed and to show which subjects and objectives need to be reviewed again. The evidence recorded in minutes can be used for serious purposes. For example, they may be used during legal action, such as a disciplinary process and need to be truthful and accurate. Minutes can also help when managing projects and tasks, to provide evidence of decisions and agreed actions.

Other key documentation needed will depend on the purpose of the meeting, who is attending and the format that is most suitable for sharing information.

The following table shows examples of documents, type of meeting where they might be used and when they might be circulated:

Documents:	Examples of their purpose:	Type of meeting where they might be useful:
Agenda	To list the points to be covered during the meeting	Any meeting, especially formal meetings or if several people are expected to attend
Minutes	Detailed notes that need to be agreed at formal meetings	Meetings between directors, trustees or shareholders, or when there is a statutory or regulatory requirement to log and approve the minutes
Briefing notes or handouts	Detailed information that people need to read before or after the meeting – e.g., about new products and services	Any meeting, especially management, sales or training meetings
Reports – including graphics, pictures, graphs and tables	Formal or informal reports about any business function – e.g., sales figures; production data sheets; organisational operations; market research analysis; feedback questionnaires and data	Any meeting, especially management, videoconferences, sales, team and directors' meetings
Workbooks	Training materials – e.g., to give to learners to use during training meetings as samples to discuss when planning and organising training with other team leaders or managers	Team, training and management meetings
Forms	To collect information in a structured manner – e.g., order forms or application forms	Meetings with customers or suppliers; team meetings for HR or training purposes
Contracts or agreements	Legally binding documents between parties	Meetings with customers, suppliers or members of staff
Instructions	To include within operational procedures and training manuals	Team or training meetings
Brochures and other marketing materials	To provide detailed information about the organisation's products and services	Meetings with customers or suppliers

Communication

Some key documents need to be made available before the meeting so that people can be fully prepared, for example:

- *the agenda*
- *briefing notes*
- *reports and materials for people who have been involved with their preparation* *– e.g., so that they can get to know their material before they present their part of the report during the meeting*

Many key documents only need to be made available during the meeting to support the information being discussed. These could include, for example:

- *copies of the agenda for people who have not seen it*
- *reports*
- *handouts, workbooks and other training materials*
- *contracts*
- *samples of marketing materials*

All of the key documents can also be circulated to appropriate people after the meeting. If people have not attended the meeting, they may need to be informed about all of the points, decisions and information that were discussed so that they can comment and stay up to date. If people did attend the meeting, they may need additional documents after the meeting that confirm what was agreed and what follow-up actions are needed. These could include, for example:

- *minutes* *– draft or agreed*
- *forms* *– that need to be completed*
- *further reports* *– to show progress and update follow-up actions*

When circulating key documentation, it is important to make sure that it is appropriate to share it. For example, care needs to be taken to make sure that:

- *the recipient is authorised to receive it*
- *the information is relevant to them*
- *confidentiality is not breached*
- *the information is current and correct*
- *the documents are sent out at the right time*
- *the information is sent in a suitable format* *– e.g., secure email or by post*

Communication

Preparing for a Meeting

There are several things that need attention when preparing for a meeting and these should be set out in the organisation's procedures. When arranging a meeting, we need to know the answers to the following questions:

When will the meeting take place?
The date, time and duration of the meeting are important so that:

- *people can be invited to the meeting*
- *the room can be booked or reserved*
- *resources can be arranged*
- *people know how long the meeting is expected to run*
- *time zones can be checked for international video conferences*

Why is the meeting happening?
It helps to know why the meeting is taking place as it enables us to:

- *make sure that standard procedures are being followed*
- *plan to deal with typical problems and issues*
- *answer questions about the purpose of the meeting* – e.g., if people call for details or to check if they should come

The meeting could be, for example:

- *an information meeting* – e.g., to cascade information down to the attendees whose primary involvement is to take notes and maybe ask relevant questions
- *a decision-making meeting* – e.g., where people need to prepare their reports, data and arguments to make their contribution to the group
- *a combination* – e.g., team or divisional meetings that involve sharing information, drawing conclusions and making decisions

Who is coming to the meeting?
We need to know who is supposed to attend the meeting so that:

- *the right people can be invited* – e.g., with written invitations, by email, using a list on the wall in the staff room or electronic meeting planners
- *resources can be planned* – e.g., the right size of meeting room, car parking capacity, or the right number of coffee cups
- *an attendance list can be prepared*
- *name badges can be prepared if needed*
- *special requirements can be accommodated* – e.g., wheelchair access, hearing loops for those with impaired hearing, or translation services
- *someone can be tasked to take notes for the minutes*

Communication

Where will the meeting happen?

Details of the location of the meeting need to be considered so that:

- *people can be told where the meeting will be*
- *maps and directions can be sent out if necessary*
- *planners can make sure that the location is big enough and has all the necessary equipment*
- *parking and transport can be arranged if needed*
- *any security and access issues can be dealt with in advance* – e.g., getting security passes for people who do not normally have access to the location
- *people with access problems can be informed and assisted as required*

Which resources and facilities are needed?

As we find out more about the 'when, why, who and where' of the meeting, the resources and facilities that are needed start to become clear. Once the venue has been established, planners who organise the meeting might need to consider the following:

- **invitations** – asking the person to accept and state any special access or dietary requirements
- **furniture** – e.g., the number and placement of chairs and tables
- **technical equipment** – e.g., PowerPoint, screens, microphones, sound system, videoconferencing system, other audio-visual aids (known as AV)
- **special access requirements** – e.g., ramps and space for wheelchairs
- **catering** – e.g., tea, coffee, water, snacks or meals
- **security and car passes** – e.g., to gain access to a secure site such as a military base
- **name badges and attendance lists** – e.g., a list of names and contact details so that colleagues can see who attended and follow them up
- **agenda** – a list of points to be covered, usually produced by the person holding the meeting
- **copies of the minutes of the last meeting** – e.g., to hand around in a formal meeting to be agreed and signed; for people to check that previously agreed points have been actioned
- **briefing notes** – e.g., detailed information that people need to read before or after the meeting
- **stationery** – e.g., pads and pens
- **literature** – e.g., notes, reports, workbooks, forms or brochures
- **the budget for resources** – e.g., the food budget per head

Some of these things need to be organised and planned well in advance of the meeting and the chairperson, or chair, needs to be aware of the whole process. They need to be confident that all points are being covered.

By preparing thoroughly, we can make sure that:

Communication

- *there is a suitable environment*
- *the right people are invited*
- *people can prepare themselves and contribute effectively*

Facilitating a Meeting

Having taken care of the practicalities of preparing for and arranging a meeting, the chairperson needs to use their skills to make sure that the meeting is effective. The need to, for example:

- *use leadership skills*
- *use effective communication skills*
- *follow the organisation's procedures*
- *guide the meeting*
- *manage time*
- *control speakers when necessary*
- *make sure that information has been recorded*

Leadership skills

Leaders inspire and motivate people – they focus on people and set new directions for a group to follow. When chairing a meeting, the leadership skills used can include, for example:

- *personal and interpersonal skills to get the most out of the people at the meeting*
- *analysing results and trends, forecasting, innovating and giving direction for change*
- *communicating visions and plans*
- *encouraging, praising, developing and inspiring team members*

The chairperson's leadership style can be important. For example, using Kurt Lewin's theory of leadership styles, the chairperson may employ one or all of the following styles:

- **autocratic** – *expecting others to do things in their way*
- **democratic** – *allowing other people to be involved in the decision-making process*
- **laissez-faire** – *trusting their team's capabilities, willing to stand back and let the team get on with the tasks*

A mixture of all three styles will often be needed when chairing a meeting. Strong, autocratic leadership can be used to keep things on time and to make sure that the points on the agenda are covered. The democratic style can help to involve and engage other people, gaining their trust and commitment and making the most of what they have to offer. The laissez-faire style is important when delegating tasks and can be used when the chairperson knows that they can trust people to take ownership of tasks and follow-up actions.

Communication

Using effective communication skills

Communication skills are covered in detail in another workbook, but the skills that are useful when chairing a meeting can include, for example:

- **questioning techniques** – *e.g., using a mixture of open, closed, probing, leading and rhetorical questions*
- **listening skills** – *e.g., using active listening techniques*
- **building rapport** – *e.g., developing working relationships and gaining the confidence of others*
- **emotional intelligence** – *e.g., recognising, understanding, managing and influencing emotions*

Good communication skills help to ensure that all participants take an active role in the meeting and contribute effectively.

Following the organisation's procedures

Organisations often have procedures about how meeting should be run. These are the ground rules that everyone needs to accept and follow to make the meeting productive and effective. For example, procedures could ask people to:

- *switch off mobile phones*
- *introduce themselves*
- *avoid interrupting other people*
- *stick to the agenda*
- *not talk amongst themselves*
- *start on time and stay until the end*

Some meetings are run on a formal basis where all questions go 'through the chair'. This means that all participants have to address their questions and comments to the chairperson, then wait for the chair to give them their turn.

Guiding meetings and managing time

The most important tasks for the chairperson are to guide meetings and keep them running to time. People attending meetings become irritated, uncomfortable and resentful if meetings are not run well. For example, nobody appreciates spending their time in a meeting that:

- *goes on too long*
- *does not have clear objectives*
- *does not cover all of the items on the agenda*
- *does not stick to the agenda – except for time allocated to 'any other business'*
- *does not allow people to speak and get important points across*
- *feels boring and irrelevant*
- *wastes time by letting some people speak for too long, or in too much detail*
- *gets out of hand with too many interruptions, inappropriate language or emotional outbursts*

Communication

- *does not have clear outcomes about decisions, changes, future actions or new responsibilities*

The chairperson needs to plan well, be focused on the objectives and be aware of people's expectations. They need to take command every so often to keep the meeting on track and make sure that time is spent effectively. For example, the chairperson needs to:

- *make sure that the right people are invited to attend* – e.g., to present and share information and take part in making decisions
- *make sure that everyone has access to the information they need* – e.g., to be able to prepare, share information and take away material that needs to be studied later
- *make sure that everyone is clear about the objectives of the meeting* – e.g., to keep everyone focused and engaged; to manage expectations
- *follow the agenda and cover all of the points listed* – e.g., make sure people do not get side-tracked too much by irrelevant topics and details
- *use good listening and questioning techniques* – e.g., to encourage people to contribute effectively and share information fully
- *guide the speakers* – e.g., to introduce themselves, make their points and stick to the agenda
- *summarise decisions and future actions* – e.g., to set the date and objectives of the next meeting; to clarify what has been agreed and what follow-up actions are required Controlling the meeting can be quite difficult as there needs to be a balance between getting enough information from people without getting too much. The amount of time given to each item on the agenda will depend on its complexity and the information that people need to discuss. If an item is taking too long, for example, the chairperson can announce that they will allow five more minutes of discussion, bring the matter to a close, move on to the next item and arrange for the matter to be discussed again in another meeting, if necessary.

Controlling speakers when necessary

This can be the hardest task for the chairperson and they need to make sure that the meeting is balanced and that everyone gets a chance to contribute.

To keep the meeting in balance, the chairperson needs to be ready to take command and not be afraid to chair the meeting. The following table gives some examples of problems that may occur, along with some suggested solutions:

Communication

Problem:	Suggested solutions:
New or shy people do not contribute to the meeting	*Invite new people to introduce themselves* *Ask questions – their silence may not mean that they agree with what others are saying*
People from minority groups or who have unpopular views are not heard	*Make sure that they are invited to air their views* *Insist that others give them time to speak, even if they disagree* *Ask if anyone who has not spoken yet wishes to comment*
People interrupt each other	*Be firm and consistent* *Acknowledge the interruption but avoid being drawn in* *Ask the person who is interrupting to wait until the first person has finished, then go back to them to air their points of view*
People talk amongst themselves	*Stop the chatter politely at first, then firmly – it is distracting and discourteous* *Be firm about them waiting for their turn to speak* *Emphasise the importance of listening to what the speaker has to say*
Speakers talk for too long or get side-tracked away from the topic	*Again, be firm and consistent* *Thank them for their contributions and for raising interesting points, then explain you want to ask others to comment*
People criticise decisions or each other in a negative way	*Be firm about looking for solutions not problems* *Ask for suggestions about how things could be improved* *Ask the critic what they would do to resolve the issue*
People argue or make emotional outbursts	*Stop the discussion* *Identify areas where there is agreement* *Summarise the issues and suggest ways forward* *Take the focus away from individuals and concentrate on the broader issues*

Recording information

The chairperson needs to work with the person taking the minutes to make sure that an accurate record is kept. Minutes need to be written up in line with the organisation's procedures, especially if there is a legal requirement to have a true representation of the points covered and agreed in the meeting.

The chairperson needs to make sure that a suitable minute-taker:

- *attends the meeting*
- *is fully briefed and able to handle the information*
- *keeps up with all of the points made and agreed*
- *writes up their notes as soon as possible after the meeting*

Communication

The chairperson and other participants can openly ask for certain, important points to be noted in the minutes during the meeting – e.g., to record a disagreement with a decision or to highlight points that affect people who could not attend the meeting.

Follow-up actions

After meetings, the chairperson's managerial input continues. They need to:

- *communicate recorded actions*
- *take follow-up action, when required*
- *make sure other people complete follow-up actions*

Communicating recorded actions

The chairperson needs to make sure that information has been circulated after meetings. This is important for:

- **people who attended the meeting** – *e.g., so that they can go ahead and action the points that are their responsibility, as shown in the minutes*
- **people who did not attend the meeting** – *e.g., so that they can see what was agreed and what they have to follow up*
- **compliance** – *e.g., as part of a legal process where people need to be informed of decisions and agreed actions*

Documents could include minutes and any other relevant key documents and can be sent in the paper-based or electronic format set out in the organisation's procedures. If it is critical to know that people have received minutes and documents, there may be procedures where the recipient needs to acknowledge receipt.

Taking follow-up action

As a leader, the chairperson needs to make sure that they follow up decisions and actions that affect them. For example, if the chairperson has agreed to research something and report their findings within a week of the meeting, they need to make sure that they do this on time or report why they are late if there is a problem. They need to lead by example to maintain credibility and other people's trust and confidence.

Making sure other people take follow-up action

The chairperson needs manage other people to make sure that they follow up decisions and agreed actions. If they have delegated responsibility for follow-up actions, the chairperson needs to keep an eye on progress and help to provide support and resources if there are problems.

The minutes are a useful guide as to who needs to take action, the details of what they should do and the timescale they need to follow. The chairperson, other managers, leaders or decisionmakers can use them as a tool when planning and monitoring progress.

Communication

The agenda of the next meeting is another useful tool to encourage people to complete agreed actions. It usually includes a reference to the actions agreed in the previous meeting and this provides a focus to make sure that follow-up actions are not overlooked.

Active Listening in Meetings

Active listening is an integral part of effective communication. You will need to demonstrate active listening with your team members, colleagues, hire managers, customers and stakeholders in the position work for.

Demonstrating active listening involves:

- *giving your full attention to the individual without interrupting them*
- *encouraging them to open up*
- *listening to what they say*
- *penitentiary and reacting appropriately to their body language*
- *using your own body language, for example, head nodding, leaning forward and using gestures*
- *understanding their viewpoint and not your interpretation of it*
- *asking questions, if necessary, to gather further information*
- *repeating back phrases to provide confirmation that your listening*
- *summarising what they have told you to check that you fully understood them*
- *giving them the opportunity to let you know if you have not got it quite right*
- *empathising with them*

An effective chairperson needs to:

- *take ownership and not be afraid of chairing the meeting*
- *set high standards*
- *be on time*
- *be courteous*
- *encourage contributions*
- *listen carefully*
- *be fair but firm*
- *be able to work with, lead and manage people, especially during meetings*

Communication

Summary

When chairing meetings, you need to think about:

- *key documentation* – that supports the participants before, during and after the meeting
- *how to prepare for the meeting* – planning a suitable environment and physical resources, inviting the right people and making sure everyone can prepare effectively
- *following the organisation's procedures* – establishing ground rules for the structure of the meeting
- *making the meeting effective* – keeping it to time and controlling the flow
- *following up after the meeting* – checking that everyone is following up on the decisions and agreed actions

Chapter 4: Leading People

Leading People

Leadership

The term 'leadership' can be used in many different ways.

It can be defined as:

> ### *the capacity to influence people to achieve a common goal*

There is, however, no single definition or concept of leadership that satisfies all situations. Leaders adopt many different approaches to each task and can operate at any level. As a result, identifying and developing leaders can be challenging.

When leadership is skilfully demonstrated, it can bring positive outcomes for individuals, teams, organisations and wider communities. It is therefore important to develop leaders to meet the current and future needs of an organisation, as well as investing in other areas which enable leaders and teams to be effective.

What is clear is that leadership covers three integral elements:

- **Self** - *skilful expression of personal qualities.*
- **Other people** - *staff, line managers, peers but also senior management and other stakeholders.*
- **The job to be done** - *specifying, defining, clarifying, reviewing and revising when needed, the task to be achieved.*

The leader must address the question 'what we are doing this job for.'? This identifies the purpose of the task and when purpose is shared, people become collaborators, offering insights of their own.

> ### *'Climb that hill!' becomes 'Climb that hill - so we can get a better view of the river'.*

When people see a point to their efforts, the work itself may become more meaningful.

A leader is involved in shaping and moulding the behaviour of the group towards accomplishment of organisational goals.

There is no best style of leadership. Leadership is linked to the situation. Successful leadership depends on tackling the problems appropriately, which each situation presents.
A leader must have many and diverse qualities, skills and traits to ensure they are effective in all situations. The following are some of the pre-requisites needed to be a good leader:

- **Physical appearance** - *A leader must have a pleasing appearance. Physique and health are very important for a good leader.*
- **Vision and foresight** - *A leader cannot maintain influence unless they exhibit that they are forward looking. They must visualise situations and thereby frame logical programmes.*

Leading People

- **Intelligence** - *A leader should be intelligent enough to examine problems and difficult situations. They should weigh up the pros and cons and then summarises the situation. A positive frame of mind and mature outlook is very important.*
- **Communicative skills** - *A leader must be able to communicate the policies and procedures clearly, precisely and effectively. This can be helpful in persuasion and stimulation.*
- **Objective** - *A leader has to have an open outlook which is free from bias and which does not show any favouritism towards a particular individual. They should develop their own opinion and should base any judgement on facts and logic.*
- **Knowledge of work** - *A leader should know the nature of the work of those they lead so they can win the trust and confidence of the people they lead.*
- **Sense of responsibility** - *A leader must have a sense of responsibility towards organisational goals in order to gain maximum benefit from their endeavours. Thy must be able to motivate themselves in order to motivate team members to give their best.*
- **Self-confidence and will-power** – *Self-confidence helps to earn the confidence of those they lead. A leader should be trustworthy and should handle challenging situations with the will power self-confidence brings.*
- **Humanist** - *This is essential in a leader. They deal with human beings and need to have close interpersonal contact with them. They must address the personal problems of those they lead with great care and attention. Therefore, treating the human beings at a humanitarian level is essential for building a relaxed, comfortable, working environment.*
- **Empathy** - *This is very important because fairness and objectivity comes from the ability to see issues from another person's perspective. A leader must be able to understand the problems and complaints of employees and be able to recognise the needs and aspirations of the employees. This helps in improving human relations and personal contacts with the employees.*

Recognising the need for these qualities in a leader, underpins the scope of leadership and its importance for a business. A leader cannot have all of these qualities, skills and traits all at one time, but having at least some of them, helps in achieving effective results.

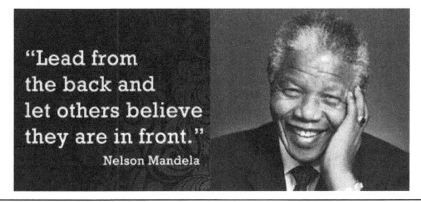

"Lead from the back and let others believe they are in front."
Nelson Mandela

Leading People

In summary, a good leader needs to:

1. ***Provide Guidance***. *Guidance involves training, instructing team members along with the vision or goal of the organisation and ensures no deviation from the vision or goal even though it may be challenging.*
2. ***Encourage Creativity***. *Good leaders abandon their egos and give room for their subordinates to express themselves in order to encourage new ideas, innovations that can trigger an organisation to new levels of success.*
3. ***Motivate***. *Motivation is vital to the achievement of an organisation. A good leader ensures team members' energy is high to perform the job to the very best of their ability.*
4. ***Communicate***. *Co-ordination of work in an effective and efficient manner requires excellent communication between the team leaders and team members.*
5. ***Foster Good Values***. *The exhibition of good values is vital to the achievement of an organisation.*
6. ***Resolve Conflict***. *A productive leader manages the conflicts that pose a threat to the unity of team members, productivity and motivation.*

Management and Leadership

People often mistake leadership and management as the same thing, but in reality, they are very different. The main difference between the two, is that leaders have people that follow them, while managers have people who simply work for them.

Leadership is about getting people to understand and believe in the vision of the organisation and to work with the leader to achieve those goals, whilst management is more about administering and making sure the day-to-day activities are happening as they should.

Leadership and management, though different, must still go hand in hand as they are necessarily linked and one complements the other. Any attempt to separate the two is likely to cause more problems than it solves. For an organisation to be successful, it needs management that can plan, organise and coordinate its staff, while also inspiring and motivating leadership to help them perform to the best of their ability.

Leadership is about inspiring and management is about planning

Leaders tend to praise success and drive people, whereas managers work to find fault. Leaders paint a picture of what they see as possible for the company and work to inspire and engage their people in turning that vision into reality. Rather than seeing individuals as just a particular set of skills, they think beyond what they do and activate them to be part of something much bigger. Leaders are well aware of how teams can accomplish a lot more when working together, than individuals working alone can ever achieve.

Leading People

One way to decipher which of the two you may be is to count the number of people outside your reporting hierarchy who come to you for advice. The more that do, the more likely it is that you are perceived to be a leader.

Management	*Leadership*
Managers give directions	**Leaders ask questions**
Managers have subordinates	**Leaders have followers**
Managers use an authoritarian style	**Leaders have a motivational style**
Managers tell what to do	**Leaders show what to do**
Managers have good ideas	**Leaders implement good ideas**
Managers react to change	**Leaders create change**
Managers try to be heroes	**Leaders make heroes of everyone around them**
Managers exercise power over people	**Leaders develop power with people**

You must think of one without the other to truly see the differences that exist between them.

Not everyone who is in charge of a team is both a leader and a manager. In order to have a successful organisation, there needs to be a mixture of both.

Many people are both, having managed people but realised that you cannot buy people to follow you down a difficult path and so act as leaders too. The challenge lies in making sure you are both leading your team as well as managing your day-to-day operation. Those who are able to do both, will be at an advantage over others.

One big difference between leadership and management and often overlooked, is that leadership always involves (leading) a group of people, whereas management need only be concerned with responsibility for things (for example IT, money, advertising, equipment, promises, etc).

Many management roles have major people-management responsibilities, but the fact that management does not necessarily include responsibility for people, whereas leadership definitely always includes responsibility for people, is a key difference.

Management is a function or responsibility within leadership, but not vice-versa.

Leadership is actually a much bigger and deeper role than management - a useful way to understand the differences between leadership and management is to consider some typical skills and responsibilities of leading and managing and determine whether each is more a function of leading, or of managing.

Leading People

Management	Leadership
• Implementing tactical actions • Detailed budgeting • Measuring and reporting performance • Applying rules and policies • Implementing disciplinary rules • Organising people and tasks within structures • Recruiting people for jobs • Checking and managing ethics and morals • Developing people • Problem-solving • Planning • Improving productivity and efficiency • Motivating and encouraging others • Delegating and training	• Creating new visions and aims • Establishing organisational financial targets • Deciding what needs measuring and reporting • Making new rules and policies • Making disciplinary rules • Deciding structures, hierarchies and workgroups • Creating new job roles • Establishing ethical and moral positions • Developing the organisation • Problem-anticipation • Visualising • Conceiving new opportunities • Inspiring and empowering others • Planning and organising succession and... • All management responsibilities, including all listed left, (which mostly and typically are delegated to others) ideally aid motivation and people-development

Broadly speaking:

- **Managers plan, organise, coordinate and facilitate** – they organise people, materials and budgets to pursue objectives
- **Leaders inspire and motivate people** – they focus on people and set new directions for a group to follow

> *Good managers need leadership skills to be able to perform all of the functions of management.*

Leading People

Four Core Theory Groups

Leadership has been studied from ancient times through to modern day. During that time, many different aspects have been studied and leadership has been examined from many angles and perspectives. As a result of this, there have been many conflicting and contrasting theories. These can be generalised into four principal groups based on the question each one asks:

1. Trait Theories – *What type of person makes a good leader?*
Trait theories argue that effective leaders share a number of common personality characteristics, or "traits."

Early trait theories said that leadership is an inbuilt, instinctive quality which people either have or don't have. Thankfully, we have moved on from this idea and we are learning more about what we can do to develop leadership qualities within ourselves and others.

Trait theories help us identify traits and qualities (for example, integrity, empathy, assertiveness, good decision-making skills and likability) that are helpful when leading others.

However, none of these traits, nor any specific combination of them, will guarantee success as a leader.

Traits are external behaviours that emerge from the things going on within our minds – and it is these internal beliefs and processes that are important for effective leadership.

2. Behavioural Theories – *What does a good leader do?*
Behavioural theories focus on how leaders behave. For instance, do leaders dictate what needs to be done and expect cooperation? Or do they involve their teams in decision-making to encourage acceptance and support?

In the 1930s, Kurt Lewin developed a framework based on a leader's behaviour. He argued that there are three types of leaders:

Autocratic leaders make decisions without consulting their teams. This style of leadership is considered appropriate when decisions need to be made quickly, when there is no need for input and when team agreement is not necessary for a successful outcome.

Democratic leaders allow the team to provide input before deciding, although the degree of input can vary from leader to leader. This style is important when team agreement matters, but it can be difficult to manage when there are lots of different perspectives and ideas.

Laissez-faire leaders do not interfere; they allow people within the team to make many of the decisions. This works well when the team is highly capable, is motivated and does not need close supervision. However, this behaviour can arise because the leader is lazy or distracted; and this is where this style of leadership can fail. Clearly, how leaders behave affects their performance. Researchers have realised, though, that

Leading People

many of these leadership behaviours are appropriate at different times. The best leaders are those who can use many different behavioural styles and choose the right style for each situation.

3. Contingency Theories – *How does the situation influence good leadership?*
The realisation that there is no one correct type of leader led to theories that the best leadership style depends on the situation. These theories try to predict which style is best in which circumstance.

For instance, when you need to make quick decisions, which style is best? When you need the full support of your team, is there a more effective way to lead? Should a leader be more people-oriented or task-oriented? These are all questions that contingency leadership theories try to address.

Popular contingency-based models include House's Path-Goal Theory and Fiedler's Contingency Model.

You can also use the Leadership Process Model to understand how your situation affects other factors that are important for effective leadership and how, in turn, these affect your leadership.

4. Power and Influence Theories – *What Is the source of the leader's power?*
Power and influence theories of leadership take an entirely different approach – these are based on the different ways that leaders use power and influence to get things done and they look at the leadership styles that emerge as a result.

Perhaps the best-known of these theories is French and Raven's Five Forms of Power. This model highlights three types of positional power – legitimate, reward and coercive – and two sources of personal power – expert and referent (your personal appeal and charm). The model suggests that using personal power is the better alternative and that you should work on building expert power (the power that comes with being a real expert in the job) because this is the most legitimate source of personal power.

Another leadership style that uses power and influence is transactional leadership. This approach assumes that people do things for reward and for no other reason. Therefore, it focuses on designing tasks and reward structures. While this may not be the most appealing leadership strategy in terms of building relationships and developing a highly motivating work environment, it often works and leaders in most organisations use it on a daily basis to get things done.

Similarly, leading by example is another highly effective way of influencing your team.

Leading People

Lewin's Leadership Styles

In 1939 psychologist Kurt Lewin set out to identify different styles of leadership. This early study was very influential and established three major leadership styles and these have been a steppingstone for more defined leadership theories.

Lewin assigned schoolchildren to one of three groups with an authoritarian, democratic, or laissez-faire leader. The children participated an arts and crafts project while their behaviour in response to the different styles of leadership was observed. The researchers found that democratic leadership tended to be the most effective at inspiring the children to perform well.

Autocratic Leadership (Authoritarian)

The phrase most associated with an autocratic leader is "Do as I say." Generally, they believe they are the smartest person at the table and know more than others. They make all the decisions with little input from team members.

Autocratic leaders provide clear expectations of what needs to be done, when it should be done and how it should be done. This leadership style is strongly focused on both command by the leader and control of the followers. Authoritarian leaders make decisions independently, with little or no input from the rest of the group. This command-and-control approach is typical of leadership styles of the past, but it does not have much credibility with the employees of today.

Autocratic leadership can still be appropriate in certain situations. For example, when crucial decisions need to be made on the spot, the leader should have the most knowledge about the situation and is best positioned to make decisions. Similarly, when dealing with inexperienced and new team members and there is no time to wait for team members to gain familiarity with their role.

An authoritarian leader will:

- *make all the important decisions*
- *not consider input from team members*
- *dictate all the working methods and processes*
- *not trust your team members with important decisions*
- *have a highly structured working environment*
- *discourage creativity and out-of-the-box thinking*
- *want to instigate rules and make sure everyone follows*

Leading People

Using an Authoritarian Style

The authoritarian style can be beneficial in some settings, but also has its shortcomings. If this tends to be your dominant leadership style, there are things that you should consider whenever you are in a leadership role.

Listen to the team

You might not change your mind or implement their advice, but team members need to feel that they can express their concerns. Autocratic leaders can sometimes make team members feel ignored or even rejected. Listening to people with an open mind can help them feel like they are making an important contribution to the group's mission.

Define the Rules

If you want team members to follow your rules, you need to ensure that guidelines are clearly established and that each person on your team is fully aware of them.

Provide Training

Once the team understand the rules, you need to be sure that they have the education and capability to perform the tasks you set. If they need additional assistance, offer training to fill in this knowledge gap.

Reliability

Inconsistency can quickly lead to the loss of respect of the team. Enforce the rules you have defined. Establish that you are a reliable leader and your team is more likely to follow your guidance because you have built trust with them.

Recognise Success

The team will quickly lose motivation if they are criticised when they make mistakes but never recognised for their successes. Try to recognise success more than pointing out mistakes. By doing so, the team will respond much more favourably to the correction.

Leading People

The negative effects of Autocratic Leadership

While autocratic leadership has some benefits, it also has some serious issues which certainly cannot be ignored. People who are autocratic leaders tend to be bossy and dictatorial in nature. Being bossy is great for some situations; however, it can create some strong resentment among team members. They have no input or no say in how things are done. This can become problematic when highly skilled and fully capable members are left feeling that their experience and information is undermined.

Autocratic leadership:

- *discourages group input*
- *has a detrimental effect on the morale of the group*

While autocratic leadership does have some potential pitfalls, leaders can learn to use elements of this style selectively. Instead of wasting valuable time consulting with less knowledgeable team members, the expert leader can quickly make decisions that are in the best interest of the group. Autocratic leadership is often most effective when it is used for specific situations. Balancing this style with other approaches including democratic or transformational styles can often lead to better group performance.

Participative Leadership (Democratic)

Lewin found that participative leadership, also known as democratic leadership, is commonly the most effective style. Participative leaders offer guidance to group members, but they also participate in the group and allow input from other group members. Lewin found the children in this group were less productive than the members of the authoritarian group, but their contributions were of a higher quality.

This type of leadership can be applied to any organisation, from private businesses to public bodies and the third sector.

Everyone is given the opportunity to participate, ideas are exchanged freely and discussion is encouraged. While the democratic process tends to focus on group equality and the free flow of ideas, the leader of the group is still there to offer guidance and control.

Participative leaders are more likely to ask, "What do you think?" They share information with employees about anything that affects their work responsibilities. They also seek employees' opinions before approving a final decision.

Participative leaders encourage group members to participate in decision making, but retain the final say in the decision-making process. Group members feel engaged in the process and are more motivated and creative. Democratic leaders tend to make followers feel like they are an important part of the team, which helps foster commitment to the goals of the group.

There are numerous benefits to this participative leadership style. It can develop trust, promote team spirit and cooperation from employees. It allows for creativity and helps employees develop. A participative leadership style gets people to do what needs to be done but in a way that they *want* to do it.

The democratic leader will decide who is in the group and who gets to contribute to the decisions that are made. Researchers have found that the democratic leadership style is one of the most effective types and leads to higher productivity, better contributions from group members and increased group morale.

Some of the primary characteristics of democratic leadership include:

- *Group members are encouraged to share ideas and opinions, even though the leader retains the final say over decisions.*
- *Members of the group feel more engaged in the process.*
- *Creativity is encouraged and rewarded.*

Research suggests that good democratic leaders possess specific traits that include honesty, intelligence, courage, creativity, competence and fairness. Strong democratic leaders inspire trust and respect among followers.

These leaders are sincere and make decisions based on their morals and values. Followers tend to feel inspired to act and contribute to the group. Good leaders also tend to seek diverse opinions and do not try to silence dissenting voices or those that offer a less popular point of view.

Strengths of Participative Leadership

Because group members are encouraged to share their thoughts, democratic leadership can lead to better ideas and more creative solutions to problems. Group members also feel more involved and committed to projects, making them more likely to care about the end results. Research on leadership styles has also shown that democratic leadership leads to higher productivity among group members.

- *More ideas and creative solutions*
- *Group member commitment*
- *High productivity*

Weaknesses of Participative Leadership

While democratic leadership has been described as the most effective leadership style, it does have some potential downsides. In situations where roles are unclear or time is of the essence, democratic leadership can lead to communication failures and uncompleted projects.

In some cases, group members may not have the necessary knowledge or expertise to make quality contributions to the decision-making process. Democratic leadership can also result in team members feeling like their opinions and ideas are not considered, which may lower employee satisfaction and morale.

Leading People

- *Communication failures*
- *Poor decision-making by unskilled groups*
- *Minority or individual opinions overridden*

When to use Participative Leadership
Participative Leadership works best in situations where group members are skilled and eager to share their knowledge. It is also important to have plenty of time to allow people to contribute, develop a plan and then vote on the best course of action.

Participative Leadership is usually effective because it allows lower-level employees to exercise and use authority they will need in future positions. In a team meeting, a democratic leader might give the team a few decision-related options, they could then discuss each option. After discussion, the leader might take the teams thoughts and feedback into consideration or may open the decision to a vote.

Delegative Leadership (Laissez-Faire)
The laissez-faire leadership style is at the opposite end of the scale to the autocratic style. Of all the leadership styles, this one involves the least amount of control. The autocratic style leader stands as firm as a rock on issues, while the laissez-faire leader lets people swim with the current.

Delegative leaders offer little or no guidance to group members and leave the decision-making up to group members. Lewin also noted that laissez-faire leadership created groups that lacked direction, members blamed each other for mistakes, refused to accept personal responsibility, made less progress and produced less work.

Under delegative leadership, Lewin found that children were the least productive. The children also made more demands on the leader, showed little cooperation and were unable to work independently.

On the surface, a laissez-faire leader may appear to trust people to get on with the task, but it can also leave the disassociated leader appearing aloof. Whist it is beneficial to give people the opportunity to spread their wings, with a total lack of direction, people may unwittingly drift in the wrong direction - away from the critical goals of the organisation.

This style can work however, if the team comprises highly skilled, experienced employees who are self-starters and motivated. To be most effective with this style, monitor team performance and provide regular feedback.

Characteristics of Laissez-Faire Leadership

- *Hands-off approach*
- *Leaders provide all training and support*
- *Decisions are left to employees*
- *Comfortable with mistakes*
- *Accountability falls to the leader*

Leading People

Pros and Cons of Laissez-Faire Leadership

Laissez-faire leadership means the leaders has a hands-off role and allows group members to make the decisions. This leadership style has been found to deliver the lowest productivity among group members.

However, this leadership style can have strengths as well as weaknesses. There are certain settings and situations where a laissez-faire leadership style might be the most appropriate.

Strengths of Laissez-Faire Leadership

Like other leadership styles, the laissez-faire leadership style has its advantages:

- *It encourages personal growth. Because leaders are so hands-off in their approach, employees have a chance to be hands-on. This leadership style creates an environment that facilitates growth and development.*
- *It encourages innovation. The freedom given to employees can encourage creativity and innovation.*
- *It allows for faster decision-making. Since there is no micromanagement, employees under laissez-faire leadership have the autonomy to make their own decisions. They can make quick decisions without waiting weeks for an approval process.*

To benefit from these strengths, certain preconditions must be met. The team should be full of highly skilled and experienced people, capable of working on their own, meaning they are capable of accomplishing tasks with very little guidance.

This style is particularly effective in situations where group members are more knowledgeable than the group's leader. The laissez-faire style allows them to demonstrate their deep knowledge and skill surrounding that subject. This level of autonomy can be motivating to some group members and help them feel more satisfied with their work.

Weaknesses of Laissez-Faire Leadership

Because the laissez-faire style depends so heavily on the abilities of the group, it is not very effective in situations where team members lack the knowledge or experience, they need to complete tasks and make decisions.

This is leadership style is also not suitable for situations where efficiency and high productivity are the main concerns. Some people are not good at setting their own deadlines, managing their own projects and solving problems on their own. Under this leadership style, projects can go off-track and deadlines can be missed when team members do not get enough guidance or feedback from leaders.

Weaknesses of the laissez-faire style include:

- *Lack of role clarity:* The laissez-faire style leads to poorly defined roles within the group. Since team members receive little or no guidance, they might not really be sure about their role within the group and what they are supposed to be doing.
- *Poor involvement with the group:* Laissez-faire leaders are often seen as uninvolved and withdrawn, which can lead to a lack of cohesiveness within the group. Since the leader seems unconcerned with what is happening, followers sometimes pick up on this and express less care and concern for the project.
- *Low accountability:* Some leaders take advantage of this style to avoid responsibility for failure. When goals are not met, the leader can blame members of the team for not completing tasks or living up to expectations.
- *Passivity: At its worst,* laissez-faire leadership represents passivity or even an outright avoidance of true leadership. In such cases, these leaders do nothing to motivate followers, do not recognise the efforts of team members and make no attempt at involvement with the group.

If team members are unfamiliar with the process or tasks, leaders are better off taking a more hands-on approach. They can switch back to a more delegative approach as team members gain more experience.

Where Laissez-Faire Leaders can succeed

Working in a creative field, where people tend to be highly motivated, skilled, creative and dedicated to their work, can be conducive to obtaining good results with this style.

Laissez-faire leaders typically excel at providing information and background at the start of a project, which can be particularly useful for self-managed teams. By giving team members all that they need at the outset of an assignment, they will then have the knowledge they need to complete the task as directed.

"I don't feel like getting out of bed today — Just tell everybody to go with laissez-faire."

A leader with this style may struggle in situations that require oversight, precision and attention to detail. In high stake and high-pressure work settings, where every detail needs to be perfect and completed in a timely manner, a more authoritarian or managerial style may be more appropriate. Using a laissez-faire approach in this scenario can lead to missed deadlines and poor performance.

Leading People

Other Leadership Styles and Models

In addition to the three styles identified by Lewin and his colleagues, researchers have described numerous other characteristic patterns of leadership. A few of the best-known include:

Strategic Leadership Style

This is a desirable leadership style in many organisations because strategic thinking supports multiple types of employees at once. However, leaders who operate this way can set a dangerous precedent with respect to how many people they can support at once and what the best direction for the company really is, if everyone is always getting their way.

Leaders must first understand their organisation's mission to be strategic. This means fully grasping why the company exists, who its customers are and how exactly it can provide value for them. Strategic leadership requires the potential to foresee and comprehend the work environment. It requires objectivity and potential to look at the broader picture. Then, strategic leaders need to create a vision of what that mission will look like at a specified time in the future. Finally, leaders must craft a strategy to put that vision into action. The strategy should map out the steps a company needs to take or the changes it needs to make to get from its current state to its desired state.

Strategic leadership can be defined as utilising strategy in the management of employees. Strategic leaders create organisational structure, allocate resources and express strategic vision.

Strategic leaders sometimes make use of rewards or incentive programs to encourage employees and help them reach their goals.

Key Traits of Strategic Leaders

> *Strategic leaders are visionary, open, focused, courageous and prudent.*

What are the distinguishing characteristics of a strategic leader? How do you recognise one? And how do you acquire the traits of a strategic leader? Based on experience, the following five traits may be considered essential for strategic leadership:

Vision

Great strategic leaders have a clear and compelling vision that is going far beyond the current reality. These leaders can communicate their vision in an effective and inspiring way to mobilise commitment within their organisation and sector.

There have been several strategic leaders with such a clear and compelling vision such as Steve Jobs and his vision of the iPod and iPhone.

Leading People

Openness
Strategic leaders are attuned to the fast pace of change and recognise that they cannot know it all. Their antennae are always on, as a seemingly minor detail may challenge their current strategic plans and be the trigger for changing the strategy for the organisation or department.

Strategic leaders are open to learn about new trends in their own or other sectors as well as about developments within their organisation. Their openness promotes a culture of openness in their whole organisation, which in turn facilitates the flow of information and the capacity of the organisation to adapt to a changing environment and turn challenges into opportunities.

Focus
Strategic leaders can focus their attention and energy on what they perceive as the most important activities and projects. Apple co-founder Steve Jobs is a prime example of a leader with a relentless focus. Instead of producing a range of smartphones, he insisted on just having one iPhone model. Keeping it simple and focusing on making one product the best on the market at the time it was launched, had incredible benefits for product management and marketing.

There is no conflict between openness and focus. Openness is required in the decision-making phase. Once a decision is taken there is a need to focus relentlessly on implementation.

Courage
In the face of complexity and uncertainty, a strategic leader can never be sure if their strategic decisions will be successful, despite all the information gathering and due diligence. The strategic leader therefore needs to have the courage to act and push for changes they consider necessary, even if their decisions are not popular with some stakeholders.

An example of a leader having the courage to make unpopular decisions is Marissa Mayer, President and CEO of Yahoo Inc. In November 2013, she introduced a performance review system based on ranking of employees by managers, with employees at the low end of the scoring being fired. Employees complained about the process and the media criticised her, too. She had the courage to stick to her decision.

Prudence
Strategic leaders must act prudently. While being ready to take calculated and courageous risks, they avoid gambling and strive to minimise risks where possible.

Leading People

Transformational Leadership Style

Transformational leadership is often identified as the single most effective style. This style was first described during the late 1970s and later expanded upon by researcher Bernard M. Bass.

Transformational leaders can motivate and inspire followers and direct positive changes in teams.

These leaders tend to be emotionally intelligent, energetic and passionate. They are not only committed to helping the organisation achieve its goals, but also to helping team members fulfil their potential.

Research shows that this style of leadership results in higher performance and more improved group satisfaction than other leadership styles. One study also found that transformational leadership led to improved well-being among group members.

Characteristics of Transformational Leadership

The following are some of the characteristics of transformational leaders:

Keep their ego in check

In transformational leadership, it is important for the leader to keep their ego under control and not let it interfere with the best interest of their team or the organisation. By keeping their ego in check, the transformational leader can put the organisation before their own personal gain and obtain the best performance from others.

Self-management

Transformational leaders need little direction from others and manage themselves well. They are highly motivated and use it to direct the organisation to the right path. These leaders do what they love and those values align with those of the organisation that they lead.

Ability to take the right risks

The transformational leader will trust their instinct and use the intelligence gathered by team members to make informed decisions. A transformational leader's team is right behind them and is ever willing to do the necessary research to evaluate the situation appropriately. The transformational leader seeks inputs from the team to make risky decisions that facilitate growth.

Make difficult decisions

Transformational leaders do not shy away from difficult decisions. They make their decisions with a clear focus on the values, vision, objectives and goals of the organisation.

Leading People

Share organisational awareness
A transformational leader understands and shares their awareness of the entire organisation. This makes them particularly attuned to the feelings of their team members and gives them a clear idea of what actions to take to elicit the desired actions from the employees.

Since they have a complete awareness of the organisation, they can make decisions that stimulate growth and create a shared vision for the organisation that all employees feel a part of.

Inspirational
People want to be inspired and transformational leaders are perhaps the most inspiring of all. They can motivate others to rise to the occasion. The inspiration is not just limited to formal acknowledgement of a job well done, they will treat each employee as a valued individual and take the time to understand what motivates them.

Entertain new ideas
Transformation cannot be achieved if the leader is not open or receptive to new ideas. Transformational leaders understand that success is dependent on the effort of the entire team and growth happens only in an organisation with a culture of openness to new ideas from all levels. A transformational leader makes deliberate efforts to solicit new ideas from team members and use their insights in making decisions.

Adaptability
The transformational leader knows that it is vital to constantly adapt to changing market conditions to keep moving forward. They are always willing to adapt to new situations and seek creative ways to respond to the dynamic business environment.

Proactive
The transformational leader is proactive in their approach. These leaders take risks and take an active role in growing the organisation.

Lead with vision
Transformational leaders set a realistic and achievable vision for the organisation. They then communicate the vision to their followers and inspire a sense of commitment and purpose. By getting everyone to buy into the common vision, transformational leaders can drive the organisation in the direction that they want.

Transformational leadership is always "transforming" and improving the organisation. Employees might have a basic set of tasks and goals that they complete every week or month, but the leader is constantly pushing them outside of their comfort sone.

When starting a job with this type of leader, all employees might get a list of goals to reach, as well as deadlines for reaching them. While the goals might seem simple at first, this manager might pick up the pace of deadlines or give you more and more challenging goals as you grow with the company.

Leading People

This is a highly encouraged form of leadership among growth-minded companies because it motivates employees to see what they are capable of. But transformational leaders can risk losing sight of everyone's individual learning curves if direct reports do not receive the right coaching to guide them through new responsibilities.

Cross-Cultural Leadership

As workforces become increasingly multicultural and businesses continue to expand overseas, the homogenous workforce has become a thing of the past. In such a global economy, cross-cultural leadership skills are critically important. Many companies today operate on international projects with multi-cultural teams located in multiple countries. It is also common to find these are led by managers who come from many different countries that adds diversity to the teams and creates a need for a greater amount of collaboration and need for leadership at multiple levels.

The ability of a leader to motivate diverse teams to manage change effectively is a critical issue in the international environment. It cannot be assumed that a manager who is successful in one country will be successful in another.
Cross-cultural leadership involves the ability to influence and motivate people's attitudes and behaviours in the global community to reach a common organisational goal.

Implicit Leadership Theory (ILT)

This theory asserts that people's underlying assumptions, stereotypes, beliefs and schemas influence the extent to which they view someone as a good leader. Since people across cultures tend to hold different implicit beliefs, schemas and stereotypes, it would seem only natural that their underlying beliefs in what makes a good leader differ across cultures.

Hofstede conducted a study into Cross Cultural leadership and identified what he calls Cultural Dimensions. This is one of the most prominent and influential studies to date regarding leadership in a globalised world. The study reveals similarities as well as differences across cultures and emphasises the need to be open-minded to understand the

Leading People

differences in other cultures. As per this theory, there are five dimensions of culture to compare cultures, to help leaders with an understanding of how to adjust their leadership styles accordingly.

- *Individualism/Collectivism,*
- *Feminine/Masculine,*
- *Power Distance,*
- *Uncertainty Avoidance,*
- *Long Term/ Short Term orientation*

Traits of a Cross-Cultural Leader:

Below is a list of traits found to be associated with successful international executives by different researchers:

General Intelligence	*Drive*
Business Knowledge	*Language Skills*
Interpersonal Skills	*Multicultural Perspective*
Commitment	*Taking*
Courage	*Knowledge and cognition*
Ease in dealing with cross-cultural issues	*Cultural Awareness*
	Cross-cultural Schema
Open Personality	*Cognitive Complexity*
Flexibility	

An effective cross-cultural leader must have a well-rounded skillset and understanding of the differences that exist among people from different backgrounds.

Facilitative Leadership

Facilitative leadership is about aligning people in the same direction, so they can achieve a shared goal.

What makes facilitative leadership different from the other forms of leadership is the involvement of others at the decision-making stage. Traditionally managers, team leaders, or bosses decide on their own and then introduce it to the group. Facilitative leadership is different. The decisions are made together as a group.

A facilitative approach recognises the synergy of bringing together the different strengths of individuals.

The three key benefits of facilitative leadership are **commitment**, **alignment** and **innovation.**

Leading People

Strengths of Facilitative Leadership

- *Enables self-leadership*
- *Helps employees see and understand the big picture*
- *Increases employee motivation and commitment via participatory decision making*
- *Helps employees align tasks*
- *Facilitated meetings can help create innovation and new ideas*
- *Very effective in dealing with complexity*

Weaknesses of Facilitative Leadership

- *Allows idea creation by employees and may seem chaotic*
- *Requires group facilitation skills to deal with the chaos of group decision making*

This concept of facilitative leadership is captured in the words accredited to Mother Theresa:

> *"You can do what I cannot do.*
> *I can do what you cannot do.*
> *Together we can do great things."*

Facilitative leadership is particularly important with teams. Whether it is a team meeting, an away day, a conference, a team set up to solve a significant problem, or a continuous improvement team, their effectiveness is often determined by how well they are facilitated. This can make all the difference.

Think about the value gained when:

- *Everyone feels involved and engaged in a meeting on how to take things forward*
- *Ideas flow at a meeting*
- *You leave a meeting feeling it had purpose and direction and it achieved something*
- *A clear set of actions are agreed and everyone feels motivated to make them happen.*

Facilitative leadership brings people together to help them achieve more.

A facilitative leadership style involves:

Leading People

- **Building rapport** – *establishing credibility to enable people to contribute with ease.*
- **Communicating effectively verbally and non-verbally** – *Being supportive and engaged*
- **Active listening** – *demonstrating your interest by your body language*
- **Questioning techniques** – *you can use questions as a very powerful facilitation skill: check understanding; seek clarification, or for a view to be expanded.*

The potential of a facilitative leadership style

Too often the knowledge and potential that exists in a team is not recognised. In many cases knowledge of how to solve a problem or identify an innovative solution is already there in the team. The skill to unlock that knowledge and expertise is often found in form of facilitation.

Transactional Leadership Style

The transactional leadership style views the leader-follower relationship as a transaction. By accepting a position as a member of the group, the individual has agreed to obey the leader. In most situations, this involves the employer-employee relationship and the transaction focuses on the follower completing required tasks in exchange for monetary compensation.

The "transaction" usually involves the organisation paying team members in return for their effort and compliance on a short-term task. The leader has a right to "punish" team members if their work does not meet an appropriate standard.

Transactional leadership is present in many business leadership situations and it does offer some benefits. For example, it clarifies everyone's roles and responsibilities. Because transactional leadership judges team members on performance, people who are ambitious or who are motivated by external rewards – including compensation – often thrive.

The downside of this style is that, on its own, it can be chilling and amoral. It can lead to high staff turnover. It also has serious limitations for knowledge-based or creative work. As a result, team members can often do little to improve their job satisfaction.

One of the main advantages of this leadership style is that it creates clearly defined roles. People know what they are required to do and what they will be receiving in exchange. This style allows leaders to offer a great deal of supervision and direction, if needed.

Transactional leaders are common today. These managers reward their employees for precisely the work they do. A marketing team that receives a scheduled bonus for helping generate a certain number of leads by the end of the quarter is a common example of transactional leadership.

When starting a job with a transactional boss, you might receive an incentive plan that motivates you to quickly master your regular job duties. For example, if you work in marketing, you might receive a bonus for sending 10 qualified marketing emails. On the other hand, a transformational leader might only offer you a bonus if your work results in a large amount of newsletter subscriptions.

Transactional leadership helps establish roles and responsibilities for each employee, but it can also encourage bare-minimum work if employees know how much their effort is worth all the time. This leadership style can use incentive programs to motivate employees, but they should be consistent with the company's goals and used in addition to *unscheduled* gestures of appreciation.

Bureaucratic Leadership

Bureaucratic leaders go by the book. This style of leadership might listen and consider the input of employees - unlike autocratic leadership - but the leader tends to reject an employee's input if it conflicts with company policy or past practices.

Bureaucratic leadership still exists especially at a larger, older or traditional company. When a colleague or employee proposes a strong strategy that seems new or non-traditional, bureaucratic leaders may reject it. Their resistance might be because the company has already been successful with current processes and trying something new could waste time or resources if it does not work.

Employees under this leadership style might not feel as controlled as they would under autocratic leadership, but there is still a lack of freedom in how much people are able to do in their roles. This can quickly close down innovation and is not encouraged for companies who are chasing ambitious goals and quick growth.

As a style it is widely regarded as outdated and is seldom successful.

Situational Leadership style

Situational leadership theories stress the significant influence of the environment and the situation on leadership. Hersey and Blanchard's leadership styles are one of the best-known situational theories. First published in 1969, it describes four primary styles of leadership, including:

- *Telling:* Telling people what to do
- *Selling:* Convincing followers to buy into their ideas and messages
- *Participating:* Allowing group members to take a more active role in the decision-making process
- *Delegating:* Taking a hands-off approach to leadership and allowing group members to make the majority of decisions

Blanchard later developed the original Hersey and Blanchard model to emphasise how the developmental and skill level of learners influence the style that should be used by leaders. Blanchard's SLII leadership styles model also described four different leading styles:

- **Directing:** *Giving orders and expecting obedience, but offering little guidance and assistance*
- **Coaching:** *Giving lots of orders, but also lots of support*
- **Supporting:** *Offering plenty of help, but very little direction*
- **Delegating:** *Offering little direction or support*

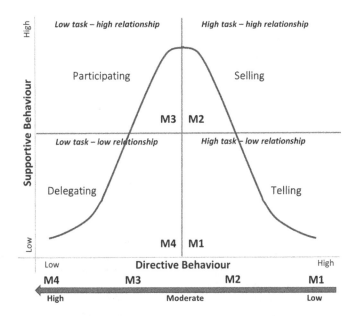

Coaching Leadership

A coaching leadership style implies there is a "consider this" approach. A leader who coaches views people as a reservoir of talent to be developed and seeks to unlock that potential.

Like a sports coach, a coaching leader focuses on identifying and nurturing the individual strengths of each member of the team. They focus on strategies that will enable their team to work better together.

This style offers strong similarities to strategic and democratic leadership but places more emphasis on the growth and success of individual employees.

Rather than forcing all employees to focus on similar skills and goals, this leader might build a team where each employee has an expertise or skillset in something different. In the long term, this leader focuses on creating strong teams that can communicate well and embrace each other's unique skillsets to get work done.

A manager with this leadership style will help employees improve on their strengths by giving them new tasks to try, offering them guidance, or meeting to discuss constructive feedback. They might also encourage one or more team members to expand on their strengths by learning new skills from other teammates.

Affiliative Leadership Style

A phrase often used to describe this type of leadership is "People come first." Of all the leadership styles, the affiliative leadership approach is one where the leader gets up close and personal with people.

This type of leadership was first developed by famous D. Goleman in the early 21st century. He said that an affiliative category is designed for managers who are well-versed in the situation and can recognise the maturity levels of their staff. Rewards or sanctions recede into the background in comparison to the inner satisfaction that wage-earners receive from realising their potential and creative capabilities.

Under this style employees are spared constant monitoring and are trying, independently, to find ways to reach the desired objectives within the framework of the delegated powers. They do not accept that the boss has already thought of everything necessary for success or provided the necessary conditions for the process.

A leader practicing this style pays attention to and supports the emotional needs of team members and strives to bridge the gap between themselves and their team.

Ultimately, this style is all about encouraging harmony and forming collaborative relationships within teams. It is particularly useful, for example, in smoothing conflicts among team members or reassuring people during times of stress.

Traits of Affiliative Leaders

Affiliative Leadership refers to emotional supervision because it directly affects the feelings of team members. An affiliative leader will typically display the following characteristics.

- *Focus on conflict-free.* *Strive to eliminate hostility and create an atmosphere of calm.*
- *Constructive criticism.* *Provide constructive feedback to maintain focus.*
- *A skilled psychologist.* *Strong emotional intelligence awareness*

Leading People

- **The flexibility of thinking.** *Create a trusting relationship between staff and managers, it is necessary to be kind-hearted about new ideas and procedures that are offered by to relieve tension and contribute to creativity.*
- **Faith in an initiative.** *Affording team members the right to adjust the company's strategic aims meaning they cooperate with maximum efficiency, without fear of mistakes or punishments*
- **Persistence.** *Effective leadership in stressful or extreme conditions when the morale of the team is significantly affected.*
- **An empathic connection.** *Demonstrate empathy when dealing with issues.*

Affiliative leadership could be considered one of the most effective ways of creating a reliable team of like-minded people truly interested in the organisation's prosperity. It will help to cope with a low level of morale due to stress or other factors. It is not effective on its own and should be combined with authoritarian and democratic methods as well.

Charismatic Leadership

Charismatic leadership resembles transformational leadership: both types of leaders inspire and motivate their team members.

The difference lies in their intent. Transformational leaders want to transform their teams and organisations, while leaders who rely on charisma often focus on themselves and their own ambitions and they may not want to change anything.

Charismatic leaders may believe that they can do no wrong, even when others warn them about the path that they are on. This feeling of invincibility can severely damage a team or an organisation, as was shown in the 2008 financial crisis.

Leading People

Servant Leadership

A "servant leader " is someone, regardless of level, who leads simply by meeting the needs of the team. The term sometimes describes a person without formal recognition as a leader.

These people often lead by example. They have high integrity and lead with generosity. Their approach can create a positive corporate culture and it can lead to high morale among team members.

Supporters of the servant leadership model suggest that it is a good way to move ahead in a world where values are increasingly important and where servant leaders can achieve power because of their values, ideals and ethics.

However, others believe that people who practice servant leadership can find themselves "left behind" by other leaders, particularly in competitive situations.

This style also takes time to apply correctly: it is ill-suited to situations where you must make quick decisions or meet tight deadlines.

Identifying Leadership Style

At first glance, we may think that some leadership styles are better than others. The truth is that every leadership style has its place in the leader's toolkit. The prudent leader knows to adapt from one style to another as the situation demands.

There are many tests online which can be used to identify your natural leadership style. This is the style you will use naturally and tend to revert to when placed under pressure.

It is important that you know what this natural leadership style is so you can understand how your style may be regarded and interpreted by those who report to you or by those who oversee what you do. That does not mean that you will live or die by your natural style – remember we know great leaders are not born!

Knowing your natural leadership style is a key step in the process to become a more effective and efficient leader. If you know the benefits of your leadership style, you can use these to your advantage. Similarly, if you are mindful of the weaknesses of your natural style, you can ensure that you do not use this style in situations where it can have a negative effect, but rather adopt an alternative style which is better suited to the situation.

Choosing Leadership Styles

Knowing which of the leadership styles works best for you is part of being a good leader. Developing a signature style with the ability to stretch into other styles as the situation warrants may help enhance your leadership effectiveness.

Leading People

Know yourself.
Start by raising your awareness of your dominant leadership style. You can do this by asking trusted colleagues to describe the strengths of your leadership style. You can also take a leadership style assessment.

Understand the different styles.
Get familiar with the repertoire of leadership styles that can work best for a given situation. What new skills do you need to develop?

Practice makes a better leader.
Be genuine with any approach you use. Moving from a dominant leadership style to a different one may be challenging at first. Practice the new behaviours until they become natural. In other words, do not use a different leadership style as a "point-and-click" approach. People can smell a fake leadership style a mile away—authenticity rules.

Develop your leadership agility.
Traditional leadership styles are still relevant in today's workplace, but they may need to be combined with new approaches in line with how leadership is defined for the 21st century.

Today's business environments are fraught with challenges due to the changing demographics and the employee expectations from a diverse workforce. This may call for a new breed of leader who is an amalgam of most of the leadership styles discussed here.

As the Chinese proverb says:

> *the wise adapt themselves to circumstances, as water moulds itself to the pitcher.*

Over time and as you become more aware and experienced, you will begin to use the benefits of more leadership styles eliminating the negative aspects, as necessary. An agile leadership style may be the ultimate leadership style required for leading today's talent.

Leadership Models

Tannenbaum and Schmidt Leadership Continuum
The Tannenbaum and Schmidt Continuum is a simple model of leadership theory which shows the relationship between the level of freedom that a manager chooses to give to a team and the level of authority used by the manager. As the team's freedom is increased, so the manager's authority decreases. This is a positive way for both teams and managers to develop.

As a manager, one of your responsibilities is to develop your team. You should delegate and ask a team to make its own decisions to varying degrees according to their abilities. There is a rising scale of levels of delegated freedom that you can use when working with your team.

Tannenbaum and Schmidt argued that there are three factors to consider when selecting a leadership style

---

Leading People

You:
- *What is your preferred style?*
- *What are your values?*

The team:
- *What is your relationship with your team?*
- *Are they ready and enthusiastic to take responsibility?*

The situation:
- *How important is the work being undertaken?*
- *How important or tight are deadlines?*
- *What is the organisational culture?*

The continuum of leadership behaviours is shown in the diagram below.

As can be seen from the diagram, the Continuum shows the relationship between the level of authority you use as a leader and the freedom this allows your team.

The far left and far right of the diagram represents two extremes of leadership. Autocratic leaders act like dictators and tell their team what to do. On the other extreme, the leader removes themselves fully from all decision making giving complete freedom to the team.

Within these two extremes, the leadership style a manager uses can fall at any point on the continuum. However, Tannenbaum and Schmidt described seven points on the continuum to make it easy to understand how different leaders behave at different points on the continuum.

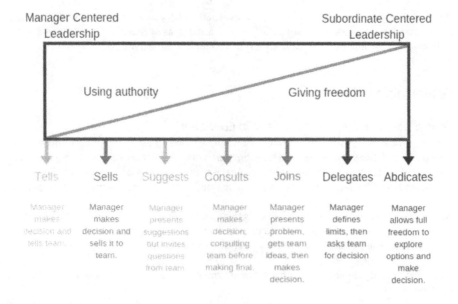

Leading People

1. Tells
The leader that tells is an authoritarian leader. They tell their team what to do and expect them to do it. This style is useful when you urgently need to turn around a department or business and also in situations where deadlines are critical. However, this extreme style can be frustrating for experienced subordinates as it takes no account of team members welfare. Because of this, make sure you only use this style when the situation calls for it.

2. Sells
The leader that sells makes their decision and then explains the logic behind the decision to their team. The leader is not looking for team input, but they are looking to ensure the team understands the rationale behind the decision. A key aspect of this approach is for the leader to explain how the decision will benefit the team. In this way, the team will see the manager as recognising their importance.

3. Suggests
The leader that suggests makes their decision, explains the logic behind the decision and then asks team members if they have any questions.

Through asking questions, the team can more fully understand the rationale behind the decision than the previous approaches. The leader is not going to change their decision, but they do want the team to fully understand the rationale behind it.

4. Consults
The leader that consults presents their provisional decision to their team and invites comments, suggestions and opinions. This is the first point on the continuum where the team's opinion can influence or even change the decision.

The leader is still in control and the ultimate decision maker, but open to any good ideas the team may have. With this style, the team feels they can influence the decision-making process. Once the leader has finished consulting with their team, their decision is finalised

5. Joins
The leader who joins presents the problem to their team and then works with the team in a collaborative manner to make the decision as to how the problem is going to be solved.

This point on the continuum differs from the previous four, as it is the first point the leader is not presenting their decision. Instead, they are simply presenting the problem to be solved.

This obviously will require plenty of input from the team, making this approach suitable when the team is very experienced or has specialist knowledge. Because this style involves greater input and influence form the team it can lead to enhanced feelings of motivation and freedom.

6. Delegates
The leader that delegates asks their team to make the decision, within limits that the leader sets.

Although the team makes the decision, it is still the leader that is accountable for the outcome of the decision. It might seem very risky to let your team decide even though you will be held accountable for the outcome. However, you can limit the risk by specifying constraints. You should use this style only with very experienced teams.

7. Abdicates
The leader who abdicates lets the team decide what problems to solve and how to solve them.

Abdication is the total opposite of telling the team what to do using an autocratic style. Here the team must shape and identify the problem, analyse all the options available, before deciding as to how to proceed. They will then implement the course of action without necessarily even running it by the leader. This style can be the most motivating but can be disastrous if it goes wrong. Because of this, you should only use this approach with very experienced and senior people. This style is often the way the executive boards of companies will run. Under the CEO, each of the division heads will have complete autonomy as to how they choose to execute the company's strategy.

All seven options are available to leaders depending on the situation. The 'situation' is most commonly a combination of:

- *the capability of the group (in various respects* - skills, experience, workload, etc)
   and
- *the nature of the task or project (again in various respects* - complexity, difficulty, risk, value, timescale, relevance to group capability, etc).

Example:

the leader of an inexperienced army platoon under enemy fire will tend to be more effective at stage 1 on the Continuum, whereas, the head of a product innovation team, under no great pressure, leading an experienced and capable group, will tend to be more effective acting at stage 7 on the Continuum.

Bennis – Leadership Qualities
Warren Bennis focuses on the work of leaders and what leadership means.

He is seen as a founder of modern thinking and has identified six leadership qualities: integrity, dedication, magnanimity (giving credit where it is due), humility, openness and creativity.

In his 1989 book, Bennis composed a list of the differences between managers and leaders.

These include:

Leading People

The manager administers; **the leader innovates.**

The manager is a copy; **the leader is an original.**

The manager maintains; **the leader develops.**

The manager focuses on systems and structure; **the leader focuses on people.**

The manager relies on control; **the leader inspires trust.**

The manager has a short-range view; **the leader has a long-range perspective.**

The manager asks how and when; **the leader asks what and why.**

The manager has his or her eye always on the bottom line; **the leader's eye is on the horizon.**

The manager imitates; **the leader originates.**

The manager accepts the status quo; **the leader challenges it.**

The manager is the classic good soldier; **the leader is his or her own person.**

The manager does things right; **the leader does the right thing.**

"Failing organisations are usually over-managed and under-led."
Warren G. Bennis

Bennis focuses on the work of leaders within an organisation. He sees leaders as innovators who outperform all others and work at the cutting edge. They know themselves, learn from their past and move towards their future. They communicate their vision, encourage and praise their followers.

"Leaders should always expect the very best of those around them. They know that people can change and grow."
Warren G. Bennis

Adair's Action-Centred Leadership Model

John Adair developed a simple management and leadership model that is practical and can be applied to any organisation. The action-centred leadership model is based on three overlapping areas:

Leading People

- *Achieving the task*
- *Building and maintaining the team*
- *Developing the individual*

The circles overlap because everything is interdependent:

- *the task needs a team because one person cannot accomplish it alone*
- *the team's needs must be met, or the task will suffer and the individuals will not be satisfied*
- *the individual's needs must be met, or the team and performance of the task will be impaired*

Adair states that there are eight leadership functions that need to be met and constantly developed to ensure success:

1. *Defining the task*
2. *Planning*
3. *Briefing*
4. *Controlling*
5. *Evaluating*
6. *Motivating*
7. *Organising*
8. *Setting a good example*

According to Adair, leadership and management are not the same, although they should work together.

Hersey and Blanchard's Situational Leadership Model

Paul Hersey and Ken Blanchard first published their Situational Leadership® Model in their 1982 book, Management of Organisational Behaviour: Utilising Human Resources. The concept has become perhaps the best known of all the Situational/Contingency models.

The Situational Leadership® model is sophisticated. Its notable features are briefly that the model:

- *Focuses on followers, rather than wider workplace circumstances.*
- *Asserts that leaders should change their behaviour according to the type of followers.*
- *Proposes a 'continuum' or progression of leadership adaptation in response to the development of followers.*

Situational Leadership® theory is commonly shown as classifying followers according to a 2x2 matrix, using the highs and lows of two criteria, thereby giving four types of follower groups.

Leading People

Task / Ability			
		Low	*High*
Relationship / Willingness	*High*	Participating *(Supporting)* M3	Selling *(Coaching)* M2
	Low	Delegating M4	Telling *(Directing)* M1

Notably, where members of a group possess different levels of capability and experience, Hersey and Blanchard's model requires a more individualistic approach, rather than a broad group approach.

Accordingly, this summary refers mainly to 'follower' or 'followers', rather than a 'group', in explaining how the model is best appreciated and used.

Notably, where members of a group possess different levels of capability and experience, Hersey and Blanchard's model requires a more individualistic approach, rather than a broad group approach.

Accordingly, this summary refers mainly to 'follower' or 'followers', rather than a 'group', in explaining how the model is best appreciated and used.

The criteria of the followers are:

> *Competence*
> *Confidence and commitment*

Alternatively:

> *Ability*
> *Willingness*

Logically the four group types are:

Leading People

Groups formed	Or .....more simply
Low Competence/Low Confidence	Unable and Unwilling
Low Competence/High Confidence	Unable but Willing
High Competence/Low Confidence	Able but Unwilling
High Competence/High Confidence	Able and Willing

Extending the logic of this, Hersey and Blanchard further described and presented these four follower 'situations' as requiring relatively high or low leadership emphasis on the Task and the Relationship.

For example, a high task emphasis means giving very clear guidance to followers about aims and methods. A low task emphasis means giving followers freedom in deciding methods and perhaps even aims.

A high Relationship emphasis means working closely and sensitively with followers. A low Relationship emphasis means detachment or remoteness and either a trust in people's emotional robustness, or a disregard for emotional reactions. This 'low relationship' aspect is also called 'separated'.

High Task means followers have Low Ability.
Low Task means followers have High Ability.
High Relationship means followers are Willing.
Low Relationship means followers are Unwilling.

(Note that 'Unwilling' may be because of lack of confidence and/or because the aims/goals are not accepted. It is possible for a group of followers to be good at their jobs, but not committed to the aims/task.)

The logic can be represented helpfully as a simple practical concise 'leadership styles guide', as below, including the continuum, by which the leader changes styles in response to the growing/different maturity of followers.

Follower 'situation'	Leadership style emphasis	H & B terminology	Quick description	Continuum
Unable and Unwilling	high task - low relationship	Telling	instruction, direction, autocratic	M1
Unable but Willing	high task - high relationship	Selling	persuasion, encouragement, incentive	M2
Able but Unwilling	low task - high relationship	Participating	involvement, consultation, teamwork	M3
Able and Willing	low task - low relationship	Delegating	trust, empowerment, responsibility	M4

Leading People

The model also proposes a 'continuum' or progression of leadership adaptation in response to the typical development of followers. See the S1-S4 continuum on the grid above.

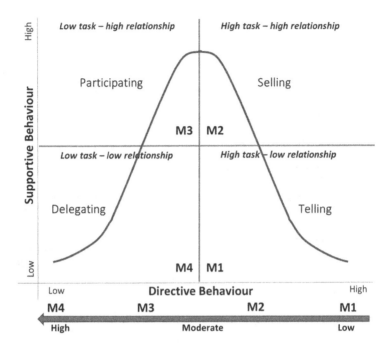

Hersey and Blanchard used the word 'maturity' in referring to the continuum of follower development, requiring and enabling a leader to change leadership style through the stages outlined above. Here 'maturity' entails experience, skills, confidence, commitment, etc - a combination of the two main 'follower' criteria, namely Ability and Willingness (Competence and Confidence/Commitment), which we can also interpret to be the follower's ability to self-manage or self-lead.

Hersey and Blanchard clearly mapped a progression of changing leadership styles in response to the tendency for people's maturity to increase over time.

This part of the theory is similar to the Tannenbaum and Schmidt Continuum model, specifically limited to where both models can apply to group maturity/capability development. That is, under certain circumstances, a leader adapts his/her behaviour progressively, in response to followers' growing maturity/capability, usually over many months, potentially from the inception or inheritance of a new team, ultimately to when the team can self-manage, perhaps even (and some would say ideally) to be led by a new leader who has emerged from the team to succeed the departing leader.

Hersey and Blanchard's 2x2 matrix, or four-square grid, has become a much-referenced tool and proprietary training method, for teaching and applying the Situational Leadership® model, notably matching the four leadership behaviours/styles to corresponding follower situations

Leading People

(or to 'entire group' situations, subject to the provisions already explained, that followers must possess similar levels of ability and experience as each other):

Hersey and Blanchard's matched sets of four follower types with four corresponding leadership styles, in order of the suggested continuum or progression coinciding with increasing follower maturity:

Followers and Leaders

Follower type	Leadership Style or Behaviour	
M1	Follower lacks experience or skill and confidence to do the task and may also lack willingness.	*Telling* - *Leader gives precise firm instructions and deadlines and closely monitors progress.*
M2	Follower lacks the ability, perhaps due to lack of experience, but is enthusiastic for the work.	*Selling* - *Leader explains goals, tasks, methods and reasons and remains available to give support.*
M3	Follower is capable and experienced but lacks confidence or commitment and may question the goal or task.	*Participating* - *Leader works with follower(s), involved with group, seeks input and encourages efforts.*
M4	Follower is capable, experienced, confident and committed to the goals.	*Delegating* - *Leader gives responsibility to followers for setting goals, planning and execution.*

Leading People

Fiedler's Contingency Model

Fred Fiedler's Contingency Model was the third notable situational model of leadership to emerge. This model appeared first in Fiedler's 1967 book, A Theory of Leadership Effectiveness.

The essence of Fiedler's theory is that a leader's effectiveness depends on a combination of two forces:

the leader's leadership style,
and
'situational favourableness'

Fiedler called this combination (of leadership style and 'situational favourableness'): Situational Contingency.

Fiedler described two basic leadership styles - task-orientated and relationship-orientated:

Task-Oriented Leaders
These leaders have a strong bias towards getting the job done without worrying about their rapport or bond with their followers. They can, of course, run the risk of failing to deliver if they do not engage enough with the people around them.

Relationship-Oriented Leaders
These leaders care much more about emotional engagement with the people they work with, but sometimes to the detriment of the task and results.

Fiedler said neither style is inherently superior. However, he asserted that certain leadership challenges suit one style or the other better.

Situational Favourability
Fiedler defined three factors determining the favourability of the situation:

- *How much trust, respect and confidence exists between leader and followers.*
- *How precisely the task is defined and how much creative freedom the leader gives to the followers.*
- *How much the followers accept the leader's power.*

Fiedler believed the situation is favourable when:

- *There is high mutual trust, respect and confidence between leader and followers.*
- *The task is clear and controllable.*
- *The followers accept the leader's power.*
- *The situation is unfavourable if the opposite is true on all three points.*

Leading People

Effectiveness

Fiedler said that task-orientated leaders are most effective when facing a situation that is either extremely favourable or extremely unfavourable. In other words:

- *when there is enormous trust, respect and confidence,*
- *when the task is very clear*
- *when followers accept the leader's power without question,*

and also, when the opposite is true, i.e.:

- *when trust and respect do not exist,*
- *when the challenge people face is vague and undefined*
- *when the atmosphere is anarchic or even rebellious (for example, an emergency or crisis)*

Fiedler concluded that relationship-orientated leaders are most effective in less extreme circumstances. That is, in situations that are neither favourable nor unfavourable, or situations that are only moderately favourable or moderately unfavourable.

Situation Favourability		Most Effective Leadership Style
high	=	task-oriented leader
intermediate	=	relationship-oriented leader
low	=	task-oriented leader

Fiedler's theory took a significant and firm view about personality: He said that a leader's style reflected his or her personality, (which incidentally he assessed in his research using a psychometric instrument).

Fiedler's view about personality - and indeed the common notion of the times - was that individual personality is fixed and does not change during a leader's life/career. Consequently, Fiedler's theory placed great emphasis on 'matching' leaders to situations, according to the perceived style of the leader and the situation faced (by the organisation).

Fiedler's Contingency Model is therefore a somewhat limited model for effective leadership. Notably, it is not a useful guide for helping people become better leaders; nor is it an efficient or necessarily flexible model for modern leadership in organisations, given the dynamic variety of situations which nowadays arise.

A further implication of Fiedler's theory is potentially to require the replacement of leaders whose styles do not match situations, which from several viewpoints (legal, practical, ethical, etc) would be simply unworkable in modern organisations.

Nevertheless, despite its limitations, Fiedler's theory was an important contribution to leadership thinking, especially in reinforcing the now generally accepted views that:

Leading People

- *There is no single ideal way of behaving as a leader and*
- *Matching leadership behaviour (or style) to circumstances (or situations) - or vice-versa - is significant in effective leadership.*

Personality

And as already suggested, Fiedler's theory also encourages us to consider the leader's personality and the leader's behaviour from these angles:

the extent to which (a leader's) personality is fixed
the extent to which (a leader's) personality controls (a leader's) behaviour.

Clearly, if a model such as this is to be of great value, then these questions need to be clarified rather more than they have been to date, which is not easy given the complexity of human nature.

Robert House - Path-Goal Theory

The next significant leadership theory to emerge in the Situational/Contingency category was Robert House's Path-Goal theory, in his 1971 paper: A Path-Goal Theory of Leader Effectiveness, which he refined three years later in cooperation with T R Mitchell.

House said that the main role of a leader is to motivate his followers by:

- *Increasing or clarifying the (group's/followers') personal benefits of striving for and reaching the group's goal.*
- *Clarifying and clearing a path to achieving the group's goals.*

Hence the theory's name: Path-Goal Theory.

House's theory matched four ways of behaving to four sets of circumstances, or 'situations'.

The circumstances in Path-Goal theory are driven by 'follower characteristics' and 'workplace characteristics.

Follower characteristics

What they believe about their ability - *Do they feel they are capable of fulfilling the task well?*

Where control resides - *Do group members believe they have control over the way they approach the task and the chances of achieving the goal? Or do they see themselves as being controlled by other people and outside events?*

Attitude to power and those in power - *Do members want to be told what to do and how to do it... or not? What do they think of those in the organisation who have more official power than they do, especially the leader?*

Leading People

Workplace characteristics

The kind of task - *Is it repetitive? Is it interesting? Is it predictable or structured? Is it unpredictable, creative or unstructured?*

The leader's formal authority - *Is it well-defined?*

Group cohesion - Do those working in the group feel a sense of unity?

House took these two external dimensions and matched them with four leadership behavioural styles, as this diagram summarises:

Leadership Style	Workplace Characteristics	Follower Characteristics
Directive	Unstructured interesting tasks Clear, formal authority Good group cohesion	Inexperienced followers They believe they lack power They want leader to direct them
Supportive	Simpler, more predictable tasks Unclear or weak formal authority Poor group cohesion	Experienced, confident followers They believe they have power They reject close control
Participative	Unstructured, complex tasks Formal authority could be either clear or unclear Group cohesion could either be good or poor	Experienced, confident followers They believe they have power They reject close control, preferring to exercise power over their work
Achievement-orientated	Unstructured, complex or unpredictable tasks Clear, formal authority Group cohesion could either be good or poor	Experienced, confident followers They think they lack some power They accept the idea of the leader setting their goals and have a lot of respect for the leader

Essentially, House's work implies that leaders need to adapt their leadership style based on both the characteristics of the workplace environment and also the characteristics of the team. By implication, Path-Goal theory assumes that a leader can vary his or her mindset and behaviour as needed.

Unlike Fiedler's Contingency model, House's Path-Goal theory asserts that leaders can and should vary their behaviour according to the situation and the problems or opportunities that each situation presents.

In this way, Path-Goal theory is similar to Tannenbaum and Schmidt's Continuum and to Kurt Lewin's Three Styles model. It is a situational or contingency theory that in addition to matching leadership styles to given situations, also advocates switching leadership styles according to changing situations.

Leading People

Bolman and Deal - Four-Frame Model

Lee Bolman and Terry Deal outlined their Four-Frame model in their book, Reframing Organisations: Artistry, Choice and Leadership (1991).

Bolman and Deal stated that leaders should look at and approach organisational issues from four perspectives, which they called 'Frames'.

In their view, if a leader works with only one habitual Frame (frame of reference), the leader risks being ineffective.

Structural	*This Frame focuses on the obvious 'how' of change. It is mainly a task-orientated Frame. It concentrates on strategy; setting measurable goals; clarifying tasks, responsibilities and reporting lines; agreeing metrics and deadlines; and creating systems and procedures.*
Human Resource	*The HR Frame places more emphasis on people's needs. It chiefly focuses on giving employees the power and opportunity to perform their jobs well, while at the same time, addressing their needs for human contact, personal growth and job satisfaction.*
Political	*The Political Frame addresses the problem of individuals and interest groups having sometimes conflicting (often hidden) agendas, especially at times when budgets are limited and the organisation has to make difficult choices. In this Frame you will see coalition-building, conflict resolution work and power-base building to support the leader's initiatives.*
Symbolic	*The Symbolic Frame addresses people's needs for a sense of purpose and meaning in their work. It focuses on inspiring people by making the organisation's direction feel significant and distinctive. It includes creating a motivating vision and recognising superb performance through company celebrations.*

Implications

Bolman and Deal proposed that a leader should see the organisation's challenges through these four Frames or 'lenses', to gain an overall view and to decide which Frame or Frames to use.

The leader may use one Frame (implying a behavioural approach) for a time and then switch to another. Or instead, the leader might combine and use a number of Frames, or all four, at the same time.

A crucial aspect of Bolman and Deal's model seeks to avoid the temptation for leaders to become stuck, viewing and acting on conditions through one lens or Frame alone.

Bolman and Deal assert that because no Frame works well in every circumstance, then a leader who sticks with one Frame is bound eventually to act inappropriately and ineffectively.

Leading People

Instead, it is the leader's responsibility to use the appropriate Frame of reference and thereby behaviour, for each challenge.

Central to this methodology is asking the right questions and diagnosing the vital issues.

Examples

Where a leader ascertains that the biggest problem in a group is lack of motivation and commitment, the leader should probably adopt a Symbolic and/or Human Resource (Frame) approach.

If the main group challenge is instead confusion around priorities and responsibilities, then the leader will probably be more successful adopting Structural and Political (Frames) orientation.

If the group is experiencing uncertainty and anxiety about direction, then Symbolic and Political (Frames) leadership behaviours are more likely to produce effective results.

Essentially, the leader should adopt a multi-Frame perspective before choosing how to act. Organisations tend naturally to use the Structural Frame but pay less attention to the other three Frames.

According to Four-Frame theory, this is due either to:

- *lack of awareness of the need for multi-Frame thinking and behaviour*
  or
- *behavioural rigidity due to unconscious limiting beliefs* (controlling the leader's perceived priorities or capabilities).

Reddin's 3D Leadership Model

Reddin's 3D Leadership Model is a simple framework for utilising managerial styles in various situations in order to maximise effectiveness.

The four basic leadership styles as identified by Reddin were:

Related. *A related leader enjoys team-based, cooperative working. They do not focus on directing or dictating orders to staff and allows much more freedom and responsibility.*

Integrated. *An integrated leader retains the cooperative nature of the group and encourages two-way communication. They emphasise the effectiveness of this communication and building a strong team capable of completing tasks to the best of their potential.*

Dedicated. *A dedicated leader is only truly concerned with the end result of the task and focuses on improving the production process. They retain power and responsibility with themselves, allowing them to dictate roles and requirements to others.*

Leading People

Separated. *A separated leader focuses on correcting deviations from the norm. They formulate policies and rules and impose them on others but do not take a direct, commanding role on themselves.*

Each of these was separated by its position along two major axes:

Task Orientation and Relationship Orientation.

This is referring to the proportion of concern that the leader in question has for either the results of the task, or for the needs and development of the individuals involved.

The central matrix in the diagram below represents Reddin's initial model, showing the four major leadership styles and their positions along the Task-Relationship axis.

Reddin later expanded on his initial theory, adding in the third dimension of Effectiveness. This effectiveness was defined by the appropriateness of the particular leadership style in any given situation and he argued that this should be the main focus of any manager's efforts.

As you can see in the diagram, the appropriate versions of the initial styles can be seen in the upper-right (Developer, Executive, Benevolent Autocrat, Bureaucrat) and the inappropriate styles (Missionary, Compromiser, Autocrat, Deserter) in the bottom-left. These are not new styles in themselves, only the primary styles when applied to appropriate or inappropriate situations.

> *"Any managerial style has a situation appropriate to it and many situations inappropriate to it..."* - William Reddin

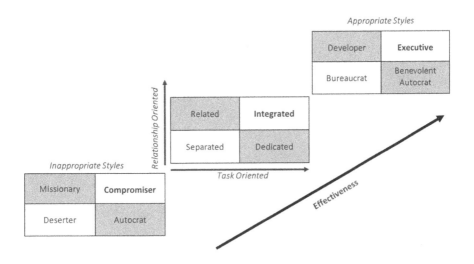

Leading People

The true strength of a leader or manager is to know when to utilise each of the basic leadership styles and how to apply them to appropriate situations. Also discussed were two other key concepts - flexibility and rigidity - which refer to how malleable the individual's style was in various scenarios.

The primary styles are fairly broad and all-encompassing and also highlighted are that leadership style could not necessarily be identified purely by examining the effectiveness of the situation.

Choosing the Appropriate Style

The most difficult part of applying Reddin's theory is for leaders to understand when to employ each of the different styles. In general, this is something which can only be understood through experience and close examination of the situation. A leader with a strong awareness of the requirements of tasks and demands of a situation will be capable of interpreting the necessity of greater task orientation or greater people orientation.

Task-orientated approaches generally are most effective in scenarios when the group is constrained by resources or time, when there is disorganisation which needs to be brought back into order, or when the leader is working with inexperienced or low-skilled team members. People-oriented approaches are often more effective in more open, creative tasks, or when the leader sees the opportunity to develop their staff's leadership or skills over the long term or motivate them through new experiences and greater responsibility. The leader may also see fit to work on a more people-centric basis in times when they have a highly experienced, skilled and competent team.

Leaders, as people, will likely have a natural predisposition towards certain approaches to the task. However, it is still possible to understand that sometimes it is beneficial to be more flexible in their approach, allowing them to maximise the rewards of the situation at hand.

Leading People

Organisational Culture

The term "Organisational culture" refers to the values, beliefs history and hidden rules of an organisation.

The principles, ideologies as well as policies followed by an organisation, form its culture.

It is the culture of the workplace which decides the way individuals interact with each other and behave with people outside the company. The employees must respect their organisation's culture for them to deliver their level best and enjoy their work. Problems crop up when individuals are unable to adjust to a new work culture and thus feel demotivated and reluctant to perform.

When we are immersed in a workplace culture, we often just go along with things without questioning them too closely. We want to fit in with other people, especially if we are new. If the culture is positive, productive, fair and trustworthy, we will usually do our best to work hard to meet the standards and become an effective member of the organisation and team. On the other hand, if the culture is based on negative and generally unacceptable values, we can feel uncomfortable about challenging things that do not seem quite right.

The underlying positive or negative cultural elements have a significant effect on the whole organisation.

Organisational culture can affect many different functions including, for example:

- *Health and safety* – e.g., a manufacturing company has a good safety culture that keeps accidents and incidents to a minimum.
- *Working hours* – e.g., employees in a City finance firm always work longer hours than are shown in their contracts; subcontractors tend to finish on time and leave tasks unfinished each evening.
- *Sales targets* – e.g., an insurance company's call centre's culture is to do a very hard sell to make sure targets are met, regardless of quality; a specialist furniture supplier's culture focuses on the quality and profitability of sales and not the quantity.
- *Quality management* – e.g., a car company's culture is to strive for consistent excellence and 100% accuracy in production; a food factory's staff do not really care about high levels of wastage as these have always been ignored.
- *Employees' health and work/life balance* – e.g., a small company's culture is to always support its loyal and hard-working employees if they are sick or have serious personal problems; another company's culture is for staff to turn up for work even if they are ill.
- *Delivering on promises* – e.g., a retail company's culture is to treat its customers and other stakeholders with honesty and integrity; a plumbing business's culture is to not care if customers complain about missed appointments or staff turning up later than promised.

Leading People

An organisation can have clearly-stated objectives and a mission statement, but these may not be in line with the reality of its culture – how things are actually done. It is part of the leadership role to work to align the organisation's culture with its overall vision and goals – to aim to make the unwritten rules match the written ones.

Consider:

- *different cultures that exist within organisations*
- *internal and external factors that can affect the culture*
- *the effect the organisation's culture can have on individuals and teams*

Organisational culture is based on people's assumptions, values and beliefs about how they should behave and interact at work, how decisions are made and how work activities should be performed. In the manufacturing company with a good attitude to health and safety, their culture could be based on, for example:

- *assumptions – that all employees will follow its well-planned policies and procedures; that suppliers provide goods and services that are fit for purpose*
- *values – that the safety of staff, customers and other visitors to the workplace is always top priority*
- *beliefs – that risks need to be eliminated, or reduced to an absolute minimum; that training and awareness need to be kept up to date*

A number of management thinkers have studied organisational culture and attempted to classify different types of culture. The following approaches may be helpful in assessing and understanding the culture of an organisation, but also illustrate its inherent complexity. Observers should recognise that an organisation's culture can be viewed from multiple angles and that its characteristics can be reflected in a number of overlapping dimensions.

Edgar Schein

Schein believed that culture is the most difficult organisational attribute to change and that it can outlast products, services, founders and leaders.

According to Edgar Schein - Organisations do not adopt a culture in a single day, instead it is formed over time as the employees go through various changes, adapt to the external environment and solve problems. They gain from their past experiences and start practicing it every day thus forming the culture of the workplace. The new employees also strive hard to adjust to the new culture and enjoy a stress-free life. Schein believed that there are three levels in an organisation culture.

Leading People

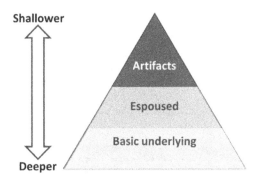

Artifacts

The first level is the characteristics of the organisation which can be easily viewed, heard and felt by individuals collectively known as artifacts. The dress code of the employees, office furniture, facilities, behaviour of the employees, mission and vision of the organisation all come under artifacts and go a long way in deciding the culture of the workplace.

Organisation A

No one in organisation A is allowed to dress casually.

Employees respect their superiors and avoid unnecessary disputes.

The individuals are very particular about the deadlines and ensure the tasks are accomplished within the stipulated time frame.

Organisation B

The employees can wear whatever they feel like.

Individuals in organisation B are least bothered about work and spend their maximum time loitering and gossiping around.

The employees use derogatory remarks at the workplace and pull each other into controversies.

In the above case, employees in organisation A dress in a way that exudes professionalism and strictly follow the policies of the organisation. On the other hand, employees in organisation B have a laid-back attitude and do not take their work seriously. Organisation A follows a strict professional culture whereas Organisation B follows a weak culture where the employees do not accept the things willingly.

Values

The next level according to Schein which constitute the organisation culture are the values of the employees. The values of the individuals working in the organisation play an important role in deciding the organisation culture. The thought process and attitude of employees have deep impact on the culture of any particular organisation. What people actually think matters a lot for the organisation.

The mindset of the individual associated with any particular
organisation influences the culture of the workplace.

Assumed Values

The third level are the assumed values of the employees which cannot be measured but do make a difference to the culture of the organisation. There are certain beliefs and facts which stay hidden but do affect the culture of the organisation. The inner aspects of human nature come under the third level of organisation culture. Organisations where female workers dominate their male counterparts do not believe in staying late as females are not very comfortable with such kind of culture. Male employees on the other hand would be more aggressive and would not have any problems with staying long after normal hours.

The organisations follow certain practices which are not discussed often but understood on their own. Such rules form the third level of the organisation culture.

Robert A. Cooke - Model of Organisation Culture

Every employee has a way of behaving at the workplace which they feel is the correct way and would help them survive in the organisation for a longer duration. Such perceptions of employees form the culture of the organisation.

According to Robert A Cooke, the culture of an organisation is:

... the way employees behave at the workplace to ensure stable future and growth.

Cooke proposed three types of culture in the organisation:

Constructive Culture

There are certain organisations which encourage healthy interaction amongst the employees. The individuals have the liberty to share their ideas, exchange information and discuss things to come to an innovative solution beneficial to all. Conflicts arise when employees feel neglected and are not allowed to speak their minds. People crib amongst themselves when queries remain unattended leading to severe demotivation. A constructive culture encourages discussions and exchange of ideas amongst employees. Constructive culture motivates the employees and eventually extracts the best out of them.

The key features of a constructive culture are:

Achievement: *A constructive culture helps the employees to achieve the targets within the stipulated time frame.*

Self-Actualising: *In this kind of culture, an employee stays motivated and realises his full potential.*

Encouragement: *A Constructive culture encourages employees to deliver their level best and strive hard for furthering the image of the organisation.*

Affiliative: *The employees avoid conflicts and unnecessary disputes and promote a positive ambience at the workplace.*

Passive Culture

In a passive culture, the employees behave in a way contrary to the way they feel is correct and should be the ideal way. In a passive culture, the main motive of the employee is to please the superiors and make his position safe and secure in the organisation. In such a culture, employees unhappily adhere to the guidelines and follow the rules and regulations just to save their job.

The characteristics of a passive culture are:

Approval: *In such a culture, employees cannot make decisions on their own. They need to have their boss's approval before implementing any idea.*

Conventional: *Employees are bound by rules and regulations of the organisation and act according to the prescribed standards only.*

Dependent: *In such a culture, the performance of the employees is dependent on the superior's decisions and they blindly follow their boss's orders.*

Avoidance: *Employees tend to avoid their own personal interests, satisfaction and simply act according to the company's policies.*

Aggressive Culture

Organisations following an aggressive culture promote competition amongst the employees. They encourage the employees to compete against each other so that each one performs better than his fellow worker. In such a culture, employees seeking their colleague's assistance are often considered to be incompetent employees. Every individual vies for power, attention and strive hard to win appreciation.

The key features of such a culture are:

Opposition
Power
Perfectionist
Competitive

In the above culture, employees are aggressive, compete against each other and try to become perfectionist by identifying their mistakes and eventually minimising them.

Leading People

Geert Hofstede Cultural Dimensions Theory

The Hofstede's Cultural Dimensions Theory, developed by Geert Hofstede, is a framework used to understand the differences in culture across countries and to discern the ways that business is done across different cultures. In other words, the framework is used to distinguish between different national cultures, the dimensions of culture and their impact on a business setting.

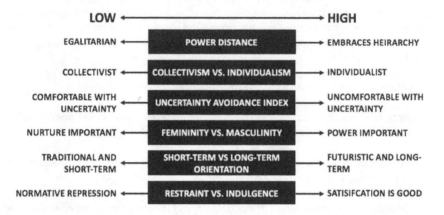

Hofstede identified six categories that define culture:

> *Power Distance Index*
> *Collectivism vs. Individualism*
> *Uncertainty Avoidance Index*
> *Femininity vs. Masculinity*
> *Short-Term vs. Long-Term Orientation*
> *Restraint vs. Indulgence*

Power Distance Index

The power distance index considers the extent to which inequality and power are tolerated. In this dimension, inequality and power are viewed from the viewpoint of the followers – the lower level.

> *High power distance index indicates that a culture accepts inequity and power differences, encourages bureaucracy and shows high respect for rank and authority.*

> *Low power distance index indicates that a culture encourages organisational structures that are flat, decentralised decision-making responsibility, participative style of management and places emphasis on power distribution.*

Individualism vs. Collectivism

The individualism vs. collectivism dimension considers the degree to which societies are integrated into groups and their perceived obligation and dependence on groups.

Leading People

Individualism indicates that there is greater importance on attaining personal goals. A person's self-image in this category is defined as "I."

Collectivism indicates that there is greater importance on the goals and well-being of the group. A person's self-image in this category is defined as "We".

Uncertainty Avoidance Index

The uncertainty avoidance index considers the extent to which uncertainty and ambiguity are tolerated. This dimension considers how unknown situations and unexpected events are dealt with.

High uncertainty avoidance index indicates a low tolerance for uncertainty, ambiguity and risk-taking. The unknown is minimised through strict rules, regulations, etc.

Low uncertainty avoidance index indicates a high tolerance for uncertainty, ambiguity and risk-taking. The unknown is more openly accepted and there are lax rules, regulations, etc.

Masculinity vs. Femininity

The masculinity vs. femininity dimension is also referred to as "tough vs. tender," and considers the preference of society for achievement, attitude towards sexuality equality, behaviour, etc.

Masculinity comes with the following characteristics: distinct gender roles, assertive and concentrated on material achievements and wealth-building.

Femininity comes with the following characteristics: fluid gender roles, modest, nurturing and concerned with the quality of life.

Long-Term Orientation vs. Short-Term Orientation

The long-term orientation vs. short-term orientation dimension considers the extent to which society views its time horizon.

Long-term orientation shows focus on the future and involves delaying short-term success or gratification in order to achieve long-term success. Long-term orientation emphasises persistence, perseverance and long-term growth.

Short-term orientation shows focus on the near future, involves delivering short-term success or gratification and places a stronger emphasis on the present than the future. Short-term orientation emphasises quick results and respect for tradition.

Leading People

Indulgence vs. Restraint

The indulgence vs. restraint dimension considers the extent and tendency for a society to fulfil its desires. In other words, this dimension revolves around how societies can control their impulses and desires.

Indulgence indicates that a society allows relatively free gratification related to enjoying life and having fun.

Restraint indicates that a society suppresses gratification of needs and regulates it through social norms.

Charles Handy's Model of Organisational Culture

Charles Handy and Roger Harrison followed various organisations and examined how power was distributed and the levels of cooperation. The level of power distributed from low to high is placed on the y-axis, and the level of cooperation is placed on the x-axis. The various combinations then result in four different organisational cultures.

- *Power*
- *Role*
- *Task*
- *Person*

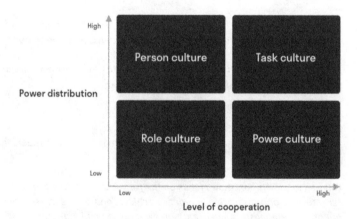

Power distribution is about the extent to which the top of an organisation (management or owner) is open to working with either a bottom-up or top-down approach. In case of a bottom-up approach, the power distribution is very high; employees are expected to take their own responsibility, determine their tasks and make independent decisions.

In case of a complete top-down approach, there is hardly any power distribution; management or the owner is completely in control and is the only person making decisions.

Leading People

The cooperation level, as the name suggests, is about the degree of cooperation between the various departments and employees. A lower cooperation level means everyone works for themselves and hardly requires the help of colleagues.

A high cooperation level, on the other hand, involves close, indispensable cooperation between colleagues.

Power Culture
In an organisation with a power culture, power is held by just a few individuals whose influence spreads throughout the organisation.

There are few rules and regulations in a power culture. What those with power decide is what happens. Employees are generally judged by what they achieve rather than how they do things or how they act. A consequence of this can be quick decision-making, even if those decisions are not in the best long-term interests of the organisation.

A power culture is usually a strong culture, though it can swiftly turn toxic. The collapse of Enron, Lehman Brothers and RBS is often attributed to a strong power culture.

Control radiates from the centre
Concentrates power among the few
Few rules and little bureaucracy
Swift decisions are possible

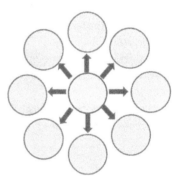

- *Firm control is the key element*
- *a specified number of individuals hold power*
- *decisions are made by these individuals*
- *rules and regulations are minimal*
- *decisions may not always be the most appropriate and can be detrimental to the business*
- *can lead to frustration among team members were unable to express their opinions*

Role Culture
Organisations with a role culture are based on rules. They are highly controlled, with everyone in the organisation knowing what their roles and responsibilities are. Power in a role culture is determined by a person's position (role) in the organisational structure.

Leading People

Role cultures are built on detailed organisational structures which are typically tall (not flat) with a long chain of command. A consequence is that decision-making in role cultures can often be painfully slow and the organisation is less likely to take risks. In short, organisations with role cultures tend to be very bureaucratic.

-People have clearly delegated authorities
within a highly defined structure
-Hierarchical bureaucracy
-Power derived from a person's position
-Little scope exists for expert power

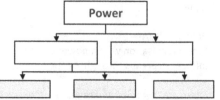

- *Based on a hierarchy of people in specific roles*
- *individual roles will be assigned specific duties*
- *clear lines of accountability and responsibility*
- *enables large organisations to ensure key tasks are addressed but not duplicated*
- *Paris designated according to a person's role and position in the hierarchy*
- *decisions can take time to make as they must go up through the correct channels*
- *the organisation will really take risks*
- *team member skills are acknowledged and valued*

Person Culture
In organisations with person cultures, individuals very much see themselves as unique and superior to the organisation. The organisation simply exists in order for people to work. An organisation with a person culture is really just a collection of individuals who happen to be working for the same organisation.

-People believe themselves to be
superior to the business
-Business full of people with similar
training and expertise
-Common in firms of lawyers,
accountants, etc.
-Power lies in each group of

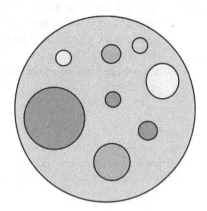

Leading People

- *More about individuals than the organisation rivers within it*
- *not working towards common goals*
- *everyone has power*
- *employees are not often loyal and work just to get paid*

Task Culture

According to Charles Handy's model, there are four types of culture which the organisations follow

Task culture forms when teams in an organisation are formed to address specific problems or progress projects. The task is the important thing, so power within the team will often shift depending on the mix of the team members and the status of the problem or project.

Whether the task culture proves effective will largely be determined by the team dynamic. With the right mix of skills, personalities and leadership, working in teams can be incredibly productive and creative.

-Teams are formed to solve particular problems
-Power derives from expertise as long as team needs it
-No single power source
-Matrix organisation
-Risk is, Team may develop own objectives

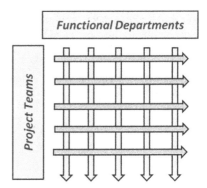

- *Task oriented teams concentrate on specific projects or problems*
- *power can shift between and within teams*
- *requires the right leadership, skill set and personalities of team members to make it work*
- *each team will have its own objectives that need to be in line with the organisations to be successful*
- *innovation is encouraged*

Leading People

Johnson and Scholes' Cultural Web Model

Strategy and development in an organisation are influenced heavily by the culture and environment.

This is often positive, but it can also act as a hinderance, or even a barrier to growth and success. When trying to drive change, managers and other figures of responsibility may find it difficult to break out of the systems, structures and routines embedded in the company's culture and politics or individual relationships often play a huge role in deciding strategy.

Published by authors and academics in the fields of business, leadership and management, Kevan Scholes and Gerry Johnson in 1992, the Cultural Web is a useful tool for analysing and altering assumptions surrounding the culture of a company. It can be used to highlight specific practices and beliefs and to subsequently align them with your company's preferred culture and strategy. It is a representation of the taken-for-granted assumptions of an organisation which helps management to focus on the key factors of culture and their impact on strategic issues. This can identify blockages to and facilitators of change in order to improve performance and competitive advantage.

Johnson and Scholes identified six distinct but interrelated elements which contribute to what they called the "paradigm", equivalent to the pattern of the work environment, or the values of the organisation. They suggested that each may be examined and analysed individually to gain a clearer picture of the wider cultural issues of an organisation.

The six contributing elements (with example questions used to examine the organisation at hand) are as follows:

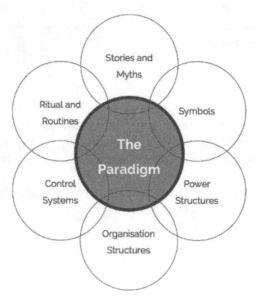

Leading People

1. Stories and Myths

These are the previous events – both accurate and not – which are discussed by individuals within and outside the company. Which events and people are remembered by the company indicates what the company values and what it chooses to immortalise through stories?

What form of company reputation is communicated between customers and stakeholders?
What stories do people tell new employees about the company?
What do people know about the history of the organisation?
What do these stories say about the culture of the business?

2. Rituals and Routines

This refers to the daily actions and behaviours of individuals within the organisation. Routines indicate what is expected of employees on a day-to-day basis and what has been either directly or indirectly approved by those in managerial positions.

What do employees expect when they arrive each day?
What experience do customers expect from the organisation?
What would be obvious if it were removed from routines?
What do these rituals and routines say about organisational beliefs?

3. Symbols

This is the visual representation of the company; how they appear to both employees and individuals on the outside. It includes logos, office spaces, dress codes and sometimes advertisements.

What kind of image is associated with the company from the outside?
How do employees and managers view the organisation?
Are there any company-specific designs or jargon used?
How does the organisation advertise itself?

4. Control Systems

These are the systems and pathways by which the organisation is controlled. This can refer to many things, including financial management, individual performance-based rewards (both measurement and distribution) and quality-control structures.

Which processes are strongly and weakly controlled?
In general, is the company loosely or tightly controlled?
Are employees rewarded or punished for performance?
What reports and processes are used to keep control of finance, etc?

5. Organisation Structures

This refers to both the hierarchy and structure designated by the organisation. Alongside this, Johnson and Scholes also use it to refer to the unwritten power and influence that some members may exert, which also indicate whose contributions to the organisation are most valued by those above them.

How hierarchical is the organisation?
Is responsibility and influence distributed in a formal or informal way?
Where are the official lines of authority?
Are there any unofficial lines of authority?

6. Power Structures

This is the genuine power structures and responsible individuals within the organisation. It may refer to a few executives, the CEO, board members, or an entire managerial division. These individuals are those who hold the greatest influence over decisions and generally have the final say on major actions or changes.

Who holds the power within the organisation?
Who makes decisions on behalf of the company?
What are the beliefs and culture of those as the top of the business?
How is power used within the organisation?

Using the Cultural Web to Change

The first step of changing the culture of the organisation is to analyse elements of the Cultural Web as they are in the present. The next step is to repeat the process, examining each element, but this time considering what one would like the culture, beliefs and systems to be. This can then subsequently be compared with the ideal culture and the differences between the two can be used to develop achievable steps towards change within the company. One will likely only then realise the true strengths and weaknesses of the organisation's current culture, what the various hinderances are to growth and how to go about changing specific elements to develop and achieve success.

A new strategy can evolve from this by looking at introducing new beliefs and prioritising positive reinforcement of current, successful ones. Hopefully, by integrating this system of analysis, managers can find themselves able to break free of ritual and belief systems within a company to achieve real change and innovation.

Influences on Organisational Culture

Culture represents the beliefs, ideologies, policies, practices of an organisation. It gives the employees a sense of direction and also controls the way they behave with each other. The work culture brings all the employees on a common platform and unites them at the workplace.

There are several factors which affect the organisation culture:

The first and the foremost factor affecting culture is the individual working with the organisation. The employees in their own way contribute to the culture of the workplace. The attitudes, mentalities, interests, perception and even the thought process of the employees affect the organisation culture.

Example

Organisations which hire individuals from army or defence background tend to follow a strict culture where all the employees abide by the set guidelines and policies. The employees are seldom late to work.

It is the mindset of the employees which forms the culture of the place. Organisations with majority of youngsters encourage healthy competition at the workplace and employees are always on their toes to perform better than the fellow workers.

The sex of the employee also affects the organisation culture. Organisations where male employees dominate, the female counterparts follow a culture where working late is a normal feature. The male employees are more aggressive than the females who instead would be caring and soft-hearted.

The nature of the business also affects the culture of the organisation. Stockbroking industries, financial services, banking industry are all dependent on external factors like demand and supply, market cap, earning per share and so on. When the market crashes, these industries have no other option than to terminate the employees and eventually affect the culture of the place. Market fluctuations lead to unrest, tensions and severely demotivate the individuals. The management also feels helpless when circumstances can be controlled by none. Individuals are unsure about their career as well as growth in such organisations.

The culture of the organisation is also affected by its goals and objectives. The strategies and procedures designed to achieve the targets of the organisation also contribute to its culture.

Individuals working with government organisations adhere to the set guidelines but do not follow a procedure of feedback thus forming its culture. Fast paced industries like advertising, event management companies expect the employees to be attentive, aggressive and hyperactive.

The clients and the external parties to some extent also affect the work culture of the place.

Organisations working with UK and US Clients have no other option but to work in shifts to match their timings, thus forming the culture.

The management and its style of handling the employees also affect the culture of the workplace. There are certain organisations where the management allows the employees to take their own decisions and let them participate in strategy making. In such a culture, employees get attached to their management and look forward to a long-term association with the organisation.

The management must respect the employees to avoid a culture where the employees just work for money and nothing else. They treat the organisation as a mere source of earning money and look for a change in a short span of time.

Leading People

Internal and external factors that can affect organisational culture

There are many internal and external factors that can affect an organisation's culture.

Internal factors are generally under the control of the organisation and can include, for example:

- *The position in the marketplace* – e.g., a leading high-street retailer; an online trade supplier; a UK base for an international consultancy company; a freelance computer specialist who works at home or on the customer's site; a government department or agency
- *Policies, procedures and working practices* – e.g., operational routines; customer service policies; anti-discrimination, equality and diversity policies; career development policies and appraisal procedures; communication methods and techniques; incentive schemes
- *History and traditions* – e.g., procedures that have been ignored or followed for years
- *Management hierarchy* – e.g., the line management system for making decisions, sharing information and solving problems
- *Leadership styles* – e.g., autocratic, democratic or laissez-faire
- *Values, beliefs and assumptions* – e.g., of individuals or teams; of the organisation as a whole, as set out in a mission statement

External factors are generally outside the control of the organisation and can include, for example:

- *Market forces* – e.g., price changes that affect the supply of raw materials and labour that make task-based projects more difficult to manage
- *Changes in technology* – e.g., increased Internet sales leading to a reduction in the need for shops on the high street
- *Competitors' activities* – e.g., phone providers competing to keep up with demand for new technology, cheaper packages and faster operation speeds
- *Changes in customer expectations* – e.g., expecting hotels to provide low-cost, high-quality rooms as standard
- *New legislation, regulations or standards* – e.g., changes in health and safety, data protection or equality and diversity laws that affect operations, or the provision of goods and services

Leading People

Equality, Diversity and Inclusion in the Workplace

In the UK, there have been serious efforts over many years to reduce discrimination and prejudice and the phrase 'equality and diversity' is quite widespread now. The Equality Act came into force in 2010 and it brought together various pieces of anti-discrimination legislation. The Act forms the legal framework to help to reduce discrimination in many parts of our lives and to protect people:

- *in the workplace* – *during recruitment and employment – e.g., in care homes, offices, retail, voluntary workplaces*
- *in education* – *e.g., schools, colleges, training companies*
- *as consumers* – *e.g., in shops, on the Internet, in cafes and restaurants, when buying or renting property*
- *when using public services* – *e.g., healthcare, libraries, transport, councils, civil service*
- *in clubs with more than 25 members* – *although the law does not stop clubs for people who share a protected characteristic – e.g., men-only or women-only clubs, or social clubs for Turkish people*

Definition of terms

Equality

Definition:

the state of being equal, especially in status, rights or opportunities.

Equality is the 'state of being equal'. It means that something is the same value, quantity or quality. It is even, balanced and fair.

Equality is about making certain that people are treated fairly and are given fair chances. However, equality is not about treating everyone in exactly the same way. It is about recognising the importance of treating each person as an individual and making sure that their needs are met in a variety of ways. Equality is based on the principles of:

- *fairness* – *working and living in ways that do not discriminate against anyone*
- *respect* – *encouraging a culture where everyone receives respect and can express their views and be heard*
- *honesty* – *ensuring that policies and practices are transparent (clear) and open to scrutiny*
- *providing opportunities* – *working and living in a culture where everyone has the opportunity to reach their full potential*

Leading People

Diversity

Definition:

> *the condition or fact of being different or varied; variety.*

Diversity refers to the wide range of attributes, backgrounds and skills that are in our society. In the UK, we have people of many races, religions, colours, abilities, ages and so on. They bring a diverse and colourful range of cultures, traditions, ceremonies, skills, languages, backgrounds, experience and other attributes to our society.

A diverse approach aims to recognise, harness and manage differences, so that everyone can contribute to society and realise their full potential. Diversity challenges us to recognise and value all sorts of differences in order to make society more inclusive, fair and comfortable for everyone.

Inclusion

Definition:

> *the action of including or of being included within a group or structure.*

When our work environment is inclusive, the policies, procedures and organisational culture focus on including people whenever possible. This is in line with treating people equally, regardless of their diversity. On a day-to-day level, treating colleagues inclusively helps to bond a team and make new members feel welcome and valuable.

There will be times when inclusion is not appropriate – e.g., in certain meetings where some people do not have the authority to attend or be party to sensitive information.

In the workplace, we need to take active steps to attract, develop and promote people from diverse backgrounds. For example, we can:

- *make sure that we appoint people from diverse backgrounds*
- *avoid asking the same people all the time when we allocate extra duties or responsibilities*
- *invite people to join a group that might help them and the organisation* – e.g., when meeting colleagues for lunch; when there is a conference or presentation that would be of benefit or interest to them
- *get to know team members well as individuals* – *e.g., to find out about their strengths, expectations and ambitions*

Leading People

Discrimination

Definition:

the unjust or prejudicial treatment of different categories of people, especially on the grounds of race, age or sex.

Discrimination occurs when a person is treated less favourably than another person in the same situation because of their race, gender, disability, religious beliefs etc. For example, in the past, sex discrimination was tolerated and it was legal to pay men and women at different rates for the same job.

This became illegal in the UK in 1970.

Discrimination can be seen in many forms, such as:

- **excluding people** – *e.g., from jobs, promotion, education or other opportunities*
- **making assumptions** – *e.g., about different abilities*
- **physical assault**
- **verbal and non-verbal abuse**
- **avoiding people** – *e.g., refusing to mix with people from different races or religious backgrounds*

Prejudice

Definition:

preconceived opinion that is not based on reason or actual experience.

Prejudice is based on preconceived and unfounded opinions, where someone does not know all of the facts about a person, group or situation. It is the act of prejudging someone or something, usually judging them to be of less worth or value and it can lead to dislike, hostility or unjust behaviour. Examples of prejudice include:

- **racial prejudice (racism)** – *e.g., when individuals or groups direct prejudice, discrimination or antagonism against someone of a different race, based on the belief that their own race is superior*
- **sexual prejudice (sexism)** – *e.g., prejudice, stereotyping or discrimination, often against women, on the basis of their gender*

Leading People

Protected Characteristics

The Equality Act 2010 means that all people are now protected from discrimination due to their:

- *age* – *young (but over 18) or old are protected at work and in work training*
- *disability or impairment* – *organisations must make 'reasonable adjustments' to accommodate staff, customers and visitors with disabilities*
- *gender* – *equal pay, training and opportunity for males and females*
- *gender reassignment* – *people changing from male to female, or female to male*
- *marriage or civil partnership* – *preventing discrimination on the grounds of being married or in a civil partnership at work or in work training*
- *pregnancy or maternity (including breastfeeding)* – *only reasons of safety are not covered – e.g., equality may not be possible for pregnant women in some circumstances if the activity could harm them or the baby*
- *race* – *wherever they were born, their parents' and their own race, colour, ethnicity are protected*
- *religion or beliefs* – *any religion, lack of religion or personal belief is protected*
- *sexual orientation* – *heterosexual, gay, lesbian and bisexual people are covered*

Under the Act, these are called protected characteristics. These characteristics are protected in most circumstances and organisations need to have sound operational reasons for discrimination.

The Legal Responsibilities of the Organisation

Organisations are required to make sure that good practices, procedures and policies are in place.

Organisations will have an equality and diversity policy that sets out their procedures and guidelines on all aspects of equality and diversity. Subjects can include, for example:

- *the commitment* to *equality and diversity in the workplace*
- *equality training* – *e.g., guidelines about expected behaviour*
- *recruitment and induction* – *e.g., using accurate and lawful job descriptions, person specifications, job advertisements, interviews and induction courses*
- *training, development and promotion* – *e.g., all staff having access to the same opportunities*
- *equal pay* – *e.g., between men and women*
- *harassment and bullying policies* – *e.g., describing what they mean and how they will be dealt with working conditions and adapting working practices – e.g., making reasonable adjustments to give people with disabilities equal opportunities*
- *flexible working* – *e.g., job sharing or part-time working*
- *dealing with customers, suppliers and others* – *e.g., how to avoid discrimination and prejudice*

- *discipline and grievance procedures* – e.g., how breaches of the policy will be dealt with

Organisations have to make sure that staff, trainees and job applicants are treated equally and with respect and dignity. They have to monitor the situation often and act if there is a problem. These requirements apply to the workplace and to the recruitment process, to make sure that everything is as fair as possible.

Consequences of non-compliance

There can be many serious consequences for organisations that do not try to create and maintain an equal and diverse environment, including:

- *legal consequences*
- *extra costs*
- *a bad reputation within the community, as an employer and in the world of business*

Legal consequences

If an organisation fails to create or maintain equality and diversity at work, or if they discriminate, people can make a legal complaint. The organisation can either deal with the complaint to the satisfaction of the claimant, or the complaint can be taken to an employment tribunal. This is like a court case and is heard by a judge and can be very costly in terms of time, money, human resources and reputation.

Extra costs

Costs arise when there are complaints, especially if a case goes to a tribunal. For example, an organisation can suffer financially from:

- **legal fees**
- *lost productivity* – e.g., if the complainant is suspended on full pay
- *failure to meet deadlines and maintain quality* – e.g., if the rest of the team lose focus and reduce their output or quality during an investigation or tribunal
- *staff recruitment and retention costs increase* – e.g., if staff keep leaving

Reputation

There can also be economic, business, social and moral consequences if an organisation has a bad reputation for equality, diversity and inclusion. Customers, staff and suppliers are likely to go elsewhere, which can affect, for example, sales, recruitment of high-quality staff, the number of jobs and the overall success of the business.

All staff have a responsibility to comply with the anti-discrimination legislation, so it is important to be aware of the ideas behind it and the things we need to do to comply.

Leading People

Communicating Organisational Strategy

The following list comprises some communications approaches that will help communicate the strategy message to employees and encourage behaviours that advance your strategy and improve your results.

1. Keep the message simple
The senior executives who define organisational strategy have a deep and clear understanding of where and what they want the business to be. It is vital that this message is also understood by the employees.
The message must be presented in such a way that employees understand the strategy and can relate what they do to the success of the organisation. It should encourage them to care about what they do and the organisation.

2. View it from the customer perspective
To help employees understand the strategy, they should be encouraged to understand it from the customer perspective. This helps to bring the strategy to life. The message should be cascaded down the organisation, so the message is understood at all levels.

3. Structure the message.
Messages can become confused and misunderstood if they are not delivered clearly and in a structured manner.

The message must be sent with a clear intent. It should inspire the recipient and it should inform and educate.

Communication should meet the following criteria.

Inspire.
A message should inspire the reader to respond. It should stimulate an emotional response from the recipient which in turn will enable them to recognise the significance to the organisation and its strategy.

Educate
Once the message has inspired the reader, they will become more receptive to the message. It is at this point that the message should explain the reason why decisions have been made. It should educate and update the reader.

Reinforce
Once the reader has been informed the message should be linked back to the strategy. This gives justification for the decision and encourages buy in. The message should then be further underpinned and reinforced in all other messages which are being sent from other departments and sections across the organisation.

4. Encourage shop floor discussions
It is important that the message is heard at all levels across the organisation. After all, the strategy is defined by a few people at the top of the organisation, yet most of the people are at the bottom of the organisation. To encourage the message to spread and be

understood at shop floor level, representatives from different levels should be encouraged to work together to spread the message among their peers.

Employees will be more receptive to the message when they hear similar arguments from colleagues and these can be far more persuasive than a directive from senior management.

5. Honesty is the best policy

The message needs to be in a language the recipient can understand and be presented in a manner to which they can relate. The use of boardroom jargon will not be understood by those who need to understand the message the most.

6. Make it real

The use of real experiences will help employees to understand the message and link it directly to their role. By citing examples of good performance employees can relate to the example and adopt the behaviours themselves

7. Use innovation in delivery

Most people today have smart telephones, laptop computers, tablets etc. never has the human race been so connected and yet many organisations continue to issue staff messages in paper form as memos or corporate newsletters. Some have ventured into the world of the intranet, but ow many people go surfing on the company website? The communication needs to reflect modern society. Personal emails, text messages and social media are all channels which are widely used and therefor highly effective. Do the unexpected.

It is vital that employees are onboard with corporate strategy. They are the people who put the strategy into practice in front of the customers. They are the ones who receive the customers feedback and have first-hand experience of how effective the strategy is. They are source of feedback for the organisation to monitor and evolve its strategy.

If employees are feeding back this information, the organisation is deaf to the needs and expectations of the customer. If the employee does not understand the strategy, the organisation is blind to what is doing and if the employees are not deploying the strategy the voice of the organisation is lost. In short, the organisation becomes deaf, dumb and blind.

Key Leadership Behaviours

Great leaders may not be born that way, but the behaviours that mark the best and lead to success can be developed and refined over time. Seven of the most important:

Being grounded in ethics and integrity.

Both are hallmarks of the most successful leaders – those who are deeply committed to doing the right things for the right reasons, even when it is difficult or unpopular to stay the course. This underscores the importance of adhering to high principles and professional standards and doing so with consistency.

Building trust. This is not something that just comes automatically to a leader. It is something the most successful know they must earn. To that end, they take actions that

Leading People

gain them respect. They involve others in decisions that affect them rather than making unilateral calls. They are transparent and consistent, so subordinates know what to expect (and can count on it). Successful leaders act in a way that makes others proud to be associated with them.

Bringing others along.
It is important to help others grow and achieve and the best leaders serve as both coaches and teachers in pursuit of that goal. It takes looking at individuals and treating them as such in understanding their distinct needs, abilities and goals. At the same time, it takes working with people to help them uncover what they do best and ways to strengthen their assets.
Inspiring those around you. The most successful leaders have a vision that motivates people to follow. But it is not just the vision – for whatever future or goal or purpose – that inspires. It is expressing it with passion and energy and backing it with strong beliefs and values that count. It is a matter of exciting people to be equally engaged and uplifted at being a part of something bigger and better.

Making decisions.
Anybody can make a decision. But it takes a great leader to take on the hard decisions with authority and confidence. Success here comes from balancing emotion with reason, enlisting input from others to ensure the move forward is well-informed yet acting with authority. Even when decisions may be unpopular, a leader who honestly communicates the rationale behind them is in a better position for long-term success.

Encouraging innovation.
Innovative organisations give their people the space to stretch their creative wings. The culture to make this happen is set by leaders who encourage the art of "possibility" thinking and looking at issues from different perspectives – and who share how such practices have worked for them. The most successful leaders also understand the importance of training people in being more innovative through questioning, observing, experimenting and networking and to that end ensure that employees get work time each week to do outside-the-job creative endeavours.

Reward achievement.
No one likes to see their hard work and accomplishments go unrecognised. The best leaders make a habit of calling out people who make contributions to the organisation and they do it in in both a timely and appropriate manner. This may be expressed through a tangible reward or a public acknowledgement. Either way, it is a function of a leader who not only sets and shares specific expectations but shows what happens when individuals meet them. Most importantly, the best leaders deliver what they promise when that happens.

Leading People

Coaching

There are significant differences between training and coaching.

Generally speaking, training is driven by the trainer who controls the process and the content of the sessions. It focuses on learning and often takes place in groups. Training is useful when team leaders and managers need to teach specific skills or knowledge.

Coaching, on the other hand, is a two-way process where the team member takes an active part and the coach acts as a facilitator. It focuses on development and is usually done on a one-to-one basis, although it can be used for small groups or teams.

Benefits of Coaching

Coaching is the art of improving the performance of others. It focuses on specific skills and goals and it can have an impact on an individual's attributes, such as social interaction or confidence. The process generally takes place over a relatively short period.

Coaching enables people to become happier and more fulfilled at work. It can enhance decision-making and problem-solving skills and increase the productivity and effectiveness of individuals, teams and organisations. It increases self-awareness and makes career options and direction clearer. It can also help people to become reconciled when they have to deal with a tricky issue.

Benefits for the individual can include:

- *a focus on the individual's needs, skills and goals*
- *access to a more experienced colleague who can guide and advise*
- *a short-term commitment to improvement*
- *enhanced job satisfaction*
- *career development opportunities*

Benefits for the team and organisation can include:

- *increased productivity from the individual*
- *increased staff retention – due to increased job satisfaction and career development*
- *a good reputation as a team or employer – making it easier to attract and retain good-quality team members*
- *a smoother transition during periods of change*

Leading People

Coaching Techniques and Models

There are many different coaching techniques and a well-known one is the GROW model.

The GROW Model

One useful and well-used coaching model that looks at how to structure a coaching plan is the GROW model. It was developed in the 1980s by performance coach, John Whitmore and has been developed since then by others, including Alan Fine and Graham Alexander.

The elements of the GROW model are Goal, Reality, Options and Will:

Goal – *establishing the goal*

- *looking at the element that needs to be changed* – *e.g., behaviour, performance level or skills gap*
- *turning it into a goal that the individual wants to achieve*
- *establishing and agreeing SMART targets (Specific, Measurable, Achievable, Realistic and Timebound)*
- *ensuring that the goal fits in with the personal, team and organisational objectives*

Reality – *examining the current reality*

- *asking the team member to describe their current reality to establish and understand the starting point*
- *examining steps that have already been taken and evaluating the outcomes*
- *checking that the goal does not conflict with other current objectives and demands on the individual's time and capacity*

Options – *exploring the options*

- *discussing the different options to determine what is possible*
- *brainstorming as many options as possible*
- *looking at what else can be done to remove barriers or constraints that have prevented progress so far*
- *comparing advantages and disadvantages*
- *developing effective strategies and behaviours that achieve success*

Will – *establishing the will to go forward*

- *committing to the process* – *the individual now has a good idea about how to achieve the goals and now needs to commit to the process by working out the 'how, why, where, what and when'*
- *preparing for change* – *mentally and practically*
- *considering what may stop progress and how obstacles will be overcome*
- *looking at how to stay motivated*

- *working out how and when to review and track progress* – to encourage accountability and allow original plans to be adjusted if necessary

When using this coaching model, it is important to remember that the team leader or manager is the facilitator and not the advisor. The idea is that the manager helps the individual to find their way and select the best options but does not offer advice or direction.

Coaching techniques that support the GROW model

When developing and delivering a coaching plan, team leaders and managers need to find and use techniques that will stretch individuals and help them to fulfil their potential. They might make use of, for example:

- *psychometric and development tests* – designed to assess the individual in detail
- *one-to-one sessions and structured interviews* – useful for reviews, appraisals, counselling and feedback sessions
- *mini projects* – to develop their skills and experience in a supported environment and to try them out before 'going live'
- *role play* – an extremely useful coaching method to practise tackling problems
- *video training sessions* – can be invaluable when coaching staff for roles that require presentation skills
- *workplace training sessions, workshops and demonstrations* – especially valuable when staff need to learn or improve physical skills
- *reading and study materials* – activities that the team member can do to support the coaching sessions

ARROW

Other techniques use different headings but follow similar ideas and principles. One is known as ARROW. This includes reflection as part of the process and was developed by Matt Somers. It stands for:

Aims

Reality

Reflection

Opportunities

Ways forward

Leading People

OSCAR

The OSCAR coaching model was developed by Andrew Gilbert and Karen Whittleworth. It builds on and enhances the GROW model. The steps of the OSCAR model are:

> Outcome - *helping the team member to clarify their outcomes*
>
> Situation - *where the team member is right now*
>
> Choices and consequences - *helping the team member to generate as many choices as possible, whilst raising awareness of consequences of each choice*
>
> Action - *supporting the team member as they clarify the action they will take*
>
> Review - *an ongoing review process to help the team member stay on track*

FUEL

The FUEL coaching model is also used. The framework was developed by John Zenger and Kathleen Stinnett and stands for:

> *Frame the conversation*
>
> *Understand the current state*
>
> *Explore the desired state*
>
> *Lay out a success plan*

Coaching Skills needed by Leaders

Coaching is usually done by team leaders and line managers, although small organisations may appoint external coaches. A certain degree of impartiality is required in successful coaching and managers need to be aware of the distance and objectivity that may be required.

Individuals need structured opportunities to reflect on their practice, in one-to-one or group sessions. The flow of information and the level of confidentiality need to be established early on in the process, to establish trust.

Productive, positive and supportive working relationships are based on several important factors, including:

- **clear lines of communication** – *so that people can use and understand the career development process with confidence*
- **openness** – *so that development can be seen, measured, monitored and adjusted as required*
- **mutual trust and respect** – *where people show that they are dependable and trustworthy, especially in sensitive situations*

Leading People

These factors apply to the coaching process as well and managers need a variety of coaching skills when developing their team members.

The spectrum of coaching skills goes from 'push' to 'pull':
- *push* – *where the manager provides the solutions to the team member's problems for them – e.g., instructing, giving advice or making suggestions*
- *pull* – *where the manager helps the team member to solve the problem on their own – e.g., listening, reflecting and summarising the team member's points*

It is important to remember that coaching is focused on goals and asking questions to encourage the team member to find solutions.   The coaching skills required include:

One-to-one meeting skills
As coaching is often done on a one-to-one basis, the manager needs to be able to:

- *create an environment where the individual feels comfortable, safe and free to express themselves*
- *plan and run the sessions in an organised way* – *to focus on goals and issues*
- *pay attention to the individual* – *making sure that they feel valued*

Listening skills
As the manager is a facilitator, rather than an advisor, it is important to listen to the individual and help them to find their own way and select the best options. Managers can assist by:

- *listening with real focus*
- *listening in detail to the individual before making any judgements or forming opinions*
- *using active listening skills* – *e.g., using eye contact, nodding, making notes*
- *allowing plenty of time for answers and using silence to encourage the individual to reflect before answering*

Questioning and speaking skills
Questioning focuses the attention on the individual, encourages commitment and enables new ideas to develop. Selecting the right questioning or speaking technique for the situation can make the session more effective, for example:

short and open questions that cannot be answered with a 'yes' or 'no' – *useful when the manager wants the individual to reflect and come up with their own ideas, opinions and suggestions – e.g., "Tell me about..." or "What are your feelings about the project?"*
questions aimed at progress towards a goal – *e.g. "What do you want?", "What's important?" and "What's the first step?"*
probing questions – *to find out more detail*

Leading People

leading questions – *useful when the manager wants to guide the team member to reflect on a particular problem or aspect – e.g. "If we've covered all of your points, are we ready to agree the objectives?"*

rhetorical questions that do not need an actual answer – *useful to help the team member to reflect and maybe commit to a course of action – e.g., "Wouldn't it be great to gain the next level of the qualification?"*

allowing the team member plenty of time to think of their answers – *only offering a suggestion, prompt or guidance when the individual becomes uncomfortable*

using language that shows support and empathy for the individual – e.g., using sympathetic language if dealing with a difficult problem; setting the level of vocabulary or technical terms to suit the individual

Offering appropriate goal setting

Coaching focuses on specific goals and skills and managers need to make sure that goals:

- *are stretching but achievable and realistic*
- *are important to the team member*
- *focus on solutions*

Seeing different perspectives and possible solutions

As a facilitator, the manager needs to guide the individual to see different perspectives and consider different solutions. They can do this by:

- *exploring information* – *guiding the team member through different options and encouraging them to research the possibilities and make suggestions*
- *offering perspective* – *guiding the team member to consider different points of view, or sharing information about other similar experiences that may help to show the issue in a different light*
- *reviewing possible solutions by reflecting at logical points of the coaching plan* – *maybe using the EARS model (Empathise, Acknowledge, Reflect, Summarise)*
- *showing empathy for the individual* – *to build and maintain trust as they seek possible solutions*
- *encouraging and supporting as required* – *guiding rather than advising when possible*

Using feedback effectively

As we have already seen, feedback techniques are extremely important when reviewing progress and planning the next stage. The manager needs to handle positive and negative feedback in a constructive and useful way so that the individual can benefit from the experience.

Leading People

Coaching to Improve Performance

By following a structured approach that has strategies to measure progress, we can make sure that coaching is used effectively to improve performance in individuals. As with training, there is little point in investing considerable resources in coaching if there is no benefit – to the individual, the team or the organisation. It is an expensive and time-consuming process and it needs to be used wisely.

There are a few steps to follow when using coaching to improve the performance in the workplace. We need to:

- *identify coaching needs*
- *create a coaching plan*
- *give feedback*
- *evaluate the effectiveness of the coaching*

Identifying coaching needs
Coaching can be needed for a variety of reasons, for example:

- *to help individuals reach higher levels of performance* – e.g., to improve decision-making skills
- *to help to increase job satisfaction and personal growth* – e.g., by giving support during implementation of delegation to increase motivation
- *to address shortcomings* – e.g., poor performance or under-confidence
- *as part of continuous professional development (CPD)*
- *to assist with challenges posed by organisational change* – e.g., possible redundancy or changes to the organisational structure
- *to support an individual who has challenges due to personal issues* – e.g., getting back to work after a long and serious illness

A manager can identify needs in several ways when:

- *discussions take place during career development appraisals*
- *an individual asks for support*
- *they become aware of poor performance*
- *the organisation announces plans that will affect the workforce*

Creating a coaching plan
Not surprisingly, we often think of sport when we think about coaching sessions. The steps for sports coaching are virtually the same as with business coaching. When developing a coaching plan, the manager/coach needs to help the individual to:

- *analyse the existing situation*
- *explore the options*

Leading People

- *take action to implement the learning*
- *generate and use effective feedback*

As for many other management functions, coaching requires us to look at where we are now, work out where we need to be, then work out how to get there.

When developing a coaching plan, it is important to remember that the manager is the facilitator helping the individual to find their way and select the best options.

Following the GROW model mentioned earlier is a very good way of structuring a coaching plan for an individual as it focuses the planning on the key areas.

The coaching plan needs all four aspects for it to be successful. The manager needs to work with the individual to help them to:

- **establish their goals** – *e.g., to be ready for promotion within six months*
- **define the reality of their current skills, knowledge, experience and attributes** – *e.g., using a skills audit or SWOT analysis*
- **work out their best options** – *e.g., courses, shadowing, volunteer work or mini projects*
- **check that they really do want to make the commitment** – *e.g., to doing evening classes and homework for 15 hours a week for 4–6 months*

When planning coaching sessions, managers need to think in detail about:

- **the meeting or learning environment, resources and timing** – *e.g., booking a private room at a time of day that fits in with work commitments, arranging equipment and other resources*
- **setting and agreeing objectives** – *e.g., discussing and agreeing training and resources to address skills gaps, setting SMART targets*
- **learning activities** – *e.g., arranging workbooks, courses, workshops or observations of experienced colleagues at work*
- **reviewing the learning** – *e.g., checking progress against targets*
- **further action planning** – *e.g., arranging future coaching sessions, resources, courses and progress reviews*

Giving feedback

Feedback is a very useful and important part of the coaching process. It is used to:

review progress, check understanding and evaluate learning – *maybe against SMART targets or course materials*
enable the individual to report and evaluate their own progress towards the goals – *their personal input can be as valuable as progress measured objectively against a target*
form the basis for planning the next stages of the coaching plan – *the manager and individual can identify strengths and weaknesses of the development and learning activities and adjust them if necessary*

Leading People

reinforce positive behaviours – *praising the individual for success and good progress is very empowering and good for morale*

support best practice – *if an individual is on track, they need to know this so that they can maintain or continue to improve standards*

challenge problems constructively – *if there are shortcomings, tactful and constructive criticism can be given by the manager as part of the coaching plan*

check that the individual is happy with progress and the coaching plan – *and that all bases have been covered*

Evaluating Coaching

To check the effectiveness of coaching, it is necessary to evaluate it. This is not always straightforward and it can be hard to quantify evidence of the organisation's return on investment (ROI).

When the coaching takes place for positive reasons, such as career development, it can be evaluated by reviewing the learning and development that has taken place or is likely to take place.

Learning can be reviewed in several ways, including, for example:

- *discussions about the learning that has taken place*
- *active listening by the manager along with good questioning techniques to establish the level of understanding of the new material*
- *questionnaires, quizzes, tests and examinations to measure retention of information*
- *trial activities in the workplace* – *to test the learning under supervision*
- *feedback forms* – *completed by the team member and others*
- *formal or informal discussions with other managers and supervisors about progress*
- *checking the individual's performance regularly to see if the learning has been put into practice*

Development can be evaluated by, for example:

- *discussions and appraisals*
- *seeing how individuals have been promoted, or improved their chances of promotion*
- *observing the improvement and development of attributes in action* – *e.g., confidence or decision-making skills*
- *measuring better productivity and observing better interaction* – *e.g., team members responding positively to a team leader's improvement in motivation skills*

When coaching has been provided to address issues of poor performance, this can be evaluated by using the performance indicators that triggered and identified the original need for it – e.g., productivity records, sales figures or customer feedback. When the coaching

Leading People

takes place for negative reasons, such as redundancy, or as a result of having to overcome problems, the effectiveness can be harder to evaluate and might be reviewed by, for example:

- *monitoring levels of sickness and absenteeism*
- *studying feedback from specialist retirement and redundancy coaches*
- *discussions with the individuals who are being coached* – e.g., to see if the plan is working to get the person who had cancer to return to full employment and productivity; to ask if the coaching is helping them to prepare for changes of location, job and so on
- *feedback forms and questionnaires*
- *formal or informal discussions with the people involved with the process of change management for the organisation*
- *discussions with other agencies involved with the individuals* – e.g., with Jobcentre services about how coaching is helping to prepare employees to move on

Effectiveness of coaching generally needs to be measured against the objectives that formed part of the plan and coaching sessions. The objectives might have been set out as SMART targets or SWOT analyses, for instance and it will be possible to measure progress and identify ongoing gaps that may need to be addressed in other ways. Coaching is usually intensive and short term, so other forms of support may need to be introduced to support it.

Chapter 5: Managing People

Managing People

Managing People

Management can be defined as:

> *"the achievement of an organisation's objectives through people and other resources"*

Put simply, management is the achievement of an organisation's objectives through people and other resources. Managers use their time, energy and expertise to achieve the best return from the organisation's resources – people, materials and a budget.

Managing a High-Performing Team

A "high-performing work team" refers to a group of individuals with specialised expertise and complementary skills who collaborate, innovate and produce consistently superior results. The group relentlessly pursues excellence through shared goals, shared leadership, collaboration, open communication, clear role expectations and group operating rules, early conflict resolution and a strong sense of accountability and trust among its members.

The ability to manage teams, which are able to communicate effectively and overcome barriers to achievement, is a critical skill for any manager. High performing teams are created in an environment where there is a collective understanding of values, goals and objectives.

Business Directory defines a team as:

> *"A group of people with a full set of complementary skills required to complete a task, job, or project. Team members operate with a high degree of interdependence, share authority and responsibility for self-management, are accountable for the collective performance and work toward a common goal and shared rewards. A team becomes more than just a collection of people when a strong sense of mutual commitment creates synergy, thus generating performance greater than the sum of the performance of its individual members"*

The purpose of creating teams is to provide a framework that will increase the ability of employees to participate in planning, problem-solving and decision-making to better serve customers.

Increased participation promotes:

- *A better understanding of decisions*
- *More support for and participation in implementation plans*
- *Increased contribution to problem-solving and decision making*
- *More ownership of decisions, processes and changes*

Managing People

- *More ability and willingness to participate in performance evaluation and improvement*

For a team to fulfil its role of improving organisational effectiveness, it is vital that the team develops into a working unit which is focused on their goal, mission, or reason for existing.

The Differences between People Management and Team Management

There are a number of differences between people management and team management.

People Management refers to a manager's role when working with individuals on their team. This involves any management activities that focus on the individual team member, for example:

- *inspiring and motivating* – e.g., identifying and focusing on an individual's motivating factors
- *allocating tasks* – e.g., matching activities to the individual's strengths and abilities
- *monitoring and managing individual performance* – e.g., informal chats in the work area or formal feedback in annual appraisals
- *training, coaching and career development* – e.g., arranging training courses or coaching sessions to improve particular skills
- *supporting team members* – e.g., during periods of illness or change

Team management refers to the manager's role when coordinating a group of individuals to perform tasks as a team. This involves management activities that focus on the group and its activities, for example:

- *promoting teamwork and cooperation* – e.g., with team-building exercises
- *setting and agreeing shared objectives* – e.g., engaging all team members in the process of agreeing deadlines
- *motivating the team to achieve objectives* – e.g., to meet deadlines and quality standards
- *allocating, directing and coordinating work activities* – e.g., allocating human and physical resources to support tasks, objectives and deadlines
- *appraising performance for the team as a whole* – e.g., tracking sales figures for the team
- *dealing with conflict and problems within the team* – e.g., intervening and communicating with team members who disagree strongly about work allocation

The distinction is important as managers need to balance the requirements of individual people with the requirements of the team. There are many different roles that individuals bring to a team and many different types of teams, so there are many variables that managers need to consider when planning and performing work functions.

Managing People

Individual Roles in Teams

Individuals bring a wide range of personal skills, preferences and attributes to the workplace. Some people like to take risks and work on unplanned tasks, whereas others function best when work is completely organised and predictable. Team members need to play a variety of roles and bring a balance of personal skills, preferences and attributes for a team to function effectively.

The different roles that people play within a team were identified by Dr Meredith Belbin in the 1970's. During the research, Belbin discovered that a team's success was dependent on behaviour and how team members relate to each other in working towards a common objective.

How team roles can improve team performance

When a team is performing at its best, you will usually find that each team member has clear responsibilities. Just as importantly, you will see that every role needed to achieve the team's goal is being performed fully and well.

Often, despite clear roles and responsibilities, a team will fall short of its full potential. How often does this happen in the teams you work with? Perhaps some team members do not complete what you expect them to do. Perhaps others are not quite flexible enough, so things "fall between the cracks." Maybe someone who is valued for their expert input fails to see the wider picture and so misses out tasks or steps that others would expect. Or perhaps one team member becomes frustrated because he or she disagrees with the approach of another team member.

Dr Meredith Belbin studied teamwork for many years and he famously observed that people in teams tend to assume different "team roles." He defined a team role as "a tendency to behave, contribute and interrelate with others in a particular way" and named nine such team roles that underlie team success.

Creating More Balanced Teams

Belbin suggests that, by understanding your role within a particular team, you can develop your strengths and manage your weaknesses as a team member and so improve how you contribute to the team.

Teams can become unbalanced if all team members have similar styles of behaviour or team roles. If team members have similar weaknesses, the team as a whole may tend to have that weakness. If team members have similar team-work strengths, they may tend to compete (rather than cooperate) for the team tasks and responsibilities that best suit their natural styles.

Belbin's theory classifies the roles people play in a team as:

- *Chair/coordinator* – able to get others working to a shared aim; confident, mature; good at making decisions and delegating. They tend to have a dominant personality and often extrovert.

Managing People

The coordinator clarifies group objectives, sets the agenda, establishes priorities, selects problems, sums up and is decisive, but does not dominate discussions.

Advantages	Disadvantages
Mature	Can be seen as manipulative
Good chairperson	
Good at delegating	
Clarifies goals and objectives	
Often confident	
Make decisions	

- *Shaper* – motivated, energetic, assertive and competitive; thrives under pressure; achievement-driven, keeping the team focused. They are normally challenging people with a dominant personality.
  - *The shaper gives shape and energy to the team effort. They can 'steamroller' the team but can get results.*

Advantages	Disadvantages
Thrives on pressure	Can be easily wound up
Driven to overcome obstacles	Can accidentally offend people
Challenging	
Often courageous	

- *Innovator/plant* – innovative, inventive, creative, original, imaginative, unorthodox. They have good problem-solving skills in a team.
  - *The innovator/plant is the source of original ideas, suggestions and proposals.*

Advantages	Disadvantages
Imaginative	Sometimes does not communicate effectively
Creative	Can ignore issues that are too small to them, but significant to others
Good at solving challenging problems	
Often unorthodox	

- *Monitor evaluator* – serious, prudent, critical thinker, analytical, impartial and even-tempered. They are normally logical thinkers and are not passionate about the plans, making them impartial in decision making.
  - *The monitor evaluator contributes a measured and dispassionate analysis and, through objectivity, stops the team committing itself to a misguided task.*

Managing People

Advantages	Disadvantages
Strategic	Sometimes lacks drive to get things done
Can see different viewpoints	Not always inspirational to others
Good at judging	

- *Implementer/company worker* – systematic, loyal, structured, reliable, dependable, practical, disciplined, efficient; uses common sense but can be inflexible about change. They tend to be social individuals, which help to gain information from others.
  - *The implementer turns decisions and strategies into defined and manageable tasks, sorting out objectives and pursuing them logically.*

Advantages	Disadvantages
Highly disciplined	Can be inflexible
Reliable	Once heading in one direction, can be slow to respond to new options
Efficient	
Turns ideas into reality	

- *Resource investigator* – good communicator, enthusiastic, networker, outgoing, affable, seeks and finds options, negotiator. They tend to be social individuals, which help to gain information from others.
  - *The resource investigator goes outside the team to bring back ideas, information and developments. This person is the team's salesperson, diplomat, liaison officer and explorer.*

Advantages	Disadvantages
Outgoing	Might be over-optimistic
Enthusiastic	Not always inspirational to others
Good at judging	Can lose interest once the initial enthusiasm has passed
Explores opportunities	
Develops contacts	

- *Team worker* – supportive, sociable, flexible, adaptable, perceptive, listener, calming influence, mediator, dislikes confrontation, hard working. They use their conflict management skills to defuse potential conflict and keep a happy working relationship.
  - *The team worker operates against division and disruption in the team, maintaining harmony, particularly in times of stress and pressure.*

Advantages	Disadvantages
Mild mannered	Can be indecisive in crunch situations
Perceptive of others	Can struggle when faced with demanding deadlines
Good listener	
Good at spotting and then reducing team friction	
Co-operative	

- **Completer finisher** – attention to detail, accurate, high standards, quality orientated; delivers to schedule and specification; good at finding errors. The completer finisher is usually a perfectionist who checks the product at the end for quality. They scrutinise work for errors and maintain a high-quality control check.
  - *The completer finisher maintains a permanent sense of urgency with relentless follow-through and attention to detail.*

Advantages	Disadvantages
Methodical	Anxious
Conscientious	Inclined to worry
Seeks mistakes and corrects them	Does not like to delegate, especially to people not like themselves
Delivers on time	

- **Specialist** – technical expert, highly focused capability and knowledge, driven by professional standards and dedication to personal subject area. They are the technical specialist with the technical knowledge to deal with queries.
  - *This ninth role was added later to the original 8 team roles for an effective team. This role is the person with in-depth knowledge of the subject area.*

Advantages	Disadvantages
Dedicated	Contributes on a narrow front
Has specialist knowledge	Dwells on technical details, sometimes losing sight of bigger picture

These classifications can help managers to work out who might be best for each activity or task when managing the team as a whole. For example, managers could allocate:

Team Role		Contribution	Allowable Weaknesses
Plant		Creative, imaginative, free-thinking. Generates ideas and solves difficult problems.	Ignores incidentals. Too preoccupied to communicate effectively.
Resource Investigator		Outgoing, enthusiastic, communicative. Explores opportunities and develops contacts.	Over-optimistic. Loses interest once initial enthusiasm has passed.
Co-ordinator		Mature, confident, identifies talent. Clarifies goals. Delegates effectively.	Can be seen as manipulative. Offloads own share of the work.
Shaper		Challenging, dynamic, thrives on pressure. Has the drive and courage to overcome obstacles.	Prone to provocation. Offends people's feelings.
Monitor Evaluator		Sober, strategic and discerning. Sees all options and judges accurately.	Lacks drive and ability to inspire others. Can be overly critical.
Teamworker		Co-operative, perceptive and diplomatic. Listens and averts friction.	Indecisive in crunch situations. Avoids confrontation.
Implementer		Practical, reliable, efficient. Turns ideas into actions and organises work that needs to be done.	Somewhat inflexible. Slow to respond to new possibilities.
Completer Finisher		Painstaking, conscientious, anxious. Searches out errors. Polishes and perfects.	Inclined to worry unduly. Reluctant to delegate.
Specialist		Single-minded, self-starting, dedicated. Provides knowledge and skills in rare supply.	Contributes only on a narrow front. Dwells on technicalities.

- *Research activities to team members who are classified as Resource investigator, Specialist or Innovator/plant*
- *Repetitive, everyday activities to members who are considered to be classified as Team worker, Implementer/company worker or Completer finisher*
- *Quality control tasks to members who are Completer finishers or Specialists*
- *Liaison and coordinating tasks to people who are seen as Resource investigators*

Managers use team role theory to help create balanced teams. If team members have similar styles of behaviour, they can have similar weaknesses that weaken the team as a whole. If members have similar strengths, they might compete rather than cooperate, unbalance the team and affect productivity.

Managing People

Creating a Team

When recruited or promoted into a leadership role it is likely you a team will be inherited which has been created by someone else. An effective leader will need to quickly adapt their ideas and plans to those of the team in order to become effective quickly as changing the skills, ideas and knowledge of the team will take much longer. When working on special projects, the opportunity to create a team from scratch sometimes arises and when it does it is important to consider the following steps.

1. **Identify the task**
   If the task is unclear, the knowledge and skills needed by team members will be vague and undefined. The temptation will be to recruit people with equally vague and varied skills which will result in a team of nice people, but none of whom have the specific skills to deliver on the task. It is essential to know in detail, what the task involves so specialists can be recruited to deliver the best possible results.

2. **Define the skills**
   Both hard and soft skills needed by team members should be defined. They may be the best programmer in the word, but if they don't have the skills to communicate and interact with customers, peers and senior management – how do they contribute to the team? Alternatively, an intermediary who has profound skills in communication could be hired to operate as the interface between the programmer and others

3. **Identify the individual**
   A team is made up of individuals who complement each other. Recruiting the wrong person could have a catastrophic effect on the team. When creating a team internally the personalities and skills of those being recruited is known. Individuls who may lack the skills or personality to be an effective team member can be avoided. The downside is that it may be difficult to fix any known weakness, and this may also weaken the team. Internal politics could also lead to conflict which will have a negative effect on the team.

   When recruiting outside the organisation care must also be taken to ensure the ideal candidate is appointed. Care should be taken to ensure the new employee is as close a fit as possible. These decisions also come at a cost. Recruiting the best candidate will inevitably incur a high salary and care should be taken to ensure the whole budget is committed to one individual leaving little money for the rest of the team.

4. **Recruit in order**
   There may be a temptation to get the routine appointments out of the way first and concentrate on the more important roles later – don't!

   Start with the most senior person and work down through the rest of the team members. The most senior person has a pivotal role and will also expect to have some input into those they will be working with. It is vital that the team is able to work together effectively from day one, rather than losing time whilst relationships are being built and maybe broken.

Managing People

5. **Say it as it is**

    The temptation is to paint a very rosy picture of the organisation, the team, the project, etc. This is good from a recruitment point of view as it will attract and encourage people to accept the offer of a role with the organisation, but what happens when the realities become apparent? It is important to honest ad frank in discussions with prospective employees. It is important that they are not under any illusion about the challenges, problems and irritations they may face as a member of the team. If they are fully aware of what to expect, it will not be a surprise when it happens.

6. **A great team still needs leading**

    Once the team is formed, it still has to be led and managed. Great teams need a great leader. A great deal of work will still be required to develop the team and the leader must be seen to do more than everyone else.

    A team which has been put together with care will have a huge advantage of one which has been formed without care or thought. It gives the team a head start and gives its leader fewer headaches!

Approaches to People Management

Managers need to consider the different aspects of people management when developing their approach, to get the best out of each individual. They need to analyse each team member's skills, knowledge, experience and attributes, their suitability and availability for the task and their career development needs, to find the best approaches for each individual when:

- *inspiring and motivating team members*
- *planning and allocating tasks*
- *monitoring and managing performance*
- *training, coaching and supporting career development*
- *supporting team members*

Preparing a SWOT analysis is a useful tool when looking at skills and development needs:

The following questions will help to develop a SWOT which will help make those challenging decisions:

Managing People

S	Strengths	What are my strengths? What am I good at already? What qualifications do I have? What have I achieved already? What do people praise? When do I get positive feedback?
W	Weaknesses	What areas of weakness do I have? What mistakes did I make, or nearly make? What are the gaps in my skills, knowledge, understanding and experience?
O	Opportunities for improvement	How can I improve? What training can I do to improve? What support do I need? Which work opportunities can I find that will help me to develop?
T	Threats to such progress	What might stop me? Finance? Time? Support from others? Lack of information? What can I do to minimise these potential problems?

Inspiring and motivating team members

Successful motivational factors that work for individuals include, for example:

- *job enjoyment and interesting work* – *an important factor for many workers*
- *a good basic salary and pension plan* – *stability and long-term security are valued highly*
- *good working relationships* – *with fellow team members, managers and other colleagues*
- *full appreciation and recognition* – *from a simple thank you to a formal scheme that rewards innovation and commitment*
- *fair treatment* – *clear command structures and procedures with regular feedback and support, especially in times of difficulty*
- *higher levels of autonomy* – *the ability to take responsibility and make decisions*
- *the opportunity to innovate* – *having ideas and suggestions taken seriously*
- *financial performance bonus* – *not as attractive and important as we would expect*

Research shows that fear and money are not good motivational factors. They might work in the short term, but the same repeated criticism or threat can have a negative impact quite quickly. If people are unhappy in their work, extra money will soon become less attractive – especially if the individual can move to another employer or department where they will enjoy interesting work in a positive working environment.

Managers need to identify the appropriate motivational factors for team members so that they can target their approach to inspire and motivate each individual.

Planning and allocating tasks

If managers are not familiar with each team member's skills, knowledge and experience, they might need to do a skills audit. This could be in the form of a questionnaire or an informal

Managing People

interview, to assess the capacity and capabilities of each person before tasks are planned and allocated.

Work needs to be allocated on a fair basis and managers need to consider, for example:

- *each individual's skills, knowledge and experience* – *e.g., to match tasks to the individual's skills and capabilities as far as possible*
- *each team member's role and attributes* – *e.g., to allocate tasks and responsibilities that suit their role as defined by Belbin, if possible*
- *the apportionment of the tasks* – *e.g., how the tasks are shared between different team members*
- *the volume of work* – *e.g., the amount that each individual needs to do*
- *the difficulty of each task* – *e.g., allocating complex and demanding tasks to team members with appropriate skills, attributes and capabilities*
- *setting stretching tasks when appropriate* – *e.g., when team members want to be challenged and develop their career and skills*

To get the best out of team members, managers need to tailor their approach to planning and allocating tasks and responsibilities to suit each individual, where possible. Even if short-term plans cannot satisfy individual needs and preferences, long-term plans and work allocations can reflect the team member's overall career development requirements.

Monitoring and managing performance

Managers and team leaders monitor and manage performance of team members in a variety of ways that may include, for example:

- *agreeing and setting individual targets* – *e.g., for output, quality, attendance or to improve skills*
- *monitoring the flow and quality of work* – *e.g., checking progress against targets or key performance indicators (KPIs)*
- *recognising and acknowledging good performance* – *e.g., with praise or a bonus*
- *taking action to improve weaker areas* – *e.g., increasing training or supervision*

Training, coaching and supporting career development

Approaches to career development need to focus on the individual and be based on, for example:

- *identifying training needs for individuals* – *e.g., performing a training needs analysis (TNA); discussing the individual's career options, plans and ambitions*
- *basing activities on preferred learning styles* – *e.g., choosing activities that suit the individual, where possible*

Managing People

- *organising training and development activities* – *e.g., courses, shadowing colleagues, working on different teams or performing new tasks under supervision*
- *evaluating effectiveness* – *e.g., of training and development activities*
- *maintaining training records* – *e.g., as part of the formal appraisal process*

Supporting team members

Part of a manager's role is to support their team members. They may need help with, for example:

- *operational queries and problems* – *e.g., how to complete a task or solve a problem, their standard of work*
- *their task allocation* – *e.g., if their tasks are too difficult or not challenging enough*
- *personal and health problems* – *e.g., issues that affect productivity and well-being*
- *conflicts in the workplace* – *e.g., problems with shift changes; bullying or harassment*

By looking at each team member as an individual, the manager or team leader can assist in their day-to-day work and long-term development, thereby improving the overall welfare and productivity of their team.

High-Performing Teams

A high-performing team is a group of people who work together for a common goal and are able to achieve extraordinary results. High performance teams are created on a solid foundation of:

- *building productive communication*
- *creating innovative solutions*
- *delivering great performance*

In other words, high performing teams are equipped with a high-performance, team culture.

Building a High-Performing Team

Teams do not simply happen. Indeed, teams are much more than groups of people. They occur when there are common goals, values and behaviours. Every leader/manager has a part to play in building teams.

These are key factors in team development:

Managing People

1. Model Excellence

You have probably heard the phrase: Behaviour breeds behaviour. This saying is illustrated by a simple model called the Betari Box.

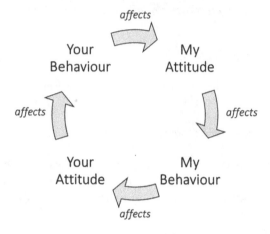

The Betari Box helps us to understand how our attitudes and behaviours directly affect the attitudes and behaviours of others.

When a team or individual is stuck in a cycle — mistrust, not taking responsibility, positive attitude and so on — it is up to the team leader to break the cycle and change attitudes.

Inevitably this has a positive impact on those around us. When we take charge and change our behaviour our team is more likely to follow our lead.

2. Open and Honest Communication

A hallmark of the high-performing team is a high level of open, honest, robust and transparent communication.

High performance teams increase trust by building a culture of partnership and shared values. This starts with open and honest communication.

When honesty and transparency are lacking there can be no trust.

Without trust teams fail to solve problems or make decisions. Without trust teams are crippled by conflict.

3. A Supportive Environment

High Performing team meets regularly to discuss progress, concerns and ideas for improvement.

Managing People

Likewise, the team leader meets the individual to talk about their objectives, development and performance. The high-performance team supports its members by:

- *accepting difference and diversity*
- *encouraging each other's strengths*
- *supporting its members at times of personal or professional challenge*

4. Understand the Expertise
Know your team's strengths and talents.

Motivation and positive attitude is more valuable to high performance teams than experience and negative character. The high-performing team motivates and coaches the individual. It helps and develops the less experience colleague. Moreover, the team listens to everyone and creates a sense of belonging. The team understands what each player has to offer and how they help achieve shared business objectives.

5. Celebrate Success
Share good news. Make noise about successes. Let everyone know when the team or a team member does something exceptional.

Finally, … encourage extracurricular activities for team members to forge close-knit relationships and build high levels of mutual trust and friendship

Characteristics of a High Performing Team

When identifying what makes a high performing team, it is important to recognise that there is far more to it, than simply achieving the KPIs' which have been set.

As well as having a clear vision and direction, there are many things that define a high performing team including:

Goal sharing
Where team members may have individual targets and KPIs, these goals are still shared – they understand the purpose of their team and its vision and what they need to do to work towards achieving it. The team know what their objectives are and are committed towards attaining them.

> *A high performing team plays together and wins – or loses - together.*

Able to communicate
The team is able to discuss and share ideas, feedback on their performance and build relationships with one another that establish a sense of social community.

Cohesive

The team members work together towards a common goal, supporting one another in pursuit of
success.

Participative

Each member of the team is able to contribute and has a sense of place within the team. Roles within the team may often be shared and occasionally members of the team may take the lead.

Problem solving

The team is able to respond to challenges positively and identify suitable solutions.

Cross-functional

The team does not work in isolation and are able to build working relations with other teams and departments that benefit the service they provide.

Autonomous

Team members feel empowered and able to take responsibility. They are able to act and make
decisions without the involvement of a leader when necessary.

Able to replicate success

The team performs consistently and is able to take on new challenges. It is able to learn from its successes as well as its failures in pursuit of continuous improvement.

Motivating a Team

People are the primary and most important resource of every organisation. To achieve great results, a leader needs to have a motivation strategy to create and maintain the spirit of enthusiasm among employees. Below are some effective ways to motivate staff and ensure the continuous growth of the team.

Share the organisational vision with each member

If everyone is aware of the collective vision, which will lead to prosperity and success of each team member, motivation and enthusiasm become the indivisible parts of all activities. Make sure that staff continuously concentrate on the glory of reaching that powerful vision.

Communicate with staff

You cannot learn about ideas, attitude or concerns of team members without constant communication. Use every opportunity to interact with them and you will discover hundreds of new ways of organising your activities more successfully.

Managing People

Make people feel appreciated
One of the greatest needs of an individual is the need to be appreciated. Very often appreciation is a greater reward than money. Show your sincere gratitude for the unique contribution everyone makes to the organisation.

Support new ideas
Each team member will feel empowered by the opportunity to not only implement day to day tasks, but also to suggest new ideas and make them a reality. Give people a chance to take initiative and you will be amazed by their ability to create brilliant ideas.

Give challenging tasks
People cannot grow if they are constantly doing what they have always done. Let them develop new skills by giving challenging tasks. At the same time make sure the tasks are reachable and in the frames of the person's interests.

Encourage Creativity
Supervising does not mean controlling each and every step. It means making sure that all the organisational activities are being implemented at the highest level. Give people the freedom to find their own unique ways of solving issues. Challenge them to think out of the box.

Give them the opportunity to grow
If people know that everything is going to be the same way all the time, they will definitely lose the motivation to put their maximum efforts in work. They should be sure that the devotion and hard work will lead to new personal and professional achievements.

Empower each individual
Very often people need just a little encouragement to believe in themselves and to realise that they have a greater potential within. Always show your confidence in the unique abilities and potential of your team members.

Give as much support as you can
Even if people in your organisation are self-disciplined and creative enough for finding solutions to various problems, they will still need your guidance. Support them as much as you can and they will be inspired to do the same for you and for the organisation.

Manage them individually
Every person has their strengths and weaknesses. Someone may be amazing at public speaking, while the other one has great writing skills. Give people a chance to operate in the frames of their strengths and they will be more confident and motivated in their activities.

Do not let them become bored
If you want your team to be enthusiastic and productive you must avoid routine. Routine is the enthusiasm killer. Let people explore and discover. Make the work as interesting and engaging as you can.

Managing People

Create healthy competition

For this purpose, you can effectively use the famous reward system. People contribute their efforts and ideas to the maximum when they know that outstanding excellence will lead to rewards. Just make sure that the reward system is absolutely transparent to everyone.

Celebrate each success

Even the smallest achievements are worth being celebrated. The road to success consists of thousand small steps. Glorify each and every goal achieved. Show to your team that all of you made one more important step forward.

Make sure there is a good working environment

Research showed that environment is more important to employees than money. This is a great chance for you to create extra motivation for your staff by making the work environment a beautiful place to work, rest and have fun at the same time.

Create and maintain a team spirit

A team is like a family, where mutual support and trust are the most important values. Organise team activities both during working time and after. You will have the half of success by creating and maintaining a powerful team spirit at the workplace.

Managing People

Types of Teams

In addition to the different types of people on a team, there are many ways of categorising types of teams. Types can include, for example:

management	temporary
operational	contract or project teams
support	virtual
functional	matrix
cross-functional	self-managed

Management teams
The leaders and managers from different departments work together to make strategic decisions for the whole organisation – e.g., long-term business development plans.

Operational teams
These teams perform ongoing activities to provide goods and service. They have well-defined roles and responsibilities – e.g., to provide a full call centre service to bank customers. Very often, the team members work in the same location, although they can be split into sub-teams if they work in several locations.

Support teams
These teams perform tasks that enable other teams to do their jobs - e.g., the physiotherapy team that supports a football team; a helpline team that deals with IT problems for the whole company.

Functional teams
These people work together and carry out the same or similar functions. The structure is relatively rigid and some projects need to be passed from one functional team to another – e.g., the marketing team has an idea that it passes to the research and development team for design and trial manufacture.

Cross-functional teams
Workers from different functions or specialities work together. These teams can be put together to work on a task, problem or project that needs a mix of specialists from different functions.

Temporary teams
These are teams that are brought together for a specific task or project – e.g., for the Olympic and Paralympic Games in London in 2012. Temporary teams are also put together to cover a limited period of abnormal activity – e.g., by delivery companies to cover the Christmas rush only.

Contract or project teams
Contract teams can be brought in from outside the organisation to perform project work and the responsibility lies with the project manager. Strong relationships between the contract team and the client are extremely important. These teams are becoming more

common – e.g., specialist consultants working with a bank to update and review its IT systems.

Virtual teams
Virtual team members can do the same work but be separated by time – e.g., working different shifts or in different time zones. They can also be separated by distance – e.g., staff working at different regional centres for the same company. There can also be cultural differences that separate people even though they are united by who they work for – e.g., people from different countries working together by using interpreters.

Matrix structures in teams
Matrix structures are often found in project teams. Individual staff report to different managers for different aspects of their work – e.g., an events team leader reports to the customer service manager when dealing with the public at an event and the marketing manager for issues concerning the sponsors. This can be confusing and good communication is critical. The team leader needs to know which manager is their main line manager, dealing with appraisals, training, career development and routine tasks.

Self-managed teams
Members take collective responsibility for ensuring that the team operates effectively to meet targets. Once the levels of responsibility and limits of authority have been established, the team can decide how the work is to be done, discuss performance issues, solve problems etc.

Teams can be classified using more than one heading – e.g., a team can be a cross-functional, virtual, project team for the duration of a collaborative, international project.

Developing Teams

Tuckman's four-stage model
Psychologist Bruce Tuckman first came up with the memorable phrase "forming, storming, norming and performing" in his 1965 article, "Developmental Sequence in Small Groups." He used it to describe the path that most teams follow on their way to high performance. Later, he added a fifth stage, "adjourning" (which is sometimes known as "mourning").

Forming a team takes time and members often go through recognisable stages as they change from being a collection of strangers to a united group with common goals. Bruce Tuckman's Forming, Storming, Norming and Performing model describes these stages. When you understand it, you can help your new team become effective more quickly.

Look at each stage in more detail.

Managing People

Forming

In this stage, most team members are positive and polite. Some are anxious, as they have not fully understood what work the team will do. Others are simply excited about the task ahead.

As leader, you play a dominant role at this stage, because team members' roles and responsibilities are not clear.

This stage can last for some time, as people start to work together and as they try to get to know their new colleagues.

Storming

Next, the team moves into the storming phase, where people start to push against the boundaries established in the forming stage. This is the stage where many teams fail.

Storming often starts where there is a conflict between team members' natural working styles. People may work in different ways for all sorts of reasons but, if differing working styles cause unforeseen problems, they may become frustrated.

Storming can also happen in other situations. For example, team members may challenge your authority, or jockey for position as their roles are clarified. Or, if you have not defined clearly how the team will work, people may feel overwhelmed by their workload, or they could be uncomfortable with the approach you are using.

Some may question the worth of the team's goal and they may resist taking on tasks.

Team members who stick with the task at hand may experience stress, particularly as they do not have the support of established processes or strong relationships with their colleagues.

Norming

Gradually, the team moves into the norming stage. This is when people start to resolve their differences, appreciate colleagues' strengths and respect your authority as a leader.

Once team members know one another better, they may socialise together and they are able to ask one another for help and provide constructive feedback. People develop a stronger commitment to the team goal and you start to see good progress towards it.

There is often a prolonged overlap between storming and norming, because, as new tasks come up, the team may lapse back into behaviour from the storming stage.

Performing

The team reaches the performing stage, when hard work leads, without friction, to the achievement of the team's goal. The structures and processes that you have set up support this well.

As leader, you can delegate much of your work and you can concentrate on developing team members.

Managing People

It feels easy to be part of the team at this stage and people who join or leave will not disrupt performance.

Adjourning
Many teams will reach this stage eventually. For example, project teams exist for only a fixed period and even permanent teams may be disbanded through organisational restructuring. Team members who like routine, or who have developed close working relationships with colleagues, may find this stage difficult, particularly if their future now looks uncertain.

Typical behaviour can be positive or negative, for example: being happy that the team is moving on to a new project together; being pleased with success and relieved that goals have been achieved; feeling sad about the team being broken up; feeling uncertain and worried about what will happen next. Team leaders and members need to conduct assessments and reviews about the previous project, recognise contributions and plan for new temporary or permanent roles.

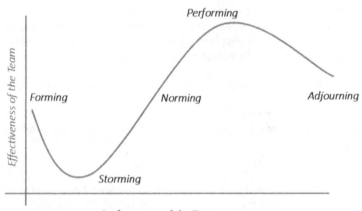

The ways in which the team develops have an effect on the dynamics of the team. The relationships change and develop within the group as the team matures and goes through the various processes identified by Tuckman.

People and Team Management Models

There are a number of management theories and models available when considering team management and an even larger number of authors who have written their interpretation of these theories.

Elton Mayo, Robert Blake, Jane Mouton and Henry Mintzberg, to name but a few. The recognised management theories include:

Managing People

- *The contingency theory* - *which identifies that managers make decisions based on the here and now, the current situation rather than the bigger picture.*
- *The systems theory* - *which recognises that different systems or teams have an impact on other systems. By utilising this model, managers can coordinate to ensure work is collective rather than being isolated.*
- *The chaos theory* - *which recognises that change is constant and not everything can be controlled - managers adapt and change as required.*

Elton Mayo published his perception that social interaction with workers is important and that people work well if they feel valued, whether this be in the form of consultation about the environment or a sound appreciation for a job well done.

Peter Drucker's management by objectives, as the title suggests, indicates that all tasks should be objective driven, however this brings with it both advantages and disadvantages.

Advantages

- *objectives are discussed prior to making an agreement*
- *full participation from all*
- *improved relationships*
- *objective linking can be implemented*
- *can be applied to any organisation*

Disadvantages

- *It is formal and systematically undertaken*
- *increased importance on goalsetting than the outcome*
- *time-consuming to implement*
- *not everything falls within easy identification as an objective*

Drucker said:

> *"management is doing things right; leadership is doing the right things"*

He also identified the emergence of the knowledge worker and identified that,

> *"one does not manage people; the task is to lead people. The goal is to make productive the specific strengths and knowledge of every individual".*

Henry Mintzberg believed that for a team to be successful, trust and information sharing is vital. He also identifies that the higher up the management level you go, the longer the time

---

Managing People

frames for specific tasks to be completed become. While there are defined roles and structures in place, communication throughout teams, both disseminated down as well as up those structures, is paramount to efficiency and good working relationships.

Team Dynamics

The term 'team dynamics' refers to the behaviour and relationships between members of a group of people who perform connected tasks within an organisation.

> *Team dynamics are the unconscious, psychological forces that affect how a team behaves and performs.*

A team consists of 2 or more people who are brought together as a distinct group, with the purpose of working on one or more tasks. The team is often led by a manager or Team Leader.

Team dynamics are created by:

- *the nature of the team's work*
- *the type of team*
- *the individual personalities within the team*
- *relationships between the team and other teams and stakeholders*
- *the working environment* – e.g., the office layout
- *communication methods used* – e.g., email or face-to-face conversations
- *organisational culture* – e.g., traditions about how people mix or communicate

Team dynamics can be a positive force – helping to bond the team and focus everyone on team objectives and achievements. They can enhance performance, improve productivity and increase job satisfaction and staff retention rates. Team members trust one another, work with a shared sense of purpose and hold each other accountable.

Team dynamics can also be a negative force if not managed effectively. If the team dynamics are negative, people's behaviour can disrupt work, affecting productivity, job satisfaction etc.

Poor team dynamics can be caused by, for example:

- *weak leadership* – enabling a dominant team member to take charge, which can lead to a lack of direction, conflict or a focus on inappropriate priorities
- *excessive reliance on leaders* – where people hold back too much because they want to defer to the leader
- *blocking* – when team members behave in a way that stops the flow of information or creativity within the team

Positive team dynamics can be encouraged by the manager being aware of potential problems, using their leadership skills and taking appropriate action. For example, they may need to:

Managing People

- *get to know their team members better – e.g., using Belbin's theory to analyse the roles team members play and making sure that tasks and responsibilities are suitable, where possible*
- *define roles and responsibilities – e.g., to make sure individuals understand their position; to give team members focus and direction*
- *develop communication skills and techniques – e.g., working with team members to improve how they handle conversations, meetings and presentations; reviewing how documents and reports are shared; reducing the number of emails*
- *review how work areas are organised – e.g., changing furniture around to make it easier for team members to work together; building or removing physical barriers to help team members create a better work environment*
- *tackle problems quickly – e.g., challenging unhelpful behaviour quickly, showing the impact of the behaviour and encouraging reflection on how behaviour could be improved*
- *work to break down barriers – e.g., using team-building exercises and encouraging people to communicate and appreciate each other's roles*

Approaches to team management

Managers need to consider the different functions of team management when developing their approach, to maximise the efficiency and effectiveness of their team. The wide range of skills are used in team management when, for example:

- *promoting teamwork and cooperation*
- *setting and agreeing shared objectives*
- *motivating the team to achieve objectives*
- *allocating, directing and coordinating work activities*
- *appraising performance for the team as a whole*
- *dealing with conflict and problems within the team*

Promoting teamwork and cooperation

Effective teamwork and cooperation can help organisations to improve productivity, quality and innovation. It also improves the motivation and commitment of team members, especially when individuals have a degree of control over their own work and have a positive and responsible attitude towards their team.

The manager's approach to developing teamwork and cooperation could include:

- *strong leadership – to show that the manager cares and is keen to develop and support working relationships within the team*
- *leading by example – e.g., excellent attendance and timekeeping; effective communication; being reliable and approachable; being open, fair and cooperative*

Managing People

- *having clear methods of communication* – *e.g., so that team members can discuss and understand each other's roles; to keep up to date with plans, targets and changes; for escalating problems and cascading information*
- *having clear roles and responsibilities* – *e.g., job and task descriptions; allocations of duties, shifts and areas of responsibility*
- *involving all team members* – *e.g., to discuss options and opportunities; encouraging team members to recognise each other's roles, strengths and weaknesses*
- *allocating and rotating the tasks fairly* – *especially if tasks are repetitive, boring, tiring, demanding or very popular, so that everyone shares the good and the bad aspects of the job*

Setting and agreeing shared objectives

When setting and agreeing objectives and targets with the team, it is important to see how the efforts of the individual team member, team and organisation fit together to achieve overall objectives. Realistic targets need to be set, performance needs to be measured and the results need to be analysed, reviewed and amended if necessary.

Many organisations use SMART targets as they provide a logical and simple template of how to set and monitor targets, objectives and activities. The targets need to be:

Specific – *to identify the target and desired outcome clearly and to show the actions and resources required.*
Measurable – *so that everyone can see the schedule of work, track progress and measure success.*
Achievable – *to make sure that the target is within the scope of the team's abilities and available resources.*
Realistic – *to make sure that everything is achievable with the time, working methods and resources that are available.*
Time-bound – *deadlines that are aligned with the organisational targets give a focus for individuals, the team and the organisation.*

Targets that are set and agreed for teams can include, for example:

- *group performance and output* – *e.g., sales or production targets for the whole team to achieve; targets to meet deadlines that affect other teams*
- *quality* – *e.g., to improve the average for the whole team*
- *spreading the workload* – *e.g., aiming for a fair distribution of tasks*
- *improved skills, experience and knowledge* – *e.g., training up certain team members to improve the overall dynamics of the team; giving certain members specialist training that they can share with the team*

By using a collaborative approach, managers can encourage team members to engage in the process, take responsibility and credit for their contribution to the team's achievements.

Managing People

Motivating the team to achieve objectives

The motivation of the individual is essential for successful motivation of the team. The individual motivational factors need to be satisfied for individuals to commit to the team and its goals.

Team motivational factors can be put into four categories:

Task – *sharing a common sense of purpose to perform tasks to achieve objectives*

Structure – *collaborative and communicative environment; sharing knowledge and support; good methods of communication*

Goals – *short-term task-orientated goals; long-term organisational goals; regularly reviewed and amended to remain relevant, on time and when goals are accomplished*

Team members – *the balance of people with different strengths and areas of expertise is important; individuals move in and out of the team and changes can affect the dynamics and balance of the whole team*

One of the most important skills that a manager can have is the ability to motivate the team. Managers need to use their skills to:

- *identify the motivating factors for each team member*
- *structure their approach around each team member to ensure that they stay engaged, motivated and happy with their work*
- *gain team members' commitment to achieve objectives*
- *help them to maintain their commitment*

When gaining commitment to objectives, a strong leader will adapt their approach to make sure that:

- **the team goals are realistic and achievable** – *so that they can 'sell' the objective to the team with confidence*
- **the team has access to the resources and the time it needs to achieve the objectives** – *so that the team knows that it will be fully supported by the organisation*
- **objectives are kept up to date** – *and modified as they change*
- **team members are kept fully informed** – *so that they remain engaged and involved in the whole process*
- **they work with team members' individual strengths and motivational factors** – *to keep the team balanced and efficient as a whole*
- **team members are aware of their part in the overall objectives** – *so that they target their efforts for the benefit of the whole team*
- **effort and input are recognised and appreciated**
- **there is continuity of leadership** - *continuity in leadership is important when gaining and maintaining commitment from the team. Keeping the same person in charge helps the team members to focus on their team goals rather than on keeping a new leader happy. Leaders that are seen to 'jump ship' early for whatever reason affect the team members' belief in success.*

Managing People

Allocating, directing and coordinating work activities

Managers need to consider many factors when allocating work, so that objectives and responsibilities can be set, agreed, briefed and achieved. There are many things to consider when planning a team's work to achieve objectives, including:

- **details about the objectives that need to be achieved** – e.g., whether the tasks are new or familiar repeats of everyday activities, budgets, equipment and deadlines
- **the range of skills and knowledge of the different team members** – e.g., some team members may already have the skills and some will need training and support
- **their level of experience** – e.g., some team members will be very experienced and used to doing things a certain way, whereas others will be new and inexperienced, but may bring fresh ideas and enthusiasm to the team
- **the capacity of the team** – e.g., whether the team has time to fit in new objectives, whether current projects need to be reprioritised
- **versatility of team members** – e.g., their ability to be moved around to perform different tasks

A team needs a good balance of skills and knowledge to be as efficient and effective as possible. The tasks need to be allocated to match each individual's capacity, skills, knowledge and abilities, as far as possible. The manager's approach needs to focus on:

- **making the most of team members' strengths**
- **minimising the effect of their weaknesses**

Managing People

Dealing with problems and conflict within the team

Problems that can occur within a team can be caused by, for example:

- *loss of team members* – *e.g., popular members with valuable skills and experience*
- *new team members who upset the balance* – *e.g., an imbalance within the Belbin team roles, due to inexperience*
- *poor leadership* – *e.g., weak or authoritarian leadership styles*
- *poor planning* – *e.g., resources not being available when needed; targets being unrealistic*
- *reduced productivity* – *e.g., due to low morale or poor working practices*
- *signs of stress* – *e.g., increased rates of sickness and absenteeism*
- *missed deadlines* – *e.g., due to technical problems or poor team skills*
- *conflict between team members* – *e.g., about standards or levels of output*
- *lack of motivation, team spirit and direction* – *e.g., not engaging with shared objectives*

Having identified the causes of problems or conflict, managers can develop an approach to tackle the issues. For example, they may need to facilitate:

- *one-to-one discussions* – *e.g., for private meetings about confidential information and opinions*
- *team review meetings and briefings* – *e.g., for open discussions about options and exchanges of views*
- *different opportunities for team members to pass on their views* – *e.g., via email or suggestion boxes*
- *meetings with other managers and team leaders* – *e.g., to discuss problems that affect people outside the team*

Once the suitable environment for discussion has been selected, managers need to think about their approach to solving the problems. Approaches could include, for example:

- *negotiation* – *e.g., to solve disputes between team members about workload or working practices*
- *mind-mapping or brainstorming* – *e.g., to involve team members in thinking about how to solve problems*
- *succession planning* – *e.g., to work out how to replace team members and develop the skills and team roles to rebalance the team*
- *reviewing, agreeing and setting targets* – *e.g., to change deadlines or output levels to help the team cope with external changes*
- *coaching and training sessions* – *e.g., to develop individuals, maybe with close monitoring, shadowing or one-to-one mentoring sessions*
- *rotating team members between different tasks* – *e.g., to be as fair as possible and develop skills and experience*

Managing People

- **improving resource management** – *e.g., order extra physical or human resources to support the team*

Appraising team performance

Managers need to align several elements when monitoring and controlling planned activities, such as, for example:

- **the agreed working standards** – *so that results can be measured against them*
- **performance indicators** – *measures that show the achievement of objectives, sometimes called key performance indicators (KPIs)*
- **work schedules** – *to show the work hours that have been used when achieving the objectives and any staff problems or changes*
- **quality control checks** – *to benchmark against successful projects and organisational standards*
- **budgets** – *to see if the objectives are being met within the allocated budget*

When measuring and assessing performance, managers need to compare the projected levels of achievement against the reality of what has been achieved.

This can be done in several ways, for example:

- **using the agreed SMART targets** – *e.g., to measure actual output against the projected output*
- **using Gantt charts or other graphs** – *e.g., to see the volume of work on an hourly, daily or weekly basis for each team function*
- **visual inspections** – *e.g., to see what has been done and to what standard*
- **analysing reports and data** – *e.g., looking at printouts of daily activity reports; studying spreadsheets that log production data; computer-generated reports*
- **discussions in progress review meetings** – *e.g., for the team to discuss output, problems and the next stages of the objectives*
- **formal one-to-one meetings** – *e.g., to discuss individual performances*

Once data has been collected and analysed, managers can adapt and target their approach to support the team's strengths and address their weaknesses.

Managing People

Motivating Teams

Understanding People's Motivations

What do you think motivates your people to come to work each morning? Do you believe that they get great satisfaction from their work and take pride in doing the best possible job? Or do you think that they see it as a burden and simply work for the money?

Your assumptions about your team members can have a significant influence on how you manage them.

There are numerous motivation theories. Here are outlines of some of the most well respected and well known:

McGregor X and Y theories
Maslow's Hierarchy of Needs
Hertzberg's Two-Factor Theory
McClelland's Acquired Needs Theory
Adams' Equity Theory
Vroom's Expectancy Motivation Theory

McGregor's Theory X and Theory Y
In the 1960's, social psychologist Douglas McGregor developed two contrasting theories that explained how managers' beliefs about what motivates their people can affect their management style. He labelled these Theory X and Theory Y. These theories continue to be important even today.

Theory X and Theory Y were first explained by McGregor in his book, "The Human Side of Enterprise," and they refer to two styles of management – authoritarian (Theory X) and participative (Theory Y).

If you believe that your team members dislike their work and have little motivation, then, according to McGregor, you will tend to use an authoritarian style of management. This approach is very "hands-on" and usually involves micromanaging people's work to ensure that it gets done properly. McGregor called this Theory X.

On the other hand, if you believe that your people take pride in their work and see it as a challenge, then you will be more likely adopt a participative management style. Managers who use this approach trust their people to take ownership of their work and do it effectively by themselves. McGregor called this Theory Y.

The approach that you take will have a significant impact on your ability to motivate your team members. So, it is important to understand how your perceptions of what motivates them can shape your management style.

Managing People

Theory X

Theory X managers tend to take a pessimistic view of their people and assume that they are naturally unmotivated and dislike work. As a result, they think that team members need to be prompted, rewarded or punished constantly to make sure that they complete their tasks.

Work in organisations that are managed like this can be repetitive and people are often motivated with a "carrot and stick" approach. Performance appraisals and remuneration are usually based on tangible results, such as sales figures or product output and are used to control staff and "keep tabs" on them.

This style of management assumes that workers:

- *Dislike their work.*
- *Avoid responsibility and need constant direction.*
- *Have to be controlled, forced and threatened to deliver work.*
- *Need to be supervised at every step.*
- *Have no incentive to work or ambition and therefore need to be enticed by rewards to achieve goals.*

According to McGregor, organisations with a Theory X approach tend to have several tiers of managers and supervisors to oversee and direct workers. Authority is rarely delegated and control remains firmly centralised. Managers are more authoritarian and actively intervene to get things done.

Although Theory X management has largely fallen out of fashion in recent times, big organisations may find that adopting it is unavoidable due to the sheer number of people that they employ and the tight deadlines that they have to meet.

Theory Y

Theory Y managers have an optimistic, positive opinion of their people and they use a decentralised, participative management style. This encourages a more collaborative, trust-based relationship between managers and their team members.

People have greater responsibility and managers encourage them to develop their skills and suggest improvements. Appraisals are regular but unlike in Theory X organisations, they are used to encourage open communication rather than control staff.

Theory Y organisations also give employees frequent opportunities for promotion.

This style of management assumes that workers are:

- *Happy to work on their own initiative.*
- *More involved in decision making.*
- *Self-motivated to complete their tasks.*
- *Enjoy taking ownership of their work.*

Managing People

- *Seek and accept responsibility and need little direction.*
- *View work as fulfilling and challenging.*
- *Solve problems creatively and imaginatively.*

Theory Y has become more popular among organisations. This reflects workers' increasing desire for more meaningful careers that provide them with more than just money. It is also viewed by McGregor as superior to Theory X, which, he says, reduces workers to "cogs in a machine," and likely demotivates people in the long term.

Most managers will use a mixture of Theory X and Theory Y. You may, however, find that you naturally favour one over the other. You might, for instance, tend to micromanage or, conversely, you may prefer to take a more hands-off approach. Although both styles of management can motivate people, the success of each will largely depend on your team's needs and wants and your organisational objectives.

You may use a Theory X style of management for new starters who will likely need a lot of guidance, or in a situation that requires you to take control such as a crisis. But you would not use it when managing a team of experts, who are used to working under their own initiative and need little direction. If you did, it would likely have a demotivating effect and may even damage your relationship with them.

However, both theories have their challenges. The restrictive nature of Theory X, for instance, could cause people to become demotivated and non-cooperative if your approach is too strict. This may lead to high staff turnover and could damage your reputation in the long term. Conversely, if you adopt a Theory Y approach that gives people too much freedom, it may allow them to stray from their key objectives or lose focus. Less-motivated individuals may also take advantage of this more relaxed working environment by shirking their work. If this happens, you may need to take back some control to ensure that everyone meets their team and organisational goals.

Circumstance can also affect your management style. Theory X, for instance, is generally more prevalent in larger organisations, or in teams where work can be repetitive and target driven. In these cases, people are unlikely to find reward or fulfilment in their work, so a "carrot and stick " approach will tend to be more successful in motivating them than a Theory Y approach.

In contrast, Theory Y tends to be favoured by organisations that have a flatter structure and where people at the lower levels are involved in decision making and have some responsibility.

Your assumptions and how you assess your people's needs and wants will likely be the biggest influencers on your management style. However, it is important that you challenge your assumptions and review your team members' individual requirements regularly. This will allow you to adapt your approach appropriately.

Your choice can also be shaped by several other factors. These include your organisational structure (tiered or flat), the type of work that your people do (repetitive or challenging) and their skill level (amateur or experienced) skills you need for a happy and successful career.

Managing People

Maslow's Hierarchy of Needs

In the 1940-50's in America, Abraham Maslow developed a motivation model known as the Hierarchy of Needs. It has been developed over the years and is often used by managers, team leaders, teachers and trainers.

It is based on a pyramid of five stages of intrinsic needs. As the individual achieves the requirements of one level, they move onto the next. They cannot move up to the next stage until all of the needs have been met.

People can also come down the pyramid if something happens, inside or outside the workplace.

Stage 1 – physiological needs
These are the basic, intrinsic survival needs – *e.g., bodily functions and needs such as air, food, water, sleep, reproduction.*

Stage 2 – safety and security
Once humans know that they can rely on food, water and so on, they can concentrate on personal and financial security – *e.g., physical safety of the body, security of employment, family members, health and property.*

Stage 3 – love and belonging
Once they feel secure about their job, health, home and so on, people can concentrate on feeling part of a group – *e.g., a family, a sports or work team, a department or a group of friends.*

Stage 4 – esteem
With physical needs, security and belonging sorted, humans move on to wanting feelings of esteem – *e.g., self-esteem, confidence, a sense of achievement, respect for others or respect from others.*

Stage 5 – self-actualisation
The top level is where people truly become themselves and are totally fulfilled. They are confident in their own opinions and place in the world. Here they can experience morality, creativity, spontaneity, problem-solving, lack of prejudice and acceptance of facts.

Managing People

It helps to think of these stages as a pyramid so that it is easier to visualise the climb up and the slide down these levels of needs. It also helps to clarify the importance of the needs lower down the pyramid. Unless the lower needs are met, humans cannot move up to the next stage.

Maslow's Hierarchy of Needs has survived because it still applies to the 21st century, for individuals and teams. For example:

> *if a well-respected individual is at stage 4 at work (esteem) and they are suddenly faced with the threat of redundancy, they will slip down quickly. They will feel that they no longer belong to the work group, they will feel that their job security has vanished, their health will suffer and they will probably have trouble with sleep, eating etc. They are back down to the bottom stage 1 in no time.*

The same problem could be applied to the whole team as well, especially is job security and job satisfaction are under threat. The whole team can be disrupted and disengaged it they are worried about redundancy or a new work regime.

Some people often think that money is the only motivation to work, but this is clearly not the case. Looking at Maslow's theory, money is at the second stage and supports the higher stages if it is sufficient to live on.

This is important when looking at motivating individuals and teams as it shows that offering money is not always the best option, especially if other needs have not been met.

Clayton Alderfer's ERG theory

In common with many other theories, Clayton Alderfer's ERG (Existence, Relatedness, Growth) theory is based on Maslow's hierarchy of needs. He collapses the five levels into three:

- **Existence needs** – *for psychological and material well-being*
- **Relatedness needs** – *for interpersonal relationships*
- **Growth needs** – *for continued growth and development*

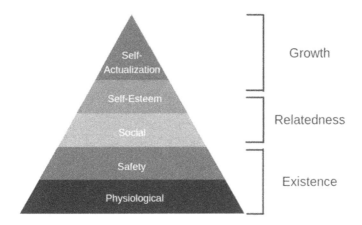

Managing People

Hertzberg's Two-Factor Theory

This theory from 1959 is also known as Frederick Herzberg's Motivation-Hygiene Theory. He was the first to show that satisfaction and dissatisfaction at work nearly always arise from different factors, the hygiene and motivator factors.

There are hygiene factors that need to be addressed to help prevent dissatisfaction at work, such as:

- *salaries and financial packages*
- *working conditions*
- *the organisation's policy and administration*
- *the quality of supervision and management*
- *feelings of job security*

If these are considered inadequate by individuals, they can become dissatisfied. This is magnified if the whole team feels the same and will affect their attitude to work and the organisation.

The motivator factors relate to the individual's need for personal growth, such as:

- *status*
- *opportunity for advancement*
- *gaining recognition*
- *responsibility*
- *challenging and stimulating work*
- *a sense of achievement and personal growth in the job*

These factors can motivate individuals to give above-average performance and effort. Again, the positive aspects of motivators will be amplified when shared by the whole team as the team dynamics will be boosted by positive opportunities and recognition.

Motivators	Hygiene factors
Achievement	Company Policies
Recognition	Supervision
The work itself	Relationships
Responsibility	Work conditions
Advancement	Remuneration
Growth	Salary
	Security

Managing People

McClelland's Acquired Needs Theory

David McClelland's Acquired Needs Theory from the early 1960's identified three motivators that we all have. He claimed that these needs are learned through life, hence the title of the theory and that people will have different characteristics depending on their dominating motivating need.

The three motivators are:

achievement

affiliation

power

People motivated by achievement need to:

- *set and accomplish challenging goals*
- *take calculated risks to achieve these*
- *receive regular feedback to see that they are on track*
- *work alone often*

These people are motivated by challenging but not impossible projects. They thrive on overcoming difficult problems, alone or with other high achievers. When receiving feedback, achievers want a fair and balanced appraisal so that they know what they are doing right and how they can improve their weaker areas.

The theory applies to individuals as people need to receive feedback about their personal performance to be clear about what they have achieved. This can be extended to team motivation, by being very public about what the team has achieved.

People motivated by affiliation:

- *want to belong to a group and be liked*
- *often go along with whatever the group wants to do*
- *favour collaboration over competition*
- *dislike high risk and uncertainty*

These people work best in a group and prefer less risky and uncertain tasks. Personal feedback is best for these people, with an emphasis on how they are trusted and valued. They are often best praised in private rather than in front of others.

Managers can apply this theory to teams and individuals by helping to build strong bonds within the team, maybe with team-building exercises, uniforms, logos or signs, if applicable. They need to recognise the team's efforts without pointing out contributions made by individual members. Individuals gain from being associated with a successful team, so it is in their interests to make sure that their team achieves excellence whenever possible.

People motivated by power:

Managing People

- *want control and to influence others*
- *like to win arguments*
- *enjoy competition, winning, status and recognition*

These people work best when they are in charge and do well on tasks that are goal oriented. They can be effective negotiators. Feedback needs to be direct and they are motivated by help with their career goals.

This part of the theory applies to individuals as teamwork is not a major factor when gaining recognition.

Recognising these motivators helps managers to influence how they set goals, allocate work, give feedback and reward individuals and teams to increase motivation levels.

Adams' Equity Theory
This theory was developed in 1963 by John Stacey Adams, a behavioural psychologist and it concentrates on balancing the employee's inputs and outputs:

> **inputs** – e.g., *hard work, enthusiasm, skills, knowledge, commitment, adaptability, flexibility, determination, trust, acceptance of others, loyalty and personal sacrifice*
> **outputs** – e.g., *salary, benefits, recognition, sense of achievement, praise, stimulus, job security and a sense of growth and development*

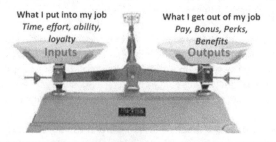

Managing People

The theory looks at achieving a fair balance between the two to improve employees' satisfaction and motivation levels. Although these inputs and outputs can be hard to quantify, the theory argues that employees should be content if they perceive these to be in balance.

Managers need to work to keep these in balance as far as possible. If the balance is too much in favour of the employer, some employees may react by, for example:

- *bringing balance between inputs and outputs on their own*
- *asking for more compensation or recognition*
- *feeling demotivated*
- *seeking alternative employment*

Vroom's Expectancy Motivation Theory

Vroom's theory separates effort (the result of motivation) from performance and outcomes. It assumes that behaviour comes from conscious choices to maximise pleasure and minimise pain and discomfort.

The theory is based on three variables:

- *expectancy* – **the belief that increased effort leads to increased performance** – *e.g., harder work will result in better outcomes*
  - *Having the right resources, skills and support to get the job done well are extremely important for expectations to be achievable.*
- *instrumentality* – **the belief that a successful outcome will be well received** – *e.g., receiving rewards for achieving targets or sales bonuses*
  - *Clear understanding of performance-related rewards and praise are important here, along with trust in the decision-makers and transparent processes*
- *valence* – **the importance that an individual gives the expected outcome** – *e.g., someone motivated by money might not be motivated by extra time off*
  - *Being aware of factors that motivate each individual is important here.*

The theory can help managers to be aware of how people are not always motivated by rewards. They can often feel motivated by their expected outcomes and how they will feel about making their contribution towards these outcomes.

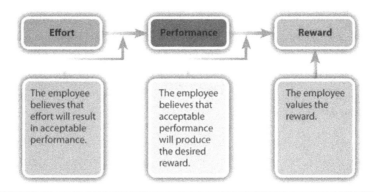

Managing People

Human Resources

The Humans Resources (HR) Department plays a pivotal role in a company because it is responsible for overseeing important aspects of employment including:

- *compliance with employment legislation*
- *administering benefits*
- *training and development*
- *annual leave*
- *sickness, recruitment*
- *disciplinary hearings and dismissal*

Team leaders today must have a firm understanding of the HR departments systems because they will be required to liaise with it on certain occasions as part of their role, especially when it comes to advising your employees on procedures and policies and on compliance with the law.

The relationship between HR and other parts of the organisation is a many faceted one. HR is the only department that interacts with all other departments. It acts in an advisory capacity regarding HR issues and maintains a good understanding of the business.

HR provides guidance on how specific situation should be dealt with and manages recruitment at the company, working in partnership with other heads to ensure the most appropriate individuals are employed. Usually, policies and procedures fall within HR and therefore it works collaboratively with other departments to present policies and procedures that are relevant and valid and that can be implemented effectively and measured appropriately.

Legislation Affecting Employment

Employment law, while designed to protect the rights of the employee, covers most of the aspects regarding the relationship between the employer and the employee. The business must comply with all aspects of employment law to avoid the negative impact of not doing so, including costly fines, employment tribunal's, adverse publicity and loss of their brand reputation, for example.

The HR Department will ensure that all policies and procedures within the business are written in line with the relevant employment law and meet with all legislation imposed on employers.

Consideration to the relevant employment laws must be given when devising contracts of employment, how employees are treated, pay and working hours as well as working conditions, among other things.

Eample:

- *recruitment*

Managing People

- *data protection*
- *holiday entitlement*
- *working time*
- *parental rights*
- *health and safety*
- *terms and conditions of employment*
- *equality and inclusion*
- *whistleblowing*

There are several pieces of legislation that can be connected with the legal requirements of HR, including:

- *Employment Rights Act 1996*
- *Equality Act 2010*
- *Working Time Regulations*
- *The General Data Protection Regulation 2016*
- *Health and Safety at Work Act 1974*
- *Other legislation and regulations*

Employment Rights Act 1996

The main employment legislation in the UK is the Employment Rights Act 1996. This law is very detailed and deals with a huge number of aspects about employment. Some of the main points covered by the Act are:

- *the employee's right to have a statement or contract of employment*
- *the employee's right to have an itemised pay statement*
- *protection of wages*
- *protection from suffering detriment in employment from taking time off work –* **e.g., taking time off for jury service, family reasons or antenatal care**
- **sickness**
- *maternity, paternity and adoption payments and leave*
- *suspension from work*
- *procedures for discipline, grievance, dismissal and redundancy*
- *Sunday working and time off*

Employment law is constantly under review and revision, with additions and changes happening every year, so it is important for managers and their organisations to keep up to date with the latest legislation and regulations.

Managing People

It helps if line managers are aware of their rights and those of their team members, so that they can apply disciplinary processes fairly and act if the employer does not comply with this Act.

Equality Act 2010

The Equality Act 2010 is the current legislation that deals with equality and discrimination in the UK. The Act gives individuals rights as it is unlawful to discriminate against anyone because of a protected characteristic:

The Equality Act 2010

- **age** – *all people over 18 are protected at work or in work training*
- **disability or impairment** – *organisations must make 'reasonable adjustments' to accommodate staff, customers and visitors with disabilities*
- **gender** – *equal pay, training and opportunity for males and females*
- **gender reassignment** – *people changing from male to female, or female to male*
- **marriage or civil partnership** – *preventing discrimination on the grounds of being married or in a civil partnership, at work or in work training*
- **pregnancy or maternity (including breastfeeding)** – *only reasons of safety are not covered – e.g., equality may not be possible for pregnant women in some circumstances if the activity could harm them or the baby*
- **race** – *wherever they were born, their parents' and their own race, colour, ethnicity are protected*
- **religion or beliefs** – *any religion, lack of religion or personal belief is protected*
- **sexual orientation** – *heterosexual, gay, lesbian and bisexual people are covered*

If there are special operational reasons, such as carers in a nursing home needing to be able to lift residents, there are exceptions to the rule, but the employer must take great care to be as fair as possible.

Individuals are protected from discrimination in these situations:

- **in the workplace** – *e.g., during recruitment and employment*
- **in education** – *e.g., schools, colleges, training companies*
- **as consumers** – *e.g., in shops, on the Internet, in cafes and restaurants, when buying or renting property*
- **when using public services** – *e.g., healthcare, libraries, transport, councils, civil service*
- **in clubs with more than 25 members** – *although the law does not stop clubs for people who share a protected characteristic – e.g., men-only or women-only clubs, or social clubs for Turkish people*

Individuals are also protected from discrimination if:

- **they are associated with someone who has a protected characteristic** – *e.g., a family member or friend*
- **they have complained about discrimination or supported someone else's claim**

Managing People

If people have a problem with discrimination at work that cannot be sorted with the employer, they have the right to act at an employment tribunal. The judge has the authority to award compensation, to stop the employer discriminating, or allow a dismissed person to come back to work. The judge can also make recommendations that affect other employees, as well as the individual.

There are many things that organisations need to observe.

Employers have a responsibility to:

- *avoid discriminating against employees, trainees and job applicants on the grounds of any of the protected characteristics*
- *make 'reasonable adjustments' to accommodate staff, job applicants, trainees, customers and visitors with disabilities or impairments*
- *make sure that discrimination is not tolerated and take steps to deal with bullying, harassment, victimisation or other forms of discrimination in the workplace*
- *give men and women equal pay and treatment in the terms and conditions of their employment contract if they are employed to do work that is the same, broadly similar or of equal value in terms of effort, skill or decision-making*
- *train and monitor their workforce and put in place policies and procedures for dealing with problems and complaints*
- *make sure that all employees, customers, job applicants and visitors know where to find information about their equality policies and procedures*
- *avoid asking job candidates about their health, age, absences due to pregnancy-related illnesses etc. during the application and interview processes – health questions can only be asked after a job offer has been made*

Employees have a responsibility to make sure that they do not breach their employer's equality and diversity policies, codes of conduct or guidelines. The law requires each individual to take responsibility and avoid discrimination and the employer needs to give clear guidelines in contracts of employment, equality and diversity policies, training sessions and so on.

If an individual fails to follow the guidelines, the organisation can implement disciplinary action or claim breach of contract (the employment contract).

In terms of disciplinary procedures, managers could be involved with HR procedures and legislation if, for example:

- *the employer discriminates and is taken to an employment tribunal*
- *a team member discriminates against someone illegally and has to be taken through the disciplinary process*

Working Time Regulations

The Working Time Regulations generally provide rights for employees to have:

Managing People

- a limit of an average 48-hour working week, although individuals may choose to work longer by 'opting out'
- 5.6 weeks of paid leave a year
- 11 consecutive hours' rest in any 24-hour period
- a 20-minute rest break if the working day is longer than 6 hours
- 1 day off each week
- a limit on the normal working hours of night workers to an average 8 hours in any 24-hour period and an entitlement for night workers to receive regular health assessments

There are special regulations for young workers, which restrict their working hours to 8 hours per day and 40 hours per week. The rest break is 30 minutes if their work lasts more than 4 and a half hours and they are entitled to 2 days off each week.

The General Data Protection Regulation 2016

GDPR stands for General Data Protection Regulation. The GDPR is a regulation from the Data Protection Act and covers any information related to a person or data subject that can be used to directly, or indirectly, identify them. It can be anything from a name, a photo and an email address to bank details, social media posts, biometric data and medical information. It also introduces digital rights for individuals.

When it came into effect on May 25, 2018, the GDPR set new standards for data protection and kickstarted a wave of global privacy laws that forever changed how we use the internet.

Why Do We Need the GDPR?

Personal data is highly valuable — in fact, it supports a trillion-dollar industry. Companies like Facebook and Google make their profits by selling personal information to advertisers. With this much money at stake, do you trust them to have your best interests at heart?

The GDPR defines what companies of all sizes can and cannot do with customer information.

What Is Classified as Personal Data Under GDPR?

Personal data is information that can be used to identify you. Put simply, it is any private details that you would not want to fall into the wrong hands.

Here are some examples of personal data:

Name	social media posts
phone number	geotagging
address	health records
date of birth	race
bank account	religious and political
passport number	opinions

Managing People

Think of personal data like a jigsaw. One piece alone might not say much but connected together they reveal a vivid picture of your life.

What Is a 'Breach' Under GDPR?
Any incident that leads to personal data being lost, stolen, destroyed, or changed is considered a data breach. Unfortunately, breaches happen all the time.

Here are some newsworthy examples from before the GDPR started cracking down:

- *Almost half the population of the US had their name, date of birth and social security number stolen from credit reporting agency Equifax as the result of a data breach.*
- *Political consulting firm Cambridge Analytica secretly took information from 50 million Facebook profiles and gave it to the 2016 Trump presidential campaign.*

Both of these incidents illustrate how data breaches have serious real-world consequences. This is exactly what GDPR and similar laws hope to regulate.

What Are the Penalties for Violating the GDPR?
The GDPR threatens would-be violators with some severe penalties. To make sure companies handle your personal data in a legal, ethical way, the fines for noncompliance are:

Up to €20 million or 4% of annual global turnover.

Some big names have already been hit with these noncompliance fines:

- **British Airways** — *£161 million. The UK airline set the record for fines when the booking details of 500,000 customers were stolen in a cyberattack.*
- **Marriott** — *£86 million. After buying the Starwood Hotels group, Marriott failed to update an old system belonging to the group. This system was hacked, revealing information about 339 million guests.*
- **Google** — *£40 million. Important information was hidden when users set up new Android phones, meaning they did not know what data collection practices they were agreeing to.*

Although smaller businesses would not be hit for such high amounts, they are held to the same standards.

A business owner now has to make sure their operations comply with the GDPR.

The only thing most people will need to do is read the cookie consent banners that now appear on websites and click agree (or not). The GDPR affects everything people do online, but it is mostly working behind the scenes.

Managing People

Core GDPR Concepts

The following are two of the most common GDPR terms used by security analysts. Understanding them is a vital part of becoming familiar with data protection in general.

Privacy by Design

Privacy by Design GDPR (PbD) is the name of an approach toward privacy that all businesses should now take when creating products and building websites. PbD involves keeping data collection to a minimum and building security measures into all stages of a product's design.

Consent

Obtaining consent simply means asking users for permission to process their data. Companies must explain their data collection practices in clear and simple language and then users must explicitly agree to them.

These new standards of consent prohibit the use of sneaky pre-selected settings in apps, as well as pre-checked boxes on websites.

These are some of the main user rights outlined by the GDPR:

- *You are entitled to know exactly how your data is collected and used*
- *You can ask what information has been collected about you (without paying anything)*
- *If there are mistakes in your data, you can request to have them corrected*
- *You can have your data deleted from records (just in case you need to disappear!)*
- *You are allowed to refuse data processing, for example, marketing efforts*
- *Keep in mind that these rights can be limited if they are misused or used excessively.*

GDPR Compliance

GDPR compliance can be costly and time consuming. Getting a grip on what is involved can save you money if you run a business, or just protect you if you spend a lot of time online.

42% of US news sites are still blocking EU users because they have not figured out how to comply with the GDPR yet!

GDPR Terminology

- ***What is a data subject?*** *- A data subject is anyone who has their data collected by a company. (Basically, everyone who has ever used the internet.)*
- ***What is a data controller?*** *- A data controller is any entity that gathers and stores data — for example, a business.*
- ***What is a data processor?*** *- This is who a large corporation hires to process data on their behalf. Usually, it is a payroll company.*
- ***What is a supervisory authority?*** *- Each country in the EU has its own supervisory authority.*

- *What is a data protection officer (DPO)?* - *Companies and public bodies that process lots of data need to appoint an officer (DPO) to handle all their GDPR activities and paperwork.*

Data Protection Impact Assessments (DPIAs)

If a company's data processing activities are high-risk and could affect people's freedoms, they will need to fill out a DPIA.

Examples of high-risk activities include:

- *Using new technology*
- *Tracking anyone's location*
- *Processing genetic or biometric data (think 23andMe or DNA testing)*
- *Marketing to children*
- *Data Breach Notifications*

When a data breach occurs, the affected company has 72 hours to inform their supervisory authority. They also have to tell users as quickly as possible.

Privacy Policies

All businesses are required to have a privacy policy that explains what they do with users' information.

Privacy policies must:

- *Include contact details of the company and its representatives*
- *Describe why the company is collecting the data*
- *Say how long the information will be kept on file*
- *Explain the rights users have*
- *Be written in simple language*
- *Name the recipients of the personal data (if the company shares data with another organisation)*
- *Include contact details for an EU representative and the DPO (if necessary)*

GDPR - Dos and Don'ts:

Do	Do not
Collect information legally and use it fairly	Mislead users about what you will do with their private details
Collect as little data as possible	Collect lots of data just because you can
Protect data with strong security systems	Assume data will take care of itself
Only store data for as long as necessary	Keep old data you do not need anymore

Managing People

Health and Safety at Work Act 1974

This Act deals with the employer's duty of care to all staff, customers and other people connected with the organisation, plus employees' rights and responsibilities. HR procedures, especially disciplinary actions, could arise if, for example, a member of staff:

Health and Safety at Work Act 1974
Anyone entering these premises must comply with regulations covered by the above act

- *refuses to wear the personal protective equipment (PPE) that has been issued that they are required to wear for their job*
- *does not follow manufacturers' instructions and training about how to use and operate materials, equipment or machinery*
- *abuses or misuses equipment or machinery*

It is a legal requirement for health and safety procedures to be in place in the workplace. Organisations have a responsibility for the welfare of their employees, customers and anyone else who comes to the workplace and employees have a responsibility to follow the procedures.

Employers and employees share responsibility for security, health and safety. In general terms, employers need to put all of the procedures and equipment in place and employees need to follow instructions and use everything correctly.

Other Legislation and Regulations

There are numerous other regulations and pieces of legislation that apply to certain industries or circumstances. Managers need to check their own organisation's policies and procedures to find out which ones affect them and what their responsibilities might be. These might include:

- *Trade Union and Labour Relations (Consolidation) Act 1992 – the ACAS code is issued under this Act*
- *National Minimum Wage Act 1998 – dealing with the minimum wage for different age groups*
- *Pensions Act 2014 – dealing with contributions to occupational pension schemes and state pensions*
- *Modern Slavery Act 2015 – dealing with people trafficking and slavery*
- *Part-Time Workers (Prevention of Less Favourable Treatment) Regulations 2000*
- *Fixed-term employees (Prevention of Less Favourable Treatment) Regulations 2002*
- *Statutory Paternity Pay and Statutory Adoption Pay (General) Regulations 2002 – and later amendments*
- *Work and Families Act 2006*
- *Enterprise and Regulatory Reform Act 2013*

Managing People

Recruitment and Selection of Staff

The anti-discrimination measures also apply to the recruitment and selection process under the Equality Act 2010. Job applicants have to be treated fairly as well as employees and trainees. If an applicant believes that they have been discriminated against unfairly during the recruitment process, they can also take the organisation to an employment tribunal.

Employers need to avoid discrimination during the recruitment and selection process by, for example:

- *advertising the job correctly*
- *making the interview process and location accessible*
- *avoiding certain questions when recruiting*
- *avoiding certain topics during the application process*

Advertising the job correctly
Employers must not state or imply that they will discriminate against anyone. Phrases such as 'recent graduate' or 'highly experienced' should be used only if they are actual requirements of the job. These phrases could discriminate against younger or older people who have not had the opportunity to get certain qualifications, so the criteria must be essential for the job. Indirect discrimination can occur by advertising the job only in men's magazines, for instance.

Making the interview process and location accessible
Employers need to make practicable adjustments to make sure that the widest number of people have access. For example, candidates in wheelchairs or with mobility problems might need to use ramps and lifts to reach the interview room and workplace.

Avoiding certain questions when recruiting
Employers cannot ask applicants about protected characteristics, their health, their marital status, if they have children, or if they plan to have children. Employers can only ask about these things if:

- *there are necessary requirements of the job that cannot be met by reasonable adjustments*
- *they are finding out if someone needs help to take part in a selection test or interview*
- *they are using 'positive action' to recruit people who are disabled or from another minority group*

Avoiding certain topics during the application process
Certain topics are avoided during the selection process that may influence a decision unfairly and cause discrimination. For example:

- *the candidate's date of birth – this can be used for monitoring only and is not allowed on the main application form*

Managing People

- *criminal convictions if they are spent – some employers are exempt from this rule, such as schools*
- *trade union membership*

Employers can discriminate, but only if it is a requirement for the job. For example, people under 18 cannot sell alcohol, so it would not be illegal to put a lower age limit on the job specification.

Discipline and Grievance

When considering HR procedures and legal requirements, managers need to be aware of:

- *the Advisory, Conciliation and Arbitration Services (ACAS)*
- *employment tribunals*
- *legal aspects of the disciplinary process*

ACAS

This is a non-departmental government public body that is sponsored by the Department for Business, Innovation and Skills. It provides information, advice, training, conciliation and other services for employers and employees to help prevent or resolve workplace problems.

The website contains a great deal of information about a wide range of employment-related subjects – e.g., rights and responsibilities at work, good practice, disputes and problems. The website is: www.acas.org.uk

ACAS has a statutory Code of Practice on discipline and grievance, which gives basic, practical guidance to employers, employees and their representatives. It gives guidance about how to proceed fairly with disciplinary and grievance issues.

Managing People

Employment Tribunals

A tribunal is like a court. Employment tribunals are independent, public bodies with statutory powers to hear many kinds of disputes between employers and employees. The most common disputes are about unfair dismissal, redundancy and discrimination.

Employment tribunals are less formal than a court, but they are open to the public and evidence is given under oath or affirmation. If the tribunal finds that the employer has breached the employee's employment rights, they can order the employer to pay penalties on top of any award made to the claimant.

Employment tribunals are legally required to take the ACAS Code of Practice into account when considering relevant cases. Before lodging a claim, ACAS must be notified first to see if conciliation is possible, which is faster, cheaper and less stressful.

Legal Aspects of the Disciplinary Process

In addition to legislation, we have the ACAS statutory Code of Practice on discipline and grievance. This gives basic, practical guidance to employers, employees and their representatives and deals with:

- *disciplinary situations* – *including misconduct and poor performance*
- *grievances* – *concerns, problems or complaints that employees raise with their employers*

The Code does not deal with redundancy dismissals or the non-renewal of fixed-term contracts.

The law on unfair dismissal requires employers to act reasonably when dealing with disciplinary issues. What is classed as reasonable behaviour will depend on the circumstances of each case and is ultimately a matter for employment tribunals to decide. However, the core principles are set out in the ACAS Code of Practice

Organisations do not have to follow the Code, but a tribunal can increase any award they have made by up to 25% if it feels that an employer has unreasonably failed to follow the guidance set out in the Code. It can also reduce any award they have made by up to 25% if they feel an employee has unreasonably failed to follow the guidance set out in the Code.

The Code supports fairness and transparency, especially when following the disciplinary process:

- *employers and employees should raise and deal with issues promptly and should not unreasonably delay meetings, decisions or confirmation of those decisions*
- *employers and employees should act consistently*
- *employers should carry out any necessary investigations, to establish the facts of the case*

Managing People

- *employers should inform employees of the basis of the problem and give them an opportunity to put their case in response before any decisions are made*
- *employers should allow employees to be accompanied at any formal disciplinary or grievance meeting*
- *employers should allow an employee to appeal against any formal decision made*

To make sure that they comply with legal requirements, organisations usually base their disciplinary process on the ACAS Code of Practice. The main themes are to be fair and consistent and to deal with things without any unreasonable delays.

The Code recommends that employers carry out investigations as soon as possible to establish the facts and keep suspension periods with pay as brief as possible.

Investigations do not necessarily have to lead to a disciplinary hearing. If they can, in the interests of fairness, employers should arrange for one set of people to do the investigation and one set to do the disciplinary hearing for cases of misconduct.

When dealing with a disciplinary situation, the ACAS Code of Practice recommends that employers:

- *establish the facts of each case*
- *inform the employee of the problem*
- *hold a meeting to discuss the problem*
- *allow the employee to be accompanied at the meeting*
- *decide on appropriate action*
- *provide employees with an opportunity to appeal*

Sickness and absence

Managing attendance problems often means that managers have to tackle the causes of absence. People are absent from work for three main reasons:

- *sickness*
- *family or caring responsibilities*
- *authorised leave* – e.g., holiday, maternity leave or a training course

As well as organising and coordinating these absences, managers may need to deal with problems such as lateness and poor timekeeping, plus unauthorised absence, which may eventually lead to disciplinary action.

There are legal requirements under the Employment Rights Act 1996 that managers need to be aware of, as employers must:

- *protect employees when taking time off work in certain situations*

Managing People

- *pay Statutory Sick Pay (SSP)*
- *pay maternity, paternity and adoption payments*
- *allow maternity, paternity and adoption leave*
- *deal with suspension from work correctly*

Managers are required to comply with these regulations when dealing with HR matters, to make sure that the individual's and the organisation's rights are protected. This helps to maintain good working relationships and avoid grievances and possible legal action or tribunals. Full details can be found on the ACAS website.

Protection from suffering detriment in employment and taking time off work
This protects employees' rights to not suffer from, for example:

- *doing jury service or public duties*
- *having time off for study or for family or domestic reasons*
- *taking time off for antenatal care*

Managers need to be aware of this protection so that they can arrange reasonable time off, support a team member, inform HR when appropriate and monitor the situation.

Sickness
Employers must pay Statutory Sick Pay (SSP) when employees have been off work sick for four or more days in a row (including non-working days). Managers may be involved with contacting and supporting the team member who is unwell, keeping sickness records for the payroll and HR departments and escalating the problem to HR when appropriate.

Maternity, paternity and adoption payments and leave
Pregnant women have several rights, including Statutory Maternity Pay (SMP), maternity leave, time off for appointments and the right to return to work. Fathers have paternity rights that include paid paternity leave, Statutory Paternity Pay (SPP) and additional paternity leave. Statutory Adoption Pay (SAP) was added in a later amendment to the Act. Parents can also have the right to paid time off for family emergencies, flexible working and for adoption leave.

Suspension from work
There are rights to remuneration when someone is suspended from work on medical or maternity grounds.

Harassment and bullying
Bullying is not actually against the law, but harassment is unlawful under the Equality Act 2010 when the unwanted behaviour is related to one of the protected characteristics.

Organisations will often be very clear about what behaviour is considered inappropriate in their equality and diversity policy. Details often appear under the heading of harassment and bullying policies.

Managing People

Examples of inappropriate behaviour include:

- *insulting and putting down others*
- *abusing, hurting, mistreating or harassing others*
- *making rude or insulting comments*
- *making unwanted personal comments about a person*
- *making fun of others*
- *taking advantage of other people*
- *holding back information that people need to enable them to make decisions*
- *stopping other people expressing themselves or practising their own attitudes, beliefs or values*

Managers and team leaders can address inappropriate behaviour in the workplace by, for instance:

- *reducing the chances of inappropriate behaviour occurring*
- *helping people to value themselves and others*
- *encouraging good communication skills*
- *encouraging politeness and tolerance*
- *following the organisation's procedures*
- *seeking external advice and guidance*

Reducing the chance of inappropriate behaviour occurring at all

It is better to prevent problems and inappropriate behaviour than to have to deal with a complaint or an unpleasant situation. Training and awareness of equality and diversity are key to avoiding discrimination in the workplace. By educating the workforce and encouraging a sense of shared purpose to refuse to allow discrimination, the chances of inappropriate behaviour reduce considerably.

Managers and team leaders need to monitor their staff as a normal part of their duties, to make sure that team members are putting the equality and diversity policy into practise.

Helping people to value themselves and others

Managers and team leaders can help others to value themselves by using motivational strategies. People cannot be forced to respect each other, but we can respect each other's differences. We can remain open-minded and learn to accept differences, even if we do not agree with them personally.

Encouraging good communication skills

Communication is a two-way process, so it is important to take responsibility for getting a message across in a way that works for the other person and to not make them feel inadequate or incompetent if at all possible.

Some people may be unable to read and write, due to language or educational difficulties and we need to be sensitive to this and remember to respect them as individuals. We can use speech, gestures and pictures to help.

Managing People

Body language can vary between cultures and individuals. Some people do not like physical contact, for instance and will be offended by it, whilst others touch as a normal part of everyday communication. We all just need to be aware of possible differences and respect the boundaries, especially while we get to know each other.

Encouraging politeness and tolerance

Mocking someone due to differences, particularly something that people have no control over, like disability, can be incredibly hurtful. People have every reason to be proud of themselves, their religion, differences, beliefs and skills.

Employers might allow time for prayers, or colleagues might cover each other for different national or religious festivals and holidays, so that some people can take time off to observe their own customs. If health and safety are not compromised, employers might be flexible about dress codes at work, to allow people to wear items of clothing or jewellery that have social, cultural or religious significance for them.

Following the organisation's procedures

Managers will have procedures to follow when there is a breach of a policy or contract and they need to take fair and swift action. The procedures may include, for example:

- *taking the team member aside to ask them to explain their words or actions – such meetings need to be conducted in private*
- *reminding them about the organisation's commitment to equality and referring them to policies and procedures*
- *taking evidence statements from the person who has been bullied or harassed or from witnesses*
- *giving a verbal or written warning – following guidelines closely*
- *giving the team member equality and diversity training, or arranging a refresher course*
- *monitoring and reviewing the situation*

Sometimes, an employee's inappropriate behaviour is beyond the team leader or manager's authority. If this happens, the team leader or manager will need to follow the organisation's equality disciplinary and grievance procedures, which may direct them to refer the matter to a more senior manager or the HR department.

Seeking external advice and guidance

There are several sources of useful information about equality and diversity, for example:

- *ACAS (Advisory, Conciliation and Arbitration Service) – dealing with all aspects of employment, disputes, equality law – www.acas.org.uk*
- *EHRC (Equality and Human Rights Commission) – an independent statutory body that helps to eliminate discrimination and reduce inequality – www.equalityhumanrights.com*
- *Stonewall – a charity working for equality and justice for lesbians, gay men and bisexuals – www.stonewall.org.uk*

Managing People

Performance Management

Formal and Informal Assessment

Performance management consists of two processes that work together to help managers to monitor, analyse and implement changes to improve or maintain high standards and quality in the workplace. These are:

- *formal* assessments to assess the performance of individuals and teams within a framework of standards and procedures at set intervals
- *informal* assessments that are done by the line manager as part of their day-to-day management activities

Methods for assessing work performance need to be fair and transparent. Looking at performance measurements over a period of time can help the managers to see if performance is increasing or decreasing, identify peaks and troughs and any seasonal, monthly, weekly or even daily variations.

The data helps managers to look at past performance, analyse current performance and plan ahead – e.g., allocating physical and human resources at the right time; controlling stock and budgets; identifying and planning training and development; monitoring customer satisfaction; reviewing progress against set objectives.

Formal Assessment methods

Formal performance assessment methods focus on personal appraisals and reviews with individual team members. They take place at regular intervals, maybe every six or twelve months, or at the end of a project or contract.

The organisation will have a formal performance assessment process based on its own culture, activities and objectives and this will consider, for example:

- *time frames* – how often the reviews will take place
- *the people involved* – e.g., the team member and their line manager
- *agreed standards and objectives* – against which performance can be measured and assessed
- *procedures* – e.g., how the review will take place and what will be tested
- *outcomes* – what happens as a result of the formal assessment, such as revised targets or training activities
- *supervision of standards* – to make sure that different team members and managers work to fair and transparent guidelines to standardise what is expected
- *rewards, if applicable* – e.g., performance-related bonuses, promotion, or increased responsibilities following a trial period

The advantages of formal assessment include:

- *a fair, transparent, standardised and predictable system of measurement* – e.g., working to agreed working standards and practices
- *an individual approach for the team member* – from having concentrated attention and feedback from the manager
- *opportunity to fine-tune development activities that suit the individual*

Disadvantages can include:

- *a nerve-wracking and stressful time for the team member* – especially those who are nervous about being tested and watched closely
- *using a great deal of management time to prepare, conduct, review and standardise the formal assessments*

It can be difficult to know which factors need to be measured to assess an individual's performance – a formal review system might not be able to take into account unusual circumstances or work activities.

Informal Assessment methods

Informal performance assessment methods are based more on day-to-day activities rather than a structured review. The managers can observe their team members at work, doing what they do all of the time. The formal assessments are typically based on what should be normal, everyday good practice.

Informal assessment activities can include, for example:

- *taking a quick look at the team member's work output to see if everything seems satisfactory on the surface*
- *asking the team member how things are going and if they have any problems*
- *observing the team member as part of a group to see if they are doing their fair share*
- *asking customers and others for informal feedback about the service they were given*

Advantages can include, for example:

- *the assessment is based on real-life working situations*
- *the activities are not forced or staged, they are part of normal everyday activities*
- *assessment and feedback can be instant – especially praise and encouragement*
- *when there are negative performance issues, these can be addressed quickly in private before the problems escalate*
- *the atmosphere will usually be relaxed and positive*

Disadvantages can include, for example:

Managing People

- *the review can be superficial* – with only one or two activities monitored for only one or two team members in any given session
- *the review can be very subjective* – with the outcome of the review based on what the manager observed over a short period of time, which might not be representative of the whole job role

The manager's role in performance management is to:

- *treat every team member as an individual*
- *follow the organisation's policies and procedures on performance management*
- *monitor individual and team performance against accepted standards or benchmarks*
- *give useful feedback and support to each individual*
- *facilitate or provide training, mentoring or coaching to maintain or improve performance*
- *do follow-up monitoring to check that standards have improved or been maintained*
- *follow formal procedures where poor performance does not improve*

Establishing Performance Standards

Managers need to establish the required performance standards so that everyone knows what to expect. These provide benchmarks against which to measure and assess performance.

Team members are more engaged with their work if they are part of the decision-making process and this applies to performance standards too. To gain maximum cooperation to improve performance, the team member needs to be involved so that they understand:

- *the reasons behind the standards* – e.g., to see how they tie in with other aspects of the organisation's activities
- *exactly what they are supposed to do and why* – e.g., so that they are clear about what is wanted
- *their responsibility to work to those standards* – e.g., to achieve consistency throughout the workforce
- *how they can support their team's efforts* – e.g., by working to consistently high standards that feed into the system and reduce problems and extra work for others

When setting standards, managers can make reference to, for example:

- *the organisation's policies and procedures* – e.g., on how to answer telephone calls
- *training manuals and other materials* – e.g., notes from a course on customer service skills
- *manufacturers' instructions* – e.g., on how to operate the telephone equipment
- *industry and legal standards* – e.g., etiquette and rules about confidentiality when dealing with calls

Managing People

- *organisational objectives* – e.g., to improve answer times and success rate of dealing with the customers' queries

The team member's performance standards can be set by concentrating on 'what', 'how', 'when' and 'why' they need to do certain things. Based on answering business calls when on reception, this could mean, for example:

What does the team member need to do exactly?

The standards could require them to:

- *Answer the calls within five rings*
- *Use the standard response* – *'good morning/afternoon, Smith and co, how can I help you?'*
- *Put the caller through to the right person, using the directory to find the extension number*
- *Apologise if there is a delay in answering or the caller cannot be put through*
- *Take messages if this is not possible and pass them on to the correct person*

How does the team member need to perform?

The standards could require them to:

- *Use a cheerful and positive voice*
- *Speak clearly and slowly*
- *Be prepared to repeat and spell words*
- *Use the telephone system correctly (in accordance with the manufacturer's instructions) so that calls are held and put through properly*

When do they need to do these things?

The standards could require them to:

- *Answer calls personally between 09:00 and 17:30, Monday to Friday*
- *Leave the answering machine on for the rest of the time*
- *Liaise with colleagues to cover breaks and days off*
- *Answer calls in the standard format every time*
- *Ask for assistance if there is a problem with the telephone system*

Why are the standards important?
Answers can include, for example:

Managing People

- *To deliver excellent customer service*
- *To improve and maintain the organisation's positive and professional image*

Setting Goals and Objectives for Individuals

The next stage is to set and agree goals and objectives with individual team members and discuss how performance will be measured against the standards and objectives. SMART targets or objectives are a useful tool that can help the manager and team member focus on individual aims and plans to assess and improve performance.

Setting SMART objectives

SMART objectives are clear and focused. When agreeing objectives with a team member, managers can set SMART objectives to help the individual to see what they need to do in a logical and useful way.

Collaboration when setting objectives helps to ensure the individual's success and achievement of goals. When team members have been part of the planning process, they are more engaged and determined to see a satisfactory outcome, which benefits the team members, managers and organisation.

Example:

> *A manager in charge of a supermarket's frozen produce department sets an objective with an experienced team member to "work towards promotion and becoming their deputy as a fresh produce supervisor". This is too vague and does not show in detail when or how they are going to achieve their objective.*

SMART objectives break down the goal into focused tasks and steps and they map a way for moving up into the more senior role. SMART objectives can cover a very broad picture, to give a studied but general overview of the goals and how they will be achieved. They can also be small and very detailed about one particular minor goal and how to achieve it.

The supermarket's department manager could set this as the general SMART objective for the team member:

Managing People

S – Specific	Get promoted to the next level and become one of three frozen produce supervisors in current store, or in new stores about to open
M – Measurable	Success would be measured by selection for interview then promotion to the desired grade Need to complete Team Leading level 2 qualification to qualify
A – Achievable	Nearly finished Team Leading level 2 Can broaden experience by shadowing other supervisors Company is expanding and opening 2 more stores locally, needing 6 more frozen produce supervisors
R – Realistic	Timescale is realistic for fitting in the study Can be ready for promotion by the time new stores open Current supervisors have agreed to mentor and support
T – Time-bound	Level 2 to be completed in 2 months New stores open in 3-4 months

Goals and objectives for individual team members need to align with team and organisational objectives.

Measuring Work Performance

Having identified, discussed and implemented performance standards and personal objectives for the team member, managers need to be able measure the work against those standards. This helps them to evaluate the team member's performance and see if there are any areas that need improvement or support.

Managers can use a variety of methods to measure work performance, including:

- *performance indicators*
- *performance ratings*
- *management by objectives (MBO)*
- *behaviourally anchored rating scales (BARS)*

Performance indicators

When measuring progress against performance indicators, managers will assess areas such as:

- **quality** – e.g., against set standards laid down in policies, procedures and training materials
- **quantity** – e.g., keeping a log of output, sales, commission or services provided over a long period of time and analysing trends
- **timeliness** – e.g., checking to see how many services and products are delivered on time, checking for delays within the internal production processes
- **cost-effectiveness** – e.g., looking at new and old systems and measuring actual cost differences; measuring actual costs against forecasts

- *absenteeism* – e.g., to find patterns of absenteeism, analyse the causes and look for solutions

Performance indicators, sometimes referred to as Key Performance Indicators (KPIs), can be set for non-time-based targets in qualitative terms, as well as obvious physical measurements. For example, they can be designed to measure response times or accuracy.

Performance can be measured against objectives or reports and need to take into account things that may affect performance – e.g., critical incidents, such as accidents, emergencies or bad weather, downtime, from broken machinery

Performance ratings

Ratings systems are all around us. The hospitality and catering industries, for instance, have used stars for many years to indicate the quality of the food, service and accommodation. Similarly, when we complete surveys and feedback forms, we are often asked to rate our reactions – e.g., 1, for very satisfied, down to 5, for very dissatisfied.

Organisations can use ratings scales internally too, for a skills audit, for example. The employee can have a questionnaire to assess details about their role, objectives and skills. The employee can tick two boxes if they are unsure, or give two ticks if they feel strongly about an answer:

1. = agree strongly
2. = agree
3. = neutral, neither agree nor disagree
4. = disagree
5. = disagree strongly

Performance Scorecard

Personal Audit Questionnaire		1	2	3	4	5
1	I lack confidence in expressing my needs			✓	✓	
2	I manage time effectively			✓	✓	
3	I am not confident to lead			✓		
4	I cope well with stress				✓	
5	I manage a number of tasks well			✓	✓	
6	I do not have the confidence to give presentations				✓	
7	I am patient when imparting knowledge and skills to others			✓	✓	
8	I do not have confidence to influence others		✓	✓		
9	I motivate people to perform			✓	✓	
10	I do not direct people to do tasks		✓			

Even though extra ticks can be used, ratings scales can be quite a blunt way of measuring performance. If they are treated as multiple-choice forms and processed electronically, extra comments on surveys and questionnaires will not usually be considered. Background

Managing People

information, creativity or critical incidents that affect performance cannot be explained in this format – e.g., a flood at a hotel that affected service for a few weeks; or an employee being off on parental leave and being unavailable to achieve certain objectives.

However, they can be a useful starting point for discussion or research and will give a good idea about the level of achievement or quality.

Management by Objectives (MBO)

The MBO theory was developed by management theorist, Peter Drucker. He identified a six-stage process that links the actions and responsibilities of individuals, teams, managers and the organisation:

Stage 1	Senior level – clearly define objectives for the organisation
Stage 2	Analyse and evaluate management tasks, identify and allocate responsibilities to specific managers
Stage 3	Discuss and set out performance standards
Stage 4	Agree and set out the objectives to the individuals
Stage 5	Devise and set individual targets that relate to the organisation's objectives
Stage 6	Monitor achievement of the objectives by implementing and developing a management information system

Having set and agreed the objectives in the early stages, performance is measured in Stage 6.

Managing People

Behaviourally Anchored Rating Scales (BARS)

The BARS method bases evaluation on specific behaviours for each task or position within an organisation. Each key task is analysed and the grades are allocated according to how that task should be completed.

Customer service in a restaurant, for instance, will have detailed standards:

Score	Rating	Standard
5	Exceptional	gives customers genuine and warm welcome, attends to drinks order immediately, takes food order as soon as customers are ready, attends to customers' requests immediately, takes initiative to sort requests and problems
4	Excellent	welcomes customers warmly, takes drinks orders straightaway and food orders within 4 minutes, engages with customers throughout, can deal with 4-5 sets of customers
3	Satisfactory	welcomes customers, takes order within 5 minutes, all correct, liaises effectively with colleagues and customers, can deal with 4 sets of customers
2	Nearly satisfactory	takes customers' orders within 10 minutes, gets orders right, reasonably polite, able to deal with 2 sets of customers at the same time
1	Unsatisfactory	ignores customers, gets orders wrong, does not engage with customers, rude to colleagues and customers

BARS can be very detailed and centred on the individual, but they can also be very time-consuming for managers to develop and perform. A high degree of monitoring and maintenance is required.

Ensuring fair and objective formal assessment

Managers need to take great care that the formal assessment process is fair and objective for everyone concerned. They need to measure performance against agreed standards, be openminded and treat each person as an individual.

The people involved in the process may have their views and decisions influenced by, for instance:

- *lack of objectivity*
- *prejudices*
- *unconscious judgements*
- *prior knowledge*
- *recollections of previous actions or communication*

Other factors can impact the performance management process too, including:

Managing People

- *time issues* – e.g., not having enough time to look at all off the evidence in detail before making a judgement
- *insufficient or inaccurate data*
- *inexperience*
- *lack of meaningful and usable feedback* – e.g., a feedback questionnaire where the customer has ticked 'very dissatisfied' without making any comments about what actually happened to make them so unhappy
- *direct experience dominating abstract information* – e.g., seeing a large crowd of frustrated train passengers and thinking that the station staff are at fault, whereas a fatal accident on the railway line 50 miles away has stopped all trains running

When managing team and individual performance, managers need to be aware of common pitfalls that can distort the standards achieved and make the process unfair and unreliable. For example:

A tendency towards the halo and horns effect

This means that a lack of objectivity can lead to:

- *rating a person highly on all performance factors due to a global impression* – e.g., marking someone up because they are popular, even though elements of their performance are weak
- *rating a person low on all performance factors due to global impression* – e.g., marking someone down on all counts because they are generally considered to be a poor performer, even though they may be satisfactory or excellent in some areas

This lack of objectivity can arise due to, for example: prejudices, personal judgements and subjective bias; memories of previous actions and standards; prior knowledge about the person rather than their actual performance; influence from other people.

A tendency to take the central line

This is where managers avoid extreme ratings, either good or bad, unless there are known complaints that they cannot ignore. Whilst marking everything as 'average' or 'satisfactory' may avoid complaints from team members about negative ratings, it is neither transparent nor fair to ignore areas of excellence, or areas for improvement.

This pitfall can occur easily if:

- *the performance standards are not clearly defined – and managers feel it will be easier to take the middle ground rather than challenge the standards*
- *there is a fear of being challenged* – e.g., by the team member who may be unhappy that their achievements have not been recognised; or by the organisation in a standardisation exercise to compare standards reported in reviews made by all managers

Managing People

Team members who have performed well but have only received an average or satisfactory rating will be demotivated and this will probably have a negative effect on the whole team and on the individual's personal career development.

A tendency to be influenced by inappropriate factors

It is possible for managers to be unduly influenced by inappropriate factors when managing performance. By not giving sufficient objective scrutiny to the details of the actual performance, there is a danger that the results of the evaluation and the decisions that follow, may be unsound.

Examples of when this pitfall could occur include:

- *giving a member of a weak team a low rating* – e.g., *marking them down as an individual because of the low performance of the whole team, rather than because of their own failings within that team*
- *basing current performance ratings on past performance* – e.g., *looking at historical data rather than evaluating the current situation and achievements, which is potentially damaging to the individual, team and organisation because increases and decreases could be missed*
- *allowing recent ratings to mask overall performance* – e.g., *giving someone a high rating due to a couple of recent big sales, even though they were underachieving on their sales all year*
- *if the manager is a perfectionist and works to their own standards instead of the organisation's standards* – e.g., *marking everyone down even though they do not deserve a low rating*

When managing work performance, objectivity is key. It is important to remove personal ideas and irrelevant facts and opinions from the management process. If possible, managers need to make sure that the appropriate standards are used to measure each individual. For example, if a team member is new and inexperienced, or if they have been off sick or doing other duties for a few months, the manager needs to take these factors into account when assessing them and reviewing their work.

Preparing for Appraisals

The following questions should be considered before undertaking an appraisal. By considering these areas, consideration will be given to whether targets which have been set are realistically achievable with the skills and resources available or are they simply unrealistic?

- *Does the team have clear actions?*
- *Does the team monitor its progress using concrete milestones?*
- *Are the team's successes acknowledged?*
- *Is the team the right size to achieve its objectives?*
- *Does the team have the right resources (skillsets, money, time, people, authority)?*

Managing People

- *Does the team meet regularly?*
- *Do team members understand their roles and are they able to carry them out effectively?*
- *Does the team have good and clear lines of communication with internal and external stakeholders and management?*
- *Is conflict effectively managed within the team?*
- *Is the team open and motivated?*

Conducting appraisals

When conducting appraisals, managers need to consider all aspects of performance management so that the appraisal can be effective. They need to:

- *refer to established performance standards*
- *refer to the individual's goals and objectives* – *based on the standards*
- *measure their performance* – *against evidence, goals, objectives and standards*
- *use formal and informal assessment procedures* – *as appropriate*
- *ensure that formal assessment is fair and objective*

For the appraisal process to be effective, it needs to be a two-way process and good communication skills are essential. When running appraisal sessions, managers need to concentrate on:

- *the content of the appraisal meeting* – *especially for a formal appraisal*
- *communication techniques*

Appraisal Meetings

Appraisals provide a structured way to look at all aspects of the role and the team member's position within the organisation. Features of appraisals include:

- *identifying current skills* – *e.g., doing a skills audit or analysis*
- *identifying strengths and weaknesses* – *e.g., preparing a SWOT analysis (Strengths, Weaknesses, Opportunities for development, Threats that may affect progress)*
- *reviewing and evaluating progress* – *e.g., using evidence-based data and information; referring to informal and formal assessments that have been done; comparing performance against standards and objectives*
- *identifying training needs*
- *discussing methods and developmental activities* – *e.g., mentoring and shadowing; college and skills centre courses; e-training and distance learning*
- *providing ongoing support* – *e.g., reviewing progress at regular intervals; establishing how and when to review progress; providing access to resources and advice*

Managing People

Working to an agenda helps to focus the team member and the manager and make sure that important information is not overlooked. Practical issues need to be well-planned so that the interview runs smoothly – e.g., booking a room; allocating time; informing the people concerned; having the correct documents, data, reports and assessments to hand.

Communication techniques

Managers need to be very aware of the impression that they need and want to make and to adapt their communication skills to make the most of the opportunity to work with the team member and to reinforce their messages. They need to use, for example:

- *open body language and confident eye contact*
- *active listening skills* – e.g., nodding, taking notes and repeating keys points
- *effective questioning techniques* – e.g., a range of open and probing questions to encourage the team member to speak
- *a high standard of written communication* – e.g., good grammar and spelling to demonstrate attention to detail
- *speaking clearly and using appropriate language* – e.g., speaking slowly if necessary; using the right level of jargon for the individual team member
- *an appropriate tone of voice* – e.g., a calm tone to indicate patience and understanding, or a sharp tone to indicate impatience or frustration

Reviewing performance

An important element of performance management is to review progress in a planned way. Assessments need to be done on a regular basis to ensure that:

- *standards are being met or exceeded on a consistent basis*
- *problems are dealt with promptly*
- *measures are put in place as soon as possible*
- *changes are monitored to make sure that they are effective*

This applies to the performance of each individual, each team or department and the organisation as a whole. For individuals, it is important to make it clear about how and when performance will be reviewed again so that they can prepare and have a focus for development and learning activities.

Managing People

Improving Performance

Where performance fails to meet the expected criteria appropriate training and development should be provided for the individual. It is important to recognise that the individuals preferred learning style should be taken into consideration where possible. Selecting the appropriate method or combination of methods of developing skills will help motivate the learner to achieve the desired outcome.

Development Choices

Activity	Advantages	Disadvantages
Coaching	• can be arranged very quickly • does not always detract from the workload • specific to the individual	• personality clashes • difference of opinions • maybe time constraints due to logistics
Internal training course	• usually low-cost • can be arranged fairly quickly	• Time away from workload • Familiarity
External training course	• usually leads to a formal qualification • individual can take some time away from the office environment	• Cost • time away from work
On-the-job shadowing	• immediate • sharing ideas and resources	• Personality clashes • difference of opinions • possible conflict
Secondment	• retained within the business • broadens experience within the company	• Time away from main work role • possible conflict-of-interest, dependent on work areas involved
Special assignment	• provides ownership and accountability • interesting and varied	• Time required to monitor and review

Managing Absence

Absenteeism puts a burden on teammates who have to cover for the individual who has not turned up for work, leading to resentment, stress and missed deadlines. This can affect the overall performance of the team and the organisation, so managers need to take action to manage staff absence.

When managing absence, managers need to:

Managing People

- *monitor absence and attendance levels*
- *follow the organisation's policies and procedures*
- *make sure that team members know what is required*
- *identify organisational causes of absence that need to be addressed*
- *offer support to the team members*

Monitoring absence and attendance levels

Organisations need to track attendance records for a variety of reasons, including:

- **for health and safety** – *e.g., to have an accurate record of people in the building in case there is an emergency evacuation*
- **for payroll records** – *e.g., to work out overtime and bonuses; to pay statutory payments for sickness, maternity or paternity*
- **to monitor absence levels** – *e.g., to look for patterns of behaviour that need to be addressed*
- **to check manning levels – e.g., to see if enough human resources are allocated to projects and tasks**
- **to calculate attendance rewards** – *e.g., bonuses for good attendance*

The Bradford Factor

A useful system that can be used to monitor absence and attendance levels is the Bradford Factor. It generates a score to measure unplanned absences to identify patterns of behaviour that may be causes of concern. The formula is:

$$B \quad = \quad S2 \quad \times \quad D$$

| *Bradford Factor Scoring* | = | *The number of separate instances of absence over a set period* | × | *The number of days of absence in the same period* |

Policies and Procedures

Organisations need a clear policy on absenteeism to show, for example:

- *how they deal with absenteeism in terms of sick pay and compassionate leave*
- *how much notice staff need to give when they cannot come to work*
- *how to ask for help when there are problems with getting to work as required*
- *rewards for good attendance*

Managing People

Managers need to follow procedures when dealing with team members' absences. These might include, for example:

- *keeping attendance records*
- *obtaining a 'Fit Note' from the team member's GP*
- *running 'return to work' interviews when people come back*
- *disciplinary processes for dealing with unauthorised absences*

Make sure that the team members understand what is required

People have personal problems that affect their work from time to time – e.g., their own health issues and sickness, bereavement, illness, separation or divorce. They can also be unhappy with their working conditions and relationships.

Managers and team leaders need to be aware of the causes of unplanned absence and make sure that team members understand their responsibilities for reporting issues and asking for help. Team members need to know:

- *their job and task descriptions, as set out in their employment contract* – e.g., to confirm the employee's responsibilities
- *expected attendance standards*
- *exactly how to report unplanned absences* – e.g., by telephoning a helpline or their line manager before the shift is due to start
- *how to report problems and ask for help* – e.g., by having contact details for HR, the line manager, a helpline or the duty manager for out-of-hours help

Identify organisational causes of absence that need to be addressed

According to ACAS, organisations can cause absenteeism by not taking care of their employees' physical and emotional well-being. Causes can include, for example:

- *a negative business culture* – e.g., where people are generally hostile, unsupportive and in the habit of taking unplanned absences whenever they want without any consequences
- *difficult working patterns* – e.g., with insufficient time to recover from changes in shifts
- *inadequate physical resources* – e.g., insufficient equipment; ongoing equipment failure; unsafe equipment; lack of investment in new technology
- *inadequate human resources* – e.g., not enough staff to cover all tasks; overworked or overloaded team members; staff not having sufficient skills, knowledge or experience for the tasks; poor-quality agency staff who do not work to the expected high standards; lack of training and development activities
- *unreasonable deadlines or bad time management* – e.g., original and revised deadlines are found to be unrealistic
- *inadequate leadership and management* – e.g., poor leadership skills that leave the workforce without vision and direction, inadequate delegation and accountability

Managing People

- *lack of communication* – e.g., *misunderstandings between colleagues and departments; lack of praise, encouragement and guidance*
- *lack of awareness of legal guidelines and compliance requirements* – e.g., *using unacceptable discriminatory language with colleagues; using equipment incorrectly and not following the manufacturer's instructions*

Offer support to the team member

If a team member is often absent and the manager suspects that this is due to personal problems, they may need to enquire about private matters if performance is affected. This can help the individual deal with their problems, show support, improve morale and help the rest of the team to function. The manager may need to, for example:

- *reassure and support the team member*
- *reduce their workload*
- *arrange for them to change their shifts or hours until the personal issues are sorted*
- *ask other team members to help out*
- *engage agency staff to cover*
- *get additional support from other managers and the HR department*

The Importance of Constructive Feedback

We all need feedback to find out how well we are doing. When feedback is good, it gives us positive reinforcement and gives us the confidence to carry on and develop our strengths further. The negative aspects of feedback are useful too because they show us where we need to make changes.

When working to improve performance, feedback needs to be collected over time to allow time for objectives to be achieved or to take effect. If the time period is too short, there may not be enough data available to be able to measure progress. If too long, energy and motivation to achieve objectives may decrease and opportunities to improve may be missed.

Feedback can be formal or informal. Formal feedback will usually be documented and more detailed and be given in meetings or on forms. Informal feedback is often unplanned and can be a brief message or comment, verbal or written.

If we do not give and receive feedback, we have no way of knowing how we are doing from an objective point of view. Our efforts need to be measured against outside standards and opinions to reflect a realistic, three-dimensional picture of our performance in the workplace.

When improving performance, managers and team members need to work together to:

- *collect feedback*
- *use the feedback that has been collected*
- *reflect on work activities*

- *reflect on training activities*
- *develop a plan to improve skills, experience and knowledge*

The team member needs to:

- **assimilate the feedback** – *e.g., think objectively about the comments, digest them and get the ideas into some sort of logical order*
- **update their SWOT analysis and SMART objectives** – *to incorporate the things that have been learned or adapted from the feedback process*
- *decide on the details about how they are going to achieve their revised objectives*
- *investigate details of courses and learning programmes to improve their knowledge*
- *initiate changes in work activities to improve experience and skills take advantage of offers for support and help that arose during the feedback process – e.g. develop opportunities to shadow experienced colleagues; develop relationships with mentors generally, use the confidence gained as a spur to rise to new challenges and chances to prove themselves*

Giving feedback

When giving feedback it is important to consider the person receiving the feedback. If the feedback is positive, it is a good opportunity to give praise and encouragement. This empowers and motivates the team member to continue doing well and not lose focus. They feel valued and respected and will benefit from feeling appreciated and recognised.

If some of the feedback is negative, this needs to be delivered carefully and objectively. The best way can be to use a 'sandwich' technique, where negative news is put between two bits of positive news, for example:

- *praise the team member for a good aspect of their performance*
- *mention and explain areas that need to be improved and give guidance and support about how to improve*
- *finish on a high note about positive aspects, plans and hopes for future developments and improvements*

When we are asked to give feedback about someone else, it can be a good idea to only say things that we would say to that person's face. This helps us to keep our comment's objective, fair, valid and useful. When delivered tactfully, constructive criticism and genuine praise are both valuable and welcome.

There are many different ways of giving feedback to team members, including:

Managing People

Formal reviews with the team member

These provide valuable, organised and focused opportunities for the team member to have detailed conversations with the line manager. They can give and receive feedback, review progress so far, discuss current strengths and issues and set goals and targets for the next stage.

Informal feedback during work activities

Informal feedback can be given at any time – e.g., during on-the-job training; when a task is completed, when something good or bad happens at work. Opportunities to give informal feedback are usually unplanned and can just be a quick email, discussion or passing comment.

Feedback from peers and other team members

Team members can ask peers and other team members to give them formal or informal feedback. It can be useful to have feedback from anyone who can give valuable and valid information that can be used to make future improvements, but the feedback needs to be given carefully and tactfully.

Following a feedback model

Following a feedback model can help to focus the conversation in a positive and useful way. One established theory of how to give constructive and effective feedback is CORBS, which states that feedback needs to be:

- *Clear* – *useful, brief, concise and jargon-free*
- *Owned* – *feedback comes from our own experience, not just hearsay*
- *Regular* – *given regularly and as soon as possible after an event*
- *Balanced* – *negative and positive feedback addressed by constructive and objective advice*
- *Specific* – *with examples, if possible, to back up the comments made*

Managing People

360-degree appraisal

Some organisations use a 360-degree model for formal appraisal, where performance feedback is given from a full circle of people at work – senior managers, line managers, colleagues, team members, customers and the person being appraised. The idea is to give a rounded view of performance from many angles that gives more valuable and detailed feedback than might be gained from just one-line manager. It takes into account the importance of a wider circle of work relationships.

Self-appraisal can feel awkward or uncomfortable and people usually prefer their line manager to take responsibility for scoring their performance. Keeping a reflective diary to monitor activities is useful, however and can be brought into appraisals and reviews with the line manager.

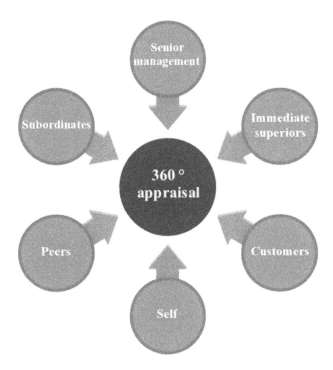

Chapter 6: Building Relationships

Building Relationships

Business Relationships

Organisations have business relationships with many different people and agencies. They can be customers or other stakeholders.

Traditionally, we think of customers as people who buy products or services from a shop or business. However, customers can be:

internal **(other teams and departments within the organisation)**
or
external **(individuals or organisations outside the organisation)**

The term stakeholder refers to anyone who has an interest or concern in the organisation and its activities. They can include, for example, employees, suppliers, shareholders, government agencies, contractors, local residents and customers. Stakeholders are affected by decisions made by the organisation, so it is important to have good business relationships with them.

Some stakeholder relationships are straightforward and are between people that we work with regularly or every day – e.g., team members or line managers. Some stakeholder relationships are more irregular and complicated, especially when different stakeholders are brought together for a project.

Relationships can be sensitive and difficult as we rely on stakeholders to use their influence to help achieve objectives – e.g., approaching lenders for finance, liaising with residents about a proposed housing estate in their area.

Building relationships with stakeholders can be quite challenging and there can be many variables.

For example:

- *the relationship might be formal or informal*
- *the manager might need to take a leadership role with some stakeholders and a subservient role with others*
- *stakeholders may be directly involved with the organisation, or have no connection at all*
- *stakeholders might influence the decision-making process or only be affected by the decisions*

When building and managing stakeholder relationships, it is important to:

- *prepare a stakeholder analysis – to identify stakeholders and their expectations, needs and influence*

Building Relationships

- *communicate with stakeholders*
- *negotiate and influence stakeholders*

Regardless of whether it is a small business or a multinational organisation, the importance of building effective business relationships should never be underestimated.

To conduct business and manage successfully, effective relationships must be established and maintained with employees, teams, suppliers and various other internal and external stakeholders.

Successful stakeholder relationships can enhance the business profile, create potential career opportunities, additional services and overall business success.

Successful stakeholder relationships can be built by:

1. Building trust
Rule number one in the stakeholder game – successful and influential partnerships are ultimately built on trust. Give people a reason to trust you by always doing what you say you are going to do. Be honest and open about project progress and never over-promise or feel pressurised to say yes to unreasonable demands. Stakeholders will respect you more for being transparent about situations and this will ultimately build trust.

2. Think in 'win/win' solutions
Being able (and willing) to put yourself in another person's shoes and understand how they feel is key to building strong stakeholder relationships. Try to understand business situations from a stakeholder's perspective and be committed to sourcing solutions that will benefit all parties. The idea of a win/win solution is not based on compromise but on the understanding that mutual benefit can actually be drawn from every project.

3. Respond
Whether a potential supplier has been in touch (but you do not need anything from them at the moment) or your largest and most important client – remember - always respond. You can obviously prioritise your communications in order of importance, so you do not need to respond straight away, but simply ignoring people shows you have little or no regard for building strong relationships. You never know whether that supplier or client might actually be useful in the future so always send a quick email response or phone call to acknowledge contact. It is vital.

4. Ask questions
The most effective stakeholder relationships are built on people asking purposeful questions whether it be to check understanding of a particular project or prompt discussion. Asking questions, in particular open questions, also develops rapport and encourages conversations. It also gives stakeholders a sense of ownership over particular projects. So, ask away!

Building Relationships

5. Continuously demonstrate your competence

Building great stakeholder relationships is by no means a one-off exercise. You should continuously develop these relationships by demonstrating your competence and reliability, keeping updates on track and communicating key agreements and decisions. Perhaps try treating your stakeholders like you would a valued client; take time to have one-to-one conversations and engage with them regularly. Take interest in their world and you will earn respect, demonstrate your competence and ultimately build strong, meaningful stakeholder relationships

Skills Required for Building Business Relationships

A range of skills are necessary when building and maintaining business relationships. These include:

- *effective communication skills*
- *organisational and planning skills*
- *awareness of objectives and expectations*

Effective communication skills

Effective communication skills are extremely important when managing and developing business relationships. We need to have a wide range of verbal, written and body language skills to perform management and business functions, many of which involve dealing with other people. For example, we need to be able to:

- **collect information about others** – *asking questions about customers' requirements to identify their needs and expectations*
- **use good listening skills** – *when listening to customers, colleagues or other stakeholders to demonstrate understanding*
- **use good speaking skills** – *when making presentations to team members; when serving customers, when discussing business with banks*
- **use effective body language** – *to reinforce verbal messages in meetings, interviews and presentations*
- **use good writing skills** – *using correct grammar, spelling and techniques when writing emails, reports, letters or publicity materials*
- **use emotional intelligence** – *using our ability to see the situation from the customer's point of view*

It is crucially important to any manager to work closely with stakeholders whose opinions and actions will directly impact on the success of the organisation. It is "crucial" because around 55% of organisations that experience failure do so due to poor communication.

Communication styles and methods will need to be adapted to suit each situation and each person. Everyone has a responsibility to make sure that messages and information are clear and easy to understand.

Building Relationships

Effective communication skills enable us to:

- **influence decision-making** – *when making sales to customers, when seeking agreement from stakeholders*
- **establish trust and build a rapport** – *when developing a team or working with new customers*
- **maintain engagement** – *communicating items of interest on a regular basis to keep people informed and engaged*
- **solve problems** – *agreeing to compromise or finding a win-win solution*
- **maintain good records that help with management** – *notes about someone's private news or celebrations that we can mention next time we meet*

Organisational and Planning Skills

When building and maintaining business relationships, it is important to be organised. There is a need to:

- **plan ahead** – *devising a marketing strategy for attracting new customers and retaining established ones*
- **be on time** – *for meetings or training sessions*
- **keep accurate and useful records** – *to track progress of a project or complaint; when producing reports for directors, when sending in returns and information to government departments*
- **organise meetings and events** – *to deliver information about new products or services to customers and other stakeholders*
- **give other people regular attention** – *having monthly telephone calls or meetings to keep everything up to date*

Awareness of Objectives and Expectations

When building relationships, there is a need to keep an eye on objectives. Actions and words need to support organisational, team and individual objectives, so that activities are focused.

Awareness must also be maintained of the other person's expectations, so that resources and the approach can be adapted to satisfy their needs and requirements. Expectations usually need to be met or exceeded, and it helps to be clear about them when we build and maintain business relationships.

Being aware of objectives and expectations enables us to, for example:

- *establish and agree objectives – when planning work tasks for the team*
- *meet deadlines – to deliver reports on time; to complete tasks that affect other people*
- *communicate and allocate tasks effectively – to suit team members' skills and needs as well as the organisation's requirements*
- *ensure that expectations are met where possible – calling people back when we promised; dealing with problems as agreed*

Building Relationships

Stakeholders

A stakeholder is anybody who can affect or is affected by an organisation, strategy or project. They can be internal or external and they can be at senior or junior levels.

Stakeholders are crucial to the success of an organisation. Neglect them and they will actively work against you. Manage them well and they will actively promote you and the organisation.

Importance of Stakeholder Management

Organisations exist to serve and provide for their general stakeholders including customers and shareholders. There are three key principles why any organisation exists.

- *To survive*
- *To make a profit*
- *To expand and develop*

Without customers and stakeholders common none of the three purposes of an organisation are achievable and thus the organisation will fail. The provision of a service or product of the very highest quality, within the given budget and within the required time limits, is expected and even rightly demanded by the stakeholders, thus the relationship between quality and stakeholders become self-evident.

The more people who are affected by the work you do, the more likely it is that some of them will have significant power and influence over your work.

These people are your stakeholders. They could be strong supporters of the work being done – or they could block it. It is therefore essential to identify who the stakeholders are and win them over as soon as possible.

A stakeholder-based approach to business delivers four key benefits:

Getting a business into shape
The opinions of the most powerful stakeholders can help define the operation at an early stage. These stakeholders will then more likely support the organisation and their input can also improve the quality of the business.

Winning resources
Gaining support from powerful stakeholders can help win more resources, such as people, time or money. This makes it more likely that the operation will be successful.

Building Relationships

Building understanding
By communicating with stakeholders early and often, they will fully grasp what you are doing and understand the benefits the organisation may be able to offer. This means that they can more actively support the organisation when necessary.

Getting ahead of the game
Understanding stakeholders means that you can anticipate and predict their reactions to the operation as it develops. This allows the planning of actions that will be more likely win their support.

The way in which stakeholders are managed depends on:

- *The size and complexity of the organisation.*
- *The amount of help needed to achieve the results required.* - *This could include sponsorship, advice and expert input, physical resources, reviews of material to increase quality and so on.*
- *The time available to communicate.* - *Consider how to manage the time spent on communication, particularly if the organisation requires a lot of stakeholder input. It is often better to allocate more time to communicating with stakeholders, rather than trying to "get by" without all the help or input that needed.*

Identifying Stakeholders

The first step in stakeholder management is to identify your stakeholders. List everybody that you can think of who is, or will, be affected by the organisation. Ask as many people as possible and capture every name, organisation or type of stakeholder they can think of. Common examples of stakeholders include employees, customers, shareholders, suppliers, communities and governments.

Stakeholders are often classified into three groups which are primary comment secondary or tertiary.

- *Primary stakeholders* - *are those who influence the actual route of the business, including business managers, external regulatory bodies and employees.*
- *Secondary stakeholders* - *those who receive the benefits of the organisation less directly. This could include businesses who benefit from the existence of the organisation.*
- *Tertiary stakeholders* - *include corporate clients as they are affected more indirectly than those within the primary and secondary groups.*

Types of Stakeholders

Customers
Many would argue that businesses exist to serve their customers. Customers are actually stakeholders of a business; in that they are impacted by the quality of service/products and

---

Building Relationships

their value. For example, passengers traveling on an airplane literally have their lives in the company's hands when flying with the airline.

Stake: Product/service quality and value

Employees
Employees have a direct stake in the company in that they earn an income to support themselves, along with other benefits (both monetary and non-monetary). Depending on the nature of the business, employees may also have a health and safety interest (for example, in the industries of transportation, mining, oil and gas, construction, etc.).

Stake: Employment income and safety

Investors
Investors include both shareholders and debtholders. Shareholders invest capital in the business and expect to earn a certain rate of return on that invested capital. Investors are commonly concerned with the concept of shareholder value. Lumped in with this group are all other providers of capital, such as lenders and potential acquirers. All shareholders are inherently stakeholders, but stakeholders are not inherently shareholders.

Stake: Financial returns

Suppliers and Vendors
Suppliers and vendors sell goods and/or services to a business and rely on it for revenue generation and on-going income. In many industries, suppliers also have their health and safety on the line, as they may be directly involved in the company's operations.

Stake: Revenues and safety

Communities
Communities are major stakeholders in large businesses located in them. They are impacted by a wide range of things, including job creation, economic development, health and safety. When a big company enters or exits a small community, there is an immediate and significant impact on employment, incomes and spending in the area. With some industries, there is a potential health impact, too, as companies may alter the environment.

Stake: Health, safety, economic development

Governments
Governments can also be considered a major stakeholder in a business, as they collect taxes from the company (corporate income taxes), as well as from all the people it employs (payroll taxes) and from other spending the company incurs (sales taxes). Governments benefit from the overall Gross Domestic Product (GDP) that companies contribute to.

Stake: Taxes and GDP

Building Relationships

Stakeholders may be further classified into internal and external stakeholders. Internal stakeholders being those who have a direct involvement with the organisation and external stakeholders are those who are affected by the organisation and or its activities and may include shareholders, the local community, those with whom who the organisation has a contract and customers. It will also comprise those who feel they are negatively affected by the presence and activities of the organisation as a consequence, there may need to be trade-offs in trying to please all of them.

A fuller list might typically include:

Internal	External
team members line managers senior managers board members	potential employees customers suppliers pressure groups government agencies and regulatory organisations general public shareholders suppliers partners contractors

Building Relationships

Stakeholder Analysis

Stakeholder analysis is a useful tool that helps identify the people who will affect and influence an organisation and those who will be influenced by it. The analysis helps managers to tailor their approach to get the most out of each relationship.

One method to accomplish this is to list the stakeholders and then determine the degree of their interest and influence in the business. If stakeholders have a high degree of interest, the business needs to communicate with them on a regular basis and keep them informed about its activities. The business also needs to keep them placated.

Stakeholder Analysis is an effective three-step process for identifying, prioritising and understanding your stakeholders

The first step is to work out who stakeholders are, usually during a brainstorming or mind-mapping session. They can include:

- *line managers*
- *team members*
- *colleagues in other departments and teams*
- *customers and potential customers*
- *shareholders and owners of the organisation*
- *suppliers and manufacturers*
- *media contacts*
- *government departments and agencies*
- *lenders and other financial consultants*
- *analysts and other outside professionals*
- *the general public and local community*
- *family and friends*

The second step is to prioritise the stakeholders and work out who has the most influence for a particular project or objective. This enables the organisation to target its attention and tailor the approach.

For example, if we need to find and develop the customer base, the main stakeholders who can influence the outcome may include established customers, potential customers, media contacts and our colleagues in the sales and marketing department.

 The third step is to get to know the relevant stakeholders, so it becomes clear exactly how to target the approach.

For example, there is a need to find out about their motivation, plans, values, contacts and objectives. This step also helps identify the stakeholders who could have a negative effect on the organisation – e.g., those who have a conflict of interest or want to undermine others.

Building Relationships

Prioritising Stakeholders

Having produced a list of people and organisations that are affected by the work. Some of these may have the power either to block that work or to advance it. Some may be interested in what you are doing, while others may not care, so you need to work out who you need to prioritise.

You can map out your stakeholders and classify them according to their power over your work and their interest in it, on a Power/Interest Grid

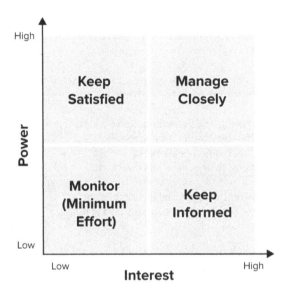

The position that you allocate to a stakeholder on the grid shows you the actions you need to take with them:

- *High power, highly interested people (Manage Closely):* you must fully engage these people and make the greatest efforts to satisfy them.

- *High power, less interested people (Keep Satisfied):* put enough work in with these people to keep them satisfied, but not so much that they become bored with your message.

- *Low power, highly interested people (Keep Informed):* adequately inform these people and talk to them to ensure that no major issues are arising. People in this category can often be very helpful with the detail of your project.

- *Low power, less interested people (Monitor):* again, monitor these people, but do not bore them with excessive communication.

Building Relationships

Understanding Stakeholders

All business relationships tend to be two-way relationships, where each party needs and wants something. Being aware of the other party's needs and expectations, then balancing them with
personal and organisational requirements, is an ongoing process that needs to be tackled with an
open mind, a willingness to adapt, confidence and skill.

Once an organisation has identified its stakeholders and their importance to the business, it can begin to plan based on their needs and expectations. Each stakeholder has concerns that it expects to be met by the business. For example, the business's owners expect it to be profitable and to distribute that profit to them while local and central government expect it to obey the law and pay its taxes on time.

The importance of each stakeholder to the business determines the degree to which the business attempts to accommodate the stakeholder in the course of planning its actions.

The impact of stakeholder needs and expectations on businesses is inescapable and ubiquitous.
Businesses exist to meet the expectations of one specific
stakeholder in the sense that businesses are set up and
operated to produce profit for their owners and investors.

Businesses also must consider the needs and expectations of
other stakeholders because of their ability to help and hinder
their operations.

For example, a business should be considerate of the
community in which it is based because it can improve its
reputation and strengthens its market presence.

On the other hand, if the business chooses to ignore its local community, that disregard becomes a negative mark on its reputation and can result in other sanctions if relations become bad enough.

The only stakeholders that businesses can ignore are the ones with little interest and influence on their operations.

Organisations often struggle to prioritise stakeholders and their competing interests. Where stakeholders are aligned, the process is easy. However, in many cases, they do not have the same interests.

Example:
if the company is pressured by shareholders to cut costs, it may lay off employees or reduce their wages, which presents a difficult trade off.

Jack Ma, the CEO of Alibaba, has famously said that, in his company, they rank stakeholders in the following priority sequence:

Building Relationships

Customers
Employees
Investors

Much of the prioritisation will be based on the stage a company is in.

Example:
if it is a start-up or an early-stage business, then customers and employees are more likely to be the stakeholders considered foremost. If it is a mature, publicly traded company, then shareholders are likely to be front and centre.

At the end of the day, it is up to the organisation, the CEO and the board of directors to determine the appropriate ranking of stakeholders when competing interests arise.

Managing Stakeholder Expectations

The most important part of operational management may be getting the business done, but the way you manage stakeholder expectations will directly affect your results.

- *Staff expect they will have all the time, tools and support they need to get their job done without burning out*
- *Top management expect the job to be completed successfully*
- *Clients expect requirements followed and executed.*
- *Plenty is expected from you as a leader, too.*

However, sometimes, communication falls short and one side is left expecting more than the other side can offer.

The trick to making sure that the business runs smoothly is in managing stakeholder expectations.

Around 57% of organisations fail because the communication was not up to standard; there was not enough transparency on either end, client or delivery team.

Not managing expectations leads to obstacles such as:

- *Team and stakeholder disengagement*
- *Unclear objectives and goals*
- *Poor prioritisation*
- *Inadequate risk management*
- *Performance issues.*

Building Relationships

It is much easier to manage a business when everyone is on the same page and that's exactly what expectation management is all about.

Fortunately, managing stakeholder expectations does not have to be complicated.

There are 9 key areas you should focus on:

1. Engage from the beginning and plan well
Planning is the key to success. However, the majority of people rush through planning, eager to get to work and get the clients off their backs. This is often what leads to expectation mismanagement, as the rules, objectives and metrics have not been properly outlined.

In order to manage everyone's expectations in the planning phase, you should communicate clearly and transparently with the clients, operational teams and top management regarding:

> *Objectives*
> *Goals*
> *Scope*
> *Changes*
> *Expectations.*

Make sure you fully understand what their expectations are and that you are clear on which expectations you will and will not meet.

Then document it in your planning documents. Later on, if there is any confusion, you can simply reference them. You should put in the maximum amount of effort and attention into the planning. If you have done everything properly, the rest of your work will be much easier.

2. Manage team expectations
It is best to include your team in any planning phase. If that is not possible, the work requirements should still be discussed with them. When requirements and roles are unclear, staff often feel like they are taking on too much once the task is underway. To avoid any confusions and unrealistic expectations:

> *Define roles and responsibilities clearly and early*
> *Define schedules and task dependencies within the team*
> *Establish KPIs and metrics that will be used*
> *Set up a communication plan.*

3. Understand stakeholder expectations
A manager, must also be a psychologist who constantly asks:

> *"Why do they want what they want?"*

Building Relationships

A manager must understand why stakeholders have expectations they have.

For example, why do clients expect different scope? Do they expect to be highly engaged with the business or simply briefed periodically? When managing expectations, it is important to ask what the team, top management and the clients are expecting from the organisation and if it can give that to them.

The most important part of managing expectations is understanding them.

Everyone has clear goals which they state, but it is vital to understand what they are really hoping to get on completion. For team members, that might be a rise. For top management, improved public esteem. Whatever it is, understand it and then approach those expectations accordingly.

4. Define levels of engagement
Some stakeholders will naturally be more engaged with the business. For example, the delivery team. However, others may want to be engaged more or less than might be assume they would like.

It is important to define levels of engagement, as well and create a communication plan for each stakeholder group. Encourage stakeholders to be proactive. If they have questions, create a forum or channel to ask them. Schedule ample time for status updates.

5. Changes and escalation
Make sure the scope is defined early on, as well as the change policy:

- *What type of changes would the organisation be willing to implement?*
- *What type of changes does the organisation lack the resources for?*
- *Have the change document available so you always know how to proceed.*

If an issue gets out of hand, it should be clearly defined who it can be escalated to. If there is a need to escalate, guide the team through the process and ensure that everyone's expectations are still being met.

6. Manage conflict
When there is conflict, a natural reaction may be to stop it immediately and decide on the course of action. However, it is much better to manage it, keeping the goals of each party in mind.

If team members are butting heads, take the time to sit down with them and understand what the problem really is. Assess whether the conflict is a professional or a personal issue.

Building Relationships

Encourage team members to communicate and offer their feedback on everything from progress to suggestions.

7. Record issues, changes and activity
Recording issues, changes and stakeholder activity is a must if expectations are to be successfully managed. Not only will recording them help understand stakeholders' motivations, but it will also help assess own performance.

It will allow the creation of better strategies in the future if it can be seen what worked and what did not.

8. Manage perceptions
Own perception of the business is one thing. The way the stakeholders perceive the business is an entirely different thing. Make sure that everyone's perception of the business is similar, if not exactly the same.

Communicate with stakeholders to ensure their perception is realistic.

9. Do not micromanage (but manage)
A team may be taking on more than they can handle, which is why it is important not only to manage the business but help them manage their time as well.

Let the team know that there is support to help them. Keep an eye on workflows to ensure they are not pushing harder than they can. In the long term, this will earn their respect and subsequent communication will be much better.

After all, it all comes down to communication.

Understand everyone's expectations, plan to meet them, or be honest about why you can't. - A business will be all the better for it

EXPECTATIONS

Building Relationships

Communicating with Stakeholders

As with all business relationships, good communication skills are essential when building and managing relationships with stakeholders. Well-chosen questioning and listening techniques, body
language, emotional intelligence and good writing skills help managers to communicate effectively.
Assertiveness, tone of voice, posture and the language used also need to be adapted to suit each
situation as the manager's role in each relationship can vary.

The approach may be different when dealing with:

- **team members** – *the manager may have more of a leadership role, be more assertive and confident and use work-based jargon*
- **established customers** – *the manager probably needs to be relaxed, well-informed and confident and treat the customers as equals*
- **potential customers** – *good questioning and listening skills are needed to learn about their needs and expectations and a quieter approach may be required*
- **senior managers and directors** – *the manager needs to be seen as being trustworthy, capable and aware of the influence of the more senior staff and confident but not too assertive*
- **media** – *as a spokesperson for the organisation, the manager usually needs to be friendly, approachable, extremely knowledgeable and well-briefed and avoid the use of jargon*
- **lenders and other outside professionals** – *the manager needs to be confident and well prepared, to show that they understand the stakeholders' influence and knowledge of the subject and use appropriate language and posture*

The communication skills used with customers are also important when dealing with stakeholders.

Effective communication skills enable managers to:

- **influence decision-making** – *e.g., by showing knowledge and confidence when pitching for finance or support*
- **establish trust and build a rapport** – *e.g., by demonstrating good speaking and listening skills when handling queries and problems effectively in the boardroom*
- **maintain engagement** – *e.g., by being consistent and confident and able to see beyond immediate problems and setbacks when negotiating with local residents and councillors*
- **solve problems** – *e.g., by showing good negotiation skills to find a compromise or win-win solution when agreeing tough objectives with team members*
- **maintain good records that help with management** – *e.g., by keeping track of progress in a format that can be understood and appreciated by the stakeholders*

Building Relationships

Effective communication skills are extremely important when managing and developing business relationships There is a need to have a wide range of verbal written and body language skills to perform management and business functions, many of which involve dealing with other people.

It is important to be able to:

- *Collect information about others* - *e.g., asking questions about customer requirements to identify their needs and expectations*
- *Use good listening skills* - *e.g., when listening to customers colleagues or other stakeholders to demonstrate understanding*
- *Use good speaking skills* - *e.g., when making presentations to team members; When serving customers, when discussing business with banks*
- *Use effective body language* - *e.g., to reinforce verbal messages in meetings, interviews and presentations*
- *Good writing skills* - *e.g., using correct grammar, spelling and techniques when writing emails, reports, letters or publicity materials*
- *Use emotional intelligence* - *e.g., using the ability to see the situation from the customers point of view*

The communication style and method will also need to be adapted to suit each situation and each person, wherever possible. There is responsibility to ensure that all messages and information are clear and easy to understand

Organisation and Planning skills

When building and maintaining business relationships, it is important to be organised in order to:

- *Plan ahead* - *e.g., devising a marketing strategy for attracting new customers and retaining established ones*
- *Be on time* - *e.g., for meetings or training sessions*
- *Keep accurate and useful records* - *e.g., to track progress of a project or complaint; when producing reports for directors, when sending in returns and information to government departments*
- *Organise meetings and events* - *e.g., to deliver information about new products or services to customers and other stakeholders*
- *Give other people regular attention* - *e.g., having monthly telephone calls or meetings to keep everything up to date*

You can start to devise a plan for communicating with your stakeholders once you have mapped them on a Power/Interest Grid.

Establishing ground rules for effective stakeholder communication will save time, remove obstacles and ultimately, put the business in the place it seeks to be. There are several

Building Relationships

communication methods you should implement when communicating with stakeholders in your company.

All methods of communication described below have their upsides and downsides, so make sure you pick the right one depending on the message you are trying to send to your stakeholders.

Schedule a meeting

Stakeholder meetings are the most common communication method in place for corporations, especially since they can save time in conveying the message to a large number of people. Best ways to communicate the message would be PowerPoint, Prezi or any of the mind mapping software solutions available online. Being in the same room with stakeholders should avoid misinterpretation issues.

However, beware that with growing distributed teams, scheduled meetings are becoming a thing of the past. With growing online platforms that ensure real-time transparency, clients are no longer passive consumers of information. Delivering periodic reports without continuous communication will not cut it anymore.

Send out a newsletter

Using the company's intranet or collaboration platform already in place, you can act proactively and define a newsletter to be sent out to stakeholders at given time periods. It can be great for including even stakeholders who are not directly involved with your project. Beware that e-mail is a one-way communication channel, so you should avoid it for issues that require immediate feedback.

Separate online "screen to screen" meetings

As time-consuming as they can be separate face to face meetings are the best way to get the message across stakeholders. Not everyone responds to your presentation style equally, so by meeting stakeholders separately, you can address their concerns in more detail and with greater control. Of course, again, as a result of the graphically dispersed teams and the growing trend of including independent contractors in projects "screen to screen" is becoming the new "face to face", since so many of the meetings are held via online communication and collaboration platforms. Having a presentation is optional; you are better off focusing on the dialogue.

Project summary report

Project summary reports are usually sent out in predefined periods (weekly, monthly). The protocol is already agreed upon here, so if your project is running on time and within budget, you should not have any concerns. Backed up with data and statistics you should highlight the top performing parts of your project and reassure the stakeholders you have the situation in control.

Schedule a conference call

Conference calls are most commonly used in situations where the issue is too urgent for a meeting. So, whenever you feel there is an obstacle that needs to be resolved immediately you can schedule a conference call, which can be arranged in the matter of minutes/hours. Have in mind that conference calls are better for one-way communication so it would be a good idea to have an agenda prepared before the conference call starts.

Building Relationships

Lunch meetings

Lunch meetings would fall into the informal communication category of stakeholder meetings. They would be a great idea for getting honest feedback or getting stakeholders to sign off on a particular idea you have in mind. Have in mind that informal meetings can be just as effective as the official ones.

It is recommended that you approach your choice of communications channels with an open mind. Consider which channels will be most effective to reach and engage your audiences. Resist the impulse to revert automatically to channels that you have used previously, or that you are familiar with, unless and until you know they are the right channels for your project and your audiences.

There are three questions that can guide your choice of communications channels:

- *What channels do your target audiences already use and trust?*
  Think about their existing behaviour. What sources of information do they already use/respond to? Do not invest in channels that your audience do not, or will not, use and trust.

- *What is the purpose of your communication?*
  Some channels lend themselves to communicating complex information; some are efficient ways of delivering short pieces of relevant information. The model below illustrates this on a spectrum.

- *What resources do you have?*
  Social media and 'owned' media that you may have access to (existing organisational websites, e-news, newsletters, etc.) are free to use but will need a combination of set-up time and regular maintenance.

  Events, printed materials, videos and media coverage will need time and budget and you may need to bring in specialist skills. Your choice of channels will need to match the resources you have.

  The channels you use to reach and engage people should depend on what you need to achieve with your communications, the preference of your target audience and the resources and budget you have available.

Building Relationships

Richest Channel

Leanest Channel

Best for engaging, creating
trust/connection and
emotional/complex messages

Best for transfer of
data, clarity,
longevity

Physical presence	Personal interactive	Impersonal interactive	Impersonal static
(one-to-one meetings, events)	*(phone, webinar, targeted social media)*	*(email, social media)*	*(letter, report, e-news updates, newsletters)*

If you have a need to communicate a complex issue, then most of your channels will be on the left of the spectrum above. However, do all your channels lie at one end of the spectrum? One-to-one meetings may need to be reinforced by regular e-news updates. Mass social media communications may be augmented by carefully targeted events.

You may need to use a range of channels to achieve all your objectives. Some channels you may want to consider are set out in the table below:

Building Relationships

Communications Channel	Good For	Consider
Group meetings, workshops, conferences	*Listening, brainstorming, relationship building, building and sharing purpose, exchange of complex learning and information, building trust and loyalty, engaging early adopters.*	*Time and cost resource; do participants have sufficient time/ motivation to attend? Timing and location: make it easy/ appealing to attend or piggyback on existing meetings.*
Launch events	*Internal morale, stakeholder awareness, can provide a hook for media coverage.*	*Time and cost resource; do target audiences have sufficient interest/ motivation to attend? Timing and location: make it easy/ appealing to attend. Media coverage: do you have something genuinely newsworthy?*
1:1 meetings	*Engaging influencers/stakeholders; building knowledge and trust; building or maintaining key relationships.*	*The messages you want to give in the meeting and how to follow up to ensure the relationship is maintained.*
Webinars	*Exchange of complex information or learning; maintaining relationships; project management among dispersed teams.*	*Scheduling: think of a time likely to be convenient to most participants. Promoting: make sure people know about it and remind them. Organising: give it some leadership and structure. Ensure the content is engaging.*
Social media *(e.g., Twitter, Facebook, LinkedIn)*	*Finding or creating networks with niche specialisation or interests; building a profile; directing to other communications (website or blog); brief, real-time updates; maintaining relationships; exchange of information/learning; place for like-minded to interact; reaching early adopters.*	*Content: who will post and regularly update/respond. Need to focus more time on reacting/ responding to others to build relationships. How can you use this to cross-promote another comms (i.e., an online blog)?*
Media coverage *(professional and consumer media)*	*Credibility (a third-party endorsement) and reputation; internal morale; improving awareness; influencing debates and agendas.*	*Time and skills required; need to be able to respond to any interest in very short timeframes; lack of ability to 'control' the message. Plan any media activity with the knowledge of senior sponsors and their comms leads.*
Film/animation	*Creating an emotional connection with a cause; telling stories that can illustrate complex issues; longevity (can be used more than once).*	*Resource and budgets; how will you promote/distribute/make it available to ensure return on investment. Length: online films should be as short as possible (one–three minutes as a general rule).*

Building Relationships

Communications Channel	Good For	Consider
Website (and/or intranet sites)	Credibility; demonstrating full range of work; attracting new members/audiences; information exchange; accessibility.	Time and cost resource for initial and ongoing development; ability to keep up to date; analytics for evaluating use/impact. Consider creating a web page hosted on the web site of the sponsor organisation/partners.
Blogs	Demonstrating expertise, learning and knowledge transfer; content for social media; can boost traffic to website; place for like-minded to interact.	Content: a catchy title; a subject your audience cares about; a central point, argument or call to action. Promoting the blog through social media channels. Blogging through existing sites with an established audience.
Email	Low cost, regular updates; driving traffic to website or blog.	Writing style and visuals: emails are easy to delete. Ensure that content and look of yours is audience-focused and stands out from crowd.
Letter	Now more unusual/distinctive than email; easy to personalise if small print run.	Language, layout, audience focus – all usual principles for good communications apply.
Leaflet, brochure, flyer, quick reference cards	Longevity; visual impact; means of communicating quite detailed information; control of message/s.	Resource for production and effective distribution (too often they are produced without sufficient thought/budget for distribution).
Merchandise or display materials (posters, mouse mats, wall charts, screensavers, pens, certificates, infographics)	Longevity; visual impact; thanking and recognising supporters and celebrating success.	Budget: is the cost justified? How will it be perceived by others? Developing tools that combine your message with useful content for your audience in a format they will use.
Online network	Facilitating information exchange; building a community.	Cloud-based technology make this possible and affordable. Easy to set up groups through social media, e.g., LinkedIn, but they need to be actively maintained.
Advertising	Communicating a strong, clear sales message; controlling how your message is received.	Can you measure its effectiveness and justify the costs involved? Can the channel owner demonstrate good return on investment and data on the readership among your audience?
Newsletters (e-news/hard copy)	Keeping a defined group of people up to date with your activities; keeping in touch.	Can you achieve more impact submitting content to existing newsletters run by others?
Mobile technology/ SMS/mobile apps	Flagging new content. Quick delivery of short, simple messages or tools.	Is the content valued and does it address a genuine need?

Building Relationships

Here are some digital and online multimedia tools and channels to consider using in your communications.

Format	Uses, Benefits and Considerations
Video	• Good for showing at meetings and events and provides a legacy for the project. • Brings life to ideas and concepts and an engaging way of telling a story and sharing the perspective of staff/patients. • Combinations of film locations – as opposed to a 'talking head' – generally more engaging. • Increasingly produced by amateurs - can be expensive if involving a film production company – around £1,500 for 'talking head', up to maybe £4,000 if location filming (e.g., in workplace) is included. • You can create very short (6 seconds) video clips using Vine (a free app) – they have a 'homemade' feel to them provide a visual snapshot. • People are increasingly used to watching video online, especially with rise of mobile and tablet use. Upload films to YouTube which increases visibility of content in Google searches.
Audio slideshow	• Quick-win content, especially if a presentation has already been prepared for offline use (e.g., at a conference). • Cheap to produce (around £300) and fairly quick to turn around. • Can help to explain and illustrate ideas at the same time (through voice and visual). • Slideshows can also be uploaded to SlideShare (open-source software) which increases visibility of content.
Audio clip	• Cheap to produce (around £300) and quick to turnaround. • Should not be too long (max 5 mins) unless it is very engaging. • You can create free audio clips using the Audioboom app (on all platforms, www.audioboom.com).
Animation	• Can be creative with visual to convey complex ideas, especially when you are doing lots of referring to and interpreting of figures. • Expensive and resource-intensive to produce. Around £7,000 and upwards.
Infographic	• Visual way of communicating data rather than simple chart or written copy – great for illustrating what data means, quickly. • Can be flat infographics or interactive • Good for sharing on social media, especially Facebook where image-led updates get highest levels of engagement. • Costs would be around £300 for non-interactive but increase significantly for interactive.
Prezi	• Interactive presentations. • Good for presenting content that is detailed and joins up in various ways – plays in a linear way but you can explore however you like. • Can simply be a more engaging way to do a presentation compared to PowerPoint. • Can embed videos, links etc which you cannot do in an audio slideshow.

Building Relationships

Benefits of Effective Stakeholder Engagement

Learning
Engaging with different perspectives provides opportunities for learning and potentially changing an approach to ensure it fits the needs of stakeholders.

On decision-making
Understanding the views and interests of stakeholders can lead to more effective decision-making.
This is more than just getting the language right. In understanding issues and concerns, it provides an opportunity to reflect on what will and will not work and why.

Saving time and money
Engaging early can lead to savings of both time and money in the long term. Stakeholder engagement is not only critical to developing a robust policy or product, but to develop a real understanding of needs.

Risk management
Being open to different can improve risk management through potentially highlighting previously unknown issues and help with prioritisation.

Accountability
Engaging with stakeholders is central to improving accountability within an own organisation as well as to the wider market. Transparency is important – be clear about the planned outcomes and the steps on the way.

Understand needs
Understanding the full range of needs and views can let to better policy making and better outcomes.

Building Relationships

Managing Stakeholder Meetings

Every business or organisation has individuals and groups who are interested in the activities of the business and have a stake in its success. Keeping stakeholders informed is the best way to keep them engaged and up to date on topics having a potential impact on the business. By involving stakeholders in decision-making and communicating regularly through meetings and other channels, it will be easier to get their approval for new ideas and their support if problems do arise.

Stakeholders

Internal stakeholders can include employees, managers, departments, demographic groups, the board of directors or any group or individual potentially affected by a program or policy or with a need to know. External stakeholders include shareholders (or stockholders), who own stock in the company, customers, suppliers, labour unions, community groups and the government. Stakeholders differ depending on the topic.

Meeting Participants

When a stakeholder meeting is scheduled, a representative from each of the stakeholder groups is invited to attend. Others from the stakeholder group also might participate depending on their need to know and ability to contribute to the discussion. One or more staff members from the department responsible for stakeholder relations also are present to facilitate the discussion, take notes and attend to meeting logistics. Internal or external subject-matter experts are invited to give presentations on a specific topic or answer questions.

Meetings

The frequency of stakeholder meetings depends on the nature of overall stakeholder communication. When stakeholders are kept informed through newsletters, email and periodic reports through a website, a meeting might only be necessary for an annual progress report or to vote on a specific topic. Meetings also are held when stakeholders need to be made aware of a new program or give feedback on an issue. Standing committees made up of stakeholders are sometimes created to meet on a regular basis and serve as decision-making bodies or advisory boards to a business or organisation.

Topics

Stakeholder meetings cover a broad range of topics. Negotiation sessions between labour unions and companies are one type of stakeholder meeting. Community members, legislators and local businesses are stakeholders in zoning laws and would attend a meeting involving rezoning for new construction. A department planning to revise the company website would meet with content owners and others who rely on the Internet for business purposes to get their input about the process.

Meeting Outcome

Meeting proceedings typically are recorded and distributed to all stakeholder groups and individuals in attendance at the meeting. Effective meeting minutes include when and where it was held, participants and their roles, topics discussed, decisions reached, action items and responsibilities and items carried over for future discussion.

Building Relationships

Stakeholder meetings give all of those with an interest in your business a chance to stay involved in the operations of the company. The meetings are typically targeted at the most influential stakeholders, such as shareholders, executives or partnering companies.

Meetings for different types of stakeholders are also an option so you are able to tailor the information presented based on how the stakeholder influences the company. Meetings are often educational and informational, covering general topics or new changes coming to the company. A well-organised meeting is key to make a positive impression on stakeholders.

1. *Identify the specific purpose of the stakeholder meeting, as well as the specific audience. For example, plan a meeting for your suppliers to address changes in your purchasing process or a meeting with shareholders to keep them updated on an upcoming corporate merger. Use this purpose and the specific audience as a planning tool for the meeting.*

2. *Write an agenda that covers each portion of the meeting. Determine how you will start the meeting, present the information and wrap up the meeting. Include key points on the agenda that you plan to cover to serve as an outline for yourself and the meeting attendees.*

3. *Write a list of questions or discussion topics that enables you to gain feedback from the stakeholders. Determine what type of information you want to learn from them beforehand. An example of information you might seek is feedback on your current products or services, as well as suggestions for how to improve them going forward.*

4. *Assemble documents you plan to pass out to stakeholders at the meeting. Provide handouts for relevant information, such as the past year's financial information for shareholders or investors.*

5. *Schedule the meeting for a time and location that works for the majority of the stakeholders involved. Choose a location with enough space to comfortably hold the number of people and facilitate the type of activities you plan to do.*

6. *Call the meeting to order on time so it does not run long. Follow the agenda and stay on schedule as much as possible while allowing stakeholders the chance to provide input.*

7. *Send out a copy of the minutes to all who attended the meeting as a method of following up. Encourage the participants to contact you with any questions or concerns after the conclusion of the meeting.*

Building Relationships

Managing Stakeholder Conflict

Conflict is an emotive word and its meaning can vary. In the Oxford Dictionary, definitions include:

- *a serious disagreement or argument, typically a protracted one*
- *a serious incompatibility between two or more opinions, principles or interests*
- *to be incompatible or at variance with something or someone*

Types of Conflict

The first step after identifying a conflict has arisen, is to determine the nature of the conflict. There are a number of common types of conflicts that occur which are closely related to the reasons they occur.

Data Conflict
The first type of conflict is a "data conflict". This is typically where stakeholders are not agreeing to a requirement that is specified in a certain way. For example, the business stakeholder might want to retrieve 1000 records at a time in real-time, whereas the technology stakeholder knows this is practically impossible and not feasible.

Conflict of Interest
The second type of conflict is a conflict of interest. This type of conflict arises when two or more stakeholders have different priorities or goals within their own business area, which is determining the requirements they are asking for. An example of this could be that the customer services stakeholder is asking to be able to see all personal customer data when supporting a customer on the phone where the organisation's Data Privacy stakeholder is saying that the personal information of customers is sensitive and should not be available in its entirety to the customer services representatives.

Conflict of Value
The third type of conflict is referred to as a "conflict of value". This type of conflict arises when the stakeholders have different values or beliefs about what is acceptable or not acceptable. For example, one stakeholder might believe it is acceptable to ask a customer to enter their cultural heritage, as a mandatory field on the screen during an online application for life insurance, whereas the other stakeholder might believe this is an unacceptable request and should only be an optional field for the customer to provide if they choose to.

Relationship Conflict
The fourth type of conflict is referred to as relationship conflict. This is the type of personal relationship conflict where two stakeholders simply do not get along. This causes some emotional anxiety during meetings and often these types of stakeholders will try and force requirements on to the organisation purely based on "winning" the conflict with another stakeholder.

Building Relationships

Structural Conflict

The fifth type of conflict is a "structural conflict" which is when a more senior team member or stakeholder continuously rejects the requirements contributions made by their less senior colleagues.

In most cases the conflicts which arise in organisations are a combination of these different types of conflicts. It is however important to understand the different types of conflicts to be able to effectively resolve the conflicts.

Causes of Conflict

According to Advisory, Conciliation and Arbitration Service (ACAS), conflict falls into two broad categories:

- *conflict between individuals* – *e.g., between colleagues or between team members and their managers*
- *conflict between groups* – *e.g., between teams or between large groups of employees and management*

Examples of causes of conflict at work could include:

- *dissatisfaction with the workload or work slippages* – *e.g., increased workloads or missed deadlines*
- *lack of appreciation and perceived unfairness* – *e.g., someone feeling that they have not received appropriate credit for their efforts*
- *misunderstandings and poor sharing of information* – *e.g., concerned discussions and arguments due to not knowing what is happening*
- *external problems that affect the team or individuals* – *e.g., a supply problem leading to the team's failure to finish on time and receive a bonus*
- *differences of opinion* – *e.g., between individuals, teams or organisations about working methods*
- *people having different objectives* – *e.g., some want to do overtime to finish the task on time whilst others want to leave and get home on time*
- *incompatible objectives and rivalry* – *e.g., between different teams*
- *bullying, harassment or personality clashes between individuals*

Conflict Development

There are many ways of measuring the stages of how a conflict develops, one straightforward process is to put the actions into five stages:

- *latent* – *potential opposition or incompatibility*

Building Relationships

- **perceived** – *people become aware that conflict exists*
- **intentions** – *stress and anxiety are felt*
- **behaviour** – *conflict is open and can be observed*
- **outcomes** – *how the conflict is resolved*

Latent
At this stage, nothing happens; people just become aware of opposition or incompatibility. This could be for a variety of reasons that may or may not be a sign of potential conflict – e.g., being excluded from a conversation; team members disagreeing about how to allocate work.

Perceived
At this stage, people become aware that conflict exists – e.g., a team member overhears comments that confirm that there is opposition or incompatibility.

Intentions
At this stage, people feel stress and anxiety as they think about what their intentions are and what the other person's intentions are.

Behaviour
In this fourth stage, the conflict escalates and people take action. They might react in a challenging way or they might withdraw completely. Typical responses to conflict are:

- **fight** – *people react in a challenging way – e.g., shouting or losing their temper*
- **flight** – *they turn their back on what is going on, ignoring a problem and hoping it will go away*
- **freeze** – *they are not sure how to react and become very passive – they might begin to deal with the issue, but things drift or become drawn out through indecision*
- **face** – *they approach a problem in a calm and rational way with a planned approach*

Outcomes
There can be several outcomes, including, for example:

- **resolution through consent** – *e.g., through negotiation, arbitration, compromise, retraining and discussions to resolve the issues that caused the conflict*
- **enforced resolution** – *e.g., if the organisation goes out of business as a result; if things escalate to such a point that people are dismissed*
- **stalemate** – *where the problem is unresolved and neither party will give in or compromise*

Conflict cannot be sustained indefinitely and eventually the issues 'run out of steam'. The costs might not be worth further arguments – in terms of money, time, stress and resources – and both sides will usually agree to find a workable compromise.

Building Relationships

For resolution to be complete, both parties need to be able to work together harmoniously again.

The Impact of Conflict

Conflict in the workplace can be very damaging. Heated exchanges, isolation and failing to communicate can lead to a decrease in motivation, morale and productivity, changes in behaviour and an increase in sickness and absenteeism.

Negative effects of conflict
The negative effects of conflict on individual and team performance include, for example:

- *negative emotions that affect morale* – e.g., *feelings of disrespect or fear high levels of tension and unhealthy stress levels*
- *inappropriate behaviour* – e.g., *aggressive outbursts, arguments and altercations reduced motivation to achieve objectives and do well*
- *loss of productivity*
- *poor staff retention*
- *instability within the organisation*
- *loss of trust*
- *increased costs*
- *customer dissatisfaction*

Positive impact of conflict
Although it is generally considered to be a negative effect, conflict can have a positive impact in the workplace if it is handled well.

If the causes of the conflict are detected and acted upon in the early latent and perceived stages of development, managers and their teams can act and sort things out for the benefit of everyone.

Initial causes of conflict can often be valid complaints – e.g., about how things are done or how the workload is shared. By listening and acting early, managers can use these complaints to review the operation, discuss problems with colleagues, identify the weak areas, find possible solutions and make improvements.

Symptoms of conflict
Before conflict develops, there may be symptoms that managers can detect that will indicate that there are underlying problems (in the latent and received stages of conflict development).

Example:

- *a drop in motivation* – e.g., *fewer people volunteer to take on new tasks; there is less input during team meetings*

Building Relationships

- *changes in behaviour* – e.g., people make negative remarks towards each other; there are fewer social events being organised
- *productivity falls* – e.g., time is taken up with queries and complaints, which leads to a drop in productivity
- *increased sick leave and absenteeism* – e.g., due to stress or depression as a result of high stress levels
- *staff indicate dissatisfaction* – e.g., making negative comments in staff surveys

Any of these symptoms will affect individual and team performance if they are not identified and dealt with appropriately.

If conflict escalates or continues at a low level for a long time, teams will suffer from, for example:

- *further drops in productivity and an increasing failure to meet objectives* – as relationships and the willingness to work together break down
- *disharmony and low morale* – with people no longer wanting to be part of the team
- *increased sickness and absenteeism* – making it hard for the team to work at full capacity
- *high turnover of staff as people resign and leave* – making it even harder to build and maintain an effective and efficient team

Similarly, individuals will suffer from, for example:

- *lack of job satisfaction*
- *lack of motivation*
- *lack of desire to improve skills and develop careers within the organisation*
- *increasing levels of stress and anxiety*
- *fatigue, depression and other health-related problems*
- *disappointment from being associated with a poorly performing, unhappy team or organisation*

The Importance of Conflict Management

Conflict management is extremely important in the workplace. Managers need to be aware of what they can do to prevent conflict occurring and how to take action when conflict has been identified, preferably as early as possible before things get out of hand. The main aim is to promote a positive atmosphere in the workplace as this will help to minimise the adverse effects of conflict.

There are three main things that managers can do:

- *put systems and procedures in place*
- *develop relationships*
- *get people working together*

Building Relationships

Put systems and procedures in place

To minimise or solve conflict, managers can, for example:

- *establish formal procedures* – *for grievances, disciplinary issues and resolution*
- *explain organisational and team plans and changes* – *linking individual performance targets to overall plans, to make everyone feel involved*
- *listen* – *consultation is the key to involving employees in decision-making*
- *reward fairly* – *to help make people feel secure and appreciated*
- *work safely* – *think about use of computers, smoking, stress and drugs as well as noise, dust and chemicals*

Develop relationships

Effective communication and positive working relationships are essential when managing and preventing conflict and managers need to, for example:

- *value employees* – *people feel more motivated and involved if they feel valued*
- *treat everyone fairly* – *managers need to be fair, transparent and consistent*
- *encourage initiative* – *managers can work to develop and encourage individuals to be innovative and take initiative*
- *help people to balance personal and work needs* – *flexible working patterns can help to improve the work-life balance of employees and the effectiveness of the business*
- *encourage the development of new skills* – *managers, team leaders and team members could benefit from learning and development activities to improve their skills, knowledge and experience and to improve communication*

Get people working together

Managers need to work to build trust between different members of the workforce. They need to encourage people to, for example:

- *identify and discuss problems and possible causes of conflict early on*
- *use mediation and negotiation skills to find an early, informal compromise if possible*
- *create a positive environment where they feel confident about talking and listening to each other*
- *agree solutions collectively*
- *reflect on actions or behaviours*

Managers might need to find extra opportunities for team members to develop working relationships if normal work activities do not provide many chances to promote communication.

They could, for example:

- *arrange social or team-building activities*
- *encourage interaction during training courses or sessions*

Building Relationships

- *encourage input during team meetings and briefings*
- *delegate new tasks for team members to try together, under supervision to begin with*

To keep progress on track, managers need to monitor problem areas closely and intervene if problems or tensions arise. A quiet word early on minimises the adverse effects of conflict and can bring problems to quick and simple resolution.

There are mediation training courses that can help people to develop communication skills, problem-solving skills, awareness of team dynamics and knowledge of employment law.

Conflict Management - Models and Techniques

There are numerous conflict management techniques and models. A few of these are shown below:

- *problem-solving cycles*
- *the Thomas-Kilmann conflict mode Instrument (TKI)*
- *Interest-Based Relational (IBR) approach*
- *Lederach theory of conflict transformation*

Problem-Solving Cycles

According to ACAS, problem-solving cycles are practical models to follow when working out problems and conflicts in a systematic way. They give managers the chance to gather thoughts, consider all the options and make a plan of action.

Having clear steps to follow helps managers to break a problem into manageable parts and tackle each element separately. If the conflicted parties can also see the structure, they can

Building Relationships

appreciate that all concerns will be addressed and evaluated, which should relieve some of the tension and stress that often accompany conflict. The ACAS cycle is as follows:

Thomas-Kilmann Conflict Mode Instrument (TKI)

Kenneth W Thomas and Ralph H Kilmann created the TKI as an assessment to measure a person's
behaviour in conflict situations. It is based on a person's:

- **assertiveness** – *how much they attempt to satisfy their own concerns*
- **cooperativeness** – *how much they attempt to satisfy the other person's concerns*

These relate to the five different modes for responding to conflict, which are:

- **competing** – **assertive and uncooperative** – *the person pursues their own concerns at another's expense*
- **accommodating** – **unassertive and cooperative** – *the individual neglects their own concerns to satisfy others' requirements*
- **avoiding** – **unassertive and uncooperative** – *the person does not pursue anybody's concerns and they fail to deal with the conflict*
- **collaborating** – **assertive and cooperative** – *working through disagreements to find a creative solution that suits everyone*
- **compromising** – **moderately assertive and cooperative** – *addresses issues in less depth than collaborating by splitting the difference, giving and receiving concessions*

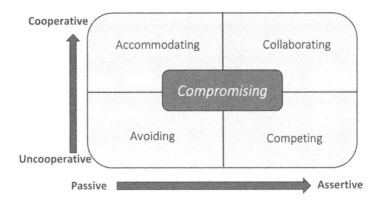

Interest-Based Relational (IBR) approach

The IBR approach was developed by Roger Fisher and William Ury and they published it in 1981 in their book Getting to Yes. The main points of the IBR approach are to:

- *separate people and their emotions from the problem*

Building Relationships

- *build mutual respect and understanding*
- *resolve conflict in a united and cooperative manner*
- *ensure team members feel respected and understood*
- *everyone behaving courteously and collaborating to reach a compromise or agreement*
- *use active listening skills, empathy, body language and emotional intelligence*

They claim that there are six steps that the conflicting parties need to follow:

1. *Make sure that good relationships are a priority*
2. *Separate people from problems*
3. *Listen carefully to different views and interests*
4. *Listen first, talk second*
5. *Set out facts*
6. *Explore options together*

Separating people from the problem can be hard to achieve, but it is very important. People are often upset if they are involved in a conflict and some can find it hard to step back from the issues and detach their feelings and personal views.

Lederach Theory of Conflict Transformation

American Professor of International Peacebuilding, John Paul Lederach, has devised a conflict resolution theory, often referred to as conflict transformation. It is based on the attitudes and orientations that people need to use in their approach to conflict resolution:

- **to envision and respond** – *based on a positive orientation towards conflict and a willingness to engage*
- **ebb and flow** – *rather than looking at isolated episodes of conflict, looking at the 'bigger picture' and accepting that the 'ups and downs' are part of a natural pattern*
- **life-giving opportunities** – *looking at the conflict as a valuable opportunity to grow and increase understanding, rather than as a threat*
- **constructive change processes** – *based on a central goal to build constructive out of the energy of conflict*
- **reduce violence and increase justice** – *concentrating on how to address obvious issues and causes, then making sure that people have access to political procedures*
- **direct interaction and social structures** – *concentrating on the value of sustained discussions between parties and face-to-face interaction*
- **human relationships** – *the key to understanding being based on less-visible aspects of human relationships rather than the actual content of the conflict*

The theory focuses on how to end something destructive and build something positive, based on relationships and constructive change.

Building Relationships

Strengths and weaknesses of other techniques

There are several techniques that a manager can use to minimise and resolve conflict at work.

Way to manage conflict	Strengths	Weaknesses
Win-win or collaborating Confronting and solving the problem by working with other parties Useful when: • the long-term relationship is important • consensus and commitment of others is important • environment is collaborative • addressing interests of multiple stakeholders • there is a high level of trust	• solves the actual problem • leads to win-win situation with mutually beneficial results • reinforces positive relationships, mutual trust and is a basis for future collaboration • responsibility is shared • less stressful • there is more respect for the manager as a good negotiator	• requires commitment from all parties and trust cannot be lost • may take more effort and time • a win-win solution might not exist, or it may not be easy to find
Forcing or competing The individual firmly pursues their own concerns. Useful when the manager: • finds that less forceful methods do not work, • and this is the last resort • needs to resist aggression and pressure • needs a quick resolution	• quick resolution • can increase self-esteem • can gain respect for being able to deal with hostility and aggression	• can have negative effect on relationships • can cause opponent to react in the same way • cannot compromise and accept the good points made by the opponent • approach requires a lot of energy and courage; can be exhausting to some
Smoothing or accommodating The individual soothes others and accommodates their views. Useful when manager: • wants to put other people's concerns first • is in the wrong • needs temporary relief whilst finding long term solutions • has no choice and continued competition would be damaging	• can protect more important interests while giving up on smaller issue • gives opportunity to reassess from a different angle	• can be abused as opponent can try to take advantage • can affect confidence about dealing with aggressive situations • difficult to move to the win-win situation • supporters may consider the manager as weak

Building Relationships

Way to manage conflict	Strengths	Weaknesses
Compromising Looking for a mutually acceptable solution that satisfies all parties. Useful when: • goals are only moderately important • a temporary or fast settlement is needed for complex issues • it is used as a first step • collaboration or forcing do not work	• faster resolution of issues • can provide temporary solution • reduces stress and tension	• parties might all be dissatisfied with the outcome • does not contribute to trust in the long term • might need close control and monitoring to see it through
Withdrawing or avoiding Ignoring or stepping away from the conflict. Useful when the manager: • believes the issue is trivial and not worth the time or effort • considers other priorities more important • needs more time to consider solutions • thinks the time and place are inappropriate • does not want to deal with hostility • cannot deal with hostility due to personal issues • passes the problem on to someone else for action	• can withdraw until time and place more appropriate • can take time to gather information, evidence, etc. • can concentrate on more important priorities first	• can lead to losing or weakening the position • where multiple parties involved, can affect relationship with parties who expect action

Conflict can be managed within the organisation, following the policies and procedures, or by using outside agencies. Depending on the nature of the conflict, these could include:

- **ACAS** (Advisory, Conciliation and Arbitration Service)
- **Citizen's Advice**
- **industry governing bodies or professional associations**
- **trade unions**
- **lawyers, accountants, consultants or counsellors**
- **the police or social services**

Building Relationships

Collaborative models, techniques and approaches do not work in all situations, especially if there are crises that require fast action. In these situations, the manager may have to make autocratic decisions to resolve disputes and conflicts quickly, then seek collaboration and long-term solutions once everything has calmed down.

Customer Relationships

Whilst it is clear that positive, effective relationships between all stakeholders is vitally important, the relationship with the customer is of greatest importance and significance. Without a customer, there is no business!

The relationship includes all aspects of customer care such as:

- *the quality, image and presentation of products and services*
- *the quality, image and presentation of staff*
- *promotion of services and products*
- *contact and communication with customers*
- *delivery of products and services to customers*
- *monitoring and improving products and services*
- *finance*
- *compliance with legislation and regulations*
- *supporting the organisation's aims and objectives*

The relationship with the Customer is a major element of customer service. Care must be taken especially with regard to contact, communication and delivery of products and services to internal
and external customers. There is a need to consider:

- *different types of customer*
- *why relationships are important*
- *customer needs and expectations*
- *approaches for building and managing customer relationships*

Types of Customer Relationship

There are many different types of customer relationship, for example:

- *Some customer relationships are very brief* – e.g., at the till in an electrical retail outlet or department store.
- *Some customers become regulars and build a rapport with staff* – e.g., in a small, local supermarket where the same customers go to shop several times a month.

Building Relationships

- *Some customer relationships are quite close for a short time only* – e.g., when a customer needs in-depth advice about buying the right mobile telephone or computer.
- *Some relationships are intensive for a few weeks or months but are not repeated very often* –e.g., between homeowners and their builders during a house renovation or building project.
- *Some relationships between customers and organisations develop over many years* – e.g. between accountancy staff and their clients; between GPs and their patients.
- *Some organisations have customer relationships with people they never meet* – e.g., online suppliers who serve customers all over the world, telephone call centres and helplines.

In any organisation, it is important to establish and develop a relationship with each customer, whether it is a one-off, brief transaction or an ongoing, long-term business relationship.

Money does not always need to change hands directly between customers and the organisation for there to be a business relationship. For example, patients at a hospital or service users who benefit from a charity's work still have a customer relationship, even though money is not charged at the point of delivery. The relationship is valuable even if the financial aspect is small or non-existent.

Whatever the customer service role or financial impact, developing relationships with customers is important to:

- *promote or maintain customer loyalty* – e.g., making customers feel valued so that they want to use a certain brand or service and recommend it to others
- *encourage or improve customer retention* – e.g., inspiring customers to stay with the organisation because they receive good service
- *encourage referrals* – e.g., giving customers incentives and the confidence to introduce their friends, family and other contacts
- *maintain or increase revenue* – e.g., developing repeat business to secure future sales and job security
- *improve and maintain high levels of customer satisfaction* – e.g., to reduce the number of complaints and rejected goods
- *maintain and improve and organisation's reputation* – e.g., portraying a good image of how an organisation treats and values its customers
- *create and maintain a competitive advantage* – e.g., delivering better products and services than competitors
- *enhance links with internal customers* – e.g., delivering good-quality support and service to other teams within the organisation

Retaining customers and encouraging them to remain loyal is critical to long-term planning and development for the organisation. If customers do not feel loyal towards an organisation, they are far more likely to leave it and take their business elsewhere.

As the saying goes

Building Relationships

"If you don't look after your customers, someone else will".

By creating an emotional bond and a valuable relationship with each customer, an organisation can help its customers to feel satisfied with their service offer and inspired to return to them in the future.

Loyal customers are also far more likely to recommend an organisation or brand to their contacts.

Customer Needs and Expectations

It is important to identify customers' needs and expectations when building relationships with them.

The facts gathered, especially at the beginning, form the foundations of the business relationship, giving it direction and purpose. The details help to manage expectations and focus on developing a long-term bond with people who are essential to the organisation.

All customers have needs and expectations and generally want:

- *efficient and polite service* – *before, during and after buying or using a product or service*
- *good-quality products and services* – *in line with the standards promised in catalogues, brochures, customer charters, company policies and on websites etc.*
- *complaints and problems to be dealt with properly* – *politely and quickly, with an effective outcome*
- *their opinion and feedback to matter* – *when dealing with staff, giving feedback or discussing a problem*

Organisations work to identify their customers' needs and expectations in several ways, including:

- *using good questioning and listening techniques*
- *details in contracts and purchase orders*
- *collecting and using feedback*
- *looking at sales and usage figures*
- *monitoring complains*
- *arranging focus groups and market research*

Once the expectations and needs have been established, they need to be managed and developed. The process of managing expectations does not mean that all expectations have to be met, especially if they are unrealistic or unreasonable. It is important to take into account the organisation's needs and expectations during the process as well.

Building Relationships

Managing customers' expectations broadly means:

- *respecting each customer's individual needs and expectations*
- *liaising with each customer to match their expectations with the right service offer for them*
- *suggesting or offering alternatives and compromises when needed*
- *keeping each customer informed at all stages*
- *keeping the organisation informed about any issues, so that changes can be discussed and implemented if necessary*

Building and Managing Customer Relationships

When building and managing customer relationships, managers need to be able to:

- *communicate with customers*
- *make sure that excellent products and services are delivered*
- *manage situations when customer expectations cannot be met*
- *deal with complaints and feedback effectively*
- *solve problems and make decisions*
- *make the customers' views count*

Communicating with Customers

Communication with customers is extremely important before, during and after a transaction. When developing approaches to customer relationships, the organisation's guidelines and the individuals' own skills need to focus on, for example:

Before the transaction:

- *understanding different customers*
- *identifying different needs and expectations*

During the transaction:

- *welcoming and greeting the customer*
- *engaging with the customer and taking genuine interest*
- *giving accurate, up-to-date and relevant information*
- *using the best communication methods and techniques for the customer and the situation*
- *dealing with queries, comments and complaints*
- *ensuring that the customer's legal rights are respected and protected*
- *ending the transaction with positive comments and body language*

Building Relationships

After the transaction:

- *giving after-care service*
- *respecting and protecting legal rights*
- *providing ongoing maintenance*
- *asking for feedback from customers*
- *dealing with complaints and feedback*

Regular communication is important when developing relationships with internal (people within the same organisation) and external customers.

Communication with internal customers helps to, for example:

- *keep staff from different departments up to date*
- *develop a unified, high-quality customer service relationship that benefits the organisation and external customers*
- *promote a sense of shared goals*
- *make staff from different departments take ownership and be accountable*

Communication with external customers helps to, for example:

- *develop openness and honesty*
- *enhance feelings of loyalty and trust*
- *make them feel valued and respected*
- *keep them informed about changes and potential problems*
- *make sure that the organisation can monitor changes in customer expectations*

Managing situations when customer expectations cannot be met

There are times when we need to tell customers that the organisation cannot meet expectations.

This can be due to delays or problems, or it can happen because the organisation simply does not offer that particular product or service. To maintain a good customer relationship, we need
to manage the situation proactively and offer suitable alternatives. For example, our approach can be to:

- *apologise for the inconvenience* – the customer has come to the organisation in the hope of getting the service or product that they want, so they need to be handled politely, even if their complaint is based on information that is incorrect explain why this cannot be offered and give information about what the organisation does offer – this reassures the customer and gives them information about the organisation that can be useful in the future

Building Relationships

- *offer alternatives if possible* – *maybe offering an alternative product or service that the organisation can provide, or suggesting other suppliers who can help the customer thank the customer for their enquiry and express a hope that the organisation can help with other things – this leaves a positive relationship experience and encourages the customer to come back in the future if a solution cannot be found immediately*

Dealing with complaints

Complaints can arise for a variety of reasons, including:

- *poor-quality or faulty products*
- *incorrect or incomplete delivery of items*
- *bad service* – *e.g., from rude or unhelpful staff the service or product does not matching the description – not meeting the customer's expectations*
- *delays and missed deadlines* – *maybe leading to fines and interest charges*
- *lack of information* – *e.g., when transport is delayed*
- *inefficient systems* – *e.g., call centres passing customers from one advisor to another when they call for help; long queues that are badly managed*

When dealing with complaints, it is essential to handle the situation well so that the customer relationship can recover and move forward again. For example, we need to:

- *listen to or read the details of the complaint* – *maybe making notes about the details*
- apologise to the customer – *and show that we understand and sympathise with them*
- *explain the background to the problem or issue* – *or offer to investigate if the cause of the problem is not obvious*
- *keep the customer informed at all stages of the process* – *even if it takes many weeks to resolve the problem apologise again, reassure and thank the customer for their patience and custom*

The HEAT method can be useful:

- *Hear* – *listening to the customer's complaint properly*
- *Empathise* – *showing that we understand the customer's position, frustration, etc.*
- *Apologise* – *saying sorry is incredibly important*
- *Take ownership* – *taking the problem seriously, seeing it through to a satisfactory end, keeping the customer informed, passing on feedback to the organisation*

Complaints need to be dealt with quickly and effectively to defuse the anxiety and stop the complaint becoming more serious.

When dealing with complaints and other awkward subjects, we need to be aware of potential communication problems. For example, the customer may be nervous and a little aggressive due to being nervous about making the complaint. They may also have visual, speech, reading,

Building Relationships

writing or hearing problems, or not have English as their first language. It is important to take these factors into account when responding, to keep the anxiety levels as low as possible and maintain good working relations.

Solving problems and making decisions

Managers need to be able to solve problems and make decisions when working on customer relationships. Problem-solving and decision-making skills enable us to, for example:

- *deal with queries*
- *find solutions that satisfy or exceed customer expectations*
- *use teamwork skills to solve more complex issues* – e.g., when help is needed from another department
- *work with colleagues and other stakeholders* – e.g., to deliver products and services
- *work with manufacturers or suppliers* – e.g., to make sure quality standards are as expected
- *promote goodwill and customer loyalty*
- *lower the chances of complaints and a bad reputation*

Making the customers' views count

Every customer likes to feel valued and we all like our opinions to matter. We want our complaints
to be taken seriously and our feedback to be respected and put to good use. When building and
maintaining customer relationships, our approach can be to, for example:

- *engage in conversation* – e.g., whilst serving someone face-to-face, online or on the telephone
- *use active listening and questioning skills* – e.g., when dealing with feedback from a customer
- *reassure customers* – e.g., if they are making a complaint to show that their views are being taken seriously
- *ask for feedback and react to it in a genuine way* – e.g., showing empathy and taking notes
- *follow up as promised* – e.g., when sourcing products for an established customer or returning a phone call promptly

Building Relationships

Active Listening

Listening is one of the most important skills you can have. How well you listen has a major impact on your job effectiveness and on the quality of your relationships with others.

For instance:

> *We listen to obtain information.*
> *We listen to understand.*
> *We listen for enjoyment.*
> *We listen to learn.*

Given all the listening that we do, you would think we would be good at it! In fact, most of us are not and research suggests that we only remember between 25 percent and 50 percent of what we hear, as described by Edgar Dale's Cone of Experience. That means that when you talk to your boss, colleagues, customers, or spouse for 10 minutes, they pay attention to less than half of the conversation.

Turn it around and it reveals that when you are receiving directions or being presented with information, you are not hearing the whole message either. You hope the important parts are captured in your 25-50 percent, but what if they are not?

Clearly, listening is a skill that we can all benefit from improving. By becoming a better listener, you can improve your productivity, as well as your ability to influence, persuade and negotiate. What is more, you will avoid conflict and misunderstandings. All of these are necessary for workplace success!

Good communication skills require a high level of self-awareness. Understanding your own personal style of communicating will go a long way toward helping you to create good and lasting impressions with others.

The way to improve your listening skills is to practice "active listening." This is where you make a conscious effort to hear not only the words that another person is saying but, more importantly, the complete message being communicated.

In order to do this, you must pay attention to the other person very carefully.

You cannot allow yourself to become distracted by whatever else may be going on around you, or by forming counter arguments while the other person is still speaking. Nor can you allow yourself to get bored and lose focus on what the other person is saying.

If you are finding it particularly difficult to concentrate on what someone is saying, try repeating their words mentally as they say them – this will reinforce his message and help you to stay focused.

To enhance your listening skills, you need to let the other person know that you are listening to what they are saying.

Building Relationships

To understand the importance of this, ask yourself if you have ever been engaged in a conversation when you wondered if the other person was listening to what you were saying. You wonder if your message is getting across, or if it is even worthwhile continuing to speak. It feels like talking to a brick wall and it is something you want to avoid.

Acknowledgement can be something as simple as a nod of the head or a simple "uh huh." You are not necessarily agreeing with the person, you are simply indicating that you are listening. Using body language and other signs to acknowledge you are listening can also help you to pay attention.

Try to respond to the speaker in a way that will encourage him to continue speaking, so that you can get the information that you need. While nodding and "uh huhing" says you are interested, an occasional question or comment to recap what has been said also communicates that you are listening and understanding his message.

Be aware that active listening can give others the impression that you agree with them even if you do not. It is also important to avoid using active listening as a checklist of actions to follow, rather than really listening. It may help to practice Mindful Listening if you find that you lose focus regularly.

Becoming an Active Listener

There are five key active listening techniques you can use to help you become a more effective listener:

1. Pay attention

Give the speaker your undivided attention and acknowledge the message. Recognise that non-verbal communication also "speaks" loudly.

Building Relationships

Look at the speaker directly.
Put aside distracting thoughts.
Do not mentally prepare a rebuttal!
Avoid being distracted by environmental factors. For example, side conversations.
"Listen" to the speaker's body language.

2. Show that you are listening

Use your own body language and gestures to show that you are engaged.

Nod occasionally.
Smile and use other facial expressions.
Make sure that your posture is open and interested.
Encourage the speaker to continue with small verbal comments like yes and "uh huh."

3. Provide feedback

Our personal filters, assumptions, judgments and beliefs can distort what we hear. As a listener, your role is to understand what is being said. This may require you to reflect on what is being said and to ask questions.

Reflect on what has been said by paraphrasing. "What I am hearing is...," and "Sounds like you are saying...," are great ways to reflect back.
Ask questions to clarify certain points. "What do you mean when you say...." " "Is this what you mean?"
Summarise the speaker's comments periodically.

If you find yourself responding emotionally to what someone said, say so. Ask for more information: "I may not be understanding you correctly and I find myself taking what you said personally. What I thought you just said is XXX. Is that what you meant?"

4. Defer judgment

Interrupting is a waste of time. It frustrates the speaker and limits full understanding of the message.

Allow the speaker to finish each point before asking questions.
Do not interrupt with counter arguments.

5. Respond appropriately

Active listening is designed to encourage respect and understanding. You are gaining information and perspective. You add nothing by attacking the speaker or otherwise putting her down.

Be candid, open and honest in your response.
Assert your opinions respectfully.
Treat the other person in a way that you think she would want to be treated.

Building Relationships

Stakeholder Feedback

The term 'feedback' is used to describe the helpful information or criticism about prior action or behaviour from an individual, communicated to another individual (or a group) who can use that information to adjust and improve current and future actions and behaviours.

Feedback occurs when an environment reacts to an action or behaviour. For example, 'customer feedback' is the buyers' reaction to a company's products, services, or policies; and 'employee performance feedback' is the employees' reaction to feedback from their manager – the exchange of information involves both performance expected and performance exhibited.

Who would dispute the idea that feedback is a good thing? All can benefit from feedback. Both common sense and research make it clear – feedback and opportunities to use that feedback helps to improve and enhance, whether an individual, group, business, business unit, company, or organisation – and that information can be used to make better informed decisions. It also allows us to build and maintain communication with others.

Effective feedback, both positive and negative, is very helpful.

Feedback is valuable information that will be used to make important decisions. Top performing companies are top performing companies because they consistently search for ways to make their best even better. For top performing companies 'continuous improvement' is not just a showy catchphrase. It is a true focus based on feedback from across the entire organisation – customers, clients, employees, suppliers, vendors and stakeholders. Top performing companies are not only good at accepting feedback, they deliberately ask for feedback. And they know that feedback is helpful only when it highlights weaknesses as well as strengths.

Effective feedback has benefits for the giver, the receiver and the wider organisation. Here are five reasons why feedback is so important.

1. Feedback is always there
If you ask someone in your organisation when feedback occurs, they will typically mention an employee survey, performance appraisal, or training evaluation. In actuality, feedback is around us all the time. Every time we speak to a person, employee, customer, vendor, etc., we communicate feedback. In actuality, it is impossible not to give feedback.

Businesses do not need to go through a lot of hassle in order to gather feedback. It is always available for them and they just need to look for a way in order to gather and manage feedback in an appropriate manner. Businesses can also gather feedback in many different ways. It is up to the business owners to think about the most convenient method that needs to be followed in order to gather feedback.

2. Feedback is effective listening
Feedback is similar to effective listening

Building Relationships

"Employees don't leave bad companies; they leave bad managers."
Marcus Buckingham

A recent survey uncovered the top ten reasons why people quit their jobs.

The top three included feeling undervalued, having a bad manager and poor communication. All of which can be fixed with a strong internal feedback system.

It does not matter how well your employees are performing, how well they are liked, or how great they treat your customers. If your business does not meet the feedback expectations of your employees, you could be putting the entire future of your business at stake.

Feedback can be gathered in different ways. Collecting verbal feedback via a survey is one of the most popular techniques out of them. In fact, collecting verbal feedback is almost similar to effective listening. The business owners can gather a lot of information from feedback, which can help them to focus on future development.

Whether the feedback is done verbally or via a feedback survey, the person providing the feedback needs to know they have been understood (or received) and they need to know that their feedback provides some value. When conducting a survey, always explain why respondents' feedback is important and how their feedback will be used.

3. Feedback can motivate
Feedback has the potential to motivate business owners as well. Through feedback, the business owners will be able to get to know where they are not doing well. It is possible for the business owners to trust feedback that they get from the customers as well. Then they can think of making required changes in the business in order to adapt accordingly and provide more value to the customers. This is one of the most convenient methods available for the businesses to increase the potential customer base as well. That is because it can help the businesses to cater the specific needs and requirements of the customers.

By asking for feedback, it can actually motivate employees to perform better. Employees like to feel valued and appreciate being asked to provide feedback that can help formulate business decisions. And feedback from client, suppliers, vendors and stakeholders can be used to motivate to build better working relations

4. Feedback can improve performance
Most of the businesses do not have a clear understanding whether they are performing in an effective manner or not. Feedback can assist them to get to know about it. However, the business owners need to be careful not to ignore feedback as criticism. What is viewed as negative criticism is actually constructive criticism and is the best kind of feedback that can help to formulate better decisions to improve and increase performance.

5. Feedback is a tool for continued learning
For an employer/employee relationship to work well, both parties need to be willing to learn from each other. Seizing learning opportunities can provide an exceptional

Building Relationships

springboard for business and personal growth. It is possible to get feedback from customers on a regular basis. Therefore, it can be considered as an excellent tool available for the businesses to engage with continuous learning. In other words, businesses can develop new products or services or rebrand the existing products based on feedback.

Regular feedback sessions, both scheduled and impromptu, allow us to reflect on our behaviours and, if appropriate, upgrade or change the way we do things. Seeing ourselves from someone else's point of view can be a truly enlightening experience.

Negative feedback, however, can have the opposite effect. Using feedback as a tool to berate a colleague or staff member, should never be employed as a leadership tactic. If someone is awful at their job, making them feel horrible about themselves will only serve to make things worse. In cases of poor performance, a more formal feedback stance or training route should be considered.

Feedback initiates change

Business processes need to change for many reasons; to make cost savings, to create efficiencies, to provide better service to clients... the reasons for change are endless.

When a business is experiencing a period of change, feedback is a crucial element of the change process. If change is not the direct result of external feedback, then it is important to source opinions from those who matter to your business: employees, customers and stakeholders.

Invest time in asking and learning about how others experience working with your organisation.

Continued feedback is important across the entire organisation in order to remain aligned to goals, create strategies, develop products and services improvements, improve relationships and much more.

Continued learning is the key to improving

Most of the world's most prominent organisations use customer and stakeholder feedback to make improvements to their products and services. No matter what the size of your business, do not lose sight of the opinion of those that spend their time, money and resources with you.

Gathering Stakeholder Feedback

Gathering feedback from internal stakeholders in your organisation is fundamental to developing a successful product. Remember that team members are also internal customers, and will likely be as or more vocal than your external customers about your product — they have a lot to say, but where and how should they say it? Let us look at some ways to gather feedback from stakeholders.

Building Relationships

While product teams rely on a combination of several communication channels to share feedback with colleagues, others find it better to pick one and stick with it. Here are a few common feedback communication channels and a brief look at the pros and cons of each so you can make a considered choice about what works best for you:

1. Interviewing Stakeholders

Interviewing stakeholders individually allows managers to gather feedback privately from people who have the ability to impact the organisation. Managers should use this opportunity to handle both negative and positive input in a more controlled environment. Taking the time to interview stakeholders or sponsors makes sense when a stakeholder cannot attend a group meeting due to time constraints or other scheduling conflicts. This method of grading stakeholder satisfaction with progress allows managers to receive potentially sensitive information out of public view, such as a recommendation that resources be terminated, or the organisation's scope be significantly altered.

Pros:	Cons:
Convenient for stakeholders to use. Feedback can be shared virtually anytime.	*Does not aggregate data or provides analytics.*
You can search feedback later.	*Requires extra manual work to extract the feedback.*

2. Focus Groups

Running brainstorming sessions to get input from stakeholders involves scheduling meetings and facilitating discussions about the team's progress toward achieving the organisation's goals. Topics typically include the presentation of status reports, quality data and project outcomes, such as prototype products.

Conducting an effective focus group usually involves comprehensive planning including setting an agenda, preparing specific questions to ask stakeholders, encouraging collaboration, and calling for action from participants. Project managers should encourage all participants to provide candid input reflecting their perspective. This method of measuring stakeholder satisfaction with progress allows project managers to get timely input for all stakeholders at once, enabling the project team to avoid costly mistakes or rework later.

Pros:	Cons:
Opportunity to provide product updates/share what is next on your roadmap.	*Getting everyone in the room at the same time can be hard and inconvenient.*
Allows you to ask follow-up questions. You can clarify feedback with those who have shared it	*Can lead to confusion if stakeholders have to hold onto feedback for a month before relaying it..*

3. Feedback Reports

In lieu of (or in addition to) facilitating a feedback meeting, have every team generate a customer feedback report every two weeks or so and share it with your team.

Pros:	Cons:
Contains both qualitative and quantitative data.	*Time-consuming and possibly inconvenient for customer teams to produce.*
It is a resource you can return to for information when you need it.	*Does not look at long-term feedback trends.*

4. Collaborative Spreadsheets

You can ask customer-facing teams to enter feedback directly into a spreadsheet within Google Sheets or a similar tool.

Pros:	Cons:
Customer teams can share feedback at any time.	*May be inconvenient for customer teams to use, which could result in them sharing less feedback.*
Good for gathering and both qualitative and quantitative feedback.	*Hard for customer teams to know whether the product team is reading their feedback*

5. Feedback Collection Platforms

Using surveys to gather and measure stakeholder satisfaction with project progress involves selecting a tool, such as Zoomerang, SurveyMonkey or Qualtrics, to create and deploy an online survey. To design an effective survey, the manager should generate a short list of questions to gather input. The manager should provide a menu of choices, such as a satisfaction rating scale including the options "Completely Satisfied," "Satisfied," "No Opinion," Dissatisfied," and "Completely Dissatisfied." Then, the manager must provide clear instructions on how to complete the survey, when feedback is requested and how the feedback will be used. This method of measuring stakeholder satisfaction allows project managers to create sophisticated charts of responses and analyse input to take decisive action.

Pros:	Cons:
Highly scalable.	*Cost may be a concern if your budget is tight.*
Can aggregate qualitative and quantitative data from every feedback source in one place, making it easy to access and use to make decisions.	*Customer teams may require a bit of training to help them understand how the system works.*

All of these communication channels come with their benefits and disadvantages, and the right approach is probably some combination of several. It is up to you and your team to decide which recipe of channels works best for you.

Building Relationships

Value of Stakeholder Feedback

Understanding your stakeholders is vital in modern-day business. This includes listening to the views and beliefs of stakeholders as well as seeking their feedback. After all, these are the people who will shape and influence future successes (or failures).

A stakeholder is anyone with an interest in the business, either having an effect on the business or being affected by it. Typically, stakeholders can be categorised into two groups: internal and external stakeholders. Examples of internal stakeholders are employees, managers and directors. External stakeholders include customers, suppliers, shareholders and funders. Keeping every stakeholder on-side can be difficult but can be hugely beneficial.

What is it?
The key to keeping stakeholders on-side is consultation. This involves the development of constructive and productive long-term relationships. Stakeholder consultation aims to build relationships based on mutual trust and benefits. Listening to and understanding the views and feedback from stakeholders can help shape and improve the overall operations of a business.

Stakeholder consultation can be project-based or on-going. Specific project-based consultation is generally used for the development of new products and services. For example, a company may consult with customers to establish specific needs of the target market. On-going consultation, however, is generally used to track the progress of a company in regard to stakeholder expectations and to maximise buy-in. For example, a company may consult with stakeholders regarding changes to the company's direction or its branding.

What are the benefits?
The benefits of stakeholder consultation are clear, with some of the most significant reasons listed below:

- *Enable more informed decision making*
- *Lead to greater stakeholder satisfaction*
- *Improves chances of project/initiative success*
- *Promote open, two-way communication*

The 4-step process
The stakeholder consultation process is an opportunity for key groups to be kept informed and for their views and feedback to be heard. It is important that any consultation is thoroughly planned with clear objectives set at the beginning.

Regardless of the aims and objectives of the stakeholder consultation, the process typically consists of four steps:

Planning, Process, Presentation and Promise (the 4Ps).

Building Relationships

Planning

The "planning" stage is where the aims and objectives of the stakeholder consultation are discussed and agreed upon. After the aims and objectives have been determined, the "planning" stage is used to discuss how the process will be carried out. Process owners allocate resources and select an appropriate consultation method. Several questions need to be asked at this stage to ensure every facet of the process is considered.

Why do we need to consult?
Who are we consulting?
What resources do we have?
How are we going to do it?
What materials will be needed?

Process

The "process" stage is where the stakeholder consultation is actually carried out. It is important at this stage to develop effective two-way communication with the stakeholders in order to promote open and honest sharing of views and beliefs. The process and data will then need to be accurately recorded for the final stages.

Presentation

The "presentation" stage is where the data gathered is analysed and reported on. The aims of this stage are to ensure the data is an accurate representation of the stakeholder views and to prepare the report ready for presentation. The report is typically presented to the process owners, such as the company itself or policy makers. However, feedback will also be provided to those who took part in the process.

Promise

Lastly, the "promise" stage is where actions are put in place in response to the information gathered. The 'promise' of action on the back of the stakeholder consultation process helps drive the development of a long-term relationship based on transparency and collaboration.

How is it done?

Methods of stakeholder consultation are largely the same as those used for market research. The key question is whether the consultation requires depth of knowledge or breadth of knowledge. The answer generally determines which method will be chosen.

If **depth** of knowledge is required, a qualitative study is usually appropriate. These are studies which encourage open styles of discussion and debate. The most common methods used to gather depth of information are focus groups, individual depth interviews and observation (or ethnography).

If **breadth** of knowledge is required, a more quantitative study is usually appropriate. These are studies which encompass large number of respondents but are restricted to closed style questions, aimed at providing generalist viewpoints. The most common methods used to gather breadth of information are online surveys, telephone surveys and short street interviews.

Building Relationships

As understanding stakeholders becomes more and more important for businesses, stakeholder consultation will become a vital process to maximise success. Stakeholder consultation can be used to evaluate reactions and to track the perceptions of a company's activities and ensure collaboration and partnership with all stakeholders. The long-term effectiveness of an organisation can depend on its relationships with stakeholders, ensuring commitment and buy-in to any future strategies and challenges. This makes for a more informed organisation that is responsive to the needs of all its users and stakeholders.

The Importance of Feedback

Getting different perspectives on our behaviour and performance can be a powerful method for self-reflection. It can be a driving force behind understanding ourselves, increasing our choices and making decisions about any changes we may wish to make.

Stakeholder feedback differs slightly from 360-degree Feedback due to the audience being targeted.
Unless designed as such, stakeholder feedback does not need to seek views from people you interact with at different hierarchical levels. Instead, questions are asked which normally relate to a specific role or service provided and/or behavioural and attitude factors. You would then identify stakeholders who would be best placed to respond to that question, regardless of their level.

Responses are normally analysed using a scoring or value judgement system. This allows you to gain a set of standardised results, which you can then analyse to help you reflect upon your performance. You should also assess yourself using the same feedback method.

Some areas for consideration when undertaking stakeholder feedback:

- *Open, honest feedback can sometimes be hard to hear. It is important to identify and agree the criteria you will use, your respondents and how the process will work.*
- *Consider the tool you are going to use to best analyse your results. For example, if you are using a numerical scoring system for responses (such as 1 – do not agree, to 6 – Agree totally) it may be a spreadsheet is the best way of recording the information to analyse. You may find numerical feedback more appropriate than descriptive feedback in most instances.*
- *You should ensure your respondents are aware of any confidentiality, equality and discrimination issues when making their responses.*
- *Once you have received your feedback, it is important you analyse this so you can look for positive feedback and possible future developmental areas where the feedback may not be so positive.*

Giving good, constructive feedback is probably one of the most important things a leader can do for their team.

Whether providing feedback to encourage improvements or simply praising a job well done, feedback is an underrated, underutilised management tool that can make a world of difference to staff and business performance.

Building Relationships

The rules of delivering feedback and interpreting it.

- **Be specific.** *Leave no room for doubt about who your feedback applies to.*
- **Be timely.** *If a performance issue arises, provide feedback as soon as possible after the event or situation.*
- **Be in the right place at the right time.** *Choose your timing and your venue carefully.*
- **Be human and humble.** *Do not let your ego or your position of authority cloud your judgement.*
- **No ifs, buts, or maybes.** *Be firm, assertive and fair. Your feedback and intentions should be crystal clear.*

And finally...

- *Be prepared to ask for help from an expert.*

By properly managing the stakeholders' expectations from the outset, the chances for a smoother journey are much greater.

Identify the stakeholder's preferred method of communication.
By using the most effective manner of communication you will help ensure the stakeholder remains content. If you make the mistake of using the wrong method (or non-preferred method) it will cause frustration and lack of confidence. It will show you did not listen to their initial direction.

Keep stakeholders engaged throughout the process with timely updates.
Ask the right questions, of the right people, at the beginning and throughout the project.

Accurately map expectations.
Be crystal clear on the expectations from the stakeholder's point of view. Ask them how they will measure success of the project. Inevitably you will discover conflicting definitions of success. Some will consider meeting the final deadline their number one priority. Another might consider end user functionality of the final product as most important. How do you manage these conflicts? One way would be to facilitate a meeting of all stakeholders (where practical) and help them come to mutually satisfying agreements.

Classify the level of communication for each stakeholder.
Understand who requires hand holding and insists on receiving all details. Who prefers a basic, occasional overview? Who wants daily or weekly communication?

Identify which stakeholders will be advocates and which will be road blockers.
Map your strategy accordingly.

Engage the stakeholders in decision making.
Stroke their egos. You probably have already identified the best course of action but present your findings in such a way that you leave room for the stakeholders to feel they have been involved in the process.

Building Relationships

Stakeholders will remember the overall mood of the entire process. Their measure of success is not just the finished product, but the way you attained the end goal.

Building Relationships

Teamworking

When people work together, there can be benefits for the individual team members, teams and the organisation. For a team to work effectively, they have to develop productive and positive working relationships that are based on:

- *clear lines of communication* – *so that people know where to go to ask questions, or report and discuss issues*
- *openness* – *giving and receiving correct and appropriate information*
- *mutual trust and respect* – *where everyone listens to each other and acknowledges feelings and opinions*

For individual team members
Individuals can benefit from:

- *feeling proud to be associated with a successful and effective team* – *e.g., a sense of belonging and job satisfaction*
- *feeling supported when tackling tasks or learning new skills* – *e.g., being able to develop their skills and stretch their talents with the help of others*
- *feeling secure and confident* – *e.g., from knowing that they are delivering high-quality goods and services*
- *other team members' knowledge, skills and experience* – *e.g., making the whole team more successful*
- *opportunities for creativity and career development* – *e.g., from team members supporting each other and being innovative*
- *increased motivation* – *e.g., to stay on a good team and help it to succeed by doing their best*
- *feeling valued* – *e.g., knowing that their input is important and that their opinions matter*

For teams
Teams can benefit from:

- *working towards shared objectives* – *e.g., working together effectively towards agreed, shared goals*
- *team members who are flexible and able to do several tasks* – *e.g., multi-skilled team members who can be moved around between tasks or cover for each other's holidays or periods of sickness*
- *a balanced and supported environment* – *e.g., from being a happy team where the members support each other and tackle objectives and problems together*
- *bringing together expertise of team members for the benefit of the whole team* – *e.g., having people with different strengths and attributes*

Building Relationships

For the organisation

The benefits of effective team working can be considerable for an organisation, for example:

- *successful achievement of organisational objectives* – e.g., to meet or exceed sales or production targets
- *access to a wide range of talents and strengths within the workforce* – e.g., pooling different talents that work together well to achieve major goals
- *good internal communications* – e.g., where team members and different teams communicate well with each other to improve operational productivity
- *increased efficiency and less duplication of work* – e.g., where teams understand each other's tasks and needs, then work together to streamline their operations
- *a more flexible workforce* – e.g., where team members can cover for each other and perform a variety of tasks to maintain consistency and continuity
- *better relationships with customers* – e.g., from offering consistently high-quality customer service
- *better relationships with others connected to the organisation* – e.g., from having a reputation for being a reliable, consistent and smooth-running operation

Cross-team Working

As an extension of teamwork, some organisations also have cross-team working. This is based on collaboration between different teams and is a useful way of working when there is a shared project or objective. The number of people involved in cross-team working will depend on the scale of the collaboration.

Some teams with different functions work together all the time. For example, in a car manufacturing company, functional teams that work together all the time could include separate teams who:

- *build the bodywork of the cars*
- *install the engines*
- *install the electronics and trim*
- *do the paint finishing*

Each team's work is very dependent on input from other teams, so they need to liaise on a regular basis about subjects that include, for example:

- *the speed of production* – so that the cars flow steadily from one team to the next without any delays, backlogs or excessive waiting times
- *quality* – so that all the teams work to a recognised standard
- *problem-solving* – so that they have agreed procedures on what to do when things go wrong to minimise the knock-on effect on other teams

Sometimes, different functional teams only come together for a specific project. For example,

Building Relationships

a wedding planning company works with over a hundred different suppliers and brings together different teams for each event. The requirements are unique for each couple and they can choose from several suppliers for each function, including, for example:

- *venue*
- *catering*
- *waiting and bar service*
- *floristry*
- *music and entertainment*
- *table and room decoration*

The wedding planner then has to bring together the different functional teams to work together just for the one wedding. Some of the supplier teams may know each other and work together from time to time, but each wedding will be different.

In cross-team working, it can help to smooth the process by having some individuals move from
one team to the other. This can be on a temporary or permanent basis. It can help to ease problems by having an expert on hand to answer queries and help solve problems. For example, in the car manufacturing company, a paintwork specialist could work with the bodywork team to help them to prepare the metal to a suitable standard to accept the paint well. This would be particularly useful when:

- **a new procedure or product is introduced** – *e.g., they need to work out new methods together when designing the quality standards for a new model*
- **there have been quality issues** – *e.g., to make sure that adjustments and improvements are effective*

Moving individuals from one team to another can also be of great benefit to their career development and working relationships. For example, in a large hotel or restaurant, kitchen team members and front of house team members rely on each other to deliver excellent products and service to the guests. To really appreciate what the other team does and needs, it can be useful and enlightening to work with them for a short while.

Benefits and challenges of effective cross-team working
Cross-team working on any scale can be complicated as there are a number of variables that have to be considered. Relationships need to be carefully managed as a range of skills, knowledge, experience, expectations and goals need to be brought together to achieve a shared objective.

As we can see in a hospital, for example, difficult and complicated tasks are performed by several different teams working together. The staff are interdependent and no team could run the hospital on its own for long. For example:

Building Relationships

- *the surgeons need the operating theatres to be fully cleaned and maintained by the facilities management team*
- *the surgeons also need a fully qualified team of nurses, doctors and technicians to work with them*
- *high-quality, sterile equipment used in theatre needs to be ordered, stored and managed by a procurement team*
- *patients need to be prepared, processed and cared for by ward and outpatient clinic staff*
- *some emergency patients need to be brought in by the ambulance service and may have been treated by a paramedic at the scene*
- *staff on the occupational health team may help to rehabilitate the patient after surgery*
- *social workers may be involved with getting support and care for the patient once they have been discharged*

When teams work together, sophisticated and complex tasks can be coordinated and performed to provide an effective service. The organisation skills and input are considerable, but they are necessary if complicated, cross-functional activities are to take place and be successful.

Benefits of cross-team working include:

- *having a shared purpose and capacity to achieve complex and difficult objectives* – that could not be done by one team on their own
- *opportunities to discuss shared goals* – and how to achieve objectives together
- *improved relationships between different teams* – from enhanced understanding of each team's issues and expectations
- *diverse and flexible team members* – who can perform a variety of tasks, work on more than one team and enhance their career development potential
- *good internal communication* – from establishing joint procedures and keeping each other informed at every stage
- *consistent standards of quality and output* – from collaboration about standards and how to achieve excellence
- *a broader team spirit* – bringing different teams together and reducing friction between them

Challenges of cross-team working include:

- *conflict* – e.g., unease between individuals or teams when they cannot agree about objectives or standards, when one team's problems have a knock-on effect on the other team
- *conflicts of interest* – e.g., when teams have incompatible goals or standards; when one team focuses on quality and takes its time, while another focuses on fast production

Building Relationships

- *practical difficulties* – e.g., when working together becomes difficult or impossible due to management, logistical or time-management issues
- *lack of shared understanding* – e.g., due to lack of preparation, information or briefing time
- *stress and anxiety* – e.g., when working on another team is in addition to normal duties and becomes too much to cope with; when team members think that arrangements are unnecessary or unreasonable, when tasks are allocated unfairly

When planning and managing cross-team working, managers need to think very carefully about the different aspects of each situation or project, making sure that individuals are not stretched too far in the quest for achieving organisational objectives. They need to employ excellent organisational skills and be able to stand back to gain an overview of the whole situation.

Building relationships across teams to achieve organisational objectives

Good communication is important when building relationships across teams to achieve organisational objectives. It can be very difficult to 'get everyone onside', especially if some team members are, for example:

- *resistant to change*
- *worried about their job security*
- *sceptical about the organisation in general*
- *sceptical about particular managers or strategies*

This is especially true if they have experienced failures in the workplace and do not have faith in the organisation's leaders and managers.

However, good, clear communication will assist greatly when a manager needs to develop relationships with other teams. Collective and collaborative decisions that are agreed by all the teams concerned are more powerful and much more likely to be successful, rather than decisions that are imposed by one team's manager, so managers need to:

Establish a command structure

This is needed so that everyone knows how to escalate problems to the right people and cascade information down to all concerned. The manager in charge of building relationships might have to work with, for example:

- *team leaders from different teams*
- *managers from other teams* – who may be senior, junior or the same level as them
- *groups of team members from different teams*
- *a mixture of employee teams, outside contractors and suppliers* – e.g., a hotel's own waiting and bar staff plus freelance teams of florists and musicians
- *internal and external teams* – e.g., the organisation's own planning team and the local council's planning team

Building Relationships

Clear lines of communication, authority and responsibility need to be established at the beginning of the relationship-building process.

Involve the teams in agreeing goals and objectives
Collaboration is the best way to go forward as it will:

- *enable team members to share their values and vision*
- *develop a joint team spirit*
- *develop mutual trust, honesty and respect*

Effective collaboration is achieved through effective communication.

Use appropriate communication techniques for messages
Effective communication is usually simple and to the point. Managers need to:

- *use appropriate language* – so that everyone can understand without feeling that they are being 'talked down to'; avoiding jargon that only some people will understand
- *use the right method of communication* – such as emails for general information, but private meetings and face-to-face discussions for sensitive or personal matters
- *present information that is clear, concise and at the right level of detail*
- *speak and write clearly* – to minimise misunderstanding
- *use good listening skills and eye contact*
- *allow people to respond and listen to what is being said*
- *be prepared to discuss issues*
- *check that everyone has understood the information*

Lead by example
Managers need to demonstrate professional and supportive behaviours at all times. By developing an atmosphere of professionalism and mutual support, members of all the teams are encouraged to perform well and to enjoy the shared tasks and to commit to the common purpose and cross-team
working.

Keep everyone informed on a regular basis
Effective communication is reinforced by regular updates about progress, goals, purpose, objectives and so on. Regular information helps to keep the purpose of the cross-team working and organisational objectives in focus. This needs to happen while relationships are getting established and later on to flag up successes and problems as they occur.

Empower team members and make them accountable for their actions – as teams and as individuals
The manager needs to make sure that the members of the different teams get the credit when things go well and feel empowered to make decisions that are within the limits of their authority.

Building Relationships

This encourages people to take pride in their work and be accountable for their actions. By taking ownership, team members will be more proactive when problems arise and should enjoy better job satisfaction when things go well.

When there are problems, support needs to be given early to keep teams on track with achieving their objectives – e.g., reviewing all relevant processes; allocating more resources; retraining or arranging help from more experienced colleagues; letting team members go back to their original team.

If team members know that they will be supported if there are problems, they are more likely to commit to the common sense of purpose and organisational objectives. They will see that issues are considered in detail for each team and that they will not be left alone to struggle.

Building Relationships

Emotional Intelligence

Emotional intelligence is the capacity to be aware of, control and express our emotions and use them effectively in interpersonal relationships.

Emotional intelligence is the ability to 'step into someone else's shoes' and see things from their point of view.

It was developed as a psychological theory by Peter Salovey and John Mayer in 1997:

"Emotional intelligence is the ability to perceive emotions, to access and generate emotions so as to assist thought, to understand emotions and emotional knowledge and to reflectively regulate emotions so as to promote emotional and intellectual growth."

The ability to understand how people feel and react can be extremely useful when building relationships in the workplace and it can be applied on two levels:

- *personal* – *understanding our own feelings or reactions*
- *interpersonal* – *understanding other people's feelings and reactions*

As managers and leaders, we often have to work as a team or develop relationships with colleagues, customers and other stakeholders. A reasonable degree of emotional intelligence can help managers be, for example:

- *empathetic* – *e.g., able to put themselves in other people's shoes*
- *sensitive to others* – *e.g., able to sense and respond to their needs, problems and feelings*
- *understanding and sympathetic* – *e.g., able to understand the complexities of life and make allowances when things go wrong*
- *good at reading other people's emotions correctly* – *e.g., able to identify the less obvious causes for emotional outbursts*

These skills give managers a great advantage, especially when they are involved with functions that rely on relationship management. Managers with good emotional intelligence skills instinctively know how to manipulate situations, inspire and motivate people and get the best out of them.

Building Relationships

Goleman's Theory of Emotional Intelligence

One model that explains emotional intelligence was developed by Daniel Goleman, a psychologist
and science journalist, following on from Salovey and Mayer's theory. The theory identifies four
components:

- **Self-awareness** – *the conscious knowledge of our character, beliefs, emotions, qualities and desires*
- **Self-management and motivation** – *the ability to stay calm under pressure and stay motivated to achieve goals*
- **Social awareness** – *the ability to have empathy and understand other people's emotions and feelings*
- **Relationship skills** – *the ability to influence, negotiate, communicate, build rapport and develop networks*

As the Goleman theory shows, the main focus for emotional intelligence is relationship management.

The Importance of Awareness of Emotional Intelligence

When building relationships in the workplace, emotional intelligence is a very useful 'soft' skill as it helps people to:

- *read each other's feelings and reactions more accurately*
- *adapt their approach*
- *employ appropriate skills*

Building Relationships

It can provide an extra insight into how to get the best out of people, how to develop leadership skills and how to deal with difficult situations effectively.

Following on from the Goleman theory, we can see how self-awareness is the starting point for building and developing relationships with others. We need self-awareness to be able to show empathy and sensitivity towards others. Our ability to manage ourselves, particularly our emotions, enables us to remain calm under pressure and be understanding and sympathetic when required.

Good social awareness helps us to read other people's emotions correctly.

By being self-confident, calm and non-judgmental, we can use our emotional intelligence to see beyond the obvious. For example, if a customer is very stressed and irate about a product or service, their strong reactions could be due to something in their personal life, rather than the problem they are complaining about. By staying calm and polite, we can use our empathy and understanding to get to the root of the problem, help diffuse the tension and address the customer's real concerns.

Managers can work to improve the emotional development of themselves and their team members by, for example:

- *running team-building exercises*
- *coaching individuals*
- *taking and running training courses in negotiation and communication skills*

According to Goleman, the higher someone goes in an organisation, the more the emotional skills matter. Senior managers and directors can hire people with the skills and knowledge that the organisation needs, but they need to be very competent in emotional intelligence themselves.

Good relationship capabilities become more critical as careers progress.

We also need to be aware that some people find it extremely hard to use and understand emotional intelligence – e.g., due to cultural or personal development issues. We cannot assume that we all have the same ability to 'put ourselves in someone else's shoes' when we are building relationships.

An awareness of the importance of emotional intelligence in the workplace enables us to:

- *make the most of the advantages the skill can offer*
- *recognise different levels of emotional intelligence in others*
- *be aware that not everyone has the skill*
- *adapt our approach when required*

Chapter 7: Operational Management

Operational Management

Mission, Vision and Values Statements

The Vision, Mission and Values statements are the foundation for all the activities of an organisation.

The Vision statement describes what the organisation hopes to become in the future. It is a broad and inspirational statement intended to engender support from stakeholders.

The Mission statement defines how the organisation differentiates itself from other organisations in its sector. It is more specific than the Vision statement and is intended to show how stakeholders' needs will be satisfied.

The Values statement defines how people in the organisation should behave. It provides guidance when making decisions.

The Vision Statement

A Vision statement is a statement of an organisation's overarching aspirations of what it hopes to achieve or to become in the future. Here are some examples of Vision Statements:

> **Disney:** *To make people happy*
> **IKEA:** *To create a better everyday life for the many people*
> **British Broadcasting Company (BBC):** *To be the most creative organisation in the world*
> **Avon:** *To be the company that best understands and satisfies the product, service and self-fulfilment needs of women—globally*
> **Sony Corporation:** *To be a company that inspires and fulfils your curiosity*

The Vision statement does not provide specific targets. Each of the above examples could apply to many different organisations. The vision is a broad description of the value an organisation provides. It is a visual image in words of what the organisation is trying to produce or become. It should inspire people and motivate them to want to be part of and contribute to, the organisation.

> *Vision Statements should be clear and concise, usually not longer than a short paragraph.*

The Mission Statement

The Mission statement is constructed from the Vision Statement. It identifies the action the organisation must undertake to achieve the vision. This is more detailed than the Vision Statement and is objective based, in that it, distinguishes actions or objectives linked to the achievement of the vision. Again, these are not detailed plans.

The Vision statement and Mission statement are often confused and many companies use the terms interchangeably. However, they each have a different purpose.

Operational Management

- *The Vision statement describes where the organisation wants to be in the future*
- *The Mission statement describes what the organisation needs to do now to achieve the vision.*

The Mission Statement defines how the organisation will be different from other organisations in its industry. Here are examples of Mission Statements from successful businesses:

> **Adidas:** *We strive to be the global leader in the sporting goods industry with brands built on a passion for sports and a sporting lifestyle.*
> **Amazon:** *We seek to be Earth's most customer-centric company for four primary customer sets: consumers, sellers, enterprises and content creators.*
> **Google:** *To organise the world's information and make it universally accessible and useful*
> **Honest Tea:** *To create and promote great-tasting, truly healthy, organic beverages*
> **Jet Blue Airways:** *To provide superior service in every aspect of our customer's air travel experience*
> **The New York Times:** *To enhance society by creating, collecting and distributing high-quality news and information*

Each of these examples indicates where the organisation will compete (what industry it is in) and how it will compete (what it will do to be different from other organisations). The Mission statement conveys to stakeholders why the organisation exists. It explains how it creates value for the market or the larger community.

Because it is more specific, the Mission statement is more actionable than the Vision statement.

The Mission statement leads to strategic goals.

Strategic goals are the broad goals the organisation will try to achieve. By describing why, the organisation exists and where and how it will compete, the Mission Statement allows leaders to define a coherent set of goals that fit together to support the mission.

The Values Statement

The Values Statement, also called the code of ethics, differs from both the Vision and Mission Statements.

The Vision and Mission state where the organisation is going (vision) and what it will do to get there (mission). They direct the efforts of people in the organisation toward common goals whilst the Values Statement defines what the organisation believes in and how people in the organisation are expected to behave - with each other, with customers and suppliers and with other stakeholders.

Operational Management

It provides a moral direction for the organisation that guides decision making and establishes a standard for assessing actions. It also provides a standard for employees to judge behaviour.

However, managers cannot just create a Values statement and expect it to be followed. For a Values Statement to be effective, it must be reinforced at all levels of the organisation and must be used to guide attitudes and actions. Organisations with strong values follow them even when it may be easier not to. Levi Strauss & Co is an excellent example of a company that is driven by its values.

When Levis Strauss began to source its manufacturing overseas, the company developed a set of principles called the Global Sourcing and Operating Guidelines for overseas operations and suppliers. One of the principles covered the use of child labour:

Use of child labour is not permissible. Workers can be no less than 15 years of age and not younger than the compulsory age to be in school. We will not utilise partners who use child labour in any of their facilities. We support the development of legitimate workplace apprenticeship programs for the educational benefit of younger people.

Levi Strauss found that one of its contractors was employing children under 15 in a factory in Bangladesh. The easy solution would be to replace those workers, but in Bangladesh, the children's wages may have supported an entire family. If they lost their jobs, they may have had to resort to begging on the streets.

Levi Strauss came up with a different solution, one that supported its values of empathy, originality, integrity and courage: it paid the children to go to school. Levi Strauss continued to pay salaries and benefits to the children and paid for tuition, books and supplies. Even though it would have been easier to just fire the child workers and consider the problem settled, Levi Strauss was driven by its values to find a better solution.

Together, the Vision, Mission and Values Statements provide direction for everything that happens in an organisation. They keep everyone focused on where the organisation is going and what it is trying to achieve.

They define the core values of the organisation and how people are expected to behave. They are not intended to be a straitjacket that restricts or inhibits initiative and innovation, but they are intended to guide decisions and behaviours to achieve common ends.

Operational Management

Organisational Strategies

The organisational strategy is used to set out the organisations vision and purpose and it is this which will be used to base and build all future and long-term developments.

The Strategic Plan is a formalised document that describes the organisations goals and the actions needed to achieve them.

The Strategic Plan provides an operational framework for managers which directs how they plan and deliver products and services and how teams and department should be managed. It will also cover the resources, activities and performance measures that will be necessary in order to achieve the objectives which are set out in the strategy and these will be included in the operational plans.

An organisational strategy is the sum of the actions a company intends to take to achieve long-term goals.

Strategic planning is a systematic process that helps set the ambition for the business' future and determines how best to achieve it. Its primary purpose is to connect three key areas:

- **the mission** - *defining the business' purpose*
- **the vision** - *describing what is to be achieved*
- **the plan** - *outlining how to achieve the ultimate goals*

Strategic planning requires taking a step back from day-to-day operations and articulating where the business is heading, by setting long-term goals, objectives and priorities for the future.

Strategic Alignment

Strategy alone is not enough to make a business successful.

Research suggests that having a strategy has no real effect on the performance of an organisation.

It is ensuring the alignment of the organisations activities to the strategies that makes the difference.

Consider.....

deciding you want a cup of coffee (your strategy) is not the same as getting up and making a cup of coffee (aligning your actions to your strategy).

Operational Management

This gets to the heart of what strategic alignment is. Most people think of strategic alignment as a noun *("the state of having everything aligned to strategy")*, but it is better to think of strategic alignment as a verb - it is about action.

Definition:

> *Strategic Alignment (verb): The process of aligning an organisation's decisions and actions such that they support the achievement of strategic goals.*

Note that the definition talks about decision-making and actions. Actions typically follow decisions so if the organisation does not have the ability to make well-aligned decisions, it really cannot take well-aligned actions.

Also implicit in the definition, is the fact that strategic alignment involves **NOT DOING** some of the things that the organisation might currently be doing... things that do not support the realisation of strategic goals

> *Understanding strategic alignment starts with understanding what strategy really is.*

Most people think of Vision Statements and Mission Statements as being "strategy", but they are only a small part of the strategy story. The Mission and Vision are simply statements about what the organisation is for and where the senior management would like to take it.

> *Strategy - in the context of "strategic alignment" - is the "how".*

A Vision and Mission statement might propose something like:

> *We want to be the most profitable widget manufacturer in the world!*

The key question which needs to be asked before any action is taken to implement this strategic vision is,

> *"How should we do that"?*

In the role of a widget manufacturer, the decision must be taken.........

> *"Are we going to be the lowest cost provider and take massive market share... or should we be the one that offers the highest level of Widget Service, but does so at a high margin?"*

Operational Management

The **"how"** question leads the organisation to strategic goals - the specific targets they must hit to achieve the vision/mission.

If they decide they are going to be the low-cost, high volume widget maker, the strategic goals might be:

- *Reduce costs to supply widgets*
- *Increase distribution channels*
- *Manage cash flow (as volume grows, the organisation will need more cash to hold stock, etc.)*

In the real world, it would be preferable to put some specific numbers on the goals, but this "big picture" of what is trying to be achieved *(be the most profitable widget company)* combined with a high-level statement of how we're going to achieve it *(by being low cost, increasing distribution while managing cash)* is the "strategy".

It is also important to consider the internal and external factors which affect the organisation and how these may impact on the business in the medium and long term. Internal factors which can affect the strategy and hence the strategic plans might include, but are not limited to:

- *physical resources – e.g., equipment, machinery, premises, availability of components or resources*
- *human resources – e.g., skill set of current employees, demand or need for new skills*
- *opportunity – e.g., operating hours, trading times, delivery lead times and production capacity*
- *stakeholders – e.g., internal stakeholders across the organisation*

External factors which impact on strategy and the strategic planning process include:

- *customers – e.g., people who use or buy the products or services*
- *suppliers – e.g., offering different products or delivery options*
- *commodity prices – e.g., in oil, metal or minerals*
- *stakeholders – e.g., community, government, or local authority*
- *competitors – e.g., marketing activity, product development, pricing strategy*
- *legislation and regulation – e.g., changes to legislation which may adversely affect the organisation*
- *natural events/act of God – e.g., floods or snowfall, land slip, etc.*

A PESTLE analysis is commonly used to assess the factors which may influence the organisations strategy and this is explained below.

Strategic plans typically take at least a year to complete, requiring involvement from all company levels.

Operational Management

Senior management create the larger organisational strategy, while middle and lower management adopt goals and plans to fulfil the overall strategy step by step.

Defining Strategic plans

A high level, overarching strategy will be defined first by the senior management. They will ask themselves three questions.

- *Where are we now?*
- *Where do we want to be?*
- *How will we get there?*

The first question requires the senior management to analyse where the organisation is in terms of finance, performance, market share, customer feedback, etc. They must then substantiate this with evidence in the form of accounts, reports etc. They will need to identify, recognise and define ways to mitigate existing problems and also plan to mitigate against problems which may arise in the future and pose risk to the organisation.

The second question helps the management team to focus on its vision. They need to consider why the business exists and what it wants the organisation to become. "Where do we want to be?" must be very clearly defined including the plans for the future. This may include relocating the business or expanding the business into a regional format.

The third question – the "How", will form the operational plan itself. They will need to consider budgets, resources, sources of funding, financial forecasts, identify ways to engage customers, investors, new employees, etc. Physical and Human resources will need to be scoped and planned for and timescales for the vision to become a reality must be clearly and realistically defined. Milestones must be set throughout the plan with metrics identified to measure progress and assess success or failure at every stage.

Strategy Development Tools

Strategy development tools include, among other things, quality, analysis and action planning. Strategy development plans must reflect the route the business is to take and the steps included to get there.

As part of the planning process an analysis of the strengths weaknesses opportunities or threats should be undertaken to ensure that all aspects will be addressed, progressed, monitored and reviewed.

SWOT Analysis

A SWOT is basically an analytical framework that assesses the business, both internally and externally and will determine what needs to happen to assist the business to achieve its objectives.

Operational Management

Strengths and weaknesses are within the organisation, while opportunities and threats are external. Once completed, the organisation can analyse all aspects of its situation and make clear decisions. It can also help to identify opportunities for the progression of your area of operational control or department and to manage or eliminate threats.

	Strengths	*Weaknesses*
Internal	*Strengths are positive characteristics which provide an advantage over the competition.* *If an organisation fails to monitor its strengths it will not know when these become weaknesses and become a problem for the business*	*Weaknesses are the inadequate aspects of the business, that if ignored can compromise the organisation.* *If the business addresses its weaknesses, they can become strengths in the future*
	Opportunities	*Threats*
External	*Opportunities are favourable conditions in the external market which the organisation can take advantage of.* *Economic situation, interest rate fall, changes to legislation, etc.*	*Threats are conditions in the external market which could cause problems for the organisation.* *These could include changes to legislation, the economic forecast, trends, competitor activity, etc.*

Performing a SWOT analysis will identify any weaknesses in the operation and allow action to be taken before they become threats. It also highlights how the organisations strengths can be used to open opportunities and is a useful way of identifying which areas can better contribute to the ongoing success of the organisation.

PESTLE Analysis

A PESTLE Analysis identifies factors which are external to the business, but which can have a direct impact on operations. The PESTLE analysis collects, collates and presents information about external factors that may have an impact on the business.

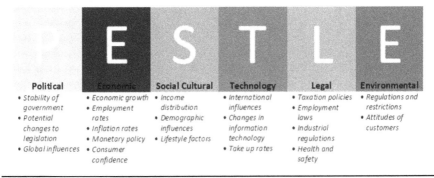

Political	Economic	Social Cultural	Technology	Legal	Environmental
• Stability of government • Potential changes to legislation • Global influences	• Economic growth • Employment rates • Inflation rates • Monetary policy • Consumer confidence	• Income distribution • Demographic influences • Lifestyle factors	• International influences • Changes in information technology • Take up rates	• Taxation policies • Employment laws • Industrial regulations • Health and safety	• Regulations and restrictions • Attitudes of customers

Political	considers what is happening or changing in the political backdrop of the organisation. This includes trade controls, import and export regulations, government agendas and policies, reforms and the political stability in which the organisation operates.
Economic	assess the economic situation - is their economic decline or growth? What is the current inflation rate and are interest rates likely to go up or down? Do exchange rates affect the organisation? How does a rising minimum wage affect staffing levels and profits?
Socio-cultural	this covers what is changing in the socio-cultural backdrop of the organisation. How are customers buying habits changing? What attitudes and beliefs are affecting their buying habits? How do customers feel about green issues? Are they more health-conscious? How is a population growth rate change in the socio-cultural diversity of the customer base affecting how the organisation is operated and the products or services it delivers. There are many socio-cultural aspects of an organisation's operational success and all need to be considered.
Technological	how does the organisation keep up with technological advances? In what ways are customers choosing to interact with the organisation through technology? Are you equipped to respond to those changes? How do you need to update your products and services to maintain a market share?
Legal	changes in legislation can have an impact on employment, access to resources, health and safety management, data management and a long list of other aspects of the organisation. Not compliance with the law can have serious consequences for an organisation, so it is imperative to keep up to date with changes in legislation and more importantly, to successfully implement those changes in the organisation.
Environmental	Environmental issues are now very important to all organisations as any changes can have a direct consequence on the organisation. Many environmental factors will not have an immediate or direct impact on the organisation, but organisations are likely to see changes in the socio-cultural and economic aspects of its operations because of these environmental issues, Customers respond to knowledge about changes in the environment by purchasing products and services organisation that demonstrate a green conscience, while not in non-environmentally friendly products and services are discarded

Operational Management

Devolving the High-Level Strategic Plan

The plan at this stage is an overarching plan which defines the strategy for the whole organisation. As a consequence, much of it will have little relevance to an individual division or department within the organisation. The production department, for example, will have little interest in how the volume of sales will treble over the next three years as that is a challenge for the sales department However, they will be very interested in how they will find the space, the tools, equipment, human resources, source of supply of commodities, etc to enable them to manage the three-fold increase in production which will be necessary to satisfy the demands of the strategic plan.

Individual divisions of the organisation will be assigned specific objectives developed from the strategic plan. These will address the areas relevant to that division and will be used to construct a more detailed plan of action. This will identify the activities the division must undertake and achieve, to contribute to the achievement of the organisation's overall strategic plan and thus its vision.

Similarly, business units or departments lower down the hierarchy will have objectives assigned by the divisions above them for their areas of operation, down through the teams of each business unit or department and finally, the individuals within those teams.

The assignment of objectives is critical to the success of the strategy.

Objectives must be SMART to ensure clarity of intent and to define the timescales in which the objective must be achieved and how success or failure will be measured.

This process of devolving strategy down through the hierarchy, naturally aligns the activities of the entire organisation from senior management down to individuals on the shop floor with the Strategic Plan and the Vision Statement. It also allows the setting of key performance indicators (KPI) at every level to ensure the achievement of organisational objectives or goals.

This entire process, however, relies on those at the top of the hierarchy, clearly communicating the objectives and the construction an objective plan which ensures the objectives are met by those at each level of the hierarchy.

The diagram below shows how the objectives are linked.

Operational Management

The KPIs' created from the objectives at each level must be clearly linked to the objectives of the level above, which in turn are linked to those of the level above that and so on.

This will ensure:

1. *It will ensure the whole organisation is working towards objectives which are aligned to the common organisational goals*
2. *Individual members of staff can clearly identify how the achievement of their actions and objectives are contributing to the achievement of the common objective or goal*
3. *It can define expectations of what must be delivered and how it should be delivered*
4. *It ensures that all staff are aware of what constitutes high-performance and what they must do to achieve it*
5. *It can enhance motivation and commitment by recognising achievement and the provision of feedback*
6. *It provides the basis for personal development planning and improvement plans*
7. *It allows staff to monitor own performance as well as those for whom they are responsible*
8. *It encourages dialogue about what needs to be done to improve performance by mutual agreement rather than having it imposed from above*

Strategic planning therefore is necessary to determine the direction of the organisation. It focuses effort and endeavour and ensures that everyone in the organisation is working towards a common goal.

Operational Management

It also helps to:

- *agree actions that will contribute to business growth*
- *align resources for optimal results*
- *prioritise financial needs*
- *build competitive advantage*
- *engage with your staff and communicate what needs to be done*

Another significant purpose of strategic planning is to help manage and reduce business risks. Growing a business is inherently risky. Detailed planning will help to:

- *remove uncertainty*
- *analyse potential risks*
- *implement risk control measures*
- *consider how to minimise the impact of risks, should they occur*

This unified effort can be likened to a journey.

The journey starts at the point where the organisation is today and ends at the destination – where it wants to be. The route that it takes to get there will be formulated and the challenges which need to be overcome, are the road conditions which must be overcome to complete the sequential legs of the journey, eventually leading to the ultimate destination.

The strategy for an organisation can include growth or expansion, diversification, acquisition or sustaining its current outputs. The way the strategy is implemented will depend on its direction and this will be determined by the strategy writers.

Operational Management

Operational Business Plans

In contrast to strategic planning, the purpose of an operational plan is to illustrate how the strategy will be executed month by month, week by week.

Turning a Strategy into an Operational plan is not about doing more things right – it is about doing more of the right things.

An actionable operational plan answers questions like:

- *What milestones do we need to hit?*
- *Who will work on what?*
- *Where might we run into bottlenecks and how can we avoid them?*
- *How will we define success?*
- *What early indicators will tell us we are on the right track?*

In order to answer these questions, the person developing the plan must consider the following areas in order to ensure every eventuality is considered:

- *the objectives and targets set*
- *timescales for delivery*
- *budgets allocated*
- *physical resources needed / available*
- *human resources needed / available*
- *SMART targets to be assigned for the team*
- *allocation of tasks*
- *monitoring, controlling and assessing performance*
- *identifying problems and resolving them*

Once an actionable plan has been drafted, feedback should be gathered from the team involved, as well as stakeholders and incorporated. Do not be surprised if a few different versions are needed before a plan is identified which everyone can relate to.

Difference Between Strategic Plan and Business Plan

Both strategic and business plan documents are essential planning tools for an organisation. However, depending on business stage and goals, one may be more useful than the other.

A strategic plan is usually for a 3-5-year period and sets out the tasks, the milestones and the steps needed to drive the business forward.

A business plan focuses on a shorter term, usually no more than a year and serves a specific goal – e.g., starting a business, getting funding, or directing operations.

Operational Management

Setting Key Performance Indicators (KPIs)

The KPIs' will be different between organisations and across departments, but it is always important to ensure performance measures are appropriate.

Being able to set SMART objectives will enable team members to work towards their KPIs and gives them the support they need to help the team succeed. Spending time and effort to develop smart objectives for team members ensures everyone has the knowledge and understanding needed to contribute effectively and comfortably to the team and the business.

The best places display information regarding KPIs, benchmarking and continuous improvement activities would be in public places that are accessible to everyone along with team boards and the intranet. These should also be displayed to give employees a fuller picture of what is going on, so they buy into the process and take ownership of it.

Leaders will have their own KPIs and objectives to achieve and may be reluctant to release any staff or contribute to anything that may increase that burden. Therefore, careful planning and excellent communication is the key to ensuring that all involved are fully aware of the importance of the change and a real need to work in co-operation.

Decisions will need to be made as to the most effective ways plans can be implemented and this should include discussions with all those involved. Sharing good practice is a great way of allowing all team members the opportunity to add their own experiences to allow for an effective and relevant way forward to be identified. Team meetings are an appropriate forum to hold these types of discussions and can be noted and documented to be referred to again in the future.

Resources should also be considered. Resources are not infinite and must be allocated appropriately to gain the most effective results. Resources can include people, machinery and facilities and quite often there will be times when one or the other will be required to be diverted for some reason.

Operational Management

Managing Performance

A variety of management tools can be used across the Operational plan to ensure that KPIs' are being met and that the assigned objectives are being achieved and therefore that the contribution from the team, department, division, etc. is meeting with the needs of the strategic plan and the organisation is moving towards realising its vision. They might be used, for example:

Tools can include, for example:

- *SWOT analyses*
- *Work Breakdown Structures (WBS)*
- *PERT Diagrams*
- *SMART objectives*
- *Gantt charts*
- *Plan on a Page*
- *RACI matrix*
- *Time management techniques*
- *Kotter's 8-stage change model*

SWOT Analyses

In the workplace, a SWOT analysis can be used in many different situations to identify and measure:

- **Strengths of a team** – *e.g., well supported; well financed*
- **Weaknesses of a team** – *e.g., very short on time; not enough trained staff to do all the tasks effectively*
- **Opportunities to improve** – *e.g., recruitment drive to bring in the staff needed*
- **Threats to progress** – *e.g., competition from other employers who need to recruit staff with the same skills*

The SWOT analysis can be applied at any level and can be simple or more detailed. It acts as a snapshot and does not track progress or interdependency of tasks, goals or resources. It can be used in any part of the project that needs a simple, focused analysis on where we are now, where we need to be and how we are going to get there.

Work Breakdown Structures (WBS)

A WBS is a useful management tool that breaks down tasks into smaller components.

The tasks and responsibilities are broken down into manageable sections that align to ensure that overall objectives can be met.

A WBS is useful in the earlier stages of planning so that:

Operational Management

- *tasks can be broken down into small pieces*
- *an overall picture of how elements will work together can be seen at a glance*
- *different people can see how the tasks may overlap and work together*

Below is a small sample of a simple WBS planner for a Charity Dinner. It could be developed to go into more detail about the actual days of the month and names and contact details for all of the internal and external team members.

	February	March	April	May	June	July	August
Tickets	Print tickets by 1st April				Launch sales 5th June	Last boost for tickets	
Caterers	Identify potential candidates	Meet shortlisted companies	Appoint caterers			Finalise menu	
Volunteers			Publicise and start recruitment	Recruit & do phone interviews	Recruit & do interviews Provisional order of uniforms by 16 Jun	In-house training Final order for uniforms by 22 Jul	Training at venue Give out uniforms
Performers	Confirm bookings and contracts		Make contact to stay in touch		Check rehearsal dates are OK	Contact about special requests – food, drink etc. Book transport	Venue rehearsals 20, 21, 22 Aug Event 23rd Aug
Transport		Research taxi & limo companies	Reserve transport for performers, guest speakers			Confirm transport bookings OK	3 limos, 6 taxis, 1 minibus needed 22, 23 Aug

PERT Diagram

Another management tool is a PERT diagram, which stands for Programme Evaluation Review Technique. This is a graphic representation of a schedule and it is used to schedule, organise and coordinate functions within a task. It was developed in the 1950s by the US Navy to manage the Polaris submarine, an extremely complex project.

A PERT diagram usually shows:

- *the sequence of tasks and milestones*
- *how these are prioritised*
- *a three-point estimation technique that shows the duration of each task as being 'optimistic', 'pessimistic' or 'most likely'*

Operational Management

The main feature of a PERT diagram, made using software, is the instant calculation of timelines with every change in the workflow. The manager can instantly see how one changed timescale affects other parts of the task. Its primary benefit is to have an overall view of the whole task, rather than individual details, showing how parts of the task can move and impact each other.

Below is a simple PERT diagram about making and packing a teddy bear that has a customised T-shirt:

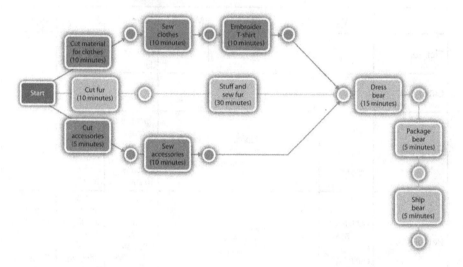

Gantt Charts

Another tool is a Gantt chart, which is a useful and flexible device for illustrating a task's progress. It could be used to represent activity across the whole Operational plan or the individual tasks within it. It makes the timeline very clear and can be simple or complicated and can be adapted to match the complexity of the task. A Gantt chart illustrates the breakdown structure of the task in terms of cascading horizontal bars that show, for example:

- *start and finish dates*
- *various relationships between activities*
- *how tasks track and influence each other*

Below is a simple example of a Gantt chart which reflects the data in the Pert chart above:

Operational Management

Activity/Day	1	2	3	4	5	6	7	8	9	10	11	12	13
Cut fur	■												
Stuff and sew fur			■	■	■	■							
Cut material	■	■											
Sew clothes			■	■									
Embroider T-shirt					■	■							
Cut accessories	■												
Sew accessories		■	■										
Dress bears										■	■		
Package bears												■	
Ship bears													

Lot size: 100 bears

All activities are scheduled to begin at their earliest start time.

■ Completed work

▨ Work to be completed

RACI Matrix

The RACI model is a straightforward tool that is used in management to identify roles and responsibilities. It stands for:

- **Responsible** – *the person who does the work to achieve the task*
- **Accountable** – *the person who is accountable for the correct completion of the task – e.g., the project manager who approves the Responsible person's work*
- **Consulted** – *the people who provide information for the project in two-way communication – e.g., subject specialists*
- **Informed** – *the people who are affected by the outcomes of tasks and need to be kept informed about progress in one-way communication – shareholders, directors or senior managers who are not involved with the day-to-day running of the project*

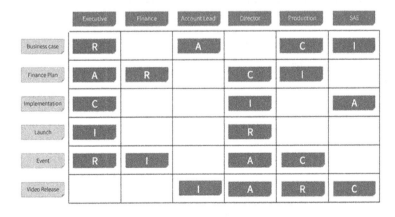

	Executive	Finance	Account Lead	Director	Production	SAE
Business case	R		A		C	I
Finance Plan	A	R		C	I	
Implementation	C			I		A
Launch	I			R		
Event	R	I		A	C	
Video Release			I	A	R	C

Operational Management

This helps to avoid confusion about the decision-making process by providing a clear illustration for all relevant stakeholders to see who is responsible for tasks and who needs to be informed along the way. A RACI model can help manage expectations and identify roles and responsibilities in the task.

Time Management Techniques

The tools used for project management help managers to:

- *plan ahead for each element and stage*
- *keep elements of the task on time*
- *predict busy and quiet times*
- *prioritise human and physical resources to meet deadlines*

Time management techniques can be extremely valuable as they will:

- *allow time each day to plan activities*
- *prioritise communications – e.g., deal with urgent messages and accept that some emails and telephone calls do not have to be answered immediately*
- *factor in some time for interruptions and unplanned activities*
- *plan meetings and be firm about time spent*
- *remove distractions when focus is needed*

Eisenhower Grid

An Eisenhower grid or matrix can be designed to give an overview for personal time management, for example:

	Urgent	Not urgent
Important	**1) DO NOW** emergencies complaints planned tasks and projects due now staff needs problem-solving	**2) PLAN TO DO** planning preparation research networking system development strategy planning
Not Important	**3) REJECT AND EXPLAIN** trivial requests from others ad hoc interruptions distractions pointless routines or activities	**4) RESIST AND CEASE** 'comfort' activities – computer games, excessive breaks chat, gossip daydreaming and doodling reading irrelevant material unnecessary travel

Kotter's 8-stage Change Model

Operational Management

Developed in 1996, the stages of Kotter's change model can be used as a tool as an overall change management framework when managing tasks. The eight stages are:

- *Establish a sense of urgency* – *when initiating the task and presenting the operating plans.*
- *Create a guiding coalition* – *convince people that the task has value and benefits; bring together a strong coalition or team of people from different departments to guide the team.*
- *Develop a shared vision* – *create a strategy to deliver the objectives of the task.*
- *Communicate the vision* – *communicate the purpose, aims and objectives of the task efficiently, address concerns openly.*
- *Empower people to act on the vision* – *remove obstacles that may stop progress.*
- *Create short-term wins to motivate with success* – *set smaller objectives that can be achieved, praised and rewarded.*
- *Consolidate and build on the changes made by the project* – *analyse each 'win' for success and areas for improvement; set goals to continue the momentum.*
- *Institutionalise the change* – *talk about progress; include relevant lessons learned during the task within the organisation's training and recruitment practices.*

Management tool/ method	*Suggestions of how this could be applied to monitoring progress*
SWOT analysis	*To track the strengths and weaknesses of recruitment policies compared to expected targets; to review the opportunities for finding the right people if there are issues; to review the threats to progress to make sure that they are still relevant*
Work Breakdown Structures (WBS)	*To monitor the job descriptions set out in the initial WBS to make sure that the right people are being selected; to monitor training programmes set out in the WBS to make sure that they are relevant and suitable*
PERT diagrams	*To have a visual record about how a delay in advertising vacancies has a knock-on effect on applications, interviews and training*
SMART objectives	*To review levels of recruitment and training against the SMART targets on a regular basis*
Gantt charts	*To see how the recruitment and training elements of the project are progressing in relation to all other aspects of the project, such as physical resources and finance*
Plan on a Page	*To prepare a quick overview for progress meetings and interim management reports*
RACI matrix	*To use as a guide to make sure that communication is as expected and agreed between different stakeholders – to ensure that the relevant directors and external stakeholders are being informed of progress*

Operational Management

RAG

Another useful tool to use when monitoring progress is to use the RAG status – red, amber, green. During the planning stage, the team can set parameters about what the colours mean, for example:

Red – *major problems that will affect the viability of the whole project and cannot be resolved by the project manager – the matter should be escalated to the project board member*

Amber – *problems that have a negative effect on one or more aspects of the project's viability and performance – problems can be dealt with by the project manager and their team, who then notify the board about progress*

Green – *the project is performing to plan – all problems are within tolerances and expectations and can be dealt with within normal limits of authority*

There can be drawbacks to the traffic-light system; it can oversimplify a progress and it is very dependent on the integrity of the information that can turn an element from red to amber or green.

As a visual aid, it is effective as it draws attention to the problem areas and shows when everything is on track.

It can really help to keep everyone involved and motivated by letting them know how things are going. If the news is not very good, it can help to reassure everyone, so that they work harder to get back on track and understand the problems behind problems and potential issues. If things are going well, the team and other stakeholders benefit from knowing and getting some positive praise and feedback. This lifts morale and helps to keep people motivated and focused.

Operational Management

Managing Resources

Resource management is the process by which businesses manage their various resources effectively.

Those resources can be intangible such as people and time – and tangible such as equipment, materials and finances. It involves planning so that the right resources are assigned to the right tasks.

Managing resources involves schedules and budgets for people, projects, equipment and supplies.

While it is often used in reference to project management, it applies to many other areas of business management. A small business will pay attention to resource management in a number of areas, including:

- **Finances** – *Can it meet current expenses or afford to invest in new equipment or staff training?*
- **Staffing** – *Does it have the right people for the work at hand? Will it need to hire if it gets that new client and if so, what skills will those people need to have?*
- **Physical space** – *Is the company's office or manufacturing space configured so that other resources can be managed for maximum efficiency?*
- **Equipment** – *Does it have the tools needed to do what is required?*
- **Technology** – *What does the business need to do succeed and should financial resources be reallocated to fund what is missing?*

What are the advantages of resource management?

Avoids unforeseen hiccups: *By understanding your resources upfront and planning how to use them, you can troubleshoot gaps or problems before they happen.*

Prevents burnout: *Effective resource management allows you to avoid "overallocation" or "dependency" of resources by gaining insight into your team's workload.*

Provides a safety net: *Let us say the project was not successful due to lack of resources (it happens). Resource planning and management establishes that you did everything you could with what you had.*
Builds transparency: Other teams can gain visibility into your team's bandwidth and plan accordingly if your team is at maximum capacity or available to take on new projects.

Measures efficiency: *With a high-level understanding of what is needed to manage and execute an upcoming project, you can effectively plan and measure ROI.*

Operational Management

Resource Management Techniques

1. Resource Allocation
Resource allocation helps get the most from the available resources. Based on team members' skills and capacity, resource allocation is the process of tackling projects using the resources available in the most efficient manner possible.

To get a clear view into allocation, managers will often use resource allocation reports. These can give information from a high-level view to a detailed run down of resource availability — helping to avoid schedule delays and going over budget. The better the reporting capabilities, the more transparency and efficiency there will be.

2. Resource Levelling
Another type of resource management is resource levelling. This technique aims to discover underused or inefficiently used resources within the organisation and utilise them to advantage. An example of resource levelling is having a bar person who has experience in food service help in the restaurant by taking on small service tasks that require completing. If a bar person can use their skills, the restaurant team will not need to hire agency staff if they suddenly get busy in the restaurant.

3. Resource Forecasting
Having a resource management plan is critical to optimising people, materials and budget efficiency. Resource forecasting allows future resource requirements to be predicted before they are needed. During the planning stages of a project, resource forecasting determines the project's scope, possible constraints, unforeseen costs and potential risks.

Management of resources is essential to ensure that objectives and KPIs' are met on time and to the desired quality. Good management will ensure that:

- *resources are available on time*
- *problems and potential risks are identified as soon as possible*
- *solutions are found to address problems, issues and risks*
- *appropriate decisions about how to reallocate resources are made*
- *evidence to support requests for increased resources and timescales is produced*
- *evidence is available to senior decision-makers how the task is being managed*

When managing resources, the objectives for the task need to be very clear. This gives a focus so that time, human and physical resources can be geared up to achieve goals without unnecessary waste.

Operational Management

Human Resources

When managing human resources, it is necessary to perform the usual functions associated with people management, for example:

- *planning and allocating work to match the skills, experience and knowledge of team members*
- *developing and maintaining a common sense of purpose and a positive working environment*
- *working to retain team members*
- *recruiting and training team members*
- *making sure everyone understands aims and objectives*
- *supporting team members in career and skills development*
- *ensuring compliance with legislation* – *e.g., health and safety, data protection and equality and diversity*
- *monitoring work and taking action to improve performance*

In addition to these management tasks, it is essential to make sure that people with the right skills are available when required for each stage of the task. During the planning stages, they can:

- *identify exactly which human resources are going to be needed for specific parts of the task*
- *work out the lead times for preparing and recruiting staff*
- *ensure that existing team members have the right skills*
- *recruit new team members, from inside or outside the organisation*
- *train and brief all team members in time*
- *emphasise the importance of timescales and quality* – *and how these can affect other areas of the task*
- *ensure that team members have the equipment they need to perform their duties* – *e.g., Hi-Viz jackets, stationery, laptops, tablets, travel tickets, radios or mobile phones*

Operational Management

Physical Resources

The strategic objectives are very focused and visible, which often means that the resources are constantly scrutiny. As there is interdependency between objectives at every level of the organisation, physical resource needs to be planned and allocated with care.

The leader is accountable and responsible for managing resources effectively and may have to answer to:

- *senior managers and directors* – *who need the team to make a profit for the organisation*
- *clients* – *customers who have commissioned and paid for the work*
- *sponsors* – *companies who have associated their brand with the organisation*
- *government agencies* – *enforcing regulations on the environment or health and safety*

Every resource has a cost and a lead time, so careful management is required to make sure that:

- *each item is fit for purpose and satisfies regulatory requirements*
- *it is available on time*
- *the quality is as agreed and expected* – *as set out in a service level agreement*
- *waste is kept to a minimum*
- *there is a plan for all resources*– *surplus equipment or that which has become obsolete may be sold off to recover some of the financial investment made.*

Financial Resources

Budgets are always strictly controlled and the leader is accountable and responsible for agreeing, controlling and managing budgets. Consideration is needed for:

- *timescales* – *to show when money is due to come in and out* – *when money from sales and sponsors is likely to be available*
- *priorities* – *to target resources correctly to support the efficiency and effectiveness of the organisation* – *prioritising workforce costs, assessing and arranging payments for urgent, planned and essential purchases*
- *financial resources* – *to match funding with anticipated income and expenditure* – *helping to arrange business loans to finance long-term projects; dealing with increases and decreases in revenue and expenses*
- *contingencies* – *negotiating and setting aside budgets and resources for unpredictable and unforeseen circumstances*

Operational Management

Evaluating Performance

The leader needs to evaluate progress and look at all of the data that has been collected, so that the team can, for example:

- *compare the outcomes with the original objectives* – *to see if the progress has achieved its intended aims and the correct quality standards*
- *understand how the task has achieved its purpose* – *or why it has failed*
- *identify how the task utilised human resources* –*to analyse the skills used and identify career development opportunities*
- *identify how efficiently physical resources were used* –*comparing budget forecasts with actual costs, reviewing the levels of waste*
- *identify problems and potential improvements*
- *advise stakeholders and decision-makers* – *about how to repeat, develop or improve actions and plans for future activity*
- *identify needs for further development work* –*to set up a new plan to solve major issues that were discovered when working on the earlier objectives*

When evaluating progress, the data needs to be reliable and relevant to be of use. Consider what needs to be identified and how it will be measured, what data is needed and how it will be collected.

Organisations will have their own ways of evaluating progress, which may include:

- *comparing estimated costs with actual costs* – *to evaluate the budget allocations and identify the causes of variance*
- *collecting and reviewing feedback from customers and other users of the services and products covered in the plan* – *e.g., independent surveys, feedback forms, forum comments, focus groups or satisfaction surveys*
- *analysing operational data* – *e.g., looking at patient records in a hospital to evaluate changes in services*
- *reviewing progress reports* – *e.g., reports from staff and other stakeholders about their experiences and recommendations*
- *analysing sales patterns* – *e.g., to see when tickets were purchased and by whom; to see if business changes have affected sales as expected*
- *analysing changes in activity and comments on websites and social media* – *e.g., to illustrate a change towards Internet shopping following a plan to develop on online sales*

The methods selected will depend upon who needs and wants to see the evaluation of progress and performance. The media, for example, might only be interested in the initial financial impact of changes made by the plan, whereas the organisation's HR department will be more interested in evaluating the impact on staff skills, experience, training and career development. Reviews of performance need to be presented in ways that satisfy the needs of stakeholders.

Operational Management

In general, reviews need to:

- *show the successes of the objective*
- *praise everyone who contributed to the success*
- *identify areas of weakness and lessons that can be learned for future plans*
- *illustrate the team's value for future plans*

Operational Management

Contingency Planning

The aim of contingency planning is to minimise the impact of a foreseeable event and to plan for how the business will resume normal operations after the event.

Contingency planning involves:

- *Preparing for predictable and quantifiable problems*
- *Preparing for unexpected and unwelcome events*

Contingency planning is one of the three approaches a business can take to manage risk. These are:

Risk management: *identifying and dealing with the risks threatening a business*
Contingency planning: *planning for unforeseen events*
Crisis management: *handling potentially dangerous events for a business*

The process of contingency planning involves:

- *Identifying what and how things can and might go wrong*
- *Understanding the potential effects if things go wrong*
- *Devising plans to cope with the threats*
- *Putting in place strategies to deal with the risks before they happen*

Almost by definition, contingency planning should focus on the most important risks; those that have the greatest potential for significant business disruption or damage. Risks vary in terms of their significance to the business.

Contingency planning is not required for every eventuality. However, risks of strategic significance cannot be ignored.

Risk
Risk can be:

- *The possibility of loss or business damage*
- *A threat that may prevent or hinder the ability to achieve business objectives*
- *The chance that a hoped-for outcome will not occur* (e.g., customers do not respond well to a new product launch)

Risk is ever-present in business and there are a variety of possible responses to it:

- *Ignore it* (wait and see)
- *Share/deflect the risk* (e.g., take-out insurance)
- *Make contingency plans* - prepare for it
- *Embrace risk as an opportunity* - particularly if it also affects other competitors

Operational Management

Some examples of how action can be taken to reduce risk include:

Marketing
- *Avoid over-reliance on customers or products*
- *Develop multiple distribution channels*
- *Test marketing for new products*

Operations
- *Hold spare capacity*
- *Rigorous quality assurance & control procedures & culture*

Finance
- *Insurance against bad debts*
- *Investment appraisal techniques*

People
- *Key man insurance – protect against loss of key staff*
- *Rigorous recruitment & selection procedures changes.*

Revising Plans

It is seldom the case that every plan progresses without hinderances or unexpected events of some kind.

It is clear that Strategic and Operational plans are totally interdependent and the objectives set at intermediate and senior management levels are totally reliant on the performance and events at the bottom of the hierarchy.

It may not be the fault of the team leader or those they lead that an objective is not achieved, however, this could impact on every other objective in the organisation. As a consequence, there will be a need for some flexibility in the plans to adapt to missed objectives and events as they arise.

Leaders will need to respond to these events by:

- ***identifying and analysing the changes needed*** - *e.g., causes, problems and possible solutions*
- ***negotiate and make appropriate revisions to the original plan***
- ***use good communication skills throughout*** - *to minimise the impact of revisions*

It should be noted that it is not enough to simply make changes to the objectives at the level where the problem arose, the impact of the problem will affect all levels in the hierarchy.

> *A one-week delay in the development of a new product may lead to a six-week delay in the production of the new product, which may lead to a six-month delay in the desired sales targets being met by the sales and marketing division, which in turn may mean a delay of up to one year in the realisation of the overall vision.*

Operational Management

It is essential that when a need for change is identified, it must be carefully analysed and the change must be negotiated in full and in detail by all stakeholders who are affected by the change. The following list identifies examples of areas where negotiation may be necessary in order to implement the change and assess the overall impact on the strategic plan:

- *timescales* – e.g., negotiating with suppliers to receive goods earlier or later than expected, agreeing new deadlines with senior managers, discussing delays with customers who are expecting deliveries
- *physical and human resources* – e.g., needing to change staffing levels if there is a long delay, recruiting at short notice to increase production, sourcing additional equipment to deal with the changes, liaising with other team leaders and managers about redeploying staff to cope with demand
- *budgets* – e.g., putting recruitment on hold; negotiating overtime to meet production targets, recruiting extra staff, renegotiating budgeted income and expenditure.

Changes should generally be kept to a minimum so that the impact is kept to a minimum for all concerned. Vigilant monitoring and assessment of performance will significantly reduce the need for change at all levels.

All possible alternatives should be considered before change is authorised.

A shortfall in production on one day due to bad weather and staff being unable to get to work, can be quickly and easily resolved over the next day or two by allowing overtime and goodwill and by the end of the week, production is back on track with only a minor additional cost from the overtime needed. A knee jerk reaction could lead to an over-reaction to the problem leading to substantial unnecessary costs. If this drop in production is not picked up quickly, however, the problem could become far greater and have a much greater impact on the organisation.

Consider all possibilities and consider the knock-on effect of each option before making any final decisions. In some industries, changes are part of the daily routine and policies and procedures will be geared to deal with such eventualities. In other industries and organisations, change will not be expected and given the continuity of the status quo, exceptional negotiation skills will be essential given the impact the unplanned change with have on stakeholders.

Operational Management

Change Management and Project Management

Project management and change management are often confused.

Although they both involve managing people and processes (and often work together to meet organisational goals), they are quite different disciplines.

Understanding what those differences are and how both practices can (and should) work together to manage change, is crucial for the success of an organisation.

Whereas project management focuses on the processes and activities needed to complete a project (such as a new software application), change management focuses on the people affected by those projects or other changes within the organisation.

Project management is about the process required to bring a team or product from point A to point B and will be dealt with in detail later.

A project team is often made up of stakeholders from various departments and backgrounds. However, the stakeholders on the team are not always able to address the impact the project may have on stakeholders outside of that isolated team. This is where Change Management comes into effect.

This uncertainty can lead to anxiety, confusion and resistance from the people on the ground who may not fully understand the need for the changes or how to adopt and adapt to new processes. Without buy-in from the rest of the organisation, a project's outcomes can be limited.

Change management is the solution to this employee resistance problem

Change managers help the people affected by a project to transition smoothly. They fulfil this goal through three process stages:

- *Planning for change*
- *Managing change*
- *Reinforcing change*

In many ways, change managers are the cheerleaders for a project. They must craft and deliver the messaging around the project and communicate the reason for the changes with employees and other stakeholders. Additionally, they will work with stakeholders to help them understand how those changes may impact different departments and roles and how to move forward effectively and efficiently.

Operational Management

Because projects can have a significant and lasting impact on the business and its stakeholders, project and change management often work hand in hand to ensure a project's long-term success.

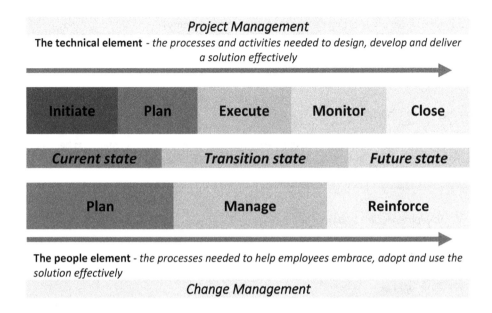

Because each discipline focuses on different aspects of a project (and ultimately its success), both project management and change management should work in tandem to ensure a project's intended outcomes and overall organisational success.

Change Management

When people talk about business change, what they mean is change management, which is the process used to ensure that changes to a business are smoothly implemented, with as little resistance as possible to achieve lasting benefits.

Definition:

> *Change management is the overarching approach taken in an organisation to move from the current to a future desirable state using a coordinated and structured approach in collaboration with stakeholders.*

Operational Management

This type of change is not the organic evolution which happens, inevitably, over time in every organisation, but the planned and considered change an organisation will undertake to significantly change the way it operates. The important term here being the word planned.

Business change should never be considered without extensive planning having taken place before hand and every effort made to identify potential problems which could arise and undermine or prevent the change from taking place or being successful.
The net effect of a failed program of business change can devastate an organisation and lead to the loss of substantial amounts of money.

The Need for Change

With all the changes happening in the business world today, change management has become one of the most important business functions an organisation undertakes.

Change management will be necessary to successfully implement changes including:

- *Implementation of a new technology*
- *Mergers & acquisitions*
- *Change in leadership*
- *Change in organisational culture*
- *Time of crisis*

Types of Change
The change undertaken can be relatively small, such as improving the organisation's invoicing procedures, to a complete transformation, such as changing the entire product and service offerings in response to unexpected competition. In most instances though, it will cause major disruption to daily operations.

There are three principal types of change in a business context: developmental, transitional and transformational change.

Developmental Change
A developmental change occurs when an organisation wishes to improve a process or procedure, such as updating the payroll system or refocusing its marketing strategy. These changes are small and incremental – you are not redesigning the entire workflow but are simply refining it to make it better.

Developmental change usually occurs in response to technology upgrades or efforts to reduce costs that aim to improve the efficiency of a work process. Staff must be given the training, they need to implement the changes, there should be minimal upheaval associated with this type of change.

Operational Management

Transitional Change
A transitional change is an act of replacing major processes with new ones, such as automating a manual production line or adopting a new IT system. It also includes mergers and acquisitions and other such courses of action. Transitional changes are usually caused by a desire to remain competitive in the marketplace. The organisation is not moving into the unknown when executing a transitional change, but it may have to reconsider its job functions, processes, culture and relationships to manage the change effectively. If handled badly this can cause doubt and insecurity in staff.

Transformational Change
Transformational change is the most disruptive since it requires a fundamental shift in the way an organisation operates. An organisation might decide to completely change direction or restructure the whole organisation using new, proprietary operating systems. Because of the upheaval caused, these types of changes happen only rarely.

Managing a transformational change is complex, requiring significant skill from the management team and outside help from change specialists. When the change process is complete, the organisation is unrecognisable from what it was before.

The Impact of Change Management

Change management is needed whenever an organisation undertakes a program or event that interrupts day-to-day operations. Such an undertaking will impact on:

The work content of individual jobs.
Many jobs require individuals or groups to perform tasks repeatedly. An accounts department has daily, weekly, monthly and annual activities. Over time, most people become comfortable with the tools provided and the rhythm of the work calendar. Even simple changes may disrupt the workflow and be disconcerting for the staff.

The roles of individual employees.
Many people view their value to the organisation as being a good technician, administrator, or data entry clerk. When asked to take on a different role, they may become very uncomfortable. People with excellent technical skills often struggle when asked to become managers. Rather than performing all the tasks, they have to learn to work through other people. Once they are no longer rewarded for the skills that made them successful, employees may question their purpose.

The organisation itself.
Management teams debate major changes for months before making final decisions, enabling each member of the team to gain a deeper understanding of the effects the change will have on the organisation. Even if they do not agree with the final decision, they have time to determine whether to accept the new direction or to depart gracefully. Individuals lower in the hierarchy rarely have time to process major changes. Managers do not want employees to worry about events that may never happen until it is clear the change will take place. If the change involves a merger, acquisition, or divestiture there will

also be strict controls on sharing information to prevent the possibility of insider dealing. As a result, individuals who are not part of the management team have much less time to prepare for the planned change and may decide to leave while the change is undertaken, making change management even more difficult.

In today's marketplace it is essential that organisations from multinational corporations to small businesses are able to flex and change with the demands customers place upon them.

This change may not be voluntary and it may also be unwanted, however, it must be addressed and responded to quickly and effectively if the business is to survive.

Some businesses today are only successful because of their ability to change at short notice or on a regular basis. Technology companies are constantly developing products to meet the ever-increasing needs of the customer base. The demand for new experiences drives change in theatre, television, film and gaming industries. The leisure sector is constantly striving to develop its product offer to build loyalty and attract new customers. The demands placed upon national security mean that defence and military engineering is fighting a constant battle to stay ahead of the challenges we face in the modern World. We are currently witnessing the race to deliver pollution free transport utilising alternative fuels such as electricity, hydrogen and even nuclear options.

Change in the 21st century is everywhere and all around us.

These industries offer employees excitement and challenge on a daily basis as they strive to innovate and stay ahead in the marketplace. The negative side to all this is that some employees are resistant to change. They do not want an ever-changing work environment.

Resistance to Change

People do not like change – they enjoy routine as it allows them to operate within their comfort zone. The moment change is proposed, the status quo is under threat and people automatically react negatively to the prospect of change.

A major part of the change process is making sure the change is accepted and adopted by the people who are affected by it.

Without proper buy-in, there is a risk that employees will reject or even sabotage the change project, resulting in wasted time and money.

Managing the people-side of the change can help to reduce fear and anxiety and ensure the new goals being set are embraced.

Research shows that only 38% of people like to leave their comfort zone.

Operational Management

When these people are presented with a change, they think, "This is exciting!" Those positive interpretations of change result in positive emotional reactions, such as happiness and satisfaction, which result in greater employee productivity.

The other 62%, however, look at the same statement and immediately feel fear and discomfort. They may think, "Oh great, this change will slow my career development." or "I will not enjoy my job anymore." or "Will they keep me on?".

The acceptance and adoption of change by employees at all levels is the biggest problem to overcome when managing change.

When supporting a team and individuals through a period of change, it is vital to communicate freely and openly by informing, educating and emphasising the benefits of the change for them as individuals.
At the time of change staff will want empathetic and supportive leadership. They need to be engaged in and part of the change process, by encouraging them to take an active role in the process itself. There will need to be negotiation with those who remain resistant to change.

Initiate and Manage Change

Change management and project management are two critical disciplines that are applied to most organisational changes to improve the likelihood of success of the organisation and maximise the return on investment.

The first question asked when senior managers begin the strategic planning process is – "where are we now?" This is also the first question asked in change management and the answers are just the same. By identifying what is available today, becomes the platform to plan what will need to change tomorrow to ensure the goals are reached.

In the same way, the second question "Where do we want to be?" provides the reasons why the change is needed. This sets the targets and objectives that the change will deliver.

The third question "How do we get there?" defines the change process itself. By answering this question, the change process becomes clear and planning for the change can begin.

Operational Management

When change is introduced to an organisation, it will impact on one or more of the following:

- *Processes*
- *Systems*
- *Organisation structure*
- *Job roles*

While there are numerous approaches and tools that can be used to improve the organisation, all of them ultimately result in adjustments to one or more of the four parts of the organisation listed above.

> *Change typically results as a reaction to specific problems or opportunities the organisation is facing based on internal or external stimuli.*

While the notion of becoming "more competitive" or "closer to the customer" or "more efficient" can be the motivation to initiate change, at some point these goals must be transformed into the specific impacts on processes, systems, organisation structures or job roles. This is the process of defining the change.

Change Management Plan

A change management plan can support a smooth transition and ensure employees are guided through the change journey. The harsh fact is that approximately 70 percent of change initiatives fail due to negative employee attitudes and unproductive management behaviour. In order to identify what needs to be incorporated into the change management plan – the following steps should be followed.

1. Clearly define the change and align it to business goals.

It might seem obvious, but many organisations miss this first vital step. It is one thing to state the change required and entirely another to conduct a critical review against organisational objectives and performance goals to ensure the change will carry the business in the right direction strategically, financially and ethically. This step can also help determine the value of the change, which will quantify the effort and inputs to be invested.

Key questions:

- *What do we need to change?*
- *Why is this change required?*

2. Determine impacts and those affected.

Once it is known exactly what is to be achieved and why, the impacts of the change at various organisational levels must be determined. Review the effect on each business unit and how it cascades through the organisational structure to the individual. This information will start to form the blueprint for where training and support is needed the most to mitigate the impacts.

Key questions:

- *What are the impacts of the change?*
- *Who will the change affect the most?*
- *How will the change be received?*

3. Develop a communication strategy.

Although all employees should be taken on the change journey, the first two steps will have highlighted those employees to whom the change absolutely must be communicated to. Determine the most effective means of communication for the group or individual that will bring them on board. The communication strategy should include a timeline for how the change will be incrementally communicated, key messages and the communication channels and mediums it is planned to use.

Key questions:

- *How will the change be communicated?*
- *How will feedback be managed?*

4. Provide effective training.

With the change message out in the open, it is important that people know they will receive training, whether structured or informal, to teach the skills and knowledge required to operate efficiently and effectively as the change is rolled out. Training could include a suite of online modules, or a blended learning approach incorporating face-to-face training sessions or on-the-job coaching and mentoring.

Key questions:

- *What behaviours and skills are required to achieve business results?*
- *What training delivery methods will be most effective?*

5. Implement a support structure.

Providing a support structure is essential to help employees to adjust to the change emotionally and practically and to build proficiency of behaviours and technical skills needed to achieve desired business results. Some change can result in redundancies or restructures, so consider providing support such as counselling services to help people navigate the situation. To help employees adjust to changes to how a role is performed, a mentorship or an open-door policy with management to ask questions as they arise could be set up.

Key questions:

Operational Management

- *Where is support most required?*
- *What types of support will be most effective?*

6. Measure the change process.

Throughout the change management process, a structure should be put in place to measure the business impact of the changes and ensure that continued reinforcement opportuniencies exist to build proficiencies. Evaluate the change management plan to determine its effectiveness and document any lessons learned.

Key questions:

- *Did the change assist in achieving business goals?*
- *Was the change management process successful?*
- *What could have been done differently?*

Identifying barriers to change and overcoming them

It should be recognised there are 2 types of organisational change - imposed and self-generated, both of which are influenced internally and externally to the organisation. To implement a coaching or mentoring scheme to bring about organisational change, the desired outcomes must be identified, even if they are obvious.

> *It must be recognised that change means that many things will be unfamiliar, uncertain and ambiguous.*

A system once in place, is familiar, establishes patterns of work and interaction and generates its own momentum; it is, by its very nature, long-term. Change on the other hand, is new and may only be temporary. Information may be uncertain, the authority to control may have to be indirect and exactly who is in charge may be ambiguous. Thus, people managing change also need to understand their environment and not just the technical requirements and objectives that appear on the change documents. The forces that prompted the change, the people that will make the change happen and the forces that will support and obstruct the change must be understood.

To avoid conflict when implementing any type of change, it is essential to ensure that all people involved understand the reasons behind the changes. As a Team Leader, you will need to be able to avoid conflict, which can be achieved by ensuring that clear lines of communication and authority are always identified.

There are several things should be considered when conflict or barriers are being displayed. The effective leader should be prepared and have adequate information to hand to be able to provide a full picture of the situation, together with the perceived benefits and advantages.

You should be able to consider the impact the change will have on team members:

- *empathise with them and be prepared to provide alternatives if required*
- *ensure that discussions made that may lead to conflict are held in an appropriate location and in a positive atmosphere*
- *ensure that the concerns or barriers presented by team members are taken seriously and listen attentively*
- *do not dictate to them, instead, encourage the team to expand on its thoughts*
- *asked them how they think the situation could be overcome or resolve to take the ideas on board*
- *if you are unable to comply with them, explain why and ensure your explanation is understood*

The Change Curve

The Change Curve is based on a model originally developed in the 1960s by Elisabeth Kubler-Ross to explain the grieving process. Since then, it has been widely utilised as a method of helping people understand their reactions to significant change or upheaval.

Kubler-Ross proposed that a terminally ill patient would progress through five stages of grief when informed of their illness. She further proposed that this model could be applied to any dramatic life changing situation and, by the 1980s, the Change Curve was a firm fixture in change management circles.

The curve and its associated emotions can be used to predict how performance is likely to be affected by the announcement and subsequent implementation of a significant change.

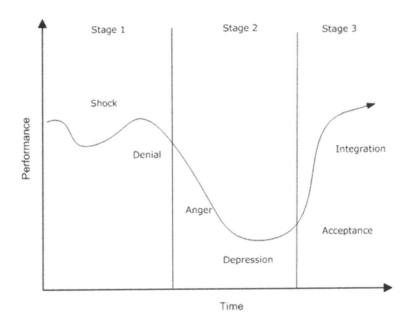

Operational Management

The original five stages of grief – denial, anger, bargaining, depression and acceptance – have adapted over the years.

There are numerous versions of the curve in existence. However, most of them are consistent in their use of the following basic emotions, which are often grouped into three distinct transitional stages.

Stage 1 – Shock and denial
The first reaction to change is usually shock. This initial shock, while frequently short lived, can result in a temporary slowdown and loss of productivity.

Performance tends to dip sharply, individuals who are normally clear and decisive seek more guidance and reassurance and agreed deadlines can be missed.

The shock is often due to:

- *lack of information*
- *fear of the unknown*
- *fear of looking stupid or doing something wrong*

After the initial shock has passed, it is common for individuals to experience denial. At this point focus tends to remain in the past. There is likely to be a feeling that as everything was OK as it was, why does there need to be a change?

Common feelings include:

- *being comfortable with the status quo*
- *feeling threatened*
- *fear of failure*

Individuals who have not previously experienced major change can be particularly affected by this first stage. It is common for people to convince themselves that the change is not going to happen, or if it does, that it will not affect them. Performance often returns to the levels seen before the dip experienced during the initial shock of the change. People carry on as they always have and may deny having received communication about the changes and may well make excuses to avoid taking part in forward planning.

At this stage, communication is key. Reiterating what the actual change is, the effects it may have and providing as much reassurance as possible, will all help to support individuals experiencing these feelings.

Stage 2 –Anger and depression
After the feelings of shock and denial, anger is often the next stage. A scapegoat, in the shape of an organisation, group or individual, is commonly found.

Focussing the blame on someone or something allows a continuation of the denial by providing another focus for the fears and anxieties the potential impact is causing.

Operational Management

Common feelings include:

- *suspicion*
- *scepticism*
- *frustration*

The lowest point of the curve comes when the anger begins to wear off and the realisation that the change is genuine hits. It is common for morale to be low and for self-doubt and anxiety levels to peak. Feelings during this stage can be hard to express and depression is possible as the impact of what has been lost is acknowledged. This period can be associated with:

- *apathy*
- *isolation*
- *remoteness*

At this point performance is at its lowest. There is a tendency to fixate on small issues or problems, often to the detriment of day-to-day tasks. Individuals may continue to perform tasks in the same way as before, even if this is no longer appropriate behaviour.

People will be reassured by the knowledge that others are experiencing the same feelings. Providing managers, teams and individuals with information about the Change Curve underlines that the emotions are usual and shared and this can help to develop a more stable platform from which to move into the final stage.

Stage 3 –Acceptance and integration

After the darker emotions of the second stage, a more optimistic and enthusiastic mood begins to emerge. Individuals accept that change is inevitable and begin to work with the changes rather than against them.

Now come thoughts of:

- *exciting new opportunities*
- *relief that the change has been survived*
- *impatience for the change to be complete*

The final steps involve integration. The focus is firmly on the future and there is a sense that real progress can now be made. By the time everyone reaches this stage, the changed situation has firmly replaced the original and becomes the new reality.

The primary feelings now include:

- *acceptance*
- *hope*
- *trust*

During the early part of this stage, energy and productivity remain low, but slowly begin to show signs of recovery. Everyone will have lots of questions and be curious about possibilities and opportunities. Normal topics of conversation resume and a wry humour is often used when referring to behaviour earlier in the process.

Individuals will respond well to being given specific tasks or responsibilities; however, communication remains key. Regular progress reports and praise help to cement the more buoyant mood. It is not uncommon for there to be a return to an earlier stage if the level of support suddenly drops.

Individual reactions

Each person reacts individually to change and not all will experience every phase. Some people may spend a lot of time in stages 1 and 2, whilst others who are more accustomed to change may move swiftly into stage 3.

Although it is generally acknowledged that moving from stage 1 through stage 2 and finally to stage 3 is most common, there is no right or wrong sequence.

Several people going through the same change at the same time are likely to travel at their own speed and will reach each stage at different times.

Summary

The Change Curve is a very useful tool when managing individual or team change. Knowing where an individual is on the curve will help when deciding on how and when to communicate information, what level of support someone requires and when best to implement final changes. Furnishing individuals with the knowledge that others understand and experience similar emotions is the best way to return, with as little pain as possible, to optimal performance.

Managing change within the team will entail the sharing of information and perhaps asking for ideas as to how the relevant change can be managed or implemented. If it is a change in a process, for example, encouraging team members to come forward with their own ideas should be considered.

A quality circle may be formed and can be a more formal approach to the generation of ideas, although adding quality to the standing agenda for a team meeting can often produce effective results for ideas of how to change. A quality circle is a participatory management technique within the framework of an organisation wide quality system, which small teams of usually 6 to 12 employees voluntarily form to define and solve the quality or performance-related problem.

Discussing the change in detail, the reason for it, the benefits from its implementation and the resources and costings involved, will engage with the team members and provide them with their understanding of why this must happen. Through engagement, the team is more likely to feel empowered and valued and hence any changes made will be transitioned to smoothly

When plans and priorities change, the team members need to be flexible in their approach and attitude to be to confront those changes and adapt accordingly however on certain occasions,

Operational Management

there will be issues that are beyond your control that impact on their ability to amend priorities and plans.   These constraints may include:

- *cost- are there any additional costs that will be incurred from making these amendments and if so, how will they be met? Are these cost hard costs for any tangible resources required or do they include the cost of the time it would take to?*
- *Time- can the plan be executed in the given timeframe or are extensions required? What will be the implications of the business of extensions are required?*
- *Support- is the relevant support available to ensure the plan/priority can be met and achieved? Again, at what cost?*
- *Competence- is there sufficient capacity and capability within the available resources to ensure the amendments can be considered?*

Change Management Models

There are many change management models, but the most common ones are as follows:

Kotter's change management theory
This change management theory is one of the most popular and most adopted ones in the world. It is divided into eight stages where each one of them focuses on a key principle that is associated with the response of people to change.

- **Increase urgency** – *Create a sense of urgency among the people to motivate them to move forward towards objectives.*
- **Build the team** – *Get the right people on the team by selecting a mix of skills, knowledge and commitment.*
- **Get the vision correct** – *Consider not just the strategy but also creativity, emotional connect and objectives.*
- **Communicate** – *Openly and frequently communicate with people regarding the change.*
- **Get things moving** – *Get support, remove the roadblocks and implement feedback in a constructive way.*
- **Focus on short term goals** – *Set small goals and achievable parts is a good way to achieve success without too much pressure.*
- **Do not give up** – *Be persistent while the process of change management is going on, no matter how tough things may seem.*
- **Incorporate change** – *Reinforce and make it a part of the workplace culture.*

The change management model is easy to follow and incorporate. It focuses on preparing employees for change rather than change implementation itself. The focus on employee experience and proper workplace communication is one of the reasons why this is one of the most used change management models.

Operational Management

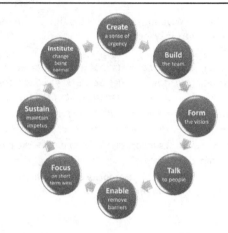

McKinsey 7-S Change Management Model

McKinsey 7-S framework or model is one of the longest lasting change management models out there. This model consists of **7 crucial categories** that companies should be aware of when implementing change:

- **Strategy** – *Strategy is the change management plan that should consist of a step-by-step procedure or future plan.*
- **Structure** – *This factor is related to the structure in which the organisation is divided or the structure it follows.*
- **Systems** – *This stage focuses on the systems that will be used to complete day-to-day tasks and activities.*
- **Shared values** – *Shared values refer to the core or main values of an organisation according to which it runs or works.*
- **Style** – *The way change is adopted or implemented is known as 'style'.*
- **Staff** – *The staff refers to the workforce or employees and their working capabilities.*
- **Skills** – *The competencies as well as other skills possessed by the employees working in the organisation.*

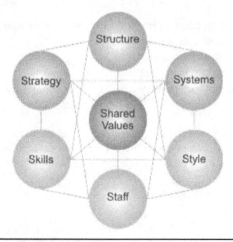

Operational Management

Unlike most other models, this model focuses on all the important factors that change may impact.

While most other models represent some kind of a process or workflow, McKinsey's model simply reminds us of all the business aspects that should be defined before the change strategy is implemented.

ADKAR Model

This powerful model is based on the understanding that organisational change can only happen when individuals change. The ADKAR model or theory of change is goal oriented. This makes it possible for change management teams to focus on activities that are directly related to the goals the company is trying to achieve. It guides individuals through change and addresses any roadblocks or barriers along the way.

The model can be used by change managers to find out the various challenges in the process of change management so that effective training can be offered to the employees.

ADKAR Model stands for:

- *Awareness* – *of the need and requirement for change*
- *Desire* – *to bring about change and be a participant in it*
- *Knowledge* – *of how to bring about this change*
- *Ability* – *to incorporate the change on a regular basis*
- *Reinforcement* – *to keep it implemented and reinforced later on as well.*

Pre-contemplation	Contemplation	Preparation	Action	Maintenance
A	D	K	A	R
Awareness	**Desire**	**Knowledge**	**Ability**	**Reinforcement**
Why is change necessary?	How do you motivate people to want to change?	What will be their involvement in the change?	Address issues which may prevent someone from changing	Maintain the change – do not let them slip back top old ways
Make employees aware of the change.	*Instil a desire to change*	*Teach employees how to make the change*	*Transform knowledge into the ability to make the change.*	*Make the change permanent by reinforcing new methods*

This change management model is a good solution for organisations that are trying to look at both the business and people dimensions of change. Unlike other change management

Operational Management

models, this model focuses on the identification and evaluation of the reasons why change is working or not and why desired results are not being obtained.

Kübler-Ross Five Stage Change Management Model

This model is different from the others in a sense that is 100% employee oriented. The model can also be applied to other life situations such as loss of job, changes in work and other less serious health conditions.

This model helps employers better understand their employees and empathise with them. This model consists of five stages through which your employees may be going during organisational changes.

Denial – *In this stage, employees are not willing to or unable to accept change. This happens because most people show resistance towards change and may not want to believe what is happening.*

Anger – *This model assumes that when the news first gets absorbed, anger follows. Denial converts into anger when employees realise that the change is actually happening.*

Bargaining – *During the bargaining stage, employees try to get to the best possible solution out of the situation or circumstance. Bargaining is a way for people to avoid ending up with the worst-case scenario.*

Depression – *When employees realise that bargaining is not working, they may end up getting depressed and may lose faith. Some of the symptoms include low energy, non-commitment, low motivation and lack of any kind of excitement or happiness.*

Acceptance – *When employees realise that there is no point in fighting change any more, they may finally accept what is happening and may begin to resign to it.*

This is a good change management model because of its focus on employees, their feelings, concerns and needs. Organisations that manage to understand their employees are much more likely to eliminate some of the biggest barriers towards successful change management.

Because most employees go through the above-mentioned feelings, it is extremely important to keep employees informed and to have an effective business communication strategy.

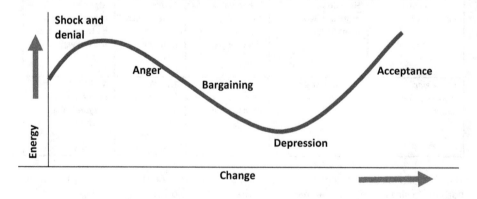

Operational Management

Lewin's Change Management Model

Lewin's Change Management Model is one of the most popular, most accepted and most effective models that make it possible for companies to understand organisational and structured change.

This model consists of three main stages which are: **unfreeze, change and refreeze**.

- *Unfreeze: The first stage of the change process is the preparation for change. Here, employers must get prepared for the change and explain to people why the change is necessary. As most people are resistant to change, this step helps to break this status quo.*
- *Change: In this stage, the change process takes place. Good leadership and effective employee communications are crucial for this step.*
- *Refreeze: In this stage, the change has been accepted. This is the time when the employees start going back to their normal pace and routine. This last step requires leaders to make sure that the changes are adopted and used even after the change management objectives have been achieved.*

Unfreeze	Change	Refreeze
• *Recognise the need for change* • *Determine what needs to change* • *Encourage the replacement of old behaviours and attitudes* • *Ensure there is strong support from management* • *Manage and understand the doubts and concerns*	• *Plan the changes* • *Implement the changes* • *Help employees to learn the new concept or points of view*	• *Changes are reinforced in stabilising* • *Integrate changes into the normal way of doing things* • *Develop ways to sustain the change* • *Celebrate success*

Lewin's change management model describes in a very simple way the three main stages that every change management process has to go through: pre-change, during change and post-change. Because of its simplicity, many organisations choose to follow this model when implementing change.

Operational Management

Open Communication

Another key to successful change management is to ensure there is open communication throughout the business.

Operating on a need-to-know basis is a costly choice for any businesses. Business needs the complete commitment and participation of all its employees. Creating an atmosphere of open communication contributes to a more vibrant, creative workforce where all employees have a deep understanding of the goals of the business and what needs to be done to accomplish those goals. Open communication gives everyone equal participation in the success of the business.

1. *Start with commitment from the top.* *Ensure that all managers are committed to open communication. Be visible and available to employees. Evaluate the systems of communication and ensure that processes are in place that allow for vital information to be communicated regularly throughout the business.*

2. *Keep your message positive.* *Motivate employees by pointing out accomplishments and exemplary work. State messages in terms of what needs to be done and what is being done well rather than what should not be done or what is being done poorly.*

3. *Make your communication process transparent.* *Hold open-ended meetings that give each team member the opportunity to share concerns, accomplishments and ideas. Set clear expectations for all work tasks and what you expect employee behaviour to be. Avoid springing surprises on your employees when it comes to what they are expected to do.*

4. *Take inventory of the diversity of employees in your workplace.* *Analyse how different groups of employees receive information. Avoid using slang or jargon that might not be understood by subcultures within your workplace. Provide employees with mentors if they lack communication skills common to the greater group -- for example, international workers may be unfamiliar with communication techniques.*

5. *Establish a grievance system through which employees can make complaints in a protected manner.* *Give complaints serious consideration when warranted and always let employees know that they have been heard. Take action on complaints and communicate those actions to all involved parties.*

Encouraging open communication

Many organisations today champion a culture of honest and open communication, but unfortunately most of them do not get down to creating it. They must walk the talk if they truly want managers and employees to share ideas and opinions.

Many employees are reluctant to disagree with their company's leadership and management out of fear of retribution. Many companies have a forced, "happy" culture that names "open communication" as a corporate value while managers actively and/or passively discourage dissenting opinions.

Operational Management

As a result, employees will avoid voicing their concerns at all costs and prefer to continue doing things as instructed by their bosses even when they suspect (or know) that there is a better way.

Most organisations have room for improvement when it comes to encouraging open communication. Employees often struggle to open up and speak freely when communicating with their managers and some of the most common reasons why they feel this way are:

- *managers not bothering to ask for employees' thoughts, views and opinions*
- *managers not listening, responding, or taking any action based on employee input*
- *managers not stopping to look at the employee and acknowledge what they are saying*
- *managers condescendingly discounting employees' ideas, views and concerns*
- *managers getting angry and/or confrontational thus inspiring fear of retaliation*

Employees are much more likely to believe the communications environment they experience in their day-to-day work at the office, no matter how glossy the "openness and honesty" posters that they see in reception are.

This means the organisation must create an environment where managers clearly know the company values communication and employees feel comfortable speaking up.

Opening up communication takes commitment and intentional effort, but the results are totally worth it.

Acknowledge that your employees' views are important
The first step in opening up communication is to admit that staff members have a unique and yet very important viewpoint of what is going in the organisation and the industry as a whole.

- *Improve your employee engagement*
- *Improve your employee engagement in less than two minutes*
- *Get started for free today.*

Free sign up
Employees are right on the front line of customer service, so they are always the first to notice the future needs and demands of customers. When leaders and managers take the time and energy to gather their thoughts and observations, they increase the organisation's chances of staying agile and innovative.

Ask employees for input
Unfortunately, many managers often respond to an employee's interest in providing input by saying they do not have the time for it. It should be made clear that the managers must make time to ask employees for suggestions.

Operational Management

This may sound simple and obvious, but it is important to communicate unambiguously that management, in fact, wants to hear from employees: ideas, concerns as well as questions.

Listen to employees reflectively
Encourage managers to clearly show that they have heard employees' opinions. One way to do this is to pause a bit before replying and perhaps repeat back to the employee what they said instead of rapidly firing back an opinion without any indication that their view has been heard or considered.

Show employees that not only are they being heard, but that the emotions behind it are recognised and understood. Tell them the particular emotions being detected in their tone or body language are not being discounted or ignored but rather they should be affirmed and validated. Reflect on their behaviour by saying "I hear the concern in your voice," instead of "There's no need to be concerned" or "I can see how agitated you are by this," instead of "You need to relax."

Engage employees on a personal level
Greet employees. There is no need to know every employee's name, but a simple, "Good morning!" or "Beautiful day, isn't it?" helps create a more relaxed and comfortable environment in which employees can feel confident enough to be more open.

Make an effort to get to know employees beyond their role in the organisation. Ask what they did over the weekend, how their children or parents are doing or how their favourite sports team are performing.

Showing interest in employees communicates that they are valued beyond their work — as human beings.

Be respectful to employees
When employees come with problems or suggestions, stop all other activity, look them straight in the eye, listen and ask questions about what they are saying.

Do not give employees the impression that they are not important by not acknowledging them, continuing to type, checking email, taking phone calls, or rummaging through your files.

Acknowledge the employees' input
Managers do not have to act on every suggestion. Employees understand that not every idea is appropriate or realistic, but they do want to know that their ideas were heard and considered.

Even if it is not possible to act on a suggestion, sharing the employees' input in the next company publication, for example goes a long way. They key is to show employees that their opinions are heard and respected.

Operational Management

Recognise employees
When employees say they want more recognition, company leadership often assumes they are talking about money – that they want a bonus or raise. In fact, they are most often talking about two simple words, "Thank you."

Expressing gratitude employees for taking the lead on a project, staying late, or putting in extra time goes a long way toward encouraging open communication in your company.

Make a schedule and stick to it
Schedule regular times for small meetings with employees and honour those commitments. Employees often complain about managers announcing a series of bi-weekly staff meetings, holding the first few and then becoming "too busy" for any further sessions.

Do not suggest a schedule that will be unrealistic – you are better off arranging for fortnightly meetings that can be consistently honoured.

Describe instead of judging
When discussing an employee's behaviour or a decision they made, avoid judging their behaviour or the reasoning behind their decision. Instead, describe what has been observed.

For example, "I noticed the reports have been a few days late for three weeks now," instead of, "You've become lazy and don't seem to care about your work." The former leaves room for the employee to explain themselves and/or commit to improving while the latter simply pushes them to disengage and feel ashamed or agitated.

Do not shy away from problems
Should a problem arise in the workplace or an employee's performance weaken, have the courage to see the situation for what it really is and address it in its nascent stages before it grows too big to handle instead of shying away from it or pretending it does not exist.

Furthermore, when avoiding addressing performance issues, everyone else on the team knows they will not be held accountable, which in turn undermines their trust and confidence in their leaders.

Summary
Encouraging honest and open communication takes more than just talking about it in your Mission statement and press releases. It requires putting in place active measures that foster an open exchange of information and ideas among employees at every level of your organisation.

Operational Management

Communicating Organisational Strategy

The following list contains some approaches that will help communicate organisational strategy to employees and encourage behaviours which advance the strategy and improve results.

1.   Keep the message simple, but deep in meaning.
Most organisations have a deeper meaning as to why they exist. This tends to influence strategy, decision-making and behaviours at senior management levels, but often is not well explained in a way employees can understand.

What it is called does not matter, the purpose, the why, the core belief, the centre.

What does matter is its relevance with employees If they understand it, they will care more about the organisation and the job they do. It should be at the core of all your communications, a simple and inspiring message that is easy to relate to and understand. By linking messages about strategy to the purpose of the organisation helps employees connect their day-to-day work with the aspiration of the company.

2.   Build behaviour based on market and customer insights
For employees to fully understand how strategy is different and why the organisation is better than the competition, they need to be in touch with the commercial aspects of the business. The challenge is in how to make them aware so they can act on them. Internal promotional campaigns based on market and customer insights brings the strategy to life for employees.

Package the promotional content so it can be shared across all departments in the organisation. Communicate with managers and leaders first providing them with easy-to-implement resources which will help them to spread the word amongst their teams. This in turn will encourage the development of department-specific responses, generate new ideas and develop new behaviours based on what they have learned.

3.   Use the discipline of a framework.
Communication with employees can have differing results, however, by using a framework to design the communication, the message will usually be more clearly defined.   The Inspire/Educate/Reinforce framework is a great tool to map and deliver messages. Always consider the purpose of the communication and try to address the points below in every communication which is made.

Inspire.
Inspiration is important when you are sharing a significant accomplishment or introducing a new initiative that relates to strategy. Content should demonstrate progress against goals, showcase benefits to customers and be presented in a way that gets attention and signals importance. The medium is less important than the impression that you want to leave with employees about the company.

Whether you are looking to build optimism, change focus, instil curiosity, or prepare them for future decisions, you will have more impact if you stir some emotion and create a lasting memory.
Educate.

Operational Management

Once the team has been energised with the inspirational messages, explanations of the organisation's strategic decisions and plans for implementing them will carry more weight. To ensure that the teams gain the maximum benefit makes sure the message is supported with information and detail which they can relate to their day-to-day responsibilities. These messages to be delivered through dialogues not monologues.

Reinforce.
It is not enough to simply explain the connection between the organisation's strategy and purpose— and between the strategy and its delivery. The message must be repeated to increase understanding, instil belief and lead to genuine change overtime. These reinforcing messages need to come in a variety of methods, channels and experiences and ultimately, they must immerse employees in important content and help them to connect with the strategy.

4. Often corporate communications has a strictly top-down approach.

Employees are more likely to believe what leaders say when they hear similar arguments from their colleagues and those conversations can be far more persuasive and engaging than a simple one-way presentation.

Create a team of employees who are responsible for delivering important messages at all levels. Rotate the members of the group annually to get more people involved in being able to represent the strategy inside the company. Integrate regular communications into daily routines through detailed planning against the messages created using the Inspire/Educate/Reinforce framework.

5. Speak openly

Not many people are particularly inspired by the communication organisations issue. Much of it ignores reality. The use of jargon is hollow and lacks meaning. Authentic, honest and open messages will help employees view the challenges and opportunities as you see them and will understand and care about the direction in which the organisation is heading.

6. Tell a story.

Facts and figures won't be remembered. Stories and experiences will. Stories help bring humanity to the organisation and helps employees understand the relevance of the strategy and factual examples of progress and shortfalls against it. Stories and the conversations they prompt will be a strong influence on positive culture-building behaviour that relates to the core purpose and strategic goals.

7. Do the unexpected.

The method of delivering the message is as important as the content. Most organisations use methods embedded in the days of memos and formal corporate announcements. The chance of employees reading this is remote. Social media, networking, blogs and games to get the word out in ways that employees are far more used to engaging with but are probably least expecting a corporate communication to appear there. The result of the unexpected is that they read it!

8. Make the necessary investment.

Most leaders recognise the importance of the employee audience. They represent the single biggest expense to the organisation. They communicate directly with customers. They control the perceptions that consumers have about the brand. Why then, are organisations so reluctant to fund internal promotional campaigns?

Deciding not to invest leaves the organisation vulnerable to a serious risk. If employees are not on side, the organisation certainly won't succeed in winning with customers, as the employees ultimately hold that relationship in their hands.

Operational Management

Data

Data is a collection of facts, such as numbers, words, measurements, observations or even just descriptions of things.

Data can exist in a variety of forms — as numbers or text on pieces of Paper, as bits and bytes stored in electronic memory, or as facts stored in a person's mind.

Since the mid-1900s, people have used the word data to mean computer information that is transmitted or stored.

Although the terms "data" and "information" are often used interchangeably, but these terms have distinct meanings.

Data is simply facts or figures — bits of information, but not information itself.

A list of dates — data — is meaningless without the information that makes the dates relevant (dates of holiday)

The history of temperature readings all over the world for the past 100 years is data. If this data is organised and analysed to find that global temperature is rising, then that is information.

The number of visitors to a website by country is an example of data. Finding out that traffic from the U.K. is increasing while that from Australia is decreasing is meaningful information.

Often data is required to back up a claim or conclusion (information) derived or deduced from it. For example, before a drug is approved by the Government, the manufacturer must conduct clinical trials and present a great deal of data to demonstrate that the drug is safe

When data is processed, interpreted, organised, structured, or presented to make them meaningful or useful, they are called information.

Information provides context for data.

Data is employed in scientific research, businesses management (e.g., sales data, revenue, profits, stock price), finance, governance (e.g., crime rates, unemployment rates, literacy rates) and in virtually every other form of human organisational activity (e.g., censuses of the number of homeless people by non-profit organisations).

Operational Management

Data is measured, collected and reported. It can then be analysed and then used in graphs, images, or other analysis tools. Data as a general concept refers to the fact that some existing information or knowledge is represented or coded in some form suitable for better usage or processing.

Sourcing Data

Good data is the life blood of any business.

Definition

Data Sourcing (or Data Collection) is the process of extracting data from external or internal systems, which form an organisations IT Infrastructure for diverse purposes of informing business objectives.

Data is one of the most valuable resources today's businesses have. The more information held about customers, the better the understanding of their interests, wants and needs. This enhanced understanding helps organisations to meet and exceed customers' expectations and allows communication with them through messaging and products that appeal to them.

Types of Data

First Party Data

Primary or First-party data is the information gathered directly from the audience. It could include data gathered from external online sources, data in inhouse systems or non-online data collected from customers through surveys and various other sources, rather than data which has been gathered by someone else.

First Party data is information obtained directly from the source.

The organisation will be the first party to use this exact set of data.

When it comes to the data businesses collect about their customers, primary data is also typically first-party data.

Operational Management

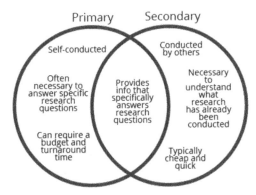

Second party data

Second-party data is the first-party data of another company. Second-party data can be purchased directly from the organisation that collected it or buy it in a private marketplace.

Third party data

Third-party data is information a company has pulled together from numerous sources. This kind of data can be bought and sold on a data exchange and it typically contains a large number of data points.

It is this thirst for data that has led to the massive increase in computer hacking as criminals try to steal data, which is legally stored by organisations, but which might be of value to others.

Because first-party data comes directly from inhouse data sources, there can be high confidence in its accuracy, as well as its relevance to the business.

Second-party data has many of the same positive attributes as first-party data. It comes directly from the source, so you can be confident in its accuracy, but it also gives you insights you couldn't get with your first-party data.

Third-party data offers much more scale than any other type of data, which is its primary benefit.

Different types of data can be useful in different scenarios. It can also be helpful to use different types of data together. First-party data will typically be the foundation of your dataset. If first-party data is limited, though, it may be supplemented with second-party or third-party data. Adding these other types of data can increase the size of the audience or help reach new audiences.

Operational Management

Sources of Data

Personal Data

Personal data is anything that is specific to an individual. It covers demographics, location, email address and other identifying factors. It's usually in the news when it gets leaked (like the Santander scandal) or is being used in a controversial way (when Uber worked out who was having an affair).

Lots of different companies collect personal data (especially social media sites), anytime email address or credit card details are entered personal data is being given away. Often, that data will be used to provide personalised suggestions to keep people engaged. Facebook for example uses personal information to suggest content based on what other likeminded people like.

In addition, personal data is aggregated (to depersonalise it somewhat) and then sold to other companies, mostly for advertising and competitive research purposes. That's one of the ways targeted ads and content from unknown organisations appear.

Transactional Data

Transactional data is anything that requires an action to collect. Click on an ad, make a purchase, visit a certain web page, etc., pretty much every website collects transactional data of some kind, either through Google Analytics, another 3rd party system, or their own internal data capture system. Transactional data is incredibly important for businesses because it helps them to expose variability and optimise their operations for the highest quality  results. By examining large amounts of data, it is possible to uncover hidden patterns and correlations. These patterns can create competitive advantages and result in business benefits like more effective marketing and increased revenue.

Web Data

Web data is a collective term which refers to any type of data which might be pulled from the internet, whether to study for research purposes or otherwise. That might be data on what competitors are selling, published government data, football scores, etc. It's a catchall for anything on the web that is public facing (i.e., not stored in some internal database). Studying this data can be very informative, especially when communicated well to management.

Web data is important because it's one of the major ways' businesses can access information that isn't generated by themselves. When creating quality business models and making important business improvement decisions, businesses need information on what is happening internally and externally within their organisation and what is happening in the wider market.

Operational Management

Web data can be used to monitor competitors, track potential customers, keep track of channel partners, generate leads, build apps and much more. It's uses are still being discovered as the technology for turning unstructured data into structured data improves.

Web data can be collected by writing web scrapers to collect it, using a scraping tool, or by paying a third party to do the scraping for you.

A web scraper is a computer program that takes a URL as an input and pulls the data out in a structured format.

Sensor Data

Sensor data is produced by objects and is often referred to as the Internet of Things. It covers everything from a smartwatch measuring heart rate to a building with external sensors that measure the weather.

So far, sensor data has mostly been used to help optimise processes. For example, AirAsia saved £30-£50 million by using sensors and technology to help reduce operating costs and increase aircraft usage. By measuring what is happening around them, machines can make smart changes to increase productivity and alert people when they are in need of maintenance.

Big Data

Technically all the types of data above contribute to Big Data. There's no official size that makes data "big". The term simply represents the increasing amount and the varied types of data that is now being gathered as part of data collection.

As more and more of the world's information moves online and becomes digitised, it means that analysts can start to use it as data. Things like social media, online books, music, videos and the increased number of sensors have all added to the astounding increase in the amount of data that has become available for analysis.

The thing that differentiates Big Data from the "regular data" we were analysing before is that the tools we use to collect, store and analyse it have had to change to accommodate the increase in size and complexity. With the latest tools on the market, we no longer must rely on sampling. Instead, we can process datasets in their entirety and gain a far more complete picture of the world around us.

Operational Management

The Importance of Data Collection

Data collection differs from data mining in that it is a process by which data is gathered and measured. All this must be done before high-quality research can begin and answers to lingering questions can be found. Data collection is usually done with software and there are many different data collection procedures, strategies and techniques. Most data collection is centred on electronic data and since this type of data collection encompasses so much information, it usually crosses into the realm of big data.

So why is data collection important? It is through data collection that a business or management has the quality information they need to make informed decisions from further analysis, study and research. Without data collection, companies would stumble around in the dark using outdated methods to make their decisions. Data collection instead allows them to stay on top of trends, provide answers to problems and analyse new insights to great effect.

Quantitative vs. Qualitative Data

Primary data can be divided into two categories: quantitative and qualitative.

Quantitative data comes in the form of numbers, quantities and values. It describes things in concrete and easily measurable terms. Examples include the number of customers who bought a given product, the rating a customer gave a product out of five stars and the amount of time a visitor spent on a website.

Because quantitative data is numeric and measurable, it lends itself well to analytics. When you analyse quantitative data, you may uncover insights that can help you better understand your audience. Because this kind of data deals with numbers, it is very objective and has a reputation for reliability.

Data	
Quantitative	*Qualitative*
Numerical data – *two types*	**Descriptive** - *based on observation/experience*
• **Discrete** - *counting*	**Uses all five senses:**
• **Continuous** - *measurement*	**See, feel, taste, hear, smell**

Qualitative data is descriptive, rather than numeric. It is less concrete and less easily measurable than quantitative data. This data may contain descriptive phrases and opinions. Examples include an online review a customer writes about a product, an answer to an open-ended survey question about what type of videos a customer likes to watch online and the conversation a customer had with a customer service representative.

Operational Management

Qualitative data helps explains the "why" behind the information quantitative data reveals. For this reason, it is useful for supplementing quantitative data, which will form the foundation of a data strategy.

Managing Data and Information

Once data has been collected it has to be managed. If data were nails, strewn across the floor, they would soon be swept up and put into a box. Data is much the same. In its raw state it is of very little use, but there is lots of it and it needs controlling. Likewise, information, once created, suddenly becomes valuable, not just to the organisation that created it, but also to its competitors, suppliers, customers and other stakeholders.

Information Management
Information includes both electronic and physical data. For example, this may be in the form of paper records, files and folders or digital databases.

Information management therefore refers to an organisational program or system that manages the processes that controls the structure, processing, delivery and usage of information. Information management is required for business intelligence purposes.

The organisational structure of the information management system, your company has in place, must be capable of managing information through its entire life cycle. This is the case for all sources or formats of data including paper documents and electronic files. This information also needs to be accessible through multiple channels so that those who need access can gain it through the use of mobile phones and laptops no matter where they are in the world.

Data Management
Data management is a subset of information management whereby data is managed as a valuable resource. Specifically, data management refers to the process of creating, obtaining, transforming, sharing, protecting, documenting and preserving data.

The process of data management includes file-naming conventions and documentation of metadata among other things. The process ensures that all data is available, accurate, complete and secure. It also addresses the development and execution of architectures, policies, practices and procedures that manage the full data life cycle

Operational Management

Data Legislation

The Data Protection Act 2018

The Data Protection Act 2018 controls how your personal information is used by organisations, businesses, or the government.

The Data Protection Act 2018 is the UK's implementation of the General Data Protection Regulation (GDPR).

Data Protection Act 2018

Everyone responsible for using personal data has to follow strict rules called data protection principles. They must make sure the information is:

- *used fairly, lawfully and transparently*
- *used for specified, explicit purposes*
- *used in a way that is adequate, relevant and limited to only what is necessary accurate and, where necessary, kept up to date*
- *kept for no longer than is necessary*
- *handled in a way that ensures appropriate security, including protection against unlawful or unauthorised processing, access, loss, destruction, or damage*

There is stronger legal protection for more sensitive information, such as:

- *race*
- *ethnic background*
- *political opinions*
- *religious beliefs*
- *trade union membership*
- *genetics*
- *biometrics (where used for identification)*
- *health*
- *sex life or orientation*

There are separate safeguards for personal data relating to criminal convictions and offences.

Rights

Under the Data Protection Act 2018, individuals have the right to find out what information the government and other organisations stores about them. These include the right to:

- *be informed about how data is being used*
- *access personal data*
- *have incorrect data updated*
- *have data erased*

Operational Management

- *stop or restrict the processing of your data*
- *data portability (allowing data to be reused for different services)*
- *object to how your data is processed in certain circumstances*

There are also rights when an organisation is using personal data for:

- *automated decision-making processes (without human involvement)*
- *profiling, for example to predict your behaviour or interests*

The General Data Protection Regulation 2016

GDPR stands for General Data Protection Regulation. The GDPR is a regulation from the Data Protection Act and covers any information related to a person or data subject that can be used to identify them directly or indirectly. It can be anything from a name, a photo and an email address to bank details, social media posts, biometric data and medical information. It also introduces digital rights for individuals.

When it came into effect on May 25, 2018, the GDPR set new standards for data protection and kickstarted a wave of global privacy laws that forever changed how we use the internet.

Why Do We Need the GDPR?

Personal data is highly valuable — in fact, it supports a trillion-dollar industry. Companies like Facebook and Google make their profits by selling personal information to advertisers. With this much money at stake, do you trust them to have your best interests at heart?

The GDPR defines what companies of all sizes can and can't do with customer information.

What Is Classified as Personal Data Under GDPR?

Personal data is information that can be used to identify you. Put simply, it's any private details that you wouldn't want to fall into the wrong hands.

Here are some examples of personal data:

Name	*social media posts*
phone number	*geotagging*
address	*health records*
date of birth	*race*
bank account	*religious and political*
passport number	*opinions*

Think of personal data like a jigsaw. One piece alone might not say much but connected together they reveal a vivid picture of your life.

Operational Management

What Is a 'Breach' Under GDPR?
Any incident that leads to personal data being lost, stolen, destroyed, or changed is considered a data breach. Unfortunately, breaches happen all the time.

Here are some newsworthy examples from before the GDPR started cracking down:

- *Almost half the population of the US had their name, date of birth and social security number stolen from credit reporting agency Equifax as the result of a data breach.*
- *Political consulting firm Cambridge Analytica secretly took information from 50 million Facebook profiles and gave it to the 2016 Trump campaign.*

Both incidents illustrate how data breaches have serious real-world consequences. This is exactly what GDPR and similar laws hope to regulate.

What Are the Penalties for Violating the GDPR?
The GDPR threatens would-be violators with some severe penalties. To make sure companies handle your personal data in a legal, ethical way, the fines for noncompliance are:

Up to €20 million or 4% of annual global turnover.

Some big names have already been hit with these noncompliance fines:

- **British Airways — $230 million.** *The airline set the record for fines when the booking details of 500,000 customers were stolen in a cyber-attack.*
- **Marriott — $123 million.** *After buying the Starwood Hotels group, Marriott failed to update an old system belonging to the group. This system was hacked, revealing information about 339 million guests.*
- **Google — $57 million.** *Important information was hidden when users set up new Android phones, meaning they didn't know what data collection practices they were agreeing to. The Google GDPR fine shows even tech giants aren't immune to GDPR enforcement.*

Although smaller businesses wouldn't be hit for such high amounts, they're held to the same standards.

A business owner now must make sure their operations comply with the GDPR.

The only thing most people will need to do is read the cookie consent banners that now appear on websites and click agree (or not). The GDPR affects everything people do online, but it's mostly working behind the scenes.

Operational Management

GDPR - Dos and Don'ts:

Do	Don't
Collect information legally and use it fairly	Mislead users about what you'll do with their private details
Collect as little data as possible	Collect lots of data just because you can
Protect data with strong security systems	Assume data will take care of itself
Only store data for as long as necessary	Keep old data you don't need anymore

Freedom of Information Act 2000

The Freedom of Information Act 2000 provides public access to information held by public authorities.
It does this in two ways:

- *public authorities are obliged to publish certain information about their activities*
- *members of the public are entitled to request information from public authorities.*

The Act covers any recorded information that is held by a public authority in England, Wales and Northern Ireland and by UK-wide public authorities based in Scotland. Information held by Scottish public authorities is covered by Scotland's own Freedom of Information (Scotland) Act 2002.

Public authorities include government departments, local authorities, the NHS, state schools and police forces. However, the Act does not necessarily cover every organisation that receives public money. For example, it does not cover some charities that receive grants and certain private sector organisations that perform public functions.

Recorded information includes printed documents, computer files, letters, emails, photographs and sound or video recordings.

The Act does not give people access to their own personal data (information about themselves) such as their health records or credit reference file. If a member of the public wants to see information that a public authority holds about them, they should make a data protection subject access request.

Digital Economy Act (2017)

The Digital Economy Act 2017 (the Act) makes provision about electronic communications infrastructure and services, including the creation of a broadband Universal Service Order (USO), to give all premises in the UK a legal right to request a minimum standard of broadband connectivity, expected to be 10 megabits per second (Mbps). The Act also introduces reform of

Operational Management

the Electronic Communications Code and provides greater clarification on data sharing between public bodies.

The Digital Economy Bill was introduced in the House of Commons on 5 July 2016, completed its parliamentary stages and received Royal Assent, becoming law, on 27 April 2017.

The Bill followed an announcement made in the Queen's Speech to introduce legislation seeking to make the United Kingdom a world leader in the digital economy.

The Act is made up of six parts as follows:

1. *Access to digital services*
2. *Digital infrastructure*
3. *Online pornography*
4. *Intellectual property*
5. *Digital government*
6. *Miscellaneous.*

Collecting Data

There are many different techniques for collecting different types of quantitative data, but there's a fundamental process you'll typically follow, no matter which method of data collection you're using. This process consists of the following five steps.

Decide what information you want to collect
The first thing you need to do is choose what details you want to collect. You'll need to decide what topics the information will cover, who you want to collect it from and how much data you need. Your goals — what you hope to accomplish using your data — will determine your answers to these questions. As an example, you may decide to collect data about which type of articles are most popular on your website among visitors who are between the ages of 18 and 34. You might also choose to gather information about the average age of all the customers who bought a product from your company within the last month.

Set a timeframe for data collection
Next, you can start formulating your plan for how you'll collect your data. In the early stages of your planning process, you should establish a timeframe for your data collection. You may want to gather some types of data continuously. When it comes to transactional data and website visitor data, for example, you may want to set up a method for tracking that data over the long term. If you're tracking data for a specific campaign, however, you'll track it over a defined period. In these instances, you'll have a schedule for when you'll start and end your data collection.

Determine your data collection method
At this step, you will choose the data collection method that will make up the core of your data-gathering strategy. To select the right collection method, you'll need to consider the

type of information you want to collect, the timeframe over which you'll obtain it and the other aspects you determined. We'll go over various methods you can use in the next section of this article.

Collect the data

Once you have finalised your plan, you can implement your data collection strategy and start collecting data. You can store and organise your data in a database or on a software package specifically designed for the purpose. Be sure to stick to your plan and check on its progress regularly. It may be useful to create a schedule for when you will check in with how your data collection is proceeding, especially if you are collecting data continuously. You may want to make updates to your plan as conditions change and you get new information.

Analyse the data and implement your findings

Once you've collected all your data, it's time to analyse it and organise your findings. The analysis phase is crucial because it turns raw data into valuable information that you can use to enhance your marketing strategies, products and business decisions. You can also use the analytics tools built into data management solutions to help with this step. Once you've uncovered the patterns and insights in your data, you can implement the findings to improve your business.

Methods of Collecting Data

There are various methods of collecting primary, quantitative data. Some involve directly asking customers for information, some involve monitoring your interactions with customers and others involve observing customers' behaviours. The right one to use depends on your goals and the type of data you're collecting. Here are some of the most common types of data collection used today.

Surveys

Surveys are one way in which you can directly ask customers for information. You can use them to collect either quantitative or qualitative data or both. A survey consists of a list of queries respondents can answer in just one or two words and often gives participants a list of responses to choose from. You can conduct surveys online, over email, over the phone or in person. One of the easiest methods is to create an online survey you host on your website or with a third party. You can then share a link to that survey on social media, over email and in pop-ups on your site.

Online Tracking

A business' website and apps if you have one, are excellent tools for collecting customer data. When someone visits your website, they create as many as 40 pieces of data. Accessing this data allows you to see how many people visited a site, how long they were on it, what they clicked on and more. A website hosting provider may collect this kind of information and you can also use analytics software. You can also place pixels on your site, which enables it to place and read cookies to help track user behaviour

Operational Management

Transactional data tracking
Whether you sell goods in-store, online or both, transactional data can give you valuable insights about your customers and your business. You may store transactional records in a customer relationship management system. That data may come from your web store, a third party you buy data from or an in-store point-of-sale system. This information can give you insights about how many products you sell, what types of products are most popular, how often people typically purchase from you and more.

Online marketing analytics
You can also collect valuable data through your marketing campaigns, whether you run them on search, webpages, email or elsewhere. You can even import information from offline marketing campaigns that you run. The software you use to place your advertisements will give you data about who clicked on the adverts, what times they clicked, what device they used and more. about your campaigns.

Social media monitoring
Social media is another excellent source of customer data. You can look through your follower list to see who follows you and what characteristics they have in common to enhance your understanding of who your target audience should be. You can also monitor mentions of your brand on social media by regularly searching your brand's name, setting up alerts or using third-party social media monitoring software. Many social media sites will also provide you with analytics about how your posts perform. Third-party tools may be able to offer you even more in-depth insights.

Collecting subscription and registration data
Offering customers something in return for providing information about themselves can help you gather valuable customer data. You can do this by requiring some basic information from customers or site visitors who want to sign up for your email list, rewards program, or another similar program. One benefit of this method is that the leads you get are likely to convert because they have actively demonstrated an interest in your brand. When creating the forms used to collect this information, it's essential to find the right balance in the amount of data you ask for. Asking for too much can discourage people from participating, while not asking for enough means your data won't be as useful as it could be.

In-store traffic monitoring
If you have a brick-and-mortar shop, you can also gather insights from monitoring the foot traffic there. The most straightforward way to do this is with a traffic counter on the door to help you keep track of how many people come into your shop throughout the day. This data will reveal what your busiest days and hours are. It may also help give you an idea about what is drawing customers to your store at certain times. You can also install security systems with motion sensors that will help you track customers' movement patterns throughout your shop. The sensor can provide you with data about which of your shop's departments are most popular.

Operational Management

Benefits of Collecting Data

Collecting data is valuable because you can use it to make informed decisions. The more relevant, high-quality data you have, the more likely you are to make good choices when it comes to marketing, sales, customer service, product development and many other areas of your business. Some specific uses of customer data include the following.

Improving your understanding of your audience

It can be difficult or impossible to get to know every one of your customers personally, especially if you run a large business or an online business. The better you understand your customers, though, the easier it will be for you to meet their expectations. Data collection enables you to improve your understanding of who your audience is and disseminate that information throughout your organisation. Through the primary data collection methods described above, you can learn about who your customers are, what they're interested in and what they want from you as a company.

Identifying areas for improvement or expansion

Collecting and analysing data helps you see where your company is doing well and where there is room for improvement. It can also reveal opportunities for expanding your business.

Looking at transactional data, for example, can show you which of your products are the most popular and which ones do not sell as well. This information might lead you to focus more on your bestsellers and develop other similar products. You could also look at customer complaints about a product to see which aspects are causing problems.

Data is also useful for identifying opportunities for expansion. For example, say you run an e-commerce business and are considering opening a brick-and-mortar store. If you look at your customer data, you can see where your customers are and launch your first store in an area with a high concentration of existing customers. You could then expand to other similar areas.

Predicting Future Patterns

Analysing the data, you collect can help you predict future trends, enabling you to prepare for them. As you look at the data for your new website, for instance, you may discover videos are consistently increasing in popularity, as opposed to articles. This observation would lead you to put more resources into your videos. You might also be able to predict more temporary patterns and react to them accordingly. If you run a clothing store, you might discover pastel colours are popular during spring and summer, while people gravitate toward darker shades in the fall and winter. Once you realise this, you can introduce the right colours to your stores at the right times to boost your sales.

You can even make predictions on the level of the individual customer. Say you sell business software. Your data might show companies with a particular job title often have questions for tech support when it comes time to update their software. Knowing this in advance allows you to offer support proactively, making for an excellent customer experience.

Operational Management

Personalising Your Content and Messaging

When you know more about your customers or site visitors, you can tailor the messaging you send them to their interests and preferences. This personalisation applies to marketers designing ads, publishers choosing which ads to run and content creators deciding what format to use for their content.

Using data collection in marketing can help you produce promotions that target a given audience. For example, say you're a marketeer looking to advertise a new brand of cereal. If your customer data shows most people who eat the cereal are in their 50s and 60s, you can use actors in those age ranges in your ads. If you're a publisher, you likely have information about what topics your site visitors prefer to read about. You can group your audience based on the characteristics they share and then show visitors with those characteristics content about topics popular with that group.

You can even go further with personalisation by adjusting your site's experience to the individual's experience. You can use cookies to determine when someone is revisiting your site or have them log in to confirm their identity and access their personalised user experience.

Data Control and Information Management

Several departments in organisations are involved in managing and governing data and information but, more often than not, the finance department is responsible, followed by IT and cross departmental groups.

The success of an organisation is usually measured in financial terms, so the finance department naturally tends to be heavily involved in defining and measuring success. For this reason, it is no surprise to see the finance department being cited by 60% as playing a prominent role in data management and governance.

While some technical input is important for data management and governance, the IT department should not manage and govern data on its own. Instead, a business function (such as finance) or a cross-departmental group such as sales and marketing should take the lead. Responsibility for data management and governance varies little when comparing top 100 companies with other organisations.

Cross-departmental alignment is crucial to successful data management and governance. The marketing department along with the production team may well define what information is required, the IT team will gather the appropriate data and that will then be further analysed by the finance team to identify what impact it may have on the business.

Organising and Managing Data

Good file and folder organisation will help you to locate, identify and retrieve your data quickly and accurately, therefore making it easier to manage your data. To do this you need to:

- *use folders to sort out your files into a series of meaningful and useful groups*

Operational Management

- *use naming conventions to give your files and folders meaningful names according to a consistent pattern*

You should establish a file organisation scheme at the start of each project to avoid having to sort out your files retrospectively:

- *if you are new to a group, or are working in a research facility, check whether there is an established procedure to follow*
- *if you are working within a research group, it essential that the whole group agrees on a file organisation structure so that everyone can find data within the group's shared storage area*
- *if you are working alone, it is still important for you to set up a scheme for yourself.*

Document your file organisation scheme in a 'readme' file, preferably in plain text and store it at the top-level folder for your project where you (or anyone in your group) will be able to access it easily.
Although these principles are aimed at digital files and folders, it is just as important to organise physical files, folders and other materials in a meaningful, consistent and documented manner.

There are many ways of organising your files so think about what makes sense for your research. If you are doing qualitative work you might want to organise your folders by topic, participant group or data collection method; if you are doing experimental work you might want to organise the results into folders by the data that you did the experiment, or by key experimental condition.

Organising Data

Use folders to group files with common properties: think about how you might want to browse your files in the future.

Apply meaningful folder names: *ensure that you use clear and appropriate folder names that concisely convey the contents of the folder.*
Keep group numbers manageable: *if you have too many sub-folders you might find this difficult to navigate but you also don't want to have to look through numerous files within a folder to find the one that you want to use.*
Structure folders hierarchically: *design a folder structure with broad topics at the highest level and then use sub-folders within these.*
Separate current and completed work: *You may find it helpful to move drafts and completed work into separate folders. This will also make it easier to review what you need to keep as you go along.*

Operational Management

Keep your raw data separate from the data you are working on: keep a 'raw data' file so that you have a copy of the file before any processing has taken place just in case you need to go back to it.

Control access at the highest level: It is easier to set access permissions near the top of the folder structure than to control permissions on sub-folders. You will need to ask Computing Services to set access permissions for folders.

Example of a folder structure. The arrows indicate the contents of that folder organised into subfolders

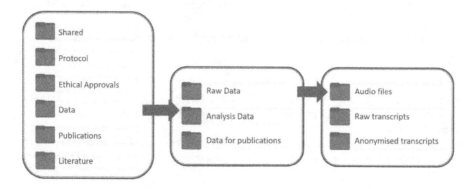

Challenges when Managing Data

Ensuring you have good data management is an obvious requirement for today's organisations. But it's harder than you'd think to get the process of measuring and managing data right.

While most businesses have a desire for data-driven insight, many are not realising that ambition. The result is that data management is often fragmented and driven by multiple stakeholders. This leaves organisations dealing with a high degree of inaccurate and disparate data and there are a number of challenges to maintaining it:

Sheer volume of data
Every day, it's estimated that 2.5 quintillion bytes of data are created. This leaves organisations continuing to face the challenge of aggregating, managing and creating value from data. The sheer amount of data being created and the numerous collection channels make good data management an important, yet elusive goal.

Taking a reactive approach to data management
One of the biggest problems, is that firms often don't realise they have a problem with their data. This means many organisations take a reactive approach to data management and will often wait until there are specific issues that need fixing.

Operational Management

Lack of processes and systems
When data is extracted from disparate databases, the inevitable result is data inconsistencies and nobody trusts the numbers. A lack of processes, data management systems and inadequate data strategies contribute towards inaccurate data.

Fragmented data ownership
A lack of data ownership is one of the key shortfalls for most organisations. Data ownership is still predominantly fragmented, with the management of data quality driven by multiple stakeholders and frequently measured at a department-by-department level, rather than across the business as a whole.

Driving a data culture
Many organisations cannot invoke enough support to improve data culture. This may be due to organisations often lacking the knowledge or skills around data management and the resources required to manage data properly.

Storing Data

Data can be stored in many ways and on many platforms

They may make use of different technologies and may include:

databases
Spreadsheets
management information systems
cloud
handheld devices
CD

reference retrieval systems
filing cabinets
folders
shared drives/servers
data repositories
data lakes
data warehouse

The Challenges of Data Management

Data quality
In a recent survey nearly one in five (18 per cent) companies said poor-quality customer data was their biggest challenge. The reasons for this were down to basic errors, such as out-of-date information and incomplete data.

The research found that problems such as duplicate data, spelling mistakes and data in incorrect fields tended to rank lower when it came to data-quality issues.

Data quickly goes out of date, meaning databases need to be regularly cleaned if they are to remain current and useful. Again, there is a gap appearing between leaders and laggards. The overall picture is that more companies are focusing on more formal, regular data cleansing – 22 per cent said they did this daily or continuously and just 11 per cent annually (down from 14 per cent last year). However, one-third (33 per cent) still had no formal processes in place to clean customer contact data, although this had dropped from 37 per cent in 2016. This means

Operational Management

a sizeable minority are putting themselves at risk of data-quality issues – and potential GDPR investigations over non-compliance.

Other factors which may affect the integrity of data are:

unstructured data and information	*integration*	*skills*
	migration of data sets	*viruses*
compatibility	*cost*	*volume*
corrupt files	*availability*	*absence of document control*
indexing	*access*	
file size	*analysis*	*confidentiality*
legal	*resources*	

Analysing and Interpreting Data

Data analysis is the process of inspecting, cleaning, transforming and modelling data with the goal of discovering useful information. This information informs and supports decision-making.

Data analysis has multiple facets and approaches, encompassing diverse techniques under a variety of names and is used throughout the whole range of different businesses. In today's business world, data analysis plays a role in making decisions more scientific and helping businesses operate more effectively.

Data mining is a particular data analysis technique that focuses on statistical modelling and knowledge discovery for predictive rather than purely descriptive purposes.

Other methods of data analysis and interpretation can include:

- *statistical analysis*
- *identifying trends and patterns*
- *anomalies*
- *benchmarking*
- *observation*
- *discussions*
- *review groups*

Presenting Data

Human beings have been hard-wired, over millions of years of evolution, to enjoy and respond to stories. It's best to work with it, not fight it, because if you tell your audience a story, they are likely to listen much more carefully and move towards a logical conclusion: the insight to which you are trying to lead them.

Operational Management

Once you understand this, the issue of using data falls into place: it is to provide evidence of how your story unfolds.

A Picture Speaks a Thousand Words

There's no record of how many numbers a picture might replace, but we can safely assume that it's quite a lot, especially if they're in a table.

There are many people in the world who do not find it easy to understand numbers.

There are also many people who will simply switch off if you show them figures in a table. But if you present data in a graph or pie chart, you make a pictorial representation of the data. It makes the numbers much easier to understand. Trends and proportions become more obvious.

Consider this set of data:

Sales	
1st Qtr	7.5
2nd Qtr	3.1
3rd Qtr	1.5
4th Qtr	1.1

Even for the highly numerate, the immediate point is only that there are lot more sales in the first quarter.

You would have to do some adding up and dividing to work out the relationships between the four numbers.

Now consider the same data in a pie chart

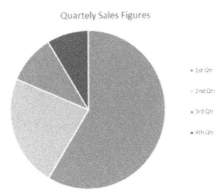

Quartely Sales Figures

- 1st Qtr
- 2nd Qtr
- 3rd Qtr
- 4th Qtr

Operational Management

It is immediately and shiningly obvious, even for those who struggle with numbers, that more of half of all sales were in the first quarter and that three quarters were in the first two quarters.

What's more, nobody is going to be straining from the back to read your figures. You really can see a lot more from a picture.

Other presentation techniques can include:

Presentations	*Tables*
Graphs	*Dashboards*
Charts	*data visualisation tools*
Graphics	*maps*
Infographics	*timelines*

Chapter 8: Problem Solving and Decision Making

Problem Solving and Decision Making

Problem-Solving and Decision-Making

There is a distinct difference between problem-solving and decision-making. Whilst they are closely linked skills that are very important in leadership and management roles, they are not the same.

The Dictionary, definitions are:

> *Problem-solving – the process of finding solutions to difficult or complex issues*
> *Decision-making – the action or process of making decisions, especially important ones*

> ### Decisions need to be made about how problems will be solved.

When a problem needs a solution, a series of decisions need to be made to find the best solution.

Example:

> *A new sofa has been ordered for delivery in six months' time, the problem is – there is no money to pay for it! Decisions need to be made about how money can be saved between now and then to pay for it.*

Problem-solving skills are needed to find possible solutions to the problem, for example:

- *using savings that are set aside for something else* – e.g., *a new car*
- *reducing current essential costs* – e.g., *money spent on bills or travel expenses*
- *reducing the money, spent on non-essential items* – e.g., *take-aways and socialising*
- *increasing earnings* – e.g., *from overtime or a second job*
- *borrowing money* – e.g., *taking out a loan*

There are many methods that could be used to solve the problem and the different options can be quantified to show much each one could add to the sofa fund. To fully solve the problem, action is needed not just writing down the options.

Before actions can be taken, decision-making skills are needed to identify the most suitable choices.

This is part of a process and all options need to be considered before deciding which will be the best one to take.

Problem Solving and Decision Making

Example:

When making a decision about increasing earnings, questions that need to be answered could include:

- *Does the employer have any extra work? Is there overtime available?*
- *How much extra would be earned after tax and national insurance?*
- *How many hours would have to be worked to make the money needed?*
- *How much would be spent on travel and parking costs for the extra shifts?*
- *How might doing so much overtime affect the work – life balance?*
- *Is there scope to take on a second job for a while to pay for the sofa?*
- *How would such a job be identified and what would be earned?*

A great deal of routine management and leadership involves solving problems and making decisions.

When managers deal with problems they need to understand as much as possible about the issues and circumstances before they can make decisions.

There are three elements to all problems which must be understood before any remedial action can be taken. These are:

- *the Scope of the problem*
- *the Nature of the problem*
- *the Impact the problem could have.*

Problem Solving and Decision Making

Nature, Scope and Impact of a Problem

Having a 360° view of a problem is critical when managers solve problems and make decisions. The more information and data they have at their disposal, the more informed they will be, making them more likely to make appropriate decisions.

When assessing a problem, a manager needs to go through a series of processes that are not dissimilar to those made by a doctor when making a diagnosis.

When diagnosing the patient, a doctor needs to:

- *examine the patient*
- *question them*
- *check mobility*
- *check temperature*
- *assess the scope and impact of the problem*
- *perform or request further tests* – e.g. *blood tests or scans*
- *research extra information if they cannot make an instant diagnosis*
- *consult with colleagues*
- *ask specialists for advice and guidance*

Very often, the diagnosis can be made and a treatment plan can be put in place. However, sometimes the diagnosis is not straightforward and the doctor will have to try different options before the best form of treatment can be found.

The same sorts of processes apply in management. Managers need to investigate and assess problems thoroughly before they can make decisions about the possible solutions.

Typical problems might include:

- *Equipment failure* – e.g. *production machinery, lifts, ITC equipment or vehicles*
- *Accidents involving equipment* – e.g. *using equipment incorrectly and damaging it*
- *Accidents involving people* – e.g., *staff or customers having slips, trips and falls in the workplace; injuries after lifting incorrectly; ladders and steps slipping*
- *Problems with physical resources* – e.g. *insufficient resources; delays in the supply chain; damaged goods; poor-quality supplies; late or missing deliveries*
- *Problems with human resources* – e.g., *insufficient skills, knowledge, or experience to be able to deal with tasks; staff absences causing delays and cancellations*
- *Missed deadlines* – e.g. *failing to deliver tasks, products, services or reports on time due to poor time management, bad weather or staff problems*

Problem Solving and Decision Making

- *Customer complaints* – e.g. faulty goods; late deliveries of products; receiving rude service; not having their telephone calls answered quickly; letters and emails not being answered
- *Difficulties with working relationships between colleagues* – e.g., arguments or disharmony within a team; harassment, bullying or discrimination; communication problems

The Nature of the Problem

When analysing problems, the first thing a manager needs to know is the nature of the problem

A manager needs to know what the problem is. They need to ask questions, such as:

- *Is the problem a life-threatening emergency?*
- *Has anyone been hurt or affected by the problem?*
- *Is the problem urgent?*
- *Have emergency procedures been put into action?*
- *What is the background to the problem?*
- *When, where and how did things go wrong?*
- *Has the problem happened before – if so, how was it handled before?*

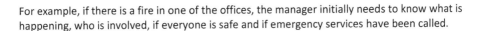

For example, if there is a fire in one of the offices, the manager initially needs to know what is happening, who is involved, if everyone is safe and if emergency services have been called.

Soon after the initial actions, managers need to look at how, when and why things went wrong.

Problems can be put into three broad categories:

- *Critical problems* – where immediate action and decisions are required
- *Non-critical problems* – not urgent and often routine, these still need early attention to stop them becoming crises
- *Opportunity problems* – where there is an element of choice that is driven by opportunity to improve rather than by routine or crisis

The Scope of the Problem

Having full details about the nature of the problem enables managers to assess the scope of the problem.

When considering the scope of a problem, managers look at the potential size of the problem. For example:

Problem Solving and Decision Making

- *exactly what is affected?* – e.g., a small work area or the whole building; the stock on a shelf or a full warehouse that contains six months' supply of materials; the budget and deadlines
- *exactly who is affected?* – e.g., one person, a small team, a large department, or the whole organisation; suppliers or customers; two people or 20,000 people
- *who might be able to solve the problem?* – e.g. are solutions within the scope of the manager's limits of authority, or will senior managers and external specialists be required?

In this process, managers will look at how big the problem is, or how big it could be. They will also look at how far reaching the problem could be:

- *the team and others in the organisation*
- *customers and suppliers*
- *production and delivery of goods and services*
- *the building, infrastructure, machinery and equipment*
- *objectives, deadlines and budgets*

INVESTIGATE THE
SCOPE OF THE
PROBLEM.

In the above example, if there is a fire in an office, there is scope for the fire to spread throughout the rest of the building, threaten the health and safety of anyone in the area, to destroy equipment, machinery and supplies and to destroy jobs, customer relations and the business.

The Impact of the Problem

The impact of the problem is the knock-on effect the problem causes.

Managers need to be able to step back and analyse everything objectively and consider the wider impact of the problem and the possible solutions. This helps them to work out plans and strategies about how to overcome the problem.

The impact of problems can vary and it might not be possible to predict every outcome. The best that managers can do if they cannot assess the full impact of a problem is:

- *work on the basis of the impact being minimal* – and plan actions and solutions for the best outcome
- *be ready for maximum impact* – and have outline plans in case they have to deal with the worst outcome

Some problems only have a short-term impact. If temporary solutions can be found, or if the problem is routine and can be fixed quickly, the short-term impact might be minimal.

Problem Solving and Decision Making

Some problems have a long-term impact. The problems might be very difficult and expensive to solve and there could be a long-term impact and far-reaching consequences on finances, jobs, customer relations, the local area and so on.

Following the office fire example again, if the fire is put out quickly with no injuries or major damage, the impact effects could include:

- *Disruption to that day's activities only*
- *Inspections by fire officers and health and safety experts before being allowed to use the office again*
- *Time spent cleaning up and redecorating if necessary*
- *Some lost materials – e.g., paperwork*
- *Staff being upset but unhurt and unaffected by smoke due to a swift exit or extinguishing of the fire*
- *Replacing fire-fighting equipment immediately*
- *Operational changes following analysis of the causes of the fire*

If the fire cannot be put out quickly and safely and spreads to the entire factory that employs 100 people, the impact effects could also include, for example:

- *Short-term emergency medical care for a large number of people*
- *Long-term health issues for some people – e.g., lung damage after smoke inhalation*
- *Destruction of the whole building and its contents*
- *Long and detailed investigations by police, fire officers, insurance assessors, health and safety specialists, legal representatives and others*
- *Serious financial and legal consequences for the organisation, directors, managers and others*
- *Loss of jobs for all employees if the business cannot recover*

This example is extreme, but it does show how far-reaching the scope and impact of a problem can be.

Solving Problems

Problem-solving and decision-making can be quite complicated processes – especially if the nature, scope and impact of the problem are considerable. When making the right decisions about which solutions to try, it can help to use a particular technique to evaluate the options.

Problem Solving and Decision Making

Model	Key Features	Best Used
Algorithm model	Analytical in nature Clear Yes or No Answers	More effective in fault finding areas as fact-based results are produced
Plus, Minus, Implications Model	Based on judgements rather than facts Involves qualitative data	More effective when a rapid response or quick decision is needed
Six thinking hats	Group decision making sessions Key roles are identified for team members and may include members who are not involved	More effective when diverse input is needed as in larger organisation

It is recognised that there are four basic rules that exist when considering potential outcomes and the impacts of decisions and that one of these rules will always apply:

1. **Pessimistic rule** - choose the option that results in the highest possible outcome for the least likely option (worst case scenario)
2. **Optimistic rule** - choose the option that results in the best possible outcome (best case scenario)
3. **Expected value rule** - choose an option based on an estimate of the likelihood of a situation occurring (what if scenario)
4. **Opportunity rule** - consider the likely or potential opportunities that can be lost by applying any of the other rules (lost opportunities scenario)

There may be occasions when more than one rule will be integral to the process for making a decision, none more so than when using the six thinking hats model.

Algorithm Method

An algorithm is a defined set of step-by-step procedures that provides the correct answer to a particular problem.

By following the instructions correctly, you are guaranteed to arrive at the right answer. While often thought of purely as a mathematical term, the same type of process can be followed to ensure finding the correct answer when solving a problem or making a decision.

An algorithm is often expressed in the form of a graph, where a square represents each step. Arrows then branch off from each step to point to possible directions that you may take to solve the problem. In some cases, you must follow a particular set of steps to solve the problem. In other instances, you might be able to follow different paths that will all lead to the same solution.

The benefit of using an algorithm to solve a problem or make a decision is that yields the best possible answer every time. This is useful in situations when accuracy is critical or where similar problems need to be frequently solved. In many cases, computer programs can be designed to speed up this process. Data then needs to be placed in the system so that the algorithm can be executed to come up with the correct solution.

Such step-by-step approaches can be useful in situations where each decision must be made following the same process and where accuracy is critical. Because the process follows a prescribed procedure, you can be sure that you will reach the correct answer each time. The downside of using an algorithm to solve the problem is that this process tends to be very time-consuming. So, if you face a situation where a decision needs to be made very quickly, you might be better off using a different problem-solving strategy.

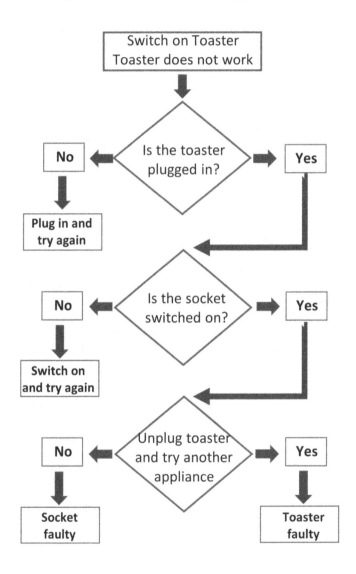

Problem Solving and Decision Making

PMI - Plus, Minus, Interesting

PMI (plus, minus, interesting) is a brainstorming, decision making and critical thinking tool. It is used to encourage the examination of ideas, concepts and experiences from more than one perspective. PMI was developed by Dr. Edward de Bono, a proponent of lateral and critical thinking.

A PMI strategy can help you to:

- *to brainstorm ideas*
- *make decisions quickly by analysing and weighing the pros and cons*
- *reflect upon or evaluate a product or processes after the fact*
- *identify strengths and weaknesses for future improvement*

To complete, make a chart of three columns - "Plus", "Minus" and "Interesting."

P	M	I

Step 1. Consider the Plus Points
Simply enumerate all of the positive things. Do not critique along the way, simply spill out all conceivable positive points.

Step 2. Consider the Minus Points
Enumerate all of the negative things. Again, do not critique. Simply spill out all the negative points.

Step 3. Consider the Interesting Points of the Situation.
List all the interesting points. Rather than positive or negative, they are simply points of interest that attention should be directed towards.

Step 4. Make the conclusion
Make the judgement based on the three important aspects: the positives, the negatives and the interesting which have been identified and organised.

It is a great tool for critical thinking, focussing your attention, evaluating and analysing. After you have used this technique, you should be in a better position to make your decision.

Problem Solving and Decision Making

Edward de Bono's - Six thinking hats

If a manager is naturally optimistic, then chances are they will not always consider potential downsides. Similarly, if they are very cautious or have a risk-averse outlook, they might not focus on opportunities that could open up. Often, the best decisions come from changing the way that people think about problems and examining them from different viewpoints.

Edward de Bono's - Six thinking hats					
Facts	Emotion	Benefit	Ideas	Planning	Judgement
neutral	emotional view	logical positive	creativity	process control	logical negative
neutral and objective, concerned with data, facts, figures and information	the intuitive view, hunches, "gut" feeling	optimistic, sunny and positive covers hope	associated with energy, fertility, growth, creativity in new ideas. Switches around the normal superiority of the Black Hat	the organising hat (start and finish) controls the use of the other hats	careful and cautious, the "judgement" hat

"Six Thinking Hats" can help look at problems from different perspectives, but one at a time, to avoid confusion from too many angles crowding thinking.

Decision makers often wear many hats in order to devise a well-rounded solution.

It is also a powerful decision-checking technique in group situations, as everyone explores the situation from each perspective at the same time. It forces thinking outside habitual styles and to look at things from a number of different perspectives and gain a more rounded view of the situation.

Successful solutions or outcomes can often be achieved from a rational, positive viewpoint, but it can also pay to consider a problem from other angles. For example, looking at it from an

Problem Solving and Decision Making

emotional, intuitive, creative or risk management viewpoint. Not considering these perspectives could lead to underestimating people's resistance to the plans, fail to make creative leaps, or ignore the need for essential contingency plans.

Using the six thinking hats model

Six Thinking Hats can be used in meetings or alone. In meetings, it has the benefit of preventing any confrontation that may happen when people with different thinking styles discuss a problem, because every perspective is valid.

Each "Thinking Hat" is a different style of thinking.

- **White Hat:** *with this thinking hat, the focus is on the available data. Look at the information to hand, analyse past trends and see what can be learnt from it. Look for gaps in knowledge and try to either fill them or take account of them.*

- **Red Hat:** *The Red Hat looks at problems using intuition, gut reaction and emotion. Also, think how others could react emotionally. Try to understand the responses of people who do not fully know the reasoning.*

- **Black Hat:** *Black Hat thinking, looks at a decision's potentially negative outcomes. Look at it cautiously and defensively. Try to see why it might not work. This is important because it highlights the weak points in a plan. It allows them to be eliminated, alter them, or prepare contingency plans to counter them. Black Hat thinking helps to make the plans "tougher" and more resilient. It can also help spot fatal flaws and risks before embarking on a course of action. It is one of the real benefits of this model, as many successful people get so used to thinking positively that they often cannot see problems in advance. This leaves them under-prepared for difficulties.*

- **Yellow Hat:** *this hat helps positive thinking. It is the optimistic viewpoint that helps see all the benefits of the decision and the value in it. Yellow Hat thinking helps to keep going when everything looks gloomy and difficult.*

- **Green Hat**: *The Green Hat represents creativity. This is where creative solutions to a problem are developed. It is a freewheeling way of thinking, in which there is little criticism of ideas.*

- **Blue Hat:** *this hat represents process control. It is the hat worn by people chairing meetings, for example. When facing difficulties because ideas are running dry, they may direct activity into Green Hat thinking. When contingency plans are needed, they will ask for Black Hat thinking.*

A variant of this technique is to look at problems from the point of view of different professionals (for example, doctors, architects or sales directors) or different customers.

Problem Solving and Decision Making

A 5-Step Approach

Some problems are small and can be resolved quickly. Other problems are large and may require significant time and effort to solve. These larger problems are often tackled by turning them into formal projects.

> *"A project is a problem scheduled for solution."*
> *- Joseph M. Juran*

Whether the problem you are focusing on is small or large, using a systematic approach for solving it will help you be a more effective manager.

This approach defines five problem solving steps you can use for most problems...

- *Define the Problem*
- *Determine the Causes*
- *Generate Ideas*
- *Select the Best Solution*
- *Take Action*

Define the Problem

The most important of the problem-solving steps is to define the problem correctly. The way the problem is defined will determine how attempts are made to solve it.

Example:

> *a complaint has been received about a team member from a client, the proposed solutions will differ based on the way the problem is defined.*

If you define the problem as poor performance by the team member you will develop different solutions than if you define the problem as poor expectation setting with the client.

Determine the Causes

Once the problem is defined, it is time to dig deeper and start to determine what is causing it. A fishbone diagram can be to help perform a cause-and-effect analysis.

If a problem is considered as the gap between where the organisation is now and where it wants or needs to be, the causes of the problem are the obstacles that are preventing it from closing that gap immediately.

This level of analysis is important to make sure the solutions address the actual causes of the problem instead of the symptoms of the problem. If the solution fixes a symptom instead of the actual cause, the problem is likely to reoccur as it was never truly solved.

Problem Solving and Decision Making

Generate Ideas
Once the hard work of defining the problem and determining its causes has been completed, it is time to get creative and develop possible solutions to the problem. Two great problem-solving methods for coming up with solutions are brainstorming and mind mapping.

Select the Best Solution
After identifying several ideas that can solve the problem, one problem solving technique which can be used to decide which is the best solution to for the problem is a simple trade-off analysis.

To perform the trade-off analysis, define the critical criteria for the problem that can be used to evaluate how each solution compares to each other. The evaluation can be done using a simple matrix. The highest-ranking solution will be the best solution for this problem.

Take Action
Once the best solution has been determined, it is time to take action. If the solution involves several actions or requires action from others, it is a good idea to create an action plan and treat it as a mini project.

Using this simple five-step approach can increase the effectiveness of problem-solving skills.

Making Decisions

Some of the decisions which need to be made will be so routine that they are made without giving them much thought. But difficult or challenging decisions demand more consideration. These are the sort of decisions that involve:

- *Uncertainty* – *Many of the facts may be unknown.*
- *Complexity* – *There can be many, interrelated factors to consider.*
- *High-risk consequences* – *The impact of the decision may be significant.*
- *Alternatives* – *There may be various alternatives, each with its own set of uncertainties and consequences.*
- *Interpersonal issues* – *You need to predict how different people will react.*

When making a decision that involves complex issues like these, problem-solving skills will be needed, as well as decision-making skills. It pays to use an effective, robust process in these circumstances, to improve the quality of the decisions and to achieve consistently good results.

One such process for combining problem-solving and decision-making strategies when making complex decisions in challenging situations is shown below.

Problem Solving and Decision Making

A Systematic Approach for Making Decisions

In real-life business situations, decisions can often fail because the best alternatives are not clear at the outset, or key factors are not considered as part of the process. To stop this happening, problem-solving and decision-making strategies need to be brought together to clarify understanding.

A logical and ordered process can help achieve this by making sure that all of the critical elements needed for a successful outcome are addressed.

Working through this process systematically will reduce the likelihood of overlooking important factors.

Our seven-step approach takes this into account:

- *Create a constructive environment.*
- *Investigate the situation in detail.*
- *Generate good alternatives.*
- *Explore your options.*
- *Select the best solution.*
- *Evaluate your plan.*
- *Communicate your decision and take action.*

This process will ensure that the best decision is made in a complex situation, but it may be unnecessarily involved for small or simple decisions. In these cases, focus on the tools in Step 5.

Step 1: Create a Constructive Environment

Decisions can become complex when they involve or affect other people, so it helps to create a constructive environment in which to explore the situation and weigh up the options.

Often, when making a decision, there is reliance on others to implement it, so it pays to gain their support. If it is most appropriate to make the decision within a group, conduct a Stakeholder Analysis to identify who to include in the process. To build commitment from others, make sure that these stakeholders are well represented within the decision-making group (which will ideally comprise five to seven people).

Use the Vroom-Yetton-Jago Decision Model to decide whether to consult stakeholders or to give them a vote.

Encourage people to contribute to the discussions, debates and analysis without any fear of the other participants rejecting their ideas. Make sure everyone recognises that the objective is to make the best decision possible in the circumstances – this is not the time for people to promote their own preferred alternative.

The Charette Procedure is a systematic process for gathering and developing ideas from many stakeholders. Alternatively, consider using The Stepladder Technique to introduce more and more people to the discussion gradually, while ensuring that everyone gets heard.

Problem Solving and Decision Making

Step 2: Investigate the Situation in Detail

Before attempting to make a decision, make sure that the situation is fully understood. It may be that the objective can be approached in isolation, but it is more likely that there are a number of interrelated factors to consider. Changes made in one department, for example, could have knock-on effects elsewhere, making the change counterproductive.

Start by considering the decision in the context of the problem it is intended to address. Use the 5Whys technique to determine whether the stated problem is the real issue, or just a symptom of something deeper. Root Cause Analysis can also be used to trace a problem to its origins.

Once the root cause is identified, define the problem to extract the greatest amount of information from what is known and use Inductive Reasoning to draw sound conclusions from the facts. The Problem-Definition Process can also be used to gain a better understanding of what is going on.

As well as this, consider using CATWOE to explore the problem from multiple perspectives and to make sure important information is not missing.

Step 3: Generate Good Alternatives

The wider the options explored, the better the final decision is likely to be.

Generating a number of different options may seem to make the decision more complicated at first, but the act of coming up with alternatives forces a deeper dig and look at the problem from different angles.

This is when it can be helpful to employ a variety of creative thinking techniques. These can help to step outside the normal patterns of thinking and come up with some truly innovative solutions.

Brainstorming is probably the most popular method of generating ideas, while Reverse Brainstorming works in a similar way, but starts by asking how the opposite outcome can be achieved from the desired one and then turning the solution on its head.

Other useful methods for getting a group of people producing ideas include the Crawford Slip Writing Technique and Round-Robin Brainstorming. Both are effective ways of ensuring that everyone's ideas are heard and given equal weight, regardless of their position or power within the team.

Do not forget to consider how people outside the group might influence or be affected by the decision. This can be done by using tools like the Reframing Matrix, which uses 4Ps (Product, Planning, Potential and People) as a way to gather different perspectives.

Ask outsiders to join the discussion as well or use the Perceptual Positions technique to encourage existing participants to adopt different functional perspectives (for example, having a marketing person speak from the viewpoint of a financial manager).

Problem Solving and Decision Making

If there are only a few or unsatisfactory options, try using Concept Fans, to take a step back from the problem and approach it from a wider perspective, or Appreciative Inquiry, to look at the problem based on what's "going right" rather than what's "going wrong." This can help when the people involved in the decision are too close to the problem.

When ideas start to emerge, try using Affinity Diagrams to organize them into common themes and groups.

Step 4: Explore Your Options

When a good selection of realistic alternatives have been identified, it is time to evaluate the feasibility, risks and implications of each one.

Almost every decision involves some degree of risk. Use Risk Analysis to consider this objectively by adopting a structured approach to assessing threats and evaluating the probability of adverse events occurring – and what they might cost to manage.
Then, prioritize the risks you identify with a Risk Impact/Probability Chart, so focus can be directed on the ones that are most likely to occur.

Another way to evaluate options is to consider the potential consequences of each one. The ORAPAPA tool helps evaluate a decision's consequences by looking at the alternatives from seven different perspectives. Alternatively conduct an Impact Analysis or use a Futures Wheel to brainstorm "unexpected" consequences that could arise from the decision.

Other considerations are whether the resources are adequate, the solution matches the objectives and is the decision likely to work in the long term. Use Starbursting to think about the questions you should ask to evaluate each alternative and assess their pros and cons using Force Field Analysis or the Quantitative Pros and Cons approach.

Weigh up a decision's financial feasibility using Cost-Benefit Analysis.

Step 5: Select the Best Solution

Once all the alternatives have been evaluated, the next step is to make the decision. If one particular alternative is clearly better than the rest, the choice will be obvious. However, if there are still several competing options, there are plenty of tools that will help decide between them.

If there are various criteria to consider, use a Decision Matrix Analysis to compare them reliably and rigorously. Or, to determine their relative importance, conduct a Paired Comparison Analysis to decide which ones should carry the most weight in the decision.

Decision Trees are also useful when choosing between different financial options. These help you to lay options out clearly and bring the likelihood of the project succeeding or failing into the decision-making process.

Group Decisions

If the decision is being made within a group, there are plenty of excellent tools and techniques to help reach a group decision.

Problem Solving and Decision Making

If the decision criteria are subjective and it is critical that you gain consensus, Multi-Voting and the Modified Borda Count can help a team reach an agreement.

When anonymity is important, decision-makers dislike one another, or there is a tendency for certain individuals to dominate the process, use the Delphi Technique to reach a fair and impartial decision. This uses cycles of anonymous, written discussion and argument, managed by a facilitator. Participants do not meet and sometimes they do not even know who else is involved.

When working with an established team, use Hartnett's Consensus-Oriented Decision-Making Model to encourage everyone to participate in making the decision. Or, if working with several different teams, or a particularly large group, assign responsibility for each stage of the decision-making process with Bain's RAPID Framework, so that everyone understands their responsibilities and any potential in-fighting can be avoided.

Step 6: Evaluate Your Plan

With all the effort and hard work already invested in evaluating and selecting alternatives, it can be tempting to forge ahead at this stage. But now, more than ever, is the time to "sense check" the decision. After all, hindsight is great for identifying why things have gone wrong, but it is far better to prevent mistakes from happening in the first place!

Before starting to implement the decision, take a long, dispassionate look at it to be sure that the examination has been thorough and that common errors have not crept into the process.

The final decision is only as good as the facts and research used to make it. Make sure that the information used is trustworthy and that every effort has been made not to "cherry pick" data. This will help avoid confirmation bias, a common psychological bias in decision making.

Discuss the preliminary conclusions with important stakeholders to enable them to spot flaws, make recommendations and support the conclusions. Listen to intuition, too and quietly and methodically test assumptions and decisions against experience. If any doubts remain, examine them thoroughly to identify what remains in doubt.

Use Blindspot Analysis to review whether common decision-making problems like over-confidence, escalating commitment, or groupthink may have undermined the process. Consider checking the logical structure of the process with the Ladder of Inference, to make sure that a well-founded and consistent decision emerges at the end.

Step 7: Communicate the decision and take action

Once the decision is made, communicate it to everyone affected by it in an engaging and inspiring way.

Get them involved in implementing the solution by discussing how and why the decision was arrived at. The more information provided about risks and projected benefits; the more likely people will be to support the decision.

Problem Solving and Decision Making

If people point out a flaw in the process as a result, have the humility to welcome their input and review your plans appropriately – it is much better to do this now, cheaply, than having to do it expensively (and embarrassingly) if the plans have failed.

Other problem-solving and decision-making techniques

Problem-solving and decision-making can be quite complicated processes – especially if the nature, scope and impact of the problem are considerable. When making the right decisions about which solutions to try, it can help to use a technique to evaluate the options.

There are many techniques that we can use to help us find suitable solutions and make effective decisions. For example:

- *SWOT analysis*
- *PESTLE analysis*
- *Root cause analysis*
- *Paired comparison analysis*
- *Weighted grid analysis*
- *Gantt charts*
- *PDCA cycle*

SWOT Analysis

One technique is to perform a SWOT analysis. Managers can produce these in a simple way to help to clarify their thinking and focus their attention on all aspects of the problem. A SWOT analysis is particularly useful for gathering, interpreting and analysing information. For each realistic possible solution, managers can analyse the following:

S – Strengths
W – Weaknesses
O – Opportunities
T – Threats to success

If your car has been breaking down and causing you problems, a SWOT analysis could show, for example:

Problem Solving and Decision Making

	Option A – have it fixed every time to keep it going for as long as possible – maybe another year	Option B – replace the car with a brand-new, up-to-date version that should last ten years	Option C – replace it with a second hand, model that should last five years
Strengths	Not too expensive to run The problems are well-known and familiar	Good reliability Up-to-date technology Good warranty support	Reasonable cost Its service history should indicate reliability Know how to operate it
Weaknesses	Cost of repairs Frequent disruption of your life that cannot be planned Drop in your efficiency and performance	Very expensive May have to make sacrifices Will be difficult to look after properly	Does not benefit from the most up-to-date technology and design Only a short warranty Could develop problems at any time
Opportunities	Easy to arrange with garage for repairs	Three possible suppliers Available in about two months	Plenty available if researched online Could be bought quickly as changes to storage arrangements not needed
Threats to success	Garage staff may refuse to repair it when it breaks again Repair costs are high Wages could be lost due to delays	Cost and budget constraints Might be outdated after a few years Personal benefits may not justify the cost	Cost might not be justifiable if planning to keep it for less than five years

Although a SWOT analysis does not give a magic answer to the problem, it does help the managers to identify the pros and cons of each option. Once they knew their budget constraints and the long-term organisational targets that could be affected by the machine in the example, the managers would be able to make the best decision to solve the problem.

Problem Solving and Decision Making

PESTLE Analysis

Another system that could be used when making well-informed decisions is a PESTLE analysis. This can be particularly useful when there are areas of concern outside of the control of the organisation and for gathering, interpreting and analysing information.

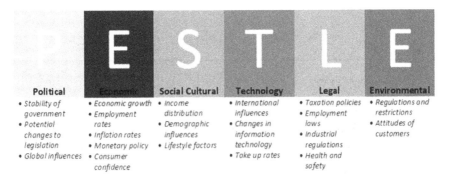

Political	Economic	Social Cultural	Technology	Legal	Environmental
• Stability of government • Potential changes to legislation • Global influences	• Economic growth • Employment rates • Inflation rates • Monetary policy • Consumer confidence	• Income distribution • Demographic influences • Lifestyle factors	• International influences • Changes in information technology • Take up rates	• Taxation policies • Employment laws • Industrial regulations • Health and safety	• Regulations and restrictions • Attitudes of customers

For example, if the problem is that the company has outgrown its present site, it will have to consider many things that are outside its control. When doing a PESTLE analysis, managers would look at these areas:

P   **Political** – e.g., government funding for expanding in the same area or setting up in a different location

E   **Economic** – e.g., the overall economic climate and whether stakeholders would support   investment and expansion if the economy is slow or in recession

S   **Social** – e.g., the effect on the local population if the company moves away/stays put and expands

T   **Technological** – e.g., the scope for using new technology as part of the expansion plans

L   **Legal** – e.g., legal requirements about redundancies or relocation of staff

E   **Environmental** – e.g., the regulations on emissions and waste management in the current area and the potential new area

Paired Comparison Analysis

This type of analysis is useful when managers need to work out relevant factors when choices are quite different from each other – rather like the classic case of comparing apples and oranges.

We will do an example based on someone having to choose which type of charity to support – an animal charity, a bequest for university, a children's charity or disaster relief.

There are six stages:

Problem Solving and Decision Making

Stage 1 – make a list of things that need to be compared, assign each option a letter – e.g. A for Animals, B for Bequest, C for Children and D for Disaster.

Stage 2 – put the letters in a grid and block out squares where data would be duplicated.

	A – Animal charity	B – Bequest for university	C – Children's charity	D – Disaster relief
A – Animal charity	XXXXXXXXXX	A1	C2	D2
B – Bequest for university	XXXXXXXXXX	XXXXXXXXXX	C2	D2
C – Children's charity	XXXXXXXXXX	XXXXXXXXXX	XXXXXXXXXX	C1
D – Disaster relief	XXXXXXXXXX	XXXXXXXXXX	XXXXXXXXXX	XXXXXXXXXX

Stage 3 – within each cell, compare the options and decided which is most important – e.g. A is more important than B in the above grid.

Stage 4 – give the letter a rating to show how important the choice is – e.g., from 0 for no importance to 3 for extremely important – A has been given rating 1 in the above grid.

Stage 5 – consolidate results by adding up the values for each of the options – maybe converting them to percentage values. In the example:

A = 1 (10%)
B = 0
C = 5 (50%)
D = 4 (40%)

Stage 6 – use common sense and manually adjust, as necessary. In the example: After comparing the results, the person decides to make their main donation to the children's charity, with some going to disaster relief.

Problem Solving and Decision Making

Weighted Grid Analysis

A grid analysis is a useful technique to use when making a decision, especially when there are numerous factors and alternatives to take into account. There are several steps:

- *Step 1* – list the options as row labels and the factors as column labels
- *Step 2* – work out the relative importance of the factors in the decision and show them as numbers to give each factor a weight – e.g., from 1 (not important) to 5 (extremely important)
- *Step 3* – work through and score each option for each of the important factors – score from 0 (poor) to 3 (very good)
- *Step 4* – multiply each of the scores to reveal the relative importance
- *Step 5* – add up the weighted scores – the highest score 'wins'

For example: a manager is deciding where to purchase a new computer to run the production line that is in operation 24 hours a day, 7 days a week. As it is a long-term investment, the quality of the machine and the back-up service from the supplier are extremely important

	Factor 1 – Cost	Factor 2 – Availability	Factor 3 – Delivery time	Factor 4 – Quality	Factor 5 – 24/7 Support	Total
Weights:	4	3	3	5	5	
Suppliers						
IBN	2	3	1	2	1	
Dill	3	2	2	2	3	
EP	2	3	2	3	0	
Toshiva	1	3	2	2	2	
Suny	2	2	3	2	2	

Then multiply the figures by the weights…. In this example, Dill come out as the favoured supplier.

Problem Solving and Decision Making

	Factor 1 – Cost	Factor 2 – Availability	Factor 3 – Delivery time	Factor 4 – Quality	Factor 5 – 24/7 Support	Total
Weights:	**4**	**3**	**3**	**5**	**5**	
Suppliers						
IBN	2 x 4 = 8	3 x 3= 9	1 x 3 =3	2 x 5 = 10	1 x 5 = 5	35
Dill	3 x 4 = 12	2 x 3 = 6	2 x 3 = 6	2 x 5= 10	3 x 5= 15	49
EP	2 x 4 = 8	3 x 3 = 9	2 x 3 = 6	3 x 5 = 15	0 x 5 = 0	38
Toshiva	1 x 4 = 4	3 x 3 = 9	2 x 3 = 6	2 x 5 = 10	2 x 5 = 10	39
Suny	2 x 4 8	2 x 3 6	3 x 3 9	2 x 5 = 10	2 x 5 = 10	43

Gantt Charts

Gantt charts are often used in project management to show activities against time. They are extremely useful when the problems are complex and interconnected, with various deadlines and targets that have an effect on each other and are frequently used as planning tools.

Managers need to start by breaking down the overall problem into smaller tasks or activities. Each activity is represented by a bar and its position and length illustrate the start and end dates. Gantt charts enable managers and others to see:

- *what the activities are*
- *when activities and whole projects begin and end*
- *how long each activity is scheduled to last*
- *where they overlap and by how much*

Task	Sept 19	Oct 19	Nov 19	Dec 19	Jan 20	Feb 20	Mar 20	Apr 20
Planning		XXXX	XXXX					
Research			XXXX	XX				
Design				XXXX				
Implementation					XXXX	XXXX		
Review							X	XX

Problem Solving and Decision Making

Gantt charts can become very large in size as well as content and depending on the problem, can become hugely complex. If this is the case, try using additional colours symbols etc to better identify the areas involved.

When making decisions, they are a flexible tool that can be used to show all of the variables and how they need to work together. In the example above, for instance, the manager can see how the design process has to be finished by the end of December, so that it does not delay the implementation start date at the beginning of January.

Root Cause Analysis (RCA)

This is a method of finding possible solutions by identifying the root causes of faults or problems. It is also referred to as cause-and-effect analysis and makes use of fishbone diagrams, herringbone diagrams and Ishikawa diagrams, named after Professor Kaoru Ishikawa, a pioneer of quality management in the 1960s.

The technique can be used to:

- *discover the root cause of problems, especially for complicated problems*
- *reveal 'bottlenecks' in a process that are causing delays*
- *identify where and why a process does not work*
- *improve quality control*

Step 1 – identify the problem – e.g., what the problem is, who is involved, where and when it occurs.

Step 2 – work out the major factors involved – e.g., systems, equipment, materials or external forces.

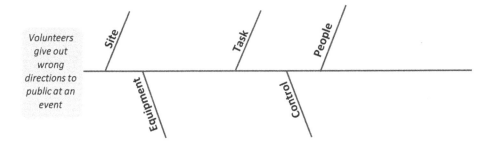

Problem Solving and Decision Making

Step 3 – identify possible causes – e.g., brainstorm the different problems in Step 2 and add them to the diagram.

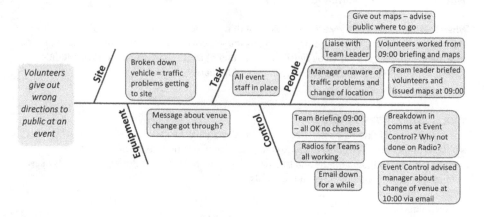

Step 4 – analyse the diagram – e.g., look at all of the possible causes and look out for problem areas that have a knock-on effect on other issues.

In this example, we can see that:

- *traffic problems caused delays*
- *volunteers worked from notes and maps given out at their 09:00 briefing*
- *the manager was informed about the change of venue at 10:00 via email*
- *email was down for a while and the message was not received or actioned*

The manager would need to make further investigations to see why the communication failed from event control and why there was no backup plan to let people know about the changes.

The Problem-Solving Cycle

The problem-solving cycle is a frame of reference for using various problem-solving methods. In this model there are six phases in problem solving:

- *Naming the problem*
- *Analysing*
- *Goal setting*
- *Searching for solutions*
- *Planning*
- *Evaluation*

The following diagram illustrates the problem-solving cycle

Problem Solving and Decision Making

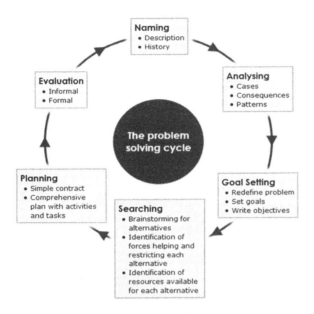

The PDCA Cycle

The PDCA cycle encourages a commitment to continuous improvement.

Imagine that the customer satisfaction score on a popular business ratings website has dipped. When studying recent comments, it is noted that customers are complaining about late delivery and that products are being damaged in transit.

It is decided to run a small pilot project for a month, using a new supplier to deliver the products to a small sample of customers and feedback from the customers is positive. As a result, a decision is made to use the new supplier for all future orders.

This short process represents once around a loop called the PDCA Cycle, which helps organisations to strive for continuous improvements in the business.

PDCA, sometimes called the "Deming Wheel," or "Deming Cycle," was developed by renowned management consultant Dr William Edwards Deming in the 1950s. Deming himself called it the "Shewhart Cycle," as his model was based on an idea from his mentor, Walter Shewhart. Deming wanted to create a way of identifying what caused products to fail to meet customer's expectations. His solution helps businesses to develop hypotheses about what needs to change and then test these in a continuous feedback loop.

The four phases are:

Problem Solving and Decision Making

Plan: identify and analyse the problem or opportunity, develop hypotheses about what the issues may be and decide which one to test.

Do: test the potential solution, ideally on a small scale and measure the results.

Check/Study: study the result, measure effectiveness and decide whether the hypothesis is supported or not.

Act: if the solution was successful, implement it.

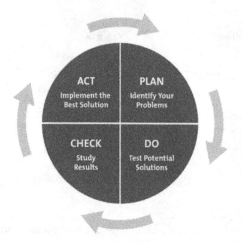

Look at the four stages in more detail, below.

The PDCA cycle helps solve problems and implement solutions in a rigorous, methodical way. Follow these four steps to ensure that the highest quality results are obtained.

1. Plan
First, you need to identify and understand your problem, or the opportunity that you want to take advantage of. Using the first six steps of The Simplex Process can help you to do this, by guiding you through a process of exploring information, defining your problem, generating and screening ideas and developing an implementation plan.

At the final part of this stage, state quantitatively what your expectations are, if the idea is successful and your problem is resolved. You will return to this in the Check stage.

2. Do
Once you have identified a potential solution, test it with a small-scale pilot project. This will allow you to assess whether your proposed changes achieve the desired outcome, with minimal disruption to the rest of your operation if they do not. For example, you could organise a trial within a department, in a limited geographical area, or with a particular demographic.

Problem Solving and Decision Making

3. Check

At this stage, you analyse your pilot project's results against the expectations that you defined in Step 1 to assess whether the idea has worked or not. If it has not worked, you return to Step 1. If it has worked, you go on to Step 4.

You may decide to try out more changes and repeat the Do and Check phases – do not settle for a less-than-satisfactory solution.

Move on to the final phase (Act) only when you are genuinely happy with the trial's outcome.

4. Act

This is where you implement your solution. But remember that PDCA / PDSA is a loop, not a process with a beginning and an end. This means that your improved process or product becomes the new baseline and you continue to look for ways to make it even better for your organisation or customers.

When to use PDCA

The PDCA framework can improve any process or product by breaking it into smaller steps. It is particularly effective for:

- *Helping to improve processes.*
- *Exploring a range of solutions to problems and piloting them in a controlled way before selecting one for implementation.*
- *Avoiding wastage of resources by rolling out an ineffective solution on a wide scale.*

You can use the model in all sorts of business environments, from new product development, project and change management to product lifecycle and supply chain management.

The Pros and Cons of PDCA

The model is a simple, yet powerful way to resolve new and recurring issues in any industry, department, or process. Its iterative approach allows you and your team to test solutions and assess results in a waste-reducing cycle.

It instils a commitment to continuous improvement, however small and can improve efficiency and productivity in a controlled way, without the risks of making large scale, untested changes to your processes.

However, going through the PDCA cycle can be much slower than a straightforward, "gung ho" implementation. So, it might not be the appropriate approach for dealing with an urgent problem or emergency.

It also requires significant "buy-in" from team members and offers fewer opportunities for radical innovation, if that is what your organisation needs.

Problem Solving and Decision Making

8D Report

The 8D Report is a problem-solving approach for product and process improvement. Furthermore, 8D Methodology is used to implement structural long-term solutions to prevent recurring problems. The 8D Report was first used in the automotive industry.

The 8D Methodology mainly focuses on solving problems and comprises 8 steps or disciplines. It helps quality control staff find the root cause of problems within a production process in a structured manner so that they can resolve the problem(s).

In addition, it helps implement product or process improvements, which can prevent problems.

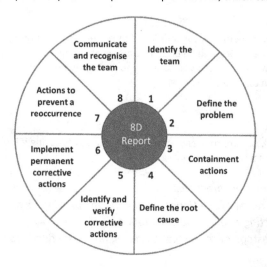

D1 – Create a team

Mobilising a good team is essential. The team must preferably be multidisciplinary. Due to a varied combination of knowledge, skills and experience, it allows the problem to be considered from different perspectives.

Besides having an effective team leader, it is also advisable to record team structure, goals, different team roles, procedures and rules in advance so that the team can begin taking action quickly and effectively and there is no room for misunderstandings.

D2 – Describe the problem

Define the problem as objectively as possible. The 5W2H analysis (who, what, when, where, why, how, how much) is a welcome addition to the problem analysis and can help to arrive at a clear description of the problem.

D3 – Interim containment action

It may be necessary to implement temporary fixes. For example, to help or meet a customer quickly or when a deadline has to be met. It is about preventing a problem from getting worse until a permanent solution is implemented.

D4 – Identify the root cause

Problem Solving and Decision Making

Before a permanent solution is found, it is important to identify all possible root causes that could explain why the problem occurred. Various methods can be used for this purpose, such as the fishbone diagram (Ishikawa) which considers factors such as people, equipment, machines and methods or the 5 whys method.

All causes must be checked and/ or proven and it is good to check why the problem was not noticed at the time it occurred.

D5 – Developing permanent corrective actions
As soon as the root cause of the problem has been identified, it is possible to search for the best possible solution. Again, various problem-solving methods can be used such as value analysis and creative problem solving.

From here, permanent corrective actions can be selected and it must be confirmed that the selected corrective actions will not cause undesirable side effects. It is therefore advisable to define contingency actions that will be useful in unforeseen circumstances.

D6 – Implementing permanent corrective actions
As soon as the permanent corrective actions are identified, they can be implemented. By planning ongoing controls, possible underlying root causes are detected far in advance.

The long-term effects should be monitored and unforeseen circumstances should be taken into account.

D7 – Preventative measures
Prevention is the best cure. This is why additional measures need to be taken to prevent similar problems. Preventative measures ensure that the possibility of recurrence is minimised. It is advisable to review management systems, operating systems and procedures, so that they can be improved procedures if necessary.

D8 – Congratulate the team
By congratulating the team on the results realised, all members are rewarded for their joint efforts. This is the most important step within the 8D method; without the team the root cause of the problem would not have been found and fixed.

By putting the team on a pedestal and sharing the knowledge throughout the organisation, team motivation will be high to solve a problem the next time it presents itself.

A key strength of the 8D Report is its focus on teamwork. The team as a whole is believed to be better and smarter than the sum of the qualities of the individuals. Not every problem justifies or requires the 8D Report. Furthermore, the 8D Report is a fact-based problem-solving process, which requires a number of specialised skills, as well as a culture of continuous improvement. It could be that training of the team members is required before 8D can work effectively within an organisation.

The team must recognise the importance of cooperation in order to arrive at the best possible solution for implementation

---

Problem Solving and Decision Making

Facts, Optimism, Cope, Understanding, Solve (FOCUS)
FOCUS Approach to Problem Solving

Facts/Problem Definition
The objective is to clearly state the problem and break it into manageable parts. Present facts in unambiguous, concrete terms, separate from assumptions and differentiate relevant from irrelevant information. Seek all available facts to answer who, what, when, where, why and how of the situation.

Optimism/Problem Orientation
The objective is to develop a sense of optimism regarding problem-solving ability. This includes instilling a belief that one is sufficiently skilled to solve problems, as well as instilling a sense of motivation to engage in problem-solving process while simultaneously regulating emotional experiences to maintain a sense of confidence.

Creativity/Generation of Alternative Solutions
The objective is to actively brainstorm multiple solutions to the problem of highest priority.

Understanding/Decision-making
The objective is to outline the process needed to make an informed, wise and appropriate choice that maximises the probability of a positive outcome. Making a decision about the "best" strategy to try and solve the problem requires a thoughtful consideration of gains and benefits of the best available strategies.

Solve/Implementation & Verification
The objective is solving the problem and then systematically reviewing the outcome to determine how the solution worked and the degree to which the actual outcome approximates the expected one. This self-monitoring is crucial for learning what made a solution effective or ineffective and how to implement a similar solution or use a different solution in the future.

Problem Definition Process
The Problem Definition Process is a tool that can be used to compare different problems, within an organisation or in a project and can highlight general problems that were previously unclear.

What initially appears to be the whole problem is often only a part or a symptom of a larger, deeper and more complex issue. The problem definition process helps to visualise the problem, by presenting it from different angles and to help define the broader context and associated problems.

Implementing the Problem Definition Process is especially effective when all stakeholders are involved. In this way, valuable insights can be developed about the size of the problem and its possible consequences. In addition, ideas can be developed about creative solutions, even if the solutions are not part of the problem definition process. However, defining the problem is essential before switching to, for

Problem Solving and Decision Making

example, a Root Cause Analysis, making an Ishikawa diagram or performing a cause-and-effect analysis.

Steps in the Problem Definition Process

1. Describe the vision
Start by describing how things should work in the most ideal situation. Before the problem is described or treated, a few sentences should be used to explain what the situation would be if the problem did not exist. Take, for example, the check-in protocol of a small airline. If every passenger has to check in at the airport, long queues develop as a result and this takes up a lot of time. An inefficient check-in protocol is time consuming and entails extra costs. This is a problem. After all, the aircraft has to depart as soon as possible. The check-in protocol must therefore be optimised, while making the situation understandable for all passengers.

2. Describe the problem
Accurately describing the problem is often half the work. Summarise the problem briefly and position the key information at the beginning of the single-phrase problem definition. In the case of the airline company, this could be that: The company's current check-in protocol is inefficient in use. By wasting man-hours, the current protocol makes the company less competitive and a slower check-in process creates an unfavourable brand image.

3. Describe the financial consequences of the problem
Once the problem is defined, it must be explained why it is a problem. After all, nobody has the means to solve every small problem. For example, if the airline transports 50 passengers per day and if the current check-in protocol wastes about 6 minutes per passenger, this results in a loss of about 5 hours per day, which amounts to £100 per day, or £36,500 per year. A cost-benefit analysis, for example, can show whether the investment into an online check-in portal can be recouped.

Lean's 5-times Why
It is advantageous to approach a problem with sufficient background information in order to spot previously unforeseen issues. When engaging in the Problem Definition Process, use Lean's "5 times why" method: who, what, where, when and why. While defining the problem definition, all five W's should be fully answered.

- *Who causes or can influence the problem?*
- *What would the situation be if the problem did not exist and what is the situation in the future if the problem persists?*
- *Where does the problem take place?*
- *When does the problem have to be solved?*
- *Why is it important to solve the problem?*
- *What are some questions that can be asked here?*
  - o *Is the problem temporary or permanent?*
  - o *How many people are affected by the problem?*

Problem Solving and Decision Making

   o *Does this analysis of the problem possibly affect existing knowledge, practices, or protocols?*

Refining the problem definition

Be concise
One thing to keep in mind when writing the problem definition is to keep it as short and clear as possible. The problem definition must not be longer than necessary and must be understood by everyone who reads it. Use clear, direct language and do not get stuck in small details. Only the essence of the problem should be dealt with.

Write for others
Since it is likeliest that different parties will be dealing with the problem, it is important that everyone interprets the problem in the same way. Therefore, adjust the tone, style and diction accordingly. Ask yourself: for whom am I writing this? Do these people know the same terms and concepts as I do? Do these people share the same attitude as I do?

Try to avoid using jargon
As mentioned above, the problem definition must be written in such a way that everyone interprets it correctly. This means that, unless it can be assumed that the reader does have the right knowledge, technical terminology should be avoided, or these terms should be explained.

Problems do not often solve themselves, which is why it is crucial to address problems without wasting time or inciting other inefficiencies. Since more than one party is usually working on a solution to the problem, the problem definition is the most important part of the solution because different interpretations of the problem cause a lot of uncertainty.

Use the Problem Definition Process to define the problem definition. By describing the ideal situation, explaining the problem and determining the consequences using the "five times why" method, one will be able to think 'outside the box' and ensure that the solution is a best fit for the problem.

Problem Solving and Decision Making

Analysing Data to Solve Problems

In most problem situations a lack of data is rarely a problem. In fact, the opposite is often the case: there is often too much information available to make a clear decision.

With so much data to sort through, more detail is needed about the data:

- *Is it the right data for answering your question?*
- *Can accurate conclusions be drawn from that data?*
- *Does the data inform the decision-making process?*

With the right data analysis processes and tools, what was once an overwhelming pile of unconnected data becomes a simple, clear piece of information to help make a decision.

When assessing the data to be used as part of the problem solving and decision-making process, there are some simple guidelines to follow. Data being used should be:

Current	*is it up to date is the data, is it the most recent data available?*
Reliable	*who and what is the source of the data, where has the data been collected from, how accurate is the data, is it misleading (intentionally or otherwise)?*
Relevant	*is it in a usable format, is it appropriate?*
Sufficient	*is there enough data to use and analyse?*
Valid	*is it pertinent to the decision, will it assist in reaching a conclusion?*
Obtainable	*is the data readily available?*
Cost-effective	*how much (money and/or time) will it take to obtain the data, is there time and money in the budget, is the cost worth the result cost benefit analysis?*

To improve data analysis skills and simplify decision making, execute these five steps in any data analysis process:

Step 1: Define the questions
Questions should be measurable, clear and concise. Design questions to either qualify or disqualify potential solutions to the specific problem or opportunity.

Start with a clearly defined problem:

> *A contractor is experiencing rising costs and is no longer able to submit competitive contract proposals.*

Problem Solving and Decision Making

One of many questions to solve this business problem might include: Can the company reduce its staff without compromising quality?

Step 2: Set Clear Measurement Priorities
This step breaks down into two sub-steps: a) Decide what to measure and b) Decide how to measure it.

a) Decide what to measure
Using the contractor example, consider what kind of data is needed to answer the key question. In this case, it would be the number and cost of current staff and the percentage of time they spend on necessary business functions. In answering this question many sub-questions may also need to be answered (e.g., are staff currently under-utilised? If so, what process improvements would help?).

Finally, the decision on what to measure, being sure to include any reasonable objections any stakeholders might have (e.g., If staff are reduced, how would the company respond to surges in demand?).

b) Decide how to measure it
Thinking about how to measure data is just as important, especially before the data collection phase, because the measuring process either backs up or discredits the analysis later on. Key questions to ask for this step include:

- *What is your time frame? (e.g., annual versus quarterly costs)*
- *What is your unit of measure? (e.g., Pound Sterling versus Euro)*
- *What factors should be included? (e.g., just annual salary versus annual salary plus cost of staff benefits)*

Step 3: Collect Data
With the question clearly defined and the measurement priorities set, now it is time to collect the data. As data is collected and organised, remember to keep these important points in mind:

- *Before you collect new data, determine what information could be collected from existing databases or sources on hand. Collect this data first.*
- *Determine a file storing and naming system ahead of time to help all tasked team members collaborate. This process saves time and prevents team members from collecting the same information twice.*
- *If you need to gather data via observation or interviews, then develop an interview template ahead of time to ensure consistency and save time.*
- *Keep your collected data organised in a log with collection dates and add any source notes as you go (including any data normalisation performed). This practice validates your conclusions down the road.*

Problem Solving and Decision Making

Step 4: Analyse Data
After the right data has been collected to answer the question from Step 1, it is time for deeper data analysis. Begin by manipulating the data in a number of different ways, such as plotting it out and finding correlations or by creating a pivot table in Excel.

Step 5: Interpret Results
After analysing the data and possibly conducting further research, it is finally time to interpret the results. As the analysis is interpreted, keep in mind that a hypothesis cannot ever be proved true, the hypothesis can only not be rejected. Meaning that no matter how much data is collected, chance could always interfere with the results.

As the results of the data are interpreted, ask these key questions:

- *Does the data answer your original question? How?*
- *Does the data help you defend against any objections? How?*
- *Is there any limitation on your conclusions, are there any angles which have not been considered?*

If the interpretation of the data holds up under all of these questions and considerations, then it is likely a productive conclusion has been reached. The only remaining step is to use the results of the data analysis process to decide the best course of action.

By following these five steps in the data analysis process, better decisions will be made because the choices are backed by data that has been robustly collected and analysed.

With practice, data analysis gets faster and more accurate – meaning better, more informed decisions are made to run the organisation most effectively.

Critical Analysis of Data

All the information used in the process of decision-making must be critically analysed and validated.

This can be undertaken in several ways including obtaining a second opinion or even a third. Cross-referencing the information provided with other sources can help to validate the information. Asking questions to relevant people, teams or companies is probably the easiest way to do this. Information gathered can be validated and its accuracy ensured by staying in touch with wider aspects of the business or trends and by reading associated journals, press releases, etc.

Other models that can be used to analyse data to support decision-making are:

- **decision trees** - *these allow you to map and consider all possible solutions to a decision you need to make*

Problem Solving and Decision Making

- *paired comparison analysis* - this allows you to compare a limited number of decisions and allocate them in order of importance.
- *grid analysis* - this allows you to compare options using the features or factors you want to consider before deciding
- *root cause analysis* - supports you to find out the root cause of a problem, you can then concentrate on finding out what happened, why it happened and act to reduce the chance of it happening again
- *cause and effect analysis* - this is a type of fishbone diagram that allows you to identify the main facts of the problem and drill down into possible causes. It was first developed in 1960 by Prof Kaoru Ishikawa.

Problem Solving and Decision Making

Escalating Problems

When a problem arises, it is important for everyone to know when and how to ask for help and escalate a problem. This could be asking a line manager for input, phoning a helpline for advice, or escalating a query to a specialist for help with a particular problem.

Organisations often specify their policies and procedures about escalation. These could cover, for example:

- *which types of issues must be escalated?*
- *who the issue should be escalated to?*
- *how and when this should be done?*
- *what happens after escalation?*

Procedures help to make sure that people do not promise or do things that could cause problems.
Even if the intentions are good, inappropriate promises, decisions or actions could be, for example:

- *illegal*
- *impossible to achieve*
- *unfair*
- *too expensive*

Identifying issues and how to escalate them

When the nature, scope and impact of a problem is analysed, issues often arise which cannot be handled by one person. There might be problems, queries, concerns, or suggestions that require input from others.

The structure of an organisation is very important, as people need to know who they should approach for the different problems which may arise. Job titles can vary, but employment contracts, job descriptions and training materials should show the hierarchy for the organisation. For example:

- *team members will usually escalate problems to their team leader, or supervisor*
- *team leaders and supervisors might refer a problem to their shift manager or a specialist from another department* – e.g., a team leader in the quality control department for help with product testing
- *managers will escalate to more senior managers or subject specialists*

Problems need to be identified and assessed as soon as possible, so they can be escalated, using the channels set out in the organisation's policies and procedures and get the help needed to finish tasks, make decisions or solve problems.
Reasons for escalating problems could include:

- *lack of authority*
- *lack of knowledge*
- *other options being exhausted*
- *organisational policies*

Lack of authority

Everyone must work within the limits of their authority. This helps make sure staff do not promise or do things that could cause further problems If the decision or action is outside the immediate area of responsibility, it must be escalated to the right person or department.

Lack of knowledge

If we lack the appropriate knowledge to deal with an issue, the matter must be referred to someone else for their assistance or input.

Other options being exhausted

When all other options have been exhausted and still unable to solve the problem, it must be escalated in order to solve the problem. Only spend so much time can be spent doing research and trying to solve problems. After a while, it becomes inefficient to spend too much time on an issue and it must be delegated to someone else. In addition, it could put oneself or others at risk of harm if responsibility is not escalated someone else.

Organisational policies

Sometimes the decision to escalate a problem is based on the procedures set out in the organisation's policies. Policies and procedures show limits of authority and give guidelines about how, when and where to escalate issues. This is particularly so when there might be financial, legal or health and safety consequences if issues are not deal with correctly.

Organisations have a duty of care towards their employees, customers and other stakeholders. They need to comply with a wide variety of legislation and regulations and they need to have robust and effective policies about when and how to escalate issues.

The following table gives some examples under each heading and suggestions about how each problem could be escalated:

Problem Solving and Decision Making

Reason for escalation	Example of type of issue to be escalated	Example of how the issue can be escalated
Lack of authority	A team leader prepares their quarterly report, but they are not authorised to submit it to the board of directors. A team member needs to make a £100 refund to a customer, but it is over their £50 authorised limit. A production manager proposes major changes to the department's budget. They do not have the authority to make final decisions about the allocation of funds.	The report needs to be escalated to their line manager to make comments and sign it off. They escalate the refund to their manager for authorisation. They need to escalate the issue to the production director to authorise the changes.
Lack of knowledge	A sales manager is drafting a new customer contract, but they need specialist legal knowledge to word it correctly. A tutor has problems with the computer network in their classroom. A new employee is unsure about an office procedure.	They escalate a draft contract to the organisation's legal department for advice and approval. They approach the in-house IT specialists and ask them to sort the problem. They escalate their query by asking an experienced colleague for help.
Other options being exhausted	An office manager has problems with a sophisticated photocopier/printer. They try the procedures shown in the instructions, look on websites and forums for advice, but cannot solve the problem. An experienced call centre employee tries everything they know to solve a customer complaint, but they are unsuccessful.	They escalate the issue by approaching the manufacturer direct and calling their helpline. An engineer is sent to sort the problem. They escalate the problem to their line manager.
Organisational policies	A production team leader spots a broken guard on a machine. They shut the machine down and stop everyone from using it. A facilities management company team member finds a used syringe in the public toilets. The organisation's policy is to report such matters to the head office helpline immediately.	They also escalate the matter to the company's safety officer, as specified in the policies and procedures. They escalate the issue straightaway and call the helpline. Specially trained staff are allocated to deal with the problem.

Problem Solving and Decision Making

Managing issues to resolution

When an issue has been escalated, it is important to be aware of what happens next and retain some ownership. We need to monitor the outcome of the problem so that we can, for example:

- **ensure the matter has been dealt with correctly** – e.g., making sure that the issue has not been forgotten
- **keep affected parties informed of progress and outcomes** – e.g., letting customers know how their problem is now being dealt with
- **help avoid further complaints or complications** – e.g., checking that improvements to products, services and procedures have been implemented as promised
- **maintain and improve good working relationships and reputations** – e.g., from handling complaints and problems well and seeing them through to resolution

When an issue is escalated, the person or department that is going to take the matter to the next stage must be trusted. This can be a difficult situation, especially if there is a good relationship with the colleague, customer or other stakeholder being helped. Therefore, to protect reputations and performance levels, make sure that the issue is dealt with properly.

Sometimes the evidence of progress will be easy to see – e.g., arranging for authorising signatures on a document that comes back to us. Sometimes progress is hard to assess and ways will need to be found to check that everything is going well – e.g., asking the line manager how they managed to resolve the issue. In other situations, there may be no further contact once an issue has been escalated and it may not be possible to gain informal feedback or information about what happened next.

Escalation is useful and necessary so that team leaders and managers can take steps to put things right and improve products, services and procedures for everyone. If issues are not escalated and progress tracked, decision-makers will not have the information they need to:

- **understand how new problems are handled** – e.g., by analysing the effectiveness of procedures
- **offer consistent standards of products and services** – e.g., by checking outcomes
- **keep complaints to a minimum** – e.g., by ensuring improvements are in place
- **support their staff and identify training and career development needs** – e.g., by identifying and addressing weaknesses in the escalation process
- **comply with regulations and legislation** – e.g., by ensuring that problems are resolved fully
- **improve and maintain standards for the organisation as a whole** – e.g., by making sure that good intentions follow through to full resolution of issues

An organisation's escalation policies and procedures tend to cover:

- **which types of issue must be escalated** – e.g., outside limits of authority or knowledge
- **who the issue should be escalated to** – e.g., line managers; HR department; health and safety manager; legal department; manufacturers and suppliers

---

- *how this should be done* – e.g., via email, telephone call or face-to-face
- *when this should be done* – e.g., immediately, within a week or on a daily basis

Chapter 9: Finance

Finance

Business

There are three principal sectors within business. These are:

- *Private Sector*
- *Public Sector*
- *Voluntary / Third Sector*

The private sector includes all the businesses who are in Private ownership and strive to make a profit. At its most simple, we have the self-employed which could be a one-man band, to a partnership of two or more individuals who work together to make money and are sometimes referred to as a firm. Such organisations are usually privately owned and the people who operate it keep all the profits and divide it between themselves in a previously agreed manner.

The next type of organisation is a Private Company. A company is essentially a legal entity in its own right. It may or may not be limited. The term limited refers to whether or not the liability of the company is limited to the value of its shares and assets or whether the directors have absolute liability for all debts. There are tax benefits depending on the structure of the company.

The next type of company is a Public Limited Company. This indicates the company is owned by shareholders and those shares are available for purchase by anyone on the stock market. People will buy the shares in order to receive a dividend. The divided is paid once or twice a year and the amount paid will depend on the success or otherwise of the company.

Organisations are legally required to take care of their financial obligations. They need to keep records that can be used to show relevant stakeholders that operations are being run properly and in accordance with legislation, regulations and rules.

Depending on the type of organisation, the internal and external stakeholders that need to be satisfied about financial issues will vary.

Internal stakeholders who need to be satisfied about how an organisation looks after its financial procedures could include, for example:

- **business owners** – *e.g., sole proprietors or partners who need to know the levels of profit and cash flow*
- **shareholders** – *e.g., employees or others who own shares in a company who need to keep an eye on their investment*
- **employees** – *e.g., who rely on the organisation to operate payroll and bonus systems*

Finance

External stakeholders could include, for example:

- *banks and other lenders* – e.g., who provide business loans to the organisation
- *national and local government agencies* – e.g., who collect taxes and provide grants
- *external customers* – e.g., individuals and companies who buy and use the organisation's products and services
- *charity commission* – e.g., who examine accounts and regulate registered charities

Government departments and agencies are also external stakeholders and are responsible for applying finance-related legislation and regulations and the collection of duties and taxes. For example:

- *HM Revenue and Customs (HMRC)* – e.g., for VAT, tax and national insurance; money laundering regulations
- *Companies House* – where accounts and reports are held for limited companies as public records
- *the Financial Conduct Authority (FCA)* – for the financial services industry
- *the Prudential Regulation Authority (PRA)* – for banks and other financial institutions
- *the Pensions Regulator* – for workplace pensions

Some finance-related legislation is covered by criminal law, such as the Bribery Act 2010.

It is important to consider finance-related governance and compliance that organisations need to follow in order to carry out their activities legally and correctly. These include:

- *the purpose of governance and compliance in finance*
- *governance and compliance processes*
- *implications of unresolved governance and compliance issues*

Finance

Governance and Compliance in Finance

All businesses must have governance – a system by which they are directed and controlled. Depending on the type of organisation, governance can be performed by, for example, proprietors, business partners, a board of directors or trustees. The organisation's systems need to focus on compliance with the various legislation and regulations that apply to its industry, environment, legal entity and circumstances.

This section will investigate:

- *key aims of governance and compliance*
- *an organisation's framework of rules and practices*
- *issues that governance and compliance aim to avoid and mitigate*
- *how governance and compliance relate to financial management*

Key Aims of Governance and Compliance

Organisations need to operate in compliance with a wide variety of financial rules, regulations and legislation that vary according to the type of organisation and their activities.

There can be internal compliance requirements where the key aims are to comply with requirements set out in the organisation's policies and procedures, for example:

- *how sales need to be recorded*
- *how often reports need to be generated*
- *how to use systems that track banking activities*
- *information needed for monthly reports sent to head office*
- *how to prepare quarterly reviews for shareholders*
- *systems to check and monitor compliance*

POLICIES & PROCEDURES

There are many more legal requirements imposed by external stakeholders. It is a requirement of all organisations to satisfy these legal requirements by, for example:

- *paying the right amounts of tax* – e.g., PAYE tax and national insurance, VAT or corporation tax
- *paying the correct level of minimum wage*
- *making contributions to workplace pensions* – e.g., to comply with the Pension Regulator's requirements
- *keeping adequate records* – e.g., audited accounts for large companies
- *using, storing and disposing of financial information correctly* – e.g., in accordance with the General Data Protection Regulations 2018 (GDPR)
- *submitting accurate returns on time* – e.g., to HMRC or Companies House
- *avoiding making bribes* – e.g., to conform with the Bribery Act 2010
- *satisfying industry-specific requirements* – e.g., FCA requirements for financial services organisations

Finance

There can also be costs associated with compliance – e.g., accountancy fees for preparing and submitting accounts; consultancy fees for compliance advice and strategy making.

To achieve compliance, organisations need good governance – the system by which organisations are directed and controlled, such as a board of directors or trustees. Financial governance is necessary to enable organisations to:

- *keep up to date with new legislation and stakeholder expectations*
- *increase efficiency and revenue*
- *lower the costs of compliance*
- *avoid fines and penalties*
- *avoid damage to their reputation*

A framework of rules and practices

The framework an organisation uses will depend on is size, type and activities. In a small company that owns and runs a single high-street shop, the rules and practices could be geared up to a part-time bookkeeper who, for example:

- *counts and banks takings from the shop*
- *deals with electronic payments made on the shop's card machine*
- *deals with payments to suppliers*
- *accounts for VAT on sales and purchases*
- *does a monthly payroll for three employees and two directors and sends the tax and national insurance to HMRC*
- *makes the company's payment into staff pensions*
- *keeps and balances banking records*
- *sends all bookkeeping records to the accountant to prepare and submit annual accounts and returns for HMRC and Companies House*

In bigger organisations, similar activities will still take place, but will be administered on a bigger scale. For a national chain of stores, for example, there will be an entire department to deal with accounts, payroll, etc. The rules and practices will be laid down in a range of policies and procedures that the staff have to follow to make sure that the organisation is compliant.

Some large organisations may outsource their administrative, payroll and financial record-keeping to specialist companies – e.g., many local councils engage companies who provide a full range of administration support services. These specialist companies' systems are geared up to full compliance, but the organisation still has responsibilities to provide the correct information.

Finance

Issues that governance and compliance aim to avoid and mitigate

Broadly speaking, governance and compliance aim to avoid and mitigate issues such as:

- *fraud* – e.g., procedures to shred documents to prevent identity theft
- *theft* – e.g., using CCTV to monitor staff using a cash till
- *tax evasion* – e.g., procedures to make sure that cash payments are declared
- *criminal activity* – e.g., taking bribes or trafficking workers
- *misuse of funds and resources* – e.g., monitoring budgets closely to reduce waste and unnecessary spending
- *inefficiency* – e.g., from not monitoring waste or opportunities to steal cash or goods

Sometimes actions are deliberate and have a criminal intent – e.g., knowingly employing people who are illegal immigrants or those who have been trafficked, stealing products or cash. Some actions are due to negligence and ignorance – e.g., from someone not realising that they need to provide workplace pensions for their employees; under-declaring VAT due to lack of knowledge about the rules.

How governance and compliance relate to financial management

When dealing with financial management, managers need to make sure that the governance and compliance procedures are in place and up to date. They need to make sure that people working for the organisation are:

- *aware of their legal obligations for their specific industry and activities*
- *following policies and procedures*
- *keeping their knowledge up to date*

Procedures need to be tested and monitored to make sure that they are robust enough to identify and deal with any non-compliance.

Finance

Governance and Compliance Processes

Organisations have a variety of processes to deal with their financial affairs. They support the organisation's activities, aid efficiency and make sure that activities are compliant with the internal and external requirements for each situation. Processes cover, for example:

- *financial reporting*
- *dealing with income*
- *record-keeping*
- *audits*

Financial Reporting

Organisations produce a range of financial reports, including:

- ***income and expenditure statements*** – *to show income, expenses and profits over a period of time – enabling the organisation to see how well it is performing.*
- ***balance sheets*** – *giving a 'snapshot' of the assets and liabilities at any given time, usually at the end of the financial year.*
- ***cash flow statements*** – *to show what cash is available and moving through the organisation, so that managers can see what they can afford to do.*
- ***annual accounts and statutory returns*** – *to show a true picture of the organisation's income, expenditure, assets and liabilities at any given time, often after being audited by registered practitioners or chartered accountants.*

Financial reports are used by managers when preparing business plans and to monitor progress. Investors and shareholders use the information to make decisions about funding and investment choices. They are also used in the preparation of statutory returns and reports, including:

- *corporation or income tax returns sent to HM Revenue and Customs*
- *VAT returns*
- *PAYE returns* – **e.g., to declare tax and national insurance for the workforce**
- *audited accounts* – *e.g., to be submitted to the Charities Commission, shareholders or lenders*
- *company returns to Companies House*

Financial reporting may be provided in paper or computer derived formats, these will be identified in their policies, procedures, training records and accounting manuals.

Finance

Dealing with Income

Various methods are used to track income and expenditure to make sure that organisations comply with internal and external requirements. Ways to safeguard income could include:

- *checking cash against till records at the end of each shift*
- *requiring employees to sign for floats when they change shifts*
- *checking income against stock levels* – e.g., to make sure that staff are not giving away stock for nothing
- *requiring supervisors or managers authorising refunds above a certain amount*
- *doing bank reconciliations against sales invoices and ledgers* – e.g., to track income and make sure everything has cleared
- *having automated stock and security systems* – e.g., bar code systems that track each item, using CCTV
- *doing spot checks* – e.g., open checks by managers; covert checks with mystery shoppers observing procedures at the point of sale
- *checking identities of new customers when large amounts of money are being spent or deposited* – e.g., to safeguard against money laundering
- *having robust procedures for international transactions*
- *using and monitoring reliable electronic payment systems* – e.g., PayPal
- *managing debtors* – e.g., chasing outstanding payments that are due from customers

Record-Keeping

It is a legal requirement that businesses need to set up and maintain records that meet the requirements of governance and compliance which apply to their situation and activities. When designing ways to keep records, organisations need to consider:

- *the type of information*
- *the people who are going to access the records*
- *the security and confidentiality of the contents*
- *how it needs to be circulated and shared*

There are many ways of organising electronic and paper-based financial information, for example:

- *in sales and purchase ledgers* – electronic and paper-based
- *in cash books* – electronic or manual
- *paper forms, reports and files*

The guidelines in the General Data Protection Regulations provide a good framework about how records need to be organised as it covers how data is used, stored and deleted. Processes need to be in place for every aspect of recording of financial information:

Finance

- *ensuring that only authorised people have access* – *e.g., by having passwords and security passes; using encryption for electronic data; vetting staff who handle sensitive information; using information for the correct purposes only*
- *storing paper-based and electronic data safely* – *e.g., with password access; locking files away in fireproof storage; archiving records safely in a secure warehouse or data management facility*
- *destroying records correctly* – *e.g., shredding paper; using a secure disposal agency; destroying backed-up information on hard drives and other IT systems securely*

In addition, organisations need to comply with requirement to keep records for different lengths of time. Some records need to be kept indefinitely and others can be destroyed securely after a short period of time, so processes need to be in place to monitor and manage this. Organisations need to make sure that they store information for the correct amount of time.

Audits

Some organisations are required to perform audits to provide stakeholders with assurance that financial statements are accurate. An audit is a three-dimensional inspection and review of all aspects of an organisation to make sure that everything balances and complies with relevant regulatory requirements.

In a medium-sized company, for instance, a registered auditor from the firm's accountants will be tasked to check samples of records to make sure that reports are accurate and truly representative. They make look at, for example:

- *sales ledgers* – *to check the level of income received*
- *cash books* – *to see that the income has been banked correctly*
- *debtors* – *to assess the amount of money owed to the company*
- *stock* – *to see that the stock records are accurate and to give the remaining stock a value as an asset*
- *purchase ledgers* – *to check that costs put through the business are correct, legal and compliant*
- *bank reconciliations* – *to see that payments in and out are all balanced or accounted for*
- *creditors* – *to see how much the company owes at the end of its financial year*
- *payroll records* – *to make sure that tax, national insurance and pension contributions have been dealt with and paid correctly*
- *VAT returns* – *to ensure that the correct amounts have been declared and paid*

During the process, the auditor will check that other regulations are complied with – e.g., money laundering or data protection.

Finance

Processes need to be robust and transparent to enable audits to be performed that can provide an accurate view of the organisation to internal and external stakeholders – e.g., shareholders, lenders and HMRC.

Implications of unresolved governance and compliance issues

There can be serious implications if governance and compliance issues are unresolved. Failure to address governance and compliance can cause internal issues that, for example:

- *result in theft and loss of income* – *e.g., if sales and transactions are not monitored correctly*
- *cause longer-term financial problems for the organisation* – *e.g., from paying compensation and having to repay money that has been taken; from a drop in share value as investors lose confidence*
- *lead to a breach of contract* – *e.g., being sued for releasing information*
- *cause a security problem* – *e.g., a personal attack or terrorist threat if security arrangements are leaked; passwords and access codes being used by unauthorised people*
- *cause embarrassment* – *e.g., if personal details or financial records are made public*
- *give competitors an advantage* – *e.g., from gaining access to confidential operational data*
- *increased compliance costs* – *e.g., restructuring costs as a consequence of prosecution or loss of reputation*
- *increased staff turnover and related costs* – *e.g., from staff not wanting to work for an employer with a poor reputation*

There can also be serious implications if an organisation's external stakeholders take action in response to governance and compliance failures – e.g., government agencies or customers who take enforcement or legal action. Actions could, for example:

- *result in fines and penalties* – *e.g., from paying insufficient tax*
- *result in compensation payments* – *e.g., to customers when financial data has been mishandled*
- *result in the organisation losing customers* – *e.g., from having a bad and unprofessional reputation*
- *cause financial problems for customers* – *e.g., if their bank accounts are hacked as a result*
- *lead to prosecution of the employer and/or employees* – *e.g., under the Data Protection Act, Bribery Act or Money Laundering regulations*

The consequences of failure can seriously affect an organisation's ability to survive and thrive due to additional costs and loss of reputation.

Finance

Value for Money

According to the Oxford dictionary, the phrase **value for money** is:

> *'used in reference to something that is well worth the money spent on it'.*

The concept of value for money encourages organisations to make the best use of their resources to achieve objectives. Today, "value for money" has changed to become a term for something which is cheap. Value for Money supermarkets are considered to sell cheap lower grade products. A better term to bring this back into context is to think of the term "value for price"

Offering value for money/price helps an organisation to have a good reputation and stand out against competitors. In the workplace, when organisations concentrate on giving value for money, this can refer to:

- *products and services that are provided for external customers* – e.g., *supermarket goods, cars or legal services*
- *services delivered to internal customers* – e.g., *credit control staff who collect money owed to the organisation; maintenance teams who look after the buildings and other facilities*

Organisations also work to receive value for money when they manage, for example:

- *operations* – e.g., *refining policies and procedures to be as efficient as possible*
- *suppliers* – e.g., *services provided by specialist contractors and consultants, suppliers of raw materials and other goods*
- *human resources* – e.g., *employees, HR departments and management costs*
- *physical resources* – e.g., *equipment and machinery; factories, offices and retail outlets*
- *finance* – e.g., *finding the best business loans for a business venture*
- *waste* – e.g., *energy, time, human and physical resources*

Achieving value for money/price helps an organisation to operate efficiently and effectively, which is an important element when delivering profits to shareholders and securing jobs for employees.

Many organisations also have a statutory responsibility to achieve value for money – e.g., when using public funds.

Finance

Achieving value for money when working with suppliers and customers
There are many things that organisations can do to give and receive value for money when
working with suppliers and customers.

Customers
Customers have expectations and they want:

- *an efficient and polite service before, during and after a transaction (buying or using products or services)*
- *good-quality and value-for-money products and services*
- *any complaints and problems to be dealt with properly*
- *their opinion to matter*

An organisation needs to offer good customer service and value for money at all times so that
it can survive and thrive. If the customers are satisfied with the products or services, they
return and they recommend the organisation to others. Quite simply, this keeps the
organisation alive and means that their employees' jobs are safer.

Organisations offer value for money to customer through, for example:

- *the range of goods and services offered* – e.g., *offering budget and luxury ranges*
- *pricing* – e.g., *offering competitive prices; grouping complementary products together as a bundle*
- *discounts* – e.g., *buy one get one free*
- *Incentives* – e.g., *10% off if customers buy today*
- *delivery options* – e.g., *free for standard delivery when customers spend above a minimum amount, charges for overnight or weekend delivery*
- *installation options* – e.g., *charges for installing household appliances like washing machines*
- *warranties* – e.g., *free or low-cost extended warranties on electrical goods that guarantee repairs or replacement if there are faults after the period covered by the manufacturer*
- *returns policies* – e.g., *rules about exchanges or refunds on returned items that are not faulty*
- *other value-added features* – e.g., *loyalty card points; membership and privilege cards*

Products and services need to be in line with the standards promised in catalogues, brochures,
websites, customer charters, company policies, etc. They may also be covered in a Service
Level Agreement (SLA) between two parties.

Finance

Suppliers

When working with suppliers, organisations can negotiate the same things because they are now the customers. In smaller organisations, managers and directors will make the decisions about how to obtain value for money when managing human and physical resources. Larger organisations can have procurement specialists and departments – e.g., in national supermarket chains or the Ministry of Defence.

Whatever the size of the organisation, the principles are the same. Physical resources need to be:

- *fit for purpose* – *of sufficient quality for the intended use*
- *sustainable* – *from sources that can maintain the supply chain for future purchases*
- *ethically and legally sourced* – *e.g., to comply with the organisation's own ethical policies*
- *able to be reused, recycled or reconditioned* – *where possible at the end of their useful working lives*

These factors are important when assessing value for money as money is not the only consideration. Even if something is incredibly cheap, if it is not fit for purpose, it will not provide value for money.

In parallel to these factors, organisations will also negotiate with suppliers to get deals – e.g., the best prices and discounts; favourable delivery and installation options; inexpensive and effective warranties and aftercare service; other added-value features that may be available.

Teams or departments delivering value for money

Teams and departments can also make the most of the organisation's resources and energy use to maximise value for money. There can be a mixture of obvious and hidden costs that need to be monitored as they all form part of the running costs that have to be met by the organisation.

Teams or departments can deliver value for money for the organisation by:

- *reviewing costs and operational activities regularly*
- *using resources efficiently*
- *using energy efficiently*

Reviewing costs and operational activities regularly

Managers need to review how their team or department spends its budgets on a regular basis, to make sure that funds are being allocated in the most efficient way to achieve objectives and maintain quality. They need to look at all aspects to make sure that everything is fit for purpose and good value for money, for example:

- *fixed costs* – *e.g., machinery and equipment*

Finance

- *variable costs* – e.g., raw materials or components
- *human resources* – e.g., to make sure that the right people are being employed at the right cost to achieve the team's objectives and quality standards
- *working practices* – e.g., to make sure that procedures are relevant and efficient
- *outsourcing opportunities* – e.g., analysing whether it is better to perform some activities in-house or to outsource them to specialist companies

Organisations need a framework for discussing and reviewing all aspects so that managers and others can:

identify areas that need improvement
address potential problems
work collaboratively to make decisions about maximising value for money

Using resources efficiently

When looking to improve the use of resources in the workplace that are related to external customers, managers need to consider, for example:

- *reducing packaging* – e.g., encouraging customers to buy loose vegetables and fruit; using smaller boxes, aerosol cans or plastic bags; cutting out unnecessary packaging; using refill packs of coffee rather than new jars every time
- *developing packaging that uses fewer resources* – e.g., boxes that stay together with folds rather than glue, reusable bags for customers
- *reducing consumables given out* – e.g., giving out one serviette per customer rather than letting them help themselves to a handful; smaller serviettes or tray liners; small hygienic packets of butter rather than a dish of butter that might be wasted

When keeping down operational costs of the team or department, managers may consider, for example:

- *reusing materials* – e.g., storage boxes and trays that can be used many times; using china mugs rather than disposable cups
- *avoiding scrap or waste* – e.g., managing portion control in a restaurant; training and monitoring production staff in a factory to help cut down on rejects and wasted materials; checking cutting patterns to make sure that they are as efficient as possible
- *reviewing, designing or adjusting procedures, products or services* – to maximise the use of resources
- *electronic communication* – rather than printed paper; emails or texts rather than paper memos
- *telephone and videoconferencing* – rather than travelling around the UK or abroad for meetings

Finance

- *using technology effectively* – e.g., using smart meters or sophisticated tills to measure consumption and target production efficiently; stock tracking systems to support Just-In-Time supply chain management; computer-based training for staff
- *working to improve staff retention* – e.g., managing the team well to avoid excessive recruitment and training costs that occur when there is a high turnover of staff
- *ensuring work practices support compliance* – e.g., to help avoid unnecessary investigations, legal proceedings, fines, penalties, compensation and loss of reputation

Managers need to be aware of changes to technology, products and processes to see if there are well-researched, better alternatives.

Using energy efficiently

When considering how to improve the use of energy and deliver value for money, managers will look at, for example:

- *more efficient buildings* – e.g., better insulation; improving weaker areas notes on the EPC (Energy Performance Certificate); good-quality glazing with thermal qualities; efficient heating and air conditioning systems; improving the layout within the building to maximise efficiency; solar panels
- *energy-efficient appliances and equipment* – e.g., heat pumps for heating and air conditioning; A-rated appliances, such as fridges; low-energy lighting where possible; reduced-energy standby modes on appliances
- *more efficient vehicles* – e.g., with low CO_2 emissions; electric vehicles, especially for short trips; with more efficient engine technology; planning routes and times of journeys to reduce mileage and time spent in traffic jams
- *switching off unnecessary electrical items* – e.g., lights, office machines, air conditioning and heating when not in use
- *using more sympathetic packaging materials* – e.g., looking at packaging with a lower carbon footprint
- *consolidation of working hours* – so that the building only has to be fully operational for a shorter time
- *home working* – e.g., reducing an organisation's costs if they can use a smaller building; saves commuter time, expense and emissions, although there is an energy cost from using the employee's home
- *telephone and videoconferencing* – e.g., using technology to hold virtual meetings, especially when participants are many miles apart
- *longer but less frequent meetings* – e.g., making the most of people having travelled to meet up so that they do not have to meet so often
- *the carbon footprint of the different options* – e.g., having a small, low-energy photocopier might seem to be a good option, but if it cannot cope with the load and has to be replaced every six months, the overall costs will be higher over a year

Finance

Budgets

The financial management process comprises three elements:

- *Planning*
- *Trading*
- *Year end*

Trading

The trading element of financial management is the recording of all the financial activity which takes place on a real-time basis.

Financial data is captured and recorded as transactions happen and is then stored until the end of the week, when it will be consolidated until a four weeks' worth of data has been captured, when the weekly records will be consolidated into monthly records. These will be further processed to produce quarterly and finally, annual records.

The trading information is captured in the Trading Account. This is a simple calculation where the costs of production are deducted from the total sales, to calculate the gross profit which the business has generated over the trading period.

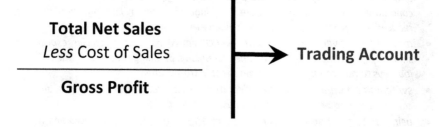

In a small business such as a café, it would not be difficult to calculate how much food has been used over a week and how much has been generated in sales and so calculate the Gross Profit for the week or month.

The process can become a little more complicated when an organisation has high stock levels as it will be more difficult to calculate exactly how much stock has been used. Similarly, if the Café were to accept credit and debit cards, although the money has been taken, it may take a day or two for the money to appear in the bank account so this may affect the financial records. When an organisation operates a sales invoicing system, the money charged for goods may not actually be received for months after they have been produced and delivered to the customer and this would also need to be reflected in some of the financial reports. All of this, however, is the concern of the accountant and not the Team Leader!

Another aspect of Trading is the recording of the costs incurred in producing a product or delivering a service. Without staff, nothing would get done and so wages and salaries are a

Finance

cost which has to be paid. Energy will be needed to produce goods and services. There may be rent and business rates to pay. Fuel will be needed to provide transport and so the list goes on. The list of costs can be extensive, even for a relatively small operation.

All of these costs are recorded in a second account called the Profit and Loss account. The profit and loss account does exactly as its name suggests – it calculates whether the business has made a profit or a loss by totalling all of the costs and subtracting them from the Gross Profit.

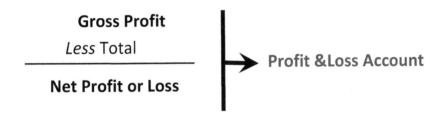

This fairly short report provides the basis for almost all financial planning. In a small business the proprietor may compile the budgets, whilst in a larger organisation there may be specific teams assigned to deal with each level of budgetary control.

Year End

The year-end accounts are the result of a year's worth of trading and therefore is a historic record of trading activity and cannot be changed.

The trading records are the tools used to produce the year end reports and are captured on a day by day, week by week basis throughout the trading period and therefore also record historical activity and likewise, cannot be changed.

Planning

The third element is the planning stage and it is this stage which is key to the success of the business.

The trading and year end elements deal with what has happened and cannot be changed. The planning stage records what we anticipate will happen during the forthcoming year.

Planning starts with a table or spreadsheet into which the values we expect to see on the Trading, Profit and Loss account are entered. By entering numbers as accurately as possible, the Trading for the next month, quarters or year can be modelled and help to envisage what may happen to the business in the forthcoming year.

Finance

This financial modelling provides many benefits for the business as it will allow a "what if" calculation to be performed. What if inflation causes prices to rise by 6%? What if the minimum wage rose by 4%? All of these scenarios can be modelled and allow plans to be put in place should that situation arise.

The problem of course, is that in the real World, calculating these values can be a challenge. Fortunately, for most Team Leaders, this work is done by other people, however, it is still important to understand the process.

What is immediately clear is that budgeting is basically one big guessing game!

Who could have foreseen or anticipated the COVID pandemic? This was an extreme situation and business as usual is typically far more stable and predictable. However, there are some things we can do to improve the "guessing game".
The first thing is to find ways to make the guesses more accurate.

Step one is to sort the costs into groups. These are known as fixed costs and variable costs. Fixed costs stay the same for a period of time, irrespective of the volume of business, whilst variable costs will rise and fall as production increases and decreases.

Fixed costs include, but are not limited to, the following:

- *Rent*
- *Rates*
- *Mortgage payments*
- *Loan repayments*
- *Insurances*
- *Maintenance contracts*
- *Licences*
- *Etc.*

These costs will remain the same for a period of time, typically at least one year, so these amounts are known with some accuracy and can be entered straight into the table. When renewing insurances, contracts, etc, there may well be some change in price, but this is fairly easy to estimate and should be fairly accurate.

The variable costs are more difficult to anticipate because they will change with the volume of business.

The million-pound question is – "What will the sales be next year?"

Finance

The simple answer is we have no idea! What we have to do is guess what we think they will be, but a business will not survive long on guesses, so we need to make educated or qualified estimates rather than out and out guessing.

Example:

Sales last year were £100,000. What may cause those sales to rise or fall? The change in social attitudes and legislation towards smoking means that there are now only very few tobacconists left on the high street – if our sales were generated from the sales of tobacco products, sales forecasts for next year may be fairly grim. Alternatively, if we manufacture components for Electric vehicle charging points - our sales forecast may look very healthy.

Inflation will affect sales too. An inflation rate of 5% means that the selling price of goods or services produced would need to increase by at least 5% - just to stand still, because the cost of components and other costs will also rise by 5%. Sales would therefore be expected to rise to £105,000, just from an inflationary price increase.

Is the marketing team planning a sales campaign, is there a new product to be launched, is demand for our product or service likely to rise, what does the Government predict will happen to business across the nation? These are all questions which must be answered to begin to make and educated "guesstimate" of the sales for the next twelve months.
The remaining figures need to be based on educated and informed estimations, based on good knowledge of the industry and marketplace, current trends, likely inflation, worldwide and domestic political events and any other relevant factors. Examples of estimations could include:

- *estimated revenue streams based on anticipated sales of a new product* – to help calculate a budget for new raw materials to make the next batch of the product
- *an estimate of the number of people likely to buy tickets for an event* – to help calculate possible revenue from the project
- *the estimated exchange rate between sterling and the Euro in a year's time* – to help calculate the value of future exports to Europe
- *the estimated number of patients likely to use NHS accident and emergency services over the winter* – to help calculate the cost of agency staff who might need to be employed short term
- *estimated birth rates in ten years' time* – to help to create a long-term budget for primary and secondary schools
- *estimates of the amount of stationery that is likely to be used by a department* – to assist when preparing the departmental budget for next year

These estimations enable people to make reasonably well-informed, calculated guesses, estimates and decisions about future activities.

Finance

Budget Structure

Budgets are estimates of income and expenditure for a set period of time. When setting realistic budgets, managers need to look at:

- **fixed costs** – *expenses that stay the same, regardless of sales rising or falling – e.g., rent and insurance*
- **variable costs** – *expenses that change according to sales volumes – e.g., raw materials used to make the products*
- **income** – *and likely income*

In addition, it is important to identify timescales, priorities and financial resources when preparing a budget to ensure that everything is accounted for:

- **timescales** – *to show when money is due to come in and out – e.g., when income is due; when sales invoices are issued; how quickly customers pay; how quickly purchase invoices need to be paid; deadlines for paying taxes*
- **priorities** – *to target resources correctly to support the efficiency and effectiveness of the organisation – e.g., prioritising workforce costs, essential purchases and urgent capital investments*
- **financial resources** – *to match funding with anticipated income and expenditure – e.g., using an overdraft for short-term cash flow problems; financing long-term projects with business loans; anticipated increases in sales revenue*

The budget tends to mirror the structure of the Trading, Profit and Loss account to simplify the process of comparing the budget to past trading.

There are standard systems of accounting practice which set out the levels at which budgets should be measured and evaluated and these will vary across different business sectors. A common standard sets seven levels of budgetary control and these are:

- *Sales*
- *Cost of Sales*
- *Gross Profit*
- *Variable Costs*
- *Operating Profit*
- *Fixed Costs*
- *Net Profit*

This slightly changes the layout of the Profit and Loss account which was discussed above and when joined to the Trading account it will look like the example below.

Finance

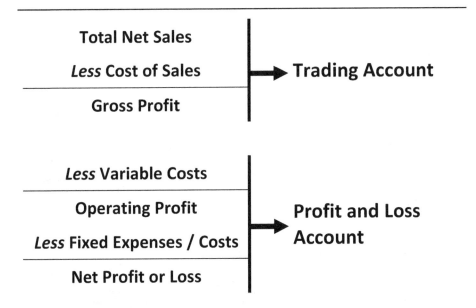

For example, the sales team may be responsible for calculating what they anticipate sales will be over the forthcoming period and the people responsible for buying the components or raw materials will be responsible for deciding what may happen to cost prices over the year and whether there will be the opportunity to obtain volume discounts based on the sales planned by the sales team. These two teams will plan what they think will happen and this will allow the budgeted Gross Profit to be calculated. It will be for the head of finance to decide if this is acceptable or whether prices need to rise, sales need to increase, or costs need to be reduced. If that is the case, the two teams will go back to the drawing board and review the figures they have calculated.

It would be foolhardy at best and downright incompetent otherwise, to try and manipulate the figures to achieve a desired outcome, without any plan or justification for how the proposed figures might be achieved.

It does not matter how grim the results are that is the realistic situation and practical ways must be identified to work around the problem.

Finance

Where there is historic information, this can be a great starting point when planning a budget. By looking at how the business behaved in the previous period, it is easier to anticipate how it might perform in the future.

Now the variable costs have to be dealt with. Variable costs are sometimes called controllable costs or controllable expenses. This is because they are controlled directly by the management. They will also change or vary in direct proportion to the business as it increases and decreases.

"Play around with these figures, Harry. I've given you the total I want them to add up to."

Trading, Profit and Loss Account		
Sales		100,000
Less Cost of Sales		30,000
Gross profit		70,000
Variable costs		
Wages	28,000	
Gas	9,000	
Electricity	7,000	
Fuel	4,000	
Less total Variable Costs		48,000
Operating Profit		22,000
Fixed costs		
Rent	15,000	
Rates	3,000	
Loan repayment	2,000	
Less total Variable Costs		20,000
Net Profit (Loss)		2,000

In the example it is clear to see what the costs were for the previous year, but it does not really help with planning for next year until percentages are added for each cost. This is the percentage of the total sales they represent. There is no reason to think that that proportion is likely to change next year unless we decide to change it. It is quick and easy therefore to simply use the same percentages for each variable cost next year

Finance

	Previous Year			Budget	
Sales	100,000	100%			100%
Less Cost of Sales	30,000	30%			30%
Gross profit	70,000	70%			70%
Variable costs					
Wages	28,000	28%			28%
Gas	9,000	9%			9%
Electricity	7,000	7%			7%
Fuel	4,000	4%			4%
Less total Variable Costs	48,000	48%			48%
Operating Profit	22,000	22%			22%
Fixed costs					
Rent	15,000	15%	15,000	
Rates	3,000	3%	3,000	
Loan repayment	2,000	2%	2,000	
Less Total fixed Costs	20,000	20%	20,000	
Net Profit (Loss)	2,000	2%		

Calculating the percentage

The calculation for working out the percentage of each cost is quite simple and can be easily entered into a spreadsheet, it is simply the value of the cost expressed as a percentage of the total sales.

$$\frac{\text{Value of the Cost}}{\text{Total Sales}} \quad X \quad 100 \quad = \quad \text{Percentage}$$

Completing the Budget

Once the budget has reached this point, the Budgeted sales value should be entered and a spreadsheet can be configured to calculate the rest of the values. The budget can then be adjusted and corrected to present a realistic forecast of what the future may look like.

It is the responsibility of the management responsible for these costs to minimise them. In much the same way as we manage of own domestic costs by switching energy supplier, using different suppliers to buy certain items, economising, etc. so, it is the responsibility of the management team to minimise the variable costs the business incurs.

Finance

By minimising variable costs the business can maximise the operating profit.

Using the budget

Once the budget has been agreed it can be converted into a working document. The first step is break down the planned budget into monthly Trading forecast. The monthly sales percentage from previous years should be reviewed and budgeted sales broken down month by month. The percentages from the budget can be entered and a spreadsheet would calculate the budget for each month.

Below is an example of the completed budget:

	Previous Year			Budget	
Sales	100,000	100%		130,000	100%
Less Cost of Sales	30,000	30%		36,400	28%
Gross profit	70,000	70%		93,600	72%
Variable costs					
Wages	28,000	28%		33,800	26%
Gas	9,000	9%		11,700	9%
Electricity	7,000	7%		9,100	7%
Fuel	4,000	4%		5,200	4%
Less Total variable costs	48,000	48%		59,800	46%
Operating Profit	22,000	22%		33,800	26%
Fixed costs					
Rent	15,000	15%		15,000	11%
Rates	3,000	3%		4,000	3%
Loan repayment	2,000	2%		2,000	1%
Less Total fixed Costs	20,000	20%		20,000	15%
Net Profit (Loss)	2,000	2%		13,800	11%

The budget can then be broken down into a monthly format by breaking down the annual sales using the percentage of sales from each month from historic records.

Finance

	Budget		Monthly Budget			
	Year		Jan	Feb	Mar	April
	100%		9%	8%	7%	9%
Sales	130,000	100%	11,700	10,400	9,100	11,700
Less Cost of Sales	36,400	28%	3,276	2,912	2,548	3,276
Gross profit	93,600	72%	8,424	7,488	6,552	8,424
Variable costs						
Wages	33,800	26%	3,042	2,704	2,366	3,042
Gas	11,700	9%	1,053	936	819	1,053
Electricity	9,100	7%	819	728	637	819
Fuel	5,200	4%	468	416	364	468
Less Total Variable Costs	59,800	46%	5,382	4,784	4,186	5,382
Operating Profit	33,800	26%	3,042	2,704	2,366	3,042
Fixed costs						
Rent	15,000	11%	1,250	1,250	1,250	1,250
Rates	4,000	3%	333	333	333	333
Loan repayment	2,000	1%	166	166	166	166
Less Total fixed Costs	20,000	15%	1,749	1,749	1,749	1,749
Net Profit (Loss)	13,800	11%	1,293	955	617	1,293

Departmental Budgets

There will be a main budget for the whole organisation, sometimes called the Master Budget and there can be several budgets within that for different departments or activities. For example, these could all have their own budgets:

- *sales and marketing department*
- *manufacturing and production department*
- *transport and packing department*
- *a project to update IT throughout the whole business*

Each department or project could have a budget of what income it expects to bring in and what expenses it expects to have – e.g., stationery, transport, materials, payroll, building costs, or one-off expenses for a specific project.

Finance

Budgets can be done for any period of time that the organisation needs for its operations – e.g., daily, weekly, monthly, quarterly, annually, or for the period covered by particular projects or activities.

A budget for one item can appear in several places and this can help provide a three-dimensional picture of the organisation. For example, staff costs can appear in:

- *each department's own budget* – *to show the wage costs for their part of the organisation*
- *the HR department's budget* – *to show the overall staff costs for the whole organisation, which include training, recruitment, pensions, employment benefits and expenses, management and HR costs as well as wage costs*
- *budgets for a project* – *to show the estimated staff costs for that project only*

The process of breaking down the total costs into departmental costs uses a process called apportionment. Some costs will naturally fall easily into each department such as wage costs and salaries some more general costs, however, may need a little more thought. There are a number of techniques for this but a common one to use for energy is by floor area. If the floor area of the building is 1,000 square feet and the finance department covers 100 square feet – they would be apportioned 10% of the energy costs in their departmental budget.

The process of apportionment will be carried out by the financial management team.

The Importance of Accurate Budgets and Forecasting

Budgets are needed to manage cash flow, control resources, plan for the future and secure financing. They are needed so that an organisation can estimate its income and expenditure in the days, months and years to come. This helps to make sure that there will be enough revenue to cover all expenditure and leave enough money to make a profit.

By making people accountable and responsible for a budget, an organisation can help to control its resources. Working to a budget helps staff to understand organisational objectives and motivate them to use resources efficiently and effectively.

Budgets can also show how a business plans to allocate its resources for the future. If a business wants to expand or make investments, it needs to know what its income and expenses are likely to be before it commits to plans.

For example, if a business wants to invest in new technology and buy a new, expensive, sophisticated machine, it needs to prepare budgets to estimate:

- *the capital cost of the new machine*
- *the running costs of the new machine*
- *the extra revenue that can be generated by using the new machine*
- *the potential savings in staff and maintenance costs from using a newer and more automated system*

Finance

- *how long it will take for the new machine to pay for itself*
- *the tax implications on investing in and operating the new machine*

Banks and other lenders will want to examine an organisation's budget before they agree to grant a loan or overdraft facility. Similarly, if an organisation applies for credit from its suppliers, it might be asked for a budget forecast so that they can negotiate discounts and payment terms based on the likely level of business.

Contingency Plans

When setting realistic budgets and planning for contingencies, managers need to take into account several elements, for example:

- *key components of a budget*
- *using information to set budgets*
- *the importance of accurate budgets and forecasting*
- *the purpose of contingency plans*

It is normal to have contingency plans to deal with unforeseen circumstances.

Sometimes it is impossible to budget exactly and managers can only estimate what may be needed to complete a particular project or objective. When renovating a building, for instance, it is not possible to get accurate costs for remedial work until some of the demolition has been done to reveal the inner fabric of the building.

Workplace and industry experience and risk assessments can help managers to estimate:

- **what may go wrong** *– e.g., machinery breakdown or severe weather*
- **unknown costs** *– e.g., changes in world prices of raw materials*
- **possible extra costs and other consequences** *– e.g., increased costs of raw materials and delays in supplies and production*
- **costs and delays when putting things right** *– e.g., paying staff whilst waiting for supplies; employing extra staff to catch up and achieve targets*
- **steps that can be taken to mitigate the risk** *– e.g., having more than one supplier for key components*
- **funds that need to be set aside** *– e.g., a 20% contingency fund when building a new factory to cover unforeseeable and variable costs*

By planning for contingencies, managers can:

- *incorporate the anticipated costs in their agreed budget*
- *reallocate funds if necessary*

Finance

- *have extra funds on standby in case they are needed*
- *avoid extra delays because the planning has already been done*
- *keep projects and progress of objectives on track*

Monitoring Budgets

It is necessary to monitor budgets to ensure effectiveness and control costs. Managers need to be able to, for example:

- *assess whether targets are being met*
- *monitor variance of actual performance against the set budget*
- *monitor internal and external factors that affect budgets and cause variance*
- *revise a budget when required*

The Budget v Actual Report provides a comparison between the budget and the actual values. The difference is fairly easy to see and can be improved further by adding the percentage columns so the variance can be assessed.

Another way of expressing the difference is by using percentage change. This expresses the degree of change between the two. This can be seen in the illustration below:

| | Budget v Actual | | | | | Feb |
| | January | | | | | |
	Budget	%	Actual	%	% Change	Budget
Sales	11,700	100	12,600	100	7.7%	10,400
Less Cost of Sales	3,276	28	4,010	32	22.4%	2,912
Gross profit	8,424	72	7,488	68	2.0%	7,488
Variable costs						
Wages	3,042	26	2,704	33	38.1%	2,704
Gas	1,053	9	936	10	23.5%	936
Electricity	819	7	728	6	-2.3%	728
Fuel	468	4	416	4	11.1%	416
Less total Variable Costs	5,382	46	4,784	54	26.7%	4,784
Operating Profit	3,042	26	2,704	14	-41.8%	2,704
Fixed costs						
Rent	1,250	11	1,250	10		1,250
Rates	333	3	333	3		333
Loan repayment	166	1	166	1		166
Less total Fixed Costs	1,749	15	1,749	14		1,749
Net Profit (Loss)	1,293	11	955		-98.4%	1,293

Finance

Assessing whether targets are being met

Organisations will have their own ways of assessing whether targets are being met, which could include, for example:

- *comparing results against SMART (Specific, Measurable, Achievable, Realistic and Timebound) targets* – *measuring progress at key stages set out in SMART targets*
- *comparing actual costs with budgeted amounts* – *to evaluate the budget allocations and identify the causes of variance*
- *analysing operational data* – *e.g., looking at productivity records to evaluate progress and output*
- *analysing sales patterns* – *e.g., to see if sales forecasts match actual sales*
- *progress reviews and team meetings*
- *flow charts, graphs and Gantt charts* – *e.g., measuring progress against specific targets*
- *internal and external audits* – *e.g., completed by managers or registered auditors*

Monitoring variance of actual performance against the set budget

As actual costs and income figures become available, managers can measure them against the estimated costs in their budgets. Fixed costs should be predictable and match forecasts and the amounts allocated in the budget. Variable and semi-variable costs need to be analysed more carefully to make sure that they are within the tolerances and amounts expected when the budgets and forecasts were prepared.

The frequency and formality of monitoring will depend on the project, objectives, activities and agreed working practices of the team, department and organisation. For example, variance of actual performance against the set budget may take place:

- *every day* – *e.g., when costs are entered into a company's accounts system that automatically compares performance against expectations*
- *monthly or quarterly* – *e.g., when departmental reports are prepared to show to the board of directors*
- *at agreed stages during a project* – *e.g., at critical review points during a building project*

By having regular reviews, causes of variance can be identified as soon as possible and actions can be planned to address issues.

Factors that cause budgetary variance

Many internal and external factors can affect budgets and cause variance. Managers need to be able to identify and respond to them to make sure that budgets and plans stay on track. Some issues will come under the manager's area of authority. Others need to be escalated so that the issues can be addressed at an organisational level.

Finance

The following table gives examples of factors and suggestions about how they might be addressed:

Reasons for changing budgets and/or plans:	Examples:	Suggestions about how to address issues. Managers may need to:
Objectives, aims and priorities change	A company decides to launch a new product A charity decides to abandon a project to run an open day for the public Business owners decide to move to larger premises An organisation decides to postpone buying new cars for staff and spend the money on a new IT system instead	Arrange discussions with decision-makers to establish revised objectives, aims and priorities Amend original budgets and plans, or prepare new ones to cover up-to-date plans once they have been agreed
Costs rise or fall	A rise in interest rates affects the plans to borrow money for expansion Weather problems and flooding damage crops and affect the cost of fruit and cereals	Make sure that there are several suppliers for key services, materials and components so that: • they work harder to be competitive • the risk of failure is spread • the manager can change suppliers Arrange to use the contingency budget to keep objectives on track
Demand for products and services rise or fall	A new tablet sells out after a successful marketing launch and the manufacturer needs to change its plans and budgets to increase production The demand for antiques and second-hand furniture drops and businesses cannot charge what they expected when selling items	Have contingency plans prepared for higher and lower volumes of output Have suppliers in the supply chain ready to cope with changes Address sales and marketing issues to boost awareness and trade Revise pricing strategies
Improvements in technology	New IT systems reduce the need for stationery and paper storage Videoconferencing technology improves and staff do not need to travel abroad for meetings so often A new website and online purchasing system increase sales dramatically	Revise operational procedures to: • incorporate relevant technology and processes • train staff in new methods • monitor their effectiveness • cope with changes in levels of production and sales

Finance

Ctd.		
Plant and machinery need to be replaced sooner than expected	*An expensive machine is expected to last 10 years and the budget is there to replace it then. However, it breaks down and is obsolete after 5 years, so it needs to be replaced early*	*Arrange discussions with decision-makers to gain agreement to:* • *gain agreement to replacing the machine* • *access the budget for replacing capital items* • *revise objectives to cope with the delay* • *revise the budget and forecasts for when the new machinery is in use*
Unforeseen circumstances and unavoidable delays	*Severe and exceptional weather affects production* *A cargo ship carrying supplies is lost at sea* *There is a fire at a factory*	*Inform relevant people* *Discuss contingency plans with other decisionmakers* *Implement contingency plans and access contingency budget if required*
Estimations are found to be unrealistic	*Estimations about sales turn out to be higher or lower than expected* *The actual running costs for new plant and machinery turn out to be much higher or lower than expected*	*Monitor data very carefully to check actual figures against estimates and look for errors* *Check the sources used when original estimates were made to test their validity Prepare revised plans, estimates and budgets* *Discuss contingency plans with other decisionmakers* *Implement contingency plans and access contingency budget if required*
Changes in legislation and regulations	*The Chancellor of the Exchequer announces a change in the rate of VAT in the Budget* *New regulations about waste management have a financial impact on a company* *New regulations dictate that all staff must have or achieve recognised industry qualifications and organisations need to invest in training*	*Inform relevant people* *Discuss contingency plans with other decisionmakers* *Implement contingency plans and access contingency budget if required*

By monitoring input and output, a business can compare figures with the budgets and identify gaps where money is going out faster than it comes in. This enables them to close gaps. For example, if a business sees in its budget that customers are paying for goods long after the business has already paid for them, it can change its credit policy and make sure that customers pay sooner and on time.

Similarly, if a business has money on deposit or invested in assets, it needs to know the cash flow requirements that are coming up so that it can move funds or sell assets at the right time, if necessary.

Finance

Managers need to monitor and review all aspects of operations and take quick action to address any issues, variances and changes in forecasts that may affect budgets and plans for their team or department. Early attention helps to keep objectives in line with the organisation's goals and budgets and minimise the impacts of changes.

Revising a Budget

When budgets are monitored, controlled and recorded, problems come to light. Managers are able to identify problems and issues when they study the figures and sometimes it is necessary to revise budgets and plans.

The organisation's policies and procedures will show what needs to be done when budgets need to be revised. For example, they may have a tolerance that is agreed in advance that the manager can use at their own discretion – e.g., a 2% or £500 increase that can be implemented without seeking permission. Or managers may have several budgets in their control and be permitted to move funds from one budget to another – e.g., taking money from their stationery budget and putting it towards increased IT costs.

The main things that need to be established before revising a budget include, for example:

- *the manager's own limits of authority for making decisions and changes*
- *the decision-making process for when decisions need to be escalated*
- *the procedures for reporting variance and issues*
- *the procedures for making revisions and merging them with organisational budgets*

Any changes made to a departmental budget may have serious repercussions for the Master Budget of the organisation. It is therefore imperative that changes are only made to department when full consultation has taken place and the Master Budget has been amended accordingly.

Any change in one departmental budget may affect the funds which have been allocated to the other department's budgets meaning that department may lose funds to meet the budget shortfall in the other.

Finance

Glossary of Financial Terms

It is important to recognise and understand terms that are used when dealing with business finance. Here are some examples of financial terminology:

Accounts – *accurate records of the business income, expenditure, assets and liabilities – e.g., annual accounts that are prepared for companies and other organisations to use when making tax returns or applying for funding.*

Apportionment – *the way funds and costs are divided between departments*

Assets – *items owned by the business – e.g., vehicles, plant and machinery, equipment and buildings.*

Balance sheet – *this shows what the organisation is worth at any given time, showing its assets and liabilities.*

Budgets – *estimates and allocations of income and expenditure for a set period of time, used to measure and estimate financial aspects of all parts of a business.*

Capital – *money that is invested into a business – e.g., from owners, banks or shareholders.*

Cash flow – *the amount of money coming into and out of the business in a given period.*

Compliance – *conforming to rules – e.g., standards, policies, regulations or laws.*

Credit – *there can be several meanings in business – e.g., a bookkeeping entry of money received; a credit note to give the customer an amount to take off their next purchase; a credit agreement for when a customer can have the goods now and pay later.*

Creditors – *people or businesses who are owed money – e.g., HM Revenue and Customs or suppliers who are waiting for payment.*

Debt – *money that is owed to someone else – e.g., if a company has a bank loan, it has a debt with the bank.*

Debtors – *people or businesses that owe money to the organisation – e.g., customers who have not paid their bills yet.*

Expenditure – *money paid out for materials – e.g., rent, payroll, marketing or travel. Capital expenditure is money spent on long-term items such as cars, buildings and machinery with a long working life.*

Fixed costs – *expenses that stay the same, regardless of sales rising or falling – e.g., rent and insurance.*

Governance – *the system by which organisations are directed and controlled – e.g., by a board of directors.*

Gross profit - *the difference between the revenue minus the cost of making the product – before deducting overheads, payroll, taxation and interest payments.*

Income, turnover or revenue – *money that comes in – e.g., from sales, planned sales, interest or investments.*

Liabilities – *the amount that a business owes to creditors – e.g., such as banks and suppliers.*

Net profit - *is the actual profit after all working expenses have been paid.*

Profit – *the amount left over that can either be distributed, held or reinvested in the business.*

Revenue – *money received – e.g., from sales, grants, government funding, interest or investments.*

Semi-variable costs - *expenses that might be influenced by changes in sales – e.g., salaries and advertising.*

Shares – *units of ownership of a company that can be offered for sale – companies usually pay dividends to their shareholders, based on the level of their profits.*

Finance

Staff costs – *all costs relating to human resources* – *e.g., wages, national insurance contributions, agency costs, welfare, uniforms and training.*

Turnover – *the amount of money taken by an organisation in a particular period* – *e.g., the annual turnover of a company.*

Variable costs – *expenses that change according to sales volumes* – *e.g., raw materials used to make the products.*

Working capital – *the amount of money left in a business once current assets and liabilities have been taken into account.*

Chapter 10: Project Management

Project Management

Projects

Each day, whether at home or work we perform a wide range of routine tasks which we often regard as being chores. At work, in addition to the chores, some tasks will not be routine and are therefore called projects.

> *A project is a planned set of interrelated and sometimes dependent tasks that must be executed over a certain period of time taking into consideration certain costs, resources and other limitations. The task must be completed in order to reach a specific goal that will ultimately satisfy the need of a customer.*

The purpose of project management is to minimise, contain or counter the risks and organise and direct the resources so that the project is finished in time, within budgeted costs and with the functional or other design objectives fulfilled. This is known as the Scope of the project.

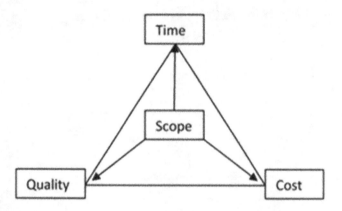

A project is a unique activity, undertaken to achieve planned objectives, which could be measured in terms of outputs, outcomes or benefits. A project is usually deemed to be a success if it achieves the objectives according to their acceptance criteria, within an agreed timescale and budget. (Quality, Cost and Time)

A key factor that distinguishes project management from just 'management' is that it has this final deliverable and a finite timespan, unlike management which is an ongoing process. Because of this, a project manager needs a wide range of skills; often technical skills and certainly people management skills and good business awareness.

Project Management

Core Components of Project Management

The core components of project management are:

Planning Phase

- *defining the reason why a project is necessary.*
- *capturing project requirements, specifying quality of the deliverables, estimating resources and timescales.*
- *preparing a business case to justify the investment.*
- *securing corporate agreement and funding.*
- *developing and implementing a management plan for the project.*

Delivery Phase

- *leading and motivating the project delivery team.*
- *managing the risks, issues and changes on the project.*
- *monitoring progress against plan.*
- *managing the project budget.*
- *maintaining communications with stakeholders and the project organisation.*
- *provider management.*

Reflective Phase

- *closing the project in a controlled fashion when appropriate*

It can also be defined as a set of inputs and outputs needed to reach a specific outcome. However, success as a project manager is dependent on how the resources of a project are optimised and it is completed on time.

Project management covers the management of projects and their running. Not all projects are the same and they vary on a number of different elements that make each project individually unique.

These factors differ in projects and must be taken into consideration so that projects can be managed efficiently and effectively regarding each project type because of the variations in their sizes and structure.

Project scope: This describes the reach and scale of the project; it sets the tone of the success of a project. Also, it specifies the details of the work to be carried out in a project.

Project scope varies depending on the number of people involved and the scale of the impact of its outcomes. Projects can be big or small depending on the scope.

Project Management

Timeframe: A project's timeframe is defined from its initiation or conception until result evaluation. It is the period that a project is anticipated to be completed. A project's timeframe can also be divided into smaller blocks which in themselves have their own timeframe.

Organisation: This is a key feature of effective project planning; the organisation of a project refers to how tasks and activities are organised and types of projects prioritised. The project workflow is calculated in each project to reach the desired objectives.

Cost: Projects can be expensive or relatively cheap depending on their overall cost.

Communication: Communication is the cornerstone of every project. Among different types of projects, communication, its frequency and its format can vary. However, without effective communication, a project will fail. Effective communication is an essential tool that propels the success of any project irrespective of its size.

Stakeholder Management: Projects can vary depending on the number of stakeholders involved. Sometimes, the only stakeholders involved in a project are the team and project manager, but more often than not, there are wider group of stakeholders involved. The more stakeholders, the more complex is the management of their expectations and communication. You can choose between these types of leadership.

Task assignation: Within the different types of projects in project management, there are many different tasks and activities. Projects can vary depending on how these tasks are assigned to team members- whether they will be completed by individual members or groups and how responsibilities will be defined. The onus is on the project manager to ensure that the tasks of the project are properly assigned to the right team members.

Quality of results: Results of projects vary among the different types of projects. They can vary depending on each client's requests. No doubt, you should strive to deliver the right quality that meets or exceeds the expectations of the clients.

Classification of a Project

Every project is different from another. Projects can be classified based on several different points. The classification of projects in project management varies according to a number of different factors such as complexity, source of capital, its content, those involved and its purpose. Projects can be classified based on the following factors.

According to complexity:

Easy: A project is classified as easy when the relationships between tasks are basic and detailed planning or organisations are not required. A small work team and a few external stakeholders and collaborators are common in this case. The tasks of the projects can be undertaken by a small team.

Project Management

Complicated: The project network is broad and complicated. There are many task interdependencies. With these projects, simplification where possible is everything. The task of executing this type of project requires proper planning.

According to the source of capital:

Public: Financing comes from Governmental institutions.
Private: Financing comes from businesses or private incentives.
Mixed: Financing comes from a mixed source of both public and private funding.

According to Project content:

Construction: These are projects that have anything to do with the construction of civil or architectural work. Predictive methods are used along with agile techniques which will be explained later on. Furthermore, construction is an engineering project and the process of planning its execution must be painstakingly done to achieve the desired outcome.
IT: Any project that has to do with software development, IT system, etc. The types of project management information systems vary across the board, but in today's world are very common.
Business: These projects are involved with the development of a business idea, management of a work team, cost management, etc. and they usually follow a commercial strategy.
Service or product production: These are projects that involve the development of an innovative product or service, design of a new product, etc. They are often used in the R & D department.

According to those involved:

Departmental: When a certain department or area of an organisation is involved.
Internal: When a whole company itself is involved in the project's development.
Matriarchal: When there is a combination of departments involved.
External: When a company outsources external project manager or teams to execute the project. This is common in digital transformations, process improvements and strategy changes, for example.

According to its objective:

Production: Oriented at the production of a product or service taking into consideration a certain determined objective to be met by an organisation.
Social: Oriented at the improvement of the quality of life of people. This can be in the form of rendering corporate social responsibility (CSR) to the people.
Educational: Oriented at the education of others. This is always done to make them better.

Project Management

Community: Oriented at people too, however with their involvement.
Research: Oriented at innovation and the gaining of knowledge to enhance the operational efficiency of an organisation.

Types of Project Manager

What is a project manager? Now that we know what a project is, the different types and its different classifications, we must consider the person responsible for bringing the goals of a project from the beginning to the end and that is the project manager. All types of projects in project management need a project manager. Like projects, there are different types of project managers. The burning question on everyone's mind is how best to grow your organisation and how best to execute a project? Depending on the type of project a certain style of project manager will be best suited to execute the project properly.

The Prophet: This type of project manager focuses on grand opportunities. This manager relies on passionate team members that are extremely determined to comply with the vision of the project. Prophets are good for challenging an existing, possibly out-of-date strategy and seeking out new opportunities for growth that previously may have been overlooked.

The Gambler: This type of project manager actively pursues business opportunities that exist within the existing strategic boundaries of the business but are not being exploited to their full potential due to a lack of trustworthy data. Essentially, this project manager takes bets on growth opportunities. In a certain light, these managers can seem risky as the likelihood of success cannot be predicted. However, they are necessary to project management as they pursue certain overlooked opportunities that have potential that can enhance the growth of an organisation.

The Expert: This type of project manager actively pursues business opportunities that lie outside the existing strategic boundaries, but contrary to the gambler and the prophet, opportunities for which there exists trustworthy data that carves a solid case. They love solid evidence that backs up their initiative to go with certain overlooked business growth opportunities. Their main challenge is to explain their vision and get everyone on the team on board while pursuing the goal.

The Executor: This project manager energetically pursues business opportunities that lie within the existing strategic boundaries and have a great case to be pursued. The sureness and confidence of this type of project manager are what gains trust from the other team members and followers of the project. Quantitative evidence is key for the executor and helps back up the pursuit of an opportunity.
Risk, uncertainty and challenge are null. They simply excel at pinpointing opportunities that need to be sought after which are not currently. It is the most certain path to success. However, the executor lacks the ability to pinpoint more obscure and maybe riskier opportunities that could potentially be exploited.

Project Management

Projects in Practice

An example of a work-based project
A project usually begins when an idea is put forward and is accepted as being a good idea, after discussion and the decision to implement this is taken. This is the start of the project after which plans and decisions will be made as to how the project should be implemented and planning will take place.

This is the beginning of the project. The next step is the middle of the project which is the plan being implemented. The project does not end when the implementation finishes, this is only the end of the middle. The project will end when the organisation has taken feedback and evaluated the whole of the project from start to finish.

A project therefore has a:

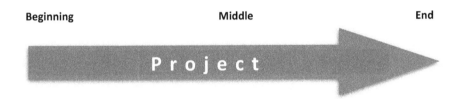

Example

A company wishes to hold a charity dinner for its stakeholders to support a local charitable organisation. Tasks for the planning team might team could include:

> **researching and planning the project** *– finding a venue, booking caterers*
> **working out timescales** *– planning when things need to be delivered*
> **finding and organising resources** *– hiring service staff on the day; seating and tables; ordering portable toilets*
> **sending out invitations the event** *– publicity materials to news agencies and media; putting up posters; arranging TV, radio and press advertisements*
> **contacting people coming to the event** *– sending invitations and tickets; dealing with telephone and email queries*
> **preparing the venue** *– decorating the venue and dealing with queries from suppliers*
> **host guests and performers** *– arranging transport or giving directions*
> **supporting staff after the concert** *– taking care of lost property; taking unused programmes back to the office; dealing with queries*
> **evaluating the success of the concert** *– reviewing sales; responding to feedback, complaints and comments; helping to sort receipts and analyse the costs; assess monies generated*

The tasks undertaken are focused on the project and follow the plans and objectives of the project. They are not part of the regular, routine work of the organisation. Once the project is over, the tasks cease.

Project Management

Working to strict timescales is critical. Things must be done on time as delays can have a knock-on effect on other people and tasks connected with the project.

Key Stages in The Lifecycle of a Project

The lifecycle of a project follows the natural sequence of the project itself. The project will need to be started, comprehensive planning will then be required before the project is delivered and subsequently it will need to be evaluated and reviewed.

The key stages in a project are therefore:

- *initiation*
- *comprehensive planning*
- *project delivery and control*
- *closure and review*

Initiation

At the initiation stage the purpose of the project needs to be clarified before planning and preparation can take place.

Working to an agreed purpose helps to focus everyone involved with the project. It helps to stop them being distracted, especially if the project becomes very intense and they are working under pressure.

In the example, the agreed purpose of the charity dinner is to raise funds for the charity. Before the planning gets fully underway, the decision-makers also need to agree the scope of the project.

The scope is defined as the broad outline of what is needed to achieve a satisfactory result. It is good practice to include details about what is not included within the scope of the project, so that people can see the parameters clearly.

In the example, the organisers need to agree, for example:

> **the size of the venue they think they can fill** – *the factory canteen can seat 75 people; a village hall can seat 125 whilst a local conference centre can accommodate 250.*
> **the catering services available** – *inhouse, outside caterers, contract caterers*
> *the type of entertainment they can afford and are able to organise – discos, local bands and entertainers or well-known bands*
> **what they can achieve** - *with the resources they have available*

Project team members, especially the main decision-makers, need to agree the scope of their particular role in the project – e.g., how much time and expertise they can contribute.

Project Management

They will look carefully at the reason for the project – the planned outcomes, costs and benefits to the organisation – and how the project fits into the activities, culture and objectives of the organisation as a whole.

The aims and objectives of the project all need to be agreed so that everyone understands where they will be going with the project and what they will have to do to make it a success at every stage.

In the example, the **purpose** of the charity dinner is to raise money for the charity.

The **aim** is to run a concert that makes a decent profit that can be given to the charity.

The **objectives** along the way could include, for example:

raising the profile of the charity
bringing public attention to the charity's work
increasing the number of supporters
giving the guests a really good and memorable night
career development for staff, by increasing their skills, knowledge and experience

All of this information will then be put into a brief, along with terms of reference to provide the basic structure for the planning stage.

Comprehensive planning

When planning and preparing for a project, there are several things that need to be agreed to make sure that:

- *the project is planned appropriately*
- *people understand what is expected of them and the project team*
- *sufficient resources are put in place*
- *sufficient budgets are put in place*
- *stakeholders' expectations are met*

In the planning stages, project managers need to consider:

timescales
resources
budgets
risk assessments
contingency plans

When planning and preparing for a project, the timescales need to be agreed so that all of the different elements can be brought together on time. Very often, different parts of the

Project Management

project are interdependent meaning one part of the project cannot go ahead until the previous stage has been completed, so a delay at any stage can delay the whole project or lead to its failure.

For the example agreed timescales could include

- *starting the planning and preparation in February*
- *booking caterers, bands, resources, etc. and a venue for a date in August*
- *having the invitations and tickets ready for April*
- *launching the publicity for the concert in March*
- *sending out tickets from June onwards*
- *recruiting and training staff and volunteers to help at the concert between July and August*

Project managers also need to plan the resources that are going to be needed, for example:

- **human resources** – *staff, volunteers and agency workers*
- **physical resources** – *accommodation, transport, seating, lighting, stationery, telephones and communication equipment*

These must be agreed at the beginning of a project as resources need to be planned in line with budgets and timescales. The project manager will need to have a total overview of resources and costs and anyone working on the project team needs to be aware of any limits or deadlines.

In the example, when planning the resources for volunteers who will help at the concert, the organisers will agree things like:

- *the number of volunteers that they are going to need*
- *the budget that is allocated for their uniforms, training, welfare, travel and other costs*
- *the locations to be used for training sessions*

When planning or preparing a project, the overall budget may already be set. The organisers might have already allocated funds and the people running the project will have to deliver it within the budget they have been given. Early in the process, they need to check the budget to make sure that they can achieve what is expected. Alternatively, the event may need to be self-financing where there is upfront funding to support the planning, but the whole costs of the event must be deducted from the money generated by the event. As a consequence, an event such as the example will only generate a charitable contribution if there is money left over after all the costs of the event have been paid.

For other projects, part of the planning process might be to research the likely costs and to forecast the budget that will be needed to deliver the project. The project managers will then negotiate and agree budgets with the organisation before starting on the main planning, preparation and delivery of the project.

Budgets need to be agreed and allocated to different elements of the project – e.g., staff costs, stationery costs, catering and hospitality.

Part of project management planning is to make contingency plans to cover unforeseen costs, last-minute problems and unforeseen events or issues that have an impact on the project. For our example, the organisers would have contingency plans for extreme weather around the time of the dinner, for example: to provide dry access to the venue, provide sufficient umbrellas, lighting for photography, etc.

Most projects have a contingency budget that is also agreed at the beginning. This is a separate budget to cover unexpected problems – last minute change to entertainment due to sickness.

Project managers need to have a contingency budget set aside to cover their contingency plans. This makes it easier to make quick decisions to get the project back on track if funds and limits of authority to use them, have been agreed in advance.

Project Delivery and Control
After a great deal of planning and many meetings, the time comes to deliver the project. This is when everything is put into practice.

Decision-making and problem-solving skills will be needed to deal with queries and problems that could threaten to alter the progress of the project.

Progress needs to be monitored and measured so that any potential problems are identified as soon as possible, maybe against SMART targets, planners, flow-charts budgets and risk assessments.

Monitoring and controlling a project can involve performing internal and external audits.

Regular progress reviews and team meetings during a project will help to identify actual and potential problems as they arise. By reviewing flow-charts, task lists, planners, project plans, objectives and so on, the team can see the problems, reprioritise and allocate resources to deal with the issues.

Closure and Review
As the project moves into its final phase, it is time to evaluate against the agreed aims and objectives to see how it met and / or exceeded expectations. Projects need to be closed down and lessons need to be learned and recorded for future research and development.

The review stage is extremely important as it gives people the chance to make notes, give and receive feedback and record information for future projects whilst issues, problems and successes are still fresh in the memory.

Project Management

Closure needs to be managed well so that:

- *people who worked on the project feel valued and appreciated*
- *the clients or other decision-makers who authorised the project appreciate its value, see what has been achieved and feel confident about commissioning further projects*
- *contacts made within the supply chain feel valued and are kept up to date*
- *all stakeholders can see the benefits and positive results of the project before they move onto the next activity*

Roles within the Project Team

Project teams can have many different members. They might work on the project full time, they might only be involved in one particular stage, or their role may only require their involvement from time to time. People on a project team can include, for example:

board members
sponsors
managers
team leaders
team members
subject specialists
administrators

Board Members
There may be board members who have direct or indirect functions on a project team. In the charity dinner example, input from board members might have included:

- **the managing director** *– providing initial ideas and overall strategy; weekly progress meetings to monitor and evaluate progress and plans; main contact to agree budgets at organisational level*
- **charity trustees** *– on the board to oversee operations from a distance and ensure compliance with regulatory requirements of the Charities Commission and the charity's own constitution*
- **shareholder representative** *– to monitor shareholders' interests and funds*
- *sales director – with an interest in sales revenue*

Sponsors
Some projects have sponsors who make contributions of finance and/or expertise. In national sports clubs, for example, sponsors pay for advertising their own businesses around the pitch, on shirts and other merchandise and in marketing materials. They also use the venue for entertaining their own guests and customers and enjoy special privileges.

Project Management

If a football club's project is to rebuild one of the stands, for example, a major sponsor may agree to cover the costs and be closely involved with the whole project, form initiation to closure and review.

Managers

Direction may come from the board, but the main planning, delivery and controlling of project plans will be the responsibilities of various managers. There may be:

- *a senior project coordinator* – *with overall authority over budgets and important decisions for several projects*
- *the project manager* – *the main manager for the project; the main point of contact for most decisions and problems; has overall control of everyday activities for the whole project*
- *department managers* – *such as an HR or health and safety manager who are only involved with certain aspects of the project*

In organisations whose core business is project management and in some other large organisations, there may be several full-time managers. Managers will deal with the different business functions and coordinate their activities with the project managers who have the overall view and control.

Team Leaders

As the project is broken down into different components, there may be team leaders in charge of each section. They will answer to the project manager and be responsible for their sub-teams and special areas only, which could include, for example:

- *induction and training* – *new team members and volunteers*
- *a catering team* – *looks after one of the food court areas in a large venue*
- *running one of the bars* – *one of ten bars in the large venue*
- *a customer service team* – *dealing with customer queries at information points*
- *a media team* – *that looks after press, TV and radio coverage*

Team Members

Team members can be, for example, employees, agency workers, freelance workers or volunteers. They might be allocated to, for example:

- *the project full time* – *working in the planning office for the whole project*
- *the project part time* – *spending a regular two days a week on the accounts and budgets*
- *short-term roles* – *directing cars in a car park for a two-day event*

They will all work within the limits of their authority and refer to the team leader for everyday queries and problems.

Project Management

Subject Specialists

Subject specialists can be called in from time to time when the project manager needs specific skills, usually during the planning and delivery stages. Specialist could be called in to deal with:

- *health and safety assessments* – e.g., *in unusual work areas or environments*
- *fireworks displays for an event, designers for stationery, posters and other marketing materials*
- *branding* – e.g., *for sponsorship coverage*
- *specialist equipment that is not normally used or owned by the organisation* – e.g., *staging, marquees, lighting or sound systems*
- *accounts and audits*

Such subject specialists might:

> *work for other departments within the organisation – and be asked to assist with specific parts of the project only*
> *work as freelancers – and be engaged for particular roles on a consultancy basis*
> *be part of specialist organisations – working as part of an independent external team that is tasked to do specific activities*
> *be a full team member for the duration of the project*

Subject specialists are often separate from the main team, so the lines of communication and responsibility need to be clearly defined. They are likely to be answerable to the project manager, who acts as a line manager and have access to more senior decision-makers when required.

Administrators

Administrators perform a wide range of tasks in project management, such as:

- *processing receipts and invoices*
- *keeping accounts records up to date*
- *processing sales records and enquiries*
- *archiving information*
- *keeping Gantt charts and other monitoring systems up to date*

Administrators might work for other departments within the organisation, such as the accounts department and be asked to assist with specific parts of the project only. Others may be part of the project team full time, performing administrative tasks for the project only.

As for other project management roles, administrators can be, for example:

- *freelancers* – *engaged for particular roles on a consultancy basis*

Project Management

- *employed by specialist external organisations* – working as part of an independent team that is tasked to do specific activities
- *employed by the organisation on a temporary basis* – for the duration of the project
- *employed by the organisation on a permanent basis* – working on the project team part or full time

Involving Stakeholders in the Project

A stakeholder is an individual, group, or organisation who may affect, be affected by, or perceive itself to be affected by a decision, activity, or outcome of a project. Stakeholders are either directly involved in the project or have interests that may be affected by the project's outcome. It normally includes the members of a project team: project managers, project sponsors, executives, customers, or users.

It is beneficial and advisable to know about good stakeholder management skill and communicate constantly with stakeholders in order to collaborate on the project because after all, they are also affected by the product.

If a project is small in size, the number of stakeholders can be small. However, if it is large and expanded to a large area, one may have a huge number of stakeholders, including communities or the general public. Also, all stakeholders are not alike. They have different expectations and needs. One must treat every stakeholder uniquely according to their needs or else the stakeholders might feel left out which can put the project in danger.

Different stakeholders often have opposing expectations that might create clashes within the project. Stakeholders may also interfere in the project, its deliverables and the project team to fulfil their strategic business objectives or other requirements.

Project Governance
Project governance is the alignment of the project with stakeholders' needs or objectives. It is critical for achieving organisational goals. It enables organisations to manage projects consistently and exploit the benefits of a project. It provides a framework which helps the project manager and sponsors to make decisions that suit both stakeholder needs and organisational objectives or deal with situations where they may not be aligned.

Type of Project Stakeholders
Project stakeholders can be classified into two types:

1. **Internal Stakeholders:** As the name suggests, these are the people involved in a project from within. They include:

Project Management

- *A sponsor*
- *An internal customer or client* (if the project started due to an internal need of the organisation)
- *A project team*
- *A program or portfolio manager*
- *Management*
- *Another team's manager of the company*

2. **External Stakeholders:** These stakeholders are not directly involved but are engaged from outside and are affected by the project outcome.

- *An external customer or client* (if project started due to a contract from external party)
- *An end user*
- *Subcontractors*
- *A supplier*
- *The government*
- *Local communities*
- *Media*

The Importance of Stakeholders

- *Stakeholders have different levels of duties and authority when contributing on a project. This level may differ as the project proceeds. It can range from occasional contributions to full project sponsorship.*
- *Some stakeholders may also detract from the success of the project, either actively or passively. These stakeholders need the project manager's attention during the whole time of project's life cycle.*
- *Stakeholder identification is a continuous process during the entire project life cycle. Identifying them, understanding their level of effect on a project and satisfying their demands, needs and expectations is essential for the success of the project.*
- *Just as stakeholders can affect a project's objectives positively or negatively, a project can be perceived by the stakeholders as having positive or negative results.*
- *One of the most important responsibilities of a project manager is to manage stakeholder expectations, which can be problematic as stakeholders often have very diverse or conflicting objectives.*

Project Management

Project Stakeholders

- **Sponsor:** *A sponsor is the person or group who provides supplies and support for the project and is liable for assisting success. He may be external or internal to the organisation.*
- **Customers and users:** *Customers are the people or organisations who will approve and manage the project's product, service, or result. Users, as clear from the name, use the product.*
- **Sellers:** *Sellers, also known as vendors, are external companies that enter into a contractual agreement to provide services or resources necessary for the project.*
- **Business partners:** *They are external organisations that have a special relationship or partnership with the enterprise.*
- **Organisational groups:** *Organisational groups are internal stakeholders who are influenced by the actions of the project team. For example, human resources, marketing, sales, legal, finance, operations, manufacturing, etc.*
- **Functional managers:** *They are key individuals who play the role of management within an administrative or functional area of the business. For example, human resources, finance, accounting, etc.*
- **Other stakeholders:** *They are additional stakeholders which include financial institutions, government regulators, subject matter experts, consultants and others, which have a financial interest in the project, contributing inputs to the project, or have in the outcome of the project.*

Stakeholders are people who get affected by your project or have any kind of interest in it. They can be internal, external, positive, negative, high power, low power, etc. However, to complete your project successfully you have to manage all these stakeholders and fulfil their prospects. If you fail to do so, your project may get jeopardised.

Whether internal or external, all projects have stakeholders. One of the main reasons' projects fail is because the deliverables were not what the customer wanted, or they did not meet the customer's needs. To ensure project success, it helps that you know all of the key stakeholders on your project, how they prefer to communicate, what their needs are and what the acceptable end results are.

Engaging stakeholders during—and especially at the beginning of—your project will help reduce and uncover risks and increase their "buy-in." When stakeholders are adequately engaged, their influence spreads far and wide. Some of the ways stakeholders are important to a project are as follows.

1. Providing Expertise
Stakeholders are a wealth of knowledge about current processes, historical information and industry insight. Many times, these team members will have been at the company or on the project longer than the project manager or project team. It is important to involve all key stakeholders when gathering and documenting requirements to avoid missing major deliverables of the project. Project managers, or others who are in charge of deliverables, may not be experts on every project. Key stakeholders can provide requirements or constraints based on information from their industry that will be important to have when understanding project constraints and risks.

Project Management

2. Reducing and Uncovering Risk

The more you engage and involve stakeholders, the more you will reduce and uncover risks on your project. When discussing initial requirements, project needs and constraints, stakeholders may bring up issues or concerns about meeting those things. Uncovering risks and then discussing a plan to mitigate them before issues arise will dramatically increase the success of your project. Involving knowledgeable stakeholders during this process will help.

3. Increasing Project Success

By gathering and reviewing project requirements with stakeholders, you will get their "buy-in," which will in turn help increase project success. If you cannot meet stakeholders' needs, due to conflicting needs or priorities, set expectations early in the project life cycle. This will help you manage the relationship throughout the project instead of there being surprises at the end. Stakeholders should always be aware of the project scope, key milestones and when they will be expected to review any deliverables prior to final acceptance.

4. Granting Project Acceptance

The more regularly you engage and involve stakeholders from the start, the more likely you will have a positive project conclusion. By the end of the project, the team members should have already been aware of delivery expectations, risks and how to mitigate the risks. They also should have reviewed draft deliverables along the way. This process should help avoid any surprises at the end of your project. The final acceptance is just their final stamp of approval during the project closure phase.

Project Management

Project Management Tools

A variety of project management tools can be used at appropriate phases of the project. They may be used:

- *during the planning phase* – *to provide a clear structure for the project*
- *when monitoring progress* – *using plans, progress charts, actions plans and risk logs when communicating with stakeholders*
- *when reviewing a project* – *to illustrate and explain progress and plans during review meetings*

Tools can include, for example:

- *SWOT analyses*
- *Work Breakdown Structures (WBS)*
- *PERT Diagrams*
- *SMART objectives*
- *Gantt charts*
- *Plan on a Page*
- *RACI matrix*
- *Time management techniques*
- *Kotter's 8-stage change model*

SWOT Analyses
In the workplace, a SWOT analysis can be used in many different situations to identify and measure:

- *Strengths of a project* – *e.g., well supported; well financed*
- *Weaknesses of a project* – *e.g., very short on time; not enough trained staff to do all the tasks effectively*
- *Opportunities to improve* – *e.g., recruitment drive to bring in the staff needed*
- *Threats to progress* – *e.g., competition from other employers who need to recruit staff with the same skills*

The SWOT analysis can be applied at any scale and can be simple or more detailed. It acts as a snapshot and does not track progress or interdependency of tasks, goals or resources. It can be used in any part of the project that needs a simple, focused analysis on where we are now, where we need to be and how we are going to get there.

Work Breakdown Structures (WBS)
A WBS is a useful project management tool that breaks down a project into smaller components. The tasks and responsibilities are broken down into manageable sections that align to ensure that overall objectives can be met.

A WBS is useful in the earlier stages of planning so that:

Project Management

- *tasks can be broken down into small pieces*
- *an overall picture of how elements will work together can be seen at a glance*
- *different people can see how the tasks may overlap and work together*

Below is a small sample of a simple WBS planner for the Charity Dinner example. It could be developed to go into more detail about the actual days of the month, and names and contact details for all of the internal and external team members.

	February	March	April	May	June	July	August
Tickets	Print tickets by 1st April				Launch sales 5th June	Last boost for tickets	
Caterers	Identify potential candidates	Meet shortlisted companies	Appoint caterers			Finalise menu	
Volunteers			Publicise and start recruitment	Recruit & do phone interviews	Recruit & do interviews Provisional order of uniforms by 16 Jun	In-house training Final order for uniforms by 22 Jul	Training at venue Give out uniforms
Performers	Confirm bookings and contracts		Make contact to stay in touch		Check rehearsal dates are OK	Contact about special requests – food, drink etc. Book transport	Venue rehearsals 20, 21, 22 Aug Event 23rd Aug
Transport		Research taxi & limo companies	Reserve transport for performers, guest speakers			Confirm transport bookings OK	3 limos, 6 taxis, 1 minibus needed 22, 23 Aug

Programme Evaluation Review Technique (PERT) diagram
Another project management tool is a PERT diagram, which stands for Programme Evaluation Review Technique.

This chart is a graphic representation of the project's schedule and it is used to schedule, organise and coordinate tasks within the project. It was developed in the 1950s by the US Navy to manage the Polaris submarine, an extremely complex project.

A PERT diagram usually shows:

> *the sequence of tasks and milestones*
> *how these are prioritised*
> *a three-point estimation technique that shows the duration of each task as being 'optimistic', 'pessimistic' or 'most likely'*

Project Management

The main feature of a PERT diagram that is made using software is the instant calculation of timelines with every change in the workflow. The project manager can instantly see how one changed timescale affects other parts of the project. Its main benefit is to have an overall view of the whole project, rather than individual details, showing how parts of the project can move and impact each other.

Below is a simple PERT diagram about making and packing a teddy bear that has a customised T-shirt:

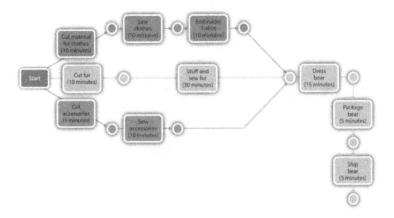

SMART targets or objectives

Another tool to use is the familiar SMART targets or objectives. As we see in many aspects of management, SMART targets are:

Specific
Measurable
Achievable
Realistic
Time-bound

As with SWOT analyses, they can be used for the project as a whole or for small tasks within the project.

Gantt Chart

The underlying concept of a Gantt chart is to map out which tasks can be done in parallel and which need to be done sequentially. If we combine this with the project resources, we can explore the trade-off between the scope (doing more or less work), cost (using more or less resources) and the time scales for the project. By adding more resources or reducing the scope the project manager can see the effect on the end date.

A Gantt chart displays information visually as a type of bar chart in a clear and easy-to-understand way and is used for the following activities:

Project Management

- *Establish the initial project schedule*
- *Allocate resources*
- *Monitor and report progress*
- *Control and communicate the schedule*
- *Display milestones*
- *Identify and report problems*

To create a chart, you need to know all of the individual tasks required to complete the project, an estimate of how long each task will take and which tasks are dependent on others. The very process of pulling this information together helps a project manager focus on the essential parts of the project and begin to establish a realistic timeframe for completion.

Project management solutions that integrate Gantt charts give managers visibility into team workloads, as well as current and future availability, which allows for more accurate scheduling. Gantt charts have been around for nearly a century, having been invented by Henry Gantt, an American mechanical engineer, around 1910. Below is a simple example of a Gantt chart which reflects the data in the Pert chart above:

Activity/Day	1	2	3	4	5	6	7	8	9	10	11	12	13
Cut fur	■	■											
Stuff and sew fur			■	■	■	■	■						
Cut material	■	■											
Sew clothes			■	■									
Embroider T-shirt					■	■							
Cut accessories	■												
Sew accessories		■	■										
Dress bears									░	░			
Package bears												░	
Ship bears													░

Lot size: 100 bears

All activities are scheduled to begin at their earliest start time.

■ Completed work

░ Work to be completed

Project Management

Disadvantages of a Gantt Chart

Gantt charts are not perfect and all too often they become overly complex with too many dependencies and activities. This is a trap many new project managers fall into when they start using planning tools.

It is much better to produce a clear and simple plan that shows the main work packages in summary, than a plan with so much detail the overall impression of project progress is lost. Let the work package manager put together the day-to-day detail of the activities within a work package, while the project schedule concentrates on the interfaces between project teams.

Neither are they good at showing the relative priorities of individual tasks and the resources expended on a task. Tasks are prioritised on the amount of float not their importance to the project. For example, they can clearly show the elapsed time of a task but cannot so easily communicate how many people may be needed to complete that task. So, if not backed up by other data they can give a misleading impression to stakeholders. This is where using additional techniques such as a precedence diagram (sometimes called a PERT chart), for instance, becomes useful

A precedence diagram is another powerful project management technique which is particularly useful for identifying complex inter-dependencies and showing relative priorities of activities and, hence, highlighting the tasks most critical to project success.

Setting up a Gantt Chart

- *When you set up a Gantt chart, you need to think through all of the tasks involved in your project and divide them into manageable components.*
- *Then decide who will be responsible for each task and delegate to the team.*
- *Identify task relationships and decide on the completion date sequence for each task, showing the expected time duration of the whole project and the sub tasks. A Gantt chart will show the tasks in a sequential order and display task dependencies (i.e., how one task relates to another).*
- *Determine and allocate your resources.*
- *Anticipate the risks and problems you may encounter and create a contingency plan for potential problems.*

Project Management

Plan on a Page

This is a simple tool that condenses the whole project down to one page of information. It is particularly useful to, for example:

- **help the project manager focus on the main points of a project** – *when making presentations to people outside the project*
- **show stakeholders a very quick overview of the entire project** – *when applying for extra funding or resources from new sources*
- **show the media the main points of the project** – *when launching a new product*
- **use as a leaflet** – *when distributing information to the local community about a project that will affect or involve them*

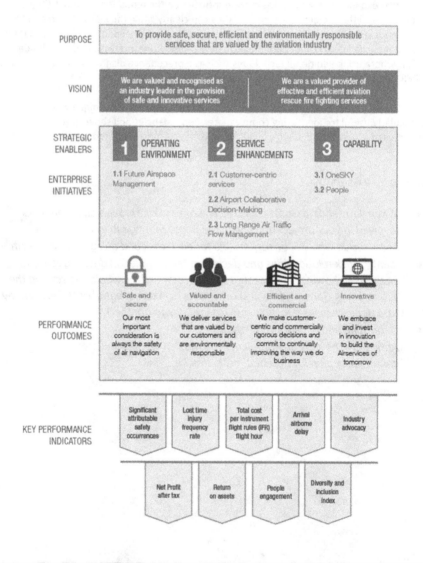

Project Management

RACI Matrix

The RACI model is a straightforward tool that is used in project management to identify roles and responsibilities. It stands for:

Responsible – *the person who does the work to achieve the task*

Accountable – *the person who is accountable for the correct completion of the task – e.g., the project manager who approves the Responsible person's work*

Consulted – *the people who provide information for the project in two-way communication – e.g., subject specialists*

Informed – *the people who are affected by the outcomes of tasks and need to be kept informed about progress in one-way communication – shareholders, directors or senior managers who are not involved with the day-to-day running of the project*

This helps to avoid confusion about the decision-making process by providing a clear illustration for all relevant stakeholders to see who is responsible for tasks, and who needs to be informed along the way. A RACI model can help the project manager to manage expectations and identify roles and responsibilities early in the project.

Time Management Techniques

The tools used for project management help managers to:

- *plan ahead for each element and stage*
- *keep elements of the project on time*
- *predict busy and quiet times*
- *prioritise human and physical resources to meet deadlines*

Time management techniques can be extremely valuable for the project manager and their team members. For example:

- *allow time each day to plan activities*
- *prioritise communications – e.g., deal with urgent messages and accept that some emails and telephone calls do not have to be answered immediately*
- *factor in some time for interruptions and unplanned activities*
- *plan meetings and be firm about time spent*
- *remove distractions when focus is needed*

Eisenhower Grid

An Eisenhower grid or matrix can be designed to give an overview for personal time management, for example:

Project Management

	URGENT	NOT URGENT
IMPORTANT	**1) DO NOW** • emergencies • complaints • planned tasks and projects due now • staff needs • problem-solving	**2) PLAN TO DO** • planning • preparation • research • networking • system development • strategy planning
NOT IMPORTANT	**3) REJECT AND EXPLAIN** • trivial requests from others • ad hoc interruptions • distractions • pointless routines or activities	**4) RESIST AND CEASE** • 'comfort' activities – computer games, excessive breaks • chat, gossip • daydreaming and doodling • reading irrelevant material • unnecessary travel

Kotter's 8-stage Change Model

Developed in 1996, the stages of Kotter's change model can be used as a tool and an overall change management framework when managing a project. The eight stages are:

1. **Establish a sense of urgency** – when initiating the project and presenting the project plans.
2. **Create a guiding coalition** – convince people that the project has value and benefits; bring together a strong coalition or team of people from different departments to guide the team.
3. **Develop a shared vision** – create a strategy to deliver the objectives of the project.
4. **Communicate the vision** – communicate the purpose, aims and objectives of the project efficiently; address concerns openly.
5. **Empower people to act on the vision** – remove obstacles that may stop progress.
6. **Create short-term wins to motivate with success** – set smaller objectives that can be achieved, praised and rewarded.
7. **Consolidate and build on the changes made by the project** – analyse each 'win' for success and areas for improvement; set goals to continue the momentum.
8. **Institutionalise the change** – talk about progress; include relevant lessons learned during the project within the organisation's training and recruitment practices.

Project Management

Project Plan

A project plan, also known as a project management plan, is a document that contains a project scope and objective. It is most commonly represented in the form of a Gantt chart to make it easy to communicate to stakeholders.

Step 1: *Understand the scope and value of your project*

At its core, a project plan defines your approach and the process your team will use to manage the project according to scope. A project plan communicates vital information to all project stakeholders. If you approach it as something more than a dry document and communicate that aspect of it differently to everyone involved, it can and will be seen as integral to your project's success. The fact is a plan is more than dates. It is the story of your project and you do not want it to be a tall tale! Like any well-written story, there are components that make it good. In fact, any solid plan should answer these questions:

- *What are the major deliverables?*
- *How will we get to those deliverables and the deadline?*
- *Who is on the project team and what role will they play in those deliverables?*
- *When will the team meet milestones and when will other members of the team play a role in contributing to or providing feedback on those deliverables?*

If your plan answers those questions and educates your team and clients on the project logistics, you are creating a viable, strategic game plan for your project.

> *At its core, a project plan defines your approach and the process your team will use to manage the project to scope.*

Step 2: *Conduct extensive research*

Before you start creating a project plan, make sure you know all of the facts. Dive into the documents and communications relevant to the project. Go over the scope of work and related documents (maybe an RFP or notes from sales calls or meetings with your client team). Be thorough. Understand the details and ask thoughtful questions before you commit to anything. A good project manager is well-informed and methodical in the way he or she decides to write a project plan. At a minimum, you will be responsible for possessing a thorough understanding of:

- *The goals of the project*
- *Your client's needs and expectations*
- *The makeup of your client team and their decision-making process (i.e., how they will review and approve your team's work), which might answer:*
- *Who is the project sponsor and how available is he or she?*
- *Who is the PM and will he or she be in constant contact with you? (They need to be).*

Project Management

- *Who are the additional stakeholders your team should be aware of?*

Set time aside with your client to ask some tough questions about process, organisational politics and risks.

Step 3: *Ask the tough questions*
In addition to all of your questions about your client team and their expectations, set some time aside with your main client contact and ask them some tough questions about process, organisational politics and general risks before creating a project plan. Doing so will convey that your team has the experience to handle any type of difficult personalities or situation and that you care about the success of the project from the start.

Questions that may impact a project plan:

- *Has your team discussed how you will gather feedback?*
- *Who is the final sign-off? Or, who owns the project?*
- *Is there a stakeholder we need to consider who is not on your list? (A president, dean, the boss's spouse?)*
- *What is the project deadline? What are the factors or events that are calling for that date? (a meeting, an ad campaign, an event?)*
- *Are there any dates when you will be closed or not available?*
- *Will there be any meetings or points in the project where you will want us to present on the current project status to a larger group (i.e., a board meeting)?*
- *Has your team been through a project like this in the past?*
- *How did it go?*
- *Is there anything that would prevent the project from being successful?*
- *Is there a preferred mode of communication and online project planning tools?*
- *Are there any points in the process that some stakeholders might not understand that we can explain?*

Step 4: *Create your project plan outline*
After getting the answers you need, take some time to think about the responses in light of the project goals and how your team might approach a similar project. Think about the tasks that are outlined in the scope of work and try to come up with a project planning and management approach by creating a high-level outline. All you need is a calendar to check dates.

A first outline can be very rough and might look something like a work breakdown structure.

Make sure your outline includes:

Project Management

- *Deliverables and the tasks taken to create them*
- *Your client's approval process*
- *Timeframes associated with tasks/deliverables*
- *Ideas on resources needed for tasks/deliverables*
- *A list of the assumptions you are making in the plan*
- *A list of absolutes as they relate to the project budget and/or deadlines*

There will always be multiple ways to execute the work you are planning and it is easy to focus on what the end product will look like. Do not go there. Instead, focus on the mechanics of how it will happen. Getting tied up in the execution will only confuse you and likely make you feel unimpressed by the final product because it is not what you envisioned.
Remind yourself: You are there to plan and guide the project, not create it.

A project outline will help you to organise your thoughts, formulate what might work for the project and then transform everything into a discussion. Take this time to build a simple project plan outline—it does not have to have all the details just yet. Doing so lays the foundations for a solid, sustainable project plan.

Step 5: *Talk with your team*
Starting a project must begin with clear communication of the project goals and the effort required to meet them. This comes with understanding the fact that a project manager cannot be the only one writing a project plan. Sure, you could try—but if you are interested in team buy-in, you will not. The reason you will not is because you do not want to put yourself or your team in an awkward position by not coming to a consensus on the approach before presenting it to your client. Doing that would be like stabbing every single one of your co-workers in the back.

It is also great to utilise the super-smart folks surrounding you to get their input on how the team can complete the tasks at hand without killing the budget and the team's morale. As a project manager, you can decide on waterfall or agile approaches, but when it comes down to it, you need to know that the team can realistically execute the plan.

You can also use your project plan review time to question your own thinking and push the team to take a new approach to the work. For instance, if you are working on a website design, can designers start creating visual concepts while the wireframes are being developed? Will it make sense for this project and for the team? Can you have two resources working on the same task at once?

Running ideas by the team and having an open dialogue about the approach can not only help you with building a project plan, it is also a big help in getting everyone to think about the project in the same terms. This type of buy-in and communication builds trust in a team and gets people excited about working together to solve a goal. It can work wonders for the greater good of your team and your project.

Project Management

Step 6: *Write your full project plan*

When you have got all the info you need and you have spoken to all parties, you should feel more than comfortable enough to put together a rock-solid project plan using whatever tool works for you. Any good online project planning tool will help you to formalise your thoughts and lay them out in a consistent, readable way.

Make it readable

To make your project plan readable, use some formatting skills to make sure tasks, durations, milestones and dates are crystal clear. Try to make a simple project plan—the more straightforward and easier to read it is, the better. No matter what tool you are using, you should include these features:

Include all pertinent project info:

- *Client Name, Project Name*
- *Version Number, Delivery Date*
- *Break out milestones and deliverables in sections by creating headers and indenting subsequent tasks.* (Reading one long list of tasks is really monotonous and can be mind-numbing even to the best of us.)
- *Call out which team is responsible for each task. (Example: "CLIENT: Provide feedback")*
- *Add resources responsible to each task so there is no confusion about who is responsible for what.*
- *Be sure to show durations of tasks clearly. Each task should have a start and end date.*
- *Add notes to tasks that might seem confusing or need explanation. It never hurts to add detail!*
- *Call out project dependencies. These are important when you are planning for the risk of delays.*
- *Include your company's logo and your client's logo if you are feeling fancy.*
- *Use your company's branded fonts if you are feeling really fancy.*

In addition to all of this, you should be as flexible as possible when it comes to how your project plan is presented. There is no absolute when it comes to how you represent your plan as long as you and your team understand what goes into one. Remember, people absorb information differently; while some people prefer a list-view, others might prefer to see a calendar, or even a Gantt chart. You can make all of those variations work if you have taken the steps to create a solid plan.

You should be as flexible as possible when it comes to how your plan is presented.

Project Management

Step 7: *Publish your plan*

You are almost finished! You have done your research! outlined your approach, discussed it with your team and built your formal project plan. Do yourself one quick favour and ask someone on your team to review it before you hand it over to your clients. There is nothing more embarrassing than being a project manager and delivering a plan with an error—like an incorrect date. It will take someone 10 minutes and you will have peace of mind.

Step 8: *Share your plan with the team and make sure they read it!*

After you have put all of that work into creating this important document, you want to make sure that it has actually been reviewed. When you are delivering your project plan, make sure you provide a summary of it in prose format. A brief message that covers the overall methodology, resources, assumptions, deadlines and related review times will help you to convey what the project plan means to the project and to everyone involved.

Do not be bashful about it: explain the thought that has gone into the process of building the project plan and open it up for discussion. It can be good to set up a call to review the plan line by line with a client. This ensures that your client will understand the process and what each step in the plan means. Sure, you might have to explain it a few more times, but at least you are making the effort to help establish good project planning standards across the board and educate your clients on how your team works. And again, it shows that you care.

Step 9: *Prepare to keep planning*

Some projects are smooth and easy to manage and others are a complete nightmare that wakes you up at 3 a.m. every other night (it happens). Regardless, plans will change. With a good team and a clear scope of work, you are on your way to making a solid plan that is manageable and well-thought-out. Having a solid project plan is your best defence against project chaos.

If you are an easy-going project manager who can adapt your approach and your plan to go with the flow while calling out the appropriate risks, you will find yourself happy. Otherwise, the daily changes will cloud your vision and you will focus on things that will not help your team, your client, or the project.

Project Management

Delivering the Project

It is true to say that no two projects are the same and everyone will have different objectives, parameters, budgets, constraints, outcomes, etc.

As a consequence, every project will need to be managed differently with different emphasis on different elements. There cannot therefore be a definitive guide as to how a project should be delivered and everyone should be assessed and planned on its own merits before a delivery plan is drawn up.

Key Project Documentation

As noted above, no two projects are the same and therefore a standard set of documentation cannot be prescribed to a project. The documentation will be unique to each project. Key pieces that may be used to deliver a project can include:

- *a brief and terms of reference*
- *project plans*
- *definitions of project roles*
- *a risk log (RAID) or register*
- *project monitoring records* – e.g., *Gantt charts or progress reports*

A brief and terms of reference
During the initiation stage, a brief and terms of reference to provide a framework for the project must be produced. By agreeing these early in the process, everyone can agree their role and commitment to it and the project managers can check whether or not the project is viable. This needs to be agreed before the organisation commits to planning and using its resources, finances and stakeholders' time.
It is important to show what is not covered by the project too. This is key in large organisations in particular, where people may look at a project and assume that it covers their area when it does not.

Project plans
The project plans will include all aspects of the project, including:

timescales, deadlines and critical review points
human and physical resources
the budgets that relate to the project
contingency plans

The plan needs to go into detail about how the different timescales and tasks will overlap and affect each other.

Project Management

Definitions of project roles

The various people involved with the project need to have their job descriptions in definitions of project roles. Having these together helps the project manager to have an overall view of who is tasked to do what, so that they can make sure that all aspects and tasks have been covered.

A risk log or register

An important element of the planning stage is to prepare a risk log or register and put in measures to minimise risk. A risk assessment needs to be performed for each aspect of the project and these are kept together in a risk log.

For example, organisations can use a RAID log for their projects:

Risks – *events that will have an adverse effect on the project*
Assumptions – *factors that are assumed to be in place*
Issues – *something that is going wrong on the project and needs managing*
Dependencies – *events or work that are dependent on the result of the project, or things on which the project will be dependent*

Risks can be defined in many ways – e.g., financial risk when investing or borrowing money; reputation when making decisions that affect the organisation's image and good name; weather or other external influences; health and safety.

According to the Health and Safety Executive, there are five main steps to risk assessment. Many organisations use these as guidelines when designing and implementing their own risk assessments:

- *Identify the hazards*
- *Decide who might be harmed and how*
- *Evaluate the risks and decide on precautions*
- *Record findings and implement them*
- *Review the assessment and update as necessary*

These risk assessment guidelines can be modified to apply to any type of risk as they help everyone to see and understand the potential hazards and to take steps to reduce the chance of harm by having control measures in place.

A risk management log could include columns such as:

risk impact – *high, medium or low*
probability of occurrence – *high, medium or low*
risk descriptions
project impact – *timescales or resources that may be affected*
risk area – *budget, resources or schedule*
symptoms – *human resources are not fully decided when a project is about to start*

---

triggers – *24 hours before bad weather is inevitable, contingency plans to cancel will come into effect*

risk response – *mitigation*

response strategy – *allocate extra resources, reschedule or cancel*

contingency plan – *bring in qualified agency staff to cover short term*

Project monitoring records

Once the project is underway, documents are needed for monitoring the project's progress against plans and objectives. These could include, for example, Gantt charts or progress reports.

Types of Project Management

All types of project in project management follow a certain approach. There exists various methodologies through which project management can be carried out.

Critical Path Method (CPM)

This method was developed in the 1950s and is based on the idea that some tasks cannot be started until others are completed. This highlights task interdependencies. The critical path method identifies the most optimised work path to follow taking these dependencies into consideration so that you can finish your project in the least time possible.

Critical Chain Project Management (CCPM)

This methodology focuses primarily on the resources needed to complete a project and its tasks. The critical chain is identified which pinpoints the project's most critical tasks. In turn, the resources are reserved for these high-priority tasks.

The PMI/PMBOK "Method"

This methodology encompasses the breakdown of different types of projects into five project groups agreed upon by the Project Management Institute (PMI). Essentially it refers to the following the project management life cycle and each phase's demands.

Agile

This methodology was developed in 2001. It focuses on effective response to change, comprehensive documentation and individuals interacting over processes and tools. Continuous collaboration is a key feature between both team members and other project stakeholders.

Scrum:

Is a variation from the Agile methodology and is its most popular framework. It is simple to implement and solves many problems that software developers have faced such as convoluted development cycles, delayed production and inflexible project plans. A small team is typically led by what is called a Scrum Master who clears all obstacles that prevent efficient work. Teams work in 'sprints' which are short cycles comprised of two weeks normally and typically meet daily to discuss the progress of the tasks of their project.

Project Management

Kanban

Kanban is a methodology based on a team's capacity to do work. It originated from Toyota in the 1940s. It is a visual approach to project management and is useful for work that requires steady output. Here, teams move through the progress of their project visually and thus allows for clearer identification of any roadblocks or bottlenecks that may occur along the way.

Project Management

Managing Project Resources

When managing the project's resources, a range of the tools above can be used. They can help to provide an up-to-date, three-dimensional view of the project at all stages, which helps the project manager to, for example:

- *make sure that resources are available on time for each stage of the project*
- *identify problems and potential risks as soon as possible*
- *find solutions to address problems, issues and risks*
- *make decisions about how to reallocate resources*
- *provide evidence to support requests for increased resources and timescales*
- *show more senior decision-makers how they are managing the project*

When managing resources, the purpose, scope, aims and objectives for the whole project need to be very clear. This gives a focus so that time, human and physical resources can be geared up to achieve goals without unnecessary waste.

Human Resources
When managing human resources for a project, managers perform the usual functions associated with people management, for example:

- *planning and allocating work to match the skills, experience and knowledge of team members*
- *developing and maintaining a common sense of purpose and a positive working environment*
- *working to retain team members*
- *recruiting and training team members*
- *making sure everyone understands aims and objectives*
- *supporting team members in career and skills development*
- *ensuring compliance with legislation* – e.g., health and safety, data protection and equality and diversity
- *monitoring work and taking action to improve performance*

In addition to these management tasks, the project manager's main focus is to make sure that people with the right skills are available when required for each stage of the project. During the planning stage, they can:

- *identify exactly which human resources are going to be needed for specific parts of the project*
- *work out the lead times for preparing and recruiting staff*
- *ensure that existing team members have the right skills*
- *recruit new team members, from inside or outside the organisation*
- *train and brief all team members in time*

Project Management

- *emphasise the importance of timescales and quality – and how these can affect other areas of the project*
- *ensure that team members have the equipment they need to perform their duties* – e.g., hi-viz jackets, stationery, laptops, tablets, travel tickets, radios or mobile phones

During the delivery and control stage, these points need to be monitored, supported and reinforced, as necessary.

Physical Resources

Projects are very focused and visible, which often means that the resources are under more scrutiny than in other business activities. As projects are usually stand-alone activities, every physical resource needs to be planned and allocated to them – e.g., venues, desks and stationery.

The project team is accountable and responsible for managing resources effectively and may have to answer to, for example:

senior managers and directors – who need the project to make a profit for the organisation

clients – customers who have commissioned and paid for the project

sponsors – companies who have associated their brand with the project

government agencies – enforcing regulations on the environment or health and safety

Due to the temporary nature of a project, with its beginning, middle and end, resources need to be flexible. This means that everything needs to be planned in great detail, which requires a considerable amount of management to keep things on track. For example, the project manager for our charity dinner example will have to manage:

the venue for the dinner – checking its capacity and suitability; booking it; setting up kitchens for the dinner; dismantling everything afterwards

resources needed at the venue – sound and lighting systems; hiring toilets and changing rooms for the artists; parking facilities for staff and artists; rest areas, training rooms and catering facilities for volunteers

office space for staff – at the venue and within the organisation's premises

office equipment – integrated IT and telephone equipment at the venue and head office

vehicles – hiring cars and vans for volunteers, artists and full-time staff to use catering and other resources for the artists– extra portable toilets; catering outlets; smoking areas

sales, marketing and ticketing – printing and distributing tickets, leaflets and posters

insurance and inspections of resources – insurance for the venue, public liability, vehicles and rented equipment; dealing with the health and safety representatives from the local council who inspect the venue

Project Management

Every item has a cost and a lead time, so careful management is required to make sure that:

- *each item is fit for purpose and satisfies regulatory requirements*
- *it is available on time*
- *the quality is as agreed and expected* - as set out in a service level agreement
- *waste is kept to a minimum*
- *there is a plan for all resources at the end of the project* –handing rented venues, equipment and machinery back in good condition; selling purchased items that are no longer required; returning equipment and supplies to head office

Financial Resources

Budgets are usually strictly controlled for projects and the project manager is accountable and responsible for agreeing, controlling and managing budgets. They need to consider, for example:

timescales – to show when money is due to come in and out – when money from ticket sales and sponsors is likely to be available

priorities – to target resources correctly to support the efficiency and effectiveness of *the organisation* – prioritising workforce costs, assessing and arranging payments for urgent, planned and essential purchases

financial resources – to match funding with anticipated income and expenditure – helping to arrange business loans to finance long-term projects; dealing with increases and decreases in revenue and expenses

contingencies – negotiating and setting aside budgets and resources for unpredictable and unforeseen circumstances

Management Tools for Monitoring Progress

By using management tools, the project manager can monitor progress and see when it is time to implement the next stage of delivery of the project. The example of the volunteers working at the charity dinner, the sequence might include:

establishing the uniform sizes needed for the new recruits
giving a provisional order to the supplier – so that they can start to prepare
finishing recruitment of volunteers
confirming the uniform sizes that are needed and making the final order a month before the dinner – the company needs two weeks to print and deliver the uniforms

Until the volunteer recruitment has been finalised, it is not possible to make the final uniform order. As a contingency, a few extras of the standard sizes will be ordered. By tracking all of this information using, for example, a PERT diagram or a Gantt chart, the project manager can identify critical points and make sure that everything is on track.

Project Management

Using the project management tools mentioned before, here are some suggestions about how they might be used to monitor progress in the recruitment and training of team members in the charity dinner example:

Management tool/ method	Suggestions of how this could be applied to monitoring progress
SWOT analysis	*To track the strengths and weaknesses of recruitment policies compared to expected targets; to review the opportunities for finding the right people if there are issues; to review the threats to progress to make sure that they are still relevant*
Work Breakdown Structures (WBS)	*To monitor the job descriptions set out in the initial WBS to make sure that the right people are being selected; to monitor training programmes set out in the WBS to make sure that they are relevant and suitable*
PERT diagrams	*To have a visual record about how a delay in advertising vacancies has a knock-on effect on applications, interviews and training*
SMART objectives	*To review levels of recruitment and training against the SMART targets on a regular basis*
Gantt charts	*To see how the recruitment and training elements of the project are progressing in relation to all other aspects of the project, such as physical resources and finance*
Plan on a Page	*To prepare a quick overview for progress meetings and interim management reports*
RACI matrix	*To use as a guide to make sure that communication is as expected and agreed between different stakeholders – to ensure that the relevant directors and external stakeholders are being informed of progress*

Another useful tool to use when monitoring a project's progress is to show the **RAG** status – **red, amber, green**. During the planning stage, the planning team can set parameters about what the colours mean, for example:

> **Red** – *major problems that will affect the viability of the whole project and cannot be resolved by the project manager – the matter should be escalated to the project board member*
> **Amber** – *problems that have a negative effect on one or more aspects of the project's viability and performance – problems can be dealt with by the project manager and their team, who then notify the board about progress*
> **Green** – *the project is performing to plan – all problems are within tolerances and expectations and can be dealt with within normal limits of authority*

There can be drawbacks to the traffic-light system; it can oversimplify a project's progress and it is very dependent on the integrity of the information that can turn an element from red to

Project Management

amber or green. As a visual aid, it is effective as it draws attention to the problem areas and shows when everything is on track.

It can really help to keep everyone involved and motivated by letting them know how things are going. If the news is not very good, it can help to reassure everyone, so that they work harder to get back on track and understand the problems behind problems and potential issues. If things are going well, the team and other stakeholders benefit from knowing and getting some positive praise and feedback. This lifts morale and helps to keep people motivated and focused.

Assigning Tasks to Individuals

You want to make sure that everyone is fully occupied but on project tasks that play to their strengths.

From time to time that might mean that someone has to work on something that is not their core area of expertise, but provided they have the support required, that could be a good development opportunity.

However, assuming you have the luxury of being able to access a range of resources with varying skills, how should you allocate tasks?

Skill
Top of the list is skill – does the person have the skills required to actually carry out this project task and complete it successfully? If so, they are probably the best person for the job.

Experience
Has the resource in question done this sort of task before? If so, they will have the relevant experience and the confidence to do it again and probably will not need much support from you.

If they have not done it before, but you believe they have the skills to do the work, then they will need more support but could still complete the task successfully.

Interest
Just because someone has the skills and experience does not mean that they are interested enough in the work to do the task well.

If they have done the same task a thousand times before and really want to spend some time building their experience in other areas then you could allocate the work to them – but it might not be done to the highest standard, or in a timely fashion.

Talk to team members before you giving them work in order to assess their level of motivation.

Cost
Yes, you do have to consider how much a resource costs before allocating tasks!

Project Management

The person best placed to do the work may be far too expensive for your project budget, so you may have to compromise.

Equally, it is not worth using a highly paid programme manager to do basic admin tasks if you have someone on the team in a project co-ordinator or PMO support role who could do those for you.

Location

Where is the task going to be carried out? With a lot of project work it does not much matter and your team members could work from anywhere.

But there are likely to be some tasks where location does play a part. For example, configuring servers on site, or working at a client location for a length of time.

You want to pick someone who is the best person for the job, but if you have a choice of resource, you could find that location plays a part in the decision-making process.

It is cheaper if you do not have to pay travel expenses and it is probably more convenient for the resource concerned if the work is local to where they are normally based.

Availability

Finally, you should take availability into account. OK, it is not the most important criteria when it comes to assigning work to team members, but it does matter.

There is not any point in assigning a task to someone who is already overloaded, while other team members sit around waiting for work to come in. Instead, it could be a good opportunity to improve the skills of someone else or to help others learn something completely new, like budget management.

In short, there are lots of factors that come into play when assigning project tasks to team members.

You probably do it unconsciously but every so often it does help to think through why you are giving a task to someone – as well as to check that they really are the most appropriate person for the job at that time.

Communicating Progress to Stakeholders

Reports are a central part of project management and there exist many different types of project management reports that are drawn up by project managers for different reasons. Project reports are important for updating the relevant stakeholders of a project about the progress of the activities of the project.

In reality, the sheer number of reports can seem overwhelming. Here are some examples of some of the different types of project reports that project managers need to fill out:

Project Management

Status Reports

Status reports are commonly drawn up to present to sponsors or certain stakeholders that will be affected by the outcome of the project and must be kept up to date on the project's progress. It is the most common type of report and one that project managers work on regularly. They can be weekly, or monthly and their frequency will depend on the stage your project is in and how much there is to say.

Risk Reports

Risk analysis and management are key parameters into project management. Risks must be analysed and kept under control so as to not cause serious damage to a project. Risks are reported at least monthly and usually come out after a risk review meeting. This report includes a risk profile of the project and how you are managing or intend to manage the risks.

Board/Executive Reports

Each report must be written bearing in mind the audience to which it will reach. For project board reports, a high level of detail should be maintained about the project. Different types of project organisation reports follow a different format for their documents, but all are always very detailed. This can help in the sense that board members can pinpoint certain problem areas that they can help with.

Resource Reports

Essentially, a resource report itself helps in identifying who is doing what with what resources and within what timeframe. It helps to ensure you have no resource clashes and makes the project more efficient as a whole. This type of report is arguably one of the most useful for project managers.

Types of Project Meeting

Meetings are another central part of different types of projects and project management. This is due to the fact that projects are carried out more often than not by teams and not individual people. They are a good way to coordinate people and get them on the same page. It is also more efficient to spread information once at a meeting rather than twenty individual times. As in the case with other aspects of project management, there are different types of project meetings:

Initiation meetings

Initiation meetings are very important for every project. They are held at the beginning of a project and include everyone involved in the project's execution. These meetings help to build trust and motivation among team members and help to ensure that everyone is on the same page and aware of what needs to be done. It is an avenue for the project team to be in the know of what is at stake in a project and understand the project scope.

Status Update Meetings

This type of meeting is one of the most common meetings in Project Management. Its aim is to align the team on project progress, challenges, changes and next moves. Problem solving, decision making and task assignments are all factors of status update meetings.

Project Management

Information Sharing Meetings

Much as the name suggests, this meeting allows team members and project managers to essentially share information. Debates, keynotes and lectures tend to appear. These meetings are very important in terms of communication as they clearly outline anything that needs to be known by the rest of the team. Visual communication tools are very useful and common in information sharing meetings.

Decision-Making Meetings

Most business decisions are made during group meetings. Decision making in general tends to be a part of every kind of meeting. The bigger and more important decisions, however, have their dedicated meeting where information sharing, gathering, brainstorming and evaluating different solutions and voting are a common occurrence.

Problem-Solving Meetings

This kind of meeting is generally known as the most complex type. Scopes and priorities are defined as well as current and potential problems that need resolution. Brainstorming is a common activity and the aim is to reach an agreement on future steps to be taken by the team.

Innovation Meetings

These are creative meetings used to motivate team members to brainstorm and come up with new innovative ideas for anything from problem resolutions to new product and service ideas. Ranking and evaluation of each idea then move on to creating a shorter and more concise list from which eventually the best option will be chosen.

Overall, projects are a complex phenomenon needed by us to achieve goals and objectives. They occur all the time around us, even if we do not consciously notice them. Projects are unavoidable, it does not matter what type of project is. Do not forget about the different types and the classification of projects in project management!

Project Management

Reviewing Project Performance

The project manager needs to evaluate a project and look at all of the data that has been collected, so that the team can, for example:

compare the outcomes with the original objectives – to see if the project has achieved its intended aims and the correct quality standards

understand how the project has achieved its purpose – or why it has failed

identify how the project used human resources –to analyse the skills used and identify career development opportunities

identify how efficiently the project used physical resources –comparing budget forecasts with actual costs, reviewing the levels of waste

identify problems and potential improvements

advise stakeholders and decision-makers – about how to repeat, develop or improve actions and plans for future projects

identify needs for further project work –to set up a new project to solve major issues that were discovered when working on the first project

When evaluating a project, the data needs to be reliable and relevant to be of use. We need to consider what we want to know and what we want to measure, to be able to identify what data we need and how we will collect it.

Organisations will have their own ways of evaluating a project, which could include, for example:

comparing estimated costs with actual costs – to evaluate the budget allocations and identify the causes of variance

collecting and reviewing feedback from customers and other users of the services and products covered in the project – e.g., independent surveys, feedback forms, forum comments, focus groups or satisfaction surveys

analysing operational data – e.g., looking at patient records in a hospital to evaluate changes in services

reviewing progress reports – e.g., final 'wash-up' reports from staff and other stakeholders about their experiences and recommendations

analysing sales patterns – e.g., to see when tickets were purchased and by whom; to see if business changes have affected sales as expected

analysing changes in activity and comments on websites and social media – e.g., to illustrate a change towards Internet shopping following a project on online sales

The methods selected will depend upon who needs and wants to see the evaluation of project performance. The media, for example, might only be interested in the initial financial impact of changes made by the project, whereas the organisation's HR department will be more interested in evaluating the impact on staff skills, experience, training and career development. Reviews of project performance need to be presented in ways that satisfy the needs of stakeholders.

Project Management

In general, the project team's review needs to:

- *show the successes of the project*
- *praise everyone who contributed to the success*
- *identify areas of weakness and lessons that can be learned for future projects*
- *illustrate the project team's value to support bids for future projects*

Managing Project Risks and Issues

A **risk** is the probability of harm happening. It is only a 'what if' and the harm may not happen at all, especially if measures are put in place to minimise the risk of harm to the project. For example, there can be a physical risk of harm from:

slips, trips and falls – *due to unsafe flooring, obstructions, wires, badly-positioned equipment or other trip hazards*
working at height – *up ladders or on scaffolds*
cross-contamination when handling food and drink – *when staff do not wash their hands and pass on germs to customers*
illness and injury – *from poor crowd control, excessive alcohol or excessive noise, if loose wires on machinery are not dealt with correctly*

Projects are also at risk due to, for example:

failure of an event or task – *from insufficient planning*
financial failure – *if revenue is too low or costs are too high*
equipment failure – *due to inadequate maintenance*
changes in external factors – *planning rules or employment laws; world prices; national or international political influence; weather; local community action*
changes in internal factors – *reorganisation of premises, workforce or management structures; organisational culture*

An issue that affects a project, has actually happened. It is something that is real and actually has an impact on the project. Despite every effort to minimise risk, there are some things that cannot be mitigated and they do cause issues for the project team.

If any one of the identified potential risks becomes a reality, it becomes an issue that the project management team needs to address. Examples of issues that affect projects include, for example:

weather – *leading to cancellation or reorganisation of an event; leading to increased costs from having to use extra resources to deal with the consequences*
inability to recruit sufficient, good-quality team members – *due to insufficient local supply or competition from other organisations*
illness or injury to team members or others – *following an accident in the workplace*

Project Management

increased prices of supplies – due to a change in world prices of raw materials
decreased revenue – as a result of bad weather
political change – the UK deciding to leave the European Union

As risks and issues can both affect how a project is run, they need to be managed and tracked. The project team need to do all that they can to minimise the risks of harm to the project and to make plans and forecasts about how they will deal with issues that do arise.

The implications of failing to mitigate risks and plan how to deal with issues can be extremely serious – from physical harm to people to the failure of the whole project or the organisation.

Identifying and Mitigating Risks

When identifying and mitigating risks, the project manager needs to, for example:

- *identify potential hazards and risks during the planning stage*
- *create a risk log or register – and use it to mitigate risk*
- *maintain awareness of potential risks*
- *consult stakeholders to agree approaches to risk management*
- *use leadership skills to manage risks that materialise*
- *amend plans when risks have an impact on the critical path or other timelines*

The following table shows some suggestions about how the risks mentioned above could be identified and mitigated:

Project Management

Area of risk	How to identify the potential risks	Suggestions about how to mitigate the risks
Slips, trips and falls	Risk assessment of hazards – e.g., wires, wet floors, obstructions Observation Accident records	Have good health and safety working practices – e.g., keep wires out of the way; put yellow hazard warning signs up; inform people about hazard; improve general hazard awareness of staff; have procedures for reporting potential hazards quickly
Working at height	Identify times and tasks where working at height will be necessary	Provide regular 'working at height' training for relevant team members and contractors Provide correct personal protective equipment (PPE) – e.g., harness, hard hat, safety boots
Cross--contamination when handling food and drink	Identify critical control points – e.g., when catering staff handle customers' food	Provide food handling training to relevant staff Insist on good hygiene – e.g., hand washing Monitor temperature control Provide equipment needed – e.g., well-maintained fridges and other storage; heat lamps; PPE; thermometers Ensure that catering contractors are properly equipped and trained
Illness and injury	Risk assessments of all areas Accident records Industry experience	Health and safety training for all team members Ensure the environment is safe Deal with potential hazards immediately Enforce noise limits Restrict access to alcohol Arrange support from security and medical specialists – e.g., door staff to keep an eye on alcohol consumption; first-aiders and ambulance crews on standby
Failure of an event	During progress checks or reviews	Improve planning and communication between project team members and other stakeholders
Financial failure	Changes in sales or costs against forecast amounts	Review finances regularly – e.g., to identify problems and act quickly Have a contingency plan and budget – e.g., to use as agreed in the planning stage Stick to budgets and escalate problems as soon as possible
Financial failure	Changes in sales or costs against forecast amounts	Review finances regularly – e.g., to identify problems and act quickly Have a contingency plan and budget – e.g., to use as agreed in the planning stage Stick to budgets and escalate problems as soon as possible
Equipment failure	Intermittent or complete breakdowns of equipment or machinery	Follow regular maintenance routines Train staff to report potential problems early – e.g., when they see a frayed wire or a crack Establish contacts who can fix and maintain equipment, especially in an emergency – e.g., IT or lighting specialists who can attend critical breakdowns that will affect delivery of the project

Project Management

Area of risk	How to identify the potential risks	Suggestions about how to mitigate the risks
Equipment failure	Intermittent or complete breakdowns of equipment or machinery	Follow regular maintenance routines Train staff to report potential problems early – e.g., when they see a frayed wire or a crack Establish contacts who can fix and maintain equipment, especially in an emergency – e.g., IT or lighting specialists who can attend critical breakdowns that will affect delivery of the project
Changes in external factors	Changes that affect the resources used in the project – e.g., an increase in fuel costs	Review factors that may affect the project regularly – e.g., to identify potential problems and act quickly Have a contingency plan and budget – e.g., to use as agreed in the planning stage Escalate problems that are outside the limits of authority as soon as possible
Changes in internal factors	Organisational meetings or communications about changes that could affect the project	Stay in touch with the whole organisation, not just the project team Check internal factors before committing to the project – e.g., to see if assumptions about resources and future plans are reliable and correct

Managing Issues

When managing issues, the project manager needs to:

understand the nature of the issue – *the reasons why recruitment of new team members is so difficult, maybe using a PESTLE analysis (to look at political, economic, social, technological, legal and environmental impacts)*
evaluate the scope of the issue – *how big a problem this could be and how the recruitment problem could either ease or get worse*
evaluate the impact on the project – *how the recruitment problems could cause extra work for current team members or complete failure of the whole project*

Doing a SWOT analysis as soon as an issue has been identified could be an effective activity to focus attention and aid the decision-making process. By looking at the strengths, weaknesses, opportunities and threats to progress of each possible solution, the project manager can evaluate the issue and work out how to limit or eliminate the impact of the issue.
For example, a project manager still needs another 50 stewards to run an event. They normally have trained volunteer stewards. However, with only one month to go, they do not have enough people to steward the event and there is a legal requirement to have sufficient stewards on duty whenever the public are in the venue. All stewards need to have a full day's training if they do not hold a current Spectator Security qualification. The project manager does a SWOT analysis to help them identify the pros and cons of each option:

Project Management

	Option A – increase publicity to attract new applications from new volunteers – e.g., advertise, make public appeals, approach organisations that place volunteers	Option B – approach another organisation that has large numbers of trained volunteers who might help for this one event	Option C – employ an event company who use qualified, paid staff
Strengths	New team members add to the pool of talent for future events and projects Control over type of person selected Control over training and monitoring Low cost	Volunteers already used to working at large events Good to have relationship between organisations that can help each other out from time to time	Staff can be provided in time Identifiable costs The company's service history should indicate reliability Staff will be qualified and will know how to operate without further training Less input required from the project team as the event company will manage the 50 staff and associated resources
Weaknesses	Time taken to deal with advertising, applications, interviews and recruitment of new volunteers No guarantee that enough people can be found, recruited and trained in time Unknown numbers for uniforms and other resources until the last-minute Cost of advertising	Volunteers might not be available or willing to work with a new project team The other organisation might not want to lose its volunteers Restricted choice in the actual individuals who join the team Staff training time required	Need to rely on the event company to choose suitable individuals High costs Volunteers might resent paid staff doing the same job as them
Opportunities	Local radio is running a volunteer campaign next week One week to advertise, then two weeks to interview and recruit Training sessions for all volunteers booked in 4 weeks' time	Three or four well-known groups in the local area that could be approached Three weeks to sort out before training is due	Plenty of event companies and staff available if researched online and using trade networks Could be arranged quickly
Threats to success	Lack of time – leading to a high chance of failure, which would put the whole event at risk Other events might be competing to recruit volunteers	Lack of cooperation from others Other events might be competing to recruit volunteers	High costs might not be covered by contingency budget Other events might be competing to recruit staff for the same day

Project Management

Following the PDCA cycle devised by J Edwards Deming can also help the project manager to focus on how to manage issues:

Plan – *identify the problem and root causes; collect data; set objectives; allocate resources and training*

Do – *implement the plan and take action*

Check – *review and measure progress against objectives; analyse strengths and weaknesses of the plan*

Act/Adjust – *praise success; identify further improvements; communicate any changes to the people involved*

The most important thing to do, though, is to act promptly when a potential or actual hazard, risk or issue is identified and to take steps to minimise or eliminate the causes before the effects become even more serious. A combination of actions may be required that might include, for example:

reallocating human resources – *e.g., to cover emergencies or sickness*

reallocating physical resources – *e.g., moving equipment to where it will be used more efficiently*

negotiating extra funds or time – *e.g., a contingency budget or an extension on a deadline*

asking people for help and advice – *e.g., team members, colleagues or industry contacts due to an emergency*

escalating issues – *e.g., when decisions are outside the limits of authority, or the project is in danger of failing*

Project Management

Reviewing Project Performance

The project manager needs to evaluate a project and look at all of the data that has been collected, so that the team can, for example:

- *compare the outcomes with the original objectives* – *to see if the project has achieved its intended aims and the correct quality standards*
- *understand how the project has achieved its purpose* – *or why it has failed*
- *identify how the project used human resources* –*to analyse the skills used and identify career development opportunities*
- *identify how efficiently the project used physical resources* –*comparing budget forecasts with actual costs, reviewing the levels of waste*
- *identify problems and potential improvements*
- *advise stakeholders and decision-makers* – *about how to repeat, develop or improve actions and plans for future projects*
- *identify needs for further project work* –*to set up a new project to solve major issues that were discovered when working on the first project*

When evaluating a project, the data needs to be reliable and relevant to be of use. We need to consider what we want to know and what we want to measure, to be able to identify what data we need and how we will collect it.

Organisations will have their own ways of evaluating a project, which could include, for example:

- *comparing estimated costs with actual costs* – *to evaluate the budget allocations and identify the causes of variance*
- *collecting and reviewing feedback from customers and other users of the services and products covered in the project* – *e.g., independent surveys, feedback forms, forum comments, focus groups or satisfaction surveys*
- *analysing operational data* – *e.g., looking at patient records in a hospital to evaluate changes in services*
- *reviewing progress reports* – *e.g., final 'wash-up' reports from staff and other stakeholders about their experiences and recommendations*
- *analysing sales patterns* – *e.g., to see when tickets were purchased and by whom; to see if business changes have affected sales as expected*
- *analysing changes in activity and comments on websites and social media* – *e.g., to illustrate a change towards Internet shopping following a project on online sales*

The methods selected will depend upon who needs and wants to see the evaluation of project performance. The media, for example, might only be interested in the initial financial impact of changes made by the project, whereas the organisation's HR department will be more interested in evaluating the impact on staff skills, experience, training and career development. Reviews of project performance need to be presented in ways that satisfy the needs of stakeholders.

Project Management

In general, the project team's review needs to:

- *show the successes of the project*
- *praise everyone who contributed to the success*
- *identify areas of weakness and lessons that can be learned for future projects*
- *illustrate the project team's value to support bids for future projects*

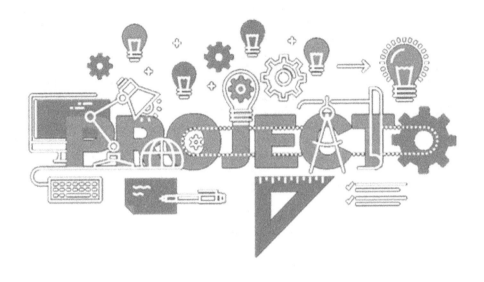

Chapter 11: Planning for a Project

Project Planning

The Project

A project will start when the sponsor (the person who has asked for the research to be done) first identifies the need for change. If the project fits in with their business plans, they will pursue it.

The next step would be to work out how much it will cost to make the change and compare it to the benefit which will be gained as a result. This is called a cost benefit analysis. A cost benefit analysis is simply a list of all the costs with a total at the bottom and a list of the benefits to be expected as a result of the change. Not all projects result in an increase in income or profit, however there are other benefits to gained from running the project which would be difficult to place a value on. A better working environment for example, might improve staff motivation resulting in less sickness, reduced stress and a happier workforce which usually leads to greater productivity. This may be difficult to work out in financial terms, it is sometimes better to look at the cost of not doing the project – in this case increasing staff turnover, more recruitment costs, low morale, poor productivity, etc. If the result is acceptable the project will be given the go ahead and the first stages of planning the project will begin.

It should be stated at this point that:

the biggest part of any project is not actually doing the work – but planning the work and how it will be done

The first document produced is the Project Charter.

Project Charter

The Charter outlines the purpose of the project, how it will be structured and how it will be executed. It will contain details about the vision, objectives, scope and deliverables along with a description of the responsibilities for the project team and stakeholders.

The charter will also list the roles and responsibilities of the project team and identify the project's customers and stakeholders.

Although it seems to contain a great deal of information, the project charter is a very brief document which covers only the headline details of the project. It may only be one or two pages, depending on the size and scale of the project.

The charter will include the following details:

- *The appointed project manager*
- *A definition of the project scope*
- *The budget*
- *The defined milestones*
- *A list of the important / key stakeholders*
- *The technical characteristics of the project deliverable*

Project Planning

The Charter is sometimes called the "Project Definition Document." It gives the project manager the authority to direct and complete the project.

> *The project manager is involved in developing the project charter,*
> *but cannot approve it*

Structure of a Project Charter

The following is the outline of a typical project charter. Not all of the content may be needed for every project, and it is the responsibility of the Project Manager to decide what should and should not be included for each project. It should be remembered that this is a document being used to "sell the idea" of the project, so the more comprehensive the document, the fewer questions may be asked, which will reduce the level of objections held by the decision makers.

Executive Summary
This section summarises each of the sections in this document concisely by outlining the project:

- *Project Definition*
- *Organisation and plan*
- *Risks and issues*
- *Assumptions and constraints*

a. Project Definition
This section describes what the project sets out to achieve. It outlines the vision for the project, the key objectives to be met, the scope of work to be undertaken and the deliverables to be produced.

Vision
Describe the overall vision of the project. The vision statement should be short, concise and achievable.

Examples of vision statements include:

> *To deliver a robust, scalable financial management system to the business*
> *To procure new work premises with adequate capacity and functional surrounds*
> *To successfully introduce new customer service processes to the marketplace*

Objectives
List the key objectives of the project. Objectives are statements which describe in more detail what it is that the project is going to achieve. All objectives listed should be Specific, Measurable, Achievable, Realistic and Time-bound (SMART).

Project Planning

Business Objectives
List the business-specific objectives to be achieved. For example:

- *To deliver new accounts payable and receivable and payroll processes, thereby reducing financial processing timescales by at least 30%*
- *To build brand new work premises with 50% more space, 30 more cark parks and 20% fewer operational costs than the existing premises*
- *To provide a new customer complaints service to enable customers to issue complaints on-line and receive a direct response from the company within 24hrs*

Technological Objectives
List the technology-specific objectives to be achieved. For example:

- *To install new accounts payable and receivable and payroll system modules within the existing accounting system, thereby achieving 99.5% system up-time*
- *To relocate existing technology infrastructure at the new building premises within 2 days elapsed time and with no impact on customer service delivery*
- *To build a new website which allows customers to enter and track complaints through to resolution.*

Scope
Define the scope of the project in terms of the business:

- *Processes which will change*
- *Organisational areas which will be affected*
- *Locations which will be impacted on*
- *Data which will be altered*
- *Applications which will be installed and/or altered*
- *Technologies which will be deployed and/or decommissioned*

Where relevant, identify the related business areas which will <u>not</u> be affected as a result of this project.

Deliverables
Summarise the key project deliverables in a table as shown below which includes examples

Project Planning

Item	Components	Description
New premises	New physical building Interior fit-out Telecommunications	• *1200 sq. m premises near city centre with outdoor facilities, parking and signage* • *Open plan environment with 5 offices, 3 meeting rooms and a staff games room* • *Voice / data telecoms infrastructure and video conference facilities*
New financial system	Accounts payable module Accounts receivable module Payroll module	• *A new system module which enables staff to quickly enter accounts payable transactions* • *A new system module which enables staff to quickly enter accounts receivable transactions* • *A new system module which enables staff to quickly enter payroll information*
New customer complaints process	Complaints website Complaints resolution process Complaints measurement process	• *New website with customer complaints forms, a complaint tracking page and company contact information* • *New full-time staff complaints role and process for resolving complaints made* • *New process for assessing complaint characteristics (such as numbers, business areas and resolution timescales)*

b. Project Organisation

Customers

Describe the customers who will use the deliverables produced from the project. Customers may be individuals or groups within or outside of the company. The success of the project will be primarily based on whether or not the deliverables produced match the requirements of the customers identified in this table.

Customer	Representative
Customer Group	**Customer Name**

Project Planning

Stakeholders

List the key stakeholders for this project. A 'stakeholder' is simply a person or entity outside of the project who has a key interest in the project. For instance, a company financial controller will have an interest in the cost implications of the project, a CEO will have an interest in whether the project is conducted in accordance with the vision of the company. Examples of stakeholders include:

- *Company Executives*
- *Legislative bodies*
- *Regulatory bodies.*

Complete a similar table to the one below (includes examples):

Stakeholder	Interested in
CEO	Alignment with company vision and strategy
Financial Controller	Alignment with company budget
Health and Safety Office	Alignment with health and safety standards
Government body	Compliance with legislation
Industry body	Compliance with codes of practice

Roles

Identify the roles required to undertake the project. Examples of typical roles include project:

- *Sponsor*
- *Review Group*
- *Manager*
- *Team Member*

For each role identified, list the resource likely to fill each role and their assignment details by completing the following table:

Role	Organisation	Resource Name	Assignment Status	Assignment Date
Role	Organisation	Person	Unassigned / Assigned	xx/yy/zz

Project Planning

For larger projects with more than 10 resources, list only the key roles in the above table. Include a detailed listing and description of all roles within a separate Resource Plan document if required.

Responsibilities

List the generic responsibilities for each role identified. A full list of the responsibilities, performance criteria and skills required should be documented within a separate *Job Description* for each project role.

Project Sponsor

The Project Sponsor is the principal 'owner' of the project. Key responsibilities include:

- *Defining the vision and high-level objectives for the project*
- *Approving the requirements, timetable, resources and budget*
- *Authorising the provision of funds / resources (internal or external)*
- *Approving the project plan and quality plan*
- *Ensuring that major business risks are identified and managed*
- *Approving any major changes in scope*
- *Receiving Project Review Group minutes and taking action accordingly*
- *Resolving issues escalated by the Project Manager / Project Review Group*
- *Ensuring business / operational support arrangements are put in place*
- *Ensuring the participation of a business resource (if required)*
- *Providing final acceptance of the solution upon project completion.*

Project Review Group

The Project Review Group may include both business and 3rd party representatives and is put in place to ensure that the project is progressing according to plan.

Key responsibilities include:

- *Assisting the Project Sponsor with the definition of the project vision and objectives*
- *Undertaking Quality Reviews prior to the completion of each project milestone*
- *Ensuring that all business risks are identified and managed accordingly*
- *Ensuring conformance to the standards and processes identified in the Quality Plan*
- *Ensuring that all appropriate client/vendor contractual documentation is in place prior to the initiation of the project*

Project Planning

Project Manager

The Project Manager ensures that the daily activities undertaken on the project are in accordance with the approved project plans. The Project Manager is responsible for ensuring that the project produces the required deliverables on time, within budgeted cost and at the level of quality outlined within the Quality Plan.

Key responsibilities include:

- *Documenting the detailed Project Plan and Quality Plan*
- *Ensuring that all required resources are assigned to the project and clearly tasked*
- *Managing assigned resources according to the defined scope of the project*
- *Implementing the following project processes: time / cost / quality / change / risk / issue / procurement / communication / acceptance management*
- *Monitoring and reporting on project performance (re: schedule, cost, quality and risk)*
- *Ensuring compliance with the processes and standards outlined in the Quality Plan*
- *Reporting and escalating project risks and issues*
- *Managing project interdependencies*
- *Adjusting the detailed plan as necessary to provide a complete picture of the progress of the project at any time.*

Project Team Member

A Project Team member undertakes all tasks necessary to design, build and implement the final solution.

Key responsibilities include:

- *Undertaking all tasks allocated by the Project Manager (as per the Project Plan)*
- *Reporting progress of the execution of tasks to the Project Manager on a frequent basis*
- *Maintaining all documentation relating to the execution of allocated tasks*
- *Escalating risks and issues to be resolved by the Project Manager.*

Structure

Depict the reporting lines between each of the key roles described above within a Project Organisation Chart. An example follows:

Project Planning

Summary Project Plan

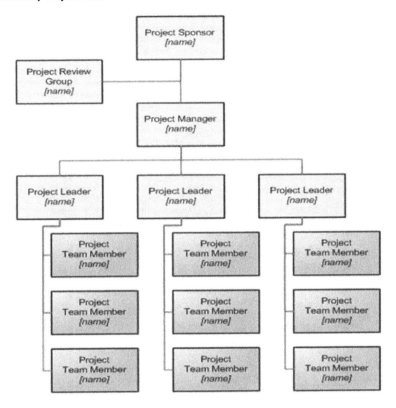

Approach

Describe the approach to be taken to implement each of the phases within the project.

Phase	Approach
Initiation	Outline the method by which the project will be further defined, the project team appointed and the Project Office established.
Planning	Define the overall planning process to ensure that the phases, activities and tasks are undertaken in a co-ordinated fashion.
Execution	Describe the generic phases and activities required to build, test and implement the deliverables of the project.
Closure	Describe the steps required to release the deliverables to the business, close the project office, reallocate staff and perform a Post Implementation Review of the project.

Project Planning

Overall Plan

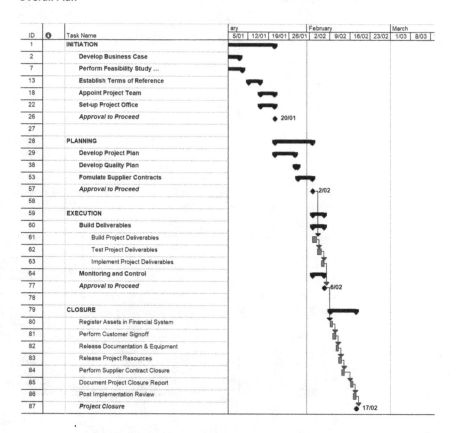

A more detailed Project Plan will be drawn up during the "Planning" phase of the project.

Milestones

List the major project milestones and the required delivery dates. A 'milestone' is a significant event or stage to be completed. Explain why each milestone is critical to the project, as follows:

Milestone	Date	Description
Milestone Title	xx/yy/zz	Explain why milestone date is critical to business

Project Planning

Dependencies

List any project activities which:

- *Will impact on another activity external to the project*
- *Will be impacted on by the non/delivery of another activity external to the project*

Project Activity	Impacts on	Impacted on by	Criticality	Date
Planned Activity	External Activity	External Activity	Low/Medium/High	xx/yy/zz

Resource Plan

Summarise the duration and effort required for each project team member, as follows:

Role	Start Date	End Date	% Effort
Project Role	xx/yy/zzzz	xx/yy/zzzz	xx/yy/zzzz

A detailed Resource Plan will be drawn up during the "Planning" phase of this project.

Financial Plan

Summarise the project budget approved (within the Business Case) as follows:

Project Planning

Category	Cost	Value
People	• Salaries of project staff • Contractors and outsourced parties • Training courses	£ x £ x £ x
Physical	• Building premises for project team • Equipment and materials • Tools (computers, cabling, phones...)	£ x £ x £ x
Marketing	• Advertising / branding • Promotional materials • PR and communications	£ x £ x £ x
Organisational	• Operational downtime • Short-term loss in productivity • Cultural change	£ x £ x Describe

A detailed Financial Plan will be drawn up during the "Planning" phase of this project.

Quality Plan

Briefly describe the various processes to be undertaken to ensure the success of the project.

Process	Description
Quality Management	**Summary of how the process will be undertaken**
Change Management	
Risk Management	
Issue Management	
Configuration Management	
Document Management	
Acceptance Management	
Procurement Management	
Financial Management	
Timesheet Management	
Project Reporting	
Project Communications	

A detailed Quality Plan will be drawn up during the "Planning" phase of this project.

Project Planning

c. Project Considerations

Risks

Summarise the most apparent risks associated with the project. Risks are defined as "any event which <u>may</u> adversely affect the ability of the solution to produce the required deliverables". Risks may be Strategic, Environmental, Financial, Operational, Technical, Industrial, Competitive or Customer related. Complete the following table:

Description	Likelihood	Impact	Mitigating Actions
Inability to recruit skilled resource	Low	Very High	Outsource project to a company with proven industry experience and appropriately skilled staff
Technology solution is unable to deliver required results	Medium	High	Complete a pilot project to prove the full technology solution
Additional capital expenditure may be required in addition to that approved	Medium	Medium	Maintain strict capital expenditure processes during the project

To complete this section thoroughly, it may be necessary to undertake a formal Risk Assessment (by documenting a *Risk Management Plan*). To reduce the likelihood and impact of each risk's eventuating, clear 'mitigating actions' should be defined.

Issues

Summarise the highest priority issues associated with the project. Issues are defined as "any event which currently adversely affects the ability of the solution to produce the required deliverables". Complete the following table:

Description	Priority	Resolution Actions
Required capital expenditure funds have not been budgeted	High	Request funding approval as part of this proposal
Required computer software is only at 'beta' phase and has not yet been released live	Medium	Design solution based on current software version and adapt changes to solution once the final version of the software has been released
Council approval must be sought to implement the final solution	Low	Initiate the council approval process early so that it does not delay the final roll-out process.

Project Planning

d. Assumptions

List the major assumptions identified with the project to date. Examples include:

- *There will be no legislative, business strategy or policy changes during this project*
- *Prices of raw materials will not increase during the course of the project*
- *Additional human resources will be available from the business to support the project*

Constraints

List the major constraints identified with the project to date. Examples include:

- *The financial budget allocated is fixed and does not allow for over-spending*
- *There are limited technical resource available for the project*
- *The technical solution must be implemented after-hours to minimise the operational impact on the business.*

e. Appendix

Supporting Documentation

Attach any other documentation which is relevant to the Project Charter, including:

- *Curricula Vitae (CVs) for key project staff*
- *Research Materials*
- *External quotes or tenders*
- *Detailed financial planning spreadsheets*
- *Other relevant information or correspondence.*

A project charter builds a solid foundation for a project. It gives a common understanding of the objectives.

Project Planning

Benefits of a Project Charter

The following are a few benefits of a project charter:

- *It gives the project manager the authority to complete the project*
- *It explains the project's existence*
- *It shows management's support for the project*
- *It defines the outcome*
- *It aligns the project with the organisation's objectives*
- *It gives team members a transparent reporting system*
- *It saves you from scope creep and gold plating*
- *It helps you avoid disputes*

The project charter is key to the project's success. It provides stakeholders with a common understanding of the project. It is an agreement between the key stakeholders, and it communicates the project manager's authority. It is at the absolute core of the project as everything else will but created from this.

Project Planning

Producing the Project Plan

A project plan is used to plan a project from its initial stages through to its planned conclusion. It is produced by the project manager who will have spent a great deal of time ensuring every detail and element of it is correct and they will use their expertise and judgement to do this.

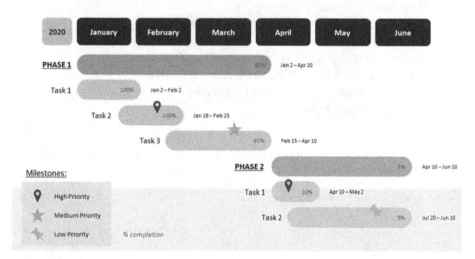

The project plan is not one single document but rather a compound document made up of a number of other documents each of which have a specific role and purpose.

Every project is unique in what it addresses, the scope, scale, value, etc. which means there cannot be a single, standard, document which can be created and tailored to suit each project, however, there are some specific elements which should be included in every project plan. This will help to avoid confusion and forced changes during the project execution phase.

Project Plan
The Project Charter
Project Goals
Project Scope
Milestones and Major Deliverables
Work Breakdown Structure
Budget
Human Resources Plan
Risk Register
Communications Plan
Stakeholder Management Plan
Change Management Plan
Timeline

Project Planning

Project Goals

Project goals are defined in the project charter, but they should be included in the project plan as well to explain the goals of the project or be included the charter as an appendix to the plan.

No matter how a project manager chooses to incorporate the goals into the project plan, the important thing is to maintain a clear link between the project charter—a project is first key document—and the project's second key document, its project plan.

> *A project goal is a tangible statement of what a project should achieve.*

The project goal defines the questions that will be asked at the end of the project. What has the project accomplished? That is the project goal.

Examples:

- *Improve employee satisfaction by introducing flexible working hours.*
- *Introduce mobile devices for sales staff to reduce average order time and increase customer satisfaction.*
- *Upgrade network infrastructure to increase bandwidth and eliminate network outages.*

A project goal should be tied to a higher purpose.

Example:

- *increase sales*
- *cut cost*
- *increase profitability*
- *increase safety*
- *protect the health of people*

This is where the goal can be linked to the Mission, Value and Goals of the organisation. If the goal is not tied to these, it may just end up as another wreck at the bottom of the sea. Simply because it did not bring the results it was supposed to deliver.

Project Planning

Project Goals		
Importance:	Goal	Ownership
1.	Build a new warehouse in the Northern region to better serve our customers in the Borders and Scotland.	Project Team

Project Scope

Like the project goals, the scope of the project is defined in the charter and should be further developed and refined in the project plan. By defining the scope, the project manager can begin to show what the project's goal or finished product will look like at the end. If the scope is not defined, it can get expanded throughout the project and lead to cost overruns and missed deadlines.

Example:

if you are leading a marketing team to create a brochure for a company's product line, you should define how many pages it will be and provide examples of how the finished product might look.

For some team members, a corporate brochure might mean two pages, while others might consider ten pages to be more appropriate. Defining the scope can get the entire team on the same page at the outset.

This should be written as a definitive of statement of what the project will achieve and what it will not achieve. It should be written in a style which can be understood by all – it should not assume and prior technical knowledge.

Project Scope

What is included:
What is Not included:

Project Planning

Milestones and Major Deliverables

The key stages in a project are called milestones and the work which is achieved at these key stages is called a major deliverable. They both represent the big components of work on a project. A project plan should identify these items, define them, and set deadlines for their completion.

If you were building a house, a key stage is when the roof is completed. So, the completed roof would be a major deliverable. This would be identified in the project plan, stating when it must be delivered (completed) by.

Following those, the project could have milestones for internal completion, electrical testing, client acceptance testing, and the date for the handover of the keys. These milestones have work products associated with them, but they are more about the processes than the products themselves.

Milestone and major deliverable deadlines do not have to be exact dates, but the more precise, the better. Precise dates help project managers break down work structures more accurately.

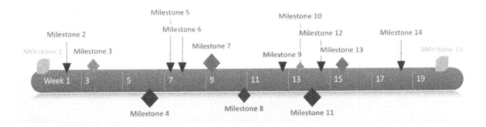

| Milestones and Major Deliverables |||
Week	Milestone	Description
1	1	**Formation Meeting**
1	2	**Planning application submission**

Typical Milestones in a Project

Project Approval
While not as commonly noted as other project milestone examples, the first milestone in the course of any project is the initial approval that allows the project to move forward.

For internal projects, this milestone often comes in the form of an approval from a department director or other high-level stakeholder. For other projects, this milestone is usually marked by the completion of a sales contract and scope of work. Once the project is approved, project managers begin inputting elements of the project into their chosen project management tool.

Requirements Review *(Major projects)*

Most enterprise projects involve a lengthy process in which the project requirements are defined and gathered through a series of meetings, review sessions, and document exchanges. The project team then typically interprets and consolidates their notes and presents the client with a detailed description of the requirements as they understand them.

When the client or customer agrees that the requirements are accurately documented, another major project milestone has been reached.

Design Approval *(Major projects)*

After gathering the customer's requirements, a project team needs to design a solution that will meet the requirements and fulfil the terms of the scope of work. When the initial design is complete (which often takes months or even years for large projects), the customer needs to review the proposed solution and confirm that it will satisfy the project objectives.

This design approval is a significant milestone for projects in fields as diverse as software, construction and marketing, just to name a few.

Project Phase Milestones

Once the project team begins to actually build or implement the proposed solution, the project manager will typically define project-specific milestones related to the components of the work being done.

In a construction project, for example, the project manager might need to mark milestones (and arrange milestone payments) for the completion of phases such as framing, concrete pouring, plumbing installation and interior finishing.

Final Approval

The most significant of all project management milestones, of course, is the one that marks the completion of a project. This milestone typically comes at the end of an extensive testing and inspection process, and a final review session in which all stakeholders agree that the work is complete and meets the project requirements.

Upon reaching this milestone, successful project managers typically hold a follow-up meeting with the team to discuss what worked, what could have been better and how to work even more efficiently and effectively on the next project.

Project Planning

Work Breakdown Structure

A work breakdown structure (WBS) breaks down the milestones and major deliverables in a project into smaller chunks so one person can be assigned responsibility for each chunk or element. In developing the work breakdown structure, the project manager will consider many factors such as the strengths and weaknesses of project team members, the interdependencies among tasks, available resources, and the overall project deadline.

Work Breakdown Structure is defined as a:

> *"Deliverable oriented hierarchical decomposition of the work to be executed by the project team."*

Project managers are ultimately responsible for the success of the project, but they cannot do the work alone. The WBS is a tool the project manager uses to ensure accountability on the project because it tells the project sponsor, project team members, and stakeholders who are responsible for what. If the project manager is concerned about a task, they know exactly who to meet with regarding that concern.

The WBS is a hierarchical reflection of all the work in the project in terms of deliverables. In order to produce these deliverables, work must be performed.

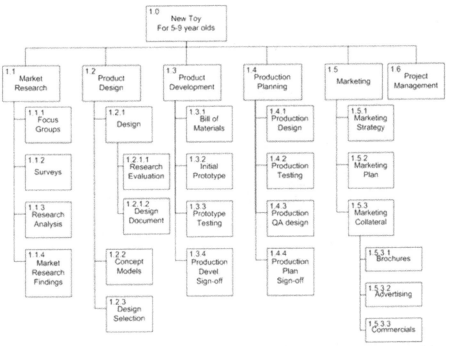

A typical approach in developing a WBS is to start at the highest level, with the product of the project. For example, you are assigned as the project manager of a New Product Development

Project Planning

project. The new product you are developing is a new toy for children. The objective of this product development project is to increase the revenue of the organisation by ten percent.

Above is an example of a WBS for this new toy. Each level of the WBS is a level of detail created by decomposition. Decomposition is the process of breaking down the work into smaller, more manageable components. The elements at the lowest level of the WBS are called tasks. In the example above, brochures, advertising and commercials are all work packages or tasks.

The decomposition of a schedule will continue at varying rates. 'Brochures' is a task identified at the fourth level of decomposition, while the 'marketing plan' is also a task but defined at the third level of decomposition.

As a project manager, the level of decomposition will be dependent on the extent to which you will need to manage. The expectation is that each task will have a single owner and the owner is expected to manage and report on the work necessary to deliver the task. This person is called the 'task owner.' If you cannot assign a single owner, or you need to have additional visibility into the progress of that task, additional decomposition is recommended.

Once all the deliverables of the project have been identified, tasks will be performed in order to create the deliverables. In some cases, these activities are the physical deliverables, but in other cases they are the actions that need to be performed. A physical deliverable, for example, might be an image (an actual file) that is needed for the brochure. Listing out each of the tasks to be performed will result in an activity list as demonstrated below.

Work Package	WBSID	Activity	Predecessor	Duration in Weeks	Resource Type
Focus Group	1.1.1.1	Identify Focus Group Targets			
Focus Group	1.1.1.2	Prepare Focus Group Objectives			
Focus Group	1.1.1.3	Perform Focus Group			
Surveys	1.1.2	Perform Survey			
Research Analysis	1.1.3	Perform Analysis			
Market Research Findings	1.1.4	Create Market Research Findings			
Research Evaluation	1.2.1.1.1	Review Market Research Findings			
Research Evaluation	1.2.1.1.2	Develop Design Options			
Research Evaluation	1.2.1.1.3	Present Design Options			
Design Document	1.2.1.2.1	Draft Design Document			
Design Document	1.2.1.2.2	Design Document Review			
Design Document	1.2.1.2.3	Final Design Document			
Concept Models	1.2.2	Develop Concept Model			
Design Selection	1.2.3	Review Concepts			
Bill of Materials	1.3.1	Create Initial Bill of Materials			
Initial Prototype	1.3.2.1	Develop Initial Prototype			
Initial Prototype	1.3.2.2	Revise Initial Prototype			
Prototype Testing	1.3.3	Test Prototype			
Production Design	1.4.1	Design Production Process			
Production Testing	1.4.2	Design Production Testing Process			
Production QA design	1.4.3	Design Quality Assurance Tests			
Marketing Strategy	1.5.1	Develop Marketing Strategy			
Marketing Plan	1.5.2.1	Develop Initial Marketing Plan			
Marketing Plan	1.5.2.2	Final Marketing Plan			
Brochures	1.5.3.1	Create Brochures			
Advertising	1.5.3.2	Create Ads			
Commercials	1.5.3.3	Create Commercials			
Production Plan Sign-off	1.4.4	Production Plan Sign-off			
Production Devel. Sign-off	1.3.4	Production Devel. Sign-off			
Project Management	1.6	Project Management Activities		LOE	

Project Planning

Budget

Project budget management is a process of formally identifying, approving and paying the costs or expenses incurred on the project. Project budget management involves using purchase order forms to state each set of project expenses, such as training, consulting services, equipment and material cost, etc. Usually in the process, the project manager plays the role of "Approver" (a person who approves a budget for a project) and the finance unit (e.g., Finance Department) acts as a "Recorder" (an organisational unit that tracks and audits budgeting activities and reports to the project manager).

Project Budget							
		Salaries & Wages		Cost		Materials & Equipment	
WBS ID.	Work Element	Rate - £/hr	Hours	Budget	Actual	Amount	Cost
1.1.1.1	Identify focus group targets	£25.75	6	£154.50			

Budgeting Process

The process of determining budget for a project is an activity of combining the cost estimates of individual activities, or a work package, to develop the total cost estimate that allows setting a formal minimum cost for that work package.

This minimum cost figure may differ from the figure which is finally recorded as the Project Manager may decide to add money into the minimum cost in case there are changes to the planned prices or the project hits a problem and is delayed. These are known as contingencies. This will be repeated for each work package until all the planned activities have been identified and funded. These values will then be used as a way to control the budget and provide valuable data to the project resource management process.

The project budgeting process is conducted at the initial steps of project planning, and typically it is performed in parallel with the project scheduling process. The steps of the process are highly dependent upon the cost estimations, task durations and allocated resources. The process is also known as "the project budgeting process". The budgeting serves as a cost control mechanism that allows comparing actual project costs to the items of the authorised project budget. The process allows developing a budget considering key cost factors associated with time durations of project tasks.

When working on the project budgeting activities, the project manager should collaborate with people responsible for managing the work efforts as well as for estimating project costs (the cost estimating team). They will develop and give the cost estimates of individual activities, or work packages, so that the project manager can actually start performing budgeting activities.

The project manager should use the Work Break Down Structure (WBS) of the project, the cost estimates, historical data and records, resource information, and policies in order to identify the monetary resources required for the project.

Budgeting and Budget Risk Management

The budgeting process will not be complete and effective if no risk assessment and assignment have been applied. Without assessing risks surrounding the project, uncertainties and threats that happen regularly during the project implementation will affect the project's bottom line. Cost estimates should be developed with reference to conducted risk assessing activities but identified risks should not be considered a factor influencing the increase in the overall price of the budget. Risk assessing activities allow representing risks as actual costs incurred over the course of project development. Usually, risk assessments cover such areas as development team experience, reliability of the technology used, time shortages, availability of project resources, etc.

Once analysed, a scope and percentage can be assigned to each identified risk.

Human Resources Plan

The human resources plan shows how the project will be staffed. Sometimes known as the staffing plan, the HR plan defines who will be on the project team and how much of a time commitment each person is expected to make. In developing this plan, the project manager negotiates with team members and their supervisors on how much time each team member can devote to the project. If additional staff are needed to consult on the project, but are part of the project team, that is also documented in the HR plan. Appropriate supervisors are consulted, as necessary.

Human Resources Plan

	Project Manager	Design Engineers	Implementation Manager	Training Leads	Functional Managers	Department Managers
Requirements Gathering	A	R	R	C	C	I
Coding Design	A	R	C		C	I
Coding Input	A	R				
Software Testing	A	R	C		I	I
Network Preparation	A	C	R		I	I
Implementation	A	C	R	C	C	C
Conduct Training	A			R	C	C

Key:

R – Responsible for completing the work

A – Accountable for ensuring task completion/sign off

C – Consulted before any decisions are made

I – Informed of when an action/decision has

Risk Register

Many things can go wrong on a project. While anticipating every possible disaster or minor hiccup is challenging, many pitfalls can be predicted. In the risk management plan, the project manager identifies risks to the project, the likelihood those scenarios will happen, and strategies to mitigate them. To formulate this plan, the project manager seeks input from the project sponsor, project team, stakeholders, and internal experts.

Mitigation strategies are put into place for risks that are likely to occur or have high costs associated with them. Risks that are unlikely to occur and ones that have low costs are noted in the plan, even though they do not have mitigation strategies.

A risk register is used to identify potential risks in a project or an organisation, sometimes to fulfil regulatory compliance but mostly to stay on top of potential issues that can derail intended outcomes. The risk register includes all information about each identified risk, such as the nature of that risk, level of risk, who owns it and what are the mitigation measures in place to respond to it.

A risk assessment needs to be performed for each aspect of the project, and these are kept together in a risk log.

Organisations can use a RAID log for their projects:

- **Risks** – *events that will have an adverse effect on the project*
- **Assumptions** – *factors that are assumed to be in place*
- **Issues** – *something that is going wrong on the project and needs managing*
- **Dependencies** – *events or work that are dependent on the result of the project, or things on which the project will be dependent*

Risks can be defined in many ways – e.g., financial risk when investing or borrowing money; reputation when making decisions that affect the organisation's image and good name; weather or other external influences; health and safety.

According to the Health and Safety Executive, there are five main steps to risk assessment. Many organisations use these as guidelines when designing and implementing their own risk assessments:

- *Identify the hazards*
- *Decide who might be harmed, and how*
- *Evaluate the risks and decide on precautions*

Project Planning

- *Record findings and implement them*
- *Review the assessment and update as necessary*

These risk assessment guidelines can be modified to apply to any type of risk as they help everyone to see and understand the potential hazards, and to take steps to reduce the chance of harm by having control measures in place.

A risk management log could include columns such as:

- **risk impact** – *high, medium or low*
- **probability of occurrence** – *high, medium or low*
- **risk descriptions**
- **project impact** – *timescales or resources that may be affected*
- **risk area** – *budget, resources or schedule*
- **symptoms** – *human resources are not fully decided when a project is about to start*
- **triggers** – *24 hours before bad weather is inevitable, contingency plans to cancel will come into effect*
- **risk response** – *mitigation*
- **response strategy** – *allocate extra resources, reschedule or cancel*
- **contingency plan** – *bring in qualified agency staff to cover short term*

Risk Register

Index	WBS	Category	Description	Effects	Probability	Impact	Risk Rank	Owner	Response Plan
001	3.2.4	Scope	Implementation depends on completion of 2.4.3	Delay	7	10	70	D Smith	Monitor closely
002									

Producing a Risk Register

Identify the Risk
Risk cannot be resolve if the risk is not known. There are many ways to identify risk. The data is collected in a risk register.

One way is brainstorming or even brainwriting, which is a more structured way to get a group to look at a problem. Use the resources to hand such as the team, colleagues or stakeholders.

Find those individuals with relevant experience and set up interviews to gather the information needed to both identify and resolve the risk.

Project Planning

Look both forward and backwards. That is, imagine the project in progress. Think of the many things that can go wrong. Note them. Do the same with historical data on past projects. This will allow the list of potential risk to grow.

As risk is identified ensure the risk register is not filling up with risks that are not really risks at all. Make sure the risks are rooted in the cause of a problem. Basically, drill down to the root cause to see if the risk is one that will have the kind of impact on the project that needs identifying.

When trying to minimise risk, it is good to trust intuition. It can point to unlikely scenarios that may be assumed could not happen. Use process to weed out risks from non-risks.

Analyse the Risk

Once potential risks are identified, they can be listed in the risk register. The next step is to determine how likely each of those risks are to happen. This information should also go into the risk register.

When assessing project risks, many impacts can ultimately and proactively be addressed, such as avoiding potential litigation, addressing regulatory issues, complying with new legislation, reducing exposure and minimising impact.

Analysing risk is hard. There is never enough information to be gathered. A lot of that data is complex, but most industries have best practices, which can help with the analysis.

The risk is analysed through qualitative and quantitative risk analysis. That means the risk factor is determined by how it impacts the project across a variety of metrics.

Those rules applied are how the risk influences the activity resources, duration and cost estimates. Another aspect of the project to think about is how the risk is going to impact on the schedule and budget. Then there is the project quality and procurements. These points must be considered to understand the full effect of risk on the project.

Prioritise the Risk

Not all risks are created equally. The risk needs to be evaluated to know what resources will be needed to resolve it when and if it occurs. Some risks are going to be acceptable. The project could grind to a halt and possibly not even be able to finish it without first prioritising the risks.

Having a large list of risks can be daunting. But this can be managed by simply categorising risks as high, medium or low. Once the risk is viewed in context, planning for how and when risks will be addressed can begin.

Some risks are going to require immediate attention. These are the risks that can derail the project. Other risks are important, but perhaps not threatening the success of the project.

Then there are those risks that have little to no impact on the overall project's schedule and budget. Some of these low-priority risks might be important, but not enough to waste time on. They can be all but ignored.

Project Planning

Assign an Owner to the Risk

All the hard work identifying and evaluating risk is for nothing if someone is not assigned to oversee the risk. Who is the person who is responsible for that risk, identifying it when and if it should occur and then leading the work towards resolving it?

That determination is up to the project manager. There might be a team member who is more skilled or experienced in the risk. Then that person should lead the charge to resolve it. Or it might just be an arbitrary choice. Of course, it is better to assign the task to the right person, but equally important in making sure that every risk has a person responsible for it. The person responsible should be identified in the risk register.

By not fulling addressing all risks at this stage leaves the project open to more risk in the event t should occur. It is one thing to identify risk, but if it is not managed then the project is not fully protected.

Respond to the Risk

For each major risk identified, there should be a plan to mitigate it. There should be a developed strategy which includes a preventative or contingency plan. The risk is acted upon by how it was prioritised. Communications should be established with the risk owner and with the project manager, decide on which of the plans to implement to resolve the risk.

Monitor the Risk

Whoever owns the risk will be responsible for tracking its progress towards resolution. The project manager will need to be updated to have an accurate picture of the project's overall progress to identify and monitor new risks.

Set up a series of meetings to manage the risks. Make sure the means of communications to do this has been agreed. There should be various channels dedicated to communication.

Face-to-face meetings may be used, but some updates might be best delivered by email or text or through a project management software tool. They might even be able to automate some, keeping the focus on the work and not busywork.

Whatever the choice, always be transparent. Everyone in the project must know what is going on, so they know what to be on the lookout for and help manage the process.

Project Planning

Communications Plan

A communications plan outlines how a project will be communicated to various audiences. Much like the work breakdown structure, a communications plan assigns responsibility for completing each component to a project team member.

In this step, it is important to outline how issues will be communicated and resolved within the team and how often communication will be opened to the team and the stakeholders or the boss. Each message has an intended audience. A communications plan helps project managers ensure the right information gets to the right people at the right time.

Communications Plan	
Project:	Project Renew
Summary:	Redesign Website to support new brand image
Communication Goals:	
Keep Stakeholders informed of project timeline, budget and project needs	
Provide a clear insight into any decision's needed or roadblocks	
Provide structured opportunities for feedback from stakeholders	
Give to stakeholders as needed to gain acceptance of the project	

Stakeholder Information				
Person	Role Title	Frequency	Format / Channel	Notes
Dave Smith	Assistant CEO	Major Milestones	High Level budget by email	Prefers audited and approved files
Joan Greaves	HR Lead	Weekly	Weekly F2F meeting & emails	Must authorise additional labour

Producing a Communications Plan

Perform a situation analysis.

Conduct an audit to evaluate the communications status. Gather and analyse all relevant information within the organisation. To conduct the communications audit, do the following:

- *Brainstorm with communication staff.*
- *Conduct surveys and focus groups.*
- *Talk to other departments in your company.*

Project Planning

Define the objectives.
After the information has been collected and evaluated, define the overall communications objectives. What results need to be achieved? What is to be accomplished by implementing this communication plan? The objectives should be SMART.

Define the key audiences.
The recipients for the messages must be identified. List all the key audiences of the organisation. These may include the following:

- *Members/non-members.*
- *Clients.*
- *Related associations.*
- *Educators.*
- *Local government officials.*
- *Media representatives.*

Identify Communication channels.
Plan to deliver messages to key recipients through multiple media channels. Decide which media channels would be the most effective to get the message delivered to the target audiences.

Establish a timetable.
In order to achieve the communications objectives, plan and time the communication steps for the best results. Based on the research and resources, develop a solid timing strategy to execute the steps of the communication plan.

Evaluate the results.
It is always important to measure the results to understand whether the objectives have been met. If the results are unsatisfactory, make necessary adjustments in order to perform better next time. The evaluation might take the form of the following:

- *Annual reports.*
- *Monthly reports.*
- *Progress reports.*
- *Reports from other departments.*

Developing a written communication plan will take some effort – but it is worth it. A communication plan is the main tool for successfully delivering the messages to the key audiences in order to develop mutually beneficial relationships.

Project Planning

Stakeholder Management Plan

A stakeholder management plan identifies how stakeholders will be used in the project. Sometimes stakeholders only need to receive information. That can be taken care of in the communications plan. If more is needed from stakeholders, a stakeholder management plan outlines how it will be obtained.

Because of how much power Stakeholders wield, the project manager needs to balance the requirements from key stakeholders with finesse.

What are their primary goals with this project? What are they hoping to invest? The more you can tease out what each of their goals and requirements are from the outset, the better.

Because there are many different types of stakeholders, you will want a well-rounded stakeholder management plan.

Stakeholder Register

Name	Title	Role	Power	Interest	Requirement	Concern
R Jones	Accountant	Sponsor	H	H	Maintain strict budget controls	Expenses only received monthly
M. Shah	Programmer	Team	L	H	Complete stage 14 by planned date	Network Issues

List the Stakeholders

Internal stakeholders are easy to identify. They are typically those within the organisation that have a key interest in the completion of a project. They are usually department heads, such as heads of Marketing, IT, Development, Operations and more. These stakeholders can affect the project either directly or indirectly by influencing the direction of their department on the given project.

External stakeholders are not typically part of the organisation itself but are made up of investors, users/customers, the media, neighbouring businesses or governmental oversight authorities.

Prioritise Your Stakeholders

Prioritise which stakeholders are going to have a bigger influence over the project and note at which stage their influence becomes lesser or greater.

Start by considering how to manage the stakeholders on your project, and then start prioritising their demands and goals. Understand that those priorities can flex at different project points. For example, at certain points, say, during a website design project, the stakeholder with a special interest in the design will have their goals prioritised. Then, as you move into the development phase, the stakeholders with a special interest in development will have their goals elevated over design.

Project Planning

Interview the Stakeholders

Working with new stakeholders can be tricky at the start—some are easier to manage than others. Depending on the type of project, there will either be many voices from outside the company with different personalities and demands, or many voices inside the company with competing goals.

Try to get a solid understanding of whether or not the stakeholders feel positively or negatively about the project, and at what stages their perspectives might shift. Also, identify which ones have a stronger set of views and which ones are more flexible and open to compromise. This will help to mitigate any possible stop gaps down the road.

Develop a Matrix

A quick mock-up of a quadrant to sort the findings will help easily distinguish those with high interest, high priority versus low interest, low priority. It will also help to sort all those in between.

For example, those with a high interest but a low priority are typically the best confidants. They are ready to get work done and will cheerlead the project on. Those with low interest and high priority might be the squeakiest wheels—keep the lines of communication open with them but keep a firm boundary so as to not spend all the time focusing on them.

They say the squeaky wheel gets the grease, so remember that even those in the low priority, low interest or high priority, low interest still need to be continually communicated with to ensure that their voices are heard throughout the project.

Set & Manage Expectations

Once the matrix is outlined and priorities and interests have been identified, create the project plan. Clearly identify which stages each key stakeholder will be involved in, and timelines by which their feedback is needed.

Include a schedule of office hours for them to easily make contact so that they can have time to provide feedback either in a private setting or in a group. As always, be realistic, transparent and honest at every project phase—the stakeholders can tell and will be thankful for it.

Risks of not having a Stakeholder Management Plan

Since stakeholders usually involve multiple key contacts across many different avenues, it is important to communicate with them effectively and efficiently. Not having interviewed them ahead of time or gauging their priority or interest, could mean spending a great deal of time trying to validate the requirements of a stakeholder with low priority and low interest, leaving those with a high priority feeling frustrated at the process.

Project Planning

Project Change Management Plan

A change management plan lays out a framework for making changes to the project. (This should not be confused with the Change management in a Human Resources context which may run in parallel to the project itself)

Although project managers tend to want to avoid changes to the project, they are sometimes unavoidable. The change management plan provides protocols and processes for making changes. It is critical for accountability and transparency that project sponsors, project managers, and project team members follow the change management plan.

There are several steps involved in writing a change management plan.

Demonstrate the reasons for the change.
Make sure that the reasons for the change effort are clearly defined. When stakeholders have a clear understanding of why the change is needed and how it will improve business or the way they work, they are more likely to support rather than resist the change.

Determine the scope
The next step in writing the change management plan is determining who the change will affect. Also determine what the change will impact, including policies, processes, job roles, and organisational structure.

Identify stakeholders
In large projects a change management team may be created to deal with changes to the project in smaller projects it will be the role of the Project Manager. The composition of this team is extremely important and it must be led by a credible leader. The change management team interacts with stakeholders, addresses concerns, and oversees a smooth change transition. Roles within the team require clear definition, including outlining each member's responsibilities.

Clarify the expected benefits
These benefits should be clearly delineated so that everyone involved understands the advantages of proceeding with the change.

Establishing well-communicated and achievable milestones are vital to the success of any change plan. These milestones become symbols to employees that the plan is working, progress is happening, the direction is still right, and the effort is worth it."

Create a change management communication plan.
There are three basic elements to communications in the context of change management.

- *Identify the stakeholders and those impacted by the change.*
- *Schedule regular face to face interactions and email communications to keep stakeholders updated on progress.*
- *Communications should be consistent, thorough, and regular. Communications should also clearly explain the change, define the reasons for change, present the benefits of the change, and always include change owner's contact information*

Project Planning

Project Monitoring

Project monitoring is a crucial element of all project management plans.

It refers to the process of keeping track of all project-related metrics including team performance and task duration, identifying potential problems and taking corrective actions necessary to ensure that the project is within scope, on budget and meets the specified deadlines. Without it, you cannot see where or why projects fail. It essentially comes down to keeping tabs on all project-related measurements, proactively recognising possible problems and taking the necessary steps to guarantee the project is completed on budget, on time and in scope.

The process of project monitoring begins during the planning phase of the project. During this phase, it is important to define how the project success will look like and how the goals can be measured using KPIs (Key performance indicators).

Project monitoring exists to make sure you are implementing a project as competently as possible. It should always be a cohesive and constant part of project management, and vital decisions should never be made without it.

The project management lifecycle has five phases: initiating, planning, executing, monitoring, and closing.

During the initiating & planning phase, the project receives the necessary approvals, a plan has been created, and the work actually begins on the tasks.

The executing phase and the monitoring phase happen concurrently. This means that you are monitoring your progress while you are completing tasks.

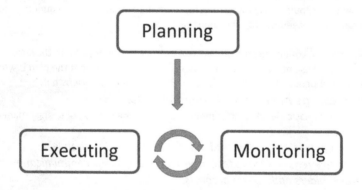

Executing and monitoring of projects happen concurrently.

Project Planning

Once the project plan is finalised and approved, the project manager monitors the progress making sure that the tasks are completed accordingly.

It is vital to monitor projects diligently and use the data you gathered both before and during the project to come up with intelligent decisions. Here are some questions answered through project monitoring:

- *Are tasks being carried out as planned?*
- *Are there any unforeseen consequences that arise as a result of these tasks?*
- *How is your team performing at a given period of time?*
- *What are the elements of the project that needs changing?*
- *What is the impact of these changes?*
- *Will these actions lead you to your expected results?*

Project Monitoring can be implemented via:

- *Staff Meetings, which can be conducted on a Weekly, Monthly or an Annual basis.*
- *Partner's meeting, Learning forums (FGD, Surveys) or Retreats.*
- *Participatory reviews by the stakeholders*
- *Monitoring and Supervision Missions that can be Self, Donor or Joint.*
- *Statistics or Progress reports*

Project monitoring aids various purposes. It brings out the problems which occur, or which might occur during the implementation of the project and which demands solutions for smoother progress in the project. Effective monitoring helps in knowing if the intended results are being achieved as planned, what actions are needed to achieve the intended results during the project execution, and whether these initiatives are creating a positive impact towards the project execution.

- *To assess the project results: To know how the objectives are being met and the desired changes are being met.*
- *To improve process planning: It helps in adapting to better contextual and risk factors which affect the research process, like social and power dynamics.*
- *To promote learning: It will help you learn how various approaches to participation influences the outcomes.*
- *To understand stakeholder's perspectives: Through direct participation in the process of monitoring and evaluation, learn about the people who are involved in the research project. Understand their values and views, as well as design methods to resolve conflicting views and interests.*
- *To ensure accountability: To assess if the project has been effectively, appropriately and efficiently executed, so that they can be held accountable.*

Project Planning

Implementing Project Monitoring and Control

Monitoring and control processes continually track, review, adjust and report on the project's performance. It is important to find out how a project's performing and whether it is on time, as well as implement approved changes. This ensures the project remains on track, on budget and on time.

On the surface this sounds simple enough, until one stops to think about the depth and breadth of the monitoring and controlling activities described throughout the PMBOK® Guide, which include:

- *Comparing planned results with actual results*
- *Reporting performance*
- *Determining if action is needed, and what the right action is*
- *Ensuring deliverables are correct based on the previously approved definitions and/or requirements*
- *Acquiring sign-off on deliverables by authorised stakeholders*
- *Assessing the overall project performance*
- *Managing risks*
- *Managing contracts and vendors*

In other words, project managers use the monitoring and controlling processes to translate project execution data from information into knowledge. This knowledge is then used to make the right management decisions and to take the right actions at the right time. Generally speaking, project managers face two choices in most situations:

- *Recommend the implementation of appropriate changes, which are planned and approved by the change management process*
  or
- *Allow the project to function "as is"*

Project Control
Project control is:

> *"a project management function that involves comparing actual performance with planned performance and taking appropriate corrective action (or directing others to take this action) that will yield the desired outcome in the project when significant differences exist."*

Project controls are a series of tools that help keep a project on schedule. Combined with people skills and project experience, they deliver information that enables accurate decision making.

Project Planning

The project control process mainly focuses on:

- *Measuring planned performance vs actual performance.*
- *Ongoing assessment of the project's performance to identify any preventive or corrective actions needed.*
- *Keeping accurate, timely information based on the project's output and associated documentation.*
- *Providing information that supports status updates, forecasting and measuring progress.*
- *Delivering forecasts that update current costs and project schedule.*
- *Monitoring the implementation of any approved changes or schedule amendments.*

Monitoring and control keep projects on track. The right controls can play a major part in completing projects on time. The data gathered also lets project managers make informed decisions. They can take advantage of opportunities, make changes and avoid crisis management issues.

Put simply, monitoring and control ensures the seamless execution of tasks. This improves productivity and efficiency.

Monitoring and Control Methods

When setting up a project's monitoring and control process, first establish the project baselines. This includes the scope, schedule and budget. Use this information to benchmark the project's progress throughout the lifecycle.

Use a Work Breakdown Structure (WBS) to break a project down into small units of work, or sub-tasks. This makes the work easier to manage and evaluate. This enables easier detection of issues, keeps the project under control and allows for easier progress verification. It also helps prevent team members from feeling overwhelmed.

There is a range of monitoring and control techniques that can be used by project managers, including:

- *A Requirements Traceability Matrix (RTM) maps or traces, the project's requirements to the deliverables. The matrix correlates the relationship between two baseline documents. This makes the project's tasks more visible. It also prevents new tasks or requirements being added to the project without approval.*
- *A control chart monitors the project's quality. There are two basic forms of control chart – a univariate control chart displays one project characteristic, while a multivariate chart displays more than one.*
- *Review and status meetings further analyse problems, finding out why something happened. They can also highlight any issues that might happen later*

CPSIA information can be obtained
at www.ICGtesting.com
Printed in the USA
LVHW081954100322
713152LV00010B/295